For 3 —

THE

WHOLE WORKS

OF THE

RIGHT REV. EDWARD REYNOLDS, D.D.

LORD BISHOP OF NORWICH;

Now First Collected

WITH HIS FUNERAL SERMON, BY B. RIVELEY,

ONE OF HIS LORDSHIP'S CHAPLAINS.

TO WHICH IS PREFIXED

A MEMOIR OF THE LIFE OF THE AUTHOR

By ALEXANDER CHALMERS, F.S.A.

———————————

IN SIX VOLUMES

VOL. III.

—————————

Soli Deo Gloria Publications
...for instruction in righteousness...

Soli Deo Gloria Publications
P.O. Box 451, Morgan, PA 15064
(412) 221-1901/FAX (412) 221-1902

*

The Works of Edwards Reynolds
was first reprinted in 1826 in 6 volumes
in London for B. Holdsworth in
St. Paul's Church-yard.

This Soli Deo Gloria Reprint is 1999.

*

Volume 3 of
The Works of Edward Reynolds
ISBN 1-57358-100-3

CONTENTS

OF

THE THIRD VOLUME.

MEDITATIONS ON THE HOLY SACRAMENT OF THE LORD'S LAST SUPPER.

SEVEN SERMONS ON THE FOURTEENTH CHAPTER OF HOSEA.

SERMON I.

SERMON II.

SERMON V.

SERMON VI.

SERMON VII.

x CONTENTS.

MEDITATIONS

ON THE

HOLY SACRAMENT

OF THE

LORD'S LAST SUPPER.

TO THE RIGHT WORSHIPFUL

SIR HENRY MARTEN, KNIGHT,

JUDGE OF THE ADMIRALTY, AND OF THE PREROGATIVE COURT
OF CANTERBURY.

Sir,

Saint Jerome having, in the heat of his youth, written an
allegorical exposition upon the prophet Obadiah, did, in his
riper age, solemnly bewail unto his friend Pammachius, both
his rashness in that attempt; and his infelicity farther herein,
that what he thought had been buried amongst his private
papers, was gotten into the hands of a certain young man,
and saw the light. The selfsame complaint am I forced
to make, touching this little manual of " Sacramental Meditations," which I humbly put into your hands. It was written with respect only to mine own private use many years
since, when I was a young student in the university, as my
first theological essay. And now lately, by means of a private copy, long ago communicated unto a friend, it had,
without my knowledge, received a license for the press.
My earnest care was, upon the first notice thereof, wholly to
have suppressed the publication : but the copy which had
been licensed, being, by I know not what miscarriage, lost,
I have found it necessary, for fear of the like inconvenience
again, to review a broken copy which I had by me, and have
rather chosen to let it pass forth with some brief and sudden
castigations of mine own, than once more run the hazard of
a surreptitious edition. Mine apology shall be no other than
that of the good Father; " Infans eram, nec tum scribere
noveram : Nunc, ut nihil aliud profecerim, saltem Socrati-
cum illud habeo, Scio quod nescio."—And now since I find
that the oblation of the first-fruits, though haply they were
not always the best and ripest, did yet find favourable acceptance with God himself; I have been emboldened to pre-

B 2

sent this small enchiridion (the very first fruits of my theological studies) unto the hands and patronage of so greatly
learned, eloquent, and judicious a person:—and that upon
this assurance; That as many times aged men, when they
walk abroad, lean upon the hand of a little child, so even
in this little and youthful treatise, such comfortable truths
may be, though weakly, delivered, as may help, in your journey towards a better country, to refresh and sustain your
aged thoughts. The blood of Christ, and the food of
life, are subjects worthy of all acceptation, though brought
unto us in an earthen vessel. Elisha [b] was not a whit the
less valued by that noble Naaman, though it were a handmaid which directed unto him. Neither was David's [c] comfort in rescuing of his wives, and recovering of the spoils
from the Amalekites any jot the smaller, because a young
man of Egypt made way for the discovery. The sovereignty
of the gospel is herein most excellently set forth, in that it
many times leadeth the soul by the hand of a child [d], and is
as truly, though not as abundantly, powerful from young
Timothy [e], as from Paul the aged. As Christ can use weak
elements to exhibit, so can he also use a weak pen to express, the virtue and comforts of his body and blood.

In this confidence, I have made bold to prefix your name
before these meditations; that therein I might make a public acknowledgment of my many deep engagements for your
abundant favours, and might, with most hearty prayers,
commend you and yours to that blood of sprinkling, which
speaketh better things for us than that of Abel. In which
desires I daily remain,

Yours, in all humble observance,

EDW. REYNOLDS.

[b] 2 Kings v. 2, 3. 2 Sam. xvii. 17.   [c] 1 Sam. xxx. 13.   [d] Isai. xi. 6.
[e] 1 Tim. iv. 12.

MEDITATIONS

ON THE

HOLY SACRAMENT.

CHAPTER I.

Man's being to be employed in working; that working directed unto some good, which is God; that good, a free and voluntary reward, which we here enjoy only in the right of a promise; the seal of which promise, is a sacrament.

THE almighty power and wisdom of God hath given unto his creatures a triple degree of perfection, their being, their working, and their good;—which three are so subordinate to each other, that working is the end and scope of being, and good is the end and scope of working: but no being can produce any work, no work reach unto any good, without something that may be a rule of working, and a way to good. And therefore Almighty God, in the work of the creation, imprinted in each creature a secret principle, which should move, govern, and uniformly direct it to its proper work and end: and that principle we call a law, which, by assigning unto each thing the kind, measure, and extent of its working, doth lead it on, by a straight and infallible line, unto that good for which it worketh. All other creatures below the sphere of reason, being not only, in the quality of their nature, of a narrow and strait perfection, but, in their duration, finite and perishable; the good unto which this law of their creation directs them, is a finite good likewise. But men and angels, being both in nature more excellent than all others, and, in continuance, infinite and immortal, cannot possibly receive from any thing, which is a mere creature, and less perfect than themselves, any complete satisfaction of their desires; and therefore must, by a circle, turn back unto God, who is as well the Omega, the end and object of their working,—as the Alpha, the cause and author of their being. Now God being most free, not only in himself, but in the diffusion and communication of himself, unto any thing created (which, therefore, he cannot be naturally or necessarily bound unto), and being also a God infinitely beyond the largest compass of the creature's merit or working,—it follows, that neither men nor angels can lay any necessary claim unto God, by a debt of nature (as a stone may unto the centre by that natural impress, which directs it thither); but all our claim is by a right of promise and voluntary donation: so that that which, in other mere natural creatures, is called the term or scope, is, in reasonable creatures, the promise or reward of their working. " Fear not, Abraham ; I am thy exceeding great reward." So then we have here our good, which is God,—to be communicated unto us, not in the manner of a necessary and natural debt, but of a voluntary and supernatural reward. Secondly, We have our working required, as the means to lead us, in a straight line, unto the fruition of that good. And inasmuch as man's will, being mutable, may carry him unto several operations of different kinds,—we have, Thirdly, A rule or law, to moderate the kind and manner of our working, whereby we reach unto our desired good : which rule when it altereth, as in the new covenant of grace it doth,—the quality of that work, whereby we reach unto our desired good, doth alter likewise. Now, Fourthly, We must farther observe, That between our working, which is the motion towards our good,—and our fruition, or resting in it,—there is a distance or succession of time. So that while we are in our estate of working, we do not enjoy God by any full real presence or possession, but only by a right of a covenant and promise ; which makes the apostle say, That, in this life, " we live by faith, and not by sight." Now promises or covenants require to have annexed unto them evidence and certainty, so far as may secure the party that relies upon them ; which, in human contracts, is done by giving our words and setting-to our seals for confirmation. And now, Lastly, Inasmuch as that duty, on condition whereof God maketh this promise of himself unto us, is the work of the whole man,—the evidence and confirmation of the promise is, by God, made unto the whole man likewise, and to each faculty of man: which it pleaseth him in mercy the rather to do, because of that dependence of our souls on the inferior and subordinate powers, and of that necessary connexion which there is between the inward reason and the outward senses. God then (pre-supposing ever the performance of conditions on our part) doth secure his church, and give evidence for the discharge of his covenant and promise,—First, To the soul alone by the testimony of his Spirit, which is both the seal and the witness of God's covenant; and, Secondly, Both to the soul and to the senses by that double bond, his Word written or preached, and his seal visibly exhibited to the eye and taste, but especially unto the taste, in which objects are, more really and with less fallibility, united to the faculty, in which there appeareth a more exquisite fruition of delight in these good things which are pleasing: and, Lastly, In which the mystical union of the church to its head, unto the making up of one body, is more naturally expressed. And these seals, annexed unto the Word or patent of God's promise, have been ever proposed unto the church in all its estates, and are nothing else but that which we call "a sacrament." So that as the testimony of the Spirit is an invisible seal, and earnest to the soul; so is the sacrament a visible seal, and earnest to the sense: both, after a several manner, ratifying and confirming the infallible expectation of that future reward, which as well the senses as the soul shall, in God's presence, really enjoy, after they have fulfilled the service which God requireth.

CHAPTER II.

Sacraments are earnests and shadows of our expected glory, made unto the senses.

THE promises and Word of grace with the Sacraments, are all but as so many sealed deeds, to make over, unto all successions of the church,—so long as they continue legitimate children, and observe the laws on their part required,—an infallible claim and title unto that good which is not yet revealed,—unto that inheritance which is as yet laid up unto that life, which is hid with God, and was never yet fully opened or let shine upon the earth.   Even in Paradise there was a Sacrament : a tree of life indeed it was, but there was but one.   Whereas Adam was to eat of all the fruits in the garden, he was there but to taste *sometimes* of life ; it was not to be his perpetual and only food.   We read of ' a tree of life' in the beginning of the Bible, and of ' a tree of life' in the end too : that was in Adam's paradise on earth; this, in St. John's paradise in Heaven : but that did bear but the first-fruits of life, the earnest of an after fulness ; this, bare life in abundance; for it bare twelve manner of fruits, and that every month ; which shows both the completeness and eternity of that glory which we expect.   And as the tree of paradise was but a Sacrament of life in Heaven, so paradise itself was but a Sacrament of Heaven.   Certainly, Adam was placed amongst the dark and shady trees of the garden, that he might, in an emblem, acknowledge that he was as yet but in the shadow of life, the substance whereof he was elsewhere to receive.   Even when the church was pure, it was not perfect : it had an age of infancy, when it had a state of innocence.   Glory was not communicated unto Adam himself, without the veil of a Sacrament : the light of God did not shine on paradise with a spreading and immediate ray : even there it was mixed with shadows, and represented only in a sacramental reflex, not in its own direct and proper brightness.   The Israelites in the wilderness had light indeed, but it was in a cloud ; and they had the presence of God in the Ark, but it was under several coverings ; and they had the light of God shining on the face of Moses, but it was under the veil ; and Moses himself did see God, but it was in a cloud : so incapable is the church, while encompassed with a body of sin, to see the lustre of that glory which is expected.   Certainly as the Son of God did admirably humble himself, in his hypostatical union, unto a visible flesh,—so doth he still, with equal wonder and lowliness, humble himself, in a sacramental union, unto visible elements.   Strange it is, that that mercy which is so wonderful, that the angels desire to look into it,—

<hr>

ᵃ 1 Pet. i. 12

so unconceivable, as that it hath not entered into the thought of man ; of such height, and length, and breadth, and depth, as passeth knowledge,—should yet be made the object of our lowest faculties : That that which is hid from the wise and prudent in man's little world, his mind and spirit,—should be revealed unto the babes, his senses. It were almost a contradiction in any thing, save God's mercy, to be so deep, as that no thought can fathom it, and yet so obvious, that each eye may see it: "Handle me and see [b]; for a spiritual substance hath not flesh," was sometimes the argument of Christ: and yet " handle and see take and eat, for a spiritual grace is conveyed by flesh," is the sacrament of Christ. So humble is his mercy, that, since we cannot raise our understandings to the comprehension of divine mysteries, he will bring down and submit those mysteries to the apprehension of our senses. Hereafter our bodies shall be over-clothed with a spiritual glory, by a real union unto Christ in his kingdom: mean time, that spiritual glory which we groan after [c], is here over-clothed with weak and visible elements, by a sacramental union at his table. Then shall sense be exalted, and made a fit subject of glory; here is glory humbled, and made a fit object of sense: " Then shall we see as we are seen, face to face ; here we see but as in a glass darkly [d];" in the glass of the creature,—in the glass of the word,—in the glass of the sacraments. And surely, these are in themselves clear and bright glasses ; yet we see even in them but darkly, in regard of that vapour and steam which exhaleth from our corrupt nature, when we use them : and even on these doth our soul look through other dark glasses, the windows of sense. But yet, at the best, they are but glasses, whose properties are to present nothing but the pattern, the shadow, the type of those things which are, in their substance, quite behind us, and therefore out of sight. So then, in general, the nature of a sacrament is to be the representative of a substance, — the sign of a covenant,—the seal of a purchase,—the figure of a body, —the witness of our faith,—the earnest of our hope,—the presence of things distant,—the sight of things absent,—the taste of things unconceivable,—and the knowledge of things that are past knowledge.

[b] Luke xxiv. 39.   [c] 2 Cor. v. 2, 4. 1 Cor. xv. 24.   [d] 1 Cor. xiii. 12.

CHAPTER III.

Inferences of practice from the former observations.

HERE then we see, first, the different state and disposition
of the church here in a state of corruption ; and, therefore,
in want of water in baptism to wash it : in a state of infancy ; and, therefore, in want of milk in the Word to nourish it: in a state of weakness ; and, therefore, in want of
bread, the body of Christ, to strengthen it: in a state of
sorrow; and, therefore, in want of wine, the blood of Christ,
to comfort it. Thus the church while it is a child, it speaks
as a child, it understands as a child, it feeds as a child,
here a little and there a little ; one day in the week, one
hour in the day, it is kept fasting and hungry. But when
it is grown from strength to strength, unto a perfect age,
and unto the fulness of the stature of Christ ; then it shall
be satisfied with fatness, and drink its full of those rivers of
pleasures, which make glad the city of God. It shall keep
an eternal sabbath, a continued festival : the supper of the
Lamb shall be without end, or satiety: " so long as the bride-
groom is with them," (which shall be for ever) " they cannot fast."

Secondly, We see here, nor see only, but even taste and
touch, how gracious the Lord is, in that he is pleased even
to unrobe his graces of their natural lustre, to overshadow
his promises ; and, as it were, to obscure his glory, that
they might be made proportioned to our dull and earthly
senses ; to lock up so rich mysteries, as lie hidden in the
sacraments, in a bason of water, or a morsel of bread. When
he was invisible, by reason of that infinite distance between
the divine nature and ours, he made himself to be seen in
the flesh : and now that his very flesh is to us again invisible, by reason of that vast distance between his place and
ours,—he hath made even it, in a mystical sense, to be seen
and tasted in the sacrament. Oh then, since God doth thus
far humble himself and his graces, even unto our senses,

let not us, by an odious ingratitude, humble them yet lower, even under our feet. Let us not trample on the blood of the covenant, by taking it into a noisome sink, into a dirty and earthy heart. He that eats Christ in the sacrament with a foul mouth, and receives him into an uncleansed and sinful soul,—doth all one as if he should sop the bread he eats, in dirt,—or lay up his richest treasures in a sink.

Thirdly, We learn, how we should employ all our senses. Not only as brute beasts do, to fasten them on the earth, but to lift them unto a more heavenly use, since God hath made even them the organs and instruments of our spiritual nourishment. Mix ever with the natural, a heavenly use of thy senses. Whatsoever thou seest, behold in it his wonder; whatsoever thou hearest, hear in it his wisdom; whatsoever thou tastest, taste in it the sweetness, as well of his love, as of the creature. If Christ will not dwell in a foul house, he will certainly not enter at a foul door. Let not those teeth that eat the bread of angels, grind the face of the poor; let not the mouth which doth drink the blood of Christ, thirst after the blood of his neighbour; let not that hand which is reached out to receive Christ in the sacrament, be stretched out to injure him in his members; let not those eyes which look on Christ, be gazing after vanity; certainly, if he will not be one in the same body with a harlot[e], neither will he be seen with the same eyes. He is really in the heaven of the greater world; and he will be nowhere else sacramentally, but in the heavenly parts of man, the lesser.

Lastly, We see here what manner of conversation we have: The church on earth hath but the earnests of glory, the earnest of the Spirit, and the earnest of the sacrament; that witnessing[f], this signifying; both confirming and sealing our adoption[g]. But we know not what we shall be[h]; our life is yet hid[i], and our inheritance is laid up for us[k]. A prince, that is haply bred up in a great distance from his future kingdom in another realm, and that amongst enemies where he suffers one while a danger, another a disgrace, loaded with dangers and discontents, — though, by the assurance of blood, by the warrant of his Father's own hand

e 1 Cor. vi. 15.   f Rom. viii. 16.   g Rom. iv. 11. Ephes. iv. 30. Rom. iv. 11.   h 1 John iii. 2.   i Col. iii. 3.   k 1 Pet. i. 4.

and seal, he may be confirmed in the evident right of his
succession,—can hardly yet so much as imagine the honour
he shall enjoy, nor any more see the gold and lustre of his
crown in the print of the wax that confirms it, than a man
that never saw the sun, can conceive that brightness which
dwelleth in it, by its picture drawn in some dark colours.
" We are a royal people [l]; heirs, yea coheirs with Christ [m];"
but we are in a far country, " and absent from the Lord [n];"
in houses ruinous and ' made of clay,' in a ' region of
darkness,' in a ' shadow of death,' in a ' valley of tears.'
Though compassed in with a wall of fire, yet do the waves
of ungodly men break in upon us : though shipped in a safe
ark, the temple of God, yet often tossed almost unto shipwreck, and ready, with Jonah, to be swallowed up of a great
Leviathan : though protected with a guard of holy angels,
which pitch their tents about us, so that the enemy without
cannot enter, yet enticed often out, and led privily, but
voluntarily, away by the enchanting lusts [o], the Dalilahs of
our own bosom. The kingdom and inheritance we expect,
is hid from us [p]; and we know no more of it, but only this,
that it passeth knowledge. Only the assurance of it is confirmed by an infallible patent, God's own promise, and that
made firm by a seal, coloured with that blood, and stamped
with the image of that body, which was the price that
bought it. What remains then, but that where the body is,
thither the eagles fly ; where the treasure is, there the heart be
also ; that we groan after the revelation of the sons of God,
when the veil of our mortality shall be rent ; the mud wall
of the flesh made spiritual and transparent ; the shadows and
resemblances of the sacraments abolished ; the glass of the
creature removed ; the riddle of our salvation unfolded ; the
vapours of corruption dispelled ; the patience of our expectation rewarded ; and from the power of the Spirit within,
and the presence of Christ without, shall be diffused on the
whole man a double lustre of exceeding abundant glory ?
The hope and assurance of this is it which, in those holy
mysteries of Christ's supper, we receive ; which if received
without dependence and relation on that glory which they

[l] 1 Peter ii. 9.   [m] Rom. viii. 17.   [n] 2 Cor. v. 6.   [o] Jam. i. 14.
[p] Eph. iii. 9.

foreshadow, and on that body which with all the merits of it they obsignate, doth no more good than the seal of a king, without any grant or patent whereunto it should be joined; in which there is no profit beyond the bare wax, and much danger in trifling with so sacred a thing.

CHAPTER IV.

Whence Sacraments derive their value and being, namely, from the Author that instituted them.

BUT why are not the instruments more glorious, where the effects are so admirable? Whence is it that there should lie so much power in the narrow room of so small and common elements? It had been worth the creating of a new creature, to be made the pledge of a new covenant. The first fruits are of the same nature with their crop; and earnest useth to be paid in coin of the same quality with the whole after-sum. If, then, sacraments are the earnests of our glory, why are not the faithful, instead of eating a morsel of bread, taken up, with St. Paul, into the third Heavens? Why are they not, instead of drinking a sip of wine, transformed with their Saviour; and have, with Stephen, a vision of him at the right hand of the Father? How discursive is foolish pride, when it would prescribe unto God! Vain man, who undertakest to instruct thy Maker, instead of praising him; to censure his benefits, when thou shouldest enjoy them; wilt thou not receive salvation without thine own counsel? or art thou so foolish as to conceive nothing precious without pomp? And to judge of the thing conveyed, by the value and quality of the instrument that conveys it? Tell me then, why it is, that water, a vulgar element, is held in a cistern of lead,—and thy wine, a more costly liquor, but in a vessel of wood? Tell me the reason why that wax, which in the shop haply was not priced at a penny, should, by cleaving unto a small parcel of parchment, be valuable unto a million of money? Tell me, why should that clay q, which while it lay under foot, was vile and disho-

q John ix. 6.

nourable dirt,—when it was applied by Christ unto the eyes
of a blind man, be advanced unto the condition of a precious
and supernatural salve ? Is not, even in works of art, the
skill of the workman more eminent in the narrowest and un-
fittest subjects ? Are not the Iliads of Homer more admirable in a nutshell than in a volume [r] ? Do not limners set the
highest value on their smallest draughts ? And is there not
matter of admiration and astonishment in the meanest and
most vulgar objects ? And what madness is it, then, by
those reasons to undervalue faith, which are the arguments
to confirm it ! As if the power of an agent were not there
greatest, where the subject on which he worketh, doth confer least ; as if the weakness of the element [s], did not add
unto the wonder of the sacrament. If it were an argument
of Christ's miraculous power, to feed five thousand with so
few loaves ; why should not the miracle of his sacrament be
equal, which feeds the whole church with so slender elements ? Certainly, they who any way disesteem the seeming meanness and emptiness of the sacrament, entertaining
but low and vulgar conceits thereof,—stumble at the same
stone of foolishness, by which the Gentiles fell from their
salvation. But wilt thou needs know both the reason why
we use no other sacraments, and why these carry with them
so much virtue ? One answer resolves both :—it is the majesty of the same king that coins his money, and that values
it : he that frames a private mint, or imposeth another rate,
is in both equally a traitor ; in the former by stealing the
king's authority, in the other by altering it. The same author did both institute the sacrament and value it; from the
same power did it receive the necessity of its being, and the
efficacy of its working [t]. In covenants or conveyances, the
articles and instruments may be haply drawn by some law-
yer; but the confirmations of them by hand and seal, are ordinarily performed by the men themselves who are interested
in them. A secretary may write the letter ; but his lord
will himself subscribe and seal it.

Thus the patent of God's covenant hath been drawn out,
for the benefit of God's church, by many selected and in-

[r] *Seneca*, Naturalium Quæst.   [s] *August*. ep. 3.—*Ambros*. Hexam. lib. 6. c. 6.
—*Chrysost*. Hom. 12. ad Pop. Antioch.—*Tertul*. de Baptis. c. 2. & contra Marc.
l. 5. c. 5.   [t] Vide *Ambros*. de Sacrament. lib. 4. cap. 4.

spired instruments, unto whom God did dictate so much of his will by divine suggestion, as his pleasure was to acquaint and edify his church withal. But when he comes to confirm this gift by hand and seal, behold then an immediate presence of his own: then comes God's [u] own finger, that is, in the phrase of scripture, his spirit to write as a witness in the soul: and then doth God stretch out his own hand, and reach unto us that supper which is the seal to obsignate unto the senses, the infallible truth of those covenants, and our evident interest in those benefits, which were before proclaimed in the patent of his word. The apostle [x] delivered nothing as it were by a second hand to the Corinthians, but what he had formerly received from the Lord. Divine things are unto us deposited [y]; we must first be receivers, before deliverers.

CHAPTER V.

Inferences of practice from the Author of this Sacrament.

HERE then we see, first, both the absurdity and the wickedness of a will-worship; when the same man who is to perform the obedience, shall dare to appoint the laws, implying a peremptory purpose of no farther observance, than may consist with the allowance of his own judgement: whereas true obedience [z] must be grounded on the majesty of that power that commands, not on the judgement of the subject, or benefit of the precept imposed. Divine laws require obedience, not so much from the quality of the things commanded (though they be ever holy and good[a]), as from the authority of him that institutes them. We are all the servants of God; and servants [b] are but living instruments, whose property it is to be governed by the will of those, in whose possession they are [c]. Will-worship, and services of

---

[u] Matth. xii. 28. Luke xi. 20. [x] 1 Cor. xi. 23. [y] 1 Tim. i. 11. and vi. 20. [z] Vid. *Tertul.* de Pœnitent. c. 4. & *Aug.* de Civit. Dei. l. i. c. 26. & de Genes. ad lit. lib. 8. c. 12. [a] Rom. 7. 12. [b] *Arist.* Polit. lib. 1.—*Plutarch* de Superstitione. [c] Δεσπότου μέν ἐστι μόνον τὸ ἐπιτάτ]ειν, δουλῶν δὲ τὸ πείθεσθαι. *Chrys.* in Rom. Hom. 2.

superstition, well they may flatter God, they do not please
him. He that requires us to deny ourselves in his service,
doth therein teach us, that his commands stand rather in
fear than in need of us; in fear of our boldness, lest we
abuse them; not in need of our judgements, to polish or alter
them. The conquest of an enemy against the prescript of
his general, cost a Roman gentleman his life[d], though his
own father were the judge. The killing of a lion contrary to
the established laws of the king's hunting,—though it were
only to rescue the king himself, whose life was set upon,—
cost a poor Persian the loss of his head[e]. The overwise industry of the architect, in bringing, not the same, but a fitter
piece of timber than he was commanded, to the Roman con-
sul, was rewarded with nothing but the bundle of rods[f]. So
jealous and displeased are even men themselves[g], to have
their own laws undervalued by the private judgements of
those, who rather interpret than obey them. And therefore
even those men who erected the fabricks of superstition and
will-worship, have yet ever endeavoured to derive the original of them on some divine revelations[h]. And that great
Roman captain Scipio, ever before the undertaking of any
business, was wont first to enter the Capitol, and pretend a
consultation with the gods, touching their allowance of his
intended designs, grounding all his attempts and governing
all his actions by the unerring judgement of their deities.
And generally in all the Roman sacrifices, the minister or
servant[i] was to attend a command, before he was to strike
the beast that was offered. Horrible then, and more than
heathenish, is the impiety of those, who mixing human inventions and ceremonies of their own unto the substance of
these sacred mysteries, and imposing them as divine duties
with a necessity of absolute obedience,—do, by that means,
wrench Christ's own divine prerogative out of his own hands,
and make themselves, shall I say, confounders and joint authors of his sacraments; nay, rather, indeed, the destroyers
of them:—since as he that receives otherwise than Christ
requires, receives not Christ, but rather damnation[k]; so he

---

d *Liv.* lib. 8.   e *Brisson.* de Reg. Pers. lib. 1.   f *A. Gell.* l. 1. c. 13.
g *Cyprian.* cont. Demetrianum.   h *Numa,* apud Liv. lib. 1.   i Semper
agatne rogat: nec nisi justus agit. *Ovid.* Fast. lib. 2.   k 1 Cor. xi.

that gives otherways than Christ instituted, doth not indeed give Christ, but an idol of his own making.

Secondly, We see here, with how great reverence we ought to approach God's temple, to receive these deep mysteries of salvation, which it pleased Christ in his own person to institute, and with his own presence to exhibit unto the church. Was a beast slain for touching the mount; and shall not a man of beastly and vile affections be punished for touching that table where the Lord is present? Was Moses[1] to put off his shoes at that bush which represented God's power; and must not we shake off our earthly and corrupt desires at those mysteries which represent his mercy? Were Nadab and Abihu destroyed before the Lord, for offering strange fire at his altar; and shall we plead immunity, if we present strange souls and a false faith at his table? Was Adam thrust out of paradise for his sin in eating of the tree of knowledge; and shall we escape, if we sin in eating of the bread of life? Even unto the institutions of mortal men, though often in their substance needless, in their observance difficult, and in their end not much beneficial, so long as they keep within the compass of indifferent things,—there is required, not only our obedience, but our reverence. The Word of God, though delivered unto us in earthen vessels, by men of like weak and frail affections with ourselves; yet, because of that native preciousness which resides in it, and of that derived glory which it brings from the spirit that revealed it, is so far to be honoured, as that the vessels that bring it, are to be had in high estimation, even for their work's sake. But the sacraments are not either of human authority, as are positive laws; nor of Divine inspiration unto holy men, as were the Scriptures: but they are by so much the more the immediate effects of Divine power, by how much they are instituted without the least concurrence of any other instrument; being reached out first unto the church of God by that immaculate and precious hand, which was itself presently stretched forth on the cross, to embrace the weary and heavy laden. Let us not, then, venture to receive so sacred things with unwashed hands, as matters of mere custom, fashion, or formality. But let us look unto that high authority that ordained them, on that holy mouth

Heb. xii. 20.

that blessed them, on that arm of mercy that exhibits them;
being ever assured, that as Christ hath one hand of bounty
and redemption, which reacheth forth life to the worthy receiver,—so hath he another of justice and power, ready to
avenge the injuries and contempt, that shall be done to his
own holy institution.

Thirdly, We see here the honourable condition of the
faithful, in that they not only receive Christ, and all the benefits of his merits and actions,—but all this they receive
from his own hands. For we may not think, that the actions
of Christ, in looking up, and blessing, and breaking, and giving, were merely temporary, local, or confined actions, ter-
minated only to the present company that were then with
him : certainly as the apostles were then the representative
church,—so was that a representative action, the virtue and
effect whereof descends and passeth through all successions
of the church. The arm of the Lord is not shortened, or
any way shrunk, that it cannot still exhibit what then it did.
If he can so lengthen the arm of faith in us, as to reach as
far as Heaven to embrace him,—he can as well stretch out
his own arm of mercy from Heaven, to present that unto us,
which he did unto his disciples. It was an admirable and
unexpected honour that was shown to Mordecai [m], when
the royal crown and the king's own apparel was put upon
him, though by the service of wicked Haman: but Christ [n]
doth not only bestow on us his kingdom in the sacrament,
which seals unto us our inheritance with him ; nor doth only
invest us with his own meritorious purple robes, his red
garments from Bozra, the garments of innocency and of
unity, but doth all this with his own immediate hand : so
that our honour must needs be so much greater than was
Mordecai's, by how much the robes of Christ are more royal
than the Persian king's, and his person more sacred than was
wicked Haman's.

m Esther vi. 10.   n 1 Pet. ii. 9. Rom. viii. 17.

CHAPTER VI.

Of the circumstances of the institution, namely, the time and place.

AND as the author, so the circumstances of the institution, do not a little add unto the excellency of this sacrament. First, For the circumstance of time: it was the same night [o] wherein he was betrayed: in the evening, and after supper. *In the evening*, or night, a time fit to prefigure a passion and eclipse,—his especially who was the Sun of righteousness, and the light of the world; a passion [p] that brought darkness on the very fountain of light, the sun, even in the mid-day. *In the evening*, to note that now the fulness of time was come, wherein Christ was to accomplish the redemption of the world. *In the evening*, or twilight, when the passover was celebrated [q]. Learn, from the condition of the time, the nature as of that legal, so, in some sort, of this evangelical sacrament; it is but a shadow and dark representation of that light which shall be revealed. It hath but the glimmerings and faint resemblances of that mercy, which redeemed us,—of that glory, which expecteth us. *In the evening*, at the eating of the paschal lamb; to note that Christ's active obedience [r] to the commands of the law, went together with his passive obedience to the curse and penalty of the law. He first celebrated the passover, that therein he might testify his performance of the law; and then he instituted his own supper, that therein he might prefigure his suffering of the law. *In the evening* after the passover, to signify the abolishing both of the evening and of the passover, the plucking away of Moses' veil, of all those dark and misty prefigurations of that light, which was within a few days to rise upon the world. He would first celebrate the passover, and there nullify it, to make it appear unto the world, that he did not abrogate that holy ordinance, because he oppugned it, but because he fulfilled it: and therefore to

---

[o] 1 Cor. xi. Matth. xxvi. 20.   [p] *Chrysost.* in Matth. xxvi.   [q] Exod. xii. 6.
[r] *Chrysost.* Tom. 5. Serm. 80. de proditione Judæ.—Id sacrificium successit omnibus sacramentis Veteris Testamenti. *Aug.* de Civ. Dei, l. 17. c. 20.

the substance he joins the shadow, the lamb of the Jews to
the Lamb of God, the true sacrifice to that which was typical;
that the brightness of the one might abolish and swallow up
the shadow of the other [s]. *In the evening*, at the time of unleavened bread ; to signify that we also (it is the inference
of the apostle [t]) should keep our feast, not with the unleavened bread of malice or of wickedness, but with the unleavened bread of sincerity and truth : that we should not
venture to play the hucksters with so divine and pure mysteries, by adulterating them with either the mixture of human inventions [u], or with the mud of our own sinful affections. *In the evening*, at the time of supper ; to note, the
most willing and ready, yea, the forward and greedy, re-
signing himself into the hands of bloody and cruel men ; to
signify, that unto him it was meat and drink, not only to do
but to suffer, his Father's will. *In the evening* [x] of that same
night wherein he was betrayed ; to give first a warrant unto
his church, of his approaching passion ; which though so
intolerable for the quality and burden of it, that it could not
but amaze his humanity, and draw from him [y] that natural
and importunate expression of the desire he had to decline
it,—yet in their elements did he ascertain the church, that as
he came to drink of the brook in the way [z], so he should not
shrink from drinking the very bitterest part of it.

And secondly, *In the night wherein he was betrayed ;* to
fore-arm his poor disciples with comfort against the present
loss of him, and against all that anguish which their tender
hearts must needs suffer at the sight of that bloody and
savage usage, which Judas and the Jews would show towards their Master. And, therefore, in these elements, he
acquaints them with the nature and quality of his passion :
that it should be as bread to strengthen, and as wine to
comfort, the faint-hearted ; to confirm the knees that tremble, and the hands that hang down.

Thirdly, *It was the night wherein he was betrayed ;* to let us
understand that these words were the words of a dying
man [a], and therefore to be religiously observed [b]; and that

[s] Καθάπερ ζωγράφοι ἐν αὐτῷ πίνακι τὴν σκιὰν γράφουσιν, καὶ τότε τὴν ἀλήθειαν τῶν χρωμάτων. *Chrysost.*   [t] 1 Cor. v. 7.   [u] 2 Cor. ii. 17.
[x] 1 Cor. xi.   [y] Matth. xxvi. 29   [z] Psal. cx.   [a] Vid. *Aug.* de
Unitate Eccl. cap. 11.—*Chrysost.* in 1 Cor. xi.   [b] "Plerique mortales postrema
meminere :" Cæsar apud *Sall.* in Catil.—Vid. *August.* Epist. 118. prope finem.

this sacrament was the work of a dying man, and therefore
in its nature a gift or legacy. In his lifetime, he gave his
church his Word and his miracles; he went about doing
good; but now, in his passion, he bestowed that which
added weight and value to all his other gifts, *himself*. Other
men use to bequeath their bodies to the earth, from whence
it came: but Christ's body was not to see corruption [c]; and
therefore he bequeathed it unto the church. It was his
body by his hypostatical and real,—but it is ours by a mystical and spiritual, union. Whatsoever fulness is in him, of
it have we all received [d]; whatsoever graces and merits flow
from him as the head, they trickle down as far as the skirts
of his garment, the meanest of his chosen. The pains of his
wounds were his [e], but ours is the benefit; the sufferings of
his death were his, but ours is the mercy; the stripes on his
back were his, but the balm that issued from them, ours;
the thorns on his head were his, but the crown is ours; the
holes in his hands and side were his, but the blood that ran
out, was ours; in a word, the price was his, but the purchase
ours. The corn is not ground, nor baked, nor broken for
itself; the grape is not bruised nor pressed for itself: these
actions rather destroy the nature of the elements than perfect
them; but all these violations that they suffer, are for the
benefit of man. No marvel then, if the angels themselves
stoop and gaze upon so deep a mystery, in which it is impossible to decide whether is greater,—the wonder, or the
mercy.

If we look unto the place where this sacrament was celebrated, even there also shall we find matter of meditation;
for we may not think that two evangelists [f] would be so express and punctual in describing the place, if there were not
some matter of consequence to be observed in it.

First, then, It was a borrowed room; he that had no hole [g]
where to lay his head in, had no place where to eat the passover. We may not then expect, in Christ's new supper, any
variety of rich and costly dishes; as his kingdom is not, so

---

[c] Acts ii. 27.   [d] John i. 16.   [e] Scivit (Latro) quod illa in corpore
Christi vulnera non essent Christi vulnera, sed latronis. *Ambros.* de Sancto La-
trone Serm. 44.   [f] Matth. xiv. 15. Luke xxii. 12.   [g] Matth. viii. 20.
Διδασκόμεθα ἐντεῦθεν ὅτι οὐκ εἶχεν οἰκίαν ἀφωρισμένην ὁ Χριστός. *Chrysost.*
Tom. 5. Serm. 30.

neither is his supper, of this world. It was not his purpose
to make our worship of him a chargeable service, and to en-
join us such a table, as should fix our thoughts on the meats,
rather than on the substance which they resembled. He
knew that where the senses are overcharged, faith lies un-
exercised : and therefore he proportioned his supper both to
the quality of his own estate, which was poor,—and to the
condition of our weakness, apt (as the church after in her
Love-feasts found[h]) to be rather tempted than edified, in too
much variety of outward meats. It was likewise an upper
room ; to note the dignity and divineness of this sacrament,
and that property of lifting up the hearts, which it should
work in the receivers of it. Our thoughts and affections
while conversant about these mysteries, should not lie
grovelling on the earth, but should be raised unto high and
noble contemplations[i].

And this particular of the place may seem to have been
imitated by the churches, in placing the Lord's table, and
celebrating the Lord's supper in the chancel, or upper room
of the temple : besides, it was a spacious and great room,
and so it should be ; for it was a great supper, the supper of
a king[k]. The disciples were then the type and representative of the whole Catholic church, which was now by them
to be begotten unto God : and therefore, the chamber must
needs be a resemblance and model of the whole world,
throughout which the sound of Christ's name, and the
memory of his passion, should, in his supper, be celebrated
until the end of all things ;—and then no marvel, if it were a
great chamber.

Lastly, It was ready spread, fitted, trimmed, and prepared.
So sacred a mystery as this may not be exhibited in an un-
fitted or unclean place, much less received into a corrupt and
unprepared soul. The body of Christ was never to see corruption ; and therefore it will never be mixed with corruption.
It lay first in a clean womb ; it was afterwards buried in a
virgin sepulchre ; it then was taken into the brightest heavens ; and it still resides in molten and purified hearts. He
that had the purity of a dove, will never take up the lodging

[h] Jude v. 12.   [i] Sursum corda.   [k] *Aug.* de Dono Perserver.—*Hieron.* ad
Hedib. quæst. 2.—*Cyprian.* de Orat. Dominica.—*Cyril.* Catech. Myst.

of a crow. Here then we see, from these circumstances, with what reverence and preparation, with what affection and high esteem, we should receive these sacred mysteries. The gift of a dying friend, though of contemptible value, is yet greatly prized for the memory of the donor; for though the thing itself be small, yet is it the pledge of a great love[1]. The words of a dying man, though formerly vile and vain, are, for the most part, serious and grave; how much more precious was the gift of Christ, who is the almoner of Almighty God, and whose only business it was "to give gifts unto men[m];" how much more sacred were his last words, who, all his lifetime, "spake as never man spake." The very presence of a dying man stamps on the mind an affection of fear and awe; much more should the words and gifts of him, who was dead and is alive again. Certainly he hath a flinty soul, whom love as strong as death[n], and death the work of that love, cannot melt into a sympathy of affection.

In sum, the time of this sacrament was a time of passion; let not us be stupid:—It was a time of passover; let not our souls be unsprinkled:—It was a time of unleavened bread; let not our doctrine of it be adulterated with the leaven of heresy; nor our souls in receiving, tainted with the leaven of malice:—It was the time of betraying Christ; let not our hands again play the Judas, by delivering him unto Jewish and sinful souls, which will crucify again unto themselves 'the Lord of glory;' let not us take that precious blood into our hands, rather to shed it than to drink it; and, by receiving the body of Christ unworthily, make it as the sop to Judas, even a harbinger to provide room for Satan.

Again, The place of the sacrament was a high room; let not our souls lie sinking in a dungeon of sin. It was a great room; let not our souls be straitened in the entertaining of Christ. It was a trimmed room; let not our souls be sluttish and unclean, when the 'King of glory should enter in:' but as the author of those mysteries was holy by a fulness of grace, the elements holy by his blessing, the time holy by his ordination, and the place holy by his presence,— so let us, by the receiving of them, be transformed, as it

[1] Debetri quippe maximo operi hanc quoque venerationem, ut novissimum esset, auctoremque ejus statim consecrandum, &c. *Plin.* Pan. Gierig. **x.** 5. [m] Ephes. iv. 7, 8, 11. [n] Cant. viii.

were, into their nature, and be holy by that union unto
Christ; of which they are as well the instrumental means
whereby it is increased, as the seals and pledges whereby it
is confirmed.

CHAP. VII.

*Of the matter of the Lord's supper, bread and wine, with their
analogy unto Christ.*

WE have considered the author or efficient of this sacrament, and those circumstances which were annexed unto its
institution. We may now a little consider the essential parts
of it : and, First, The elements or matter, of which it consisteth, consecrated bread and wine. It neither stood with
the outward poverty of Christ, nor with the benefit of the
church, to institute such sumptuous ° and gaudy elements, as
might possess too much the sense of the beholder, and too
little resemble the quality of the Saviour. And therefore
he chose his sacraments rather for the fitness, than the
beauty of them ; as respecting more the end, than the splendour or riches, of his table ; and intended rather to manifest
his divine power in altering poor elements unto a precious
use, than to exhibit any carnal pomp, in such delicious fare,
as did not agree with the spiritualness of his kingdom.
Though he be contented, out of tenderness toward our weakness, to stoop unto our senses, yet he will not cocker them :
as in his real and natural body, so in his representative, the
sacrament,—a sensual or carnal eye sees not either form or
beauty[p], for which it may be desired. Pictures ought to resemble their originals ; and the sacrament, we know, is the
picture or type of him who was a man of sorrow[q] ; and this
picture was drawn, when the day of God's fierce wrath was
upon him[r] : and can we expect from it any satisfaction or
pleasure to the senses? This body was naked on the cross ;
it were incongruous to have the sacrament of it pompous on
the table. As it was the will of the Father, which Christ both
glorifies and admires, to reveal unto babes what he hath hid-

---

° Non ad, elaborata impensis et arte, convivia populi invitantur. *Cyprian.*
[p] Isai. liii. 2.   [q] Isai liii. 3.   [r] Lam. i. 12.

den from the wise ; so is it here his wisdom to communicate, by the meanest instruments, what he hath denied unto the choicest delicates, to feed his Daniels rather with pulse, than with all the dainties on the king's table. And if we observe it, divine miracles take ever the poorest and meanest subjects to manifest themselves on. If he want an army to protect his church, flies [s], and frogs, and caterpillars [t], and lamps, and pitchers [u], &c. shall be the strongest soldiers [x] and weapons he useth ; the lame and the blind [y], the dumb [z], and the dead [a], water [b], and clay [c], these are materials for his power [d].— Even where thou seest the instruments of God weakest, there expect and admire the more abundant manifestation of his greatness and wisdom: undervalue not the bread and wine in this holy Sacrament, which do better resemble the benefits of Christ crucified, than any other the choicest delicates.

"*Bread and wine;*" the element is double to increase the comfort of the faithful, that by two things wherein it is impossible for God to deceive, we might have strong consolation who have laid hold upon him [e]. "The dream is doubled," said Joseph [f] to Pharaoh, "because the thing is certain:" and surely here the element is doubled too, that the grace may be the more certain. No marvel then, if those men who deny unto the people the certainty of grace, deny unto them likewise these double elements : so fit is it, that they which preached but a half-comfort, should administer likewise but a half-sacrament.

Secondly, *Bread and wine :* in the passover there was blood shed, but there was none drunken [g]; yea, that flesh which was eaten, was but once a-year. They who had all in types, had yet their types, as it were, imperfect. In the fulness of time [h] came Christ ; and with or in Christ came the fulness of grace; and of his fulness do we receive in the gospel, which the Jews only expected in the promise, that they without us might not be made perfect [i]. "These things have I

[s] Isai. vii. 18.　　[t] Exod. viii. 6, 24.　　[u] Judges vii. 20. Josh. vi. 4. Judges xv. 15.　[x] Joel ii. 25.　[y] John v. 23. Matth. xii. 10.　[z] John ix. 1. [a] Matth. ix. 25.　[b] Matth. xii. 22.　[c] John ii. 7.　[d] John ix. 6.　[e] Heb. vi. 18.　[f] Gen. xli. 32.　[g] Lex esum sanguinis prohibet: Evangelium præcipit, ut bibatur. *Cypr.* de Cœna Dom.—Vid. *Ambros.* Tom. 4. lib. de iis qui initiantur, c. 9.　[h] Gal. iv. 4. Col. i. 19.　[i] Heb. xi. 40.

spoken," saith Christ[k], "that your joy might be full." The
fulness of our sacrament, notes also the fulness of our salvation, and of his sacrifice who is able perfectly to save those
that come unto God by him [l].

Thirdly, *Bread and wine :* common, vulgar, obvious food ;
wine with water being the only known drink with them in
those hot countries. Amongst the Jews, a lamb was to be
slain, a more chargeable and costly sacrament, not so easy
for the poor to procure : and therefore in the offering of
purification [m], the poor were dispensed with ; and, for a
lamb, offered a pair of pigeons. Christ now hath broken [n]
down that partition wall, that wall of enclosure which made
the church as a garden with hedges [o],—and made only the
rich, the people of the Jews, capable of God's covenants and
sacraments. Now that God's table hath crumbs as well as
flesh [p], the dogs and Gentiles eat of it too ; the poorest in
the world is admitted to it, even as the poorest that are to
shift for bread, though they are not able to provide flesh.
Then the church was a fountain sealed up [q] ; but, in Christ,
there was a fountain, opened for transgressions and for
sins [r].

Fourthly, *Bread and wine;* bread to strengthen, and wine to
comfort [s]. All temporal benefits are, in divine dialect, called
" bread [t]," it being the staff of life ; and the want of which,
though in a confluence of all other blessings, causeth famine
in a land [u]. See here the abundant sufficiency of Christ's
passion:—it is the universal food of the whole church, which
sanctifieth all other blessings ; without which they have no
relish nor comfort in them. Sin and the corrupt nature of
man hath a venomous quality in it to turn all other good
things into poison, unless corrected by this antidote, this
" bread of life [x]" that came down from Heaven. And well
may it be called a bread of life, inasmuch as in it resides a
power of trans-elementation; that whereas other nourish-
ments do themselves turn into the substance of the receiver,
—this, quite otherwise, transforms and assimilates the soul
unto the image of itself. Whatsoever faintness we are in,

[k] John xv. 11.   [l] Heb. vii. 15.   [m] Levit. xii. 8.   [n] Ephes. ii. 14.
[o] Cant. iv. 12.   [p] Matth. xv. 27.   [q] Cant. iv. 12.   [r] Zach. xiii. 1.
[s] Psalm civ. 19. Matth. xi. 6. Gen. xviii. 5, 8.   [t] Levit. xxvi. 26.   [u] Amos
viii. 11.   [x] John vi. Vita Christus, et vita panis.

if we hunger after Christ, he can refresh us: whatsoever
fears oppress us, if, like men oppressed with fear, we thirst
and gasp after his blood, it will comfort us: whatsoever
weakness either our sins or sufferings have brought us to,
the staff of this bread will support us : whatsoever sorrows
of mind, or coldness of affection do any way surprise us,—
this wine, or rather this blood (in which only is true life[y]),
will, with great efficacy, quicken us. If we want power,
we have the power of Christ's cross[z]; if victory[a], we have
the victory of his cross ; if triumph[b], we have the triumph
of his cross ; if peace[c], we have the peace of his cross; if
wisdom[d], we have the wisdom of his cross. Thus is Christ
crucified a treasure to his church, full of all sufficient provision both for necessity and delight.

Fifthly, *Bread and wine,* both of parts homogeneal, and
alike ; each part of bread, bread; each part of wine, wine ;
no crumb in the one, no drop in the other, differing from the
quality of the whole. O the admirable nature of Christ's
blood, to reduce the affections and the whole man to one
uniform and spiritual nature with itself! Insomuch, that
when we shall come to the perfect fruition of Christ's glorious body[e], our very bodies likewise shall be spiritual bodies; spiritual in a uniformity of glory, though not of
nature with the soul. Sins, commonly, are jarring and
contentious[f]: one affection struggles in the same soul with
another for mastery ; ambition fights with malice[g], and
pride with covetousness ; the head plots against the heart,
and the heart swells against the head; reason and appetite,
will and passion, soul and body, set the whole frame of nature in a continual combustion; like an unjointed or broken
arm, one faculty moves contrary to the government or attrac-
tion of another; and so as, in a confluence of contrary
streams and winds, the soul is whirled about in a maze of
intestine contentions. But when once we become conformable unto Christ's death[h], it presently makes of two one, and
so worketh peace[i]; it slayeth that hatred and war in the
members, and reduceth all unto that primitive harmony, unto

[y] Levit. xvii. 11.   [z] 1 Cor. i. 24.   [a] 1 Cor. xv.   [b] Col. ii. 15.
[c] Col. i. 20.   [d] 1 Cor. i. 24. Col. ii. 3.   [e] 1 Cor. xv.   [f] Scelera dissident.
Senec.   [g] James iv. 1.   [h] Phil. iii. 10.   [i] Ephes. ii. 15, 16.

that uniform spiritualness, which changeth us all into the
same image " from glory to glory r."

Sixthly, *Bread and wine*, as they are homogeneal, so are
they united together, and wrought out of divers particular
grains and grapes, into one whole lump or vessel s : and
therefore bread and blood, even amongst the heathen, were
used for emblems of leagues, friendship, and marriage, the
greatest of all unions.   See the wonderful efficacy of Christ
crucified to solder, as it were, and joint all his members
into one body by love, as they are united unto him by
faith.   They are built up as living stones t through him,
who is the chief corner-stone, elect and precious unto one
temple : they are all united by love, by the bond or sinews
of peace unto him who is the head u, and transfuseth through
them all the same vital nourishment : they are all the flock
of Christ x reduced unto one fold, by that one chief shepherd of their souls, who came to gather those that wan-
dered either from him in life, or from one another in affection.

Lastly, *Bread and wine* severed and asunder ; that to be
eaten, this to be drunken ; that, in a loaf,—this, in a cup.
It is not the blood of Christ running in his veins, but shed
on his members, that doth nourish his church.   Impious,
therefore, is their practice, who pour Christ's blood, as it
were, into his body again ; and shut up his wounds, when
they deny the cup unto the people, under pretence that
Christ's body by being received, the blood by way of concomitancy is received together with it ; and so seal up that precious fountain which he had opened, and make a monopoly
of Christ's sacred wounds ; as if his blood had been shed
only for the priest, and not as well for the people ; or as if
the church had power to withhold that from the people of
Jesus, which himself had given them.

---

r 2 Cor. iii. 18.   s Vid. *Cyprian.* l. 1. epist. 6.—Vid. *Gul. Stuck.* in Antiq.
Convival.   t 1 Pet. ii. 5, 6.   u Ephes. iv. 16. 1 Cor. xii.   x John x.
1 Pet. v. 4.

CHAPTER VIII.

Practical inferences from the materials of the Lord's Supper.

HERE then we see, First, Inasmuch as these elements are so necessary and beneficial to that life of man, with what appetite we should approach these holy mysteries, even with hungry and thirsty souls, longing for the sweetness of Christ crucified. Wheresoever God hath bestowed a vital being, he hath also afforded nourishment to sustain it, and an inclination and attractive faculty in the subject towards its nourishment. Even the new born-babe, by the impression of nature, is moved to use the breasts before he knows them. Now us which were dead in sins [y], hath Christ quickened, and hath infused into us a vital principle, even that faith by which the just do live [z]; which being instilled into us, Christ beginneth to be formed in the soul [a], and the whole man to be made conformable unto him [b]. Then are the parts organized and fitted for their several works ; there is an eye, with Stephen, to see Christ; an ear, with Mary, to hear him ; a mouth, with Peter, to confess him ; a hand, with Thomas, to touch him; an arm, with Simeon, to embrace him ; feet, with his disciples, to follow him ; a heart to entertain him, and bowels of affection to love him. All the members are ' weapons of righteousness [c];' and thus is the ' new man [d],' the ' new creature [e]' perfected. Now he that left not himself amongst the Heathen without a witness [f], but filled even their hearts with food and gladness,—hath not, certainly, left his own chosen without nourishment [g], such as may preserve them in that estate which he hath thus framed them unto. As therefore new infants are fed with the same nourishment and substance of which they consist ; so the same Christ, crucified, is as the cause and matter of our new birth, so the food which sustaineth and preserveth

[y] Ephes. ii. 1.   [z] Hab. ii. 4. Gal. ii. 20.   [a] Gal. iv. 19.   [b] Phil. iii. 10.
[c] Rom. vi. 19.   [d] Ephes. iv. 24.   [e] 2 Cor. v. 17.   [f] Acts xiv. 17.
[g] *Clem. Alex.* Præd. l. 1. 1. cap. 6.

us in it: unto whose body and blood there must needs be
as proportionable an appetite in a new Christian, as there is
unto milk in a new infant [h]; it being more nourishable than
milk, and faith more vital to desire it than nature. And all
this so much the rather, because he himself did begin unto
us in a more bitter cup. Did he, on his cross, drink gall
and vinegar for me, and that also made infinitely more bitter by my sins; and shall not I, at his table, drink wine for
myself, made infinitely sweeter with the blood which it conveys?   Did he drink a cup of bitterness and wrath [i], and
shall not I drink the cup of blessing [k]?   Did he eat the bread
of affliction, and shall not I eat the bread of life?   Did he
suffer his passion, and shall not I enjoy it?   Did he stretch
out his hands on the cross, and shall mine be withered and
shrunken towards his table?   Certainly, it is a presumption
that he is not only sick but desperate, who refuseth that nourishment, which is both food to strengthen, and physic to
recover him.

Secondly, The benefit of Christ being so obvious as the
commons, and so sufficient as the properties of these elements declare ; we see how little we should be dismayed
at any either inward weaknesses and bruises of mind, or
outward dangers and assaults of enemies, having so powerful
a remedy so near unto us ; how little we ought to trust in
any thing within ourselves, whose sufficiency and nourishment is from without.   There is no created substance in the
world, but receives perfection from some other things : how
much more must man, who hath lost his own native integrity, go out of himself to procure a better estate ! which in
vain he might have done for ever, had not God first (if I
may so speak) gone out of himself, humbling the divine
nature unto a personal union with the human.   And now
having such an Emmanuel as is with us, not only by assuming
us unto himself in his incarnation, but by communicating
himself to us in these sacred mysteries ; whatsoever weaknesses dismay us, his body is bread to strengthen us : whatsoever waves or tempests rise against us, his wounds are
holes to hide and shelter us.   What though sin be poison ;
have we not here the bread of Christ for an antidote ? What

h 1 Pet. ii. 2.   i Matth. xxvi. 39, xx. 23.   k 1 Cor. x. 16.

though it be red as scarlet; is not his blood of a deeper colour? What though the darts of Satan continually wound us; is not the issue of his wounds the balm for ours? Let me be fed all my days with bread of affliction and water of affliction, I have another bread, another cup to sweeten both. Let Satan tempt me to despair of life, I have, in these visible and common elements, the author of life, made the food of life unto me. Let who will persuade me to trust a little in my own righteousness, to spy out some gaspings and faint relics of life in myself;—I receive, in these signs, an all-sufficient Saviour ; and I will seek for nothing in myself, when I have so much in him.

Lastly, We see here, both from the example of Christ, who is the pattern of unity,—and from the Sacrament of Christ, which is the symbol of unity,—what a conspiracy of affections ought to be in us, both between our own and towards our fellow-members. Think not, that thou hast worthily received these holy mysteries, till thou find the image of that unity which is in them, conveyed by them into thy soul. As the breaking of the bread is the sacrament of Christ's passion ; so the aggregation of many grains into one mass, should be a sacrament of the church's unity. What is the reason, that the bread and the church should be both called in the Scripture by the same name ? The bread[1] is the *body* of Christ, and the church is the *body* of Christ too ! Is it not, because as the bread is one loaf out of divers corns, so the church is one body out of divers believers : that, the representative ; this, the mystical body of the same Christ ? Even as the Word, and the Spirit, and the faithful, are, in the Scripture, all called by the same name of *seed*[m],— because of that assimilating virtue, whereby the one, re- ceived[n], doth transform the other into the similitude and nature of itself. If the beams of the sun, though divided and distinct from one another, have yet a unity in the same nature of light, because all partake of one native and origi- nal splendour;—if the limbs of a tree[o], though all several, and spreading different ways, have yet a unity in the same

[1] 1 Cor. x. 17. xi. 24.   [m] Matth. xiii. 19. 1 John iii. 9. Matth. xiii. 28.
[n] Διὰ τὴν σύγκρασιν καὶ ἀναστοιχείωσιν. *Isid. Pelus. Cyprian.* de Unit. Eccles.
[o] Jam. iii. 13. Rom. xi. 16.

fruits, because all are incorporated into one stock or root ;—
if the streams of a river, though running divers ways, do yet
all agree in a unity of sweetness and clearness, because all
issuing from the same pure fountain ;—why then should not
the church of Christ, though of several and divided qualities
and conditions, agree in a unity of truth and love ?—Christ
being the sun whence they all receive light ; the vine [p], into
which they are all ingrafted ; and the fountain [q], that is
opened unto them all for transgressions and for sins.

CHAPTER IX.

*Of the analogy and proportion between the holy actions used
by Christ in this Sacrament, and Christ himself who is the
substance of it.*

It follows now, that we enquire farther into the nature of
this holy Sacrament, which will be explained by considering
the analogy, fitness, and similitude between the signs and
the things signified by them, and conferred or exhibited together with them, which is Christ the Lord.   Now this analogy or fitness, as it hath been, in some general manner, expressed in the nature or quality of the elements substantially
or physically taken,—so, more expressly and punctually, is
it proposed unto us in those holy actions, which do alter it
in the use, and make it a sacrament [r].

And first, We find that "Christ took the bread and wine [s],
and blessed it, and gave thanks, and so consecrated it," or
set it apart unto a holy or solemn use ; which is the reason
why St. Paul [t] calls it "a cup of blessing ;" so that unto the
church it ceaseth to be that which nature had made it, and
begins to be that unto which the blessing had consecrated.
In like manner, did the eternal Son of God [u] assume, into
the subsistence of his own infinite person, the whole nature
of man, the body and the soul ; by the virtue of which wonderful union, notwithstanding the properties of the divine

p John xv. 1.   q Zach. xiii. 1.   r *Cyprian.* de Cœn.*Tertul.* cont
Marc. lib. 1. c. 23.   s Matth. xxvi. 26. Luke xxii. 19.   t 1 Cor. x. 16.
u *Ambros.* lib. de iis qui initiantur. c. 9.   Et de Sacramentis, l. l. c. 5. et l. 4. c. 4.
Justin. Martyr. in Apolog. 2.

nature remain absolutely intransient and incommunicable unto the human; yet are there shed, from that inexhaustible fountain, many high and glorious endowments, by which the humanity under this manner of subsistence is anointed, consecrated, sealed, and set apart for that work of incomprehensible love and power, the redemption of the world.

And secondly, As the bread is taken by us from Christ in the nature of a gift,—he brake it and *gave* it to his disciples [x]; —so is the human nature taken by Christ from the Father [z] as a gift from that good pleasure of God.

Thirdly, As the taking of the bread by Christ did alter only the manner of its being, the operation and efficacy, the dignity and use, but no way at all the element or nature, of the bread; even so the taking of the human body by Christ, did confer, indeed, upon it many glorious virtues, and advance it to an estate far above its common and ordinary capacity (always yet reserving those defects and weaknesses, which were required in the economy and dispensation of that great work for which he assumed it); but yet he never altered the essential and natural qualities of the body, but kept it still within the measure and limits of the created perfection, which the wisdom of God did at first share out unto it.

Lastly (to come nearer unto the cross of Christ), As he did, by prayer and thanksgiving, consecrate these elements unto a holy use; so did he, immediately before his passion (of which this is the sacrament), make that consecratory prayer and thanksgiving [a], which is registered for the perpetual comfort of his church.

The second action is the 'breaking of the bread, and pouring the wine into the cup;' which doth nearly express his crucified body, where the joints were loosed [b], the sinews torn, the flesh bruised and pierced, the skin rent, the whole frame violated by that straining, and razing, and cutting, and stretching, and wrenching, which was used in the crucifying of it, and by the shedding of that precious blood [c] which stopped the issue and flux of ours. It were infinite and intricate to spin a meditation into a controversy, about

---

[x] Isai. lxi. 1. Luke iv. 18. Heb. i. 9. John vi. 33. Matth. xi. 27. xxviii. 18.
[z] Phil. ii. 9. John 5. 26.   [a] John xvii.   [b] Psal. xxii. 14.   [c] Sanguinis fluxum de fusâ venulâ revocamus. *Tertul.* cont. Gnost. c. 5.

the extent and nature of Christ's passion : but certainly, whatsoever either ignominy or agony his body suffered (which two I conceive to comprise all the generals of 'Christ crucified') are, if not particularly expressed, yet typically and sacramentally shadowed and exhibited in the bread broken, and the wine poured out.

The third action was the giving, or 'the delivering of the bread and wine :' which, First, evidently expresseth the nature and quality of 'Christ crucified,' with these benefits which flow from him, that they are freely bestowed upon the church ; which, of itself, had no interest or claim unto any thing save death.

Secondly, We see the nature of Christ's passion, that it was a free, voluntary, and unconstrained passion [d]. For though it be true, that Judas did betray him, and Pilate deliver him to be crucified, yet none of this was the giving of Christ, but the selling of him. It was not for us, but for money that Judas delivered him : it was not for us, but for fear, that Pilate delivered him. But God delivered the Son [e], and the Son delivered himself [f], with a most merciful and gracious will, to bestow his death upon sinners ; and not to get, but to be himself, a price. The passion, then, of Christ was most freely undertaken ; without which free-will of his own, they could never have laid hold on him. And his death was a most free and voluntary expiation : his life was not wrenched nor wrung from him, nor snatched or torn from him by the bare violence of any foreign impression ; but was, with a loud voice (arguing nature not brought to utter decay), most freely surrendered and laid down by that power, which did after re-assume it.

But how then comes it to pass, that there lay a necessity upon Christ of suffering [g], which necessity may seem to have enforced and constrained him to Golgotha, inasmuch as he himself did not only shrink, but even testify his dislike of what he was to suffer, by a redoubled prayer unto his Father, that "That cup might pass from him!" Doth not fear make

---

[d] *August.* Vid. tom. 8. in Psal. xciii. et tom. 9. Tract. 7. in Epist. Johannis.
[e] Rom. viii. 32. Acts ii. 23. Gal. iv. 4.   [f] Gal. ii. 20. Phil. ii. 7. John xix. 11.
x. 11, 17, 18.   [g] *August.* tom. 9. Tract. 31. in Johan. et Tract. 47. et de Trinitate, l. 3. cap. 13.—*Tertul.* in Apolog. cap. 21.—*Cyprian.* de Cœna Dom.—Non necessitate, sed obedientiâ, urgetur ad mortem: et lib. de Dupl. Martyr.

actions involuntary, or at least derogate and detract from the
fulness of their liberty? And Christ did fear: how then is
it that Christ's passion was most voluntary, though attended
with necessity, fear, and reluctance?—Surely, it was most
voluntary still; and first therefore necessary, because voluntary; the main and primitive reason of the necessity being
nothing else but that immutable will which had fore-decreed
it. Christ's death, then, was necessary by a necessity of the
event, which must needs come to pass, after it had once been
fore-determined by that most wise will of God [h];—which
never useth to repent him of his counsels; but not by a necessity of the cause, which was most free and voluntary.
Again; Necessary it was in regard of the Scriptures, whose
truth could not miscarry; in regard of the promises made of
him, which were to be performed; in regard of prophetical
predictions which were to be fulfilled; in regard of typical
prefigurations which were to be abrogated, and seconded
with that substance which they did fore-shadow: but no way
necessary in opposition to Christ's will, which was the first
mover, into which both this necessity and all the causes of it
are to be finally resolved.

And then for the fear and reluctance of Christ:—no marvel if he, who was in all things like unto us, had his share in
the same passions and affections likewise, though without
sin. But neither of these did any way derogate from the most
free sacrifice, which he himself offered once for all [i]; inasmuch as there was an absolute submission of the inferior to
the higher will; and the inferior itself shrunk not at the
obedience but at the pain.

To explain this more clearly, consider in Christ a double
will, or rather a double respect of the same will [k].

First, The natural will of Christ; whereby he could not
but wish well unto himself, and groan [l] after the conservation
of that Being, whose anguish and dissolution did now approach; whereby he could not, upon the immediate burden
of the sin of man, and the wrath of God, but fear; and,
notwithstanding the assistance of the angels, drop down a

[h] Heb. viii. 3. Mark viii. 31. Luke xxiv. 7. xxvi. 46. Matth. xxvi. 39. Heb. v. 7.
Acts ii. 23, 33. Heb. ix. 14.   [i] Heb. ix. 12.   [k] Vid. *Hooker* l. 5. sect.
48. and Dr. *Field* of the Church, lib. 1. c. 18.   [l] Heb. v. 7.

sweat, as full of wonder as it was of torment, great drops of
blood:—and then no marvel, if we hear, "Father, if it be
possible, let this cup pass from me [m]."

But then again consider, Not the natural, but the merciful will of Christ, by which he intended to appease the wrath
of an offended, and, by any other way, unsatisfiable God.
The removal of an unsupportable curse, the redemption of
his own, and yet his fellow-creatures; the giving them access
unto a Father, who was before a 'consuming fire ;'—in a word,
the finishing of that great work which the angels desire to
look into ; and then we find that he did freely lay down his
life, and most willingly embraced what he most naturally did
abhor.   As if Christ had said (if we may venture to para-
phrase his sacred words) " Father, thou hast united me to
such a nature, whose created and essential property it is to
shrink from any thing that may destroy it; and, therefore, if
it be thy will, let this cup pass from me:—but yet I know
that thou hast likewise anointed me to fulfil the eternal decree of thy love, and to the performance of such an office,
the dispensation whereof requires the dissolution of my assumed nature ; and therefore not as I, but as thou wilt." So
then both the desire of preservation was a natural desire ;
and the offering up of his body was a free-will offering.
And, indeed, the light of nature hath required a kind of
willingness, even in the heathen's brute sacrifices : and therefore the beast was led [n], and not haled to the altar; and the
struggling of it, or flying and breaking from the altar, or
bellowing and crying, was ever counted ominous and unhappy.   Now our Saviour Christ's willingness to offer up
himself is herein declared, "In that he opened not his
mouth :" in that he suffered such a death, wherein he first
did bear the cross [o], before it bore him ; in that he dehorted
the women that followed after him, to weep or express any
passion or unwillingness for his death [p].

Thus did he, in his passion, and still doth in his Sacrament,
really, perfectly, and most willingly, give himself unto his
church : insomuch, as that the oil of that unction which
consecrated him unto that bitter work, is called an 'oil of

[m] Luke xxii. 43, 44.   [n] *Macrob.* Satur. lib. 3. c. 5.—*Pliny*, l. 8. c. 45.—
Suet. in Galb. c. 19.—*Val. Max.* l. 1. c. 6.—*Plut.* Symp. l. 8. c. 8.   [o] John
xix. 17.   [p] Luke xxiii. 28.

gladness[q].' So then Christ freely offereth, both in himself originally, and in his sacraments instrumentally, all grace sufficient for nourishment unto life, to as many as reach forth to receive or entertain it.

CHAPTER X.

Of the fourth action, with the reasons why the Sacrament is to be eaten and drunken.

THE fourth and last action, made mention of in this sacrament, is the 'eating of the bread,' and the 'drinking of wine,' after we have taken them from the hands of Christ: to signify unto us, That Christ crucified is the life and food of a Christian that receiveth him. Here are the degress of faith :—

First, We take Christ ; and then we eat him. There are none that find any nourishment or relish in the blood of Christ, but those who have received him, and so have an interest, propriety, and title to him. He must first be ours, before we can taste any sweetness in him: ours, first, in possession and claim ; and, after, ours, in fruition and comfort. For all manner of sweetness is a consequent and effect of some propriety, which we have unto the good thing which causeth it ; unto which the nearer our interest is, the greater is the sweetness that we find in it. In natural things we may observe, how nothing will be kindly nourished in any other place or means, than those unto which nature hath given it a primitive right and sympathy. Fishes perish in the air ; and spice-trees die and wither in these colder countries, because nature hath denied them any claim or propriety unto such places. We are all branches[r], and Christ is a vine : now no branch receiveth juice or nourishment, unless first it be inserted into the stock. If we are not first ingrafted into Christ, and so receive the right of branches, we cannot expect any nourishment from him. As the name that was written in that 'white stone[s],' was known unto him only that had it ; so in these mysteries, which have the impress and

[q] Heb. i. 9. [r] John xv. [s] Revel. ii.

character of Christ's passion on them, Christ is known and
enjoyed only by those, who first take him, and so have a
hold and right unto him.   But why is it that Christ, in this
sacrament, should be eaten and drunken ? Cannot the benefit
of his passion be as well conveyed by the eye as by the
mouth ? It was the joy of Abraham [t], that he saw Christ's
day ; the comfort of Simeon [u], that he had seen God's salvation ; the support of Stephen [x], that he saw Christ in his
kingdom ; the faith of Thomas [y], that he saw his resurrection :
and why is it not enough that we see the passion of Christ
in this sacrament, wherein he is crucified before our eyes [z] ?
Certainly if we look into the Scriptures, we shall find nothing
more common than the analogy and resemblance betwixt
spiritual grace and natural food.   Hence it is that we so often
read of manna from Heaven [a], water from the rock [b], trees in
paradise, apples [c] and flaggons for Christ's spouse, wisdom's
feasts [d], and the marriage-feast [e], of hungering [f] and thirsting [g],
and sucking [h] of marrow, and fatness, and milk [i], and honey,
and infinite the like expressions of Divine grace.   The reasons whereof are many and important : First, To signify the
benefit we receive by Christ crucified, exhibited unto us, in
his Last Supper, by that analogy and similitude, which is betwixt him and those things we eat and drink.   Now meats
are all either physical, common, or costly ; either for the
restoring, or for the supporting, or for the delighting of nature : and they have all some of those excellent properties
of good which Aristotle [k] hath observed, either to preserve
nature entire, or to restore it when it hath been violated, or
to prevent diseases ere they creep upon it.   And all these
benefits, do the faithful receive by Christ.

1st. His body and blood is an antidote against all infections
of sin, or fear of death.   When he said, " Fear not, it is I [l],"
it was an argument of comfort, which no temptation could
repel.

2d. It hath a purging and purifying property : " The blood
of Christ cleanseth us from all sin [m]."

t John viii. 56.   u Luke ii. 30.   x Acts vii. 55·   y John xx. 29.   z Gal. iii. 1.
a See John vi.   b 1 Cor. x. 3, 4.   c Cant. ii. 5.   d Prov. ix. 2, 5.
e Matth. xxii. 4.   f Matth. v.   g Psalm lxiii. 1. cxix. 103. xlii. 1, 2·
cxix. 131.   h Isai. lxvi. 11.   i Isai. lv. 1, 2. 1 Pet. ii. 2. Heb. v. 12. See
Jackson of Justifying Faith, sect. 1. cap. 9.   k Φυλακτικὸν, Θεραπευτικὸν,
κωλυτικὸν τῶν ἐναντίων. Rhet. l. 1. et *Eth.*   l Matth. xiv. 27.   m 1 John xvii.

3d. It hath a quickening, preserving, and strengthening power. Christ is our life[n]; and our life is hid with Christ[o]; and Christ liveth in us; and he hath quickened us[p] together with Christ; and we are able to do all things through Christ that strengthens us[q].

And lastly, It hath a joying and delighting property: "I rejoice in nothing but in the cross of Christ: I count all things dung[r], that I may win Christ;" and "I protest by our rejoicing which we have in Christ.[s]" Whether we want physic to cure us, or strong meats to nourish us, or sweet-meats to delight us, "Christ is unto us all in all," our health, our strength, our joy.

Secondly, The Sacrament is eaten and drunken; to signify the necessity we stand in of Christ crucified. Many things there are usual in the life of man, both for delight and profit; beautiful and pleasant objects, for the eye; melody and harmony, for the ear; ointments and odours, for the smell; curiosities and luxuriances of invention, for the fancy: but there is no faculty of nature that doth so immediately concur to the support and preservation of the whole man, as the sense of tasting[t], which is (as it were) the sluice and inlet to life; without which, we have not so much as a capacity of that delight, which other objects of an inferior and subordinate nature can afford. Even so many things there are, wherein the children of God may and ought to take pleasure and solace, even as many as we acknowledge from God for a blessing. But there is nothing in the world, which is the object and principle of our life, but only Christ; no quality in man, which is the instrument and organ of our life, but only a lively and operative faith[u], by which only we taste "how gracious the Lord is."—"The just shall live by faith[x];" and "I live by the faith of the Son of God[y];" and "Where the body is, thither do the eagles fly," that they may eat and live.

Thirdly, The Sacrament is eaten and drunken, to show unto us the greedy desire which is, and ought to be, in the hearts of believers towards Christ crucified. There is no one fa-

[n] Phil. i. 21.   [o] Col. iii. 3, 4.   [p] Eph. ii. 5.   [q] Phil. iv. 13. Gal. vi. 14.
[r] Phil. iii. 8.   [s] Phil. iv. 4. 1 Cor. xv. 31.   [t] Eccles. ii. 24, iii. 12, 22,
v. 17.   [u] Crede et manducasti. *Aug.* in Johan.   [x] Hab. ii.   [y] Gal.
ii. 20.   Vide *Chrysost.* in 1 Cor. Hom. 24.

culty in man's will so much put to its utmost for procuring
satisfaction, as this of tasting, if once brought into anguish
or straits. Because, as death, in the general, is most terrible[z], so much more that lingering death which consumes
with famine : and therefore no power of nature more importunate and clamorous for satisfaction, no motive stronger
to work a love, and attempt a conquest on any nation, than
an experience of such excellent commodities, as may from
thence be obtained for the relieving of this one faculty.
And therefore Almighty God, when he would provoke the
people to forsake Egypt, and comfort them with the news of
a better country, describes it by the plenty that it brought
forth: " I will bring you to a land which floweth with milk
and honey[a]." And when the people murmured against God
in the wilderness ; all that hatred of Egypt, which the tyranny of the land had wrought in them,—all the toil and
servitude that was redoubled on them,—was wholly swallowed up by the one consideration of flesh-pots and onions[b],
which they there enjoyed. And when, by God's appoint-
ment, spies were sent into Canaan, to enquire of the goodness of the land,—their commission was to bring of the fruit
of the land unto the people[c]; that thereby they might be
encouraged unto a desire of it. And we find, how the Roman emperors did strictly prohibit the transportation of
wine or oil, or other pleasant commodities unto barbarous
nations, lest they might prove rather temptations to some
mischievous design, than matters of mutual intercourse and
traffic. No marvel then, if the sacrament of Christ crucified, who was to be the desire of all nations, the desire of
whom was not only to transcend and surpass, but even (after
a sort) to nullify all other desires[d],—be received with that
faculty which is the seat of the most eager and importunate
desire.

Fourthly, We eat and drink the Sacrament, to intimate
unto us the conformity of the faithful unto Christ. As, in
all the appetites and propensions of natural things, we find
an innate amity betwixt the natures that do so incline to-

[z] Πάντων φοβερώτατον. *Arist.* Πάντες μὲν στυγεροὶ Θάνατοι δειλοῖσι βροτοῖσι,
Λιμῷ δ' οἴκτιστον Θανέειν καὶ πότμον ἐπισπεῖν. *Hom.* Odyss. lib. 12. and l. 17.
[a] Exod. iii. 17.   [b] Exod. xvi. 3.   Num. xi. 5.   [c] Num. xiii. 21, 24.
[d] Matth. xiii. 44, 45. Luke xviii. 28. Phil. iii. 7, 8.

wards, or embrace one another; so, principally, in this main appetite unto food, is there ever found a proportion between nature and its nourishment[e]; insomuch, that young infants are nourished with that very matter, of which their substance consisteth.   Whatsoever hath repugnant qualities unto Nature, she is altogether impatient of it; and is never quieted, till, one way or other, she disburden herself.   And thus is it, and ought to be, betwixt Christ and the faithful: there is a conspiracy of affections, motions, passions, desires; a conformity of being in holiness, as well as in nature; a similitude, participation, and communion with Christ in his death[f], sufferings[g], glory[h].   All other things in the world are very unsuitable to the desires of faith, nor are able to satiate a soul which hath tasted Christ; because we find something in them of a different, yea, repugnant nature, unto that precious faith by him infused.   No man, having tasted old wine, desireth new, for he saith the old is better[i]: and therefore howsoever the wicked may drink iniquity like water[k], and roll it under their tongue as a sweet thing; yet the children of God, who have been sensible of that venomous quality which lurketh in it, and have tasted of that bread[l] which came down from Heaven, never thirst any more after the deceitful pleasures, the stolen waters of sin: but no sooner have they unadvisedly tasted of it, but presently they feel a war in their bowels, a struggling and rebellion between that faith by which they live, and that poison which would smother and extinguish it, which, by the efficacy of faith, whereby we overcome the world[m], is cast out and vomited up in a humble confession, and so the faithful do regain their fellowship with Christ; who as he was, by his merits, our Saviour unto remission of sins,—so is he, by his holiness, our example[n]; and, by his Spirit, our head, unto newness of life.

[e] *Clem. Alex.* Pædag. l. 1. c. 6.   [f] Rom. vi. 4, 5.   [g] Rom. viii. 17.
[h] 1 Cor. xv. 49.   2 Cor. iii. 18.   Phil. iii. 10, 20.   [i] Luke v. 39.
[k] Job xx. 12.   [l] John vi. 48, 50, 51. iv. 14.   [m] 1 John v. 1.   [n] 1 Pet. i. 15. ii. 21.

CHAPTER XI.

*Of other reasons why the Sacrament is eaten and drunken, and
of the manner of our union and incorporation into Christ.*

FIFTHLY, We eat and drink the sacrament of Christ crucified, to signify that real and near incorporation of the
faithful into Christ their head [o] : for the end of eating [p] is the
assimilation of our nourishment, and the turning of it into
our own nature and substance : whatsoever cannot be assimilated, is ejected : and thus is it between us and Christ.
Whence it cometh that we so often read of the inhabitation
of Christ in his church [q] ; of his more peculiar presence with,
and in, his people ; of our spiritual ingrafture into him by
faith [r] ; of those more near and approaching relations of
brotherhood [s] and coinheritance between Christ and us ; that
mutual interest, fellowship, and society, which we have to
each other ; with infinite other expressions of that divine
and expressless mixture, whereby the faithful are, not only
by a consociation of affections [t] and confederacy of wills,
but by a real, though mystical, union, ingrafted, knit, and
(as it were) jointed unto Christ by the sinew of faith ; and
so made heirs of all that glory and good, which in his person was purchased for his members, and is from him diffused
on them, as on the parts and portions of himself. So that
it pleaseth God's spirit (as some do observe) so far sometimes to express this union betwixt Christ and his church,
as to call the church itself by the name of Christ ; and every
where almost to interest himself in the injuries and sufferings of his church [u], yea, to esteem himself incomplete and
maimed without it.

 And here this mystical unity between Christ and his
church being, by eating and drinking, so expressly signified,

---

 [o] Eph. iii. 17. [p] Rev. iii. 20. [q] Ephes. iv. 6. [r] Gal. ii. 20.
John xiv. 20. Rom. xi. 17. John xv. and xx. 17. [s] Matth. xxv. 40.
Mark iii. 35. Rom. viii. 17. [t] Affectus consociat et confederat voluntates.
Cyprian. de Cœna Dom.—*August.* de Peccat. Merit. et Remiss. lib. 1. c. 31. de
Genesi ad lit. l. ii. c. 24.—*Beza* in annotat. ad Ephes. i. 23.—*Hooker,* p. 306.
[u] Matth. xxv. 45. Acts ix. 4. *Hooker* l. 5. sect. 56.

and in the Sacrament so graciously obsignated unto us,—it will not be impertinent to enlarge somewhat on so divine a point. Wheresoever any thing hath so inward a relation and dependency on something else, as that it subsisteth not, nor can retain that integrity of being which is due unto it, without that whereon it dependeth,—there is necessarily required some manner of union between those two things ; by means whereof, the one may derive unto the other that influence and virtue whereby it is preserved : for broken, discontinued, and ununited parts receive no succour from those, from which they are divided ; all manner of activity requiring a contact and immediateness between the agent and the subject. And this is one proof of that omnipresence and immensity which we attribute unto God, whereby he filleth all creatures [x], bestowing on them all that general influence and assistance of his providence, " whereby they live, and move, and have their being [y]."

But besides this universal presence of God, wherewith he doth equally fill all things by his essence, which were from eternity wrapped up in his power and wisdom ; there is a more special presence and union of his unto the creature ; according as he doth, in any of them, exhibit more express characters of his glorious attributes. In which sense, he is said to be in Heaven [z], because he doth there more especially manifest his power, wisdom, and majesty : in the soft and still voice, because there his lenity was more conspicuous: in the burning bush [a], and in the light cloud, because in them his mercy was more expressed : in the Mount Sinai, because there his terror was especially declared. According unto which different diffusions of himself on the creature, and dispensation of his attributes, God (without any impeachment of his immensity) may be said to be absent, to depart, and to turn away from his creature, as the words are every where in the Scriptures used [b].

Thus is God united to the creature in general, by the

---

[x] Deum namque ire per omnes Terrasque tractusque maris cœlumque profundum. *Virg.*—Vid. *Hugo. Vict.* de Sacrament. l. 1. part. 3. c. 17.   Psal. cxxxviii. Isai. vi.   Amos ix. 1, 3.   Jer. xxiii. 24.   [y] Acts xvii. 28.   Vid. *August.* de Genesi ad lit. lib. 4. cap. 12. & Confess. l. 1. c. 2, 3.   [z] Psal. ciii. 19.   Matth. vi. 9. [a] Exod. iii. xix. 18.   [b] Vide *Tertul.* Adver. Praxeam, c. 23. et *August.* ep. 3. ad Volus.

right of a creator [c], upholding all things by his mighty Word
without the participation whereof they could not but be an-
nihilated and resolved into their first nothing : but besides,
there is a more distinct and nobler kind of union unto his
more excellent creature, man.   For as there are some things
which partake only of the virtue and efficacy, others which
partake of the image and nature, of the sun ; as the bowels
of the earth receive only the virtue, heat, and influence,—but
the beam receives the very image and form of it, light ;—so
in the creatures, some partake of God only as an agent, as
depending on his eternal power, from whence they did originally issue, and by which they do now still subsist ; and
so receive only some common impressions and foot-prints of
Divine virtue, whereby they declare his glory [d] :   Others partake of the image of God [e], of " the Divine nature," as St.
Peter speaks [f] ; and receive from him those two special properties wherein principally consists the image of God, holiness and happiness, *that* giving perfection to our working,
and *this* to our being (which two satisfy the whole compass
of a created desire), and so declare his love.   Some acknowledge God as their maker, others as their Father : in *them*, is
dependence and gubernation only ; in *these*, is recognition
and inheritance.
    The bond of this more special union of the reasonable
creature unto God, was originally the law of man's creation,
which did prescribe unto him the form and limits of his
working, and subordination unto God ; which knot he, by
his voluntary aversation, violating and untying, there did immediately ensue a disunion between God and man.   So says
the prophet [g] ; " Your sins have separated between you and
your God."   Now as the parts of a body, so long as they
are, by the natural bonds of joints and sinews, united to
the whole, do receive from the fountains of life, the heart
and the brain, all comfortable supplies for life and motion,
which are due unto them; but being once dissolved and broken off, there then ceaseth all the interest which they had
in the principal parts ;—so, as long as man, by obedience
to the law, did preserve the union between God and him
entire, so long had he an evident participation of all those

[c] Heb. i. 3.   [d] Psalm xix. 1.   [e] Ephes. iv. 24.   [f] 2 Pet. i. 4.   [g] Isai. lix. 2.

graces spiritual, which were requisite to the holiness and happiness of so noble a creature : but having once transgressed the law, and by that means broken the knot, he is no more possessed of that sweet illapse and influence of the Spirit, which quickeneth the church unto eternal life : but having united himself unto another head, and subjected his parts unto another prince, even the prince that " ruleth in the children of disobedience [h]," he is utterly destitute of all divine communion, an ' alien from the commonwealth [i],' and, by consequence, from all the privileges of Israel ; a stranger from the ' covenant of promise,' unacquainted with, yea, unable to conceive aright of spiritual things [k] ; quite shut out from the kingdom, yea, " without God in the world."

And thus far we have considered the several unions, which are between the creatures, either in general, as creatures,— or in particular, as reasonable,—and considered God in the relation of a Creator ;—which will give great light to understand both the manner and dignity of this mystical and evangelical union betwixt the church and Christ, considered under the relation of a Redeemer, by whom we have reunion and access to the Father [l] ; in whom only he hath accepted us again, and given unto us the adoption of children. Now as, in the union of God to the creatures, we have before observed the differences of it, that it was either general unto all, or special unto some ; in which he did either more expressly manifest his glory, or more graciously imprint his image ;— so also, in the union of Christ unto us, we may observe something general, whereby he is united to the whole mankind ; and something special, whereby he is united unto his church ; and that after a double manner ; either common unto the whole visible assembly of the Christians, or peculiar and proper unto that invisible company, who are the immediate members of his mystical body.

First, Then, all mankind may be said to be in Christ, inasmuch as, in the mystery of his incarnation [m], he took on him the self-same nature, which maketh us to be men ;

[h] Ephes. ii. 2.　　[i] Ephes. ii. 12.　　[k] 1 Cor. ii. 14.　　[l] Rev. xxii. 14. Ephes. ii. 13, 18. i. 5, 6.　　[m] Unius naturæ sunt vites et palmites ; propter quod cum esset Deus, cujus naturæ non sumus, factus est homo, ut in illo esset vitis humana natura ; cujus et nos omnes palmites essemus. *Aug.* Tract. 80. Joh.

and whereby he is as properly man as any of us, subject to the same infirmities [n], liable and naked to the same dangers and temptations, moved by the same passions, obedient to the same laws with us ;—with this only difference, that all this was in him sinless and voluntary,—in us, sinful and necessary.

Secondly, Besides this, there is a farther union of Christ unto all the professors of his truth, in knowledge and explicit faith ; which is, by a farther operation, infusing into them the light of truth, and some general graces which make them serviceable for his church : even as the root of a tree will sometimes so far enliven the branches, as shall suffice unto the bringing forth of leaves, though it supply not juice enough for solid fruit.   For whatsoever graces the outward professors of Christianity do receive, they have it all derived on them from Christ, who is the dispenser of his Father's bounty, and who enlighteneth every man that cometh into the world.

Thirdly, There is a more special and near union of Christ to the faithful, set forth by the resemblances of " building [o], ingrafture, members [p], marriage [q]," and other the like similitudes in the Scriptures,—whereby Christ is made unto us the original and well-spring [r] of all spiritual life [s] and motion, of all fulness [t] and fructification [u].   Even as, in natural generation, the soul is no sooner infused and united, but presently there is sense and vegetation derived on the body ;—so in the spiritual new birth, as soon as " Christ is formed in us," as the apostle speaks [x], then presently are we ' quickened by him [y],' and all the operations of a spiritual life [z], sense of sin, vegetation, and growth in faith, understanding, and knowledge of the mystery of godliness, taste and relish of eternal life, begin to show themselves in us: we are in Christ by grace, even as, by nature, we were in Adam. Now as, from Adam, there is a perpetual transfusion of

---

[n] Esuriens sub diabolo, sitiens sub Samaritide, flens Làzarum, anxius usque ad mortem. *Tert.* de Carn. Christi, c. 9. et advers. Prax. c. 27.   [o] 1 Pet. ii. 4. Eph. ii. 15. 1 Cor. iii. 16. John xv. 5. Eph. iv. 15, 16.   [p] 1 Cor. xii. 12. [q] Eph. v. 32. Psalm xlv. 2 Cor. xi. 2.   [r] John iv. 14. vi. 51.   [s] John xiv. 19. 1 John v. 12.   [t] John i. 16.   [u] John xv. 5.   [x] Gal. iv. 19. [y] Eph. ii. 5.   [z] Gal. ii. 20. Rom. v. 12, 15, 17, 18, 19. 1 Cor. xv. 22, 45, 49.

original sin on all his posterity [a], because we were all then
not only represented by his person, but contained in his
loins ; so from Christ, who, on the cross, did represent the
church of God, and in whom we are,—is there, by a most
special influence, transfused on the church, some measure
of those graces [b], those vital motions, that incorruption, purity, and holiness, which was given to him without measure ;
that he alone might be the author [c] and original of eternal
salvation, the consecrated Prince of Glory to the church :—
from which consecration of Christ, and sanctification of the
church, the apostle infers a union between Christ and the
church ; " For he that sanctifieth, and they that are sanctified, are of one [d]." And all this, both union or association
with Christ, and communion in those heavenly graces, which,
by spiritual influence from him, are shed forth upon all his
members, is brought to pass by this means originally,—because Christ and we do both partake of one and the self-
same Spirit [e] ; which Spirit conveys to the faithful, whatsoever in Christ is communicable unto them. For as the members natural of man are all conserved in the integrity and
unity of one body, by that reasonable soul which animates,
enlivens, and actuates them,—by one simple and undivided
information, without which they would presently fall asunder
and moulder into dust ; even so the members of Christ are
all firmly united unto him, and from him receive all vital
motions, by means of that common Spirit, which, in Christ
above measure, in us according unto the dispensation of
God's good will, worketh one and the self-same life and
grace : so that by it, we are all as really compacted into one
mystical body, as if we had all but one common soul. And
this is that which we believe touching our " fellowship with
the Son," as St. John [f] calls it : the clear and ample apprehension whereof, is left unto that place where both our
union and likeness to him, and our knowledge of him, shall
be made perfect [g].

[a] *August.* Enchirid. cap. 26. et Epist. 23. ad Bonifacium : " Traxit reatum,
quia unus erat in illo à quo traxit ;" et *Tert.* de Testim. Anim. c. 3. Regene-
ravit hominem in uno Christo, ex uno Adam generatum. *Aug.* Epist. 23.
[b] John i. 16.   [c] Heb. v. 9.   [d] Heb. ii. 10, 11.   [e] Rom. viii. 9.
[f] 1 John i. 3.   [g] Nam et nunc est in nobis, et nos in illo ; sed hoc nunc
credimus, tunc etiam cognoscemus : quamvis et nunc credendo noverimus, sed
tunc contemplando noscemus. *August.* Tom. 9. Tract. 75. in Johan.

Sixthly, We eat and drink the Sacrament of Christ's passion, that thereby we may express that more close and sensible pleasure, which the faithful enjoy in receiving of him.
For there is not any one sense, whose pleasure is more constant and express, than this of tasting: the reasons whereof
are manifest.

For first, It follows by the consequence of opposites, that
that faculty when fully satisfied, must needs be sensible of
the greatest pleasure, whose penury and defect brings the
extremest anguish on nature. For the evil of any thing,
being nothing else but an obliquity and aberration from that
proper good to which it is opposed,—it must needs follow,
that the greater the extent and degrees of an evil are, the
more large must the measure of that good be, in the distance
from which that evil consisteth. Now it is manifest that
the evil of no sense is so oppressive and terrible unto nature,
as are those which violate the taste and touch [h]; which latter
is ever annexed to the former. No ugly spectacles for the
eyes, no howls or shriekings for the ear, no stench or infection of air for the smell, so distasteful,—through all
which, the anguish of famine would not make a man adventure to purchase any good, though affected even with
noisome qualities.

Secondly, The pleasure which nature takes in any good
thing, is caused by the union thereof to the faculty, by means
whereof it is enjoyed : so that the greater the union is, the
more necessarily is the pleasure of the thing united. Now
there is not any faculty, whose object is more closely united
unto it, than this of tasting. In seeing, or hearing, or smell-
ing, there may be a far distance between us and the things
that do so affect us ; but no tasting without an immediate
application of the object to the faculty. Other objects satisfy, though without me; but meats never content nor
benefit, till they be taken in. Even so is it with Christ and
the faithful: many things there are, which affect them with
pleasure, but they are without, and at a distance; only
Christ it is, who, by being and dwelling in them [i], delighteth them.

[h] Moriensque recepit Quas nollet victurus, aquas, &c. Vid. *Lucan.* lib. 4.
[i] 'Εν ὑμῖν. Gal. iv. 19.—'Εν ταῖς καρδίαις ὑμῶν. Eph. iii. 17.

Lastly, We eat and drink the Sacrament of Christ crucified, that therein we may learn to admire the wisdom of
God's mercy, who, by the same manner of actions [k], doth
restore us to life, by which we fell from it. Satan and death
did first assault our ear, and then took possession of us by
the mouth : Christ and faith chose no other gates, to make
a re-entry and dispossess them.

Thus as skilful physicians [l] do often cure a body by the
same means which did first distemper it, quench heats with
heat, and stop one flux of blood by opening another; so
Christ [m], that he may quell Satan at his own weapons, doth,
by the same instruments and actions, restore us unto our
primitive estate, by which he had hurried us down from it :
that those mouths, which were at first open to let in death,
may now much more be open, not only to receive, but to
praise him, who is made unto us the author and Prince of
life.

CHAPTER XII.

Inferences of practice from the consideration of the former actions.

THESE are all the holy actions we find to have been, by
Christ and his apostles, celebrated in the great mystery of
this Supper. All other human accessions and superstructions, that are by the policy of Satan, and that carnal affection, which ever laboureth to reduce God's service unto an
outward and pompous gaudiness, foisted into the substance
of so divine a work, are, all of them, that ' straw and stubble [n],' which he who is ' a consuming fire [o],' will at last
purge away. Impotent Christ was not, that he could not,—
nor malignant, that he would not,—appoint,—nor improvi-
dent, that he could not foresee,—the needfulness of such
actions ; which are by some proposed, not as matter of ornament, comeliness, and ceremony, but are obtruded on consciences, swayed with superstitious pompousness, for matters

k *Tertul.* cont. Gnost. c. 5.　　l *Arist.* Probl. sect. 1. quæst. 45. et sect.
3. quæst. 26.　　m Vid. *August.* de Doctrina Christiana, lib. 1. c. 14.　　n 1 Cor.
iii. 12.　　o Heb. xii. 29.

substantial and necessary to be observed. As if God, who,
in the first creation of the world from nothing, did, immediately after the work produced, cease from all manner of further creations,—did, in the second creation of the world
from sin, not finish the work himself, but leave it imperfect,
to be by another consummated and finished. Certainly,
whatsoever human inventions do claim, direct, proper, and
immediate subscription of conscience, and do propose themselves as essential, or integral, or any way necessary parts
of Divine mysteries ; they do not only rob God of his honour,
and intrude on his sovereignty, but they do farther lay on
him the aspersion of an imperfect Saviour, who standeth in
need of the church's concurrence, to consummate the work
which he had begun. Away then with those actions of ele-
vation, adoration, oblation, circumgestation, mimical gestures, silent whisperings[p], and other the like encroachments,
in the supposed proper and real sacrifice of Christ in the
mass ; wherein I see not, how they avoid the guilt of St.
Paul's fearful observation, "To crucify again the Lord of
glory, and put him unto an open shame." In which things,
as in sundry others, they do nothing else but imitate the
carnal ordinances of the Jews, and the heathenish will-worship of the Ethnicks ; who thought rather by the motions of
their bodies, than by the affections of their hearts, to wind
into the opinion and good liking of their gods.

Certainly, affectation of pomp, ceremony, and such other
human superstructions on the Divine institution, which are
not used for order, with decency and paucity, but imposed
as yokes upon the consciences of the people, by an arro-
gated power of the church, to bind the conscience by them ;
—I say, all other pompous accumulations unto the substance of Christ's Sacraments, are, by Tertullian[q], made the
characters and presumptions of an idolatrous service. True
it is indeed, that the ancients make mention, out of that
fervour of love and piety towards so sacred mysteries, of
adoration at them[r], and of carrying the remainders[s] of them

<hr/>

p Dr. *Reynolds'* conference with Hart, c. 8. divis. 4.—Et *Mornay* de Eucharist.
p. 82. in fol.   q Mentior, si non Idolorum solemma de suggestu, et apparatu,
deque sumptu fidem et auctoritatem sibi exstruunt. *Tert.* de Bapt. cap. 2.
r Carnem Christi in mysteriis adoramus. *Ambros.* de Spirit. Sancto, l. 3. c. 12.—
Manducant et adorant. *Aug.* ep. 120. c. 27.   s 'Η διάδοσις καὶ ἡ μετάληψις

unto the absent Christians. But, as in other things, so here likewise, we find it most true, That things, by devout men begun piously, and continued with zeal, do after, when they light in the handling of men otherwise qualified, degenerate into superstition,—the form, purpose, end, and reason of their observation being utterly neglected : it being the contrivance of Satan to raise his temple after the same form, and with the same materials whereof God's consisteth,—to pretend the practice of the saints, for the enforcements of his own projects,—to transform himself into an angel of light[t], that he may the easier mislead unstable and wandering souls,—and to retain at least ' a form of godliness[u],' that he may, with less clamour and reluctancy, withdraw the substance. And as, in many other things, so hath he herein likewise abused the piety of the best men, unto the furtherance of his own ends. That adoration, which they in and at the mysteries did exhibit unto Christ himself (as indeed they could not choose a better time to worship him in), he impiously derives upon the creature; and makes it now to be done, not so much at, as unto, the elements; making them as well the term and object[x], as occasion of that worship, which is due only to the Lord of the Sacrament[y]. That carrying about, and reserving of the eucharist, which the primitive Christians [z] used for the benefit of those, who, either by sickness or by persecutions, were withheld from the meetings of the Christians (as in those days many were), is by him now turned into an idolatrous circumgestation; that, at the sight of the bread, the people might direct unto it that worship, which is due only to the person whose passion it representeth, but whose honour it neither challengeth nor knoweth. And certainly, if we view the whole fabric either of gentilism or heresy, we shall observe the methods and contrivances of Satan[a], most often to drive at this point,—That, either under pretence of Divine truth, or under imitation of Divine institutions, retain-

τοῖς οὐ παροῦσιν διὰ τῶν διακόνων πέμπεται. *Justin. Mart.* Apolog. 2. pro Christianis.　　t 2 Cor. xi. 14.　　u 2 Tim. iii. 5.　　x *Justin. Mart.* ut supra scriptum est.　　y Matth. iv. 10.　　z Vid. *Tert.* de Coron. Milit. c. 15. et de Baptis. c. 5. et de Præscript. cap. 40. cont. Praxeum, c. 1. et de Specta. cap. 27. et Apolog. 47. et *Johan. Stuck.* de Antiq. Convival. l. 1. c. 33. et l. 3. c. 21. a Πανουργία, 2 Cor. xi. 3.　μεθοδεῖαι, Ephes. vi. 11.　βάθη, Rev. ii. 24.　νοήματα, 2 Cor. ii.

ing the same material actions which God requires, or which
the godly have piously, or upon temporary reasons observed,
—he may convey into the hearts of men his own poison, and
imprint an opinion of holiness towards his own devices.
For howsoever his power and tyranny have done much mischief to God's church ; yet his masterpiece is that cunning
and deceit which the Scripture so often takes notice of.

Secondly, We see here what manner of men we ought to
be in imitation of these blessed actions, that we may be conformable unto the death of Christ [b].

First, As he, when he took these elements, did consecrate
them unto a holy use ; so we, when we receive them, should
first consecrate ourselves with thanksgiving [c] and prayer [d]
unto a holy life. For if, not only amongst Christians, but
even amongst heathens [e] themselves, it hath been, by the
law of nature, received for a religious custom, not to eat their
ordinary food without blessing and prayer ; with how much
more fervency of prayer should we call upon the name of the
Lord, when we take this ' cup of salvation,' this ' bread of
life,' wherein we do not only ' taste how gracious the Lord
is,' but do ' eat and drink the Lord himself !' And, therefore, the church hath, both at first and since, most devoutly
imitated our blessed Saviour in consecrating both these mysteries and their own souls, by thanksgiving and prayer, before ever they received the elements from the hands of the
deacons ; that so that same pure wine, that immaculate
blood, might be put into pure and untainted vessels [f], even
into sanctified and holy hearts,—lest otherwise the wine
should be spilt, and the vessels perish. And indeed the Sacrament is ignorantly and fruitlessly received, if we do not
therein devote, consecrate, and set apart ourselves unto God's
service. For what is a Sacrament but a visible oath ? [g]
wherein we do, in consideration of Christ's mercies unto us,
vow eternal allegiance and service unto him, against all those

---

[b] Phil. iii. 10. 1 Pet. iv. 1.   [c] 1 Cor. x. 31. 1 Tim. iv. 4, 5.   [d] Non
prius discumbitur, quam oratio ad Deum prægustetur. *Terl.* Apolog. c. 39.
[e] Inter epulas ubi bene precari mos esset. *Liv.* lib. 39. *Justinus* Martyr fuse
explicat in Apolog. 2. et *Tertul.* cont. Marc. l. 1. c. 23.   [f] Matth. ix. 17.
Vasa pura ad rem divinam. *Plaut.* in Captiv. Act. 4. Scene 1.   [g] Sacramentum visibile juramentum. *Paræus,* in Heb. vi. 17. Vid. *Aug.* ep. 57. Verbum
à militari juramento sumptum. Vid. *Dempster.* in Rosins. Antiq. l. 10. cap. 3.

powers and lusts which war against the soul, and to make our members weapons of righteousness unto him?

Secondly, As Christ brake the bread before he gave it,— so must our hearts, before they be offered up to God for a reasonable sacrifice [h], be humbled and bruised with the apprehension of their own demerits: for "a broken and contrite heart, O Lord, thou wilt not despise [i]." Shall we have adamantine and unbended souls, under the weight of those sins which brake the very rock of our salvation [k], and made the dead stones of the temple to rend asunder [l]? Was his body broken to let out his blood, and shall not our souls be broken to let it in? Was the head wounded, and shall the ulcers and imposthumes remain unlanced? Would not God, in the law [m], accept of any but pushed, and dissected, and burned sacrifices? was his temple [n] built of none but cut and hewed stones? and shall we think to have no sword of the Spirit [o] divide us; no hammer of the Word [p] break us; none of our dross and stubble [q] burned up; none of our flesh beaten down; none of our old man crucified [r] and cut off [s] from us, and yet be still living sacrifices [t], and living stones [u] in his temple? Whence did David [x] call on God, but out of the pit and the deep waters, when his bones were broken, and could not rejoice? Certainly, we come unto God, either as unto a physician, or as to a judge: we must needs bring souls, either full of sores to be cured, or full of sins to be condemned.

Again; In that this rock of ours was broken,—we know whither to fly, in case of tempest and oppression, even unto the holes of the rock for succour. To disclaim our own sufficiency, to disavow any confidence in our own strength; to fly from church, treasures, supererogations, and to lay hold on him [y] in whom were the treasures [z], the fulness of all grace [a], of which fulness we all receive [b]; to forsake the private lamps of the wisest virgins, the saints and angels, which have not light enough to shine into another's house;

---

[h] Rom. xii. 1.   [i] Psal. li.   [k] 1 Cor. x. 4.   [l] Matth. xxvii. 51.
[m] Levit. xxvi. Vid. *Tertul.* cont. Judæos, c. 14. Levit. i. 6. 9.   [n] 1 Kings vi. 7.
[o] Ephes. vi. 17.   [p] Jer. xxiii. 39.   [q] 1 Cor. iii. 13. ix. 27.   [r] Ephes.
iv. 22. Col. iii. 5.   [s] Matth. v. 29, 30.   [t] Rom. xii. 1.   [u] 1 Pet. ii. 5.
[x] Psalm lxix. and li.   [y] Cant. ii. 14.   [z] Col. ii. 3.   [a] Col. i. 19.
[b] John i. 16.

and to have recourse only to the sun of righteousness, the light not of a house, but of the world, who enlighteneth every man that cometh into it. Think when thou seest these elements broken, that even then thou appliest thy lips unto his bleeding wounds, and dost from thence suck salvation. That even then with Thomas, thy hand is in his side, from whence thou mayest pluck out those words of life, " My Lord and my God ;" that even then thou seest in each wound, a mouth open,—and in that mouth the blood, as a visible prayer to intercede with God the Father for thee ; and to solicit him with stronger cries for salvation, than did Abel's for revenge ᶜ. Let not any sins, though never so bloody, so numberless, deter thee from this precious fountain. If it be the glory of Christ's blood to wash away sin, then is it his greatest glory to wash away the greatest sins. Thy sin, indeed, is the object of God's hate; but the misery which sin brings upon thee, is the object of his pity. O when a poor distressed soul, that for many years together hath securely weltered in a sink of numberless and noisome lusts, and hath ever been environed with a hell of wickedness,—shall, at last, have received a wound from the sword of God's Spirit, an eye to see, and a heart to feel and tremble at, the terrors of God's judgements,—shall then (I say) fly out of himself, smite upon his thigh, cast away his rags, crouch and crawl unto the Throne of Grace, solicit God's mercy with strong cries for one drop of that blood which is never cast away, when poured into sinful and sorrowful souls ;—how think we, will the bowels of Christ turn within him ! How will he hasten to meet such an humbled soul, to embrace him in those arms which were stretched on the cross for him, and to open unto him that inexhausted fountain, which even delighteth to mix itself with the tears of sinners ! Certainly, if it were possible for any one of Christ's wounds to be more precious than at the rest, even that should be opened wide, and poured out into the soul of such a penitent. Yea, if it might possibly be, that the sins of all the world could be even thronged into the conscience of one man, and the whole guilt of them made proper and personal unto him ; yet if such a man could be brought to sue for grace in the medita-

tion of Christ's broken body, there would thence issue balm
enough to cure, blood enough to wash and to drown, them all.
Only let not us sin, because grace abounds ; let not us make
work for the blood of Christ, and go about, by crimson and
presumptuous sins, as it were, to pose God's mercy : the
blood of Christ, if spilt and trampled under foot, will
certainly cry so much louder than Abel's for vengeance,
by how much it is the more precious. It may be as well
upon us as *in* us. As the virtue and benefit of Christ's blood
is *in* those, that embrace it unto life and happiness ; so is
the guilt of it *upon* those, that despise it unto wretchedness
and condemnation.

Thirdly, In that Christ gave and delivered these mysteries
unto the church, we likewise must learn not to engross ourselves or our own gifts ; but freely to dedicate them all unto
the honour of that God, and benefit of that church, unto
which he gave both himself and them. Even nature hath
made men to stand in need of each other [d] ; and therefore
hath imprinted in them a natural inclination unto fellowship
and society, in one common city. By Christ we are all made
of one city [e], of one household ; yea of one church, of one
temple. He hath made us members of one body [f], animated
by one and the same spirit : stones [g] of one entire building,
united on one and the same foundation [h] : branches [i] of one
undivided stock, quickened by one and the same root [k] : and
therefore requires from us all a mutual support, succour, sustentation, and nourishment of each other, a kind of traffic
and continual intelligence from part to part ; a union of
members by the supply of nerves and joints, that so each
may be serviceable unto the whole [l]. The eye seeth not for
itself, but for the body ; and therefore if the eye be simple,
the whole body is full of light ; for the light of the body is
the eye [m]. Nay, God in each creature imprinteth a love of
community (which is that whereby one thing doth, as it
were, bestow itself on another) far above the private and do-
mestic love, whereby it labours the preservation and advancement of itself. From which general charity and feeling of

[d] *Arist.* Polit. l. 1.   [e] Eph. ii. 19, 21.   [f] 1 Cor. vi. 19. xii. 12, 13. Rom.
viii. 11. Eph. iv. 4.   [g] 1 Pet. ii. 5.   [h] Eph. ii. 20. 1 Cor. iii. 11.   [i] John
xv. 2.   [k] Rom. xi. 16, 17, 18.   [l] Eph. iv. 16.   [m] Matth. vi. 22.

communion it comes to pass, that if, by any casualty, the
whole body of the universe be like to suffer any rupture or
deformity (as in the danger of a vacuum, which is the con-
tumely of nature), each particular creature is taught to relin-
quish his own natural motion, and to prevent the public reproach, even by forsaking and forgetting of themselves.
Agreeable unto which noble impress of nature, was that he-
roical resolution of Pompey, when the safety of his country
depended on an expedition dangerous to his own particular :
" It is not (said he) necessary for me to live ; it is necessary
that I go [n]." And more honourable that of Codrus, to dedicate his own life as a sacrifice for his country's victory.
But yet more honourable that of the blessed apostle,—" I
count not my life dear unto myself, that I may finish the
ministry which I have received of the Lord[o]." But lastly,
most admirable was that of the same blessed Paul[p] and
Moses[q] whose feeling of community transported them, not
only beyond the fear, but even into a conditional desire, of
their own destruction.

In man's first creation, what was that great endowment of
original righteousness[r], but such a harmony of all man's faculties[s], as that there was no schism in the body, no part
unsubordinated, or unjointed from the rest[t]; but did each
conspire with other, unto the service of the whole, and with
the whole unto the service of God? And what was the immediate effect of that great fall of man, but the breaking and
unjointing of his faculties, the rebellion of his members each
towards other, whereby every faculty seeketh the satisfaction
of itself, without any respect unto the common good? And
as it bred in man an enmity to himself, so to his neighbour
likewise. So long as Adam remained upright, his judgement of Eva was a judgement of unity, " bone of bone[u]:"
—no sooner comes sin, but we hear him upbraid God with
" the woman that thou gavest me[x];" terms of dislike and
enmity.

---

[n] Necesse est ut eam, non ut vivam.   [o] Acts xx. 24.   [p] Rom. ix. 3.
[q] Exod. xxxii. 32.   [r] Aquin. Sum. part 1. quæst. 95. art. 1.—Zœmannus de Dei
Imagine in Hom. c. 5.   [s] Ὥσπερ τὸν παῖδα δεῖ κατὰ τὰ προστάγματα τοῦ
παιδαγωγοῦ ζῆν, οὕτω καὶ τὸ ἐπιθυμητικὸν κατὰ τὸν λόγον. Vide Arist. Ethic.
l. 3. c. 12.   [t] Καθάπερ τὰ παραλελυμένα τοῦ σώματος μόρια. Vide Arist. Ethic.
l. 1. cap. 13.   [u] Gen. ii. 33.   [x] Gen. iii. 13.

For the removal whereof, we must imitate this great example of Christ our head, whose sufferings are not only our
merit, but our example [y]; who, denying himself [z], his own
natural will, and life, bestowed himself on us, that we likewise might not seek every man his own, but every man the
good of another [a]; bestowing ourselves on the service and
benefit of the church [b], and so grow up [c], and be built up together in love, which is the concinnation or perfecting of
the saints [d].

Secondly, In that Christ gave this sacrament, and did
thereby testify his most willing obedience unto a cursed
death, we likewise should, in all our respects, back unto
him, break through all obstacles of self-love, or any temptations of Satan, and the world; and though contrary to the
bent of our own desires, to the propension of our own corrupt hearts, most willingly render our obedience unto him,
and make him the Lord of all our thoughts.

First, For our understandings; we should offer them as
free and voluntary sacrifices, ready not only to yield unto
truth out of constraint, but out of willingness and love to
embrace it, not only for the evidence [e], but for the author,
and goodness of it;—and thus to resign our judgements into
God's hands, to be (though never so much against its own
natural and carnal prejudices) informed and captivated unto
all kind of saving knowledge, even to the extirpating of all
those presumptions, prepossessions, and principles of corruption [f], which use to smother and adulterate divine truth.
For there is naturally in the minds of men, (though otherwise
eagerly pursuing knowledge) a kind of dread and shrinking
from the evidence of divine truths, (as each faculty avoideth
too excellent an object) a voluntary and affected ignorance [g],
lest, knowing the truth, they should cease to hate it [h] :—a faculty of making doubts [i], touching the meaning and extent of
such truths, whose evidence would cross the corruptions of
our practice ; and then a framing of arguments and pre-

[y] 1 Pet. ii. 21.　[z] Matth. xxvi. 39.　[a] 1 Cor. x. 2, 4. Phil. ii. 21, and ii. 17.
[b] Acts xx. 24.　[c] Ephes. iv. 15.　[d] Καταρτισμὸς τῶν ἁγίων, Ephes. iv. 12.
[e] *Tertul.* de Pœnit. cap. 4.　[f] Κακία ἐστι φθαρτικὴ ἀρχῆς. *Arist.* Eth. l. 6.
[g] Ἄγνοια ἐκ προαιρέσεως. *Arist.* Eth. l. 3. c. 1.　[h] Simul ut desinant ignorare, cessant et odisse. *Tertul.* Apolog. cap. 1.　[i] Domestica judicia, *Tertul.*
Apol. cap. 1.—*Clemens Alex.* Strom. lib. 4. Vid. *Herald.* in Tertul. Apol. c. 1.

sumptions for that part, which is most favourable and flattering unto nature; a certain private prejudice against the lustre of the most strict and practical principles; a humour of
cavilling and disputing about those parts of God's will[k],
which bring with them a more straight obligation on the conscience; a withdrawing the thoughts from acquainting themselves with the more spiritual parts of divine truth, under
pretence of more important employments, about scholastical
and sublime speculations.   All which do evidently prove,
that there is not, in the understanding, that willingness to
give up itself unto God, which there was in Christ to bestow
himself unto us.

Secondly, For our wills and affections[l]; we should be
ready to cross and bend them against all the noise of corrupt
delights; to pluck out our right eye, cut off our right hand;
to be crucified to the world; to be disposed of by God's providence, cheerfully in any course, whether of passive obedience
to have a mind submitting unto it, and rejoicing in it; or of
active obedience to obey him, contrary to the stream and
current of our natural desires; though it be to offer unto him
our Isaac[m], our closest and choicest affection; though to
shake off the child that hangeth about our neck[n], to stop our
ear to the voice of her that bare us, to throw the wife out of
our bosom, when they shall tempt us to neglect God, to spit
out the sweetest sin that lies under our tongue; briefly, to
take under Christ's banners the Roman oath[o], to go and do
where and whatsoever our great captain commanded; neither
for fear of death, or dread of enemy, to forsake service, or
resign weapon till death shall extort it.

Lastly, In that Christ gave his sacrament, and therein
himself, the author and finisher of our salvation[p]; we learn
how to esteem of our salvation,—namely, as of a free and
unmerited gift.   Christ was sold by Judas, but he was given
by God[q]; and that in the absolute nature of a gift, without

[k] Audaciam existimo de bono divini præcepti disputare; *Tert.* de Pœnit. c. 4.
[l] Qui perspicit apud te paratam fuisse virtutem, reddet pro virtute mercedem.
Cyprian. de Mortal. Vide *Tertul.* Apol. c. 49.   [m] Quid faceres si filium jubere-
ris occidere? *Cyprian.* de Mortal.   [n] Licet parvulus ex collo pendeat nepos, &c.
Hieron. ad Heliodorum.   [o] Πειθαρχήσειν καὶ ποιήσειν τὸ προστατ]όμενον ὑπὸ
τῶν ἀρχόντων κατὰ δύναμιν. Vid. *Brisson.* de Formulis, l. 4. et *Just. Martyr.*
Apol. 2.   [p] Heb. xii. 2.   [q] Deus cogitavit salutem qua redempti sumus;
Judas cogitavit pretium, &c. *Aug.* Tom. 9, Tract. 7. in Ep. 1. Johan.

so much as suit or request on our part for him. True it is, that if man had persisted in the state of his created integrity, he might, after an improper manner, be said to have merited the glory which he was after to enjoy, inasmuch as he was to obtain it in the virtue of those legal operations, unto which he was, by the abilities of his own nature, without the special influence of a supernatural infused grace, fitted and disposed; though even this was not from the dignity and value of our work, but from the indulgence of Almighty God [r], who would set no higher price on that glory, which he proposed unto man for the object of his desires, and reward of his works. For if we go exactly unto the first rule of justice unqualified with clemency and bounty, it could not possibly be, that God should be bound to requite our labours with eternal bliss; there being so vast a disproportion between the fruition of God, an infinite good, and any the most excellent, yet still limited operation of the creature. For as water in its own nature riseth no farther than the spring whence it first issueth; so the endeavours of nature could never have raised man, without a mixture of God's mercy, unto a higher degree of happiness, than should have been proportionable to the quality of his work. But now having in Adam utterly disabled ourselves to pay that small price, at which God was pleased to rate our glory [s]; all those who are restored thereunto again, must acknowledge both it, and Christ the purchaser of it, as a free gift of Almighty God, by them so far undeserved, as he was, before the promise, unknown and unexpected.

If it be here demanded, how salvation can be said to be freely given us, when on our part there is a condition required;—for the work whereby we obtain life, is not quite taken away, but only altered: before, it was a legal work; now, an evangelical; before, it was an obedience to the law; now, a belief in the promise; before, "eat not, lest ye die;" now, "eat and you shall live:"—We answer, that the hand of the beggar, without which the alms is no way received,

[r] Habemus nos aliquid Dei, sed ab ipso, non à nobis; sed ex gratiâ ipsius, non ex nostrâ proprietate; *Tertul.* cont. Hermog.—Vide *Hooker,* Eccles. Polit. l. 1. sect. 11.—See Dr. *Field* of the Church, l. 1. c. 2.   [s] Nec quisquam dicat meritis operum suorum, vel meritis fidei sibi traditam, &c. *Aug.* Ep. 46, ad Valentem. Evangelium aliud à lege, non alienum; diversum, sed non contrarium. *Tertul.* cont. Marcion. lib. 4. cap. 11.

doth not prejudice the free donation thereof, that being the instrument whereby the gift is conveyed. The labourer doth not deserve his wages, because he receives it; but he receives it, because he hath before deserved it; receiving conveyeth, it doth not merit it. Neither is salvation given us for our faith in the virtue of a work, but only because of that respect and relation, which it hath unto him who trod the wine-press alone, without any assisting or co-meriting cause. Even Adam in innocency could not be without an assent and firm belief, that the faithful God would perform the promise of life [t], made and annexed unto the covenant of works. But this faith could not be the merit of life [u], but the fruit and effect of merit, or rather obedience anteceding; for his performance of the law (in the right whereof he had interest unto glory) preceding, there should immediately from thence have issued, by faith, a prepossession (as it were) and pre-apprehension of that glory, which, by virtue of that legal obedience, he should have had interest unto. So that it is repugnant absolutely to the nature of faith, to be any way the cause meritorious of salvation, it being nothing else but the application and apprehension of that salvation; which in vain our faith layeth claim unto, unless in the right of some anteceding work, either our own, or some other's in our behalf, it be first merited for us. He which believes, and so by consequence lays hold on life, without a ground preceding for his claim thereunto, is a robber rather than a believer, and doth rather steal Heaven than deserve it, though he is not likely so to do; for in Heaven, thieves break not through nor steal [x].

Again, Suppose faith in the quality of the work should merit that, which until merited, can, in truth, be never by faith apprehended;—yet, inasmuch as nothing can merit for another any farther, than as it is his own proper work,—faith, therefore, being not within the compass, either of natural or of acquired endowment, but proceeding from a supernatural and infused grace [y], it is manifest, that even so, it cannot possibly obtain salvation by any virtue or efficacy of its own. For as he which bestows money on his poor friend, and after, for that money, sells him land, far beyond the value of the money which he gave, may be thus far said rather to multiply and change his gifts, than to receive a price for them ; so God, bestowing eternal life on man, upon the condition of believing, the ability whereunto he himself hath first bestowed [z], and between which life and faith there is an infinite disproportion of worth,—may be said rather to heap his gifts, than to bargain and compact for them ; rather to double his free bounty, than to reward man's weak and imperfect obedience, unless we take it improperly for the discharge of a voluntary debt, wherein it hath pleased God in mercy, as it were, to oblige and engage himself upon condition of our faith [a].

Neither do we herein at all make way for that cursed doctrine of Socinianism,—than which a more venomous was never sucked from so sweet and saving a truth,—That because salvation is a free gift, Christ therefore did not suffer for the satisfaction of God's wrath, nor pay any legal price for the salvation of the world, nor lay down himself in our room, as the ransomer of us, and purchaser of life for us, but became incarnate in the flesh, made under the law, obedient unto death, only for an example of patience and humility unto us, not for a propitiation to his Father, and reconcilement of the world unto God. A price was paid [b], and that so precious, as that the confluence of all created wealth into one sum, cannot carry the estimate of one farthing in comparison of it ; and indeed it ought to be a price more valuable than the whole world, which was to ransom so many souls, the loss of the least whereof cannot, by the purchase of the whole world, be countervailed. A price it was, valuable only by him that paid and received it, by us to be enjoyed and adored, by God only to be measured. Neither could it stand with the truth and constancy of God's law, with the sacredness and majesty of his justice, to suffer violation and not revenge it ; and when all his attributes are in him one and the same thing, to magnify his mercy, not by the satis-

---

[z] Gratias ago tibi, Domine, quia quod quæris a me, prius ipse donasti : *Cyprian.* de Bapt. Christi.—Remunerans in nobis quicquid ipse præstitit, & honorans quod ipse perfecit : *Cypr.* l. 3. epist. 25.   [a] Deus, promittendo, seipsum fecit debitorem. *August.*   [b] Λύτρον, *Matth.* xx. 28. ἀντίλυτρον, 1 Tim. ii. 5. προσφορὰ καὶ θυσία, Eph. v. 2. Heb. ix. 12. κατάρα, Gal. iii. 13. ἀπολύτρωσιν, 1 Cor i. 30. ἱλασμὸς, 1 John ii. 2. Matth. xvi. 26.

faction, but the destruction of his justice, and so to set his
own unity at variance with itself. Mercy and truth, righteousness and peace, they were, in man's redemption, to kiss,
and not to quarrel with each other: God did not disunite
his attributes, when he did reunite his church unto himself.
A price then was paid unto God's justice, and eternal life is
a purchase by Christ bought[c], but still unto us a gift[d],
not by any pains or satisfaction of ours attained unto, but
only by him who was himself given unto us, that together
with himself he might give us all things[e]. He unto whom I
stand engaged in a sum of money, by me ever impossible to
be raised, if it please him to persuade his own heir to join in
my obligation, and out of that great estate, by himself conferred on him for that very purpose, to lay down so much as
shall cancel the bond, and acquit me; doth not only freely
forgive my debt[f], but doth moreover commend the abundance of his favour, by the manner and circumstances of the
forgiveness. Man by nature is a debtor unto God: there is
a hand-writing against him[g], which was so long to stand in
virtue, till he was able to offer something in value proportionable to that infinite justice unto which he stood obliged;
which being by him, without the sustaining of an infinite
misery, utterly unsatisfiable, it pleased God to appoint his
own co-essential and co-eternal Son[h] to enter under the
same bond of law for us, on whom he bestowed such rich
graces, as were requisite for the œconomy of so great a
work. By the means of which human and created graces,
concurring with, and receiving value from, the divine nature,
meeting hypostatically in one infinite person,—the debt of
mankind was discharged, and the obligation cancelled; and
so as many as were ordained to life, effectually delivered by
this great ransom, virtually sufficient, and, by God's power,
applicable unto all, but actually beneficial, and by his most
wise and just will, conferred only upon those, who should,
by the grace of a lively faith, apply unto themselves this
common gift. So then, all our salvation is a gift, Christ a
gift[i], the knowledge of Christ[k] a gift, the faith[l] in Christ a

c Περιποίησις, Ephes. 1. 14.   d John iii. 16.   Gal. i. 4.   Tit. 2. 14. Isai. ix. 6.
e Rom. viii. 32.   f Matth. vi. 12.   g Col. ii. 14.   h Gal. iv. 4.   i Isai. ix. 6.
k Matth. xiii. 11.   l Jude v. 3.   Phil. i. 29.

gift, repentance [m] by Christ a gift, the suffering [n] for Christ a gift, the reward [o] of all a gift; whatsoever we have, whatsoever we are, is all from God that showeth mercy [p].

Lastly, In that Christ gives his sacrament to be eaten, we learn, first, not only our benefit, but our duty: the same Christ it is, whom, in eating, we both enjoy and obey, he being as well the institutor as the substance of the sacrament. If it were but his precept, we owe him our observance; but besides it is his body, and even self-love might move us to obey his precept: our mouths have been wide open unto poison, let them not be shut up against so sovereign an antidote [q].

Secondly, We see how we should use this precious gift of Christ crucified, not to look on, but to eat, not with a gazing, speculative knowledge of him, as it were at a distance, but with an experimental and working knowledge; none truly knows Christ, but he that feels him. " Come, taste and see," saith the prophet, " how gracious the Lord is." In divine things, tasting goes before seeing, the union before the vision: Christ must first dwell in us, before we can know the love of God that passeth knowledge [r].

Thirdly, We learn not to sin against Christ, because therein we do sin against ourselves, by offering indignity to the body of Christ, which should nourish us; and, like swine [s], by trampling under foot that precious food, which preserveth unto life those that with reverence eat it, but fatteth unto slaughter those who profanely devour it: — even as the same rain in different grounds serves sometimes to bring on the seed, other times to choke and stifle it by the forwardness of weeds [t]. For as it is the goodness of God to bring good out of the worst of things, even sin; so is it the malignity of sin and cunning of Satan, to pervert the most holy things, the word of God, yea, the very blood of Christ, unto evil.

[m] Acts v. 31. 2 Tim. ii. 25. [n] Phil. i. 29. [o] Rom. vi. 23. [p] Restat ut propterea rectè dictum intelligatur, ' Non volentis, neque currentis, sed miserentis est Dei;' ut totum Deo detur, qui hominis voluntatem bonam et præparat adjuvandam, et adjuvat præparatam. Vid. *Aug.* Enchir. cap. 32. [q] Nauseabit ad antidotum, qui hiavit ad venenum? *Tert.* cont. Gnost. cap. 5. [r] Eph. 3. 17, 18. [s] Porcis comparandi, qui ea prius conculcant, ac luto cœnoque involvunt, quæ mox avide devorant: *Parker* de Antiq. Brit. in Præfat. [t] Matth. iv. 3, 6.

Lastly, We learn, how pure we ought to preserve those doors of the soul from filthiness and intemperance, at which so often the ' Prince of glory ' himself will enter in.

CHAPTER XIII.

Of the two first ends or effects of the Sacrament, namely, the exhibition of Christ to the Church, and the union of the Church to Christ : Of the real presence.

HAVING thus far spoken of the nature and quality of this holy sacrament, it follows in order to treat of the ends or effects thereof, on which depends its necessity, and our comfort.   Our sacraments are nothing else but evangelical types or shadows of some more perfect substance.   For as the legal sacrifices were the shadows[u] of Christ expected, and wrapped up in a cloud of predictions, and in the loins of his predecessors; so this new mystical sacrifice of the gospel is a shadow of Christ, risen indeed, but yet hidden from us under the cloud of those heavens, which shall contain him until the dissolution of all things.   For the whole heavens are but as one great cloud, which intercepts the lustre of that sun of righteousness, who enlighteneth every one that cometh into the world.   Now shadows are for the refreshing of us against the lustre of any light, unto which the weakness of the sense is yet disproportioned. As there are many things for their own smallness imperceptible,—so some, for their magnitude, do exceed the power of sense, and have a transcendency in them, which surpasseth the comprehension of that faculty, unto which they properly belong.   No man can, in one simple view, look upon the whole vast frame of heaven ; because he cannot, at the same moment, receive the species of so spreading and diffused an object : so is it in things divine ; some of them are so above the reach of our imperfect faculties, as that they swallow up the understanding, and make not any immediate impression on the soul, between which and their excellency, there is so great disproportion.

Now disproportion useth, in all things, to arise from a

u Heb. x. 1.

double cause : the one natural [x], being the limited constitution of the faculty, whereby, even in its best sufficiency, it
is disabled for the perception of too excellent an object, as
are the eyes of an owl in respect of the sun.

The other accidental ; namely, by violation and distemper
of the faculty, even within the compass of its own strength ;
as in soreness of eyes in regard of light, or lameness in regard of motion. Great certainly was the mystery of man's
redemption, which posed and dazzled the eyes of the angels
themselves [y] : so that between Christ and man, there are both
these former disproportions observable.

For first of all, man, while he is on the earth, a traveller
towards that glory which yet he never saw, and which the
tongue of St. Paul himself could not utter [z], is altogether,
even in his highest pitch of perfection, unqualified to comprehend the excellent mystery of Christ, either crucified, or
much more glorified. And, therefore, our manner of assenting in this life, though in regard of the authority on
which it is grounded (which is God's own Word), it be most
evident and infallible,—yet, in its own quality, it is not so
immediate and express, as is that which is elsewhere reserved for us. For, hereafter, we shall know even as we are
known, by a knowledge of vision [a], fruition, and possession :
here darkly, by stooping and captivating our understandings
unto those divine reports, which are made in Scripture, which
is a knowledge of faith, distance, and expectation. We do,
I say, here bend our understandings to assent unto such
truths, as do not transmit any immediate species or irradiation
of their own upon them : but there our understandings shall
be raised unto a greater capacity, and be made able, without
a secondary report and conveyance, to apprehend clearly
those glorious truths, the evidence whereof it did here submit unto, for the infallible credit of God ; who, in his Word,
had revealed, and, by his Spirit, obsignated the same unto
them : as the Samaritans knew Christ at first only by the report of the woman [b],—which was an assent of faith ; but
after, when they saw his wonders, and heard his words, they
knew him by himself,—which was an assent of vision.

---

[x] Vide *Aquin.* part. 1. quæst. 62. art. 2. ad secundum.   [y] 1 Tim. iii. 16.
[z] 2 Cor. xii. 4.   [a] 1 Cor. xv.   [b] John iv.

Secondly, As the church is here but a travelling church, therefore cannot possibly have any farther knowledge of that country whither it goes, but only by the maps which describe it, the Word of God; and these few fruits [c] which are sent unto them from it, the fruits of the Spirit [d], whereby they have some taste and relish of the world to come : so moreover is it even in this estate, by being enclosed in a body of sin (which hath a darkening property in it, and adds unto the natural limitedness of the understanding, an accidental defect and soreness), much disabled from this very imperfect assent unto Christ, the object of its faith. For as sin, when it wastes the conscience, and bears rule in the soul, hath a power like Delilah and the Philistines, to put out our eyes (as Ulysses the eye of his Cyclops with his sweet wine [e]), a power to corrupt principles, to pervert and make crooked the very rule by which we work [f]; conveying all moral truths to the soul, as some concave glasses use to represent the species of things to the eye, not according to their natural rectitude or beauty, but with those wrestings, inversions, and deformities, which, by the indisposition thereof, they are framed unto ;—so even the least corruptions, unto which the best are subject (having a natural antipathy to the evidence and power of Divine truth), do necessarily, in some manner, distemper our understandings, — and make such a degree of soreness in the faculty, as that it cannot but, so far forth, be impatient and unable to bear that glorious lustre, which shines immediately in the Lord Christ. So then, we see what a great disproportion there is between us and Christ immediately presented : and from thence we may observe our necessity, and God's mercy, in affording us the refreshment of a type and shadow.

These shadows were to the church of the Jews, many ; because their weakness in the knowledge of Christ was of necessity more than ours, inasmuch as they were but an infant [g], we an adult and grown church: and they looked on Christ at a distance; we near at hand, he being already incarnate : unto us, they are the sacraments of his body and blood, in which we see and receive Christ, as weak eyes do the light

---

[c] Numb. xiii. 21.   [d] Gal. v. 22.   [e] Hom. Odyss. l. 9.   [f] Στρεβλὸν ποιεῖν τὸν κανόνα, Arist. Rh. lib. 1. cap. 1.   [g] Gal. iv. 3.

of the sun, through some dark cloud, or thick grove. So
then, one main and principal end of this Sacrament, is, to be
an instrument fitted unto the measure of our present estate,
for the exhibition or conveyance of Christ, with the benefits
of his passion unto the faithful soul; an end not proper to
this mystery alone, but common to it with all those legal
sacraments which were the more thick shadows of the Jewish
church: for even they in the Red Sea [h] did pass through Christ,
who was their way; in the manna [i] and rock, did eat and drink
Christ, who was their life ; in the brazen serpent, did behold
Christ, who was their Saviour ; in their daily sacrifices, did
prefigure Christ, who was their truth ; in their passover, did
eat Christ, by whose blood they were sprinkled.   For howsoever between the legal and evangelical covenant there may
be sundry circumstantial differences :

As first, In the manner of their evidence ; that, being obscure,—this, perspicuous ; to them, a promise only,—to us,
a gospel ;—

Secondly, In their extent and compass ; that, being confined to Judea [k],—this, universal to all creatures [l];—

Thirdly, In the means of ministration; that, by priests and
prophets [m],—this, by the Son himself, and those delegates
who were by him enabled and authorized by a solemn commission, and by many excellent endowments for the same
service;—

Lastly, In the quality of its durance ; that being mutable
and abrogated, this to continue until the consummation of
all things ;—yet notwithstanding, in substance they agree,
and, though by sundry ways, do all at last meet in one and the
same Christ, who, like the heart in the midst of the body,
coming himself in person between the legal and evangelical
church, doth equally convey life and motion to them both :
even as that light which I see in a star, and that which I
receive by the immediate beam of the sun, doth originally

[h] 1 Cor. x. 1, 2, 3, 4. *Tertul.* de Baptis. cap. 9. et cont. Marcion. lib. 3. cap. 16.
et l. 5. c. 7.   [i] Manna et aqua è petrâ habebant in se figuram futuri mysterii,
quod nunc sumimus in commemorationem Christi Domini.   *Ambros.* in
1 Cor. x.—Vid. *Mornay* de Eucharist. lib. 4. cap. 1.—Dr. *Field* of the Church,
l. 1. c. 5.   *Pareus* in Heb. cap. 8. et cap. 10, &c. 12, 18, 28. Acts xiii. 32.
Gal. iii. 17. Acts xiii. 46. Matth. x. 5, 6.   [k] Rom. iii. 2. Eph. ii. 12.   [l] Mark
xvi. 15. Isai. xlix. 6.   [m] Heb. i. 1, 2. x. 9. vii. 12, 16. vi. 20. vii. 16, 24, 28.

issue from the same fountain, though conveyed with a different lustre, and by a several means.

So then, we see the end of all Sacraments made after the second covenant (for Sacraments there were even in Paradise before the fall), namely, To exhibit Christ, with those benefits which he bestoweth on his church, unto each believing soul. But after a more especial manner, is Christ exhibited in the Lord's Supper, because his presence is there more notable. For as, by faith, we have the evidence,—so, by the Sacrament, we have the presence of things farthest distant and absent from us. A man that looketh on the light through a shadow, doth, truly and really, receive the selfsame light, which would, in the openest and clearest sunshine, appear unto him, though after a different manner. " There shall we see him," as Job speaks, " with these selfsame eyes ;" here, with a spiritual eye, after a mystical manner. So then, in this Sacrament we do most willingly acknowledge a real, true, and perfect presence of Christ,—not in, with, or under the elements, considered absolutely in themselves [n], but with that relative habitude and respect, which they have unto the immediate use, whereunto they are consecrated. Nor yet so do we acknowledge any such carnal trans-elementation of the materials in this Sacrament, as if the body or blood of Christ were, by the virtue of consecration, and, by way of a local substitution, in the place of the bread and wine,—but are truly and really by them, though in nature different, conveyed into the souls of those, who by faith receive him. And therefore Christ first said, "Take, eat," and then, "This is my body ;" to intimate unto us (as learned Hooker observeth [o]), that the Sacrament, however by consecration it be changed from common unto holy bread, and separated from common unto a divine use, is yet never properly to be called the ' Body of Christ,' till taken and eaten ; by means of which actions (if they be actions of faith) that holy bread and wine do as really convey whole Christ, with the vital influences that proceed from him, unto the soul, as the hand doth them unto the mouth, or the mouth unto the stomach. Otherwise,

[n] Secundum quendam modum Sacramentum Corporis Christi Corpus est, et Sacramentum sanguinis sanguis est. *Aug.* Epist. 23.   [o] *Hooker*, lib. 5. page 359. Οὐ γὰρ ὡς κοινὸν πόμα ταῦτα λαμβάνομεν. *Just. Mart.* Apol. 2.

if Christ were not really and corporally present with the consecrated elements, severed from the act of faithful receiving,
the wicked should as easily receive him with their teeth, as
the faithful in their soul : which to affirm, is both absurd
and impious [p].

Now Christ's presence in this holy Sacrament being a
thing of so important consequence, and the consideration
thereof being very proper to this first end of the Sacrament,
the exhibiting of Christ (for to exhibit a thing, is nothing
else but to present it, or to make it present unto the party
to whom it is exhibited ;) it will not be impertinent to make
some short digression for setting down the manner, and
clearing the truth of Christ's real presence ; the understanding whereof will depend upon the distinguishing of the several manners, in which Christ may be said to be present.

First then, Christ being an infinite person, hath, in the
virtue of his godhead, an infinite and unlimited presence,
whereby he so filleth all places, as that he is not contained
or circumscribed in them : which immensity of his making
him intimately present with all the creatures, is that whereby they are quickened, supported, and conserved by him.
For " by him all things consist;" and " he upholdeth
them all by the word of his power ;" and " in him they live,
and move, and have their being." But this is not that presence, which in the Sacrament we affirm, because that presupposeth a presence of Christ in and according to that nature, wherein he was the Redeemer of the world; which was
his human nature. Yet inasmuch as this his human nature
subsisteth not, but in and with the infiniteness of the second
person ; there is therefore, in the second place, by the Lu-
therans framed another imaginary presence of Christ's human
body (after once the Divinity was pleased to derive glory in
fulness on it); which giveth it a participated ubiquity unto
it too, by means whereof, Christ is corporally in or under the
sacramental elements.

But this opinion, as it is no way agreeable with the truth
of the human nature of Christ, so is it greatly injurious to

---

[p] Non dentes ad mordendum acuimus, sed fide sincerâ panem frangimus et
partimur. *Cypr.*—Qui manducat intùs, non forìs; qui manducat in corde, non
qui premit dente. *Aug.* Tract. 26. in Johan. et vid. de Civit. Dei, lib. 21.
cap. 25.

his divinity. For first, Though Christ's human nature was, in regard of its production, extraordinary,—and in regard of the sacred union which it had with the divine nature, admirable,—and in regard of communication of glory from the godhead, and of the unction of the Holy Ghost, far above all other names that are named in Heaven or earth ;—yet, in its nature, did it ever retain the essential and primitive properties of a created substance, which is to be in all manner of perfections finite, and so by consequence in place too. For glory destroys not nature, but exalts it; nor exalts it to any farther degrees of perfection, than are consistent with the finiteness of a creature, who is like unto us in regard of all natural and essential properties. But these men give unto Christ's body far more than his own divine nature doth ; for he glorifies it only to be the head, that is, the most excellent and first-born of every creature : but they glorify it so far, as to make it share in the essential properties of the divine nature. For as that substance unto which the intrinsecal and essential properties of a man belong, is a man necessarily (man being nothing else but a substance so qualified) ; so that being, unto which the divine attributes do belong in that degree of infiniteness, as they do to the divine person itself, must needs be God : and immensity, we know, is a proper attribute of the Divinity, implying infiniteness, which is God's own prerogative. Neither can the distinction of ubiquity communicated, and original or essential, solve the consequence : for God is by himself so differenced from all the creatures, as that it is not possible any attribute of his should be participated by any creature in that manner of infiniteness as it is in him : nay, it implies an inevitable contradiction, that, in a finite nature, there should be room enough for an infinite attribute.

We confess, that inasmuch as the human nature in Christ is inseparably taken into the subsistence of the omnipresent Son of God, it is therefore a truth to say, That the Son of God, though filling all places, is not yet, in any of them, separated or asunder from the human nature. Nay, by the virtue of the communication of the properties, it is true likewise to say, that the man Christ is in all places, though not in, or according, to his human nature. But now from the union of the manhood to the godhead, to argue a co-exten-

sion, or joint-presence therewith, is an inconsequent argument, as may appear in other things. The soul hath a kind
of immensity in her little world, being in each part thereof
whole and entire : and yet it follows not, because the soul
is united to the body, that therefore the body must needs
partake of this omnipresence of the soul : else should the
whole body be in the little finger, because the soul, unto
which it is united, is wholly there.

Again, There is an inseparable union between the sun
and the beam : so that it is infallibly true to say, the sun is
no where severed from the beam ; yet we know they both
occupy a distinct place. Again, Misletoe is so united to the
substance of the tree out of which it groweth, that (though
of a different nature) it subsisteth not but in and by the subsistence of the tree ; and yet it hath not that amplitude of
place, which the tree hath.

Letting go then this opinion, there is a third presence of
Christ, which is a carnal, physical, local presence, which we
affirm his human nature to have only in heaven ; the Papists
attribute it to the Sacrament, because Christ hath said,
" This is my body ;" and, in matters of fundamental consequence, he useth no figurative or dark speeches.—To this
we say, that it is a carnal doctrine, and a mistake like that
of Nicodemus, and of Origen, from the spirit to the letter.
And for the difficulty, it is none to men that have more than
only a carnal ear to hear it : for what difficulty is it to say,
that then the king gives a man an office, when he hath sealed
him such a patent, in the right whereof that office belongeth, and is conveyed unto him ? And if Christ be thus locally in the Sacrament, and eaten with the mouth, and so
conveyed into the stomach ; I then demand what becomes of
him, when and after he is thus received into the stomach ?
If he retire from the accidents out of a man, then first accidents shall be left without any substance at all under them to
sustain them ; and which is (if any thing can be) yet more
absurd, bare accidents should nourish, be assimilated, and
augment a substance. For it is plain, that a man might be
nourished by the bread ; yea, the priest by intemperate ex-
cess made drunk with the consecrated wine: unto which detestable effects, we cannot imagine that God, by a more
especial concurrence and miracle, would enable the bare ac-

cidents of bread and wine. But if Christ stay, and do corporally unite himself to the receiver ; then I see not how all
they that receive the Sacrament, being physically and substantially united to Christ's body, have not likewise a natural union to his person too, that being no where separated
from this, which is blasphemous to affirm.

Secondly, How Christ's body may not be said to have a
double subsistence ; infinite in the second person, and finite
in all those with whom he is incorporated.

Leaving then this as a fleshly conceit, we come to a fourth
presence of Christ, which is by energy and power.   Thus,
" Where two or three be gathered together in his name [q],
Christ is in the midst of them" by the powerful working of
his holy Spirit ; even as the sun is present to the earth, inasmuch as, by its influence and benignity, it heateth and
quickeneth it.   For all manner of operation is, by some
manner of contact, between the agent and the patient,
which cannot be without some manner of presence too :
but the last manner of presence is a sacramental, relative, mystical presence.   Understand it thus ;—The king
is in his court or presence-chamber only locally and physically ; but, representatively, he is wheresoever his chan-
cellor or subordinate judges are, inasmuch as whatsoever
they, in a legal and judicial course, do determine, is
accounted by him as his own personal act,—as being an
effect of that power, which though in them as the instruments, doth yet originally reside no where but in his own
person.   Just so, Christ is locally in Heaven, which must
contain him till " the restitution of all things :" yet having
instituted these elements for the supply, as it were, of his
absence, he is accounted present with them ; inasmuch as
they which receive them with that reverend and faithful affection, as they would Christ himself, do, together with
them, receive him too, really and truly, though not carnally
or physically, but after a mystical and spiritual manner.   A
real presence of Christ we acknowledge, but not a local or
physical ; for presence real (that being a metaphysical term)
is not opposed unto a mere physical or local absence or distance ; but is opposed to a false, imaginary, fantastic pre-

[q] Matth. xxviii.

sence. For if real presence may be understood of nothing but a carnal and local presence, then that speech of Christ, " Where two or three be gathered together in my name, there am I in the midst of them," cannot have any real truth in it ; because Christ is not locally in the midst of them.

This real presence, being thus explained, may be thus proved :—The main end of the Sacrament (as shall be shown) is to unite the faithful unto Christ ; to which union there must, of necessity, be a presence of Christ by means of the Sacrament, which is the instrument of that union. Such then as the union is, such must needs be the presence too : since presence is therefore only necessary, that by means thereof that union may be effected. Now united unto Christ we are not carnally or physically, as the meat is to the body ; but after a mystical manner, by joints and sinews, not fleshly, but spiritual : even as the faithful are united to each other in one mystical body of Christ, into one holy spiritual building [r], into one fruitful olive-tree, into a holy but mystical marriage with Christ. Now what presence fitter for a spiritual union than a spiritual presence ? Certainly, to confine Christ unto the narrow compass of a piece of bread, to squeeze and contract his body into so strait a room, and to grind him between our teeth, is to humble him (though now glorified) lower than he humbled himself: he himself, to the form of a servant ; but this, to the condition of a monster.

That presence then of Christ, which, in the Sacrament, we acknowledge, is not any gross presence of circumscription ; as if Christ Jesus, in body, lay hid under the accidents of bread and wine ; as if he who was wont to use the senses [s] for witness and proof of his presence, did now hide from them, yea, deceive them under the appearances of that which he is not ;—but it is a spiritual presence, of energy, power, and concomitancy with the element, by which Christ doth appoint, that *by* and *with* these mysteries, though not *in* or *from* them, his sacred body should be conveyed into the faithful soul. And such a presence of Christ in power, though absent in flesh, as it is most compatible with the

[r] 1 Pet. ii. 5.   [s] John xx. 20, 27. Luke xxiv. 39. Matth. xxviii. 6.

properties of a human body [t], so doth it most make for the
demonstration of his power, who can, without any necessity
of a fleshly presence, send as great influence from his sacred body on the church, as if he should descend visibly
amongst us.   Neither can any man show any enforcing reason, why, unto the real exhibition and reception of Christ
crucified, there should any more physical presence of his be
required, than there is of the sun unto the eye for receiving
his light, or of the root unto the utmost branches for receiving of vital sap [u], or of the head unto the feet [x] for the receiving of sense, or of the land and purchase made over by a
sealed deed [y] for receiving the lordship [z]; or lastly (to use an
instance from the Jesuits' [a] own doctrine out of Aristotle),
of a final cause in an actual existence, to effect its power and
casualty on the will.   For if the final cause do truly and
really produce its effect, though it have not any material gross
presence, but only an intellectual presence to the apprehension ; why may not Christ (whose sacred body, however it
be not substantially coextended, as I may so speak, in regard of ubiquity with the godhead,—yet in regard of its co-
operation, force, efficacy, unlimited by any place or subject,
it having neither sphere of activity, nor stint of merit, nor
bounds of efficacy, nor necessary subject of application, beyond which the virtue of it grows faint and ineffectual),—
why may not he, I say, really unite himself unto his church
by a spiritual presence to the faithful soul, without any such
gross and carnal descent, or re-humiliation of his glorified
body, unto an ignoble and prodigious form?

So then, to conclude this digression, and the first end of
this Sacrament together; when Christ saith, "This is my
body," we are not otherwise to understand it, than those
other sacramental speeches of the same nature, "I am that
bread of life [b],"—"Christ was that rock [c]," and the like: it
being a common thing, not only in holy Scriptures [d], but
even in profane writers also [e], to call the instrumental ele-

---

[t] Erat caro ejus in monumento, sed virtus ejus operabatur in Cœlo ; *Ambros.*
de Incarnat. cap. 5.   [u] Rom. xi. 16.   [x] Ephes. i. 22. περιποίησις.
[y] Ephes. i. 14. σφραγίς.   [z] Rom. xiv. 11.   [a] *Greg. de Valen.* tom. 1.
disp. 1. qu. 1. punct. 1.—*Hooker*, lib. 5. sect. 55. p. 303, 304.   [b] John vi. 51.
[c] 1 Cor. x. 4.   [d] Gen. xvii. 10. Exod. xii. 11.   [e] Fœdus ferire. *Liv.*
Κήρυκες δ' ἀνὰ ἄστυ, Θεῶν φέρον ὅρκια πιστὰ, Ἄρνε δύω καὶ οἶνον. *Homer.*

ments by the name of that covenant, of which they are only
the sacrifices, seals, and visible confirmations, because of
that relation and near resemblance that is between them.

The second end or effect of this Sacrament, which in order
of nature immediately followeth the former, is to obsignate,
and to increase the mystical union of the church unto Christ
their head. For as the same operation, which infuseth the
reasonable soul (which is the first act or principle of life
natural) doth also unite it unto the body, to the making up
of one man ; so the same Sacrament which doth exhibit
Christ unto us (who is the first act and original of life divine) doth also unite us together unto the making up of one
church. In natural nourishment,—the vital heat, being
stronger than the resistance of the meat, doth macerate, con-
coct, and convert that into the substance of the body : but
in this spiritual nourishment, the vital Spirit of Christ [f], having a heat invincible by the coldness of nature, doth turn us
into the same image and quality with itself, working a fellowship of affections, and confederacy of wills [g]. And as the
body doth, from the union of the soul unto it, receive
strength, beauty, motion, and the like active qualities ; so
also Christ, being united unto us by these holy mysteries,
doth comfort, refresh, strengthen, rule, and direct us in all
our ways. We all, in the virtue of that covenant made by
God unto the faithful, and to their seed in the first instant of
our being, do belong unto Christ that bought us [h]; after, in
the laver of regeneration, the sacrament of baptism, we are
farther admitted and united to him. Our right unto Christ
before was general, from the benefit of the common covenant [i]; but, in this sacrament of baptism, my right is made
personal; and I now lay claim unto Christ, not only in the
right of his common promise, but by the efficacy of this particular washing, which sealeth and ratifieth the covenant unto
me. Thus is our first union unto Christ wrought by the
grace of the covenant effectively,—and by the grace of baptism (where it may be had) instrumentally; the one giving

[f] John vi. 63. Rom. viii. 2. [g] Affectus consociat et confœderat voluntates.
Cyprian. [h] 1 Cor. iii. 16. Rom. viii. 9, 11. 2 Tim. i. 14. Eph. iii. 17. Gen.
xvii. 17. Deus ut personam non accipit, sic nec ætatem. *Cyprian.* lib. 3. Epist. 8.
[i] Tit. iii. 5. Vide *Coquæ.* Commen. ad lib. 1.—*Aug.* de Civ. Dei, cap. 27. num. 2.

unto Christ, the other obsignating and exhibiting, that right, by a farther admission of us into his body.

But now we must conceive, that as there is a union unto Christ, so there must, as in natural bodies, be, after that union, a growing up, till we come to our ἀχμὴ, the measure of the fulness of Christ [k]. This growth, being an effect of the vital faculty, is more or less perfected in us, as that is either more or less stifled or cherished. For as in the soul and body, so in Christ and the church, we are not to conceive the union without any latitude, but capable of augmentation, and liable to sundry diminutions, according as are the several means, which, for either purpose, we apply unto ourselves. The union of the soul and body, though not dissolved, is yet, by every the least distemper, slackened,—by some violent diseases, almost rended asunder; so that the body hath sometimes more, sometimes less holdfast of the soul. So here, we are in the covenant and in baptism united unto Christ: but we must not forget, that in men there is by nature ' a root of bitterness [l],' whence issue those ' fruits of the flesh [m],' a spawn and womb of actual corruptions, where sin is daily ' conceived and brought forth [n];' a ' mare mortuum,' *a lake of death,* whence continually arise all manner of noisome and infectious lusts: by means of which, our union to Christ, though not dissolved, is yet daily weakened, and stands in need of continual confirmation. For every sin doth more or less smother and stop the principle of life in us; so that it cannot work our growth, which we must rise unto, with so free and uninterrupted a course as otherwise it might.

The principle of life in a Christian, is the very same, from whence Christ himself, according to his created graces, receiveth life; and that is the Spirit of Christ [o], a quickening Spirit [p], and a strengthening Spirit [q]. Now as that great sin, which is incompatible with faith, doth bid defiance to the good Spirit of God, and therefore is more especially called, ' The sin against the Holy Ghost;' so every sin doth, in its own manner and measure, quench the Spirit [r], that it cannot

---

[k] Eph. iv. 13, 15.   Heb. xii. 15.   [m] Gal. v.   [n] Jam. i. 15.
[o] Gal. iv. 6. Rom. viii. 2.   [p] John vi. 63.   [q] Ephes. iii. 16.   [r] 1 Thess.
v. 19.

quicken, and grieve the Spirit[s], that it cannot strengthen us in that perfection of degrees as it might otherwise.

And thus is our union unto Christ daily loosened and slackened by the distempers of sin. For the re-establishing whereof, God hath appointed these sacred mysteries as effectual instruments, where they meet with a qualified subject, to produce a more firm and close union of the soul to Christ, and to strengthen our faith, which is the joint and sinew by which that union is preserved ; to cure those wounds[t], and to purge those iniquities, whose property is to separate betwixt Christ and us ; to make us submit our services[u], to knit our wills, to conform our affections, and to incorporate our persons into him: that so, by constant, though slow proceedings, we might be changed from ' glory to glory,' and attain unto the 'measure of Christ,' there where our faith can no way be impaired, our bodies and souls subject to no decay, and by consequence stand in no need of any such viaticums[x], as we here use to strengthen us in a journey so much both above the perfection, and against the corruption of our present nature.

CHAPTER XIV.

Of three other ends of the holy Sacrament: the fellowship or union of the faithful; the obsignation of the covenant of grace; and the abrogation of the passover.

Now as the same nourishment, which preserveth the union between the soul and body, or head and members, doth, in like manner, preserve the union between the members themselves ; even so this Sacrament is, as it were, the

---

[s] Ephes. iv. 30.   [t] Iste qui vulnus habet, medicinam requirit. Vulnus est, quia sub peccato sumus; medicina est cœleste et venerabile Sacramentum. *Ambros.* de Sacram. l. 5. cap. 4. Simul medicamentum et holocaustum ad sanandas infirmitates, et purgandas iniquitates. *Cyprian.* de Cœn. Dom.   [u] Potus quasi quædam incorporatio, subjectis obsequiis, voluntatibus junctis, affectibus unitis : Esus carnis hujus quædam aviditas est, et quoddam desiderium manendi in ipso. *Cyprian.* Ibid.—ἕνωσις. *Chrysost.* hom. 24. in 1 Cor.—Qui vult vivere, habet ubi vivat, accedat, credat, incorporetur, vivificetur. *Aug.* epist. 59. et vide de Civ. Dei, lib. 10. cap. 6.   [x] Sicolim Sacramentum appellatum. Vid. *Dur.* de ritibus Ecclesiæ, lib. 2. cap. 25.

sinew of the church, whereby the faithful, being all animated
by the same Spirit that makes them one with Christ, are
knit together in a bond of peace [y], conspiring all in a unity
of thoughts and desires; having the same common enemies
to withstand, the same common prince to obey, the same
common rule to direct them, the same common way to pass,
the same common faith to vindicate; and therefore the same
mutual engagements to further and advance the good of each
other. So that the next immediate effect of this Sacrament
is, to confirm the union of all the members of the church,
each to other, in a communion of saints, whereby their
prayers are the more strengthened, and their adversaries the
more resisted. For as in natural things, union [z] strengtheneth motions natural, and weakeneth violent; so, in the
church, union strengtheneth all spiritual motions, whether
upward, as meditations and prayers to God,—or downward,
as sympathy and good works towards our weak brethren:
and it hindereth all violent motions, the strength of sin, the
darts of Satan, the provocations of the world, the judgements of God; or whatever evil may be by the flesh,
either committed or deserved. And this union of the faithful, is both in the elements, and appellations, and in the
ancient ceremonies, and in the very act of eating and drinking, most significantly represented.

First, For the elements, they are such as, though naturally
their parts were separated in several grains and grapes, yet
are they, by the art of man, moulded together, and made up
into one artificial body, consisting of divers homogeneous
parts [a]. Men, by nature, are disjointed not more in being,
than in affections and desires each from other, every one
being his own end, and not any way affected with that tenderness of communion, or bowels of love, which in Christ
we recover. But now Christ hath redeemed us from this
estate of enmity; and drawing us all to the pursuit of one
common end, and thereunto enabling us by one uniform
rule, his holy Word, and by one vital principle, his holy

---

[y] Ephes. iv. 3, 4.   [z] Advancement of Learning, lib. 2.   [a] Quando
Dominus Corpus suum ' panem' vocat de multorum granorum adunatione con-
gestum, populum nostrum quem portabat, indicat adunatum, &c. *Cypr*. lib. 1.
epist. 6. Καθάπερ γὰρ ὁ ἄρτος ἐκ πολλῶν συγκείμενος κόκκων ἥνωται, &c
Chrysost. in 1 Cor. Hom. 24.

Spirit,—we are, by the means of this holy Sacrament, after the same manner, reunited into one spiritual body, as the elements, though originally several, are into one artificial mass. And for the same reason (as I conceive) was the holy passover, in the law [b], commanded to be one whole lamb, and eaten in one family, and not to have one bone of it broken; to signify that there should be all unity, and no schism or rupture in the church, which is Christ's body.

Secondly, For the appellations of this Sacrament, it is commonly called " The Lord's Supper;" which word, though with us it import nothing but an ordinary course and time of eating, yet in other language it expresseth that, which the other appellation retains, ' communion ' or ' fellowship [c].' And lastly, it was called by the ancients, ' Synaxis [d],' a collection, gathering together, or assembling of the faithful, namely, into that unity which Christ by his merits purchased, by his prayer obtained, and by his Spirit wrought in them. So great hath ever been the wisdom of God's spirit, and of his church, which is ruled by it; to impose on divine institutions such names, as might express their virtue and our duty. As Adam's sacrament was called the tree of life [e]; the Jews' sacraments [f], the covenant, and the passover; and with the Christians [g], baptism is called ' regeneration :' —and the Lord's Supper, ' communion :' that, by the names, we might be put in mind of the power of the things themselves.

Thirdly, For the ceremonies and customs, annexed unto this Sacrament in the primitive times,—notwithstanding for superstitious abuses some of them have been abolished, yet in their own original use they did signify this uniting and knitting quality, which the Sacraments have in it, whereby the faithful are made one with Christ by faith, and amongst themselves by love.

And first, They had a custom of mixing water with the wine [h] (as there came water and blood out of Christ's side),

---

[b] Exod. xii. 26.   [c] *Cæna*, ἀπὸ τοῦ κοινοῦ, à Communione vescentium. *Plut.* et *Isiod.*   [d] Σύναξις διὰ τὸ συνάγειν πρὸς τὸ ἕν. *Dionys.* in John 17.   [e] Gen. iii. 22. xvii. 10.   [f] Exod. xii. 17.   [g] Tit. iii. 5. 1 Cor. x. 16.   [h] Quando in calice vino aqua miscetur, Christo populus adunatur. Si vinum tantum quis offerat, sanguis Christi incipit esse sine nobis ; si verò aqua sit sola, plebs incipit esse sine Christo. *Cypr.* lib. 2. epist. 3.—Ποτήριον ὕδατος καὶ κράματος. *Just. Mart.* Apol. 2.—Ὁ μὲν οἶνος τῷ ὕδατι κίρναται, τῷ δὲ ἀνθρώπῳ τὸ πνεῦμα. *Clem. Alex.* Pœd. lib. 2. c. 2.—*Ambros.* de Sacra. l. 5. c. 1.

which, however it might have a natural reason, because of
the heat of the country, and custom of the southern parts,
where the use was to correct the heat of wine with water [i];
yet was it, by the Christians, used not without a mystical
and allegorical sense,—to express the mixture (whereof this
Sacrament is an effectual instrument) of all the people (who
have faith to receive it) with Christ's blood: water [k] being,
by the Holy Ghost himself, interpreted for 'people' and
' nations.'

Secondly, At the receiving of this holy Sacrament, their
custom was to kiss one another with a holy kiss [l], or a kiss
of love, as a testification of mutual dearness; it proceeding
from the exiliency of the spirits [m], and readiness of nature
to meet and unite itself unto the thing beloved. For love is
nothing else but a delightful affection arising from an attractive power in the goodness of some excellent object,
unto which it endeavoureth to cleave and to unite itself.
And therefore it was an argument of hellish hypocrisy in
Judas, and an imitation of his father the Devil (who trans-
formeth himself into an angel of light, for the enlargement
of his kingdom), to use this holy symbol of love for the instrument of a hatred: so much the more devilish than any,
by how much the object of it was the more divine.

Thirdly, After the celebration of the divine mysteries, the
Christians, to testify their mutual love to each other, did
eat in common together. Which feasts, from that which
they did signify (as the use of God and his church, is to
proportion names and things), were called ' love-feasts [n],' to
testify unto the very heathen [o], how dearly they were knit
together.

Fourthly, After receiving of these holy mysteries, there
were extraordinary oblations and collections [p] for refreshing
Christ's poor members; who, either for his name, or under
his hand, did suffer with patience the calamities of this pre-

i _Stuck._ Antiq. Conviv. lib. 3. c. 11.   k Rev. xvii. 15.   l Ἀλλήλους φιλήματι
ἀσπαζόμεθα, &c. _Justin._ Mart. Apol. 2.   m _Scalig._ de Subt. Exercit.—_Arist._
Pol. l. 2. c. 4.   n Acts ii. 26. 2 Pet. ii. 13. Jude v. 12. Cœna nostra de nomine rationem sui ostendit. _Tert._ Apol. cap. 39. Vide _Stuck._ Antiq. Conviv. l. 1.
c. 33.   o Vide (inquiunt) ut invicem diligunt! _Tertul._ et _Minut. Fel._
p Οἱ εὐποροῦντες καὶ βουλόμενοι, κατὰ προαίρεσιν ἕκαστος τὴν ἑαυτοῦ ὃ βούλεται,
δίδωσι, καὶ τὸ συλλεγόμενον παρὰ τῷ προεστῶτι ἀποτίθεται, καὶ αὐτὸς ἐπινέμει
ὀρφάνοις τε καὶ χήραις, &c. _Just. Mart._ Apolog. 2.

sent life, expecting the glory which should be revealed unto
them. Those did they make the treasures of the church,—
their bowels, the hordes and repositories of their piety[q];
and such as were orphans, or widows, or aged, or sick, or
in bonds, condemned to mine-pits, or to the islands, or desolate places, or dark dungeons (the usual punishments in
those times), with all these were they not ashamed in this
holy work to acknowledge a unity of condition, a fellowship
and equality in the spiritual privileges of the same Head, a
mutual relation of fellow-members in the same common
body; unto which, if any had greater right than other, they
certainly were the men, who were conformed unto their
Head in suffering, and did go to their kingdom through the
same path of blood, which he had before besprinkled for
them.

Lastly, It was the custom, in any solemn testimonial of
peace[r], to receive and exhibit this holy Sacrament, as the
seal and earnest of that union, which the parties, whom it
did concern, had between themselves. Such had ever been
the care of the holy church[s] in all the customs and ceremonial accessions, whether of decency or charity, which have
been by it appointed in this holy Sacrament,—That by them
and in them all, the concinnation of the body of Christ, the
fellowship, sympathy, and unity of his members, might be
both signified and professed:—That as we have all but one
sacrament, which is the food of life,—so we should have but
one soul, which is the Spirit of life; and from thence but
one heart, and one mind, thinking, and loving, and pursuing all the same things, through the same way, by the same
rule, to the same end. And for this reason, amongst others,
I take it, it is that our church doth require, in the receiving
of these mysteries, a uniformity in all her members, even in
matters that are of themselves indifferent,—that, in the sacrament of unity, there might not appear any breach or
schism; but that as at all times, so much more then, we

q Deposita Pietatis : Vide *Tert.* Apol. c. 39. ʳ Vide *Stuck.* An. Conv.
lib. 1. cap. 3. ˢ Acts iv. 32.—Phil. i. 27.—Unum signum habemus: quare
non in uno ovili sumus? *August.* Tom. 7. Serm. ad Pleb. Cæsariensem.—Ἔστι δ'
ἡ τοιαύτη ὁμόνοια ἐν τοῖς ἐπιείκεσιν· οὗτοι γὰρ καὶ ἑαυτοῖς ὁμονοοῦσι καὶ ἀλλήλοις.
Arist. Ethic. l. 9. c. 6. edit. Zell, vol. 1. p. 407.—Vide fus. de hac re *Stuck.* Antiq.
Conv. l. 1. c. 3.

should all think, and speak, and do the same things, lest
the manner should oppose the substance of the celebration.

Lastly, If we consider the very act of eating and drinking,
even therein is expressed the fellowship and the union of the
faithful to each other: for even, by nature, are men directed to express their affections or reconcilements to others in
feasts and invitations, where even public enemies[t] have con-
descended to terms of fairness and plausibility. For which
cause it is noted for one of the acts of tyrants, whereby to
dissociate the minds of their subjects, and so to break them
when they are asunder, whom all together they could not
bend, to interdict invitations and mutual hospitalities,
whereby the body politic is as well preserved as the natural,
and the love of men as much nourished as their bodies. And
therefore where Joseph[u] did love most, there was the mess
doubled; and the national hatred between the Jews and
Egyptians, springing from the diversity of religions (whose
work it is to knit[x] and fasten the affections of men), was no
way better expressed, than by their mutual abominating the
tables of each other[y]. So that, in all these circumstances,
we find how the union of the faithful unto each other, is,
in this holy Sacrament, both signified and confirmed; whereby (however they may, in regard of temporal relations, stand
at great distance, even as great as is between the palace and
the prison) yet in Christ, they are all fellow-members of the
same common body, and fellow-heirs of the same common
kingdom, and spiritual stones of the same common church,
which is a name of unity and peace[z].

They have ' one Father[a],' who deriveth on them an equal
nobility; 'one Lord,' who equally governeth them; 'one
Spirit,' who equally quickeneth them; 'one baptism,' which
equally regenerateth them; 'one faith,' which equally war-
rants their inheritance to them; and lastly, one sinew and
bond of love, which equally interesteth them in the joys and
griefs of each other: so that, as in all other, so principally

[t] Scipio et Asdrubal apud Scyphacem. *Liv.* l. 20.—*Arist.* Polit. lib. 5. cap. 11.
—Vid. *Baron.* An. 100. Num. 8.   [u] Gen. xliii. 34.   [x] Religio à religando,
Cicero.   [y] Gen. xliii. 32. Ἐκβάλλων τὴν ἀνομαλίαν τῶν ἀξιωμάτων, πᾶσι
μίαν ἐπιστέλλει προσηγορίαν. *Chrys.* in Rom. Hom. l. 2.   [z] Τὸ τῆς ἐκκλησίας
ὄνομα οὐ χωρισμοῦ, ἀλλ᾽ ἐνώσεως καὶ συμφωνίας ὄνομα. *Chrys.* in 1 Cor. Hom. 1.
[a] Ephes. iv. 5, 6.

in this divine friendship of Christ's church, there is an equality and uniformity [b], be the outward distances how great soever.

Another principal end or effect of this holy supper, is to signify and obsignate, unto the soul of each believer, his personal claim and title unto the new covenant of grace. We are in a state of corruption. Sin, though it have received by Christ a wound, of which it cannot recover; yet as beasts[c] commonly in the pangs of death, use most violently to struggle, and often to fasten their teeth more eagerly and fiercely where they light; so sin here, that ' body of death [d],' that besieging [e], encompassing evil,—that Canaanite [f] that lieth in our members, being continually heartened by our arch-enemy Satan, however subdued by Israel, doth yet never cease to goad and prick us in the eyes, that we might not look up to our future possession,—is ever raising up steams of corruption to intercept the lustre of that glory which we expect,—is ever suggesting unto the believer, matter of diffidence and anxiety, that his hopes hitherto have been ungrounded, his faith presumptuous, his claim to Christ deceitful, his propriety uncertain, if not quite desperate; till at last the faithful soul lies gasping and panting for breath under the buffets of this messenger of Satan. And for this cause it hath pleased our good God (who hath promised never to fail [g] nor forsake us), that we might not be swallowed up with grief, to renew often our right, and exhibit with his own hands [h] (for what is done by his officers is by him done) that sacred body, with the efficacy of it, unto us, that we might fore-enjoy the promised inheritance, and put, not into our chests or coffers, which may haply by casualties miscarry, but into our very bowels, into our substance and soul, the pledges of our salvation; that we might, at this spiritual altar, see Christ (as it were) crucified before our eyes [i], cling unto his cross [k], and grasp it in our arms, suck in his blood, and with it salvation; put

---

[b] Λέγεται φιλότης ἡ ἰσότης. Eth. lib. 8. c. 5. & 8.   [c] Maximè mortiferi esse solent morsus morientium bestiarum. *Flor.* 1. 2. cap. 15.   [d] Rom. vii. 24.   [e] Heb. xii. 1.   [f] Josh. xxiii. 13.   [g] Heb. xiii. 6.   [h] Καὶ γὰρ καὶ σήμερον αὐτός ἐστιν ὁ πάντα ἐργαζόμενος καὶ παραδιδοὺς ὥσπερ καὶ τότε. *Chrys.* in 1. Cor. Hom. 27.   [i] Gal. iii. 1.   [k] Cruci hæremus, sanguinem sugimus, et inter ipsa Redemptoris nostri vulnera figimus linguam, &c. *Cyprian.* Cœna Dom.

G 2

in our hands, with Thomas, not out of diffidence, but out of
faith, into his side, and fasten our tongues in his sacred
wounds ; that being all over died with his blood, we may use
boldness, and approach to the throne of grace, lifting up
unto Heaven, in faith and confidence of acceptance, those
eyes and hands which have seen and handled him,—opening
wide that mouth which hath received him, and crying aloud
with that tongue which, having tasted the bread of life, hath
from thence both strength and arguments for prayer to move
God for mercy.   This then is a singular benefit of this Sacrament, the often repetition and celebration whereof, is (as
it were) the renewing, or rather the confirming with more
and more seals our patent of life ; that by so many things,
in the smallest whereof it is impossible for God to lie [1], we
might have strong consolation, who have our refuge to lay
hold on him, who in these holy mysteries is set before us :
for the Sacrament is not only a sign to represent [m], but a
seal to exhibit that which it represents.   In the sign we see,
in the seal we receive, him ; in the sign we have the image,
in the seal the benefit, of Christ's body : for the nature of a
sign is to discover and represent that which in itself is obscure or absent, as words are called signs and symbols
of our invisible thoughts : but the property of a seal [n] is to
ratify and to establish that which might otherwise be ineffectual : for which cause, some have called the Sacrament
by the name of 'a ring,' which men use in sealing those
writings, unto which they annex their trust and credit [o].   And
as the Sacrament is a sign and seal from God to us, representing and exhibiting his benefits, so should it be a sign and
seal from us to God ; a sign to separate us from sinners [p], a
seal to oblige us to all performances of faith and thankfulness on our part required.

Another end and effect of this holy Sacrament was, to
abrogate the passover, and testify the alteration of those
former types, which were not the commemorations, but the
predictions of Christ's passion.   And for this cause our

[1] Heb. vi. 18.   [m] Gen. xvii. 11. Rom. iv. 11. Exod. xii. 13. *Aug.* de Doctr.
Christ. l. 2. c. 1.   [n] Σημεῖα καὶ σύμβολα τῶν παθημάτων. *Arist.* de Interp.
cap. 1.   [o] Plus annulis nostris quàm animis creditur. *Seneca.*   [p] Καθάπερ
ϛαλινόν τινα ἐπιτιθεὶς, οὕτω τὸ σημεῖον τῆς περιτομῆς ἔδωκε, ὥστε μὴ τοῖς
θνεσι συναναμίγνυσθαι. *Chrys.* in Gen. Hom. 39.

blessed Saviour did celebrate both those suppers at the same
time (but the new supper after the other, and in the evening,
whereby was figured the fulness of time ᑫ); that thereby the
presence of the substance might evacuate the shadow; even
as the sun doth ʳ, with his lustre, take away all those lesser
and substituted lights, which were used for no other purpose
but to supply the defect which there was of him. The passover, however, in the nature of a sacrifice, it did prefigure
Christ; yet in the nature of a solemnity and annual commemoration, it did immediately respect the temporal deliverance of that people out of Egypt, by the sprinkling of their
doors with blood, which was itself but a shadow of our freedom from Satan. So that their Sacrament was but the type
of a type, and therefore must needs have so much the weaker
and more obscure reference unto Christ: even as those
draughts do less resemble the face of a man, which are taken
from a former piece; or that light the brightness of its original ˢ, which shines weakly through a second or third reflection. Besides this small light which shined from the
passover on the people of the Jews, and by which they were
something, though darkly, enabled to behold Christ,—was
but like the light in a house or family, which could not shine
beyond the narrow compass of that small people: and therefore it was to be eaten in such a family ᵗ;—to signify, as I
conceive, that the church was then but as a handful or household, in respect of that fulness of the Gentiles, which was to
follow. Now then, the church being to enlarge its borders,
and to be co-extended with the world, it stood in need of a
greater light, even that Son of righteousness, who was now to
be as well the light to lighten the Gentiles ᵘ, as he had been
formerly the glory of his people Israel. And therefore we
may observe, that this second Sacrament was not to be
eaten in a private separated family, but the church was to
come together, and to stay one for another ˣ, that, in the
confluence of the people, and the publicness of the action,
the increase and amplitude of the church might be ex-

ᑫ Ἔνθα ὁ τύπος τὴν ἀλήθειαν ἐπιτίθησι. *Chrys.* in Mat. Hom. 81. Ἡ δὲ
ἑσπέρα τοῦ πληρώματος τῶν καιρῶν τεκμήριον. *Ib.* ʳ Est hæc natura side-
ribus, ut parva et exilia validiorum exortus obscuret: *Plin.* Paneg. xix. 1.
ˢ Cum velut è speculo in speculum tralucet imago. *Lucret.* ᵗ Exod. xii. 46.
ᵘ Luke ii. 32. ˣ 1 Cor. xi. 33.

pressed. Besides, the Gentiles were uninterested in that temporal deliverance of the Jews from Pharaoh, it being a particular and national benefit; and therefore the commemoration thereof in the paschal lamb, could not, by them,—who, in the loins of their ancestors, had not been there delivered,—be, literally and with reflection on themselves, celebrated. Requisite therefore in this respect also it was, inasmuch as the partition-wall [y] was broken down, and both Jew and Gentile were incorporated into one head,—that national and particular relations ceasing, such a Sacrament might be re-instituted; wherein the universal restoring of all mankind might be represented [z]. And certainly for a man, at midday, to shut his windows from the communion of the general light, and to use only private lamps of his own, as it is towards men madness, so it is impiety and schism in religion.

There is, between the gospel and the legal ceremonies (as I observed) the same proportion of difference, as is between household tapers and the common sunshine;—as in regard of the amplitude of their light, and of the extent of their light, so in the duration of it likewise. For as lamps, within a small time, do of themselves expire and perish, whereas the light of the sun doth never waste itself; even so Jewish rites were by God's institution perishable and temporary [a], during that infancy of the church, wherein it was not able to look on a brighter object [b]: but when, in the fulness of time, the church was grown unto a firmer sense, then, in the death of Christ, did those types likewise die, and were, together with the sins of the world, cancelled upon the cross [c]. Amongst the Persians [d], it was a solemn observation to nullify, for a time, the force of their laws, and to extinguish those fires, which they were wont idolatrously to adore, upon the death of their king, as if by him both their policy and religion had been animated: even so, at the death of our blessed Saviour, were all those legal ordinances, those holy fires, which were wont to send up the sweet savour of incense, and sacrifices unto Heaven, abolished. He (who before had substituted them in his room, and by an effectual

[y] Ephes. ii. 14.   [z] Hos. i. 10, 11.   [a] Vide *Aug.* Epist. 5. ad Marcellinum, et Epist. 19. ad Hieron. cap. 2. et *Tert.* cont. Judæ. cap. 2. et 6. et de Monogam. cap. 7. et de Orat. c. 1.   [b] Gal. iv. 3.   [c] Ephes. ii. 15, 16.   [d] Vide *Brisson.* de Reb. Pers. l. 1. p. 27.

influence from himself made them temporary instruments of that propitiation, which it was impossible for them [e], in their own natures, to have effected) being himself come to finish that work which was by them only fore-shadowed, but not begun, much less accomplished.

CHAPTER XV.

The last end of this holy Sacrament; namely, the celebration and memory of Christ's death. A brief collection of all the benefits which are, by his death, conveyed on the Church. The question touching the quality of temporal punishments, stated.

THE last and most express end of this holy Sacrament, is, to celebrate the memory of Christ's death and passion [f], which was that invaluable price of our double redemption; redemption from hell, and redemption unto glory. Great deliverances, as they have moved the church unto anniversary celebrations of them [g], which Christ himself hath been pleased to honour with his own presence; so have they drawn even heathen men [h] also, not only to solemnize the festivals, and deify the memories of those, unto whose inventions they owed the good things which they enjoy, but further to honour even brute creatures themselves [i] with solemn triumphs and memorials. Nay, beasts [k] have not been forgetful of those, unto whom they owe any way their life and safety: how much more then doth it become Christians to celebrate, with an eternal memory the Author of their redemption: a work beyond all that ever the sun saw; yea, a work, whose lustre darkened the sun itself, and which the angels cannot comprehend! Matters circumstantial, as time and place; and matters typical and representative, as ceremonies, sacrifices, and sacraments; as they receive their particular advancement and sanctification from those works

---

[e] Heb. x. 4.   [f] 1 Cor. xi.   [g] Esth. ix. 17.   [h] 1 Mac. iv. 55, 56. John x. 22.—*Cypr.* de Idol. Vanit.—*Min. Fel.* in Octav.—*Clem. Alex.* in Protreptico. [i] Anseres quotannis apud Romanos splendida in lectica sedebant, quod in obsidione Capitolii excitâssent. Vid. *Rosin.* Antiq. Rom. lib. 4. cap. 17.   [k] *Leo.* apud Aul. Gell. lib. 5. cap. 14.

which they immediately respect; so are they not by us to
be solemnly celebrated without continual memories of those
works which do so dignify them. All places, naturally being
but several parcels of the same common air and earth, are
of an equal worth. But when it pleaseth God in any place
to bestow a more special ray of his presence [1], and to sanctify any temple unto his own service, as it is then, by that
extraordinary presence of his, made a holy and consecrated
place; so are we, when we enter into it, to look unto our
feet [m], to pull off our shoes [n], to have an eye unto him that
filleth it with his presence ; or otherwise if we enter into it,
as into a common place, we shall offer nothing but the sacrifice of fools. All times are naturally equal, as being distinguished by the same constant and uniform motion of the
heavens : yet notwithstanding, when God shall, by any notable and extraordinary work of his, honour and sanctify
some certain days, as he did the Jewish sabbath with respect
to the creation, and our Lord's day, by raising up Christ
from the dead ; as they are, by this wonderful work of his,
severed from the rank of common times ;—so are we, ever
when we come unto them, not to pass them over without
the memory [o] of that work which had so advanced them :
otherwise to solemnize a day, without reference unto the
cause of its solemnization, is but a blind observance. And
for this cause, when God commands reverence to places, and
sanctification of days,—he annexeth the ground of both, and
leads us to a sight of those works, from which they receive
both their dignity and institution. So likewise in Sacraments, to eat bread and drink wine are naked, common,
simple actions, and in themselves always alike : but when
Christ shall, by that great work of his death, set them apart
unto a holy use, and make them representations of his own
sacred body,— as they are by this divine relation hallowed, so
to partake of them, without commemorating that great work
which hath so sanctified them, is not only impious, in that it
perverteth the divine institution, but absurd likewise ; it
being all one, as if a man should, with much ceremony and
solemnity, receive parchment and wax, never so much as
thinking on the land it conveys ; or look on a picture, with-

[1] Exod. xi. 34.   1 Kings viii. 11.   [m] Eccles. iv. 17.   [n] Exod. iii. 4.
[o] Εἰς ἀνάμνησιν τοῦ παθοῦς. Just. Mart. Dialog.

out any reflection on the pattern and original which it resembleth,—which is indeed to look on the wood, and not on
the picture ; it being naturally impossible to separate things
in notion, whose being do consist in relation to each other.
So then, the Sacrament being a typical service, is not, nor
can be, celebrated without a remembrance of the substance
which it resembleth : which thing, according as the preciousness, value, and importance of it doth proportionably
impose on us a greater necessity of this duty ; which is then
rightly performed, when there is a deep impression of Christ
crucified made on the soul, by these seals of his death ; than
which there is not any thing in the world more fit to fasten a
stamp of itself in the minds of men.

Permanent and firm impressions do use to be made in the
minds of men by such causes as these :—

First, If the object be wonderful[p], and beyond the common course of things, it doth then strangely affect the
thoughts ; whereas obvious and ordinary things pass through
the soul, as common people do through the streets, without
any notice at all. And this is the reason why naturally men
remember those things best, which either they did in their
childhood[q], because then every thing brings with it the
shape of novelty, and novelty is the mother of admiration ;
or those things which do very rarely fall out, which howsoever they may be in their causes natural, yet, with the
greater part of men, who use to make their observations rather on the events, than on the originals of things, they pass
for wonders. Now what greater wonder hath ever entered
into the thoughts of men, even of those who have spent
their time and conceits in amplifying nature with creatures
of their own fancying than this,—That the God of all the
world, without derivation from whose life, all the creatures
must moulder into their first nothing,—should himself die,
and expire, the frame of Nature still subsisting ? That he
who filleth all things with his presence, should be stretched
out upon a piece of wood, and confined within a narrow

---

p *Aug.* de Gen. ad liter. l. 12. cap. 11. Amant homines inexperta mirari, &c.
Ea quæ sub oculis posita sunt, negligimus : quia seu natura comparatum ita, ut
proximorum incuriosi, longinqua sectemur ; seu quod omnium rerum cupido
languescit, cum facilis occasio est. *Plin.* lib. 8. epist. 20. Magnitudinem rerum
consuetudo subducit : Sol spectatorem, nisi cum deficit, non habet ; nemo observat lunam, nisi laborantem. *Senec.* Nat. q. l. 7. c. 1.   q *Arist.* Polit. l. 2.

stone? He who upholdeth all things by his power, should be himself kept under by that which is nothing, by death? Certainly, that at which the world stood amazed,—that which against the course of nature brought darkness on the fountain of light, which could no longer shine, when his glory, who derived lustre on it, was itself eclipsed;—that which made the earth to tremble under the burden of so bloody a sin;—that which the angels stoop and look into with humble astonishment and adoration;—that which consisteth of so great a combination and confluence of wonders;—must needs make a deep impression on the soul, though hard as marble, at which the stones themselves of the temple did rend asunder.

Secondly, Those things use to make impressions on the understanding, which do move and excite any strong passion of the mind; there being ever a most near activity and intimate reference between passion and reason, by means of that natural affinity and subordination which is between them. Observe it in one passion of love, how it removes the mind from all other objects, firmly fixing it on one thing which it most respecteth. For as knowledge makes the object to be loved, so love makes us desire to know more of the object[q]. The reason whereof is that inseparable union which nature hath fixed in all things between the truth and good of them; either of which, working on the proper faculty to which it belongeth, provokes it to set the other faculty on work, either by distinction, as from the understanding to the passion,—or by insinuation, as from the passion to the understanding;—even as fire doth not heat without light, nor enlighten without heat. Where the treasure is, the earth cannot be absent; where the body is, the eagles must resort. If I know a thing to be good, I must love it; and where I love the goodness of it, I cannot but desire to know it; all divine objects being as essentially good as they are true, and the knowledge and love of them being as naturally linked, as the nerve is to the part which it moveth, or as the beam is to the heat and influence by which it worketh[r]. Now what object is there can more deserve our love, than the death of Christ? Certainly if it be natural

[q] Non patior me quicquam nescire de eo quem amem. *Plin. Epist.* [r] Dr. *Jackson*, of Faith, sect. 1. cap. 8. sect. 8.

for men to love where they have been loved before [s]; and if
in that case it be fit, that the quantity of the former love
should be the rule and measure of the latter; how can it be,
that our love to him should not exceed all other love, even
as he justly requireth ?—" since greater love than this hath
not been seen, that a man should neglect the love of himself, and lay down his life for his enemies [t]." And if we love
Christ, that will naturally lead us to remember him too;
who as he is the life, and so the object of our love, so he is
the truth likewise [u], and so the object of our knowledge.
And therefore the same apostle, who did rejoice in nothing
but Christ crucified [x] (and joy is nothing else but love perfected, for they differ only as the same water in the pipe,
and in the fountain), did likewise, notwithstanding his emi-
nency in all pharisaical learning, desire to know nothing but
Jesus Christ, and him crucified [y]. Such a dominion hath
love on the mind, to make permanent and firm impressions.

Lastly, Those things work strongly upon the memory,
which do mainly concern and are beneficial to man. There
is no man, not dispossessed of reason, who in sickness doth
forget the physician; neither did ever any man hear of any
one starved, because he did not remember to eat his meat.
Beasts [z] indeed I have heard of (but those very strange ones
too) which, upon turning aside from their meat, have forgotten the presence of it. but never were any so forsaken
by nature, as to forget the desire and enquiry after what they
wanted. And the reason is, because wheresoever Nature
hath left a capacity of receiving further perfection from
some other thing, there she hath imprinted an appetite to
that thing: and there is such a sympathy between the faculties of nature, that the indigence of one sets all the rest
on motion to supply it. Now what thing was there ever
more beneficial unto mankind than the death of Christ? In
comparison whereof, all other things are as dross and dung.
The name [a], and fruit, and hope of a Christian, would be all
but shadows, if Christ had not died. By his humility, are
we exalted; by his curse, are we blessed; by his bondage,

[s] Τοὺς πεποιηκότας εὖ φιλοῦσι. *Arist.* Rhet. lib. 2.   [t] 1 John xiv. 19. Rom.
v. 7, 8.   [u] John xv. 13.   [x] Gal. vi. 12.   [y] 1 Cor. ii. 2.   [z] *Senec.*
de Benef.   [a] Totum Christiani nominis et pondus et fructus, Mors Christi.
Tertul. cont. Marc. l. 3. c. 8.

are we made free; by his stripes, are we healed : we, who
were vessels of dishonour, had all our miseries emptied into
him, in whom dwelled the fulness of the Godhead. Whatsoever evils he suffered [b], ours was the propriety to them,
but the pain was his : all that ignominy and agony [c] which
was unworthy so honourable a person as Christ, was necessary for so vile a sinner as man.

Infinite it is, and indeed impossible, to take a full view of
all the benefits of Christ's death. Yet because the remembrance of Christ's death here, is nothing else but a recordation of those invaluable blessings, which by means of it
were, together with his holy blood, shed down upon the
church, I will touch a little upon the principal of them.

That Christ Jesus is, unto his church, the author and original of all spiritual life [d], the deliverer [e] that should come
out of Sion, that should set at liberty his people [f], spoil
principalities and powers [g], lead captivity captive [h], take
from the strong man all his armour [i], and divide the spoils ;
is a truth so clearly written with a sunbeam, that no Craco-
vian heretick dare deny it. Let us then see by what means
he doth all this. And we will not here speak of that work,
whereby Christ, having formerly purchased the right, doth
afterwards confer, and actually apply, the benefit and interest of that right unto his members, which is the work of his
quickening Spirit, but only of those means which he used to
procure the right itself; and that was, in general, Christ's
merit. The whole conversation of Christ on the earth, was
nothing else but a continued merit, proceeding from a double estate, an estate of ignominy and passion procuring,—and
an estate of exaltation and honour,—applying his benefits.

The passion of Christ was his death ; whereby I understand not that last act only of expiration, but the whole
space between that and his nativity, wherein being subject
to the law of death, and to all those natural infirmities,
which were the harbingers of death [k], he might, in that

---

[b] Illa in corpore Christi vulnera non erant Christi vulnera, sed latronis. *Ambros.* Serm. 44. de Sancto latrone.   [c] Sibi quidem indigna, homini autem necessaria, et ita jam Deo digna, quia nihil tam dignum Deo quàm salus hominis.
Tert. cont. Marc. l. 2. c. 27.— Quodcunque Deo indignum est, mihi expedit. *Id.*
de Carn. Chris. cap. 5.   [d] John vi. 47.   [e] Rom. xi. 26.   [f] John viii. 36.
Gal. ii. 4.   [g] Col. ii. 15.   [h] Ephes. iv. 8.   [i] Luke xi. 22.   [k] Esuriens
sub diabolo, sitiens sub Samaritide, &c. *Tert.*

whole space, be as truly called, ' a man of death,' as Adam
was a dead man[1] in the virtue of the curse that very day,
beyond which notwithstanding he lived many hundred years.
that which we call death, being nothing else but the consummation of it[m].

The estate of exaltation is the resurrection of Christ;
whereby the efficacy of that merit which was on the cross
consummated, is publicly declared; and his intercession
wherein it is proposed and presented unto God the Father,
as an eternal price and prayer in the behalf of his church.
Now the benefits, which by this merit of Christ's we receive,
are of several kinds. Some are privative, consisting in an
immunity from all those evils which we were formerly subject unto, whether of sin or punishment. Others are positive, including in them a right[n] and interest unto all the prerogatives of the sons of God. The one is called an ' expiation, satisfaction, redemption, or deliverance :' the other,
' a purchase, and free donation of some excellent blessing.'
Redemption, thus distinguished, is either a redemption of
grace, from the bondage and tyranny of sin; or a redemption of glory, from the bondage of corruption : and both
these have their parts and latitudes.

For the first. In sin we may consider three things : the
state or mass of sin; the guilt or damnableness of sin; and
the corruption, stain, or deformity of sin.

The state of sin is a state of deadness[o], or immobility in
nature, towards any good. The understanding is dead and
disabled for any spiritual perception ; the will is dead and
disabled for any holy propension ; the affections are dead
and disabled for any pursuit; the body dead and disabled
for any obedient ministry ; and the whole man dead, and
by consequence disabled for any sense of its own death.
And as it is a state of death, so it is a state of enmity too :
and therefore in this state, we are the objects of God's hatred and detestation. So then, the first part of our deliverance respects us, as we are in this state of death and
enmity : and it is (as I said before) a double deliverance ;
negative, by removing us out of this estate ; and positive,

[1] Vide *Zeaman* de Imag. Dei in Homine, c. 8. art. 2.   [m] *Senec.* Epist.
[n] Ἐξουσίαν, John i. 12.   [o] Ephes. ii. 1.

by constituting us in another, which is an estate of life and reconcilement.

First, The understanding is delivered from the bondage of ignorance, vanity, worldly wisdom, mispersuasions, carnal principles, and the like; and is (after removal of this darkness and veil) opened, to see and acknowledge both its own darkness, and the evidence of that light which shines upon it. Our wills and affections are delivered from that disability[q] of embracing or pursuing of divine objects, and from that love of darkness and prosecution of evil which is naturally in them[r]; and after this are wrought unto a sorrow and sense of their former estate, to a desire and love of salvation, and of the means thereof, with a resolution to make use of them. And the whole man is delivered, from the estate of death and enmity[s], unto an estate of life and reconciliation, by being adopted for the sons of God. Of these deliverances, Christ is the author, who worketh them (as I observed) by a double casualty : the one, that whereby he meriteth them ; the other, that whereby he conveyeth and transfuseth that which he had merited. This conveying cause is our vocation[t], wrought by the Spirit of Christ effectively, by the Word of life and gospel of regeneration instrumentally; by means of both which (this latter as the seed, that other as the formative virtue that doth vegetate and quicken the seed) are we, from dead men, ingrafted into Christ,—and, of enemies, made sons and co-heirs with Christ. But the meritorious cause of all this, was, that price which Christ laid down, whereby he did ransom us from the estate of death, and purchase for us the adoption of sons. For every ransom and purchase (which are the two acts of our redemption) are procured by the laying down of some price, valuable to the thing ransomed and purchased[u]. Now this price was the precious blood of Christ; and the laying down or payment of this blood, was the pouring it out of his sacred body, and the exhibiting of it unto his Father in a passive obedience. And this is to be applied in the other deliverances.

q 1 Cor. ii. 14.   r Gen. vi. 5.   s 2 Cor. iii. 5. 1 Pet. ii. 9. 2 Cor. iii. 15, 16. Acts. xxvi. 18.   t 2 Cor. iii. 8. 16, 17. Rom. x. 8. James i. 18. 2 Thes. ii. 14. 1 Pet. i. 23.   u 1 Cor. vi. 20.

The second consideration then of sin, was, the guilt of it; which is, the binding over unto some punishment, prescribed in the law. So we have here a double deliverance, from the guilt of sin, and from the bondage of the law.

First, For sin, though it leave still a stain in the soul, yet the sting of it is quite removed : though we are not perfectly cleansed from the soil, yet are we soundly healed from the mortalness and bruises of it.

Then for the law, we are first freed from the curse of the law [x]: it is not unto us a killing letter, nor a word of death, inasmuch as it is not that rule according unto which we expect life.

Secondly, We are freed from the exaction of the law; we are not necessarily bound to the rigorous performance of each jot and tittle of it, a performance unto which is ever annexed legal justification : but our endeavours, though imperfect, are accepted,—our infirmities, though sundry, are forgiven [y], for his sake,—who was under both these bondages of the law for our sakes. And as we are thus delivered from the guilt of sin [z], so are we further endued with positive dignities, interest and propriety to all the righteousness of Christ, with which we are clothed as with a garment : claim unto all the blessings which the law infers upon due obedience performed to it, and the comforts which from either of these titles and prerogatives may ensue. And this is the second branch of deliverance, conveyed by the act of justification, but merited, as the rest, by the death of Jesus Christ.

The third consideration of sin, was the corruption of it; from the which likewise we are by Christ delivered. Sin doth not any more rule, nor reign, nor lead captive those who are ingrafted into Christ,—though for their patience, trial, and exercise' sake, and that they may still learn to live by faith, and to prize mercy, the remnants of it do cleave fast unto our nature; like the sprigs and roots of ivy to a wall which will never out, till the wall be broken down and new built again. Sin is not like the people of Jericho, utterly destroyed; but rather, like the Gibeonites, it liveth still; but in an estate of bondage, servitude, and decay : and besides

[x] Gal. iii. 13.   [y] Mal. iii. 17. Gal. iv. 4, 5.   [z] Rom. v. xiii. 14.

this, we are enabled to love the law in our inner man, to delight in it [a], to perform a ready and sincere, though not
an exact and perfect obedience to it; we are made partakers
of the Divine nature; the graces with which Christ was
anointed, do from him stream down unto his lowest members, which of his fulness do all receive [b], and are all renewed after God's image in righteousness and true holiness [c].

The next part of our redemption was from the bondage of
corruption, unto the liberty of glory, which likewise is by
Christ performed for us [d], which is a deliverance from the
consequents of sin; for sin doth bind over unto punishment,
even as the perfect obedience of the law would bring a man
unto glory. Now the punishments due unto sin are either
temporary or eternal, consisting principally in the oppres-
sions and distresses of nature. For as sin is the evil of our
working, so punishment is the evil of our being: and it in-
cludes not only bodily and spiritual death, but all the in-
choations and preparatory dispositions [e] thereunto; as in the
soul, doubtings, distractions, tremblings, and terrors of conscience, hardness of heart, fearful expectation of the wrath
that shall be revealed;—in the body, sickness, poverty,
shame, infamy, which are as so many earnests and petty
payments of that full debt, which will at last be measured
out to all the wicked of the world. Even as amongst the
Romans [f], their prelusory fights with dull and blunt weapons,
were but introductions to their mortal and bloody games.
And besides this deliverance, there is in the soul peace and
serenity,—in the body [g], a patient waiting for redemption,—
and, in the whole man, the pledges of that eternal glory
which shall be revealed; of all which, the only meritorious
cause is the death of Christ [h]. This alone is it which hath
overcome our death, even as one heat cureth, one flux of
blood stoppeth, another,—and hath caught Satan, as it were,
by deceit, with a bait and a hook. This is it which hath
taken away the enmity between God and man, reconciling
us to the Father [i], and by the prayer of that precious blood,
hath obtained for us the right of children. This is it which

[a] Rom. vii. 22.   [b] John i. 16.   [c] Ephes. iv. 24.   [d] Rom. viii.
[e] *Zeaman* de Imag. Dei in Homine, cap. 8.   [f] *Lips.* Saturn.   [g] Rom. v. and viii.
[h] *Aug.* de Doctr. Christ. l. 1. c. 14.—*Tert.* cont. Gnost. cap. 5.—*Cypr.* in Symb.
[i] Ephes. ii. 16, 19.

took away the guilt of sin, and cancelled the bond that was in force against us[k], swallowing up the curse of the law, and humbling Christ unto the form of a servant, that thereby we might be made free[l]. This is it which removeth, both temporal and eternal punishment, from the faithful, it having been a perfect payment of our whole debt; for inasmuch as Christ himself said on the cross, " It is finished," we are to conclude, that the other work of resurrection was not properly an essential part of Christ's merit, but only a necessary consequent required to make the passion applicable and valuable to the church. As, in coined metals, it is the substance of the coin, the gold or silver only, that buyeth the ware, but the impression of the King's image is that, which makes that coin to be current and passable; it doth not give the value or worth to the gold, but only the application of that value unto other things;—even so the resurrection and intercession of Christ do serve to make actual applications of those merits of his to his church, which yet had their consummation on the cross.

And if it be here demanded, how it comes to pass, that, if all these consequents of sin be removed, the faithful are still subject to all those temporal evils both in life and death, which, even in the state of nature, they should have undergone,—we answer in general, That the faithful die in regard of the state, but not in regard of the sting of death; they are subject to a dissolution, but it is to obtain a more blessed union, even " to be with Christ[m]." And though a man may not take the whole world in exchange for his soul, yet he may well take Christ in exchange for his life. It is not a loss of our money, but traffic and merchandise, to part from it, for the procuring of such commodities as are more valuable[n]: and St. Paul tells us, That ' to die is gain.' The " sting," we know, " of death is sin[o];" for sin is the cause of all inward discomforts; for which cause, the wicked are often compared to the ' foaming sea[p],' which is still tossed and unquiet with every wind; and " the strength of sin is the law," with the malediction and bondage thereof: from the which we being per-

[k] Col. ii. 14.   [l] John xx. 17. Col. ii. 14. Gal. iii. 13. Phil. ii. 7. John viii. 36. 1 John i. 7.   [m] Phil. i. 23.   [n] Mercatura est pauca amittere, ut majora lucreris. Tert. ad Martyr.—Phil. i. 21.   [o] 1 Cor. xv. 56.   [p] Psalm cxxiv. 5. Isai. lv. 20. Jude v. 13

fectly delivered, by him who was himself made under the law ^q, and, by that means, became a perfect and sufficient Saviour ^r,—we are, in like manner, delivered from the penalty of death: For weaken sin by destroying the law, which is the strength of it; and death cannot possibly sting.

To examine this point, though by way of digression, something further will not be altogether impertinent, because it serves to magnify the power of Christ's passion. The evils which we speak of, are the violations of the nature and person of a man. And that evil may be considered two ways, either physically, as it oppresseth and burdeneth nature, working some violence on the primitive integrity thereof, and by consequence imprinting an affection of sorrow in the mind, and so it may be called ' pain ; ' or else morally and legally, with respect unto the motive cause in the patient, sin ; or to the original efficient cause in the agent, justice ; and so it may be called ' punishment.' Punishment being some evil inflicted on a subject for transgressing some law commanded him by his law-maker, there is thereunto requisite something on the part of the commander, something on the part of the subject, and something on the part of the evil inflicted.

In the commander, there must be first a will, unto which the actions of the subject must conform ; and that signified in the nature of a law.

Secondly, There must be a justice which will.

And thirdly, A power, which can punish the transgressors of that law.

In the subject, there must be First, Reason and free-will (I mean originally); for a law, proceeding from justice, presupposeth a power of obedience: to command impossibilities is both absurd and tyrannous, befitting Pharaoh, and not God.

Secondly, There must be a debt and obligation, whereby he is bound unto the fulfilling of that law.

And lastly, The conditions of this obligation being broken, there must be a forfeiture, guilt, and demerit, following the violation of that law.

Lastly, In the evil itself inflicted, there is required, First, Something absolute, namely, a destructive power, some way

q Gal. iv. 4, 5.   r Heb. vii. 25

or other oppressing and disquieting nature : for as sin is a violation offered from man to the law, so punishment must be a violation retorted from the law to man.

Secondly, There must be something relative, which may respect, First, The author of the evil, whose justice, being by man's sin provoked, is, by his own power, and according to the sentence of his own law, to be executed. Secondly, It may respect the end, for which it is inflicted ; it is not the torment of the creature, whom, as a creature, God loveth,— neither is it the pleasing of the Devil, whom, as a devil, God hateth,—but only the satisfaction of God's justice, and the manifestation of his wrath.

These things being thus premised, we will again make a double consideration of punishment ; either it may be taken improperly and incompletely, for whatsoever oppressive evil doth so draw its original in a reasonable creature from sin, as that, if there were not an habitation of sin, there should be no room for such an evil ; as in the man that was born blind, though sin were not the cause of the blindness, yet it was that which made room for the blindness :—Or it may be taken properly and perfectly, and then I take it to admit of some such description as this : punishment is an evil or pressure of nature, proceeding from a law-giver, just and powerful, and inflicted on a reasonable creature for the disobedience and breach of that law ; unto the performance whereof it was originally, by the natural faculty of free-will, enabled, whereby there is intended a declaration of wrath, and satisfaction of justice.

Now then, I take it, we may, with conformity unto the Scriptures, and with the analogy of faith, set down these conclusions :

First, Consider punishments as they are dolours and pains, and as they are impressions contrary to the integrity of nature,—so the temporal evils of the godly are punishments, because they work the very same manner of natural effects in them, which they do in other men.

Secondly, Take punishments improperly for those evils of nature, which do occasionally follow sin, and unto which sin hath originally opened an entrance, which declares how God stands affected towards sin, with a mind purposing the rooting out and destroying of it :—In this sense likewise may

the afflictions of the godly be called 'punishments,' as God
is said to have been exceeding angry with Aaron [s].

But now these evils, though inflicted on the godly because
of their sins, as were the death of the child to David, the
tempest to Jonah, and the like; yet are they not evils inflicted for the revenge of sin (which is yet the right nature
of a proper punishment; so saith the Lord, " Vengeance is
mine, I will repay it"); but they are evils, by the wisdom of
God and love towards his saints, inflicted for the overthrow
of sin, for weakening the violence, and abating the outrageous-
ness, of our natural corruptions.   As then, in the godly, sin
may be said to be, and not to be, in a diverse sense; [so saith
St. John in one place [t], " If we say we have no sin, we deceive ourselves;" and yet in another, "He that is born of
God, sinneth not [u]:" it is not in them in regard of its condemnation, although it be in them in regard of its inhabitation, though even that also is daily dying and crucified:]
even so punishments, or consequents of sin, may be said to
be in the godly, or not to be in them, in a different sense.
They are not in them in regard of their sting and curse, as
they are proper revenges of sin, although they be in them in
regard of their state, substance, and painfulness, until such
time as they shall put on an eternal triumph over death, the
last enemy that must be overcome.

Lastly, I conclude, that the temporal evils which do befall
the godly, are not formally or properly punishments, nor
effects of divine malediction or vengeance towards the persons of the godly; who, having obtained in Christ a plenary
reconciliation with the Father, can be by him respected with
no other affection (however in manner of appearance it may
seem otherwise) than with an affection of love and free-grace.

The reasons for this position are these :

First, Punishment, with what mitigation soever qualified,
is ' in suo formali,' in the nature of it, a thing legal, namely,
the execution of the law: for Divine law is ever the square
and rule of that justice, of which punishment is the effect
and work.   Now all those on whom the execution of the law
doth take any effect, may truly be said to be so far under the
law, in regard of the sting and curse thereof (for the curse
of the law is nothing else, but the evil which the law pro-

---

[s] Numb. xii. 9.   [t] 1 John i. 8.   [u] John iii. 9.

nounceth to be inflicted; so that every branch and sprig of that evil, must needs bear in it some part of the nature of a curse; even as every part of water hath in it the nature of water); but all the godly are wholly delivered from all the sting and malediction of the law. Christ is unto us " the end of the law x," abolishing the shadows of the ceremonial, the curses of the moral. " We are no more under the law, but under grace y :" under the precepts, but not under the covenant; under the obedience z, but not under the bondage of the law: unto the righteous there is no law, that is, " There is no condemnation to them that are in Christ a." We are dead unto the law by the body of Christ; it hath not the least power or dominion over us.

Secondly, The most proper nature of a punishment is, to satisfy an offended justice: but Christ, bearing the iniquity of us all in his body on the tree, did therein make a most sufficient and ample satisfaction to his Father's wrath, leaving nothing wherein we should make up either the measure or the virtue of his sufferings, but did himself perfectly save us. For an infinite person suffering, and the value of the suffering depending on the dignity of the person, it must needs be, that the satisfaction, made by that suffering, must be likewise infinite, and, by consequence, most perfect.

Lastly, If we consider (as it is in all matters of consequence necessary b) but the author of this evil, we shall find it to be no true and proper punishment; for it is a reconciled Father c, who chasteneth every son whom he receiveth; who as he often doth declare his severest wrath by forbearing to punish d, so doth he as often, even out of tenderness and compassion e, chastise his children; who hath predestinated us unto them f; doth execute his decrees of mercy in them g; doth by his providence govern, and by his love sanctify, them unto those that suffer them, in none of which things are there the prints of punishment.

---

x Rom. x. 4.   y Rom. vi. 14.   z Planè et nos sic dicimus decessisse legem quoad onera, non quoad justitiam. *Tert.* de Monog. c. 7.   a 1 Tim. i. 9.
b Omnis rei inspectio. auctore cognito, planior est. *Tert.* de fug. in persec. cap. 1.
c Heb. xii. 6.   d Indignantis Dei major hæc plaga est, ut nec intelligant delicta, nec plangant. *Cypr.* de Lapsis.   e O servum illum beatum, cujus emendationi Dominus instat, cui dignatur irasci. *Tert.* de Patient. c. 11. In corripiendo filio, quamvis asperè, nunquam profectò amor paternus amittitur. *Aug.* ep. 5.   f 1 Thess. iii. 3. Job. v. 6.   g 1 Cor. xi. 32.

But if Christ have thus taken away the malignity of all
temporal punishments, why are they not quite removed?
To what end should the substance of that remain, whose
properties are extinguished? Certainly, God is so good [h],
as that he would not permit evil to be, if he were not so
powerful as to turn it to good. Is there not honey in the
bee, when the sting is removed? sweetness in the rose,
when the prickles are cut off? a medicinable virtue in the
flesh of vipers, when the poison is cast out? And can man
turn serpents into antidotes, and shall not God be able to
turn the fiery darts of that old serpent into instruments for
letting out our corruptions; and all his buffets into so many
strokes, for the better fastening of those graces in us, which
were before loose, and ready to fall out?

Briefly to conclude this digression, some ends of the remaining death, and other temporal evils (notwithstanding the
death of Christ have taken away the malignity of them all)
are, amongst others, these:—

First, For the trial of our faith [i], and other graces. Our
faith in God's providence is then greatest [k], when we dare
cast ourselves on his care, even when, to outward appearances, he seemeth not at all to care for us: when we can so
look on our miseries, that we can withal look through them.
Admirable is that faith which can, with Israel, see the land
of promise through a sea, a persecution, a wilderness,
through whole armies of the sons of Anak; which can, with
Abraham, see a posterity like the stars of Heaven, through a
dead womb, a bleeding sword, a sacrificed Son; which can,
with Job, see a Redeemer, a resurrection, a restitution,
through the dunghill and the potsherd, through ulcers and
botches, through the violence of Heaven and of men, through
the discomforts of friends, the temptations of a wife, and the
malice of Satan; which can, with Stephen, see Christ in
Heaven through a whole tempest and cloud of stones;
which can, with that poor Syrophœnician woman, see

[h] Deus est adeò bonus, ut non permitteret malum fieri, si non esset adeò potens,
ut posset ex malo bonum educere. *Aug.* in Enchir.   [i] Heb. xii. 36. Zech.
xiii. 9. Deut. viii. 2. 1 Pet. iv. 12.—Conflictatio in adversis probatio est veritatis.
Cypr. de Mortal. et de Lapsis.   [k] Sed quando Deus magis creditur, nisi cum
magis timetur? *Tert.* de fuga in persec. cap. 1. et vide Apol. cap. ult.—*Aug*
epist. 28. et de Civ. Dei, lib. 10. c. 29. et *Chrys.* ad Populum Antioch. Hom. 1.

Christ's compassion through the odious name of dog; which can, in every Egypt, see an Exodus,—in every Red sea, a passage,—in every fiery furnace, an angel of light,—in every den of lions, a lion of Judah,—in every temptation, a door of escape,—and in every grave, an "Arise and sing."

Secondly, They are unto us for antidotes against sin[1], and means of humility and newness of life, by which our faith is exercised and excited[m], our corruptions pruned, our diseases cured, our security and slackness in the race which is set before us, corrected; without which good effects, all our afflictions are cast away in vain upon us. He hath lost his affliction[n], that hath not learned to endure it. The evils of the faithful are not to destroy, but to instruct them; they lose their end, if they teach them nothing.

Thirdly, They make us conformable unto Christ's sufferings[o].

Fourthly, They show unto us the perfection of God's graces[p], and the sufficiency of his love.

Fifthly, They drive us unto God for succour[q], unto his Word for information, and unto his Son for better hopes: for nothing sooner drives a man out of himself, than that which oppresseth and conquereth him. Insomuch, as that public calamities drove the heathen themselves to their prayers[r], and to consult with their Sibyl's Oracles for removing those judgements, whose author, though ignorant of, yet under false names and idolatrous representations, they laboured, as much as in them lay, to reconcile and propitiate.

Sixthly, God is in them glorified[s], in that he spareth not his own people; and yet doth so punish, that he doth withal support and amend them.

Lastly, It prepareth us for glory[t], and by these evils con-

---

[1] Heb. xii. 20. Psal. xciv. 12, 13. Sicut sub uno igne aurum rutilat, palea fumat; ita una eademque vis irruens bonos probat, purificat, eliquat; malos damnat, vastat, exterminat. *Aug.* de Civ. Dei, l. 1. c. 8. [m] Jacentem fidem et (penè dixeram) dormientem, censura cœlestis erexit. *Cypr.*—Exercitia sunt ista, non funera. *Id.* de Mor.—Sic quoties ferro vitis abscinditur, erumpentibus pampinis meliùs uva vestitur. *Id.* de Laud. Mart.—Incidisti in mantelis, sed feliciter incidisti: incidit et ille in ægritudines tuas. *Tert.* cont. Gnost. [n] Perdidistis utilitatem calamitatis, et miserrimi facti estis, et pessimi permansistis. *Aug.* de Civ. Dei, lib. 1. cap. 33. [o] Rom. viii. 17. [p] 2 Cor. xii. 9. [q] Hos. v. 15. vi. 1. [r] Vide *Brisson.* de Form. lib. 2. p. 204 and 208. [s] Levit. x. 3. 2 Sam. xii. 14. John ix. 3. xi. 4. [t] Heb. xi. 26. xii. 2. Ἵνα περὶ ἀναστά-

vincing the understanding of the slipperiness, and uncertainty of this world's delights ; and how happiness cannot grow in that earth, which is cursed with thorns and briers,— it teacheth us to groan after the revelation of that life which is hid with Christ, where all tears shall be wiped from our eyes. So that, in all temporal evils, that which is destructive, the sting and malediction of them, is, in the death of Christ, destroyed.

Having therefore so many motives to make impressions on the soul, the wonder of Christ's death, the love of it, and the benefits redounding unto us from it, there is required of us a multiplied recordation, a ruminating [u], and often recalling of it to our thoughts, if it were possible at all times, to have no word, or thought, or work, pass from us without an eye unto Christ crucified, as the pattern, or, if not, as the judge of them ; but especially at that time when the drift and purpose of our whole sacred business is the celebration of his death.

CHAPTER XVI.

Of the manner, after which we are to celebrate the memory of Christ's passion.

But we may not presume, that we remember Christ's death as he requires, when either with a historical memory, or with a festival solemnity only, we celebrate or discourse of it, except we do it with a practical memory, proportioned to the goodness and quality of the thing remembered.

And, first, We must remember Christ with a memory of faith, with an applying and assuming memory, not only in the general, that he died,—but in particular, that the reason of his death was my salvation and deliverance from death. Pilate and the unbelieving Jews, shall one day see him whom

σεως φιλοσοφῶμεν. *Chrysost.* ad Pop. Antioch. Hom. 1. Amavit quos vocaverat in salutem, invitare ad gloriam, ut qui gaudeamus liberati, exultemus etiam coronati, &c. Vide *Tert.* cont. Gnost. cap. 6.   u Celebrantes Sacramenta commovemur, quasi ungulam findens, et ruminans pecus revocare ad fauces, et minutatim commemorare Dominicæ institutionis exemplum, ut semper passio sit in memoria, &c. *Cypr.* de Cœna Dom.

they have pierced, and remember his death: Judas shall see
and remember him whom he kissed: the devil shall see and
remember him whom he persecuted; and in every one of
these, shall their remembrance produce an effect of horror
and trembling, because they remember him as their Judge [x].
If our remembrance of the love and mercy of his death, not
only testified, but exhibited and obsignated unto us, were
no other than that which the wicked spirits have of his justice and severity,—it could not be, but that we should as
readily believe, as they do tremble at his death.

And indeed (if we observe it) the remembrance of Christ's
death, and the faith in it, are one and the same thing: for
what else is faith, but a review and reflection of our thoughts
upon Christ? a multiplied, and reiterated assent unto the benefits of him crucified? And what is remembrance, but the
returning of the mind back unto the same object, about the
which it had been formerly employed? The remembrance
of Christ is nothing else but the knowledge of Christ re-
peated, and the knowledge of Christ is all one with the belief in him [y]; they which are not by faith united unto him,
are quite ignorant of him. And therefore we find that St.
Peter's second denial of Christ, is by the evangelists diversely
related [z]: in some, " I am none of his;" in others, " I know
not the man:" and certainly, if the one had been true, the
other had been true too; for all complete knowledge must
have a commensuration to the objects that are known, and
the ends for which they are proposed. Now all divine objects, besides their truth, have together annexed a goodness,
which is applicable to those that know it; so that to profess
the knowledge of it, and yet not know how to apply it to our
own use, is indeed therefore to be ignorant of it, because
there is no other end why it should be known, than that
thereby it might be applied [a]. And therefore, in the Scrip-
ture-phrase, ' a wicked man and a fool' are terms equivalent,
because the right knowledge of Divine truths doth ever infer
the love and prosecution of them: for every act in the will,
whether of embracing or abominating any object, is grounded

---

[a] James ii. 19.　　　[y] John xvii. 3.　　　[z] John xviii. 25. Matth. xxvi. 72.
[a] Nullum bonum perfecte noscitur, quod non perfecte amatur, &c. Vide *Aug.*
l. 83. quæst. Tom. 4. p. 208. q. 35.

on some precedent judgement of the understanding. Nothing that, by the ultimate dictate of each particular and practical judgement, is proposed as totally and supremely good, can possibly be by the will refused, because therein it must needs resist the impress of nature, which leads every, as well voluntary as necessary agent, unto an infallible pursuit of whatsoever is proposed unto it, as a thing able, by the accession of its goodness, to advance and perfect the nature of the other. And therefore whosoever believe not in Christ Jesus, and his death, nor do embrace and cling unto it with all the desires of a most ardent affection, cannot possibly be said to know him; because however they may have some few, broken, faint, and floating notions of him, yet he is not by this knowledge proposed unto the will, as its sole and greatest good (for then he could not but be embraced), but is in good earnest by the practic judgement undervalued and disesteemed, in comparison of other things, whose goodness and convenience, unto sensual and corrupt nature, is represented more clearly. Many men may be able to discourse of the death of Christ, after a speculative and scholastical manner, so profoundly, as that another who truly believes in him, shall not be able to understand it. And yet this poor soul, that desires to know nothing but him,—that accounts all things else dung in comparison of him,—that endeavours to be made conformable unto him in the communion and fellowship of his sufferings;—that can, in Christ's wounds, see his safety,—in Christ's stripes, his medicine,— in Christ's anguish, his peace,—in Christ's cross, his triumph,—doth so much more truly know him, as a man that is able safely to guide a ship through all the coasts of the world, doth better know the regions and situations of countries, than he who, by a dexterity that way, is able to draw most exact and geographical descriptions[b]. Boys may be able to turn to, or to repeat several passages of a poet or orator more readily than a grounded artist, who yet notwithstanding knows the elegancy and worth of them far better. And a stage-player can haply express, with greater life of passion, the griefs of a distressed man, than he can himself, although altogether ignorant of the weight and oppression of them.

b Vide *Arist.* Eth. l. 7. c. 3.

It is not therefore logical, historical, speculative remembrance of Christ, but an experimental and believing remembrance of him, which we are to use in the receiving of these sacred mysteries, which are not a bare type and resemblance, but a seal also, confirming and exhibiting his death unto each believing soul.

Secondly, We must remember the death of Christ with a remembrance of thankfulness for that great love, which by it we enjoy from him. Certainly he hath no dram of good-nature in him, who, for the greatest benefit that can befall him, doth not return a recompense of remembrance, which costs him nothing[c]. Our salvation cost Christ a precious price, his own blood ; and shall not we so much as lay up the memory of it in our minds, that we may have it forth-coming to answer all the objections, that can be made against our title to salvation? Consider with thyself the fearfulness and horror of thy natural estate, wherein thou wert exposed to the infinite wrath of Almighty God,—whom thou therefore, being both finite and impotent, wert no way able to appease, subject to the strokes and terrors, not only of thine own conscience, a bosom-hell,—but of that most exact justice, which it is as impossible for thee to sustain with patience, as with obedience to satisfy. The creatures thine enemies, thine own heart thy witness, thy Creator thy judge; eternity of expressless anguish, gnawing of conscience, despair of deliverance, and whatsoever misery the most searching understanding can but imagine, thy sentence: for according to his fear, so is his wrath : from this, and much more, hath the death of Christ, not only delivered thee,—but of a cast-away, an enemy, a deplored wretch, weltering in thine own blood, rotting and stinking in thine own grave, hath restored thee not only to thine original interest and patrimony, but unto an estate so much more glorious than that could have been, by how much the obedience of Christ is more precious, than any thy innocency could possibly have performed.

Consider the odious filthiness of sin, the pertinacious adherence thereof unto thy nature ; so that nothing but the incarnation and blood of the Son of God, the creator of the

[c] Qui meminit, sine impendio gratus est. *Senec.* de Benef.

world, could wash it out. Consider the justice, and indis-
pensable severity of our God against sin, which would not
spare the life of his own Son, nor be satisfied without a
sacrifice of infinite and co-equal virtue with itself. Consider
that it was thy sins, which were the associates with Judas,
and Pilate, and the Jews, to crucify him: it was thy hypocrisy which was the kiss, that betrayed him ; thy covetousness the thorns, that crowned him ; thy oppression and cruelty the nails and spears, that pierced him ; thy idolatry and
superstition the knee, that mocked him ; thy contempt of
religion the spittle, that defiled him ; thy anger and bitterness the gall and vinegar, that distasted him ; thy crimson
and redoubled sins the purple that dishonoured him : in a
word, thou wert the Jew that killed him. Canst thou, then,
have so many members, as weapons, wherewith to crucify
thy Saviour,—and hast thou not a heart wherein to recog-
nise, and a tongue wherewith to celebrate, the benefits of
that blood which thy sins had poured out? The fire is
quenched by that water, which by its heat was caused to run
over; and shall not any of thy sins be put out by the over-
flowing of that precious blood, which thy sins caused to run
out of his sacred body?

Lastly, Consider the immensity of God's mercy, and the
unutterable treasures of grace, which neither the provocations of thy sin, nor the infinite exactness of his own justice, could any way overcome, or constrain to despise the
work of his own hands, or not to compassionate the wretchedness of his creature, though it cost the humiliation of the
Son of God, and the examination of his sacred person to
perform it. Lay together all those considerations ; and certainly they are able even to melt a heart of adamant, into
thoughts of continual thankfulness towards so bountiful a
Redeemer.

Thirdly, We must remember the death of Christ with a
remembrance of obedience; even the commands of God
should be sufficient to enforce our obedience. It is not the
manner of law-makers to use insinuations, and plausible
provokements, but peremptory and resolute injunctions upon
pain of penalty. But our God deals not only as a Lord, but
as a Father; he hath delivered us from the penalty, and now
rather invites than compels us to obedience, lest, by persist-

ing in sin, we should make void unto ourselves the benefit of
Christ's death, yea, should crucify him afresh, and so bring
upon ourselves, not the benefit, but the guilt of his blood.
Is it nothing, think we, that Christ should die in vain, and
take upon him the dishonour and shame of a servant to no
purpose. And disobedience, as much as in it lies, doth
nullify and make void the death of Christ. Is it nothing
that that sacred blood of the covenant should be shed only
to be trodden and trampled under foot as a vile thing? And
certainly he that celebrates the memory of Christ's death in
this holy Sacrament[d] with a wilfully polluted soul, doth not
commemorate the sacrifice, but share in the slaughter of
him; and receives that precious blood, not according to the
institution of Christ, to drink it,—but with the purpose of
Judas and the Jews, to shed it on the ground;—a cruelty so
much more detestable than Cain's was, by how much the
blood of Christ is more precious than that of Abel. In the
phrase of Scripture, 'sinning against God,' and 'forgetting of
him,' or 'casting of him behind our back,' or 'bidding him depart from us,' or 'not having him before our eyes,' are all of
equal signification: neither is any thing called remembrance,
in divine dialect, which doth not frame the soul unto affections[e], befitting the quality of the object that is remembered. He is not said to see a pit, though before his eyes,
who, by star-gazing or other thoughts, falls into it; nor he
to remember Christ, though presented to all his senses at
once, who makes no regard of his presence.

Divine knowledge, being practical, requires advertence
and consideration, an efficacious pondering of the consequences of good or evil, and thereby a proportionable government of our several courses;—which whoso neglecteth,
may be properly said to forget, or to be ignorant of what
was before him[f], though not out of blindness, yet out of in-
considerateness, as not applying close unto himself the object represented; which, if truly remembered, would infallibly
frame the mind unto a ready obedience and conformity
thereunto.

---

[d] Ὥσπερ οἱ κεντήσαντες οὐχ ἵνα πίωσιν ἐκέντησαν, ἀλλ᾽ ἵνα ἐκχέωσιν, οὕτω καὶ
ὁ ἀναξίως μετιὼν, καὶ μηδὲν ἐντεῦθεν καρπούμενος. *Chrys.* in 1 Cor. Hom. 27.
[e] Verba notitiæ connotant affectus. *August.* de Gen. ad literam, l. 7. c. 20.
[f] Vide *Casaub.* Comment. in c. 8. Theophrast. Charact. p. 271.

Lastly, We must remember the death of Christ with prayer unto God: for as by faith we apply to ourselves, so by prayer we represent unto God the Father that his death, as the merit and means of reconciliation with him. As prayer is animated by the death of Christ (which alone is that character, that adds currentness unto them), so is the death of Christ not to be celebrated without prayer, wherein we do with confidence implore God's acceptance of that sacrifice for us, in which alone he is well pleased. " Open thine eyes unto the supplication of thy servants, to hearken unto all for which they shall call unto thee," was the prayer of Solomon[g] in the consecration of the temple. What, doth God hearken with his eyes unto the prayers of his people ? Hath not he that made the ear, an ear himself, but must be fain to make use of another faculty unto a different work ? Certainly, unless the eye of God be first open to look on the blood of his Son, and on the persons of his saints, bathed and sprinkled therewith, his ears can never be open unto their prayers. Prayer doth put God in mind of his covenant[h], and covenants are not to be presented without seals. Now the seal of our covenant is the blood of Christ : no testament is of force but by the death of the testator. Whensoever therefore we present unto God the truth of his own free covenant in our prayers[i], let us not forget to show him his own seal too, by which we are confirmed in our hope therein. Thus are we to celebrate the death of Christ, and in these regards is this holy work called by the ancients ' an unbloody sacrifice,' in a mystical and spiritual sense,— because, in this work, is a confluence of all such holy duties, as are in the Scripture called ' spiritual sacrifices.' And in the same sense, was the Lord's table ofttimes by them called an " altar," as that was which the Reubenites erected on the other side of Jordan, not for any proper sacrifice, but to be a pattern and memorial of that, whereon sacrifice was offered.

[g] 1 Kings viii. 52.   [h] Isai. xliii. 26.   Psal. lxxxix. 49.   Isai. lxiv. 8, 12. Jer. xiv. 8, 9, 21.   [i] *Ambros.* de Sacram. lib. 4. c. 6. et *Chrys.*—Deo litabilis hostia bonus animus, pura mens, sincera conscientia ; hæc nostra sacrificia, hæc pia sæva sunt *Minut. Felix* in Octavio.

CHAPTER XVII.

Inferences of practice from the several ends of this holy Sacrament.

HERE then, inasmuch as these sacred elements are instituted to present and exhibit Christ unto the faithful soul, we may infer with what affection we ought to approach unto him, and what reverent estimation to have of them. Happiness, as it is the scope of all reasonable desires, so the confirmation of that happiness is the solace and security of those that desire it. " He," said the prophet, speaking of Christ, " shall be the desire of all nations;" inasmuch as, without him, that happiness which all do naturally desire, is but a meteor and fiction. So then we see, that even the light of our inbred reason, seconded and directed by divine truths, doth lead us unto a desire of Christ, who alone is the author and matter of that happiness, which is the true, though unknown object of all our natural desires. Now this happiness in Christ we cannot have, till we have actual fruition of him ; enjoy this blessedness we never can, till we are united to him, no more than a dissected member enjoys the vital influences of the soul and spirits. Union unto Christ we cannot have, until it please him, by his Spirit, as it were, to stoop from that kingdom where now he is, and to exhibit himself unto those, whom it pleaseth him to assume into the unity of his body. Other way to enjoy him here, we can have none ; since no man can, at his pleasure or power, lift up his eyes with Stephen to see him, or go up with St. Paul to the heavens, to enjoy him. Now it hath pleased the wisdom of Christ (whose honour ever it is to magnify his power in his creatures' weakness [k], and to borrow no parcel of glory in his service from those earthly and elementary instruments which he useth in it), by no other means to exhibit, and confirm the virtue of his sacred body unto us, with the life and righteousness that from it issueth, but only

[k] 1 Cor. i. 21.   2 Cor. iv. 7.

by those poor and ordinary elements of bread and wine in
his sacrament; unto which therefore he requireth such reverence, such hunger and affection, as is, in reason, due to the
hand that reacheth, to the seal that secureth, to the food
that strengtheneth that spiritual life in us, without which
we cannot possibly reach unto the end of our very natural
and created desires, happiness and tranquillity. It behoves
us, therefore, to beware how we give entertainment to any
carnal thoughts, which go about to vilify and undervalue
the excellency of so divine mysteries from the outward
meanness of the things themselves. Say not, like sullen
Naaman [1], "Is not the wine in the vintner's cellar, or the
bread of mine own table, as good and as nourishing as is
any in the temple?" Certainly, if thou be commanded some
great work for the procuring of so great a good, as there
had been between the service and the reward no disproportion; so would even reason itself have dictated unto us a
necessity of obeying, rather than of disputing: how much
rather when he biddeth us only to eat and live.

True it is, that these creatures naturally have no more
power to convey Christ, than wax hath in itself to convey a
lordship : yet as a small piece of wax, when once, in the virtue of a human covenant or contract, it is made the instrument to confirm and ratify such a conveyance, is, unto the
receiver, of more consequence than all the wax in the town
besides, and is, with the greatest care, preserved ;—so these
elements, though physically the same which are used at our
own tables, yet in the virtue of that holy consecration,
whereby they are made the instruments of exhibiting, and
the seals of ascertaining God's covenant of grace unto us,—
are unto us more valuable than our barns full of grain, or
our presses full of grapes, and are to be desired with so far
distant an affection from the other that are common, as
heaven is above earth.

Secondly, In that these elements are consecrated and exhibited for confirmation of our faith, we thence see how the
church hath her degrees of faith [m], her measure of the Spirit, her deficiencies of grace, her languishings, ebbings,

l 2 Kings v. 12, 13.   m 1 Thess. iii. 10.   Luke xvii. 5.   Rom. i. 19.   1 John
i. 16.   Phil. i. 19.   Ephes. iv. 12, 13.   Col. ii. 6, 7.   Ephes. iv. 15.   1 Pet. ii. 2.

imperfections, her decays, blemishes, and falls, which make her stand in need of being perfected, builded, rooted, established in faith and righteousness. All things under the middle region are subject to winds, thunders, tempests, the continual uncertainties of boisterous weather; whereas in the Heavens there is a perfect uniform serenity and calmness: so when a Christian comes once to his own country unto Heaven, he then comes unto an estate of peace and security; to be filled with the fulness of God, where thieves do not break through nor steal, where neither flesh nor Satan have any admission, no storms of temptation, no shipwreck of conscience, but where all things are spiritual and peaceable [n]. But in this earth, where Satan hath power to go from place to place to compass the world, to raise his tempests against the church, even the waves of ungodly men, —we can have no safety from any danger, which either his subtilty can contrive, or his malice provoke, or his power execute, or his instruments further: and therefore we are here subject to more or fewer degrees of faintness in our faith, according as our strength to resist the common Adversary is less or greater [o]. As in the natural, so in the mystical body, though all the parts do in common partake of life, yet one is more vital than another, the heart and head than the hands and feet; yea, the same part is, at one time, more active and quick than at others; one while, overgrown with humours, and stiffened with distempers,—another while, free, expedite, and able for the discharge of any vital office. And this is that which drives us to a necessity of recovering our strength, and making up our breaches by this holy Sacrament; which should likewise tell us in what humble esteem we ought to have our perfectest endowments, they being all subject to their failings and decays.

Thirdly, In that these mysteries do knit the faithful together into the unity of one common body, we see what fellow-feeling the faithful should have of each other; how they should interest themselves in the several states and affections of their fellow-members, to " rejoice with those that

[n] Pars superior mundi et ordinatior, nec in nubem cogitur, nec in tempestatem impellitur, nec versatur in turbinem; omni tumultu caret; inferiora fulminant. *Sen.* de ira, l. 3. c. 6. *Ruhkopf*, i. 101.—Minimas rerum discordia turbat; Pacem summa tenent. *Luc.* ii. 272.   [o] Ephes. iii. 19. v. 13.   Job i. 7. ii. 2.

rejoice, and to weep with those that weep [p]." As we should
think the same things [q], and so agree in a unity of judgements, because all led with one and the same spirit, which
is the "Spirit of Truth [r];" so we should all suffer, and do the
same things, and so all concur in a unity of affections, because all animated by the same spirit, which is the spirit of
love too.   Where there is dissension and disagreement,
there must needs be a several law ; where the law is diverse,
the government differs too ; and in a different government,
there must of necessity be a different subjection [s].   He then
that doth not sympathize with his brother, but nourisheth
factious and uncharitable thoughts against him, doth therein
plainly testify, that he is not subject (at least totally) unto
the same prince with him, and then we know that there are
but two princes, a Prince of Peace, and a prince of darkness.
    Nature is in all her operations uniform and constant unto
herself ; one tree cannot naturally bring forth grapes and
figs [t].   Out of the same fountain, cannot issue bitter water
and sweet [u].   The selfsame vital faculty of feeling which is
in one member of the body, is in all, because all are animated with that soul, which doth not confine itself unto any
one.   The church of God is a tree planted by the same
hand [x], a garden watered from the same fountain [y], a body
quickened by the same Spirit [z] ; the members of it are all
brethren, begotten by one Father of mercy, generated by
one seed of the Word, delivered from one womb of ignorance, fed with one bread of life, employed in one heavenly
calling, brought up in one household of the church, tra-
vellers in one way of grace, heirs to one kingdom of glory ;
and when they agree in so many unities, should they then
admit any fraction or disunion in their minds?   From
Adam, unto the last man that shall tread on the earth, is the
church of God but one continued and perfected body : and
therefore we find that, as in the body, the head is affected
with the grievances of the feet, though there be a great distance of place between them ; so the holy men of God have

---

p Rom. xii. 15.   q Phil. ii. 2.   r John xiv. 26. xv. 26. Gal. vi. 2.
s Rom. viii. 11. v. 5. vii. 23.   t Luke vi. 44.   u James iii. 11, 12.
x Isai. v. 7.   Ezek. xvii. 24.   Cant. iv. 12, 13.   Ephes. v. 23.   Rom. xii. 5.
Acts xi. 1. xv. 36.   y 1 Cor. xii. 26.   z Isai. lxiv.

mourned, and been exceedingly touched with the afflictions
of the church even in after-ages, though between them did
intervene a great distance of time.

Certainly then, if the church of God lie in distress, and
we stretch ourselves on beds of ivory[a]; if she mourn in
sackcloth, and we riot in soft raiment; if the wild boar in
the forest break in upon her, and we send not one prayer to
drive him away; if there be cleanness of teeth in the poor,
and our teeth grind them still; if their bowels be empty of
food, and ours still empty of compassion; if the wrath of
God be inflamed against his people, and our zeal remain
still as frozen, our charity as cold, our affections as be-
numbed, our compassion as stupid as ever it was; in a word,
if Sion lie in the dust, and we hang not up our harps, nor
pray for her peace; as we can conclude nothing, but that
we are unnatural members, so we can expect nothing but
the curse of Meroz[b], who went not out to help the Lord.

Fourthly, In that this Sacrament is God's instrument to
ratify and make sure our claim unto his covenant, we
learn :—

First, Therein to admire and adore the unspeakable love
of God, who is pleased not only to make, but to confirm his
promises unto the church. As God, so his truth, whether of
judgements or promises, are all in themselves immutable and
infallible in their event[c]; yet notwithstanding, as the sun,
though in itself of a most uniform light and magnitude, yet,
by reason of the great distance, and of the variety of mists
and vapours, through which the rays are diffused, it often
seemeth in both properties to vary; so the promises of God,
however in themselves of a fixed and unmovable certainty,
yet, passing through the various tempers of our minds, one
while serene and clear,—another while, by the steam of passions and temptations of Satan, foggy and distempered,—do
appear under an inconstant shape. And for this cause, as
the sun doth itself dispel those vapours, which did hinder
the right perception; so the grace of God, together with
and by the holy Sacrament communicated, doth rectify the
mind and compose those diffident affections, which did before intercept the efficacy and evidence thereof.

[a] Amos vi. 4, 7.   [b] Judges v. 29.   [c] James i. 17.

God made a covenant with our fathers; and not account-
ing that enough, " he confirmed it by an oath, that by two
immutable things, wherein it was impossible for God to lie,
they might have strong consolation, who have had refuge to
lay hold on the hope that is set before them [d]."
The strength, we see, of the consolation depends upon the
stability of the covenant: and is God's covenant made more
firm by an oath than by a promise? The truth of God is as
his nature, without variableness or shadow of changing [e];
and can it then be made more immutable? Certainly as to
infiniteness in regard of accession, so unto immutability in
regard of firmness, there cannot be any accession of degrees,
or parts; all immutability being nothing else but an exclu-
sion of whatsoever might possibly occur to make the thing
variable and uncertain. So then the oath of God doth no
more add to the certainty of his word, than do men's oaths
and protestations to the truth of what they affirm: but because we consist of an earthly and dull temper, therefore
God, when he speaks unto us, doth ingeminate his compella-
tions, " O earth, earth, earth, hear the Word of the Lord [f]."
So weak is our sight, so diffident our nature, as that it seems
to want the evidence of what it sees [g]. Peradventure God
may repent him of his promise, as he did sometime of his
creature [h]. Why should not the covenant of grace be as
mutable as was that of works? God promised to establish
Sion for ever [i]; and yet Sion, the city of the great God, is
fallen. Was not Shilo beloved [k], and did not God forsake it?
Had not Coniah been as the signet of his hand [l], and has he
not yet been cast away? Was not Jerusalem a vine of God's
planting [m], and hath not the wild boar long since rooted it
up? Was not Israel the natural olive [n], that did partake of
the fat and sweetness of the root, and is it not yet cut off,
and wrath come upon it to the uttermost? Though God be
most immutable, may he not yet alter his promise? Did
the abrogation of ceremonies prove any way a change in
him, who was as well the erector as the dissolver of them?
Though the sun be fastened to his own sphere, yet may he

[d] Heb. vi. 18.   [e] James i. 17.   [f] Jer. xxii. 9.   [g] Vel præsentem
desideramus. *Plin.* Paneg.   [h] Gen. vi. 6.   [i] Psalm xlviii. 8.   [k] Jer.
vii. 24.   [l] Jer. xxii. 28.   [m] Isai. v. 1.   [n] Rom. xi. 21, 24.

be moved by another orb. What if God's promise, barely considered, proceed from his antecedent and simple way of benevolence towards the creature ; but the stability and certainty of his promise in the event depend on a second resolution of his consequent will, which pre-supposeth the good use of mine own liberty ? May not I then abuse my free-will, and so frustrate unto myself the benefit of God's promise ? Is not my will mutable, though God's be not ? May not I sink and fall, though the place on which I stand, be firm ? May not I let go my hold, though the thing which I handle, be itself fast ? What if, all this while, I have been in a dream, mistaking mine own private fancies and mis-persuasions for the dictates of God's Spirit ? mistaking Satan (who useth to transform himself) for an angel of light ? God hath promised, it is true, but hath he promised unto me ? Did he ever say unto me, " Simon, Simon [o]," or " Saul, Saul [p]," or " Samuel, Samuel [q] ?" Or if he did, must he needs perform his promise to me, who am not able to fulfil my conditions unto him ?

Thus, as unto men floating upon the sea, or unto distempered brains, the land and house, though immovable, seem to reel and totter ; or as unto weak eyes, every thing seems double ;--so the promises of God, however built on a sure foundation, his counsel and fore-knowledge [r], yet unto men, prepossessed with their own private distempers, do they seem unstable and frail,—unto a weak eye of faith, God's covenant to be (if I may so speak) double [s], to have a tongue and a tongue, a promise and a promise, that is, a various and uncertain promise. And for this cause (notwithstanding diffident and distrustful men do, indeed, deserve what they suspect, and are worthy to suffer what they unworthily do fear) doth God yet, in compassion towards our frailty, condescend to confirm his promises by an oath, to engage the truth of his own essence for performance, to seal the patent which he hath given with his own blood, and to exhibit that seal unto us so often, as, with faith, we approach

---

[o] Luke xxii. 31.   [p] Acts ix. 4.   [q] 1 Sam. iii. 10.   [r] 2 Tim. ii. 19.
[s] Duos Deos cæci perspexisse se existimaverunt ; unum enim non integrè viderant ; lippientibus enim singularis lucerna numerosa est. *Tert.* cont. *Marc.* l. 1. c. 2.—*Senec.* Epist. 3.

unto the communion of these holy mysteries. And who can
sufficiently admire the riches of this mercy, which makes
the very weaknesses and imperfections of his church, occasions of redoubling his promises unto it?

Secondly, In that this Sacrament is the instrumental cause
of confirming our faith from this possibility, yea, facility of
obtaining,—we must conclude the necessity of using so great
a benefit, wherein we procure the strengthening of our
graces, the calming of our consciences, and the experience
of God's favour. In the natural body there being a continual activity and conflict between the heat and the moisture
of the body, and by that means a wasting, depastion, and
decay of nature, it is kept in a perpetual necessity of suc-
couring itself by food: so in the spiritual man, there being,
in this present estate, an unreconcilable enmity between the
Spirit and the flesh, there is, in either part, a propension
towards such outward food, whereby each in its distresses
may be relieved. The flesh pursues all such objects as may
content and cherish the desires thereof, which the apostle
calleth " the provisions of lust." The Spirit, on the contrary side, strengthens itself by those divine helps, which
the wisdom of God had appointed to confer grace, and to
settle the heart in a firm persuasion of its own peace. And
amongst these instruments, this holy Sacrament is one of
the principal; which is indeed nothing else but a visible
oath, wherein Christ giveth us a taste of his benefits, and en-
gageth his own sacred body for the accomplishing of them;
which supporteth our tottering faith, and reduceth the soul
unto a more settled tranquillity.

Thirdly, In that in this one all other types were abrogated
and nullified, we learn to admire and glorify the love of God,
who hath set us at liberty from the thraldom of ceremonies,
from the costliness and difficulty of his service, with which
his own chosen people were held in bondage [t], under the
pedagogy and government of schoolmasters, the ceremonial
and judicial law, as so many notes of distinctions, charac-
teristical differences, or walls of separation between Jew and
Gentile [u], until the coming of the Messiah; which was the
time of the reformation of all things [x], wherein the Gentiles

[t] Gal. iv. 3. v. 1. Acts. xv. 10.   [u] Ephes. ii. 14.   [x] Heb. ix. 10.

were by his death to be ingrafted into the same stock [y], and made partakers of the same juice and fatness ; the shadows to be removed, the ordinances to be cancelled [z], the law to be abolished. For " the law came by Moses, but grace and truth by Jesus Christ [a] ;" grace, in opposition to the curse of the moral law; truth, in opposition to the figures and resemblances of the ceremonial law. The Jews in God's service were bound unto one place, and unto one form; no temple or ministration of sacrifices without Jerusalem [b], nor, without express prescription, no use of creatures without difference of common and unclean : whereas, unto us, all places are lawful and pure [c], all things lawful and pure ; every country a Canaan, and every city a Jerusalem, and every oratory a temple. It is not an ordinance, but a prayer, which sanctifieth and maketh good unto our use every creature of God [d].

But yet though we, under the gospel, are thus set at liberty from all manner of ordinances which are not of intrinsecal, eternal, and unvariable necessity; yet may this liberty, in regard of the nature of things indifferent, be made a necessity in respect of the use of them. We may not think, that our liberty is a licentious and unbounded liberty, as if Christ had been the author of confusion, to leave every man in the external carriages of his worship, unto the conduct of his private fancy. This were to have our liberty [e] for a cloak of naughtiness, and as an occasion to the flesh [f] ; but we must always limit it by those general and moral rules of piety, loyalty, charity, and sobriety.

Use all things we may, indifferently, without subjection or bondage unto the thing, but not without subjection unto God and superiors. Use them we may, but with temperateness and moderation; use them we may, but with respect to God's glory [g]; use them we may, but with submission to authority [h]; use them we may, but with avoiding of scandal [i]. Christian liberty [k] consisteth in the inward freedom of the conscience, whose only bond is a necessity of doc-

[y] Rom. xi. 17. Heb. x. 1.   [z] Col. ii. 14. 2 Cor. iii. 11, 13.   [a] John i. 17. [b] John iv. 21, 23.   [c] 1 Cor. vi. 12. Tit. i. 15.   [d] 1 Tim. iv. 5. Rom. xiv. 14. Acts x. 15.   [e] 1 Pet. ii. 16. Gal. v. 13.   [f] Gal. v. 13.   [g] 1 Cor. x. 31.   [h] Rom. xiii. 1, 2, 5.   [i] 1 Cor. viii. 9.   [k] See Dr. *Field* of the Church, l. 1. c. 32, 33.

trine; not in outward conformity or observances only, whose bond is a necessity of obedience, and subordination unto higher powers ; which obeying, though we become thereby subject unto some human or ecclesiastical ordinances, the conscience yet remains uncurbed and at liberty.

Secondly, We have hereby a great encouragement to serve our God in Spirit and in Truth [l], being delivered from all those burdensome accessions, which unto the inward worship were added, in the legal observances :—in Spirit, in opposition unto the carnal ; in Truth, in opposition unto the typical ceremonies. The services of the Jews were celebrated in the blood and smoke of unreasonable creatures ; but ours, in the gospel [m], must be a spiritual, a reasonable service of him : for as in the Word of God the letter profiteth nothing, it is the Spirit that quickeneth [n] ; so in the worship of God likewise, the knee, the lip, the eye, the hand alone, profiteth not at all ; it is the Spirit that worshippeth.

It is not a macerated body, but a contrite soul which he respecteth. If there be paleness in the face, but blood in the heart; if whiteness in the eye, but blackness in the soul ; if a drooping conscience, but an unbended conscience ; if a knee bowing down in the temple of God, and thoughts rising up against the grace of God ; the head like a bulrush, and the heart like an adamant ;—in a word, if there be but a bodily and unquickened service, a schism in the same worshipper, between his outward and his inward man ; he that is not a God of the dead, but of the living,— he that accounteth, in the Levitical law, carcases as unclean things (as being in the nearest disposition to rottenness and putrefaction), will never smell any sweet savour in such services. " What have I to do," saith God, " with your sacrifices [o] ?" and, " My soul hateth your new moons, and your appointed feasts [p]." " My sacrifices, and my sabbaths, they were by original institution [q], but your carnal observance of them hath made them yours [r]." Even the heathen

[l] John iv. 24.   [m] Rom. xii. 1.   [n] 2 Cor. iii. 6.   [o] Isai. i. 11, 13, 14.
[p] Amos v. 21.   [q] Exod. xx. 10. Ezek. xx. 12. Isai. lviii. 13.   [r] Vestra dicit, quæ secundum libidinem suam, non secundum religionem Dei, celebrando sua jam, non Dei, fecerant. *Tert.* Cont. Marcion. l. 2. c. 22.

idols [s] themselves did require rather the truth of an inward, than the pomp of an outward worship; and therefore they forbade all profane people any access to their services [t]. And God, certainly, will not be content with less than the devil.

Sixthly, In that, by these frequent ceremonies, we are led unto the celebration of Christ's death, and the benefits thereby arising unto mankind; we may hence observe the natural deadness and stupidity of man's memory in the things of his salvation. It is a wonder how a man should forget his Redeemer that ransomed him with the price of his own blood, to whom he oweth whatsoever he either is, or hath; him whom each good thing we enjoy, leadeth unto the acknowledgment of. Look where we will, he is still not only in us, but before us. The wisdom of our minds, the goodness of our natures, the purposes of our wills and desires, the calmness of our consciences, the hope and expectation of our souls and bodies, the liberty from law and sin: whatever it is in or about us, which we either know, or admire, or enjoy, or expect, he is the treasury whence they were taken; the fulness whence they were received; the head which transferreth; the hand which bestoweth them. We are on all sides compassed, and even hedged [u] in with his blessings: so that, in this sense, we may acknowledge a kind of ubiquity of Christ's body, inasmuch as it is every where even visible and palpable in those benefits which flow from it. And yet we, like men that look on the river Nile, and gaze wondrously on the streams, remain still ignorant of the head and original from whence they issue. Thus, as there is, between blood and poison, such a natural antipathy, as makes them to shrink in, and retire at the presence of each other; so though each good thing we enjoy, serves to present that precious blood, which was the price of it, unto our souls; yet there is in us so much venom

[s] Cultus Deorum optimus idemque castissimus, ut eos semper purâ, integrâ, incorruptâ et mente et voce venereris. *Cic.* de Nat. Deorum. l. 2.—Sicut nec in victimis quidem, licet opimæ sint, auroque præfulgeant, deorum est honos, sed piâ ac rectâ voluntate venerantium. *Sen.* de Benef. l. 1. c. 6. et Epist. 95.—Ad divos adeunto castè. *Cic.* de legib. lib. 2.—Animadverto etiam Deos ipsos non tam accuratis adorantium precibus, quàm innocentia et sanctitate, lætari. *Plin.* Paneg.
[t] Semper impiæ institutiones arcent profanos, &c. *Tert.* in Apol. c. 7. Οὐ γὰρ θέμις τοῖς βεβήλοις τὰ τοῦ λόγου μυστήρια διηγεῖσθαι, *Clem. Alex.*—*Jerom.* l. 5.— Vide *Brisson.* de Formulis, lib. 1.   [u] Job. i. 10.

of sin, as makes us still to remove our thoughts from so pure
an object. As, in the knowledge of things, many men are
of so narrow understandings, that they are not able to raise
them unto consideration of the causes of such things, whose
effects they are haply better acquainted with than wiser
men ; it being the work of a discursive head to discover the
secret knittings, obscure dependences of natural things on
each other ;—so, in matters of practice in divinity, many
men commonly are so fastened unto the present goods which
they enjoy, and so full with them, that they either have no
room, or no leisure, or rather indeed no power nor will, to
lift up their minds from the streams unto the fountain, or
by a holy logic to resolve them into the death of Christ ;
from whence if they issue not, they are but fallacies, and
sophistical good things ; and whatever happiness we expect
in or from them, will prove a ' non sequitur' at the last.
Remember and know Christ, indeed, such men may and do,
in some sort, sometimes, to dishonour him, at best, but to
discourse of him : but as the philosopher [a] speaks of intemperate men, who sin not out of a full purpose and uncon-
trolled swing of vicious resolutions, but with checks of
judgement and reluctancy of reason, that they are but ' half
vicious ' (which yet is indeed but a half truth), so certainly
they, who though they do not quite forget Christ, or cast
him behind their back, do yet remember him only with a
speculative knowledge of the nature and general efficacy of
his death, without particular application of it unto their own
persons and practices, have but a half and halting knowledge
of him.   Certainly a mere schoolman, who is able exactly
to dispute of Christ and his passion, is as far from the length,
and breadth, and depth, and height of Christ crucified,
from the requisite dimensions of a Christian, as a mere sur-
veyor or architect, who hath only the practice of measur-
ing land or timber, is from the learning of a geometrician.
For as mathematicks, being a speculative science, cannot
possibly be comprised in the narrow compass of a practical
art ; so neither can the knowledge of Christ, being a saving
and practic knowledge, be complete, when it floats only in
the discourses of a speculative brain.   And therefore Christ
at the last day will say unto many men, who thought them-

---

[a] ἡμιπόνηρος, *Arist*. Eth. vii. 10. 3. Zell, p. 326.

selves great clerks, and of his near acquaintance, even such as did preach him, and do wonders in his name, That he never knew them[x]; and that is an argument, that they likewise never knew him neither. For as no man can see the sun, but by the benefit of that light, which from the sun shineth on him; so no man can know Christ, but those on whom Christ first shineth, and whom he vouchsafeth to know. Mary Magdalen could not say ' Rabboni ' to Christ, till Christ first had said ' Mary ' to her. And therefore that we may not fail to remember Christ aright, it pleaseth him to institute this holy Sacrament, as the image of his crucified body, whereby we might as truly have Christ's death presented unto us, as if he had been crucified before our eyes[y].

Secondly, We see here who they are, who, in the Sacrament, receive Christ,—even such as remember his death with a recognition of faith, thankfulness, and obedience. Others only receive the elements, but not the Sacrament: as when the king seals a pardon to a condemned malefactor, the messenger that is sent with it, receives nothing from the king but paper written and sealed, but the malefactor (unto whom only it is a gift) receives it as it were a resurrection. Certainly there is a staff as well of sacramental, as of common bread: the staff of common bread is the blessing of the Lord; the staff of the sacramental is the body of the Lord. And as the wicked, which never look up in thankfulness unto God, do often receive the bread without the blessing; so here the element without the body; they receive indeed, as it is fit unclean birds should do, nothing but the carcase of a sacrament; the body of Christ being the soul of the bread, and his blood the life of wine. His body is not now any more capable of dishonour; it is a glorified body, and therefore will not enter into an earthy and unclean soul: as it is corporally in Heaven, so it will be spiritually and sacramentally in no place but a heavenly soul.—Think not, that thou hast received Christ, till thou hast effectually remembered, seriously meditated, and been religiously affected and inflamed with the love of his death: without this, thou mayst be guilty of his body; thou canst not be a partaker of it. Guilty thou art, because thou didst reach out thy

[x] Matth. vii. 22, 23.   [y] Gal. iii. 1.

hand with a purpose to receive Christ into a polluted soul, though he withdrew himself from thee. Even as Mucius Scævola was guilty of Porsena's blood, though it was not he, but another whom the dagger wounded: because the error of the hand cannot remove the malice of the heart.

CHAPTER XVIII.

Of the subject, who may with benefit receive the holy Sacrament; with the necessary qualifications thereunto; of the necessity of due preparation.

WE have hitherto handled the Sacrament itself: we are now briefly to consider the subject whom it concerneth, in whom we will observe such qualifications, as may fit and pre-dispose him for the comfortable receiving, and proper interest in these holy mysteries. Sacraments, since the time that Satan hath had a kingdom in the world, have been ever notes and characters whereby to distinguish the church of God from the ethnic and unbelieving part of men; so that they being not common unto all mankind, some subject unto whom the right and propriety of them belongeth, must be found out.

God, at the first, created man upright, framed him after his own image, and endowed him with gifts of nature, able to preserve him entire in that estate wherein he was created. And because it was repugnant to the essential freedom [z] wherein he was made, to necessitate him by any outward constraint, unto an immutable estate of integrity ; he therefore so framed him, that it might be within the free liberty of his own will to cleave to him, or to decline from him.

Man, being thus framed, abused this native freedom, and committed sin; and thereby, in the very same instant, became really and properly dead. For as he was dead judicially in regard of a temporal and eternal death (both which were now already pronounced, though not executed on him), so was he dead actually and really, in regard of that spiritual death, which consisteth in a separation of the soul from

---

[z] *Justin Martyr* in Dialog. cum Tryph.

God, and in an absolute immobility unto divine operations. But man's sin did not nullify God's power: he that made him a glorious creature, when he was nothing, could as easily renew and rectify him when he fell away.

Being dead, true it is, that active concurrence unto his own restitution he could have none; but yet still the same passive obedience and capacity which was in the red clay, of which Adam's body was fashioned unto that divine image which God breathed into it, the same had man, being now fallen, unto the restitution of those heavenly benefits and habitual graces which then he lost: save that in the clay, there was only a passive obedience; but in man fallen, there is an active rebellion, crossing resistance [a], and withstanding of God's good work in him. More certainly than this he cannot have; because howsoever, in regard of natural and reasonable operations, he be more self-moving than clay, yet, in regard of spiritual graces, he is full as dead: even as a man, though more excellent than a beast, is yet as truly and equally not an angel, as a beast is. So then, thus far we see all mankind do agree in an equality of creation, in a universality of desertion, in a capacity of restitution.

God made the world, that therein he might communicate his goodness unto the creature, and unto every creature in that proportion, as the nature of it is capable of. And man, being one of the most excellent creatures, is amongst the rest capable of these two principal attributes, holiness and happiness: which two, God, out of his most secret counsel and eternal mercy, conferreth on whom he hath chosen and made accepted in Christ the Beloved, shutting the rest either out of the compass, as heathen; or at least out of the inward privileges and benefits of that covenant which he hath established with mankind, as hypocrites and licentious Christians.

Now as, in the first creation of man, God did, into the unformed lump of clay, infuse, by his power, the breath of life, and so made man; so, in the regeneration of a Christian, doth he in the natural man, who is dead in sin, breathe a principle of spiritual life,—the first act, as it were, and the original of all supernatural motions, whereby he is constituted in the first being of a member of Christ.

[a] Acts vii. 51. Rom. vii. 23.

And this first act is faith [b], the soul of a Christian, that whereby we live in Christ; so that till we have faith, we are dead, and out of him. And as faith is the principle (next under the Holy Ghost) of all spiritual life here,—so is baptism the Sacrament of that life [c], which, accompanied and raised by the Spirit of grace, is unto the church, though not the cause, yet the means, in and by which this grace is conveyed unto the soul.

Now as Adam, after once life was infused into him, was presently to preserve it by the eating of the fruits in the garden [d], where God had placed him, because of that continual depastion of his radical moisture by vital heat, which made nature to stand in need of succours and supplies from outward nourishment;—so after man is once regenerated and made alive, he is to preserve that faith which quickeneth him by such food, as is provided by God for that purpose, it being otherwise of itself subject to continual languishings and decays. And this life is thus continued and preserved, amongst other means, by the grace of this holy Eucharist, which conveys unto us that true food of life, the body and blood of Christ crucified. So then, inasmuch as the Sacrament of Christ's supper is not the Sacrament of regeneration, but of sustentation and nourishment; and inasmuch as no dead thing is capable of being nourished (augmentation being a vegetative and vital act); and lastly, inasmuch as the principle of this spiritual life is faith, and the Sacrament of it baptism;—it followeth evidently, That no man is a subject-qualified for the holy communion of Christ's body, who hath not been before partaker of faith and baptism.

In Heaven, where all things shall be perfected and renewed, our souls shall be in as little need of this Sacrament, as our bodies of nourishment. But this being a state of imperfection, subject to decays, and still capable of further augmentation; we are therefore by these holy mysteries to preserve the life, which by faith and baptism we have received: without which life, as the Sacrament doth confer and confirm nothing, so do we receive nothing neither, but the bare elements.

Christ is now in Heaven, no eye sharp enough to see him,

---

[b] 1 John v. 13.   [c] John iii. 5. Tit. iii. 5.   [d] Gen. i. 29.

no arm long enough to reach him, but only faith. The Sacrament is but the seal of a covenant[e]; and covenants essentially include conditions, and the conditions on our part is faith: no faith, no covenant; no covenant, no seal; no seal, no Sacrament; Christ and Belial will not lodge together[f].

Having thus found out the first necessary qualification of a man for the receiving of the holy Eucharist, without which, he is absolutely as uncapable of it, as a dead man of food; we may more easily look into the next more immediate and particular, consisting in that preparatory act of examination or trial of the conscience[g], touching its fitness to communicate; because the former is to be the rule and measure, by which we proceed in the latter.

Some things there are which men learn to do by doing of them[h], and which are better performed, and the dangers incident unto them better avoided by an extemporary dexterity, than by any pre-meditation or forecast. But yet generally, since matters of consequence are never without some perplexed difficulties, not discernible by a sudden intuition; and since the minds of men are of a limited efficacy, and therefore unfit for any serious work, till first dispossessed of all different notions which might divert, and of all repugnant principles or indispositions which might oppose it in the performance of any great business, set upon with sudden, uncomposed, and uncollected thoughts;—it is very necessary before we undertake any serious and difficult work, both to examine the sufficiency, and to prepare the instruments by which we may be enabled to perform it.

Thus we see in the works of nature, those which admit of any latitude or degrees of perfection, are seldom done without many previous dispositions to produce them. In plants and vegetables, the earth is to be opened, the seed to be scattered, the rain to moisten, the sun to evocate and excite the seminal virtue, and after all this comes a fruitful harvest: and so in generation of all other natural bodies, there are ever some antecedent qualities introduced, by means whereof, Nature is assisted and prepared for her last act. So in

---

[e] Rom. iv. 11.   [f] 2 Cor. vi. 15.   [g] 1 Cor. xi.   [h] ᾁΑ γὰρ δεῖ μανθάνοντας ποιεῖν, ταῦτα ποιοῦντες μανθάνομεν. *Arist.* Eth. l. 2. c. 1.—In arena consilium. *Sen.*—Videbitur in monte. Gen. xxii. 14.

the works of art, we find how wrestlers, and runners in
races, did supple their joints with ointments, and diet their
bodies, that by that means they might be fit for those bodily exercises : how those Roman fencers, in their gladia-
tory fights [k], did first use prefatory or dulled weapons,
before they entered in good earnest into the theatre ; and
then their custom was, first, to carry their weapons to the
prince to have his allowance of the fitness of them, before
they used them in fighting. The Lacedemonians were wont
to have musical instruments before their wars [l], that thereby
their courage might be sharpened, and their minds raised
unto bold attempts. And we read of Scipio Africanus [m],
that ever before he set himself upon the undertaking of any
great business, his manner was to enter the Capitol, to submit his projects to the judgement of the gods, and to implore
their aid and allowance for the good success of such his enterprises. A thing, for the substance of it, practised by all the
ethnics, before they addressed themselves unto any work
of consequence, whose constant use it was to have recourse
unto their gods in prayers, for benediction and encouragement. And it was a religious observation in the Roman
superstitious sacrifices, for a servant that stood by, to put
the priest in mind of what he was about, and to advise him
to consider maturely, and to do with his whole mind and
endeavour that work he was to perform. And whatsoever
vessels or garments were in those solemnities used, were beforehand washed and cleansed, that they might be fit instruments for such a work. Thus far we see the light of reason, and the very blindness of superstition, enforceth a necessity of preparation unto any great, especially divine
work.

If we look into the holy Scriptures, we may find God
himself a pattern of these deliberate preparations. In
making the world, it had been as easy for him in one simple
command to have erected this glorious frame at once, as to

[k] Vide *Lipsii* Satur. l. 2. c. 19.   [l] *Aul. Gell.* Noct. Attic. lib. i. 11.
[m] *Liv.* l. 26.—*Plin.* Paneg. in initio.—*Cic.* de legib. l. 2. et in Vatinium. So-
lenne hoc ante bella ;—*Virg.* Æn. l. 8. et 11.—*Xenoph.* Cyrop. l. 7.—*Macrob.*
Satur. l. 3. c. 15.—Ante epulas; *Athenæus* l. 4.—*Liv.* l. 49.—*Virg.* Æn. l. 1.
—Ante Nuptias ; *Servius* ad Virg. Æn. l. 3.—Vid. *Brisson.* de Formulis, lib. 1.
—*Servius* ad illud Virg., ' Puràque in veste Sacerdos.' Æn. 12.

be six days in the fashioning of it : but to exhibit unto us an example of temperate and advised proceedings, he first provides the materials, and then superadds the accomplishment and perfection.   In the dispensing of his judgements, he first prepares them before he inflicts them : he hath whet his sword, and bent his bow, and made ready his arrows, before he strikes or shoots.   His eye comes before his hand : he comes down to see Sodom [n], before to consume it.   He examines before he expels : " Adam [o], where art thou ?" before he drives him out of Paradise.   Nay, in the very sweetest of all his attributes, his mercy, we find him first consider his people Israel [p], before he sends Moses to deliver them. In like manner, our blessed Saviour, though having in him the fulness of the godhead, the treasures of wisdom, and grace without measure, he was therefore perfectly able to discharge that great work unto which the Father had sealed him,—was yet pleased to prepare himself [q], both unto his prophetical and sacerdotal obedience by baptism, fasting, temptation, and prayer ; that the practice of this great work, where it is was not necessary, might be a precedent unto us, who are not able of ourselves to think, or to do any good thing.   In the building of Solomon's temple [r], the stones were perfected and hewed, before they were brought ; there was neither hammer, nor axe, nor any tool of iron heard in the house, while it was in building.   And so should it be in the temple, of which that was a type, even in the mystical body of Christ : every man should be first hewed and fitted by repentance, and other preparatory works, before he should approach to incorporate himself into that spiritual and eternal building.   In the observation of Levitical ceremonies, we may note, That before the celebration of the passover [s], the Lamb was to be taken and separated from the flock three days ere it was slain : in which time, the people might, in that figure, learn to sanctify themselves, and to be separated from sinners.   And our Saviour Christ, in the celebration of the last supper [t], would not have so much as the room unprovided, but he sent his disciples beforehand about it ; teaching us, that in sacred things there should be first a

[n] Gen. xviii. 21.   [o] Gen. iii. 9.   [p] Exod. iii. 7, 8.   [q] Matth. iii. 13. iv. 12. xxvi. 36.   [r] 1 Kings vi. 7.   [s] Exod. xii. 3, 6.   [t] Mark xiv. 13, 15.

preparation before a celebration. So then we see in general
the necessity of preparing and deliberating, before we address ourselves unto the performance of any holy work; and·
if any where, certainly in this work of the Sacrament most
necessary it is. Though God's commands by his apostle
were bond enough to enforce us the necessity of obedience,
depending rather on the Author [u], than on the emolument of
the law; yet God, who is not wanting always to win men
unto the observance of what he requires, urgeth us thereunto, not only with an argument of debt, because we are his
servants, but with an argument of profit too; because the
omission of it will not only nullify unto us the benefit of his
Sacrament, but make us guilty of that very blood, which
was shed for the salvation of the world, and turn that into
judgement which was intended for mercy.

What this danger of being ' guilty of Christ's blood ' is, I
will not stand long to explain.

Briefly, To be guilty of the body and blood of Christ, is
to offer some notable contempt and indignity unto the sufferings of Christ, to sin against the price of our redemption,
and to vilify and set at nought the precious blood of the
new covenant [x], as if it were a common and profane thing,
when men out of ignorant, sensual, secure, presumptuous,
formalizing, inconsiderate, and profane affections, approach
unto Christ's table to communicate of him. To be guilty of
blood is, in some sort or other, to shed it, and to join with
the crucifiers of Christ [y]:—a sin, which as it drove Judas to
despair, and to end with himself, who had begun with his
Master,—so doth it, to this day, lie with the heaviest curse
that ever that people endured, on the offspring of those
wicked Jews, whose imprecation it was, "His blood be on
us, and on our children." As Christ on the cross, was,
in regard of himself, offered up unto the Father, but in
regard of Pilate and the Jews, crucified;—so is his blood in
the Sacrament by the faithful received,—by the wicked, shed
and spilt on the ground; when, not discerning or differencing
the Lord's body from other ordinary food, they rush irre-
verently to the participation of it. For a man may be guilty of

[u] Prior est auctoritas imperantis quam utilitas servientis. *Tert.* de Pœnit. c. 4.
[x] Heb. x. 29. [y] *Chrysost.* in 1 Cor. Hom. 27.

the blood of Christ, though he receive it not at all ; as a man may of murder [z], though he hit not the party, against whom his weapon was directed.   It is not the event, but the purpose, which specifies the sin [a].   The anger of a dog is as great, when he barks at the moon, which is above his malice, as when at a man, whom he may easily bite.   The malice of the apostate, who shot up darts against Heaven [b], was no less, than if he had hit the body of Christ, at whom he shot. If that which is done unto the apostles of Christ, is done unto him, because they are his ambassadors ; and if that which is done unto the poor and distressed flock of Christ, is done unto him, because they are his members ;—then surely that which is done unto the Sacrament of Christ, must needs be done unto him too, inasmuch as it is his representation and image.   For a man may be guilty of treason, by offering indignity to the picture, coin, garment, or seal of a prince.   The dishonour that is done to the image (it being a relative thing), doth ever reflect on the original itself.   And therefore the Romans [c], when they would dishonour any man, would show some disgrace to the statues that had been erected to his honour, by demolishing, breaking down, and dragging them in the dirt.

Again, A man may be guilty of the blood of Christ, by reaching forth his hand to receive it, having no right unto it.   A sacrilege it is to lay hold wrongfully on the Lord's inheritance, or on any thing consecrated to the maintenance of his worship and service ; but this certainly is so much the greater, by how much the Lord's body is more precious than his portion.   To counterfeit right of inheritance unto some kingdom, hath been ever, amongst men, unfortunate and capital.   We know how ill it succeeded with the counterfeit Nero amongst the Romans [d] ; and that forged Duke of York in the time of Henry the Seventh.   And surely, no less successful can their insolence be, who having, by reason of

---

[z] Voluntas facit Homicidam.   [a] Omnia scelera etiam ante effectum operis, quantum culpæ satìs est, perfecta sunt.   *Sen.* de Const. cap. 7. 4.   [b] Quid ? tu putas, cum stolidus ille Rex multitudine telorum diem obscurasset, ullam sagittam in solem incidisse?   *Sen.* ibid. c. 4. 2.   [c] Descendunt statuæ restemque sequuntur, &c. *Juvenal.* Sat. 10. Effigies Pisonis traxerant in Gemonias, ac devellebant.   *Tac.* Hist. l. 3. 14.—Vexillarius comitantis Galbam cohortis dereptam Galbæ imaginem solo afflixit.   *Tac.* Hist. l. 1.   [d] *Tac.* Hist. l. 2.

their unworthy approach, no claim nor interest unto the
benefit of Christ's body, do yet usurp it, and take the kingdom of Heaven, as it were, by rapine and presumptuous
violence.   Certainly, if Christ will not have the wicked to
take his Word [e], much less his body into their mouths.   If
the rain that falleth to the ground, returns not empty [f], but,
according to the quality of the ground on which it falls,
makes it fruitful, either in herbs, meet for the use of men
that dressed it,—or in thorns and briers that are near unto
cursing; impossible it is, that the blood of Christ in his Sacrament should be ineffectual, whether for a blessing unto
the faithful, or for a curse to those that unworthily receive
it.   So then, necessary it is, that before the communication
of these sacred mysteries, a man prepare himself by some
previous devotions : and for this cause we find our Saviour
Christ washing his disciples' feet [g], that is, cleansing their
earthly and human affections before his institution of this
Sacrament.   And we find Joseph of Arimathea [h] wrapping
his dead body in a clean linen garment, and putting it into
a new tomb, never yet defiled with rottenness and corruption.
And can we imagine, that he that endured not an unclean
grave or shroud, will enter into a sinful and unprepared soul?
The everlasting doors must first be lifted up, before the King
of Glory will enter in.

CHAPTER XIX.

Of the form or manner of examination required, which is,
touching the main qualification of a worthy receiver, Faith:
the demonstration whereof is made, first, from the causes ;
secondly, from the nature of it.

HAVING thus discovered the necessity of preparation, and
that standing in the examination and trial of a man's conscience; it followeth, that we conclude with setting down
very compendiously the manner of this examination, only
naming some principal particulars.

_____

[e] Psalm l. 16.   [f] Heb. vi. 7.   [g] John xiii. 5.   [h] Matth.
xxvii. 59, 60.

The main query is, Whether I am a fit guest to approach God's table, and to share in the fellowship of his sufferings?

The sufferings of Christ are not exposed unto the rapine and violence of each bold intruder; but he who was first the author, is for ever the dispenser of them. And as in the dispensation of his miracles, for the most part, so of his sufferings likewise,—there is either a question premised, " Believest thou ?" or a condition included, " Be it unto thee, as thou believest." But a man may be alive, and yet unfit to eat, nor capable of any nourishment by reason of some dangerous diseases, which weaken the stomach, and trouble it with an apepsy, or difficulty of concoction. And so faith may sometimes in the habit lie smothered, and almost stifled with some spiritual lethargy, binding up the vital faculties from their proper motions. And therefore our faith must be an operative and expedite faith,—not stupified with any known and practised course of sin, which doth ever weaken our appetite unto grace, they being things inconsistent.

The matter, then, we see of this trial, must be that vital qualification, which pre-disposeth a man for the receiving of these holy mysteries; and that is Faith.

To enter into such a discourse of faith, as the condition of that subject would require, were a labour beyond the length of a short meditation, and, unto the present purpose, impertinent. We will therefore only take some generalities about the causes, nature, properties, or effects of faith, which are the usual mediums of producing assents; and propose them by way of interrogation to the conscience; that so the major and minor being contrived, the light of reason in the soul may make up a practical syllogism, and so conclude either its fitness or indisposition towards these holy mysteries.

First, For the causes of faith,—not to meddle with that extraordinary cause, I mean, miracles;—the ordinary are the Word of God, and the Spirit of God : the Word as the seed, the Spirit as the formative and seminal virtue, making it active and effectual. For " the letter profiteth nothing; it is the Spirit which quickeneth." What the formality of that particular action is, whereby the Word and Spirit do implant this heavenly branch of faith in the soul (faith itself having in its nature several distinct degrees, some intellectual of assent, some fiducial of reliance and confidence, some of abnegation, renouncing, and flying out of ourselves, as insufficient for the contrivance of our own salvation; and so, in congruity of reason, requiring, in the causes producing them, several manners of causalities), as I take it not necessary, so neither am I able to determine. I shall therefore touch upon some principal properties of either; all which, if they concur not unto the original production, do certainly to the radication and establishing of that divine virtue, and therefore may justly come within the compass of these premises; from the evidences of which, assumed and applied, the conscience is to conclude the truth of its faith in Christ.

And, first, For the Word, to let pass those properties which are only the inherent attributes, and not any transient operations thereof (as its sufficiency, perspicuity, majesty, self-authority, and the like), let us touch upon those which it carrieth along with it into the conscience, and I shall observe but two; its light [i], and its power [k]: even as the sun, wherever it goes, doth still carry with it that brightness whereby it discovereth, and that influence whereby it quickeneth, inferior bodies.

First, For the Word, the properties thereof are, First, To make manifest, and to discover the hidden things of darkness; for "whatsoever doth make manifest, is light." The heart of man naturally is a labyrinth of darkness [l]; his works, works of darkness; his prince, a prince of darkness, whose projects are full of darkness; they are depths, devices, craftiness, methods. The Word of God alone is that light which maketh manifest the secrets of the heart; that glass wherein we may see, both ourselves [m], and all the devices of Satan against us, discovered [n].

And, secondly, By this act of manifesting, doth light distinguish one thing from another. In the dark, we make no difference of fair or foul, of right or wrong ways, but all are alike unto us. And so while we continue in the blind-

i 2 Pet. i. 19. Psalm cxix.   k Rom. i. 16.   l Rom. i. 21.   m Plangendæ tenebræ, in quibus me mea facultas latet. *Aug.* Confes. l. 10. c. 32. n Ephes. v. 11. Rev. ii. 24. 2 Cor. ii. 11. xi. 3. Ephes. vi. 11. 1 Cor. xiv. 15. James i. 1 John. ii. 11.

ness of our natural estate, we are not able to perceive the distinction between divine and natural objects; but the Word of God, like a touchstone, discovereth the differences of truth and falsehood, good and evil, and, like fire, separateth the precious from the vile.

Secondly, Light is quickening, and a comforting thing. The glory of the saints[o] is ' an inheritance of light;' and they are ' children of light,' who shall shine as ' the sun in the firmament :' whereas darkness is both the title and the portion of the wicked. The times of darkness[p] men make to be the times of their sleeping, which is an image of death; it is in the light only that men work: and so ' the Word of God' is a comforting word; it was ' David's delight[q], his ' honeycomb.' And it is a quickening Word too, for it is the ' Word of life.'

Lastly, Light doth assist, direct, and guide us in our ways; and so doth the Word of God: it is " a lantern to our feet, and a light unto our paths."

Secondly, For the power of the Word, it is twofold, even as all power is : a governing power, in respect of that which is under it; and a subduing power, in respect of that which is against it.

First, The Word hath a governing power, in respect of those which are subject to it; for which cause it is every where called a ' law, ' and a ' royal,' that is, a commanding sovereign ' law:' it bears dominion in the soul, conforming each faculty to itself, directeth the righteous, furnisheth unto good works, raiseth the drooping, bindeth the broken, comforteth the afflicted, reclaimeth the straggling.

Secondly, It subdueth all enmity and opposition[r], discomfiteth Satan, beateth down the strong holds of sin[s]; it is a sword to cut off, a weapon to subdue, a hammer to break in pieces whatsoever thought riseth up against it[t]. Now then, let a man's conscience make but these few demands unto itself:—

Hath the light and power of God's Word discovered itself unto me? Have the Scriptures made me known unto myself? have they unlocked those crooked windings of my

[o] Colos. i. Ephes. v. [p] John vi. 68. xii. 35. [q] Psalm cxix. [r] Heb. iii. 12. [s] 2 Cor. x. 4. [t] Jer. xxiii. 29.

perverse heart? have they manifested unto my soul, not
only those sins which the light of reason could have discerned, but even those privy corruptions, which I could not
otherwise have known? have they acquainted me with the
devices of Satan, wherewith he lieth in wait to deceive?
have they taught me to distinguish between truth and appearances, between goodness and shadows, to find out the
better part, the one necessary thing, and to adhere unto it?
Am I sensible of the sweetness and benefits of his holy
Word? doth it refresh my soul, and revive me unto every
good work? Is it unto my soul like the honeycomb [u], like
pleasant pastures [x], like springs of water, like the tree of
life [y]? Do I take it along with me wheresoever I go, to preserve me from stumbling and straggling in this valley of darkness, and shadow of death?

Again, Do I feel the power of it like a royal commanding
law, bearing rule in my soul? Am I willing to submit and
resign myself unto the obedience of it? Do I not, against
the clear and convincing evidence thereof, entertain in my
bosom any the least rebellious thought? Do I spare no
Agag, no ruling sin? withdraw no wedge or Babylonish
garment, no gainful sin? make a league with no Gibeonite,
no pretending sin? But do I suffer it, like Joshua, to destroy every Canaanite, even the sin, which, for sweetness,
I rolled under my tongue? Doth it batter the towers of Jericho, break down the bulwarks of the flesh, lead into captivity the corruptions of nature, mortify and crucify the old
man in me? Doth it minister comforts unto me, in all the
ebbs and droopings of my spirit, even above the confluence
of all earthly happiness, and against the combination of all
outward discontents? And do I set up a resolution thus
always to submit myself unto the regiment thereof? in
one word, doth it ' convince me of sin' in myself, and so humble me to repent of it; —' of righteousness' in Christ, and so
raise me to believe in it; —of his spiritual 'judgement' in governing the souls of true believers by the power of love, and
beauty of his graces, and so constrain and persuade me to
be obedient unto it?

        [u] Psalm cxix.   [x] Psalm xxiii.   [y] Isai. xii. 3.   xlix. 10.

These are those good premises, out of which I may infallibly conclude, that I have had the beginnings, the seeds of faith shed abroad in my heart, which will certainly be further quickened by that holy Spirit, who is the next and principal producer of it.

The operations of this holy Spirit, being as numberless as all the holy actions of the faithful, cannot therefore all possibly be set down. I shall touch at some few, which are of principal and obvious observation.

First of all, The Spirit is a Spirit of liberty[z] and a Spirit of prayer; it takes away the bondage and fear[a] wherein we naturally are (for fear makes us run from God, as from a punishing and revenging judge; never any man in danger fled thither for succour, whence the danger issued; fear is so far from this[b], that it betrayeth and suspecteth those very assistances which reason offereth)—and it enableth us to have access and recourse unto God himself, whom our sins had provoked; and in our prayers, like Aaron and Hur, it supporteth our hands, that they do not faint nor fall. It raiseth the soul unto divine and unutterable petitions, and it melteth the heart into sighs and groans that cannot be expressed.

Secondly, The Holy Ghost is compared unto a 'witness,' whose proper work it is to reveal and affirm some truth, which is called in question. There is in a man's bosom, by reason of that enmity and rebellion betwixt the flesh and the spirit, and by means of Satan's suggestions,—sundry dialogues and conflicts, wherein Satan questioneth the title we pretend to salvation. In this case, the spirit of a man (as one cannot choose but do, when his whole estate is made ambiguous) staggereth, droopeth, and is much distressed: till at last the Spirit of God, by the light of the Word, the testimony of conscience, and the sensible motions of inward grace, layeth open our title, and helpeth us to read the evidence of it, and thus recomposeth our troubled thoughts.

Thirdly, The Spirit of God is compared to a seal[c]; the work of a seal is, first, to make a stamp and impression in

---

[z] Rom. viii. 2.　[a] 2 Tim. i. 7.　[b] Wisd. xvii. 11.—Timor etiam auxilia reformidat. *Q. Curt.*　[c] Ephes. iv. 30.—Cuicunque rei ponis signum, ideò ponis signum, ne confusa cum aliis à te non possit agnosci. *Aug.* in Joh. Tract. 25.

some other matter ; secondly, by that means to difference
and distinguish it from all other things : and so the Spirit of
God doth fashion the hearts of his people unto a conformity
with Christ, framing in it holy impressions, and renewing
the decayed image of God therein ; and thereby separateth
them from sinners, maketh them of a distinct commonwealth under a distinct government; that whereas, before,
they were subject to the same prince, laws, and desires with
the world,—being now called out, they are new men, and
have another character upon them.

Secondly, A seal doth obsignate and ratify some covenant, grant, or conveyance to the person to whom it belongeth. It is used amongst men for confirming their mutual trust in each other. And so certainly doth the Spirit of
God pre-affect the soul with an evident taste of that glory,
which in the day of redemption shall be actually conferred
upon it ; and therefore it is called ' a hansel, earnest, and
first-fruit of life [d].'

Fourthly, The Spirit of God is compared to an ointment.
Now the properties of ointments are, First, To supple and
assuage tumours in the body ; and so doth the Spirit of
God mollify the hardness of man's heart, and work it to a
sensible tenderness, and quick apprehension of every sin.

Secondly, Ointments do open and penetrate those places
unto which they are applied: and so the unction [e] which the
faithful have, teacheth them all things, and openeth their
eyes to see the wonders of God's law, and the beauty of
his graces. In vain are all outward sounds or sermons, unless this Spirit be within to teach us [f].

Thirdly, Ointments do refresh and lighten nature, because
as they make way for the emission of all noxious humours,
so likewise for the free passage and translation of all vital
spirits, which do enliven and comfort. And so the Spirit of
God is a Spirit of consolation, and a Spirit of life ; he is the
Comforter of his Church [g].

Lastly, Ointments in the Levitical law [h], and in the state

---

[d] Ephes. i. 14.   [e] 1 John ii. 20.   [f] Sonus verborum nostrorum aures
percutit ; magister intus est ; quantum ad me pertinet, omnibus locutus sum ;
sed quibus unctio illa intùs non loquitur, indocti redeurt: magisteria forin-
secus adjutoria quædam sunt ; cathedram in Cœlo habet, qui corda docet. *Aug.*
in Joh. Tract. 4.   [g] John xiv. 16.   [h] Exod. xxx. 25, 30.

of the Jews, were for consecration and sequestration of things unto some holy use : as Christ is said to be anointed by his Father[i] unto the economy of that great work, the redemption of the world : and thus doth the Holy Ghost anoint us to be a royal priesthood, a holy nation[k], a people set at liberty.

Fifthly and lastly, I find the Holy Ghost compared unto fire[l], whose properties are,

First, To be of a very active and working nature, which stands never still, but is ever doing something. And so the Spirit of God, and his graces, are all operative in the hearts of the faithful ; they set all where they come, on work.

Secondly, The nature and proper motion of fire is to ascend ; other motions whatever it hath, arise from some outward and accidental restraint, limiting the nature of it. And so the Spirit of God ever raiseth up the affections from earth, fasteneth the eye of faith upon eternity, ravisheth the soul with a fervent longing to be with the Lord, and to be admitted unto the fruition of those precious joys which here it suspireth after. As soon as ever men have chosen Christ to be their head, then presently, ' ascendunt de terra,' they go up out of the land[m], and have their conversation above, where Christ is.

Thirdly, Fire doth inflame and transform every thing that is combustible, into the nature of itself. And so the Spirit of God filleth the soul with a divine fervour and zeal, which purgeth away the corruptions and dross of the flesh, with the spirit of judgement, and with the spirit of burning.

Fourthly, Fire hath a purifying and cleansing property, to draw away all noxious or infectious vapours out of the air, to separate all soil and dross from metals, and the like. And so doth the Spirit of God[n] cleanse the heart, and in heavenly sighs, and repentant tears, cause to expire all those steams of corruptions, those noisome and infectious lusts which fight against the soul.

Fifthly, Fire hath a penetrating and insinuating quality, whereby it creepeth into all the pores of a combustible body. And, in like manner, the holy Spirit of God doth

---

[i] Heb. i. 9.   [k] 1 Pet. ii. 9.   [l] 1 Thess. v. 19.   [m] Hos. i. 11.
[n] Spiritus Ardoris, Isai. iv. 4.

penetrate the heart, though full of insensible and inscrutable windings; doth search the reins, doth pry into the closest nooks and inmost corners of the soul, there discovering and working out those secret corruptions which did deceive and defile us.

Lastly, Fire doth illighten, and by that means communicates the comforts of itself unto others. And so the Spirit, being a spirit of truth, doth illuminate the understanding, and doth dispose it likewise to discover its light unto others who stand in need of it: for this is the nature of God's grace, That when Christ hath manifested himself to the soul of one man, it setteth him on work to manifest Christ unto others; as Andrew to Simon[o]; and the woman of Samaria to the men of the city[p]; and Mary Magdalen to the disciples[q]. It is like ointment poured forth, which cannot be concealed[r], "We cannot," saith the apostle, " but speak the things which we have heard and seen[s]," and " they who feared the Lord," in the prophet, "spake often to one another[t]."

These propositions being thus set down, let the conscience assume them to itself in such demands as these:—

Do I find in myself a freedom from that spirit of fear and bondage, which maketh a man, like Adam, to fly from the presence of God in his Word? Do I find myself able, with affiance and firm hope, to fly unto God as unto an altar of refuge in time of trouble, and to call upon his name? and this not only with an outward battology and lip-labour, but by the spirit to cry 'Abba, Father?' Doth the testimony of God's Spirit settle and compose such doubtings in me, as usually arise out of the war between flesh and faith? Do I find a change and transformation in me from the vanity of my old conversation unto the image of Christ, and of that original justice wherein I was created? Do I find myself distinguished and taken out from the world, by heavenly-mindedness and raised affections, by renouncing the delights, abandoning the corruptions, suppressing the motions of secular and carnal thoughts? solacing my soul, not with perishable and inconstant contentments, but with that

o John i. 41.   p John iv. 29.   q John xx. 17.   r Prov. xxvii. 16.
s Acts iv. 20.   t Mal. iii. 16.

blessed hope of a city made without hands, immortal, unde-
filed, and that fadeth not away? Do I find in my heart an
habitual tenderness, and aptness to bleed, and relent at the
danger of any sin, though mainly crossing my carnal delights, and whatever plots and contrivances I might lay for
furthering mine own secular ends, if, by indirectness, sinful
engagements, and unwarrantable courses, I could advance
them? Do I find myself, in reading or hearing God's
Word, inwardly wrought upon to admire the wisdom, assent
unto the truth, acknowledge the holiness, and submit myself
unto the obedience of it? Do I, in my ordinary and best
composed thoughts, prefer the tranquillity of a good conscience and the comforts of God's Spirit, before all outside and glittering happiness, notwithstanding any discouragements that may be incident to a conscionable conversation?

Lastly, Are the graces of God operative and stirring in my
soul : is my conversation more heavenly, my zeal more fervent, my corruptions more discovered, each faculty in its several sphere, more transformed into the same image with
Christ Jesus? Are all these things in me?—or, in defect of
any, do the desires and longings of my soul after them, appear to be sincere and unfeigned, by my daily employing all
my strength, and improving each advantage to further my
proficiency in them? Then I have an evident and infallible
token, that having thus far partaken of the Spirit of life, and,
by consequence, of faith, whereby our souls are fastened
unto Christ,—I may with comfort approach unto this holy
table, wherein that life which I have received, may be further nourished and confirmed to me.

The second medium, formerly propounded for the trial of
faith, was the nature and essence of it. To find out the
formal nature of faith, we must, first, consider, that all faith
is not a saving faith ; for there is a faith that worketh a
trembling[u], as in the devils ; and there is a faith which
worketh life and peace[x], as in those that are justified.
Faith, in general, is an assent of the reasonable soul[y] unto
revealed truths. Now every medium or inducement to an
assent, is drawn either from the light which the object itself

[u] James ii. 19.   [x] Rom. v. 1.   [y] *Aquin.* 22. quæst. 1. art. 4.

proposeth to the faculty ; and this the blessed apostle ^z con-
tradistinguisheth from faith, by the name of ' light :'—or else
it is drawn from the authority and authenticalness of a nar-
rator, upon whose report while we rely, without any evidence of the thing itself, the assent which we produce, is an
assent of faith or credence. The Samaritans ^a did first assent
unto the miracles of Christ, by the report of the woman ; and
this was faith : but afterwards they assented, because themselves had heard him speak ; and this was sight. Now both
those assents have annexed unto them either evidence and infallibility, or only probability, admitting degrees of fear and
suspicion. That faith is a certain assent, and 'certitudine rei,'
in regard of the object, even above the evidence of demon-
strative conclusions, is on all hands confessed : because howsoever, ' quantum ad certitudinem mentis,' in regard of our
weakness and distrust, we are often subject to stagger,—yet,
in the thing itself, it dependeth upon the infallibility of
God's own Word, which hath said it, and, by consequence,
is nearer unto him who is the fountain of all truth ; and
therefore doth more share in the properties of truth, which
are certainty and infallibility, than any thing proved by mere
natural reason : and the assent produced by it, is differenced
from suspicion, hesitancy, or dubitation, in the opinion of
schoolmen themselves.

Now then, inasmuch as we are bound to yield an evident
assent unto the articles of our Christian faith, both intellectual in regard of the truth, and fiducial, in regard of the
goodness of them respectively to our own benefit and salvation;—necessary it is, that the understanding be convinced
of these two things :—

First, That God is of infallible authority, and cannot lie
nor deceive : which thing is a principle, unto which the
light of nature doth willingly assent.

And, secondly, That this authority, which in faith I thus
rely upon, is, indeed and infallibly, God's own authority.
The means whereby I come to know that, may be either extraordinary, as revelation, such as was made to prophets
concerning future events ; or else ordinary and common to
all the faithful.

z 2 Cor. v. 7.   a John iv.

For discovery of them, we must again rightly distinguish the double act of faith.

1st. That act, whereby we assent unto the general truth of the object in itself.

2nd. That act, whereby we rest persuaded of the goodness thereof unto us in particular, with respect unto both;—with these doth a double question arise :—

First, Touching the means, whereby a believer comes to know, that the testimony and authority within the promises and truths of Scripture he relieth upon, are certainly and infallibly God's own authority. Which question is all one with that, How a Christian man may infallibly be assured, ' ita ut non possit subesse falsum,' that the holy Scriptures are the very dictates of Almighty God.

For the resolution whereof, in a very few words, we must first agree, That as no created understanding could ever have invented the mystery of the gospel (it being the counsel of God's own bosom, and containing such manifold wisdom, as the angels are astonished at [b]) ; so it being dictated and revealed by Almighty God, such is the deepness, excellency, and holiness of it, that the natural man [c], whose faculties are vitiated by original and contracted corruption, cannot, by the strength of his own naked principles, be able to understand it : for notwithstanding the grammatical sense of the words, and the logical coherence and connexion of consequences, may be discerned by the common light of ordinary reason ; yet our Saviour's ἔλεγχος, conviction, and the apostle's ἀπόδειξις and φανέρωσις, 'demonstration and manifestation' of the Spirit, is a thing surpassing the discovery and comprehension of natural men : and therefore it is called "a knowledge which passeth knowledge." And this doth plainly appear upon this ground :—one principal end, we know, of the gospel is, " to cast down every high thing that exalteth itself against the knowledge of God, and to bring into captivity every thought to the obedience of Christ [d]." So that until such time as the light of evangelical truth have thus far prevailed over the conscience, certain it is, that the practical judgement is not yet fully convinced of it, or acquainted with

---

[b] Vide *Chrysost.* Hom. 7. in 1 Cor.   [c] Ubi ad profunditatem Sacramentorum perventum est, omnis Platonicorum caligavit subtilitas.—*Cyprian.* de Spirit. S. John xvi. 8.   1 Cor. ii. 4.   2 Cor. iv. 2.   Eph. iv. 19.   [d] 2 Cor. x. 4, 5.

it. It is an excellent speech of the philosopher[e], that according as every man is himself in the habit of his own nature, such likewise doth the end appear unto him : and therefore natural men, whose inclinations and habit of soul are
altogether sensual and worldly, never have a supernatural
good appear unto them under the formal conceit of an ultimate and most eligible end ; and, therefore, their knowledge
thereof must needs be imperfect and defective.

Again, The Scripture every where, besides the external
proposing of the object, and the material and remote disposition of the subject (which must be ever a reasonable
creature), doth require a special help of the grace of Christ
to open, and mollify, and illighten the heart, and to proportion the palate of the practical judgement, unto the sweetness and goodness of supernatural truths. He it is, who
openeth the eye to see wonders in the law; giveth a heart
to understand and to know God; teacheth all those which
come unto Christ, without which teaching they do not come;
giveth us an understanding to know him ; illighteneth the understanding to know what is the hope of our calling;
enableth us to call Jesus ' Lord ;' and draweth away the veil
from before our eyes, that we may see, with open face, the
glory of God[f].

Again, There is a vast disproportion between a supernatural light, and a natural faculty ; the one being spiritual,
the other sensual ; and spiritual things must be spiritually
discerned. Two great impediments there are[g], whereby the
minds of mere natural men are bound up, and disabled from
receiving full impressions, and passing a right sentence upon
spiritual things. First, The native and original blindness of
them, which is not able to apprehend τὸ ὕψωμα τῶν διδασκο-

* Ὁποῖός ποθ' ἕκαστός ἐστι, τοιοῦτο καὶ τὸ τέλος φαίνεται αὐτῷ. Arist.
Ethic. l. 3. c. 7.   f Psalm cxix. 18. Deut. xxix. 4. Jer. xxvii. 7. xxxi. 4. John
vi. 45. Eph. i. 17. 1 Cor. xii. 7. John xiv. 21. 1 Thes. iv. 9. 2 Cor. iii. 18.
1 John v. 20. Quisquis non venit, profecto nec didicit, ita ut Deus docet per
Spiritum gratiam, ut quod quisque didicerit, non tantùm cognoscendo videat, sed
etiam volendo appetat, et agendo proficiat. Aug. de Grat. Christi. lib. 1. c. 14.—
Et vide de præd. sect. c. 8.—Nemo potest Deum scire, nisi Deo docente.
Ireneus, lib. 4. c. 14.—A Deo discendum quod de Deo intelligendum. Hilar. de
Trin. 1. 5. Concil. Arausican. Can. 7.   g Ignorantia et difficultas. Aug.
Ἄνοια καὶ ἀσθένεια. Clem. Alex. Strom. 1. 7.—Ratio communium opinionum
consilii cœlestis incapax ; hoc solum putat in naturâ rerum esse, quod ut intra se
intelligit, aut præstare possit ex sese. Hilar. de Trin. lib. 1.

μένων, 'the height and majesty of the things which are taught.' Secondly, That which the apostle calleth φρόνημα σαρκὸς 'the wisdom of the flesh,' which is enmity against God: for as the appetite of the flesh lusteth against the spirit, so the wisdom of the flesh reasoneth and rebelleth against the spirit. For such ever as are the ways and wills of men, whereby they work; such likewise would they have the light and the law to be, which ruleth them in their working. And therefore where there is a meek spirit, and a heart devoted unto the obedience of Christ, and a purpose to do the things which the gospel requireth, there is never any swelling nor resistance against supernatural truths : for as the cleanness of the window doth much conduce to the admission of light, so doth the cleanness of the conscience to the admission of truth. "If any man will do his will, he shall know of the doctrine whether it be of God; and he will reveal his secrets to them that fear him[h]."

And yet by all this which hath been spoken, we do not go about so to disable natural reason, as to leave it no room at all in matters of supernatural assent. For though nature alone be not able to comprehend grace, yet grace is able to use nature : and being in itself a spiritual eye-salve, when it hath healed and rectified reason, it then applieth it as an instrument more exactly to discover the connexion and mutual consequences and joinings of spiritual doctrines together. Besides, thus much vigour we may safely attribute to natural reason alone, that by the force of such premises as itself can frame,—the falseness, vanity, and insufficiency unto human happiness of all other religions or doctrines which are not Christian, may, by a wise man, be evidently discovered. Neither have there been wanting, amongst infidels[i] and idolaters, men of more generous, piercing, and impartial judgements, who have made bold to confess the vanity of

[h] John vii. 17. Psalm xxv. 9, 14. John x. 4, 5. James iii. 13. 1 John ii. 20. *Aug.* de Doctrin. Christ. l. 2. c. 6.—*Hilar.* de Trin. l. 10. [i] Vide *Justin.* *Mart.* Parænes. ad Græcos.—*Clem. Alex.* in Protrept.—*Tert.* Apolog. c. 12. 17. et de Testimon. Animæ, c. 1. 2.—*Cyprian.* de Vanit. Idolorum.—Sophocles et alii apud *Clem. Alex.* Strom. l. 5.—*Theodoret* de Curand. Græc. Affectib. Serm. 2. 3.— *Cyril.* contr. Julian. l. 1.—*Aug.* de Civ. Dei. l. 4. c. 31. et *Lud. Vivem* ibi. l. 6. c. 10.—*Lactant.* l. 3. c. 3.—*Joseph.* lib. 2. contr. Apion.—*Euseb.* de Præpar. Evang. l. 13. c. 13. l. 4. c. 16.

that polytheism and corrupt worship which was amongst
them.

Natural reason then being (notwithstanding any remainders of strength or vigour in it) too impotent to discover
the certainty of God's Word, and unable alone to present
the gospel as 'objectum credibile,' and as the infallible
oracle of God;—It remaineth, that we consider by what
further means this may be effected.   And, in one word,
there is a threefold different, but subordinate casuality, requisite to the founding of this assent [k] :—

The first is, ministerial, dispositive, and introductory by
ecclesiastical dispensation, which is likewise twofold:—

1st. To those that are bred in her bosom, and matricu-
lated by baptism, and so from their infancy trained up to
have a reverend and due esteem of her authority; there is
her act of tradition, delivering to her children in this age, as
she herself, by a continued succession, hath also received:
this is an indubitate principle to be rested on, That holy
Scriptures are the Word of God.

2nd. If the church meet with such as are without her
bosom, and so will not ascribe any thing to her maternal
authority in testification and tradition, except she can,
by strength of argument, evince what she affirmeth,—she is
not in that case destitute of her 'arma prælusoria,' valid and
sufficient arguments to make preparation in minds, not extremely possessed with prejudice and perverseness, for the
entertaining of this principle.

As first, That all sciences have their hypotheses and postu-
lata; certain principles which are to be granted, and not
disputed; and that even in lower sciences, and more commensurate to human reason; yet, 'oportet discentem cre-
dere,' he must first believe principles for granted, and then,
after some progress and better proficiency in the study, he
shall not fail more clearly to perceive the infallibility of them
by their own light.   That therefore which is granted unto all
other sciences, more descending to the reach of human
judgement than divinity doth, cannot, without unreasonable
pertinacy, be denied unto it; especially considering, that
of all so many millions of men, who, in all ages, have been

[k] *Aug.* de Doctr. Christ. in Prooem.—*Hooker*, lib. 3. sect. 8.—*Camer.* de Eccles.
page 411.

thus contented to believe, first, upon ecclesiastical tradition and suggestion, there hath not, in any age, been enough to make up a number, who, upon inducements of argument and debate, have forsaken the Scriptures at the last ;—which is a strong presumption, that they all who persisted in the embracing of them, did, after trial and further acquaintance, by certain taste and experience, find the testimony and tradition of the Church to be therein faithful and certain.

Secondly, That man being made by God, and subject to his will, and owing unto him worship and obedience, which in reason ought to be prescribed by none other than by him to whom it is to be performed ; that, therefore, requisite and congruous it is, that the will of God should be made known unto his creature, in such a manner, and by such means, as that he shall not, without his own wilful neglect, mistake it : inasmuch as law is the rule of obedience, and promulgation the force of law.

Thirdly, That no other rule or religion can be assigned, either of Pagans or Mahumetans, which may not manifestly, by the strength of right reason, be justly disproved, as not proceeding from God, either by the lateness of its original, or the shortness of its continuance, or the vanity and brutishness of its rules, or the contradictions within itself, or by some other apparent imperfection. And for that of the Jews, notwithstanding it had its original from Divine ordination, yet from thence likewise it may be made appear out of those Scriptures which they confess, to have received its period and abrogation : God promising, that as he had the first time shaken the mount in the publication of the law, and first founding of the Mosaical pedagogy, so he would once again shake both the earth and the heaven, in the promulgation of the gospel. To say nothing, that force of reason will easily conclude, that, with such a God, as the old Scriptures set forth the Lord to be, the blood of bulls and goats could not possibly make expiation for sin, but must necessarily relate to some greater sacrifice, which is in the gospel revealed. And besides, whereas the Lord was wont, for the greatest sins of that people, namely, idolatry, and pollution of his worship, to chastise them notwithstanding with more tolerable punishments, (their two greatest captivities having been that of Egypt, which was not much above two hun-

dred years,—and that of Babylon, which was but seventy), yet
now, when they hate idolatry as much as ever their fathers
loved it, they have lain under wrath to the uttermost, under
the heaviest judgement of dispersion, contempt, and base-
ness, and that for fifteen hundred years together : a reason
whereof can be no other given, than that fearful imprecation,
which hath derived the stain of the blood of Christ upon the
children of those that shed it, unto this day [1].

Fourthly, The prevailing of the gospel by the ministry
of but a few, and those unarmed, impotent, and despised
men; and that too, against all the opposition which power,
wit, or malice could call up, making it appear, that Christ
was to rule in the midst of his enemies ;—when Lucian,
Porphyry, Libanius, and Julian, by their wits ; Nero, Severus,
Dioclesian, and other tyrants, by their swords ; the whole
world, by their scorn, malice, and contempt, and all the
arts which Satan could suggest, laboured the suppression
and extinguishing of it :—the prevailing, I say, of the gospel by such means, against such power, in the midst of such
contempt and danger, and that over such persons, as were, by
long custom and tradition from their fathers, trained up in a
religion extremely contrary to the truth, and very favourable
to all vicious dispositions ; and upon such conditions to deny
themselves, to hate the world and the flesh, to suffer joyfully the loss of credit, friends, peace, quiet, goods, liberties, life and all, for the name of a crucified Saviour, whom
their eyes never saw, and whom their ears daily heard to be
blasphemed ;—such a prevailing as this must needs prove
the original of the gospel to be divine : for had not God
favoured it as much as men hated it, impossible it must
needs have been for it to have continued.

Fifthly, That the doctrines, therein delivered, were confirmed by miracles and divine operations. And certain it is,
that God would not, in so wonderful a manner, have honoured the figments of men, pretending his name and authority to the countenancing of their own inventions. And
for the historical truth of those miracles, they were not in
those ages, when the church, in her apologies, did glory of
them,—and when, if feigned, they might most easily have

---

[1] Matth. xxvii. 25.

been disproved,—nor yet by those enemies, who marvellously maligned and persecuted Christian religion, ever gainsayed.

Lastly, That were it not so that ' omne mendacium est pellucidum,' and hath ever something in it to bewray itself, yet it could not be ' operæ pretium' for them to lie, in publishing a doctrine whereby they got nothing but shame, stripes, imprisonments, persecution, torments, death. Especially since the holiness of their lives, their humility in denying all glory to themselves, and ascribing all to God, must needs make it appear to any reasonable man, that they did not lay any project for their own glory, which they purposely disclaimed, refused to receive from the hands of such as offered it, yea, and registered their own infirmities upon perpetual records.

With these and many other the like arguments, is the church furnished to prepare the minds of men, swayed but with ordinary ingenuity, and respect to common reason, at the least to look further, and make some sad enquiry into the doctrine of the gospel ;—there being therein especially promises of good things, made without money or price, of incomprehensible value, and of eternal continuance.

But now though a philosopher may make a very learned discourse to a blind man, of colours, yet it cannot be, that any formal and adequate notion of them should be fashioned in his mind, till such time as the faculty be restored ; and then all that preceding lecture being compared with what he afterward actually seeth in the things themselves, doth marvellously settle and satisfy his mind. So though the church, by these and the like inducements, doth prepare the minds of men to assent to divine authority in the Scriptures ;—yet till the natural ineptitude and disposition of the soul be healed, and it raised to a capacity of supernatural light, the work is no whit brought to maturity.

Two things, therefore, do yet remain after this ministry and manuduction of the church.

1st. An act of the grace of God's Spirit, healing the understanding, and opening the eye that it may see wonders in the law, writing the law in the heart ; and so making it a fit receptacle for so great a light.

2nd. The subject, being thus, by the outward motives from the church prepared, and by the inward grace of God repaired ;

Then, lastly, the object itself, being proposed, and being maturely considered, by reason thus guided and thus assisted, doth then show forth such a heavenly light of holiness, purity, majesty, authority, efficacy, mercy, wisdom, comfort, perfection; in one word, such an unsearchable treasury of internal mysteries, as that now the soul is as fully able, by the native light of the Scriptures, to distinguish their divine original and authenticalness, from any other mere human writings, as the eye is to observe the difference between a beam of the sun, and a blaze of a candle.

The second question is, How the soul comes to be settled in this persuasion, that the goodness of these truths, founded on the authority of God, doth particularly belong unto it? Whereunto I answer in one word, that this ariseth from a twofold testimony, grounded upon a preceding work of God's Spirit:—

For, first, The Spirit of God putteth his fear into the hearts of his servants, and purgeth their consciences, by applying the blood of Christ unto them, from dead works; which affections, strongly and very sensibly altering the constitution of the mind, must needs notably manifest themselves unto the soul, when, by any reflex act, she shall set herself to look inward upon her own operations.

This being thus wrought by the grace of God, thereupon there ensueth a twofold testimony. The first, of a man's own spirit, as we see in the examples of Job [m], David [n], Hezekiah [o], Nehemiah [p], Saul [q], and others; namely, that he desireth to fear God's name, to keep a conscience void of offence, to walk in all integrity towards God and men; from which, and the like personal qualifications, arise joy in the Holy Ghost, peace of conscience [r], and experience of sweetness in the fellowship with the Father and his Son. Secondly, the testimony of the holy Spirit [s], bearing witness to the sincerity of those affections, and to the evidence and truth of those persuasions, which himself by his grace stirred up. So then, First, The Spirit of God writeth the law in the heart, upon obedience whereunto ariseth the testimony of a man's own spirit: and then he writeth the promises in the

[m] Job. xxxi.   [n] Psalm cxvi. 1. xxvi. 1. 11.   [o] Isai. xxxviii. 3.   [p] Nehem. xiii. 14. 22.   [q] Acts xxiv. 16.   [r] John xxi. 15. 17. 2 Cor. i. 12.
[s] Rom. viii. 16.

heart, and by them ratifieth and confirmeth a man's hopes and joys unto him.

I understand not all this, which hath been spoken generally of all assents unto objects divine, which (I take it) in regard of their evidence, firmness, and stability, do much differ according unto the divers tempers of those hearts in which they reside; but principally unto the chief of those assents, which are proper unto saving faith. For assent, as I said, in general, is common unto devils with men; and therefore to make up the nature of true faith, there is required some differencing property, whereby it may be constituted in the entire essence of saving faith. In each sense we may observe, that unto the general faculty, whereby it is able to perceive objects proportioned to it, there is annexed ever another property, whereby, according to the several natures of the objects proposed, it is apt to delight or be ill-affected with it. For example, our ear apprehendeth all sounds in common; but according as is the harmony or discord of the sound, it is apt to take pleasure or offence at it. Our taste reacheth unto whatsoever is the object of it; but yet some things there are which grievously offend the palate, others which as much delight it: and so it is in divine assents. Some things in some subjects bring along with them tremblings, horrors, fearful expectations, aversation of mind, unwilling to admit or be pursued with the evidence of Divine truths, as it is in devils, and despairing sinners: other assents, on the contrary, do beget serenity of mind, a sweet complacency, delight, adherence, and comfort. Into the hearts of some men, doth the truth of God shine like lightning, with a penetrating and amazing brightness; in others, like the sun, with comfortable and refreshing beams.

For understanding whereof, we are to observe [t], that, in matters practical and divine (and so in all others, though not in an equal measure) the truth of them is ever mutually embraced, and, as it were, infolded in their goodness: for as truth doth not delight the understanding, unless it be a good truth, that is, such as unto the understanding bears a relation of convenience (whence arise diversities in men's studies, because all men are not alike affected with all kinds of truth); so good doth no way affect the will, unless it be a

---

[t] Dr. *Jackson*, of Faith.

true and real good : otherwise it proves but like the banquet of a dreaming man[u], which leaves him as hungry and empty, as when he lay down. Goodness then, added unto truth, doth, together with the assent, generate a kind of rest and delight in the heart on which it shineth.

Now goodness, moral or divine, hath a double relation : a relation unto that original, in dependency on, and propinquity whereunto, it consisteth ; and a relation unto that faculty or subject, wherein it resideth, and whereunto it is proposed. Good, in the former sense, is that which bears in it a proportion unto the fountain of good : for every thing is in itself so far good, as it resembles that original which is the author and pattern of it, and that is God. In the second sense, that is good, which bears a conveniency and fitness to the mind which entertains it: good, I mean not always in nature, but in apprehension. All divine truths are in themselves essentially good ; but yet they work not always delight and comfort in the minds of men, until proportioned and fitted unto the faculty that receives them. As the sun is in itself equally light ; the water, in a fountain, of itself equally sweet : but according unto the several temper of the eye, which perceiveth the one, and of the vessel through which the other passeth, they may prove to be offensive and distasteful.

But now further, when the faculty is thus fitted to receive a good, it is not the generality of that good which pleaseth neither, but the particular propriety and interest thereunto. Wealth and honour, as it is in itself good, so is it likewise in the apprehension of most men ; yet we see, men are apt to be grieved at it in others, and to look on it with an evil eye; nothing makes them to delight in it, but possession and propriety unto it. I speak here only of such divine good things, as are by God appointed to make happy his creature, namely, our blessed Lord and Saviour Jesus Christ, his obedience, satisfaction, resurrection, ascension, intercession, glory, and whatever else it is, of which he hath been unto his church the author, purchaser, conveyor, and foundation.

Now unto these, as unto other good things, there is a double right belonging by free donation from him unto the

[u] Isai. xxix. 8.

church; a right of propriety unto the thing, and a right of possession in the thing. This latter is that which here on earth the church suspireth, and longeth after; that other only it is which here we have, and that confirmed unto us by a double title. The first, as the land of Canaan was confirmed unto the Israelites by some few clusters of grapes, and other fruits of the land; I mean, By the earnest first-fruits and pledges of the Spirit. Secondly, By the free promise of Christ, who cannot deceive. Thus then at last we have discovered the proper, ultimate, and complete object of faith, which is all divine truth and goodness; unto which there is a right and propriety given to all such as are Christ's, though not in actual possession, yet in an infallible promise; and the acts by which they entertain that object, assenting, adhering, and delighting in it as particularly good. By these two, to wit, the object and the act (as all other habits of the mind), so is this of faith to be defined. So that from these observations, I take it, we may conclude, that the nature of saving faith admits of some such explication as this :—

Faith is a particular, personal, applicative, and experimental assent unto all divine revelations, as true, and good, not in general only, but unto me,—arising out of that sweet correspondency which is between the soul, and from that relish and experience of sweetness, which the soul, being raised and enlightened by God's Spirit, doth find in them.

I have been over tedious in finding out this definition of the nature of faith; and therefore, briefly, from these grounds, let the conscience impartially examine itself in such demands as these: Do I find in myself a most willing assent unto the whole compass of divine truths, not out of constraint, nor with grief, reluctancy, and trembling of spirit? Doth God's Word shine on me, not like lightning, which pierceth the eyelids, though they shut themselves against it; but doth this find in my heart a welcome and a willing admittance? Am I glad, when I find any divine truth discovered, of which formerly I had been ignorant? Do I not of purpose close mine eyes, forbear the means of true information, stifle and smother divine principles, quench the motions and dictates of God's Spirit in me? Am I not ignorant willingly of such things, the mention whereof would disquiet me in my bosom

sin, and the enquiry whereunto would cross the reserved
resolutions and unwarrantable projects which I am peremptory to prosecute? Am I not so in league with mine own corruptions [x], that I could heartily wish some divine truths
were not revealed, rather than, being so, they should sting
my conscience, and disable me from secure enjoying some
beloved sin? Do I assent unto all divine truths as alike
precious, with equal adherence? Am I as little displeased
with the truth of God's threats as of his promises? Do they
as powerfully work upon me to reform,—as the other, to refresh me? Do I believe them all, not only in the thesis or
general, but in the hypothesis, and respectively to mine
own particular?

Again, Do I find my heart fitted unto the goodness of
divine truth? Am I forward to embrace with much affection,
and loving delight, whatsoever promises are made unto me?
Do I find a spiritual taste and relish in the food of life,
which, having once tasted of, I find myself weaned from the
love of the world? from admiring the honours, pursuing the
preferments, hunting after the applause, adoring the glories,
and selling my soul and liberty for the smiles thereof? Doth
the sweetness of those promises, like the fruits brought by
the spies from Canaan, so much affect me, as that to come
to the full possession thereof, I am at a point with all other
things, ready to encounter any Canaanite, or sinful lust that
shall oppose me, to adventure on any difficulties that might
deter me, to pass through a sea, a wilderness, through fiery
serpents, the darts of Satan; yea, if need were, by the
gates of hell? Briefly, do I find in my heart (however in
itself froward, and wayward from any good) a more than
natural liveliness and vigour, which disposeth me to approve
of the word, promises, and purchases of my salvation, as of
an invaluable jewel; so precious, as that all things in this
world are but as dung in comparison? to a most fervent
expectation and longing after them; to a heavenly persuasion of my happiness by them; and, lastly, to a sweet delight in them, working peace of conscience, and joy in the
Holy Ghost, a love of Christ's appearing, an endeavour to
be like unto him, and a desire above all things to be with

him, and enjoy him, (which are all so many secret and pure issues of the Spirit of adoption)? I may, from these premises, infallibly conclude, that I am possessed of a lively faith, and thereby of those first-fruits, which bring with them an assurance of that great harvest of glory in the day of redemption: and in the mean time, having this wedding-garment, I may, with much confidence, approach God's table, to receive there the renewal of my patent unto life.

CHAPTER XX. *

Of the third and last means for the trial and demonstration of faith; namely, from effects or properties thereof.

THE last medium which was assigned for the examination of faith, was the properties or effects of it; by which, as by steps, we raise our thoughts to the apprehension of faith itself. To assign all the consequences or effects of faith, is a labour as difficult, as it would be tedious. I decline both; and shall therefore touch upon some special ones, which if present, all the rest in their order follow with a voluntary train.

And now, as, in the soul of man, there are two kinds of operations: one primitive and substantial, which we call the act of information; others secondary and subsequent, as, to understand, to will, to desire, and the like;—so faith, being (as hath been formerly observed) in some sort the ' actus primus,' or form of a Christian, I mean, that very ' medium unionis,' whereby the soul of man is really united to Christ, hath, therefore, in it two kinds of operations: the first, as it were, substantial,—the other, secondary. The former of these is that act of vivification or quickening, by which, faith doth make a man to live the life of Christ [y], by knitting him unto Christ, as it were, with joints and sinews [z], and ingrafting him into the unity of that vine, whose fruit is life [a].

That which doth quicken, is ever of a more excellent nature, than that which is quickened. Now the soul, being a spirit, and therefore within the compass of highest created

---

* Folio edition, p. 484.   [y] Gal. ii. 20.   [z] Ephes. iv. 16.   [a] John xv. 1, 2.

perfection, cannot possibly be quickened by any but him
who is above all perfection, which the Heathen themselves
have acknowledged to be God: for St. Paul hath observed
it out of them, that " in him we live, and move, and have
our being." Now unto life, necessary it is, that there be a
union unto the principal, or original of life; which, to the
soul, is God. In regard of the essence of God, nothing can
be separated from him, he being immense and filling all
things: but yet in regard of his voluntary communication
and dispensing of himself unto the creature, the manner of
his special presence doth much vary. Unto this special union
of the creature to God (in virtue whereof, the creature is
quickened, and doth in some sort live the life of God), there
is necessarily pre-supposed some sinew or ligament, which
may be therefore called the medium and instrument of life.
This knot in the estate of man's creation, was the obedience
of the law, or the covenant of works, which, while man did
maintain firm and unshaken, he had an evident communion
with God in all those vital influences, which his mercy was
pleased to shed down upon him: but once untying this knot,
and cutting asunder that bond, there did immediately ensue
a separation between God and man, and, by an infallible
consequence, death likewise. But God, being rich in mercy,
and not willing to plunge his creature into eternal misery,
found a new means to communicate himself unto him, by
appointing a more easy covenant, which should be the second knot of our union unto him,—only to believe in Christ
incarnate, who had done that for us which we ourselves had
formerly undone. And this new covenant is the covenant of
' faith, by which the just do live '

But here a man may object, That it is harder for one to
discern that he doth live in Christ, than that he believe in
him ; and therefore this can be no good mean by which we
may find out the truth of our faith.

To this we answer, That life must be discerned by those
tokens, which are inseparable from it. And they are First, A
desire of nourishment, without which it cannot continue : for
Nature hath imprinted in all things a love of its own being
and preservation, and, by consequence, a prosecution of all
such means as may preserve, and a removal of all such, as
may endanger or oppress it. Secondly, A conversion of

nourishment into the nature of the body. Thirdly, Augmentation and growth, till we come unto that stature, which
our life requires. Fourthly, Participation of influences from
the vital parts, the head, the heart, and others, with conformity unto the principal mover amongst them : for a dead part
is ever withered, immovable, and disobedient to the other
faculties. Fifthly, A sympathy and communion in pains or
delights with the fellow-members. Lastly, A free use of our
senses and other faculties, by all which we may infallibly
conclude that a creature liveth.

And so it is in faith. It frameth the heart to delight in
all such spiritual food, as is requisite thereunto ; disposing
it upon the view, at least upon the taste, of any poisonous
thing, to be pained with it, and cast it up. The food that
nourisheth faith, is, as in little infants, of the same quality
with that which begat it, even the Word of life, wherein
there is sincere milk, and strong meat. The poison which
endangereth it is heresy, which tainteth the root of faith,
and goeth about to pervert the assent and impiety, which
blasteth and corrupteth the branches. All which, the soul
of a faithful man abhorreth.

Secondly, In faith there is a conversion likewise, the virtue
whereof ever there resides, where the vital power is. In natural life, the power of altering is in the man, and not in the
meat ; and therefore the meat is assimilated to our flesh :
but in spiritual life, the quickening faculty is in the meat ;
and therefore the man is assimilated and transformed into
the quality of the meat. And indeed, the word is not cast
into the heart of man, as meat into the stomach, to be converted into the corrupt quality of nature ; but rather as seed
into the ground, to convert that earth which is about it, into
the quality of itself.

Thirdly, Where faith is, there is some growth in grace :
we grow nearer unto Heaven, than when we first believed ; an
improvement of our knowledge in the mysteries of godliness,
which like the sun, shines brighter and brighter unto the
perfect day : an increase of willingness to obey God in all
things. And as in the growth of natural bodies, if they be
sound and healthy, so in this of faith likewise it is universal
and uniform : one part doth not grow, and another shrivel ;
neither doth one part grow too big, and disproportioned for

another; the head doth not increase in knowledge, and the heart decay in love; the heart doth not swell in zeal, and the hand wither in charity; but, in the nourishment of faith, every grace receives proportionably its habitual confirmation [b].

Fourthly, By the spiritual life of faith, the faithful do partake of such heavenly influences, as are from the head shed down upon the members. The influences of Christ in his church are many, and peradventure, in many things, imperceptible. Some principal I conceive to be the influence of his truth, and the influence of his power. His truth is exhibited in teaching the church, which is illumination; his power partly in guiding the church, and partly in defending it; that, is direction,—this, protection. Now in all these do they, who are in Christ, according to the measure and proportion of his Spirit, certainly communicate. They have their eyes more or less opened, like Paul, to see the terrors of God, the fearfulness of sin, the rottenness of a spiritual death, the preciousness of Christ and his promises, the glimpses and rays of that glory which shall be revealed. They have their feet loosened with Lazarus, that they can now rise, and walk, and leap, and praise God. Lastly, They are strengthened and clothed with the whole arms of God, which secureth them against all the malice or force of Satan.

Fifthly, Where faith is, there is a natural compassion in all the members of Christ towards each other. If sin be by one member committed, the other members are troubled for it; because they are all partakers of that Spirit, which is grieved with the sins of his people. If one part be afflicted, the other are interested in the pain; because all are united together in one head, which is the fountain and original of sense. The members of the church are not like paralytic and unjointed members, which cannot move towards the succour of each other.

Lastly, Where faith is, there all the faculties are expedite and free in their operations: the eye open to see the wonders of God's law; the ear open to hear his voice; the mouth open to praise his name; the arm enlarged towards the relief of his servants; the whole man tenderly sensible of all pressures, and repugnant qualities.

[b] Ephes. iv. 16.

The secondary effects of faith, are, amongst sundry others, such as these:

First, A love and liking of those spiritual truths, which, by faith, I assent unto. For saving faith being an assent with adherence and delight, contrary to that of devils, which is with trembling and horror (which delight is a kind of relish, and experience of the goodness of those objects we assent unto); it necessarily follows, even from the dictate of nature, (which instructeth a man to love that which worketh in him delight and comfort) that, from this assent, must arise an approbation and love of those objects, whence doth issue such sweetness.

A second effect is, affiance and hope, confidently, for the present, relying on the goodness, and, for the future, waiting on the power of God, which shall to the full in time perform what he hath in his Word promised, when once the mind of a man is wrought so to assent unto divine promises made in Christ, as to acknowledge an interest and propriety unto them; and that to be at last actually performed not by a man, who is subject both to unfaithfulness in perseverance, and to disability in performance of his promises (for every man is a liar, either by imposture, ready to deceive,—or by impotency, likely to disappoint the expectations of those who rely upon him); but by Almighty God, who, the better to confirm our faith in him, hath, both by his Word and oath, engaged his fidelity, and is altogether omnipotent to do what he hath purposed. Impossible it is but, from such an assent, grounded on the veracity, and on the all-sufficiency of God, there should result in the mind of a faithful man, a confident dependence on such promises, renouncing in the mean time all self-dependence, as in itself utterly impotent,—and resolving, in the midst of temptations, to rely on him, to hold fast his mercy, and the profession of his faith without wavering,—having an eye to the recompense of reward, and being assured, that he who hath promised, will certainly bring it to pass.

A third effect of faith is, joy and peace of conscience; for "being justified by faith, we have peace with God [d]." The

---

[c] Ὅσον γὰρ τίμιόν ἐστι τὸ πιστευόμενον, τοσοῦτον ἀγαπᾶται. *Just. Martyr.* Quæst. Orthod. q. 8.   [d] Rom. v. 1

mind is, by faith and the impression of sweetness in God's promises, composed unto a settled calmness and serenity. I do not mean a dead peace, an immobility and sleepiness of conscience, like the rest of a dreaming prisoner : but such a peace as a man may, by a syllogism of the practic judgement, upon right examination of his own interest in Christ, safely infer unto himself. The wicked often hath an appearance of peace, as well as the faithful ; but here is the difference :—between a wicked man's sin and him, there is a door shut, which will surely one day open ; for it is but either a door of error, or the door of death. For sin lieth at the door, ready to fly at his throat as soon as it shall find either his eyes open to see it, or his life to let it in upon the soul : but between a faithful man and his sin, there is a cornerstone, a wall of fire, through which Satan himself cannot break, even the merits of Christ Jesus. Briefly, the peace which comes from faith, hath these two properties in it, tranquillity and serenity too ; otherwise it is but like the calmness of the Dead Sea, whose unmoveableness is not nature, but a curse.

The last effect which I shall now name of faith, is, That general effect of fructification, purifying the heart[e], and disposing it unto holiness, and new obedience, which is to be framed after God's law. Faith unites us unto Christ: being thus united, we are quickened by one and the same Spirit ; having one Spirit and soul, we must needs agree in the same operations ; and those operations must necessarily bear conformity unto the same rule ; and that rule is the law, under which Christ himself was for our sakes, made. So that the rule to examine this effect of faith by, should be the whole compass of God's law, which to enter into, were to redouble all this labour past : " For thy law," saith David, " is exceeding wide."

Briefly therefore, in all our obedience observe these few rules :—First, The obligatory power which is in the law, depends upon the one and sole authority of the law-giver, who is God. He that breaks but one commandment, ventures to violate that authority, which, by the same ordination, made one equally obligatory with the rest. And therefore our

---

• Acts xv. 9.

obedience must not be partial, but universal unto the whole law, inasmuch as it proceeds from that faith, which, without indulgence or dispensation, yieldeth assent unto the whole compass of divine truth.

Secondly, As is God, so is his law, a spiritual and a perfect law ; and therefore requires a universality of the subject, as well as of the obedience : I mean (besides that perfect integrity of nature, which, in regard of present inherence, is irrecoverably lost in Adam, and supplied only by the imputed righteousness and integrity of Christ) an inward, spiritual, sincere obedience of the heart, from thence spreading like lines from a centre, unto the whole circumference of our nature, unto our words, actions, gestures, unto all our parts, without crooked, mercenary, and reserved respects, wherein men often, instead of the Lord, make their ends or their fears, their God. Lastly, Remember, that, in every law, all homogeneal matters to the main duty which is commanded, every sprig, or seed, or original, or degree thereof is included, as all the several branches of a tree are fastened to one and the same stock. And by these rules are we to examine the truth of our obedience.

But here, before I draw down these premises to an assumption, I will but name one caution, which is this ;—That faith, as it may be either habitual or actual, so it is the cause of these holy actions, either habitually by framing and disposing the heart unto them, or actually when it is itself, as it ought ever to be, sound and operative. But sometimes faith (so great is the corruption of our nature) admits of a decay and languor, wherein it lies (as it were) like fire under ashes raked up, and stifled under our corruptions.

Again, In some there is a weaker, in some a stronger faith ; according unto which difference, there must be a difference in the measure and magnitude of the effects : but yet it is infallibly true, that all or most of those holy fruits do, in some seasons or other, bud forth of that stock which is quickened by faith, though sometimes in some men less discernible, by reason of corruptions interposed. For it usually thus falleth out, That our graces are but like the army of Gideon, a small handful ; whereas our corruptions are like the Midianites, which lay on the ground as grass-

hoppers, innumerable. But yet, in these, God crowneth his
own meanest gifts with victory and success.

So then these things being thus proposed, let the conscience, without connivance, examine itself by such interro-
gatories as these: Do I find myself live by the faith of the
Son of God, who gave himself for me? Do I delight in his
Word, more than my appointed food, never adulterating it
with the leaven or dregs of heretical fancies, or dead works?
Doth the Word of truth transform me to the image of itself,
crucifying all those corruptions which harboured in me?
Do I find myself to grow in all graces, universally and uniformly, towards God and man, not thinking to recompense
some defects, which my nature drives me unto, with super-
erogation (as I conceive) and over-performance of such duties, as are not so visibly repugnant to my personal corruptions? Do the beams of the Sun of righteousness, shining
on my soul, illighten me with his truth, and, with his power,
sway me unto all good? Am I heartily affected with all the
conditions of God's church, to mourn or to rejoice with it
even at such times, when mine own particular estate would
frame me unto affections of a contrary temper? Have I free
use of all my spiritual senses, to see the light of God, to
hear his Word, to taste his mercies, to feel with much tenderness all the wounds and pressures of sin? Do I love all
Divine truth, not so much, because proportionable unto my
desires, but because conformable unto God? Am I resolved in all estates to rely on God's mercy and providence,
and though he should kill me, to trust in him? Do I wholly
renounce all trust in mine own worthiness, or in any concurrences of mine own naturally towards God? Do I not build
either my hopes or fears upon the faces of men, nor make
either them or myself the rule or end of my desires? Finally, do I endeavour a universal obedience unto God's law
in all the whole latitude and extent of it, not indulging to
myself liberty in any known sin? Is not my obedience
mercenary and hypocritical, but spiritual and sincere? Do
I not swallow gnats, nor stumble at straws, nor dispense
with myself for the least of sins; for irregular thoughts, for
occasions of offence, for appearances of evil, for the motions
of concupiscence, for idle words and vain conversation, and
whatsoever is in the lowest degree forbidden? And though

in any, or all these, I may be sometimes overtaken (as who is it that can say, ' I have washed my hands in innocency, I am clean from my sins ?'), do I yet relent for it, strive, and resolve against it ? In a word, doth not mine own heart condemn me of self-deceit, of hypocrisy, of halting and dissembling in God's service ? Then may I safely conclude, that I have partaken of the saving efficacy of faith, and am fitly qualified to partake of these holy mysteries, whereby this good work of faith, begun in me, may be strengthened, and more perfected against the day of the Lord Jesus.

In the receiving of which, we must use all, both inward and outward reverence, secret elevations of spirit, and comfortable thoughts touching the mercies of God in Christ, touching the qualities and benefits of his passion, and of our sins that caused it. And lastly, for the course of our life after, we must pitch upon a constant resolution to abandon all sin ; and to keep a strict hand over all our ways ; lest turning again with the swine to the mire, that which should be the badge of our honour, prove the character of our shame [f]. The Persians [g] had a festival-time one day in the year, which they called 'Vitiorum Interitum,' wherein they slew all serpents and venomous creatures; and after that, till the revolution of that same day, suffered them to swarm again as fast as ever. If we think in that manner to destroy our sins, and only one day in the year, when we celebrate this holy festival,—the evil spirit may haply depart for a day in policy, but surely he will turn again with seven other spirits, and make the end of that man worse than his beginning. But that ground which drinketh-in the rain which cometh oft upon it (and what rain comparable to a shower of Christ's blood in the Sacrament?), and bringeth forth herbs meet for the use of him that dressed it, receiveth blessings from God: a cup of blessing here; but rivers of blessedness hereafter, in that paradise which is above; where He who is in this life the object of our faith and hope, shall be the end and reward of them both for ever.

[f] Desertor de charactere damnatur, de quo militans honoratur, *Aug.*—
[g] *Brisson.* de Reg. Persic. lib. 2.

ISRAEL'S PRAYER IN TIME OF TROUBLE,

WITH GOD'S GRACIOUS ANSWER THEREUNTO;

OR AN

EXPLICATION

OF THE FOURTEENTH CHAPTER

OF THE PROPHET HOSEA,

IN SEVEN SERMONS,

PREACHED UPON SO MANY DAYS OF SOLEMN HUMILIATION.

[1645.]

TO

THE HONOURABLE HOUSE OF COMMONS

ASSEMBLED IN PARLIAMENT.*

In obedience to your commands, I here humbly present to your view what you were pleased, with patience and readiness of affection, lately to attend unto. I consider-ed, that though the choiceness of the auditory might re-quire the exactest preparation; yet both the condition of the times, and the nature of the duty, did call upon us to lay aside our ornaments. And therefore I spake with such plainness, as might commend the matter delivered, rather to the conscience of a penitent, than to the fancy of a delicate hearer. The king of Nineveh was a king as well in his sackcloth as in his robes: and the truth of God is indeed fuller of majesty when it is naked, than when adorned with the dress of any human contribution, which many times takes from it, but never adds any value unto it.

I looked upon you in your double relation, both common, as Christians, and special, as men intrusted with the manage-ing of those arduous and most pressing difficulties, under which this distemper'd kingdom is now groaning.

And for the quickening of those endeavours which belong to you in both those relations, I presented you both with the bottom of a nation's unhappiness, which is sin; and with the top of their felicity, which is God's free grace and favour : that by your serious cares to purge out the one, and to pro-cure the other, you might, by God's blessings on your con-sultations, dispel that black tempest which hangs over this kingdom, and reduce the face of things unto calmness and serenity again.

When the children struggled together in the womb of Rebekah, she was thereupon inquisitive, If it be so, why am I thus [a] ? and she addressed herself to God for a resolution.

---

* This Dedication is omitted in the Folio edition.

[a] Gen. xxv. 22.

Surely this nation is become like the womb of Rebekah, the children thereof struggling in their mother's belly together; and when God hath mercifully freed us from foreign enemies, brethren are become enemies to brethren, and by their enmities likely to tear and torment the bowels of their mother, and to ruin themselves.

And what have we now to do but to enquire the cause of these sad commotions, Why are we thus? And surely the cause is chiefly where the disease is, within ourselves. We have been, like the womb of Rebekah, a barren nation, not bringing forth fruits of so many mercies as God had filled us withal: so that now it is no wonder, if God cause us to be in pain within our own bowels, and to feel the throes and strugglings of a travailing woman [b], ready to bring forth her own confusion—a Benoni, or an Ichabod, a son of sorrow and of shame, to this hitherto so peaceable and flourishing a kingdom.

All that we can comfort ourselves with in these pangs and qualms of distemper is, that there are some Jacobs [c] amongst us, who, instead of supplanting their brethren, will wrestle and have power with God. The people have often petitioned, sometimes his sacred Majesty, sometimes this Honourable House, which are his great council; many overtures and endeavours of accommodation have been tendered; and yet we " cry out in our pangs, and have, as it were, brought forth wind; neither have we wrought any deliverance in the earth [d]."

I have here therefore presented a new petition, dictated and drawn up to our hands by God's own Spirit, unto which, both kings and parliament, peers, and prophets, and people, must all subscribe, and offer it with prostrate and penitent hearts unto him who "stands in the congregation of the mighty, and judgeth amongst the gods [e]," that he would take away all our iniquity, and receive us into favour again, and accept of a covenant of new obedience.

And this petition God is pleased to anticipate with an answer of grace, in the consequent parts of the chapter whence the text is taken; and that particularly to every branch of the petition.   He will take away iniquity.   His anger shall

[b] Hosea xiii. 13.   [c] Gen. xxxii. 24. Hosea xii. 3, 4.   [d] Isai. xxvi. 17, 18.
[e] Psalm lxxxii. 1.

not punish ; his love shall heal our back-slidings; the greatness of our sins shall not hinder the freeness of this grace.
He will do us good, and give us life, by the dew of his grace
reviving us ; and glory, clothing us, like the lily of the field,
with the beauty of holiness ; and stability, fixing us by his
grace, as the cedars of Lebanon are fastened upon their
roots ; and growth or enlargement, as the branches spread
forth themselves ; and continual vigour and plenty, as
the olive-tree, which is always green and fruitful ; and
glorious comforts, by the sweet savour [a] of the knowledge of
God, which, like the spice-trees of Lebanon, shall diffuse a
spiritual perfume upon the names and into the consciences
of penitent converts.

He will present us with the blessings of safety, as well as
of sanctity and comfort ; we shall under his shadow find
shelter and protection from all our fears. Though like corn
we be harrowed under the clods, though like a lopped vine
we seem naked and reduced to lowness, though like
crushed grapes we lie under heavy pressure ; yet he will
receive, and enlarge, and comfort us again ; and when we
are, in our own eyes, as fatherless children, he will set his
eyes upon us as a tutor and guardian ; he will hear, and observe, and answer, and pity us, enabling us to make good
our covenant by his grace, and causing the fruits of his
loving kindness to be found upon us. Thus God is pleased
to borrow the various perfections of other things, to adumbrate the united and cumulated mercies, which he promiseth
unto a converting and petitioning people.

You have the petition sent you from God, and his answer,
preventing you, in all the members of it, with the blessings of
goodness. I have nothing else to do, but to beg of you, and
of all this great people whom you represent, the subscription
of your hearts and lives unto this petition: and to beg of
God, that he would graciously incline the hearts of this
whole kingdom rather to wrestle with him for a blessing,
than to struggle and conflict amongst themselves for a curse.
With which prayer I humbly conclude, commending your
persons and your weighty affairs to his grace ; and rest
Your most humble servant in Christ,

ED. REYNOLDS.

From my Study in Braunston,
August the 8th, 1642.

[a] 2 Cor. ii. 14.

TO THE READER *

CHRISTIAN Reader, understanding that my sermon, which was preached three years since before the Honourable House of Commons, on the day of their solemn humiliation, was to be reprinted ; I thought fit to peruse, transcribe, and enlarge six other sermons, in which I had, at mine own charge, in the country, on the ensuing fast days, briefly explained and applied that whole chapter (a portion only whereof was in the first handled), and to send them forth, together with it, unto the public ; which I was the rather induced to do for these two reasons :— 1st. Because it hath pleased God, in his righteous and holy providence, to make me, by a long infirmity, unserviceable to his church in the principal work of the ministry—the preaching of the gospel, which is no small grief unto me : so that there remained no other means whereby my life might, in regard of my function, be useful to the church, and comfortable to myself, than by inverting the words of the psalmist, and as he made " his tongue the pen of a ready writer [a]," so to make my pen the tongue of an unready speaker. 2d. I considered the seasonableness and suitableness of these meditations unto the condition of the sad and disconsolate times wherein we live, very like those which our prophet threatened the ten tribes withal throughout this whole prophecy, unto which this last chapter is a kind of use and a most solemn exhortation, pressing upon all wise and prudent men such duties of humiliation and repentance as might turn threats into promises, and recover again the mercies, which by their sins they had forfeited and forsaken. Which being restored unto them according to their petition, they are here likewise further instructed in which manner to return unto God the praises due to his great name. And these two duties of humiliation and thanksgiving are the most solemn duties which, in

* This address is omitted in the Folio edition.
[a] Psalm xlv. 1.

these times of judgements and mercies, so variously inter-woven together, the Lord doth so frequently call us unto.

Places of Scripture I have, for brevity sake, for the most part, only quoted and referred thereunto, without transcribing all the words; and have usually put many parallel places to-gether, because by that means they do not only strengthen the doctrine whereunto they belong, but mutually give light unto one another.

The Lord make us all in this our day so wise and prudent as to understand the righteous ways of our God towards us; that we may not stumble at them, but walk in them, and be taught by them " to wait upon him in the way of his judge-ments[a]," and to fix the desires of our soul upon his name, as our great refuge, and upon his righteousness, as our great business; till he shall be pleased, by the dew of his grace, to revive us as the corn, to make us grow as the vine, and to let the scent of all his ordinances be over all our land, as the smell and as the wine of Lebanon.

It will be an abundant return unto my poor and weak en-deavours, if I may have that room in thy prayers which the apostle Paul desired to have in the prayers of the Ephe-sians[b], " that utterance may be given unto me that I may open my mouth boldly to preach the mystery of the gospel."

The Lord sanctify all the ways of his providence towards us, that when we are [c] chastened we may be taught; and may be greater gainers by the voice [d] of his rod, than we are sufferers by the stripes.

---

[a] Isai. xxvi. 8, 9.   [b] Ephes. vi. 19.   [c] Psalm xciv. 12.   [d] Micah vi. 9.

SEVEN SERMONS

ON THE

FOURTEENTH CHAPTER OF HOSEA.

FIRST SERMON.*

HOSEA XIV. 1, 2.

O Israel, return unto the Lord thy God; for thou hast fallen by thine iniquity. Take with you words, and turn to the Lord: say unto him, Take away all iniquity, and receive us graciously (or give good); *so will we render the calves of our lips.*

SECT. 1. The blessing of Ephraim was according to his name, 'fruitfulness[a].' The fruitfulness of the earth, a bough by a well, and the fruitfulness of the womb and of the breasts[b]. Contrary unto which two blessings, we find in our prophet two judgements threatened against him for his sins[c]. "Though he be fruitful amongst his brethren, an east wind shall come, the wind of the Lord shall come up from the wilderness, and his spring shall become dry, and his fountain shall be dried up; he shall spoil the treasure of all pleasant vessels. Samaria shall become desolate; for she hath rebelled against her God: they shall fall by the sword; their infants shall be dashed in pieces, and their women with child shall be ripped up[c]." And throughout the whole prophecy[d], if you read and observe it, you will find the judgements of God against Ephraim to be expressed by weeds, emptiness, barrenness, dryness of roots, of fruits, of branches, of springs, and by a curse upon their children[e]; as, on the other side, the blessings, here in this chapter renewed unto Ephraim repenting, are all expressed by metaphors of 'fruitfulness[f].'

From these two woful judgements, against the fruitfulness

---

[a] Gen. xli. 52.   [q] Gen. xlix. 22, 25. Deut. xxxiii. 13, 17.   [c] Hos. xiii. 15, 16.   [d] Hos. viii. 7. ix. 2, 6, 16. x. 1, 8. xi. 6.   [e] Hos. ix. 11, 14.
[f] Hos. i. 5, 6, 7.   * Folio-edition, p. 491.

of their springs, and the fruitfulness of their wombs, by the
desolations of a bloody sword, our prophet taketh occasion
once more for all, to awaken and drive them to a timely repentance, that so they may recover the blessing of their
name;—Ephraim may be Ephraim again, a plentiful, a
fruitful, a flourishing people. That when God's judgements
are in the earth [f], they would then at least 'set themselves
to learn righteousness,' that they may 'wash their feet in
the blood of the wicked.'

Of all nations under Heaven, this land of ours hath had
the blessing of Ephraim upon it,—fruitfulness of the earth,
abundance of plenty; fruitfulness of the womb, abundance
of people. But our misery is, that the abundance of our
sins hath mightily outvied the abundance both of our plenty
and of our people : sins too parallel to those of Ephraim, if
you will but read this prophet, and compare the behaviours
of this nation with him. And this parity of sins hath, no
doubt, called upon God for a parity of judgements. It is
but a very little while, since the Lord seemed to call for a
north wind, as he doth here for an east wind; two armies
there met, ready to look one another in the face. But his
heart turned, his repentings were kindled, he would not give
up Ephraim then. He seems once more to be drawing of a
sword, and having in vain 'hewed us by his prophets,' as he
complains, Hos. vi. 5, to try whether hewing us by his
judgements will work upon us. So that now, though I must
read my text, "O *Israel*," yet I must apply it, "O *England*,
return unto the Lord thy God, for thou hast fallen by thine
iniquity. Take with you words," &c.

The whole context containeth two general parts : an invitation unto repentance, *verse* 1. And an institution how to
perform it, in the *two verses* following.

SECT. 2. Before we come to the particulars of the invitation, let us first briefly observe, That, in the midst of judge-

<hr/>

f Isai. xxvi. 9. Παράδειγμά τι τοῖς ἄλλοις γίνεσθαι, ἵνα ἄλλοι ὁρῶντες πάσ-
χοντα ἃ ἂν πάσχοι, φοβούμενοι βελτίους γίνονται. *Plato* apud Aul. Gell. l. 6.
c. 14. edit. Oisel. p. 388. Famosos latrones, in his locis, ubi grassati sunt, furca
figendos compluribus placuit, ut et conspectu deterreantur alii ab iisdem facinori-
bus, ff. de pœnis l. 28. sect. famosos. Et in brutis et in rebus inanimatis obser-
vata vindicta. Vid. Pet. Et. Decr. l. 2. Tit. 14.—*Zepp.* de leg. l. 1. c. 11.—
Plut. de fort. Ro.—Psalm lii. 6. Luke xvii. 32. Acts v. 11. Luke xiii. 1, 7. Jer.
iii. 8. Dan. iii. 18, 21. Numb. xvi. 38, 40.

ments proposed against sinners that are obstinate, God doth reserve and proclaim mercy unto sinners that are penitent. When a consumption is decreed, yet a remnant is reserved to return [g]. The Lord will keep his vineyard, when he will burn up the thorns and the briers together [h]. When a day of fierce anger is determined, the meek of the earth are called upon to seek the Lord [i]. When the Lord is coming out of his place to punish the inhabitants of the earth for their iniquity, he calls upon his people to hide themselves in their chambers, until the indignation be overpast [k]. The angel which was sent to destroy Sodom, had withal a commission to deliver Lot [l]. God made full provision for those who mourned for public abominations, before he gave order to destroy the rest [m]. Men in their wrath will, many times, rather strike a friend than spare a foe: but God's proceedings are without disorder; he will rather spare his foes than strike his servants, as he showed himself willing to have done in the case of Sodom [n]. Moses stood in the gap, and diverted judgements from Israel [o]. Yea, God seeks for such [p], and complains when they cannot be found [q]. And if he deliver others for them, certainly he will not destroy them for others. However it go with the world and with wicked men, it shall go well with the righteous; there shall be a sanctuary for them, when others stumble; and they shall pass through the fire, when others are consumed by it [r].

Reasons hereof are,—God's justice: He will not punish the righteous with the wicked: he will have it appear, that there is a difference between him that serveth God, and him that serveth him not [s]. God's love unto his people: He hath a book of remembrance written before him, for them that fear him, and think upon his name: "And they shall be mine, saith the Lord of hosts, in that day when I make up my jewels, and I will spare them as a man spareth his own son that serveth him [t]." Here is a climax and gradation of arguments drawn from love. In a great fire, and devouring trouble (such as is threatened Mal. iv. 1), 'property' alone is a

---

[g] Isai. x. 22, 23.   [h] Isai. xxvii. 3, 4.   [i] Zeph. ii. 3.   [k] Isai. xxvi. 20, 21.   [l] Gen. xix. 15.   [m] Ezek. ix. 4, 6.   [n] Gen. xviii. 26.   [o] Psalm cix. 23.   [p] Ezek. xxii. 30.   [q] Ezek. xiii. 5.   [r] Isai. iii. 10, 11. viii. 14, 15, 16. Zech. xiii. 8, 9.   [s] Gen. xviii. 23. Mal. iii. 18.   [t] Mal. iii. 16, 17.

ground of care ; a man would willingly save and secure that
which is his own, and of any use unto him ; but if you add
unto this, ' preciousness,' that increaseth the care.   A man
will make hard shift to deliver a rich cabinet of jewels,
though all his ordinary goods and utensils should perish.
But of all jewels, those which come out of the body, are
much more precious than those which only adorn it.   Who
would not snatch rather his child, than his casket or purse,
out of a flame? relation works not only upon the affection,
but upon the bowels[x].   And lastly, the same excellency
that the word ' jewel ' doth add unto the word ' mine,' the
same excellency doth ' service ' add unto the word ' son.'
A man hath much conflict in himself to take off his heart
from an undutiful son.   Never a worse son than Absalom ;
and yet how doth David give a charge to the commanders
to have him spared ! how inquisitive after his safety ! how
passionately and unseasonably mournful upon the news of his
death !   But if any child be more a jewel than another, certainly it is a dutiful child, who hath not only an interest in
our love by nature, but by obedience.   All these grounds of
care and protection for God's people in trouble are here expressed, ' property,' they are ' mine ; ' ' preciousness,' they
are ' jewels ;' treasures, ornaments unto me ; ' relation,' they
are ' sons ;' ' usefulness,' they are sons that ' serve ;' none
could look on a thing so many ways lovely with the same
eye, as upon a professed and provoking enemy.

Lastly, God's name and glory : He hath spared his people,
even in the midst of their provocations, for his name's sake[y].
How much more when they repent and seek his face !   He
will never let it be said, that any " seek the Lord in vain[z]."

SECT. 3. But it may be objected, Doth not Solomon say,
that " All things happen alike unto all ?" and that " no man
can know love or hatred by that which is before him[a] ?"
And is it not certain and common, that, in public desolations, good as well as bad do perish ?   Doth not the sword
devour as well one as another ?

It is true, God doth not always difference his servants
from wicked men by temporal deliverances : troubles com-

x Jer. xxxi. 20.   y Deut. xxxiii. 26, 27. Josh. vii. 9.   z Isai. xlv. 19.
a Eccles. ix. 1, 2.

monly and promiscuously involve all sorts. But there are
these two things considerable in it:

First, That many times the good suffer with the bad, because they are together corrupted with them; and when they
join in the common provocations, no wonder if they suffer
in the 'common judgements [b].' Nay, the sins of God's people do (especially in this case) more provoke him unto outward judgements, than the sins of his professed enemies;
because they expose his name to the more contempt [c], and
are committed against the greater love [d]: and he hath future
judgement for the wicked, and therefore usually beginneth
here at his own sanctuary [e].

Secondly, When good men, who have preserved themselves
from public sins, do yet fall by public judgements, yet there
is a great difference in this seeming equality; the same affliction having, like the pillar that went before Israel, a light
side towards God's people, and a dark side towards the
Egyptians; God usually recompensing the outward evils of
his people with more plentiful evidences of inward and spiritual joy. A good man may be in great darkness, as well
as a wicked man; but in that case he hath the name of God
to stay himself upon, which no wicked man in the world
hath [f]. The metal and dross go both into the fire together;
but the dross is consumed, the metal refined:—so is it with
godly and wicked men, in their sufferings [g].

This reproveth the folly of those, who, in time of trouble,
rely upon vain things which cannot help them, and continue
their sins still. For judgements make no difference of any
but penitent and impenitent. Sickness doth not compliment
with an honourable person, but useth him as coarsely as the
base. Death knocks as well at a prince's palace as a poor
man's cottage. Wise men die as well as fools. Yet poison
usually works more violently when tempered with wine,
than with some duller and baser material. In times of
trouble, usually, the greater the persons, the closer the
judgements. When Jerusalem was taken, the nobles were
slain; but the poor of the land had vineyards and fields
given them [h].

[b] Rev. xviii. 4.   [c] 2 Sam. xii. 14.   [d] Amos iii. 2.   [e] Ezek. ix. 6.
1 Pet. iv. 17.   [f] Isai. l. 10.   [g] Zach. xiii. 9. Eccles. viii. 12, 13
[h] Jer. xxxix. 6, 10.

Therefore, in troubles, we should be more humbled for our sins than our sufferings; because sin is the sting of suffering. That mercies should not win us; that judgement should not awaken us; that the rod should speak, and we not hear[i]; that the fire should burn, and we not feel[k]; that desolation should be threatened, and we not instructed[l]; that the hand of God should be lifted up, and we not see it[m]; that darkness should be upon us, and we not give glory to God[n]: —this is that should most deject us, that in mercies we have been wanton, and, in judgements, senseless. Get repentance by an affliction, and then you may look on it as traffic, and not as a trouble; like a merchant's voyage, which hath pain in the way, but treasure in the end. No afflictions can hurt him that is penitent. If thou escape, they will make thee the more thankful; if not, they will bring thee the nearer and the sooner unto God.

The way to be safe in times of trouble, is to get the blood of the Lamb upon our doors. All troubles have their commission and instructions from God, what to do, whither to go, whom to touch, whom to pass over. Be gold; and though the fire come upon you, you shall keep pure nature and purity still. "Godliness," saith the apostle, "hath the promises of this life:" and amongst those, one special one is, that "we shall not be tempted above what we are able[o]." Neither are there indeed any distresses, against which there is not a refuge and escape for penitent sinners unto some promise or other. Against captivity:—When they be in the land of their enemies, "I will not cast them away, nor abhor them[p]." Against famine and pestilence:—"If I shut up Heaven, that there be no rain, or if I command the locusts to devour the land, or if I send pestilence among my people; if my people, which are called by my name, shall humble themselves, and pray, and seek my face, and turn from their wicked ways;—then will I hear from heaven, and will forgive their sin, and will heal their land[q]." Against sickness:— The Lord will strengthen him upon the bed of languishing, and "make all his bed in his sickness[r]." Against poverty:—"When the poor and needy seek water, and there is

i Mic. vi. 9.	k Isai. xlii. 25.	l Jer. vi. 8.	m Isai. xxvi. 11.
n Jer. xiii. 6.	o 1 Cor. xii. 13.	p Lev. xxvi. 4.	q 2 Chron.
vii. 13, 14.	r Psalm xli. 3.		

none, I the Lord will hear them [r]," &c. Against want of
friends:—" When my father and mother forsake me, then the
Lord will take me up [s]." Against oppression and imprison-
ment:—" He executeth judgement for the oppressed, he
looseth the prisoners [t]." Against whatsoever plague or
trouble [u]:—He is the God of all consolation: how disconsolate soever a man's condition is in any kind, there cannot
but, within the compass of all consolation, be some one or
other remedy at hand, to comfort and relieve him:—and so
much, by the way, of the invitation in general.

In the invitation, we have the matter of it, and the motives
to it. The matter is conversion; without that, the hand
which is lifted up in threatening [x], will fall down in punishing: and where that is, God hath a book of remembrance
for his jewels, when his wrath burneth as an oven against
the stubble [y].

Sect. 4. But this conversion then must have two conditions in it:—First, It must be 'Ad Dominum,' to the Lord;
not merely philosophical, to some low and general dictates
of reason, such as Aristotle, or Plato, or Epictetus, or Plutarch, or the like heathen moralists, could furnish us withal,
without self-denial, lowliness of Spirit, or faith in Christ [z].

Nor merely political, to credit, or profit, or secular ends,
" propter famam, non propter conscientiam [a]," as the orator
speaks; or as our prophet hath it, " for corn and for wine [b]."
As good be an empty vine, as bring forth fruit only to ourselves [c].

But it must be spiritual unto the Lord. " If thou wilt return, O Israel, saith the Lord, return unto me [d]." And not
only 'Ad Dominum,' to the Lord; for that may be done
falsely [e], and flatteringly, with a halting and divided heart.
By the force of semi-persuasions, like that of Agrippa [f], and

---

[r] Isai. xli. 17. Psalm lxviii. 10.   [s] Psalm xxvii. 10. lxxii. 12.   [t] Psalm
cxlvi. 7.   [u] 1 Kings viii. 37, 38, 39.   [x] Isai. xxvi. 18.   [y] Mal. iii. 16.
[z] Rom. x. 3. Heb. xi. 6. Non sunt bona, quæ non de radice bona procedunt.
Ea ipsa opera, quæ dicuntur ante fidem, quamvis videantur hominibus, 'lauda-
bilia,' inania sunt, ut magnæ vires et cursus celerrimus præter viam. *Aug.*
Enarr. in Psalm 31. Vide de Spirit. et Lite. c. 20, 21. 26. Contra duas Epist. Pelag. l. 3. c. 7. ep. 106. de fide et operibus, c. 14. contra Julian. l. 4. c. 3.   [a] Nihil ad ostentationem, omnia ad conscientiam refert. *Plin.* l. 1. ep. 22. 5. Nihil
opinionis causa, omnia conscientiæ faciam. *Senec.* de Vita Beata, c. 20. 3.
[b] Hos. vii. 16.   [c] Hos. x. 1.   [d] Jer. iv. 8.   [e] Jer. iii. 10.
[f] Acts xxvi. 23.

N 2

Orpah [g], complimenting with God, and then forsaking him.
By the force of compulsory impressions, like that of Pharaoh [h] and Israel [i] in the wilderness. Promises on the rack [k],
and pride when there was respite again ; thawing in the sun,
and freezing in the shade ; melting in the furnace, and out of
it returning unto hardness again,—like the prophet's cake,
burnt on the one side, and dough on the other. But it
must be,

Secondly, 'Usque ad Dominum;' so much the original
word importeth. A full, thorough, constant, continued
conversion [l], with a whole, a fixed, a rooted, a united, an
established heart, yielding up the whole conscience and conversation to be ruled by God's will in all things.

SECT. 5. The motives to this duty are two : First, His
mercy [m], he is yet *thy God;* no such argument for our turning unto God as his turning unto us. Adam looks on him
as a judge, and hides ; the prodigal looks on him as a Father, and returns. As the beam of the sun, shining on fire,
doth discourage the burning of that; so the shining of
God's mercies on us, should dishearten and extinguish lust
in us. This is the use we should make of mercy. Say not,
" He is my God ; therefore I may presume upon him ; but
he is mine, therefore I must return unto him. Because he
is God, I will be afraid to provoke him ; and because he is
mine, I will be afraid to forfeit him. He is so great, I must
not dare to offend him ; he is so precious, I must not venture to lose him."—His mercy is a holy mercy, which knows
to pardon sin, but not to protect it. It is a sanctuary for
the penitent, not for the presumptuous.

Secondly, His judgement, and that expressed rather as
our act than his, " *Thou hast fallen by thine iniquity.*" If
mercies [n] do not work upon love, let judgements work upon

g Ruth i. 14.   h Exodus viii. 8. ix. 27, 34.   i Psalm lxxviii. 34, 37.
k Semisauciam hac atque hac versare voluntatem. *Aug.* Confess. l. 8. c. 8.—
Plerique ipsius pœnitentis pœnitentiam agunt. *Ambros.* de Pœn. l. 2. c. 9.—
Ἐπάλληλοι ἐπὶ τοῖς ἁμαρτήμασι μετάνοιαι. *Clem. Alex.* l. 2. Strom. 13.—Irrisor est,
non pœnitens, qui adhuc agit quod pœnitet, &c. *Isidor.* de Summo Bono.—Mag-
nam rem puta, unum hominem agere: præter sapientem, nemo unum agit;
cæteri multiformes sunt. *Sen.* ep. 120.—*Ambros.* Offic. l. 2. c. 22.   l Joel
ii. 12. Acts xi. 23. Psalm lvii. 7. Ephes. iii. 27. Psalm lxxxvi. 11. Heb. xiii. 9.
m Joel ii. 12, 13. Isai. lv. 6, 7. Jer. xxxi. 18. Hos. iii. 5. Psalm cxxx. 4. Acts
ii. 38. Matth. iii. 2. Isai. lxiv. 9.   n Qui beneficiis non intelligitur, vel plagis
intelligatur. *Cypr.* in Demetr.

fear [o]. Extremities are a warrant unto importunities. Even heathen-mariners [p] in a storm will cry mightily upon God. When there is a deluge coming, is it not time for Noah to fear, and to prepare an ark [q]? What meanest thou, O thou sleeper, to lose the season and benefit of God's visitations [r]? When there is a tempest over the ship, heavy distresses and distractions both at home and abroad, to be so secure in thy wonted impenitency, as if thou hadst had no sins to procure these judgements, or no sense to feel them? as if there were agreements [s], and sealed covenants between thee and the sword that it should not touch thee? If thou be falling, is it not high time to consider thy ways? to search and to judge thyself? to have thine eyes like the windows of Solomon's temple, broad inwards [t], to find out thine own provocations; and as David speaks [u], to keep thyself from thine own iniquity?

Thus when, in one and the same time, mercies and judgements are intermixed, then is the most solemn season to call upon men for repentance. If we felt nothing but fears [x], they might make us despair; if nothing but mercies, they would make us secure. If the whole year were summer, the sap of the earth would be exhausted; if the whole were winter, it would be quite buried. The hammer breaks metal, and the fire melts it; and then you may cast it into any shape. Judgements break, mercies melt; and then, if ever, the soul is fit to be cast into God's mould. There is no figure in all the prophets more usual than this, to interweave mercies and judgements, like those elegancies which rhetoricians call *ὀξύμωρα* [y], to allure and to bring into a wilderness [z]. And this of all other is the *ἡμέρα κρίσιμος*, as physicians call

[o] Dant animum ad loquendum libere ultimæ miseriæ, *Liv.* l. 29. [p] Inops Senatus auxilii humani, ad Deos populum et vota vertit: jussi cum conjugibus et liberis supplicatum ire, et pacem exposcere Deum. *Liv.* l. 3. 7.—Cum stupet cœlum, et aret annus, Nudipedalia denunciantur: Magistratus purpuras deponunt, fasces retro avertunt, precem indigitant, hostiam instaurant. Vide *Tert.* adv. Psychicos, c. 16.—*Clem. Alex.* Stro. l. 6. p. 453. Edit. Heins. —*Sozom.* l. 9. c. 6.—*Brisson.* de form. l. 1. [q] Heb. xi. 7. [r] Perdidisti tot mala, si nondum misera esse didicisti. *Sen.* ad Helvid.—Perdidistis utilitatem calamitatis, et miserrimi facti estis, et pessimi permansistis. *Aug.* de Civ. Dei, l. 1. c. 33. [s] Isai. xxviii. 15. [t] 1 Kings vi. 4. [u] Psalm xviii. 23. Ἕκαστος τῶν κακούργων ἐκφέρει τὸν αὑτοῦ σταυρόν. *Plut.* de sera numin. vindicta, *Wyttenb.* p. 34. [x] Vide *Tertul.* contra Marcion. l. 2. c. 13. [y] *Voss.* Rhet. l. 5. c. 12. sect. 7. [z] Hos. ii. 14.

it [a]; the critical time of diseased people, wherein the chief
conjecture lieth, whether they be mending or ending, according to the use which they make of such interwoven mercies.

SECT. 6. I have cursorily run over the first part of the context, the invitation unto repentance, as intending to make my
abode on the second, which is the institution how to perform
it. Therein we have, First, A general instruction, "Take unto
you words." Secondly, A particular form, what words they
should take, or a petition drawn to their hands, "Take away
all iniquity, &c."

Of the former of these, I shall speak but a word. It importeth the serious pondering and choosing of requests to
put up to God. The mother of Artaxerxes [b], in Plutarch, was
wont to say, that they who would address themselves unto
princes, must use ῥήμασι βυσσίνοις, silken words.—Surely he
that would approach unto God, must consider, and look as
well to his words as to his feet. He is so holy and jealous
of his worship [c], that he expects there should be preparation
in our accesses unto him: preparation of our persons, by
purity of life [d]; preparation of our services, by choice of
matter [e]; preparation of our hearts [f], by finding them out [g],
stirring them up [h], fixing them, fetching them in [i], and calling together all that is within us, to prevail with God [k].

The services which we thus prepare, must be *taken* from
him. They must not be the issues of our own private and
fleshly hearts: for nothing can go to God, but that which
comes from him. And this phrase seemeth to import these
three things: First, We must attend unto his will [l], as the
rule of our prayers. Secondly, We must attend unto his
precepts and promises [m], as the matter of our prayers.
Thirdly, We must attend unto the guidance of his holy
Spirit [n], as the life and principle of our prayers, without which
we know not what to ask.

[a] Vide *Gorræi* Definit. Medic.   [b] *Plutarch.* Apophthegm.   [c] Josh. xxiii. 9.
John iv. 22. Eccles. v. 1, 2. Gen. xxxv. 2, 3. 1 Sam. xvi. 5. Isai. i. 15, 16.
[d] Quantum à præceptis, tantum ab auribus Dei, longe sumus. *Tertul.* de Orat.
c. 7.—Οὐδέ πη ἐστὶ, κελαινεφέϊ Κρονίωνι Αἵματι καὶ λύθρῳ πεπαλαγμένον εὐχε-
τάασθαι. *Homer.* Iliad. ζ. 267. Job. xi. 13.   [e] John ix. 1. Luke xv. 17, 18.
[f] Sacerdos parat fratrum mentes, dicendo 'Sursum corda.' *Cyprian.* de Orat.
[g] 2 Sam. vii. 27.   [h] Isai. lxiv. 7.   [i] Psalm lvii. 7, 8.   [k] Psalm ciii. 1.
2 Chron. xxx. 19.   [l] 1 John v. 14.   [m] 2 Sam. vii. 25.   [n] Rom. viii. 36.
Zach. ii. 10. Job xxxvii. 19. Vide *Aug.* Ep. 105. Et Ep. 121. c. 15.

And prayers, thus regulated, are most seasonable and sovereign duties in times of trouble; the key which openeth a door of mercy; the sluice which keepeth out an inundation of judgements. Jacob wrestled and obtained a blessing [o]. Amos prayed, and removed a curse [p]. The woman of Canaan will not be denied with a denial [q]. The people of Israel will beg for deliverance even then, when God had positively told them, that he would deliver them no more [r]. Jonah will venture a prayer from the bottom of the sea, when double death had seized upon him, the belly of the deep, and the belly of the whale; and that prayer of his did " open the doors " of the Leviathan, as the expression is, Job xli. 14, and made one of those deaths a deliverance from the other.

O let the Lord's remembrances give him no rest. There is a kind of omnipotency in prayer [s], as having an interest and prevalence with God's omnipotency. It hath loosed iron chains [t]; it hath opened iron gates [u]; it hath unlocked the windows of Heaven [x]; it hath broken the bars of death [y]. Satan hath three titles given him in the Scripture, setting forth his malignity against the church of God: a ' dragon [z],' to note his malice; a ' serpent [a],' to note his subtilty; and a ' lion [b],' to note his strength. But none of all these can stand before prayer. The greatest malice, the malice of Haman, sinks under the prayer of Esther [c]; the deepest policy, the counsel of Ahithophel, withers before the prayer of David [d]: the hugest army, an host of a thousand thousand Ethiopians, run away like cowards before the prayer of Asa [e].

How should this encourage us to treasure up our prayers, to besiege the throne of grace with armies of supplications, to refuse a denial, to break through a repulse! He hath blessed those whom he did cripple [f]: he hath answered those whom he did reproach [g]: he hath delivered those whom he

---

[o] Hos. xii. 4.   [p] Amos vii. 1, 7.   [q] Mat. xv. 24, 27.   [r] Judg. x. 13, 15. [s] Dei potentiam servi preces impediebant. *Hieron.* ad Gaudentium.   [t] Acts xvi. 25. 26.   [u] Acts xii. 5, 10.   [x] 1 Kings xviii. 41. Fulmen de cœlo precibus suis contra hostium machinamentum extorsit, suis pluvia impetrata, cum siti laborarent. *Jul. Capitolin.* in Antonino. Vide *Justin. Martyr. Apol.* 2. *Tertul. Apol.* c. 5. 39, 40. Et ad Scapulam, c. 4.   [y] John xi. 40, 43.   [z] Rev. xii. 3. [a] Gen. iii. 1.   [b] 1 Pet. v. 8.   [c] Esth. iv. 16.   [d] 2 Sam. xv. 31.   [e] 2 Chron. xiv. 9, 11, 12.   [f] Gen. xxxii. 25, 28.   [g] Matth. xv. 26, 28.

did deny [h]. And he is the same yesterday and to-day [i]. If
he save in six and in seven troubles [k], should not we pray in
six and seven extremities? Certainly, in all the afflictions
of the church, when prayers are strongest, mercies are
nearest.

And therefore let me humbly recommend to the cares of
this Honourable Assembly, amongst all your other pressing
affairs, the providing that those solemn days, wherein the
united prayers of this whole kingdom should, with strongest
importunities, stop the breaches, and stand in the gaps of
judgements which are ready to rush in upon us, may, with
more obedience and solemnity, be observed, than indeed of
late they are. It is true, here, and in other cities, and po-
pulous places, there is haply less cause to complain. But
who can, without sorrow and shame, behold in our country
towns, men so unapprehensive either of their brethren's
sufferings, or of their own sins and dangers, as to give God
quite over, to let him rest, that they themselves may work;—
to come in truth to Jehoram's resolution, ' Why should they
wait upon God any longer?' to grudge their brethren's and
their own souls and safeties one day in thirty, and to tell all
the world that indeed their day's work is of more value with
them than their day's worship, multitudes drudging and moil-
ing in the earth, while their brethren are mourning and besieging of Heaven. I do but name it, and proceed.

The second part of the institution, was the particular form
suggested unto them, according unto which their addresses
unto God are to be regulated, which consisteth of two parts,
a prayer, and a promise. The prayer is for two benefits:
the one, ' removal of sin;' the other, ' conferring good.' In
the promise or restipulation, we have first their covenant,
wherein they promise two things: 1st. ' Thanksgiving'
for the hearing and answering of their prayers. 2nd. A
' special care' for the amendment of their lives.—Secondly,
The ground of their confidence so to pray, and of their resolutions so to promise, " Because, in thee, the fatherless
findeth mercy." My meditations will be confined within the
first of these, the prayer of the church in their fears and
sufferings;—wherein I shall begin, in the prophet's order,
with their prayer against sin, *Take away all iniquity.*

ʰ Judges x. 13, 16.   ⁱ Heb. xiii. 8.   ᵏ Job v. 19.

The word signifies, 1. To expiate, and make atonement by a sacrifice. So the scape-goat (which was a sign of Christ our sacrifice as risen and living again) is said to carry the sins of the people into the wilderness [l], thereby signifying Christ's taking our sins from us [m]. 2. To forgive, which, in the court of mercy, is the taking of sin away [n]. 3. To remove or take away by destroying; so it is used, Hosea i. 6. Job xxxii. 22; and is sometimes used to express burning [o]. So sin is said to be destroyed [p], to be subdued [q], to be purged away with the spirit of judgement and burning [r]. The meaning then is, ' Take away all our sins from us; lay them upon Christ our sacrifice ; for his merit, pardon them ; by his grace, destroy and subdue them; that so the root of judgements being removed, they likewise may therewithal be removed too.'—From hence the observation which I shall insist upon, is this :—

SECT. 7. ' When God threateneth judgements, we, in our conversion unto him, should pray against sins.'—Our eye of sorrow should be more upon that which dishonoureth him, than upon that which afflicts ourselves; more upon that which is contrary to his image, than upon that which is contrary to our own nature; more upon that which defileth, than upon that which paineth us. Pharaoh [s] cares for nothing but the removal of death: Simon Magus [t] for nothing but to have perdition and the gall of bitterness kept from him. But good men, like wise physicians, cure the disease at the root, as Elisha [u] did the waters, by putting salt into the spring-head. The angel was smiting the people with a plague; David betakes himself to the right remedy, " I have sinned, I have done wickedly [x] :"—he goes not to the physicians, but to the altar, to make atonement for sin; and so the plague was stayed. Destruction was threatened against Israel for their calf, their murmurings, their rebellions; " Moses stands in the gap," to divert it [y] ; but how doth he do it? surely by praying against their sins. " O this people have sinned a great sin, O that thou wouldest forgive them [z]!" A sick man was brought to Christ to be

---

[l] Lev. xvi. 22.   [m] John i. 29. Heb. ix. 28.   [n] Psalm xxxii. 1, 5.
[o] 2 Sam. v. 21. Nahum i. 5.   [p] Rom. vi. 6.   [q] Mic. vii. 19.   [r] Isai. iv. 4.   [s] Exod. x. 17.   [t] Acts viii. 24.   [u] 2 Kings ii. 21.   [x] 2 Sam. xxiv. 17, 25.   [y] Psalm cvi. 23.   [z] Exod. xxxii. 31, 32, 34, 39.

healed [a]; Christ overlooks the disease, and begins at the sin: " Son, be of good cheer, thy sins are forgiven thee:" and, this being forgiven, the malignity of the disease was removed, though the matter should have remained. This was the usual method of David in his troubles [b], to throw over these Shebas that had wrought his woe, " Blot out, wash thoroughly, cleanse, create, renew ;" he is far more importunate for pardon and purging, than for ease and comfort. Complaining in trouble, is the work of a man [c]; but repenting, is the work of a Christian.

The reasons of this point are these three :—

SECT. 8. I. If a judgement should be removed, while sin remains, it is not removed in mercy, but in anger : for, many times, God gives over punishing in displeasure, as a man throweth away the rod, when his scholar is incorrigible. " Why should ye be smitten any more? ye will revolt more and more [d]." If men be settled on their lees, and will not be reclaimed, there cannot a heavier punishment light upon them, than to be without punishment [e], to be left to themselves, and the fury of their own wills, speedily to work out their own perdition, that their own pleasures may become their plagues,—and the liberty of their own lusts, their sorest bondage. God may take away in wrath, that which he sent in anger [f]; as, on the other side, he may punish sin then when he forgiveth it, and may visit iniquity with rods then when he will " not utterly take away his loving kindness from a people [g]."

II. If a judgement be removed, so long as sin remains, it is gone ' cum animo revertendi,' either the same or a worse is likely to succeed : for God will overcome whom he

---

[a] Matth. ix. 2.   [b] Psalm xxv. 8. xxxii. 4, 5. xxxviii. 3, 4, 51.   [c] Lam. iii. 39, 40.   [d] Isai. i. 5.   [e] Hos. iv. 14. Psalm lxxxi. 11, 12. Ezek. xxiv. 13. Rom. i. 24, 28. Rev. xxii. 11.   Exaudit propitius, non exaudit iratus : et rursus non exaudit propitius, exaudit iratus.—Non parcit propitius, parcit iratus. *Aug.* contra Jul. l. 5. c. 4.—Parci sibi putat, cum excæcetur, et servetur ad ultimam opportunamque vindictam. *Aug.* in Psalm ix.—Ad utilitatem quosdam non exaudis ; ad damnationem quosdam exaudis. In Psalm xxi.—Iratus dat amanti, quod malè amat, in Psalm. xxvi.—Magna ira est, quando peccantibus non irascitur Deus. *Hier.* ep. 33. et in Psalm cxl.—Indignantis Dei major hæc plaga. *Cypr.* de Lapsis.—O servum illum beatum, cujus emendationi Deus instat, cui dignatur irasci, &c. *Tertul.* de pat. c. 11.   [f] Hos. xiii. 11.   [g] Psalm xcix. 8, 9, 32, 33.

judgeth [h]. Pharaoh's stubbornness did not but increase his plagues. God will not endure, that the pride [i] of man should outvie his justice. If we do not take Christ's warning to go and "sin no more," we have great cause to fear his inference, that " a worse thing will come upon us [j]." If we do yet exalt ourselves, God will yet plead with us [k]. If we will walk contrary unto him [l], he threateneth to do the like unto us, and to punish us seven times more for our sins. If we do not turn unto him that smiteth us, then his anger in smiting shall " not be turned away, but his hand shall be stretched out still [m]." God can bring clouds after rain ; distresses in Ireland, after distractions in Scotland ; and distractions in England, after distresses in Ireland ; mischief upon mischief, and counsel against counsel; Manasseh against Ephraim, and Ephraim against Manasseh,—to vex and weary out a sinful people, till they pine away in their calamities.

III. Sin being removed, though the afflictions should not be removed, yet it is sanctified, and turned into good. Repentance, like the philosopher's stone, can turn iron into gold, can make golden afflictions : so the trial of our faith, that is, our affliction, is said to be " more precious than gold [n]." Whereas sin, remaining, is like copperas, which will turn wine or milk into ink : it converts the blessing of God into the provisions of lusts; cankers learning with pride, and wit with profaneness, and wealth with luxury; like leaven, which turns a very passover into pollution. As the pearl [o], which is an ornament to the woman which wears it, is a disease to the fish which breeds it; as the same perfume which refresheth a dove, is mortal to a vulture ; as the same pillar and cloud was light to Israel, but dark to Egypt ; the same deep a path to Israel, but a grave to Egypt ;—so the same blessings, which by grace are converted into comforts, by sin are abused into dishonourable services [p]. Sweet powders can make leather an ornament, when the sanies of a plague-sore will render a robe infectious. As it was said of Naaman, He was a great man, an honourable man, a mighty man of war ; but " he was a leper [q] :" so whatever other ornaments a man hath, sin stains them with the foulest *but,*

[h] Rom. iii. 4.   [i] Exod. ix. 17.   [j] John v. 14.   [k] Jer. ii. 9.   [l] Lev. xxvi. 18, 21, 24, 28.   [m] Isai. ix. 12.   [n] 1 Pet. i. 7.   [o] *Athen.* l. 3. *c.* 13. [p] Hag. ii. 13.   [q] 2 Kings v. 1.

that can be brought to deprave the fairest endowments : a learned man, a wealthy man, a wise man, an honourable man, *but a wicked man ;* this makes all those other good things tributary unto Satan.

And therefore as the gold and silver of the Canaanites [r] was to pass through the fire, before it could be used by Israel; so all other blessings, bestowed on men, must pass through the Spirit of judgement and burning, through the purifying waters of repentance, before they can bring honour to the Author, or comfort to the enjoyer of them. When Christ overcometh Satan, " he taketh from him all his armour, and divideth the spoils [s]." How doth he divide the spoils? surely he maketh use of that wit, wealth, power, learning, wisdom, interests, which Satan used against Christ's kingdom, as instruments and ornaments unto the gospel. As when a magazine in war is taken, the general makes use of those arms which were provided against him, for his own service [t].

And as sin doth thus corrupt blessings, so, on the other side, repentance doth sweeten judgements, and can turn afflictions into matter of comfort. As scarlet pulls out the teeth of a serpent, so this takes away the sting of a judgement. As wine draweth a nourishing virtue from the flesh of vipers [u]; as hot birds can feed upon iron, and purge their bodies with swallowing of stones ; so repentance, though it should not remove a judgement, yet can feed upon it ; and fetch meat out of the eater, and, out of the strong, sweetness.

There are two evils in afflictions ; their thorn in the flesh, as they are matter of pain ; and their snare to the conscience [x], as they are matter of temptation : as there are two things in a chain or fetter, the heaviness whereby it loads, and the hardness whereby it galls. Now as a prisoner, though he cannot make his chain lighter than it is, yet by lining it with wool, or other soft things, he can prevent the galling ; so repentance, though it take not away the pain of affliction from the flesh, yet by meekening and humbling the

---

r Num. xxxi. 22.   s Τεύχεα συλήσας φερέτω κοίλας ἐπὶ νῆας. *Hom.* Il. 11. Luke xi. 21.   t Qui se dedebant, arma tradebant. *Cæsar* de Bello Gallico, l. 3.   u Venenum aliquando pro remedio fuit. *Sen.* de Benef. l. 2. c. 18. Medici pedes et alas cantharidis, cum sit ipsa mortifera, prodesse dicunt. *Plut.* de Aud. Poetis.   x Isa. viii. 21. 2 Chro. xxviii. 22. Rev. xvi. 10.

soul, with silence and quietness to ' bear the indignation of the Lord [y],' and 'accept of the punishment of sin,' it removeth the temptation and malignity of it from the conscience.   And thus as Protagoras [z], by his natural dexterity, ordered the burden which he was to bear, with more ease and advantage ; so piety makes judgements, by spiritual prudence, more easy to be borne: and the light yoke of Christ, as bladders in a deep water, bears up the spirits of men from sinking, and lighteneth every other burden.   And therefore as he in Plutarch said of the Scythians [a], That though they had no music nor vines amongst them, yet they had gods ; so whatever other things may be wanting to a people, yet if God be their God, they are not destitute of any happiness.   Yea, as those roses [b] are usually sweetest, which grow nearest unto stinking weeds ; so the comforts of God's Spirit are strongest, when a man is otherwise perplexed with the greater difficulties.   It was promised unto Josiah, that he should die in peace [c] ; and yet we find, that he was slain in war [d] : his weeping and humiliation altered the very nature of trouble, and made war to be peace unto him.

SECT. 9. Now for the use and application of this point. This serveth, first, To instruct us how to deprecate calamities, when God shakes his rod over us.   There is nothing in all the world that God is angry with, but sin : for all other things are his own works, in the goodness [e] of which he rested with singular complacency and delight.   Sin is that against which God's arrows are directed ; and as the arrow sticks in the butt unto which the mark is fastened ; so the judgements which are shot at sin, must needs light upon us unto whom sin cleaveth.   The way then to divert the arrow, is to remove the mark.   It is true, God doth sometimes bring afflictions, without respect to the provocations of sin, upon his best servants.   As if a man should shape, out of a mass of gold, some excellent vessel,—though the gold be never so pure, yet it must pass through the fire and the hammer again. But it is certain too, that no afflictions come in anger, but

[y] Mic. vii. 9. Lev. xxvi. 41. Jer. x. 19.   [z] *Aul. Gell.* l. 5. c. 3.   [a] *Plut.* συμπόσ. ἑπτὰ σοφῶν.   [b] *Plut.* de Sanitate tuend.   [c] 2 Chron. xxxiv. 28.
[d] 2 Chron. xxxv. 24.   [e] Usque ad delictum hominis Deus tantum bonus, exinde Jude et severus, &c. *Tertul.* contra Marc. l. 2. c. 11, 14.

with respect to sin.   And the anger of God is the bitterest
thing in any calamity.

Now for diversion of this, there is no way but to get sin
removed.   Take the bark from a tree, and the sap can never
find way to the boughs.   Sin is the ' vehiculum,' which conveys shame and sorrow to the soul : take away that, and a
judgement hath no commission.   You may find an error in
it, if you be not the same men that you were, when it issued
forth; for God shoots no arrows to hurt the body of his Son.
It is true, Job complains, that " God's arrows did stick in
him[f];" but these were not for destruction[g], but for trial; as
men shoot bullets against armour of proof, not to hurt it,
but to praise it.   Job in this case was brought forth, not as
a malefactor to suffer, but, as a champion, to triumph.   Let a
man take what course he can, to keep off God's judgements,
and hide himself in the closest protection that human power
or policy can contrive ; so long as he keeps his sin with him,
God's arrows[h] will get through at one joint or other.   A
naked man, with innocency, is better armed than Goliah in
brass or iron.

We are apt, in our distresses, to howl and repine, to
gnaw our tongues, and tear our flesh in the anguish of our
sufferings.   Like the silly hart, which runs mourning and
bleeding, but never thinks of getting out the fatal dart
which sticks in his side.   We look upward[i], to see whether
help will drop into our mouths; and we look downward, to
see whether human succours will avail us : but we look not
inward, to find out ' the plague of our own hearts[k],' that we
may be rid of that.   And till this be done, sin doth as naturally draw and suck judgement to it, as the loadstone doth
iron, or turpentine fire.   Indefatigable have been the pains of
this High Court, to make up the breaches that threaten us,
and to heal the land.   Whence comes it, that our distractions remain unremoved ?   Certainly, our leaks are not stopped; our sins are not thrown away : we labour at the pump
to get the water out, but we do not take care to cure the pas-

   [f] Job. vi. 4.   [g] Verberat nos et lacerat ? non est sævitia ; certamen est. Sen.
de Prov. c. 4. 11.—Tentationibus non vincitur fides, sed probatur. Cypr. de Mort.
—Aug. de Civ. Dei, l. 1. c. 29, 30. l. 4. c. 3.   [h] 1 Kings, xxii. 34.   [i] Isai.
viii. 21, 22.   [k] 1 Kings viii. 38.

sage at which it enters in: we are old bottles still, and "God
will not put new wine into old bottles[1]." If men would
spend their murmurings and reproaches rather upon their
sins than upon their physicians, the work would be sooner
done. When the temple of God was to be new built, and a
public restitution of the face of things unto glory and splendour was in agitation, the prophets [m] call upon God's people
in special then to repent. Impenitency puts obstructions to
God's mercy, and to all noble enterprises. So long as our
lives are as bad as before, how can we expect that our condition should be better? In that case, mercies themselves
become no mercies: as in the case of repentance, judgements would be no judgements. If we turn from our evil
ways, God hath engaged himself by a solemn promise, that
" he will do us no harm [n]." Otherwise, to busy ourselves in
outward ceremonies of repentance, bodily fasting, and verbal praying, is indeed but to flatter God, and, if we could,
to deceive him. And God will answer such men, not according to the prayer of their lips, but according to ' the
idol of their hearts [o].'

SECT. 10. Secondly, This teacheth us how to pray against
sin; it must be against *all*, and in *all respects*. In the Hebrew text, there is a kind of a usual transposition of the
words, עון תשא—כל the word *all* is first [p]. Methinks it doth
intimate an intentness of the church upon that point, to
have, if it were possible, all taken away at the very first.
If there be one leak in a ship, one gap in a wall, one gate
in a city, unprovided for; it is enough to sink a ship, to
drown a country, to betray a city. One little boy, thrust in
at a window, can unlock the door for all the rest of the
thieves. It was but one Jonah that raised a tempest, but
one Achan that troubled a camp; and one sin, generally un-
repented of, were enough to undo a kingdom. Do not say
" It is a little one, and my soul shall live." Even the philosopher telleth us [q], that sometimes ἀδικήματα ἐλάχιστα are μέγιστα,
the smallest errors prove most dangerous. How little soever
it be in its own nature, it becomes heinous by thy allowance.
It is as much treason for a private man to coin pence as

---

[1] Matth. ix. 17. [m] Hag. i. 6. Zech. i. 2. [n] Jer. xxv. 6. [o] Ezek.
xiv. 4, 5. [p] *Duncan's* Stereotype Hebrew Bible, vol. ii. p. 233. [q] *Arist.*
Rhet. l. i. et Polit. l. 5. c. 8.

88

twenty-shilling pieces; because the royal authority is as much violated by the one as the other.

This, then, we must first and principally remember, To set ourselves against *all sin.* In confession, none to be dissembled; in supplication, none to be excepted; in conversion, none to be reserved; never give it over so long as any is left.—" O Lord, yet it works, yet it lives, yet it tempts, yet it pains me. Sin hath not done accusing of me; let not thy mercy have done forgiving of sin. Sin hath not done rebelling in me; let not thy grace have done subduing of sin."—When men kill snakes or vipers, so long as they see them pant, or offer to thrust out a sting, they strike them still. Sin, like the thief on the cross, when it is fast nailed, and kept from its old tyranny, yet will, as much as it can, revile and spit out venom upon Christ. O therefore give it not over; break the legs of it; crucify it clean through, till it be quite dead. None can pray, or turn unto God in truth, or hope to be delivered from judgements in mercy, so long as he holds fast any known sin. Can any man look to receive benefit by the blood of Christ, who hugs the villain that shed it? Is it not treason, knowingly to harbour and entertain a traitor? Whosoever loves and holds fast sin, lies unto God in every prayer that he makes.

This serveth to prove and humble us for our hypocrisy and halvings with God in our conversions from sin, and confessions of it. We are willing to pray for the pardon of them all, we would have none hurt us; but when it comes to parting, and taking all away, this we cannot away with. Some are fat, delicate, golden sins; we would fain spare these, as Saul did Agag[r]; and hide them, as Achan[s] did his wedge. Herod hears John[t] gladly in many things; but if he restrain him of his Herodias, he must expect to be himself restrained. Agrippa[u] will be almost a Christian, but altogether may chance bring a chain with it. Jehu[x] will down with Baal and his priests; but he knows not how to part with his calves, lest he venture his kingdom. Policy is ever entering caveats against piety. Thus men huck, and stand upon abatements with Christ, in the bargain of salvation; not con-

[r] 1 Sam. xv. 9. [s] Josh. vii. 11. [t] Mark vi. 20. [u] Acts xxvi. 28. [x] 2 Kings x. 30, 31.

sidering, that the purchase of Heaven is like the buying of
the Sibyl's prophecy; the longer we stand off, the dearer
every day it will cost us ; the more tears, the harder repentance, the deeper sorrow, the stronger cries.   These men
know not the price of a soul, nor the worth of a Saviour.

O ! if Christ should have served us so in dying for sin, as
many of us do serve him in turning from sin, what a condition had our souls been in ! if he had died for some sins,
and not for others; if he had been unwilling to ' save us to
the uttermost,' as we are to serve him to the uttermost; if
he should have stopped before he came to ' consummatum
est,' and left any one drop of that bitter cup for us to drink
after him; would it not have caused our belly to swell, and
our thigh to rot, and made us for ever incapable of any other
mercy, than only a less damnation?

Well, beloved, Christ expecteth, that as he died for
all sin, so we should die to all : he will be counted worthy
of all acceptation[z], before he will bestow himself: he
will not suffer his blood and his mercy to mingle with sin,
or to be a protection to it: he cannot endure mingling
of the holy seed with the profane; swearing by God, and
swearing by Malcham[a]; Samaritan services[b], to be for
the Lord in one thing, and, for the world and flesh, in another; one step straight, and another crooked ; one speech
Ashdod[c], and another Canaan ; to let our conversation be
' Yea and Nay,' a mungrel service :—' In this, I will do as you
bid me[d], but in that, I will not ;'—like the Jews, that would
buy Christ's blood with money, but not take the money into
the treasury ; they were fearful to defile their chests, but not
to defile their consciences.   This Christ cannot away with.
It is dangerous to say with the Pharisee[e], ' This I am not,
and that I am not;' or with the young man[f], ' This and that
I have done ;' and, in the mean time, to have one thing lack-
ing, to have one door locked up still, to keep Christ and

z 1 Tim. i. 15.   a Zeph. i. 5.   b 1 Reg. xvii. 33.   c Neh. xiii. 24.
d Alternæ inter cupiditatem nostram et pœnitentiam vices sunt. Sen. de Otio Sap.
c. 27. Maximum judicium malæ mentis fluctuatio. ep. 120.—Vir bonus ἀμετα-
μέλητος. Arist. Ethic. l. 9. c. 46. Τετράγωνος. 1. 1. c. 10.—Μοχθηροὶ τὸ βέβαιον
οὐκ ἔχουσιν, 1. 8. c. 3.— Οὐκ ἐφ' ὧν μὲν, ἐφ' ὧν δ' οὐ, ἀλλ' ἐν ἕξει εὐποιίας.
Clem. Alex. Strom. l. 4. Nulli servorum licet, ex his quæ dominus imperat,
quod placuerit assumere, quod displicuerit repudiare.   Salv. de Prov. l. 3
• Luke. xviii. 11.   f Mark x. 20.

salvation from us. Whosoever keeps a covetous heart for
the world, or a sensual heart for the flesh, or a proud heart
for the devil, is unworthy of Heaven by his own election,
and would not go in thither, if the door were wide open: he
would not find there any fuel for these his lusts, any Nabal,
or Cozbi, or Diotrephes to converse withal. And surely,
he that hath any one wickedness with allowance [g], in God's
construction is habitually guilty of all [h].

Therefore in this case, as Samuel said to Jesse [i], "Are
here all thy children? if any be left, we will not sit down
till he come;"—so we must conceive in our confessions and
renunciations of sin, that Christ asketh us, "Are here all?
if any be reserved, I will not take possession, till that be
cast out." There must not a hoof [k] be left in Egypt, if God
be to be served. God's law, as well as man's, disallows in-
mates in the same house; he will not endure a divided heart [l];
he is heir of all things; there lies no writ of partition in his
inheritance; his title is so good, that he will never yield to
a composition; he will have all the heart or none.

4. We should therefore be exhorted (in time of trouble
especially) to set about this great work, to fall foul upon our
sins, to complain against them to God, as the Achans that
trouble Israel, as the corrupters and betrayers of our peace;
to set ourselves in God's eye, and not to dare to lie unto his
Holy Spirit, by falseness or hypocrisy; as if we could reserve any one sin unmortified, which he should not know of.
But being in his sight, " to whom all things are naked and
open [m]," to deal in all sincerity [n], and to hate sin even as he
hates it."

SECT. 11. There are five notable duties which these three
words, ' Omnem tolle iniquitatem,' do lead us unto.

1. Sense of sin, as of ' a heavy burden,' as the prophet
David calls it [o]. Such sense our Saviour requires in true
penitents, "Come unto me, all ye that are weary and heavy
laden [p];" to conceive them heavier than a millstone [q], than

g Qui uno peccavit, omnium reus est, peccans contra caritatem, à qua pen-
dent omnia: *Aug.* ep. 29.—Si pauca simulacra circumferat, in una idololatria
est; si unam thensam trahat, Jovis tamen plaustrum est. *Tert.*—Vide *Sen.* de
Benef. 1. 4. c. 26, 27. 1. 5. e. 15.   h James ii. 10. Luke xvi. 10. Ezek. xviii.
10, 13.   i 1 Sam. xvi. 11.   k Exod. x. 26.   l Psalm xii. 2.
James i. 8. Psalm cxix. 10.   m Heb. iv. 13.   n Gen. xvii. 1. 2 Cor.
ii. 17.   o Psalm xxxviii. 5.   p Matth. xi. 28.   q Luke xvii. 2.

the weight of a mountain[r]. O! what apprehension had St. Peter's converts of sin, when they felt the nails wherewith they had crucified Christ, sticking fast in their own hearts, and piercing their spirits with torment and horror[s]! O! what apprehensions had the poor gaoler of his sins, when he came as a prisoner before his own prisoners, springing in with monstrous amazement and consternation of spirit, beseeching them to tell him, "What he should do[t]?"

Consider it in its nature: a universal bruise and sickness, like those diseases which, physicians say, are 'Corruptio totius substantiæ,' from 'head to foot[u]:' and who doth not feel such a universal languor to be a heavy burden? for a man that must needs labour, to have weights hung at his hands; that must needs walk, to have clogs fastened to his feet;—how can he choose but cry out with the apostle, "O wretched man that I am, who shall deliver me[x]?"

Consider it in the curse that belongs unto it; "a roll written within and without[y]," with curses.

Look outward; and behold a curse in the creature, vanity, emptiness, vexation, disappointments; every creature armed with a sting, to revenge its Maker's quarrel.

Look inward; and behold a curse in the conscience, accusing, witnessing, condemning, haling to the tribunal of vengeance; first, defiling with the allowance, and after, terrifying with the remembrance of sin.

Look upward; and behold a curse in the heavens, the wrath of God revealed[z] from thence upon all unrighteousness.

Look downward; and behold a curse in the earth: death ready to put a period to all the pleasures of sin, and, like a trap-door, to let down into hell, where nothing of sin will remain, but the worm and the fire.

Look into the Scripture, and see the curse there described; an 'everlasting banishment' from the glory of God's presence: an 'everlasting destruction' by the glory of his power[a]. The Lord showing the jealousy of his justice, the unsearchableness of his severity, the unconceivableness of his strength, the bottomless guilt and malignity of

---

[r] Luke xxiii. 30.   [s] Acts ii. 37.   [t] Acts xvi. 23, 30.   [u] Isai. i. 5, 6.
[x] Rom. vii. 24.   [y] Ezek. ii. 10.   [z] Rom. i. 18.   [a] 2 Thess. i. 9.

sin, in the everlasting destruction of ungodly men, and in
the everlasting preserving of them to feel that destruction [b].
" Who knoweth the power of thy anger ?" saith Moses;
" even according to thy fear, so is thy wrath [c]." It is impossible for the most trembling consciences, or the most
jealous fears of a guilty heart, to look beyond the wrath of
God, or to conceive more of it than indeed it is. As in
peace of conscience, the mercy of God is revealed unto believers from faith to faith ; so, in anguish of conscience, the
wrath of God is revealed from fear to fear.

A timorous man can fancy vast and terrible fears, fire,
sword, tempests, racks, furnaces, scalding lead, boiling
pitch, running bell-metal, and being kept alive in all these
to feel their torment ; but these come far short of the wrath
of God : for first, There are bounds set to the hurting power
of a creature ; the fire can burn, but it cannot drown ; the
serpent can sting, but he cannot tear in pieces. Secondly, The
fears of the heart are bounded within those narrow apprehensions, which itself can frame of the hurts which may be
done.   But the wrath of God proceeds from an infinite justice, and is executed by an omnipotent and unbounded
power, comprising all the terror of all other creatures (as the
sun doth all other light) eminently and excessively in it: it
burns, and drowns, and tears, and stings, and bruises, and
consumes, and can nature feel much more than reason is
able to comprehend.

O ! if we could lay these things seriously to heart, (and
yet these are but low expressions of that which cannot be
expressed ; and cometh as short of the truth itself, as the
picture of the sun, in a table, doth of the greatness and
brightness of it in its own orb,) should we not find it necessary to cry out, " Take away all iniquity ?" this sickness out
of my soul,—this sword, this nail, this poisoned arrow, out
of my heart,—this dagger of Ehud out of my belly,—this
millstone, this mountain from off my back,—these stings
and terrors, these flames and furies out of my conscience ?
Lord, my wounds stink, my lips quiver, my knees tremble,
my belly rots ; I am feeble, and broken, and roar, and lan-

---

[b] Anima in corpore erit non vivendi causa, sed dolendi. *Aug.* de Civ. Dei, l. 13.
c. 2.   Prima mors animam nolentem pellit à corpore ; secunda nolentem retinet
in corpore. *Ibid.* l. 21. c. 3.   [c] Psalm xc. 11.

guish; thy wrath lies hard upon me, and thy waves go over
my head.

O! if we had but a view of sin as it is in its native foulness, and did feel but a touch of that fury that God is ready
to pour out upon it; this would stain all the pride of man,
and sour all the pleasures of sin, and make a man as fearful
to meddle with it, as a guilty woman with the bitter water
which caused the curse.   Most true was that which Luther
spake in this point, "If a man could perfectly see his own
evils, the sight thereof would be a perfect hell unto him :"—
and this God will bring wicked men unto ; " Reprove them,
and set their sins in order before them [d]," make them take a
view of their own hearts and lives, fuller of sins than the firmament of stars, or a furnace of sparks.   " O consider this,
ye that forget me," saith the Lord, " lest I tear you in
pieces, and there be none to deliver you."

Sect. 12. The second duty is, Confession; for he that cries
to have sin taken away, acknowledgeth that it lies upon
him.   A full confession, not of many, but of all sins, either
actually committed, or habitually comprised in our body of
sin.   As he in the Comedian said [e], that he had invited two
guests to dinner, Philocrates, and Philocrates,—a single
man, but a double eater ;—so, in examination of ourselves,
we shall every one find sins enough in himself to denomi-
nate him a double and a treble sinner.   A free confession,
not as Pharaoh's, extorted upon the rack ; nor as that of
Judas, squeezed out with anguish and horror ; but ingenuous
and penitent, arising from the purpose of a pious heart, that
cometh like water out of a spring, with a voluntary freeness ; not like water out of a still, which is forced with fire.

The third duty is, Weariness and detestation of all sin ;
for we call not to have a thing removed, till we be weary of
it.   Thus we are taught in the Scripture to be ashamed and
confounded, to loathe and abhor, to judge and condemn ourselves ; to throw sin away as a detestable thing, though it
be a golden or silver sin.   A spiritual judgement looks on
all sin as filthy and stinking [f] ; showeth a man to himself as
a vessel full of dung, scum, excrements ; and makes him out

---

[d] Psalm l. 31.   [e] Athenæus l. i.   [f] Psalm xxxviii. 2.   Ezek. xvi. 63.
Ezek. vi. 9, 20, 43.   1 Cor. xi. 31.   Isai. xxx. 22.   Psalm xiv. 3.   2 Cor. vii.
Omnis quem pœnitet, vexatur secum. *Aug.* in Psal. xxxiv.

of quiet, till he be thoroughly purged. For hatred is προς τα γένη, against the whole kind of that which we hate.

The fourth duty is, an Acknowledgment of our own impotency[g] to remove sin from ourselves. We have no more power than a slave in chains hath to get out of his bondage, till another ransom him; than a dead body in a grave, till Christ raise it. Our iniquity takes hold on us, and keeps us down, that we cannot hearken or be subject to the will of God. If sin were not removed by a greater strength than our own, it would most certainly sink us into hell.

The last duty is, An imploring of God's mercy and grace, that what we cannot do ourselves, he would be pleased to do for us. In works of art[h], it is hard to build, but easy to destroy: but in works of sin, though our weakness is able to commit them, yet none but God's power is able to demolish them. None but Christ is strong enough to overcome the strong man[i]; his person only hath strength enough to bear the curse of sin; his sacrifice only merit enough to make expiation for sin; his grace only virtue enough to remove the pollution of sin. Though we should take ' nitre and much soap[k],' our sin would be marked still; but he cometh with ' refiner's fire, and with fuller's soap[l],' and can wash out all. It was his only business of coming into the world, ' to destroy the works of the devil[m].'

Now the things which we pray for in this petition, are these three : First, For remission, that God would take away the condemnation of sin from us, by not imputing the guilt thereof unto us ; but would cause it to pass over on Christ, on whom he hath ' laid the iniquity of his people[n].' Such an expression the Holy Ghost useth, העביר, the Lord hath caused thy sin ' to pass over' from thee to Christ[o]: which being obtained, all other judgements are, ' ipso facto,' removed too, so far as they import proper and vindictive punishment[p].

Secondly, For sanctification, that the virtue of Christ's

---

g Ephes. ii. 1, 5.   Psalm xl. 12.   Rom. v. 6, 7. vi. 24.   2 Cor. iii. 5.   Jer. vi. 10.   Rom. viii. 7.   h Facile est momento quo quis velit, cedere possessione magnæ fortunæ : facere et parare cum difficile atque arduum. Liv. ii. 24. Corpora lente augescunt, citò exstinguuntur. Tacit. Vit. Agric.—Arbores magnas diu crescere, unâ horâ exstirpari. Quint. Curt. l. 7.   i Luke xi. 21.   k Jer. ii. 22. l Mal. iii. 3.   m 1 John iii. 8.   n Isai. liii. 6.   o 2 Sam. xii. 13.   p Rom. iv 8. Heb. ix. 14. Mic. vii. 19.

death, and the grace of his Spirit may subdue the power of sin, and cleanse and strengthen our consciences against the commands of it, and temptations unto it.

Thirdly, For continued renovation [q], that as, in sanctification begun, we have power against all kinds of sin,—so, by the continual supplies of the Holy Spirit, we may have further power against all degrees and remainders of sin. That Christ would pursue our sin unto death, as our sin did him; and not give over mortifying it, till his blood be revenged of it to the uttermost, and our souls delivered from it to the uttermost.

SECT. 13. I shall conclude the first part of the petition with a short word of exhortation unto this Honourable Assembly. Those things which God worketh in us [r], and bestoweth upon us by his grace, he also requireth of us by his command. Sometimes he promiseth to turn us; sometimes he commandeth us to turn to him; sometimes he biddeth us put away sin; and sometimes he promiseth to take it away from us: in the one, showing us what is our duty,—and in the other, where is our help. And as this latter consideration calleth upon our faith to pray, so the former upon our obedience to work. I shall therefore, Right Honourable, humbly offer a double exhortation unto all of you :—

First, That every one of you would seriously endeavour to take away all iniquity from his own person. And unto this there lieth upon you a double obligation; one with relation to the safety of your souls; for whatever other honour, wealth, wisdom, learning, interest a man hath besides, if sin have the predominancy, they are but Satan's magazine, and that man his servant to employ them against God that gave them: and the more mercies any man hath been trusted withal, the heavier judgement will be poured out upon the breach of that trust. Better be a wooden vessel to hold wine, than a silver vessel to hold excrements : better be a beggar with the treasure of God's grace, than a prince with the load of a man's own sins.

---

[q] Ezek. xxxvi. 26.   Jer. xxi. 8.   Ezek. xviii. 31.   Isai. i. 16.   Heb. viii. 12.
[r] Lex jubet, gratia juvat.   *Aug.* ep. 95. et ep. 144. et l. 3. contr. 2. ep. Pelag. c. 7.
—Petamus ut det, quod ut habeamus jubet. In Exod. Quæst. 55. de Bono Vidui-
tatis, c. 17.

But there is a further tie upon you, with relation unto the success of that honourable employment, whereunto you are called. " Ita nati estis, ut bona malaque vestra ad Rempublicam pertineant[s]." God will be sanctified in all those that draw near unto him, as well in civil as in sacred administrations. It is very hard for a person in whom sin rules, to be constantly faithful to any public and honourable service ; for grace only ' establisheth the heart[t].' Ahithophel, a man of great wisdom, falls from David : Joab, a man of great valour, falls from Solomon. And admit he be faithful, yet the sin of his heart sends out a prohibition to the wisdom of his head, and the labour of his hand. He that will be a fit vessel for his Master's use, must first of all ' purge himself[u]; as we first cleanse a vessel, before we use it. When Joshua was to negotiate a public reformation, and to administer a public service, his ' filthy garment' must be taken from him, and he must be clothed with change of raiment[x]. Let every one of you make his public service one argument more than he had before, for his necessary reformation, and let the piety of your lives bear witness to the integrity of your honourable undertakings.

SECT. 14. Secondly, As you must take away sin from yourselves, so make it your principal work to ' take away iniquity out of the land ;' liberty, property, privileges, are sacred and precious things, not to be in the least manner betrayed : yea, in some sense we may look upon them, as the Jews upon their Masorah[y], ' tanquam legis et pietatis sepem ;' as a fence and mound unto religion herself. Arbitrary government would quickly be tampering in sacred things, because corruption in the church is marvellously subservient and advantageous to corruption in the state. But the most orient pearl of this kingdom, is our religion; and the bitterest enemies unto that, are our sins. These are the snuffs that dim our candlestick, and threaten the removal of it; these are the leaven that defile our passovers, and urge God to pass away and depart from us ; these the obstructions between his sacred Majesty and you, and between both, and the happiness of the kingdom. Think seriously what ways may be most effectual to purge out this

---

[s] *Tacit.* Annal. .4.   [t] Heb. xiii. 9.   2 Tim. ii. 21.   [x] Zach. iii. 4, 7.   [y] R. Akiba in Pirke Aboth.

leaven out of the land. The principal sacrificing knife which kills and mortifies sin, is the Word of God, and the knowledge of it. It would have been a great unhappiness to the commonwealth of learning, if Caligula [z] had (as he endeavoured) deprived the world of the writings of Homer, Virgil, and Livy. But O! what an Egyptian calamity is it, to have, in this sunshine of the gospel, thousands of persons and families (as I doubt not but, upon enquiry, it would appear) without the Writings of the prophets and apostles! A Christian soldier without his sword, a Christian builder without his rule and square, a Christian calling without the instruments and balances of the sanctuary belonging to it. O! therefore that every parish had an endowment fit for a learned, laborious, and worthy pastor,—and pastors worthy of such endowments,—that provision were made, that every family might have a Bible in it, and (if by law it might possibly be procured) the exercises of religion therewithal: this would be the surest magazine to secure the happiness of a kingdom : That all reproachful titles, which the Devil useth as scarecrows and whifflers to keep back company from pressing in upon Christ's kingdom, were, by law, proscribed: that scandalous sins were, by the awfulness and severity of discipline, more blasted and brought to shame : that the Lord's house were more frequented, and his day more sanctified, and his ordinances more reverenced; and his ministers, which teach the good knowledge of the Lord, more encouraged than ever heretofore :—in one word, that all the several fountains of the commonwealth were settled in a sound and flourishing constitution : that, in every place, we might see piety the elm to every other vine, the supporter to every other profession ; learning adorned with piety, and law administered with piety, and counsels managed with piety, and trade regulated with piety, and the plough followed with piety : that when ministers fight against sin, with the sword of God's Word, ye who are the nobles and gentry of the land, would second them, and frown upon it too ; a frown of yours may sometimes do as much service to Christ as a sermon of ours. And he cannot but take it very unkindly from you, if ye will not bestow your countenance on him, who

z *Sueton.* in Calig. c. 34, ed. Crus. vol. i. p. 529.

bestowed his blood on you:—that ye would let the strict-ness of your lives, and the piety of your examples put wick-edness out of countenance, and make it appear (as indeed it is) a base and a sordid thing.

If we would thus sadly set ourselves against the sins of the land, no power, no malice, no policies should stand between us and God's mercies. Religion would flourish, and peace would settle, and trade would revive, and the hearts of men would be re-united, and the church be as a city compacted ; and this nation would continue to be, as it hath been, like the garden of Eden, a mirror of prosperity and happiness to other people ; and God would prevent us, in the second part of our petition, with the blessing of goodness ; as soon as ever iniquity were removed, he would do us good, which is the second thing here directed to pray for, " Receive us graciously."

SECT. 15. In the original it is קח טוב, " take good," to wit, to bestow upon us ; so taking [a] is sometimes used for giving : he " received gifts for men," so in David [b] ; he " gave gifts to men," so in the apostle [c]. And it is not improbable, that the prophet here secretly leadeth us to Christ the Me-diator, who first receiveth gifts from his Father, and then poureth them forth upon his church [d].

The meaning then is, " Lord, when thou hast pardoned, weakened, mortified sin, go on with thy mercy ; and, being in Christ graciously reconciled unto us, give further evidence of thy fatherly affection, by bestowing portions upon us. They shall not be cast away upon unthankful persons ; ' we will render the calves of our lips ;' they shall not be bestow-ed upon those that need them not, or that know where else to provide themselves. It is true, we have gone to the Assy-rian ; we have taken our horses instead of our prayers ; ' and gone about to find out good : we have been so foolish as to think that the idols, which have been beholden to our hands for any shape that is in them, could be instead of hands, and of God unto us, to help us in our need : but now we know that men of high degree are but a lie [e], that horses are but a vanity [f], that an idol is nothing [g], and therefore can give

a Gen. xliii. 31.   b Psalm lxviii. 19.   c Ephes. iv. 8.   d Acts ii. 23.
e Psalm lxii. 9.   f Psalm xxxiii. 17.   xx. 7.   g 1 Cor. viii. 4.

nothing :—that power belongeth unto thee, none else can do it ; that mercy belongeth unto thee, none else will do it : therefore since in thee only the fatherless find mercy, be thou pleased to do us good."

We will consider the words, First, Absolutely, as a single prayer by themselves :—Secondly, Relatively, in their connexion, and with respect to the scope of the place.

From the former consideration we observe, that all the good we have, is from God : he only must be sought unto for it: we have none in ourselves ; " I know, that in me, that is, in my flesh, dwelleth no good [g]." We can neither think, nor speak, nor do it [h].

And missing it in ourselves, it is all in vain to seek for it in things below ourselves.

They can provide for our back and belly ;—and yet not that neither without God : the root, out of which the fruits of the earth do grow, is above in Heaven ; the genealogy of corn and wine, is resolved into God [i]. But if you go to your lands, or houses, or treasuries for physic for a sick soul, or a guilty conscience, they will all return an ' ignoramus' to that enquiry. Salvation doth not grow in the furrows of the field ; neither are there in the earth to be found any mines or harvests of grace or comfort.

In God alone is " the fountain of life [k] :" he that only " is good [l]," he only " doth good [m]." When we have wearied ourselves with having recourse to second causes, here at last, like the wandering dove, we must arrive for rest. " Many will say, Who will show us any good ? do thou lift up the light of thy countenance upon us [n]." From him alone " comes every good gift [o] :" whether temporal, it is his blessing that maketh the creature able to comfort us [p]. The woman touched the hem of Christ's garment ; but the virtue went not out of the garment, but out of Christ [q]. Or whether spiritual, sanctified faculties [r], sanctified habits [s], sanctified motions [t], glorious relations [u], in predestination, adoption,

[g] Rom. vii. 18.   [h] Gen. vi. 5. 2 Cor. iii. 5. Matth. xii. 34. Psalm xiv. 3.
[i] Hos. ii. 22.   [k] Psalm xxxvi. 9.   [l] Matth. xix. 17.   [m] Psalm cxix. 68.
[n] Psalm iv. 6.   [o] James i. 17.   [p] Prov. x. 2. Matth. iv. 4. 1 Tim. iv. 5.
[q] Luke viii. 44.   [r] 1 John v. 20. Phil. ii. 13. Jer. xxxii. 39. Rom. v. 5.
[s] Ephes. ii. 8, 9, 10. Col. ii. 11, 12.   [t] 2 Tim. ii. 25. Phil. ii. 13.   [u] Ephes.
i. 5, 6. John i. 12.

and Christian liberty : excellent gifts [x], heavenly comforts [y], all and only from him [z]. And that without change and alteration: he doth not do good one while, and evil another ; but goodness is his proper and native operation. He is not the author of sin, that entered by the devil ; he is not the author of death, that entered by sin ; but " our destruction is of ourselves [a]." And therefore though the prophet say [b], " Is there any evil in the city which the Lord hath not done?" yet he doth it not but only as it is ' bonum justitiæ,' good in order to his glory. For it is just with God, that they who run from the order of his commands, should fall under the order of his providence; and doing willingly what he forbids, should unwillingly suffer what he threateneth.

In one word, God is the author of all good,—by his grace working it: the permitter of all evil,—by his patience enduring it : the orderer and disposer of both,—by his mercy, rewarding the one,—by his justice, revenging the other,— and by his wisdom, directing both to the ends of his eternal glory.

SECT. 16. This serveth to discover the free and sole working of grace in our first conversion, and the continued working of grace in our further sanctification; whatsoever is good in us habitually, as grace inhering,—or actually, as grace working,—is from him alone as the author of it. For though it be certain, that when we will and do, ourselves are agents, yet it is still under and from him. " Certum est nos facere, cum faciamus ; sed ille facit, ut faciamus [c]," as the great champion of grace speaketh; by grace we are that we are ; we do what we do, in God's service. Vessels have no wine, bags have no money in them, but what the merchant putteth in: the bowls of the candlesticks had no oil, but that which dropped from the olive-branches.

Other things which seek no higher perfection than is to be found within the compass of their own nature [d], may, by the guidance and activity of the same nature, attain thereunto :

[x] 1 Cor. xii. 6.   [y] 2 Cor. i. 3. Rom. xv. 13.   [z] Concil. Milevit. Can. iii. 4, 5.—Concil. Arausican. secund.—*Aug.* de Grat. et Lib. Arb. c. 21.   [a] Hos. xiii. 9.   [b] Amos iii. 6. Isai. xlv. 7.—Vid. *Tertul.* contr. Marcion. l. 2. c. 14.   [c] *Aug.* de Grat. et Lib. Arb. c. 6.—de Grat. Christi c. 25. contr. 2. ep. Pelag. l. 4. c. 6.—de Perfect. Justitiæ, c. 19.   [d] *Aug.* de Civ. Dei, l. 2. c. 9.—*Field,* of the Church, l. 1. c. 2.

but man aspiring to a divine happiness, can never attain thereunto but by a divine strength : impossible it is for any man to enjoy God without God[e].

The truth of this point showeth it in five gradations :—

1st. By grace, our minds are enlightened[f] to know and believe him : for spiritual things are spiritually discerned.

2nd. By grace, our hearts are inclined to love and obey him[g]; for spiritual things are spiritually approved. He only by his almighty and ineffable operation worketh in us, " et veras revelationes, et bonas voluntates[h]."

3rd. By grace, our lives are enabled to work what our hearts do love[i]: without which, though we should will, yet we cannot perform; no more than the knife which hath a good edge, is able actually to cut till moved by the hand.

4th. By grace, our good works are carried on unto perfection[k]. Adam, wanting the grace of perseverance, fell from innocency itself : it is not sufficient for us that he prevent and excite us to will[l], that he co-operate and assist us to work, except he continually follow and supply us with a residue of spirit, to perfect and finish what we set about: all our works are begun, continued, and ended in him.

Lastly, By grace, our perseverance is crowned : for our best works could not endure the trial of justice[m], if God should enter into judgement with us. Grace enableth us to work, and grace rewardeth us for working. Grace beginneth[n], and grace finisheth both our faith and salvation. The work of holiness is nothing but grace ; and the reward of holiness is nothing but grace for grace.

SECT. 17. Secondly, This teacheth us how to know good from evil in ourselves. What we look on as good, we must see how we have derived it from God. The more recourse we have had unto God by prayer, and faith, and study of his will, in the procurement of it, the more goodness we shall find in it. A thing done may be good in the substance of

---

[e] *Aug.* de patientia, c. 18.   [f] 1 Cor. ii. 12, 14. Matth. xi. 27. Jer. xxxi. 34. Vid. *Aug.* de Grat. Christ. l. 1. c. 13, 14. et ep. 143.   [g] John vi. 45. Ezek. iii. 26. Jer. xxxii. 29.   [h] *Aug.* de Grat. Christ. c. 24.   [i] Heb. xiii. 20. Rom. vii. 18. Phil. ii. 13.   [k] 1 Thess. v. 22. 1 Pet. v. 10. Jude v. 24. John xvii. 15.   [l] Vid. *Aug.* Enchirid. c. 31. de Grat. et Lib. Arb. c. 6. et 17.—Peto ut accipiam ; et cum accepero, rursus peto. *Hieron.* ad Ctesiphont.   [m] Psalm cxliii. 2. Isai. lxiv. 6.   [n] Phil. i. 6. Heb. xii. 2.

the work, and yet evil in the manner of doing it[o]: as the substance of a vessel may be silver, but the use sordid. Jehu's zeal was rewarded as an act of justice, 'quoad substantiam operis[p];' and it was punished too as an act of policy, 'quoad modum,' for the perverse end. A thing which I see in the night, may shine, and that shining proceed from nothing but rottenness. We must not measure ourselves by the matter of things done; for there may be 'Malum opus in bona materia[q].' Doeg prays, and Herod hears, and hypocrites fast, and Pharisees preach: but when we would know the goodness of our works[r], look to the fountain, whether they proceed from the Father of lights by the spirit of love, and the grace of Christ, from humble, penitent, filial, heavenly dispositions. Nothing will carry the soul unto God, but that which cometh from him. Our communion with the Father, and the Son, is the trial of all our goodness.

Thirdly, This should exceedingly abase us in our own eyes, and stain all the pride, and cast down all the plumes of flesh and blood, when we seriously consider, that in us, as now degenerated from our original[s], there is no good to be found; our wine become water[t], and our silver dross. As our Saviour saith of the devil, when he lies, he speaks 'de suo[u],' of his own; so when we do evil, we work, 'de nostro,' of our own, and 'secundum hominem,' as the apostle speaks, "According unto man[x]." Lusts are our own[y]; our very members[z] to that body of sin, which the apostle calleth the "old man[a];" with which it is as impossible to do any good, as for a toad to spit cordials.

Men are apt to glory of their good hearts and intentions, only because they cannot search them[b]; and, being carnal themselves, to entertain none but carnal notions of God's service. But if they knew the purity and jealousy of God, and their own impotency to answer so holy a will, they would

---

[o] Phil. i. 15, 16.   [p] 2 Kings x. 30.   [q] 1 Sam. xxi. 7. Mark vi. 20. Acts xxiv. 25. Isai. lviii. 3. Matth. vi. 16. xxiii. 2, 3.   [r] Rebus, ad ima tendentibus, in imo ponitur fundamentum: Ecclesia verò, in imo posita, tendit in Cœlum ; fundamentum ergo nostrum ibi positum est. *Aug.* enarr. 1. in Psalm 29.   [s] Jer. ii. 21.   [t] Isai. i. 22. Ezek. xxii. 18.   [u] John viii. 44.   [x] 1 Cor. iii. 3.   [y] Rom. ii. 24.   [z] James i. 14.   [a] Col. iii. 5. Ephes. iv. 22.   [b] Jer. xvii. 11.

lay their hands upon their mouths, and with Job [c], abhor themselves; and with Isaiah [d], bewail the uncleanness of their lips; and with Moses [e], fear and quake, as not being able to endure the things that are commanded; and with Joshua [f], acknowledge that they cannot serve God because he is holy. They would then remember, that the law of God is a law of fire [g], and the tribunal of God, a tribunal of fire [h]; that the pleadings of God with sinners, are in flames of fire [i]; that the trial of all our works shall be by fire [k]; that the God before whom we must appear, is a consuming fire [l]. Go now, and bring thy straw and stubble, thy drowsy and sluggish devotion, thy fickle and flattering repentance, thy formal and demure services into the fire, to the law to measure them, to the judge to censure them: nay, now carry them to thine own conscience; and tell me whether that will not pass the Father's verdict upon them, " Sordet in conspectu judicis, quod fulget in conspectu operantis [m]," That which is fair in thine eye, is filthy in God's.

SECT. 18. Lastly, This serveth for exhortation unto these particular duties:—First, Unto patience and meekness under any evil, that God may bring upon us; and that not barely, because he doth us good in other things, which was Job's argument, " Shall we receive good from the Lord, and not evil [n]?" But further, because the very evils that come upon us, are oftentimes by him intended for good, as Joseph told his brethren [o]. We are not angry with the physician when he lanceth [p], dieteth, and restraineth us of our will: he denieth us our will, that we may have our will: a sick man is many times most faithfully served, when he is crossed. I lop my trees, bruise my grapes, grind my corn to fit it to the ends whereunto it tendeth. God's end is merciful when his hand is heavy, as John's roll was sweet in the mouth [q], but bitter in the belly: so troubles may be bitter to the palate, but profitable to the conscience: like hot spices that bite the tongue, but comfort the stomach.

---

[c] Job xlii. 5, 6.   [d] Isai. vi. 5.   [e] Heb. xii. 20.   [f] Josh. xxiv. 29.
[g] Deut. xxxiii. 2.   [h] Ezek. i. 27.   [i] Ezek. lxvi. 15, 16.   [k] 1 Cor. iii. 13.
[l] Heb. xii. 29.   [m] *Greg.*   [n] Job. ii. 10.   [o] Gen. l. 20.   [p] Medicina etiam invitis prodest. *Sen.* ep. 98.—Quæ per insuavitatem medentur, emolumento curationis offensam sui excusant, et præsentem injuriam superventuræ utilitatis gratia commendant. *Tert.* de pœnit. c. 10.   [q] Rev. x. 9. Heb. xii. 11. Isai. xxvii. 9. xlviii. 10.

And as it dictateth patience in suffering evil, so in doing
our duties, though we suffer contempt and reproaches for it[r].
If we were to receive our rewards from men, their frowns
might discourage us: but when we have done God's will,
God himself will be our reward, and make his promises a
comfort unto us. Moses and Aaron, though their whole
employments were for the good of Israel, were yet repaid
with murmuring and discontent; and the people, like children, 'qui cibum sumunt, sed flentes,' (to use the similitude
of the orator in Aristotle[s],) repined at the food which their
prayers obtained for them, yet nothing dismayed them from
their duty. "Etiam post naufragium, tentantur maria[t]."
The woman of Canaan prays on, when she is denied; and
Jacob holds with his hands, when his thigh is lamed. Our
first care must be to be in our way, to be doing our duties;
and then though (as Solomon speaks) we should meet "a
lion in our way," we must not be dismayed; for angels are
stronger than lions, and "he hath given his angels charge
over us, to bear us in our ways[u]." Yea, whilst we are with
him, he himself is with us[x]. So that the way of the Lord
is the surest and safest walk that any man can have; "The
way of the Lord is strength to the upright[y]."

Secondly, Unto humility: If thou be a vessel of gold, and
thy brother but of wood, be not high-minded; it is God that
maketh thee to differ[z]: the more bounty God shows, the
more humility he requires. Those mines that are richest[a],
are deepest: those stars that are highest, seem smallest: the
goodliest buildings have the lowest foundations: the more God
honoureth men the more they should humble themselves: the
more the fruit, the lower the branch on which it grows; pride
is ever the companion of emptiness. O! how full was the
apostle, yet how low was his language of himself[b]! "Least
of saints; last of apostles; chief of sinners; no sufficiency to
think;—no abilities to do; all that he is, he is by grace." Thus

[r] Quisquis volens detrahit famæ meæ, nolens addit mercedi meæ. *Aug.* contr.
literas Petiliani, l. 3. c. 7. [s] Rhet. l. 3. c. 4. [t] Sen. ep. 81. [u] Psalm
xci. 81. [x] 2 Chron. xv. 2. [y] Prov. x. 29. [z] 1 Cor. iv. 7. Rom. xi. 20.
Ille discernit, qui unde discernaris impertit, pœnam debitam removendo, indebi-
tam gratiam largiendo. *Aug.* contr. 2. ep. Pelag. l. 2. c. 7. [a] Opulentissima
metalla, quorum in alto latent venæ. *Sen.* Ep. 23. Altissima flumina minimo
sono labuntur. Q. *Curt.* l. 7. [b] Ephes. iii. 8. 1 Cor. xv. 8. 2 Tim. i. 15.
2 Cor. iii. 5. Rom. vii. 18.—Vid. *Aug.* de Grat. et Lib. Arb. c. 8.

humility teacheth us, in our operation, to draw strength from God, not from ourselves: in our graces, to ascribe their goodness to God, and their weakness to ourselves.

Thirdly, Unto dependence and continual recourse to God, as the fountain of all good, to keep an open and unobstructed passage between him and our soul. Say not, " I have light enough in my house; I may now shut up my windows;" for light within hath dependence upon immediate supplies from the sun without, and so hath grace upon continual supplies from the Sun of righteousness. God teacheth even the husbandman to plough and thresh[c]. In these things his direction is to be implored. Meddle not then with great and high affairs without recourse unto him. His name is ' counsellor[d],' and his testimonies are counsellors[e]; let them be the rule and square of all your debates. It is recorded for the honour of Scipio[f], that he went first to the Capitol, and then to the senate: but you have more noble examples: David is put to flight[g], he flees and prays: Ezekiah is at a stand in all his counsels[h], he sends to the prophet and prays: Jehoshaphat is in great distress[i], and knows not what in the world to do, but he prays: Nehemiah is sore afraid[k], and hath a petition to make to the king, but first he makes one to God, and prays. Whenever the children are come to the birth, and there is no strength to bring forth, all the world cannot furnish you with such another midwife as prayer, and recourse to God; it hath delivered even graves of their dead. Therefore let me beseech you, whenever you meet with such difficulties as put you to a stand, that you know not what to advise or resolve upon,—go to your closets, prostrate yourselves at his throne, whose honour it is to be seen in the mount; beg counsel of him in whom are hid all the treasures of wisdom and knowledge. Let it appear, that you seek his face to direct you, and his glory as the supreme end and design of all your consultations; and then try whether he be not a present help in trouble; and whether he will not magnify the wisdom of his counsel in the perplexity of yours.

---

[c] Isai. xxviii. 26.   [d] Isai. ix. 6.   [e] Psalm cxix. 24.   [f] *Liv.* l. 26.—
Aul. Gel. l. 7. 1.—*Valer. Maxim.* l. 1. c. 2.   [g] 2 Sam. xv. 26. 31.
[h] Isai. xlvii. 3, 4, 14.   [i] 2 Chron. xx. 6.   [k] Nehem. ii. 3, 4.

Fourthly, Unto fidelity, in the use of any good which God bestows upon us; for God gives not talents to men, barely to enrich men, but to employ them. Therefore, as the vessel hath one passage to let the wine into itself, and another to pour it out into the flaggon, so we should not only fill ourselves by dependence upon God, but should supply others by love and service unto our brethren.

Right Honourable, This nation hath put into your hands all that is outwardly dear unto them, their persons, posterities, liberties, estates. In these sad and woful distractions, they look upon you as binders, and healers, and standers in the gap, and repairers of waste places. God hath called you unto a high and a great trust; and the sad distempers of the Church and state, the distresses and desolations of Ireland, the doubts and fears, the shiverings and convulsions of England, and in these two the interest of all the protestant churches call upon you, like the man of Macedonia, in St. Paul's vision [1], " Come and help us." Now in this great strait, when the children are come to the birth, and there is no strength to bring forth,—stir up the graces of God in you; call together all that is within you, to call upon his name; improve the uttermost of your interests in him for the state of his church; manage every one of his gifts to the closing of those miserable breaches which threaten an inundation of calamity upon us : wisdom, and learning, and piety, and prudence, are healing things. Remember (and O that God would put it into the hearts of this whole kingdom, from the throne to the plough, to remember) the fate of a divided kingdom from the mouth of truth itself: O that we would all remember, that misunderstandings, and jealousies, and divisions of heart, are a high evidence of God's displeasure, and that " through the wrath of the Lord of Hosts, a land is darkened, and (as it were) infatuated, when Manasseh is against Ephraim, and Ephraim against Manasseh, and every man eateth the flesh of his own arm [m]." O let us all remember what it cost Shechem and Abimelech, what it cost Benjamin and the other tribes, even the loss of threescore and five thousand men. Remember Priamus and his children will laugh; Babylon will clap their hands, and wag

[1] Acts xvi. 2.   [m] Isai. ix. 9, 21.

their head ; no such time for Shishak the Egyptian to trouble Jerusalem, as when Israel is divided [n]. Let it never be said of God's own people, that they are fallen into the curse of Midianites, and Amorites, and Edomites, and Philistines, to help forward the destruction of one another. O ! that God would give this whole nation hearts to consider these things, that he would put a spirit of peace and resolved unity into the minds of this whole people, to be true to their own happiness ; and by how much the greater are the subtilties of men to divide them, to be so much the more firmly united in prayers to God, and in concord between themselves, that they may not expose their persons, estates, posterities, and (which is dearest of all) their religion, to the crafty and bloody advantages of the enemies of the protestant churches, who, in human view, could have no way to overthrow them, but by their own dissensions.

I have done with this point, and shall conclude all with a very few words of the next, which is drawn from the scope and connexion of the prayer, suggested to the judgement threatened. It is this:

SECT. 19. When temporal judgements are felt or feared, God's people should pray for spiritual mercies. Human sorrows cannot overcome, where the joy of the Lord is our strength. Thus the Lord seems to have taught his apostle : he was under some pressing discomfort ; the messenger of Satan sent to buffet him ; he prays for particular deliverance, and God answers him ' non ad voluntatem sed ad utilitatem [o],' implying a direction unto all such prayers, " My grace is sufficient for thee [p]." When thou feelest a thorn in thy flesh, pray for grace in thy heart; the buffets of Satan cannot hurt, where the grace of God doth suffice : so he directeth in time of plague and famine, to pray, and to seek his face [q]; to look more after his favour than our own ease ; to be more solicitous for the recovering of his love, than for the removing of his rod. This is a true character of a filial disposition. " In the way of thy judgements," even in that way, wherein wicked men fling thee off, and give thee over,

[n] 2 Chron. xii. 2.　　[o] Bonus, qui non tribuit quod volumus, ut attribuat quod mallemus. *Aug.* ep. 34. tom. 2. p. 42. Exaudiens cardinem desiderii ejus, non curasti quod tunc petebat, ut in me faceres quod semper petebat. *Conf.* l. 5. c. 8. tom. 8. p. 82.　　[p] 2 Cor. xii. 9.　　[q] 2 Chron. vii. 14.

and quarrell with thee, and repine against thee, even in the
way of thy judgements " do we wait for thee, and the desire
of our soul" is more to thy name, than to our own deliverance [r]. True disciples follow Christ more for his doctrine
than his loaves [s], and are willing to choose rather affliction
than iniquity [t].

The grace and favour of God is ' life [u],' ' better than life [x]:'
and therefore must needs be the most sovereign antidote to
preserve, and to bear up the soul above all other discomforts ;
whereas if he be angry, no other helps are able to relieve us.
Brass and iron can fence me against a bullet, or against a
sword : but if I were to be cast into a furnace of fire, it
would help to torment me ; if into a pit of water, it would
help to sink me. Now our God is a ' consuming fire [y],' and
his breath a ' stream of brimstone [z].' Human plaisters can
never cure the wounds which God makes : where he is the
smiter, he must be the healer too [a]. All the candles in a
country are not able to make day there, till the sun come ;
and all the contents of the world are not able to make comfort to the soul, till the Sun of righteousness arise, with healing in his wings." In a mine, if a damp come, it is in vain
to trust to your lights ; they will burn blue, and dim, and at
last vanish : you must make haste to be drawn upward, if you
will be safe. When God sharpeneth an affliction with his
displeasure, it is vain to trust to worldly succours ; your desires and affections must be on ' things above,' if you will be
relieved. There is no remedy, no refuge from God's anger,
but to God's grace. Blood-letting is a cure of bleeding [b],
and a burn a cure against a burn ; and running unto God is
the way to escape him ; as to close and get in with him that
would strike you, doth avoid the blow. In a tempest at sea,
it is very dangerous to strike to the shore ; the safest way is
to have sea-room, and to keep in the main still :—there is no
landing against any tempest of God's judgements at any
shore of worldly or carnal policies, but the way is to keep
with him still : if he be with us in the ship, the winds and
the sea will at last be rebuked.

---

[r] Isai. xxvi. 8.   [s] John vi. 29.   [t] John xvi. 21. xxxv. 9, 10.   [u] Psalm
xxx. 5.   [x] Psalm lxiii. 3.   [y] Heb. xii. 29.   [z] Isai. xxx. 33.
[a] Hos. vi. 1.   [b] Calores caloribus onerando, sanguinis fluxum defusa insuper
deprimimus et venula revocamus. *Tert.*

SECT. 20. This then should serve to humble us for our carnal prayers in times of judgements, such as the hungry raven, or the dry or gaping earth makes, when we assemble ourselves for corn and wine, for peace and safety, and be, in the mean time, careless whether God receive us graciously or no. God much complains of it, when he slew Israel, the rack made him roar, the rod made him flatter, but all was to be rid of affliction: it was the prayer of nature for ease, not of the Spirit for grace, for their " heart was not right [c]." The like he complains of after the captivity [d] : they fasted and prayed in the fifth month, wherein the city and temple had been burned ; and in the seventh month, wherein Gedaliah had been slain, and the remnant carried captive ; but they did it not out of sincerity toward God, but out of policy for themselves : and this he proves by their behaviour after their return. If you had indeed sought me, you would have remembered the words of the prophets, when Jerusalem was inhabited before, and being returned, would now have put them to practice. But Jerusalem, inhabited after the captivity, is just like Jerusalem inhabited before the captivity : so that from hence it appears, that all their weeping and separating was not for pious, but politic reasons [e]. And there is nothing under Heaven more hateful, or more reproachful unto God, than to make religion serve turns, to have piety lackey and dance attendance, and be a drudge and groom to private ends, to make it a cloak to policy, a varnish to rotten wood, silver, dross to a broken potsherd.

O then, when we weep, and separate ourselves, let us not then think to mock God with empty ceremonies of repentance ; let us not assemble ourselves only to flatter away the rod from our back, and to get peace and security to our own persons ; and then let the favour of God, the power of his grace, the comforts of his Spirit, be unregarded as before ; as if we fasted and prayed only for our backs and bellies, not for our consciences or conversations : for be we well assured, he who doth not ask the things which he ought, shall not obtain the things which he asks : such a prayer begs nothing but a denial.

We have, now many fasts together, prayed for making up

* Psalm lxxviii. 34, 37.   d Jer. xlii. 12. xli. 1.   e Zach. vii. 5, 6.

our breaches, for repairing our ruins, for composing our distractions, for reducing this kingdom unto a happy constitution, for a right understanding between the king and his
great council. These prayers we have not found yet return
like Noah's dove, with an olive-branch, a gracious answer
unto us again. What is the reason? where is the obstruc-
tion? Is not he a God that heareth prayers? Is it not his
title? Doth he not glory in it? Certainly mercies stop not
at God, but at us. "We are not straitened in him, but in
our own bowels." If there come but a little light into a
room, the defect is not in the sun, but in the narrowness of
the window : if a vessel fill but slowly, the fault is not in
any emptiness in the fountain, but the smallness of the pipe.
If mercies ripen slowly, or stop at any time in the way, it is
not because they are unwilling to come to us, but because
we are unfit to enjoy them. Our prayers doubtless, in many
of us, have not been words taken from him, but from our
own carnal dictates.

We would fain have things well in our country; but
have we hitherto looked after our consciences? The distractions without us,—have they driven us to consider the
distempers within, or to desire the things above? The un-
settledness of peace in the kingdom,—hath it awakened us
to secure our peace with God? We would fain have better
times[f]; but have we yet laboured for better hearts? We
would fain have a right understanding between the king and
his great council; but have we yet sadly set about it, to
have a more clear and sweet communion between us and
our God? We long to see more good laws ; but are we yet
come to the care of good lives ? Every one cries out, "Who
will show us any good?" but how few think on "the light
of God's countenance."

Hence, hence, beloved, is the miscarriage of all our prayers. If we would seek God's kingdom, we are promised other
things by way of overplus and accession ; as he that buyeth a treasury of jewels, hath the cabinet into the bargain.
But when we place our kingdom in outward comforts, and
let our 'daily bread' shut all the other five petitions out
of our prayers; no wonder if the 'promises of this life,'

[f] Semper dies mali in seculo, boni in Deo. *Aug.* in Psalm 33.

which are annexed unto godliness, do not answer those prayers, wherein godliness is neglected. It were preposterous to begin the building of a house at the roof and not at the foundation: piety is the foundation of prosperity. If you would have your " children like plants and like polished stones, your garners full, your cattle plenteous, no complaining in your streets ᵍ;" if you would have the king happy, and the church happy, and the state happy, and peace and prosperity flourish again; let our chief prayer be, " Lord, make us a happy people by being our God." Give us thyself, thy grace, thy favour; give us renewed hearts, and reformed lives; let not our sins confute, and outcry, and belie our prayers, and pray them back again without an answer. And when we seek thee and thy Christ above all, we know that with him thou wilt freely give us all other things ʰ.'ⁱ The spiritual good things which we beg, will either remove, or shelter and defend us from the outward evil things which we suffer.

SECT. 21. Secondly, This serveth for an instruction unto us touching a sanctified use of God's judgements, or threatenings: when we "learn obedience," as Christ did, "by the things which we suffer ⁱ;"—when παθήματα are μαθήματα, that we are chastened and taught together ᵏ;—when sufferings do quicken spiritual desires ; and the more troubles we find in our way, the more love we have to our country;—when we can say, "All this is come upon us, and yet we have not forgotten thee ˡ;"—when we can serve God as well in 'ploughing and breaking the clods,' as in 'treading out the corn ᵐ;'—when, with Jonah, we can delight in him, even in the whale's belly, and suffer not our love of him to be quenched with all the waters of the sea; when we can truly say to him, ' Lord, love me, and then do what thou wilt unto me ; let me feel thy rod, rather than forfeit thine affection;'—when we can look through the anger of his

---

ᵍ Psalm cxliv. 12, 15.   ʰ Quicquid mihi præter illum est, dulce non est; quicquid mihi vult dare Dominus meus, auferat totum, et se mihi det. *Aug.* Enarr. 2. in Psalm xxvi.—Hic quod vinum est, non potest esse panis ; quod tibi lux est, non potest esse potus : Deus tuus totum tibi erit. Manducabis eum, ne esurias; bibes eum, ne sitias ; illuminaberis ab eo, ne sis cæcus ; fulcieris ab eo, ne deficias. *Ib.* in Psalm xxxvi.   ⁱ Heb. v. 8.   ᵏ Psalm xciv. 12.   ˡ Psalm xlv. 17, 18.   ᵐ Hos. x. 11.

chastisements unto the beauty of his commands; and to the
sweetness of his loving countenance, as by a rainbow we see
the beautiful image of the sun's light in the midst of dark
and waterish clouds;—when by how much the flesh is the
fuller of pain, by so much prayers are fuller of spirit; by
how much the heavier are our earthly sufferings, by so much
the stronger are our heavenly desires;—when God threateneth punishments, and we pray for grace,—this is a sanctified
use of God's judgements. And this we should all be exhorted unto in the times of distraction, to make it the principal argument of our prayers and study of our lives, to obtain spiritual good things; and the less comfort we find in
the world, to be the more importunate for the comforts of
God, that by them we may encourage ourselves, as David
did in his calamity at Ziklag[n]; when the city Shechem was
beaten down to the ground, then the men and women fled to
the strong tower, and shut that upon them[o]. " The name of
the Lord is a strong tower; the righteous flee to it and are
safe[p]."

Herein we shall more honour God, when we set him up in
our hearts as our fear and treasure, and mourn more towards
him, than for the miseries we feel; and suspire more after
him, than all the outward contentment which we want.

Herein we shall more exercise repentance, for it is worldly
sorrow which droopeth under the pain of the flesh, but godly
sorrow is most of all affected with the anger of God.

Herein we shall more prevail with God, the more heavenly
the matters of your prayers are, the more prevalent they
must needs be with a heavenly Father. We have five spiritual petitions unto one for bread; the more suitable our
prayers are to God's will, the more easy access they will have
to his ear. The covenant of grace turns precepts into promises, and the spirit of grace turns precepts and promises
into prayers. It is not God's will, that we should live without afflictions, but ' our sanctification is God's will[q].' The
more prayers proceed from love, the more acceptable to the
God of love:—now prayer against judgements proceeds from
fear; but prayer for grace and favour proceeds from love.

Lastly, Hereby we shall more benefit ourselves: God's

[n] 1 Sam. xxx. 6.   [o] Judges ix. 51.   [p] Prov. xviii. 18.   [q] 1 Thess. iv. 3.

grace is much better than our own ease ; it gives us meekness to submit, it gives us strength to bear, it gives us wisdom to benefit by, our afflictions.

God's favour is much better than our own ease, and is a recompense for sufferings beyond all their evils. A man would be contented to be loaded with gold, so he might have it for the bearing ; though it be heavy, yet it is precious, and God's favour turns affliction into gold. "If he gives quietness, nothing can give trouble[r];" and if he keep back his grace and favour, nothing can give peace : neither wealth, nor honours, nor pleasures, nor crowns, nor all the world, with the fulness, or rather the emptiness thereof, can do us any good at all. Any thing which will consist with the reign of lust, with the guilt of sin, with the curse of the law, with the wrath of God, with horrors of conscience, and with the damnation of hell, is too base to be called the good of man. "To do judgement, to love mercy, and walk humbly with God," this is 'bonum hominis,' the good of man[s]; "to fear God, to keep his commandments," this is 'totum hominis,' the whole end, and happiness of man[t].

O! then get remission and removal of sin; get this 'bonum hominis,' the oil of grace in your lamps, peace of God in your hearts, the streams of the rivers of God in your consciences : and then, though the earth be moved, and the mountains shake, and the waters roar, whatever distractions, whatever desolations happen, 'Impavidum ferient ruinæ ;' thou shalt find a chamber in God's providence, a refuge in his promises, 'a pavilion in the secret of his presence,' to protect and to comfort thee above them all.

---

[r] Job xxxiv. 29.   [s] Mich. vi. 8.   [t] Eccles. xii. 13.

THE

SECOND SERMON.

HOSEA XIV. 2, 3.

—— *So will we render the calves of our lips.* 3. *Asshur shall not save us: we will not ride upon horses; neither will we say to the work of our hands, Ye are our gods, &c.*

In the whole context, we have before observed two general parts; 'Israel's prayer,' and 'Israel's promise.' The prayer we have handled; and do now proceed unto the promise, wherein are two things to be considered: 1. The covenant itself. 2. The ground upon which they make it; God's mercy to the fatherless.—First then, of the covenant, wherein they promise two things. 1. Thanksgiving, for God's hearing and answering of their prayers. 2. A special care for amendment of their lives.

"*We will render the calves of our lips.*"] The apostle, out of the Septuagint, reads it, " the fruit of our lips[a]." It is the use of the Scripture to describe spiritual duties by expressions, drawn from ceremonies and usages under the law; as repentance is called 'washing[b],'—and prayer, 'incense[c];' and the righteousness of saints[d], ' fine linen,' being an allusion to the garments of the priests[e]; and Christ[f], ' an altar,' whereby both our persons and services are sanctified and accepted[g]. Thus here, the spiritual sacrifices of praise are called ' calves,' to show the end of all sacrifices, which were or-

---

[a] Pro פרים legisse videntur פרי Heb. xiii. 15. [b] Isai. i. 26. [c] Psalm cxli. 2. Rev. v. 8. [d] Rev. iii. 18. vii. 14. Psalm xxxii. 9. Exod. xxviii. 2. Zach. iii. 4. Psalm xlv. 8. [e] Rev. xix. 8. [f] Vide *Reynolds'* Conference with Hart, c. 8. div. 4. et *Aquin.* in Heb. xiii. 10. Habemus altare viz. corpus Christi. *Hesych.* in Liv. l. 1. c. 4. [g] Heb. xiii. 10. Rom. xii. 1. 1 Peter ii. 5 Isai. lvi. 7.

dained for the stirring up of spiritual affections and praises unto God [h]; and also to intimate the vanity of ceremonial without real services. The beast on the altar was but a carnal,—but the faith of the heart, and the confession of the mouth, was a reasonable, sacrifice. No point more insisted on in the prophets than this [i]. They had idolatrously dishonoured God with their calves of Dan and Bethel, and they had carnally and superstitiously placed all worship and holiness in the calves of the altar: but now they resolve to worship God neither politicly, after human inventions; nor perfunctorily, with mere outward ceremonies: but spiritually and from inward affections: for the lips are moved by the heart.

Now thanksgiving is further called the ' calves,' or sacrifices ' of the lips,' to intimate, that, after all God's rich mercies upon us in pardoning our sins, and in multiplying his grace and spiritual comforts upon us,—we, like beggars, have nothing to return, but the bare acknowledgements and praises of our lips, words for wonders : and those words too his own gifts; we cannot render them to him, before we have received them from him [k].

SECT. 2. *Asshur shall not save us.*] Unto the general confession of sin, intimated in those words, " *take away all iniquity,*" here is added a particular detestation of their special sins, with a covenant to forsake them ; lest, waxing wanton with pardon and grace, they should relapse into them again. The sum is, to confess the vanity of carnal confidence, betaking itself to the aid of men, to the strength of horses, to the superstition of idols, for safety and deliverance. All which they are, now at last, by their experience and by their repentance, taught to abandon, as things which indeed cannot, and therefore they are resolved shall not, save them.

By the *Assyrian* is here intimated ' all human succour, procured by sinful correspondence;' by a synecdoche of the part for the whole. But he is particularly mentioned, 1. Because he was the chief monarch of the world ; to show, that the greatest worldly succours are vain, when they are

[h] Vide *Tertul.* contr. Judæos, c. 5, 6. et de Oratione, c. 1.—*Aug.* de Civ. Dei, l. 10. c. 5. et ep. 49.   [i] Isai. i. 15. Mic. vi. 6, 7, 8. Amos iv. 4. v. 5. ii. 1. Psalm l. 13, 15. lxix. 30, 31.   [k] Psalm cxvi. 12, 13. Matth. xii. 34. 1 Chron. xxix. 16.

relied upon without, or against God. 2. Because the Scripture takes notice often of it as their particular sin, the sending unto, relying upon, and paying tribute unto him for aid
and assistance[1]. 3. Because, instead of helping, he did
greatly afflict them. Their flying unto him, was like a bird's
flying into a snare, or a fish's avoiding the pole wherewith
the water is troubled, by swimming into the net.

By *horses* we are to understand the ' military preparations
and provisions' which they made for themselves, both at
home, and from Egypt[n].

By the *work of their hands*, are meant their ' idols,' which
were beholden to their hands for any shape or beauty that
was in them. The same hands which formed them, were
afterwards lifted up in worship unto them[o]. Time was when
we said, " These are our gods which brought us up out of
Egypt[p];" but now we will *not say so any more*; for how can
a man be the maker of his Maker ?

" *For in thee the fatherless findeth mercy.*"] This is the
ground of their petition for pardon and grace, and of their
promise of praises and amendment. God's mercy in hearing
the prayers, and in enabling the performances of his people.
It is a metaphor drawn from orphans in their minority, who
are, 1. Destitute of wisdom and abilities to help themselves ;
2. Exposed to violence and injuries ; 3. Committed, for that
reason, to the care of tutors and guardians to govern and
protect them.—The church here acknowledgeth herself an
outcast, destitute of all wisdom and strength within, of all
succour and support from without ; and therefore betaketh
herself solely unto God's tuition, whose mercy can, and
useth to, help when all other help fails.

This is the last link of that golden chain of repentance,
made up of these gradations. 1. An humble address unto
God. 2. A penitent confession of sin. 3. An earnest petition against it. 4 An imploring of grace and favour. 5.
Thanksgiving for so great benefits. 6. A covenant of new
obedience. And lastly, A confidence and quiet repose in God.

[1] Hos. v. 13. vii. 11, 12. 2 *Kings* xv. 19, 20.   [n] 2 Chron. i. 16. Isai. xxxi. 1.
o Isai. xliv. 10, 17. xlvi. 6, 7, 8. Jer. x. 3. xv. 6, 20. Acts xix. 26.   [p] Exod.
xxxii. 4. 1 Kings xii. 28. .   [q] Orphanotrophi sunt, qui, praentibus atque sub-
stantiis destitutos, minores sustentant, et educant velut affectione paterna. Cod.
de Episc. et Cleric. l. 1. Tit. 1. leg. 32. and 35.

Let us now consider, what useful observations the words, thus opened, will afford unto us. And one main point may be collected from the general scope of the place. We see after they have petitioned for pardon and grace, they then restipulate and undertake to perform duties of thankfulness and obedience.

SECT. 10. True penitents, in their conversion from sin, and humiliation for it, do not only pray unto God for mercy, but do further covenant to express the fruits of those mercies in a thankful and obedient conversation. When first we are admitted into the family and household of God, we enter into a covenant. Therefore circumcision, whereby the children of the Jews were first sealed and separated for God, is called his ' covenant[r];' because therein God did covenant to own them, and they did, in the figure, covenant to mortify lust, and to serve him; without which, they were, in his sight, but uncircumcised still. " I will punish[s], saith the Lord, all those that are *circumcised in uncircumcision*;"—so the original runs[t]: and the nations there mentioned with Judah, who are said to be uncircumcised, did yet use 'circumcision[u], as the learned have observed; but being out of covenant with God, it is accounted to them as uncircumcision: and so was that of the Jews too, when they did break covenant with God[x]. And as the Gentiles, being converted, are called ' Jews,' and said to be ' born in Sion[y];' so the Jews, living impenitently, are called ' Gentiles[z], Canaanites, Amorites, Hittites, Ethiopians, Sodomites[a].' In like manner, baptism among Christians is called, by the apostle, συνειδήσεως ἀγαθῆς ἐπερώτημα, which the learned interpret ' the answer, or covenant of keeping a good conscience' towards God[b]; the word signifying ' a question,' or ' interrogation,' which some

---

[r] Gen. xvii. 13.   [s] ' Visitabo super omnes populos incircumcisos :' Versio Chald. 'Ἐπισκέψομαι ἐπὶ πάντας περιτετμημένους ἀκροβυστίας αὐτῶν. *Septuagint.*   [t] Jer. ix. 25.   [u] *Herodot.* l. 2.—*Atapanus* apud Euseb. de Præparat. Evang. l. 9. c. 27.—*Orig.* in Rom. l. 2. c. 2.—*Cyprian.* de ratione Circumcis.—*Clem. Alex.* Strom. l. 1.—*Pierii* Hieroglyph. l. 6.—*Perer.* in Gen. xvii. 13.—*Valles.* de Sacra Philosophia.   [x] Rom ii. 18, 19. Acts vii. 51. [y] Gal. vi. 16. 1 Cor. xii. 2. Psalm lxxxvii. 4, 5.   [z] *Cameron* de Eccl. p. 34.— Nec hoc novum Scripturis figurate uti translatione nominum ex comparatione criminum, &c. *Tert.* cont. Judæos, c. 8. et contr. Marcion. l. 3. c. 8.—*Diodati.*— *Heinsius.*   [a] Ezek. xvi. 3. Hos. xii. 7. Amos ix. 7. Isai. i. 10.   [b] 1 Pet. iii. 21.

would have to be the conscience's making interpellation for
itself to God ;—others to be as much as δοκιμασία, ' the exa-
mining' of a man's self, like that before the Lord's supper c.
I rather·take it as an allusion to the manner of John's baptism, wherein the people first confessed, and consequently
renounced sin; and being taken into Christ's service, or
into that kingdom of God which was at hand, did enquire
after the work which they were to do.   And we find the
same word in Luke iii. 10., which the apostle Peter useth,
ἐπηρώτων αὐτὸν, " The people asked him, saying, What shall
we do ?" whereby is intimated an engaging of themselves,
by a solemn promise and undertaking, to the practice of that
repentance unto which John baptized them.   Whence arose
the grave form of the ancient churches, wherein questions
were proposed to the person baptized touching his ' Faith
and repentance, renouncing the world, the flesh, and the
devil,' with a solemn answer and stipulation obliging thereunto.   Which custom seems to have been derived from the
practice, used in the apostles' time, wherein profession of
faith, unfeigned and sincere repentance, was made before
baptism e. This is the first dedicating of ourselves, and
entering into a covenant with God, which we may call, in
the prophet's expression, ' the subscribing,' or giving a
man's name to God f.

Now the covenant between us and God being perpetual,
" a covenant of salt g ;" as we are to begin it in our own baptism, so we are to continue it to our lives' end, and upon all
fit occasions to repeat and renew it, for our further quickening
and remembrancing unto duties.   So did David h: so Jacob i:

c 1 Cor. xii. 28.   d Luke iii. 10.   e Acts ii. 38. viii. 37. xvi. 3. xix. 4.
f Isai xliv. 5.   Aug. lib. de fide et operibus, c. 9.—Tert. ad Martyr. c. 2. et 3. et
de coron. Milit. c. 3. et 13. de Habitu mulieb, c. 2. de Spectacul. c. 24. et lib. de
Idololatria, Apol. c. 38.—Interrogatio legitima et Ecclesiastica. Firmil. apud
Cypr. ep. 75. et ib. ep 70. et 76.—Salv. l. 6. cod. de Episcop. Audient. l. 34.
sect. 1.—Vide Danœum, in Aug. Enchirid. c. 42.—Brisson. l. Dominic. de spectac.
—Joseph. Vicecomit. de Antiq. Bapt. l. 2.—Gatak. of Lots, p. 319.—Espen. in
Tit. digres. 9. Verbis obligatio contrahitur ex interrogatione et respons. ff. de
obligationibus et Action. l. 1. sect 7. et de verborum obligat. l. 5. sect. 1.
g De pacto salis, vide Paul. Fagi. in Levit. 22. et Perer. in Gen. xix. 16, 17, 26.
Stuck. Antiq. Conviv. l. 1. c. 30.—Sal duraturæ amicitiæ symbolum. Pierius,
lib. 31.—Jer. xxxii. 2 Chron. xiii. 5.   h Psalm cxix. 106.   i Gen. xxviii.
20, 21, 22.

so Asa, and the people in his time [k]: so Hezekiah [l]: so Josiah [m]: so Ezra and Nehemiah [n].

SECT. 4. The reasons, enforcing this duty, may be drawn from several considerations. 1. From God in Christ, where two strong obligations occur, namely, the consideration of his dealing with us, and of our relation unto him. For the former, he is pleased not only to enter into covenant with us, but to bind himself to the performance of what he promiseth. Though whatever he bestow upon us, is all matter of mere and most free grace, wherein he is no debtor to us at all, yet he is pleased to bind himself unto acts of grace. Men love to have all their works of favour free, and to reserve to themselves a power of alteration or revocation, as themselves shall please. But God is pleased, that his gifts should take upon them in some sense the condition of debts [o]; and although he can owe nothing to the creature [p], yet he is contented to be a debtor to his own promise; and having at first in mercy made it, his truth is after engaged to the performance of it [q].

Again, his word is established in Heaven; with him "there is no variableness, nor shadow of change;" his "promises are not Yea and Nay, but in Christ, Amen [r]." If he speak a thing, it shall not fail [s]. He spake, and the world was made: his Word alone is a foundation and bottom to the being of all his creatures; and yet, notwithstanding the immutable certainty of his promises, when they are first uttered, for our sakes he is pleased to bind himself by further ties. [t] Free

---

[k] 2 Chron. xv. 12. 15.   [l] 2 Chron. xxix. 10. xxx. 5. 23.   [m] 2 Chron. xxxiv. 31, 32.   [n] Ezra x. 3. Nehem. ix. 38.   [o] Dignaris eis quibus omnia debita dimittis, etiam promissionibus tuis debitor fieri. *Aug.* Conf. l. 5. c. 9.— Non ei aliquid dedimus, et tenemus debitorem. Unde debitorem? quia promissor est, non dicimus Deo, ' Domine : redde quod accepisti, sed ;' ' redde quod promisisti.' *Aug.* in Psal. xxxii.—Cum promissum Dei redditur, justitia Dei dicitur; justitia enim Dei est, quia redditum est quod promissum est. *Ambros.* in Rom. 3.—Justum est ut reddat quod debet ; debet autem quod pollicitus est : Et hæc est justitia de qua prosumit Apostolus promisso Dei. *Bern.* de grat. et lib. arbit.—Licet Deus debitum alicui det, non tamen est ipse debitor, quia ipse ad alia non ordinatur, sed potius alia ad ipsum ; et ideo justitia, quandoque dicitur in Deo condecentia suæ bonitatis. *Aquin.* part. 1. qu. 21. art. 1.   Nulla alia in Deo justitia, nisi ad se, quasi ad alterum, ut sibi ipsi debitum reddat, secundum condecentiam bonitatis, et rectitudinem voluntatis suæ. *Scotus* 4. dist. 46. q.   [p] Rom. xi. 35. Job xxii. 3. xxxv. 7, 8.   [q] Mic. vii. 20.   [r] 2 Cor. i. 20.   [s] Josh. xxi. 45.   [t] Quid est Dei veri veracisque juratio, nisi promissi confirmatio, et infidelium quædam increpatio ? *Aug.* de Civ. Dei, lib. 16. cap. 32.

mercy, secured by a covenant, and a firm covenant secured by an oath [u]; that we, who, like Gideon, are apt to call for sign upon sign, and to stagger and be disheartened, if we have not double security from God; we, whose doubting calls for promise upon promise, as our ignorance doth for precept upon precept, may, by "two immutable things, wherein it is impossible for God to lie, have strong consolation." Now if God, whose gifts are free, bind himself to bestow them by his promise; if God, whose promises are sure, bind himself to perform them by his oath: how much more are we bound to tie ourselves by covenant unto God, to do those things which are our duty to do; unto the doing whereof we have such infirm principles, as are a mutable will, and an unsteadfast heart.

For the latter, our relation unto him,—we are his, not only by a property founded in his sovereign power and dominion over us, as our Maker, Lord, and Saviour [x]; but by a property growing out of our own voluntary consent, whereby we surrender, and yield, and give up ourselves unto God [y]. We are not only his people [z], but his willing people, by the intervention of our own consent. 'We give him our hand' (as the expression is [a]) which is an allusion to the manner of covenants or engagements [b]. We offer up ourselves as a free oblation [c], and are thereupon called "a kind of first-fruits [d]." We are his; the wife is her husband's [e]. Now such an interest as this, ever presupposeth a contract. As in ancient forms of stipulation, there was asking and answering, "Spondes? Spondeo. Promittis? Promitto. Dabis? Dabo:"—as in contract of marriage, the mutual consent is asked and given [f]; so is it here between God and the soul; the covenant is mutual [g]. He promiseth mercy to be "our exceeding great reward;" and we promise obedience, to be his "willing people;" and usually according as is the proportion of

[u] Deut. vii. 12. Luke i. 72, 73. Heb. vi. 17, 18. [x] Psalm c. 3. 1 Cor. vi. 19, 20. [y] Rom. vi. 19. 2 Cor. viii. 5. [z] Psalm cx. 3. [a] 2 Chron. xxx. 8. [b] Emittere manum est cautionem sive chirographum dare; ff. de probat. et presumpt. l. 15.—Junge ergo manus, et concipe fœdus: *Statius.*— Heus ubi pacta fides, commissa que dextera dextræ? *Ovid.*—Justinian. Institut. de verborum obligat. Sect. 1. l. 3. ff. de Obligat. et Action. Sect. 2.—Prov. vi. 1, 17, 18. Ezek. xvii. 18. [c] Rom. xv. 16. [d] James i. 18. [e] Hos. ii. 19. Ezek. xvi. 8. [f] Gen. xxiv. 58. [g] Gen. xvii. 2.

strength in our faith to believe God's promises of mercy to us, such is also the proportion of care in our obedience to perform our promises of duty unto him.

Sect. 5. II. From ourselves. And here covenants are needful in two respects. 1. In regard of the falseness and deceitfulness of our corrupt hearts in all spiritual duties. The more cunning a sophister is to evade an argument, the more close and pressing we frame it:—the more vigilant a prisoner to make an escape, the stronger guard we keep upon him. Our hearts are exceeding apt to be false with God: one while, they melt into promises and resolutions of obedience, as Pharaoh and Israel did[g]; and presently forget and harden again. Lot's wife goes out of Sodom for fear of the judgements, but quickly looks back again, out of love to the place, or some other curiosity and distemper of mind. Saul relents towards David, and quickly after persecutes him again[h]. This is the true picture of man's heart[i] under a strong conviction, or in a pang of devotion, or in time either of sickness, or some pressing affliction: on the rack, in the furnace, under the rod, nothing then but vows of better obedience; all which do oftentimes dry suddenly away like a morning dew, and wither away like Jonah's gourd. Therefore, both to acknowledge, and prevent this miserable perfidiousness of such revolting hearts, it is very needful to bind them unto God with renewed covenants: and since they are so apt, with Jonah, to run away, and start aside, to neglect Nineveh, and to flee to Tarshish, necessary is it to find them out, and to bring them home, and, as David did[k], to fix and fasten them to their business, that they may not run away any more.

2. In regard of the natural sluggishness, which is in us, unto duty. We are apt to faint and be weary, when we meet with any unexpected difficulties in God's service; to esteem the wilderness as bad as Egypt; to sit down as Hagar did, and cry, to think that half-way to Heaven is far enough, and almost a Christian progress enough; that baking on one side will make the cake good enough; that God will

[g] Psalm lxxviii. 34, 37.   [h] 1 Sam. xxiv. 17, 19.   [i] Inversâ occasione, ebullire saniem quæ latebat in ulcere, et excisam, non extirpatam, arborem in sylvam pullulare videas densiorem. *Bern.* Serm. 2. in Assump. Mariæ.
[k] Psalm lvii. 7.

accept of bankrupt-payment, a noble in the pound, part of
our hearts and duties for all.   We must sometimes venture
to leap the hedge, for there is " a lion in the way." Now
to correct this torpor, this acedia, and ὀλιγοψυχία, as the
apostle calls it[1]; this pusillanimity and faint-heartedness in
God's service,—we must bind them on ourselves with renewed[m] covenants, and put the more strength because of the
bluntness of the iron[n]. A covenant doth, as it were, twist
the cords of the law, and double the precept upon the soul.
When it is only a precept, then God alone commands it:
but when I have made it a promise, then I command it, and
bind it upon myself.   The more feeble our hands and knees
are, the more care we should have to bind and strengthen
them, that we may lift them up speedily, and keep them
straight[o]: and the way hereunto is to come to David's resolution, " I have purposed, that my mouth shall not transgress[p]." Empty velleities, wishings, and wouldings will not
keep weak faculties together.   Broken bones must have
strong hands to close them fast again.   A crazy piece of
building must be cramped with iron bars, to keep it from
tottering. So if we would indeed cleave to the Lord, we
must bring purposes of heart, and strong resolutions to
enable us thereunto[q].   Cleaving will call for swearing[r]. As
it should be our prayer, so also our purpose, to have hearts
" united to fear God's name[s]:" whence the phrases of " preparing, fixing, confirming, establishing, rooting, grounding,"
and other like, so frequently occurring in the Scripture[t].

SECT. 6. III. From our brethren, that by an holy association
and spiritual confederacy in heavenly resolutions, every
man's example may quicken his brother, and so duties be
performed with more vigour and fervency, and return with
the greater blessings. If fire be in a whole pile of wood,
every stick will burn the brighter; the greenest wood that
is, will take fire in so general a flame. Men usually have
more courage in the body of an army, where concurrent
shoutings and encouragements do, as it were, infuse mutual

---

[1] Masora sepes legi: decimæ divitiis ; vota sanctimoniæ : silentium sapientiæ.
Pirke Aboth.   [m] 1 Thes. v. 14.   [n] Eccles. x. 10.   [o] Heb. xii. 12, 13.
[p] Psalm xvii. 3.   [q] Acts xi. 23.   [r] Deut. x. 20.   [s] Psalm lxxxvi. 11.
[t] 2 Chron. xxx. 19. 1 Chron. xxix. 18. Ephes. iii. 17. Heb. xiii. 9. James v. 8.

spirits into one another, than when they are alone by themselves. David rejoiced in but recounting the companies
and armies of God's people, when they went up to Jerusalem in their solemn feasts [u]. And therefore most covenants
in 'scripture were general and public, solemnly entered into
by a great body of people, as that of Asa, Josiah, and Nehemiah ; the forwardness of every man whetting the face of
his neighbour [x].

SECT. 7. IV. From the multitudes, strength, vigilancy, malice, assiduous attempts of our spiritual enemies, which call
upon us for the stronger and more united resolutions. For
common adversaries usually gain more by our faintness and
divisions, than by their own strength. Therefore soldiers
use to take an oath of fidelity [y] towards their country and
service. And Hannibal's father made him take a solemn
oath [z], to maintain perpetual hostility with Rome. Such an
oath have all Christ's soldiers taken [a] ; and do, at the Lord's
supper and in solemn humiliations, virtually renew the same,
never to hold intelligence or correspondence with any of his
enemies.

The first thing in a Christian man's armour, mentioned by
the apostle, Ephes. vi. 14, is "the girdle [b]," that which
binds on all the other armour (for so we read of girding on
armour [c]), and that there is " truth :" which we may understand either doctrinally, for steadfastness and stability of
judgement in the doctrine of Christ, which we profess; not
being " carried about with every wind of doctrine, but
holding fast the form of sound words, knowing whom we

---

u Psal. lxxxiv. 7.   x Prov. xxvii. 17.   y Μήτε ἀπολείψειν τὰ σημεῖα,
μήτε ἄλλο πράξαι μηδὲν ἐναντίον τῷ δήμῳ. *Dionys. Halicarnas.* l. 10. Ποιήσειν τὸ
προσταττόμενον ὑπὲρ τῶν ἀρχόντων κατὰ δύναμιν. *Polyb.* 6.—Vid. *Veget.* de Re
Milit. lib. 2.—*Tertul.* de Corona Mil. c. 11. l. 2.—ff. de his qui notantur infamia ;
Sect. 'Miles;' et notas *Gothofridi* in l. 2. ff. de Veteranis. *Lipsii* not. ad lib. 15.
Annal. Tacit.—Praemia nunc alia atque alia emolumenta notemus Sacramentorum : *Juvenal.* Satir. 16.—*Lips.* de Milit. Rom. lib. 1. Dialog. 6.   z *Liv.*
lib. 35.—*Appian.* in Iberico et Libyco.—*Polyb.* l. 3.—*Tertul.* Apolog. c. 8.—*Flo-
rus,* lib. 4.   a Vid. *Tertul.* de Coron. Milit. cap. 11.   b ' Cingere ' est ' mili-
tare,' apud Plautum : omnes qui militant, cincti sunt. *Servius* in l. 8. Aeneid.
Unde cingulum Marti sacrum, teste Homero, Iliad. 2.—Et 'stare discinctum' erat
poenae militaris genus. *Sueton.* in *Aug.*—Vid. l. 25. 38. et 43. ff. de Testamento mi-
litis.—*Suid.* Ζώννυσθαι est καθοπλίζεσθαι et Ζῶν δύναμις : unde dicitur Deus ' Bal-
teum regum dissolvere,' Job xii. 18.—Vid.*Sluck.* Antiq. Conviv.l. 2. c. 19. et *Pined.*
in Job xii. 18.—*Tolet.* Annot. 62. in Luc. 12.   c Judg. xviii. 11. 1 Kings xx. 11.

believe, and having certainty of the things wherein we have
been instructed[d];"—or else morally and practically, for steadfastness of heart, in the faithful discharge of those promises which we have made unto God (for so faithfulness is
compared to a girdle[e]), whereby we are preserved from
shrinking and tergiversation, in times of trial, and in our
spiritual warfare. And this faithfulness, the more it is in
solemn covenants renewed, the stronger it must needs be,
and the better able to bind all our other arms upon.
Christ's enemies will enter into covenants and combinations
against him and his church[f]. And our own lusts[g] within
us, will, many times, draw from us oaths and obligations to
the fulfilling of them, and make them 'vincula iniquitatis,'
contrary to the nature of an oath[h]. How much more careful should we be to bind ourselves unto God, that our resolutions may be the stronger and more united, against so
many and confederate enemies!

SECT. 8. This point serveth, First, For a just reproof of
those, who are so far from entering into covenant with God,
that indeed they make covenants with Satan, his greatest
enemy; and do in their conversations, as it were, abuse those
promises, and blot out that subscription, and tear off that seal
of solemn profession, which they had so often set unto the covenant of obedience. Such as those, who, in the prophet's time,
were "at an agreement with hell and the grave[i]." Men are
apt to think, that none but witches are in covenant with the
devil; because such are, in the scripture, said to "consult
familiar spirits[k]." But as Samuel said to Saul, "Rebellion
is as witchcraft[l];" every stubborn and presumptuous sinner
hath so much of witchcraft in him, as to hold a kind of spiritual compact with the devil. We read of 'the serpent and

[d] Ephes. iv. 14. 2 Tim. i. 12, 13. Luke i. 4.   [e] Isai. xi. 5.   [f] Psalm
ii. 2. lxiv. 5, 6. lxxxiii. 5, 8.   Acts xxiii. 12.   Jer. xi. 9.   [g] Καὶ τούς
γε πρώτους αὐτῶν δυνατωτάτους ἐς ἀθεμίτων ὁρκωμοσιῶν ὀναγκὴν προσήγαγε.
παῖδα γάρ τινα καταθύσας, καὶ ἐπὶ τῶν σπλάγχνων αὐτοῦ τὰ ὅρκια ποιήσας, ἔπειτα
ἐσπλάγχνευσεν αὐτὰ μετὰ τῶν ἄλλων. Dion. de Catilina 1. 37.—Ita se ad Romanæ
sedis obedientiam obligant Archiepiscopi, cum pallium accipiunt.   Decret. Greg.
de election. c. 1. et ad Consilii Tridentini doctrinam Jesuitæ in voto Professionis
Hopinian. Hist. Jesuit. fol. 57.—Et Hubaldus quidam apud Augustinum juravit
se nec matri nec fratribus necessaria subministraturum; c. 12. quæst. 4. c.—Inter
cætera vid. Eus. Hist. Eccles. l. 6. c. 8.   [h] 1 Kings xix 2.   Mark vi. 23.
[i] Isai. xxviii. 15.   [k] Deut. xviii. 11.   [l] 1 Sam. xv. 53.

his seed [m];' of 'the dragon and his soldiers [n];' of some sinners 'being of the devil [o],' animated by his principles, and actuated by his will and commands [p]. Satan tempting, and sinners embracing and admitting the temptation upon the inducements suggested, hath in it the resemblance of a covenant or compact. There are mutual agreements and promises, as between master and servant; one requiring work to be done,—and the other expecting wages to be paid for the doing of it:—as in buying and selling, one bargains to have a commodity,—and the other to have a price valuable for it. Thus we read in some places, of the service of sin [q]; and in others, of the wages belonging unto that service [r]; and elsewhere, of the covenant, bargain, and sale, for the mutual securing of the service, and of the wages [s]. Wicked men sell themselves, chaffer and grant away their time, and strength, and wit, and abilities, to be at the will and disposal of Satan, for such profits, pleasures, honours, advantages, as are laid in their way to allure them; and thus do, as it were " with cords," bind themselves unto sin [t]. Ahab bought Naboth's vineyard of the devil, and sold himself for the price in that purchase. Balaam, against the light of his own conscience, and the many discoveries of God's dislike, never gives over his endeavours of cursing God's people, till he had drawn them into a snare by the Midianitish women; and all to this end,—that he might at last overtake " the wages of iniquity, which he ran so greedily after [u]." Jezebel binds herself by an oath unto murder [x]; Judas makes a bargain for his Master's blood, and at once sells a soul and a Saviour for so base a price as thirty pieces of silver [y]; profane Esau makes merchandise of his birthright (whereunto belonged the inheritance, or double portion, the princely power, and the office of priesthood, the blessing,

---

[m] Gen. iii. 15.　　[n] Rev. xii. 7.　　[o] Alterius esse non possunt nisi diaboli, quæ Dei non sunt. *Tert.* de Idol. c. 18. et de Habit. Mulieb. c. viii. 8. de cultu fœmin. c. 5.—Nemo in castra hostium transit, nisi projectis armis, nisi destitutis signis et sacramentis principis sui, nisi pactus simul perire. *Tert.* de tac. c. 24.—Mane piger stertis:—surge, inquit avaritia; eja Surge:—negas:—instat, surge, inquit;—'non queo:'—surge. *Pers.* Satir. 5. 132.　　[p] 1 John iii. 8. 2 Tim. ii. 26.　　[q] John viii. 34. Rom. vi. 16. 2 Pet. ii. 19.　　[r] Heb. xi. 25. 2 Pet. ii. 15. Jude v. 11.　　[s] 1 Reg. xxi. 25.　　[t] Prov. v. 22.　　[u] Numb. xxii. 15, 21. xxiii. 1, 14, 29. xxxi. 16. Mic. vi. 5. Rev. ii. 14. 2 Pet. ii. 15.　　[x] 1 Kings xix. 2.　　[y] Matth. xxvi. 55.

the excellency, and the government[z], all which he parts
with for one morsel of meat[a]; being therein a type of all
those profane wretches, who deride the ways of godliness,
and promises of salvation, drowning themselves in sensual
delights, and esteeming heaven and hell, salvation and perdition, but as the vain notions of melancholy men, having no
other God, but their belly or their gain[b].

So much monstrous wickedness is there in the hearts of
men, that they add spurs and whips unto a horse, which of
himself rusheth into the battle. When the tide of their own
lusts, the stream and current of their own headstrong and
impetuous affections do carry them too swiftly before, yet
they hoist up sail, and, as it were, spread open their hearts
to the winds of temptation; precipitating and urging on
their natural lusts by their voluntary engagements; tying
themselves yet faster to misery, than Adam by his fall had
tied them;—and making themselves, not by nature only, but
by compact, the children of wrath. One makes beforehand
a bargain for drunkenness; another contrives a meeting for
uncleanness; a third enters into a combination for robbery
and cozenage; a fourth makes an oath of revenge and malice; like Ananias and Sapphira, they agree together to
tempt the Spirit of the Lord[c]: like Samson's foxes, join
together with firebrands to set the souls of one another on
fire; as if they had not title enough to hell, except they
bargained for it anew, and bound themselves, as it were, by
solemn obligation not to part with it again.

O! that every presumptuous sinner, who thus sells himself
to do wickedly, would seriously consider those sad encum-
brances, that go along with this his purchase. Those who
would have estates to continue in such or such a succession,
as themselves had pre-intended, have sometimes charged
curses and execrations upon those, who should alienate, or
go about to alter the property and condition of them.
These, many times, are causeless curses, and do not come:
but if any man will needs make bargains with Satan, and be
buying the pleasures of sin, he must needs know that there

[z] Gen. xlix. 4.   2 Chron. xxix. 3.   [a] Ut Lysimachus se, ob frigidæ aquæ
potum, hostibus dedit. *Plut.* lib. de tuendâ sanitate.—Heb. xii. 16.   [b] Phil.
iii. 19.   1 Tim. vi. 5.   [c] Acts v. 9.

goes a curse from Heaven along with such a purchase, which will make it at the last but a γλυκὺ πικρὸν, ' a sweet bitter,'—like John's roll, which was sweet in the mouth but bitter in the belly: like Claudius's mushroom, pleasant but poison[d]; that will blast all the pleasures of sin in 'aurum tholosanum[e],' into such gold, as ever brought destruction to the owners of it. It is said of Cn. Seius, that he had a goodly horse, which had all the perfections that could be named for stature, feature, colour, strength, limbs, comeliness, belonging to a horse; but withal, this misery ever went along with him, that whosoever became owner of him, was sure to die an unhappy death. This is the misery that always accompanies the bargain of sin; how pleasant, how profitable, how advantageous soever it may seem to be unto flesh and blood, it hath always calamity in the end; it ever expires in a miserable death. Honey is very sweet; but it turns into the bitterest choler. The valley of Sodom was one of the most delightful places in the world; but it is now become a dead and a standing lake. Let the life of a wicked man run on never so fluently, it hath a 'mare mortuum' at the dead end of it. O then, when thou art making a covenant with sin, say to thy soul, as Boaz said to his kinsman[f], "At what time thou buyest it, thou must have Ruth the Moabitess with it." If thou wilt have the pleasures, the rewards, the wages of iniquity, thou must also have the curse and damnation that is entailed upon it; and let thy soul answer which he there doth, "No, I may not do it; I shall mar and spoil a better inheritance."

Sect. 9. II. This may serve for an instruction unto us, touching the duties of solemn humiliation and repentance, which is the scope of the prophet's direction in this place. We must not think we have done enough, when we have made general acknowledgments and confessions of sin, and begged pardon and grace from God; but we must withal further bind ourselves fast unto God by engagements of new obedience, as holy men in the Scripture have done in their

---

[d] Nemo venenum temperat felle et helleboro; sed conditis pulmentis, et bene saporatis, et plurimum dulcibus, id mali injicit. Tert. de Spect. c. 27.—Infusum delectabili cibo hoc boletorum venenum. Tacit. Annal. l. 12. 67.   [e] Vid. Aul. Gell. l. 3. c. 9.—Omnia illic seu fortia, seu honesta, seu sonora, seu canora, seu subtilia, proinde habenda sunt stillicidia mellis de libacunculo venenato; nec tanti gulam facias, quanti voluptatis periculum. Tert. ib.   [f] Ruth iv. 4, 5.

more solemn addresses unto God[g]: for without amendment
of life, prayers are but howlings and abominations[h]. "Quantum à præceptis, tantum ab auribus Dei longe sumus[i]." No
obedience, no audience. A beast will roar when he is
beaten; but men, when God punisheth, should not only cry,
but covenant.

Unto the performance whereof, that we may the better
apply ourselves, let us a little consider the nature of a religious covenant. A covenant is a mutual stipulation, or a
giving and receiving of faith between two parties, whereby
they do unanimously agree in one inviolable sentence or resolution. Such a covenant there is between God and true
believers: he giving himself as a reward unto them; and they
giving themselves as servants unto him: he willing and requiring the service, and they willing and consenting to the
reward: he promising to be their God, and they to be his
people[k]. A notable expression of which joint and mutual
stipulation we have, Deut. xxvi. 17, 18: "Thou hast avouched the Lord this day to be thy God, and to walk in his
ways, and to keep his statutes, and his commandments, and
his judgements, and to hearken unto his voice: and the
Lord hath avouched thee this day to be his peculiar people,
as he hath promised thee, and that thou shouldest keep all
his commandments; and to make thee high above all nations
which he hath made, in praise, and in name, and in honour;
and that thou mayest be an holy people unto the Lord thy
God, as he hath spoken[l]." Where we have both the mutual
expressions of intimate relations one to another, and the mutual engagements unto universal obedience on the one
side, and unto high and precious benefits on the other,
growing out of that relation. For because God is mine, I
am bound to serve him; and because I am his, he hath
bound himself to provide for me. We are not now to consider that part of the covenant, which standeth in God's promise to be our God, which, in general, importeth thus much,
God's giving himself in Christ unto us, and, together with

g Nehem. ix. 38. Psalm li. 12, 13, 14, 15.   h Hos. vii. 14. Prov. xxviii. 9.
i Tert. de Orat. c. 10.   k Heb. viii. 10.   l Duorum pluriumve in idem
placitum consensus. Ulpian. l. 1. ff. de pactis; unde mutua ex fide data et accepta oritur obligatio.—Voluntatis est suscipere, necessitatis consummare. Paul.
leg 17. ff. Commodati.

Christ, all other good things : benefits relative, in justification from sin, and adoption unto sons : benefits habitual, a new nature by regeneration, a new heart and life by sanctification, a quiet conscience by peace and comfort: benefits temporal, in the promises of this life: benefits eternal, in the glory of the next. Thus is Christ made of God unto us, ' wisdom,' in our vocation, converting us unto faith in him ; ' righteousness,' in our justification, reconciling us unto his Father; ' sanctification,' in our conformity to him in grace, and ' redemption' from all evils or enemies which might hate us here, and unto all glory, which may fill and everlastingly satisfy us hereafter [n].—But we are now to consider of the other part of the covenant, which concerneth our engagement unto God, wherein we promise both ourselves and our abilities unto him, to be his people, and to do him service.

SECT. 10. The material cause of this covenant is whatsoever may be promised unto God : and that is, first, our persons ; and secondly, our service. Our persons, " We are thine [o]." Giving our ownselves to the Lord [p] ; not esteeming ourselves [q] our own, but his that bought us [r] ; and being willing, that he which bought us, should have the property in us, and the possession of us, and the dominion over us, and the liberty to do what he pleaseth with us. Being contented to be lost to ourselves, that we may be " found in him [s]." If sin or Satan call for our tongue, or heart, or hand, or eye, to answer, ' These are not mine own, Christ hath bought them ; the Lord hath set them apart for himself [t] ; they are vessels for the Master's use [u] : I am but the steward of my-

---

[n] 1 Cor. i. 30.   [o] Isai. lxiii. 19.   [p] 2 Cor. viii. 5.   [q] Servi pro nullis habentur l. 1. ff. de Jure deliberandi; et l. 32. de regulis juris. Sunt res Domini, et quicquid acquirunt, Domino acquirunt. Instit. lib. 1. tit. 8. et leg. 1. de his qui sui aut alieni juris sunt, ff. lib. 1. et lib. 41 c. 10. sect. 1. Nihil suum habere possunt, Instit. lib. 2. T. 9. non debent saluti dominorum suam anteponere. l. 1. sect 28. ff. de Senatusconsulto Silaniano.—Xerxis servi, exorta tempestate, in mare desiliunt, ut domini sui saluti consulant. *Herodot.* lib. 8. —Socrati cum multa multi pro suisquisque facultatibus offerrent, Æschines, pauper auditor, " Nihil," inquit, " dignum te, quod dare tibi possim, invenio et hoc uno modo pauperem me esse sentio ; itaque dono tibi quod unum habeo, Meipsum. Hoc munus, rogo, qualecunque est, boni consulas ; cogitesque alios, cum multum tibi darent, plus sibi reliquisse." *Seneca* de Benef. 1. 1. c. 8. *Ruhkopf,* vol. iv. p. 23.   [r] 1 Cor. vi. 19.   [s] Phil. iii. 9.   [t] Psalm iv. 3.   [u] 2 Tim. ii. 21.

self, and may not dispose of my Master's goods without, much less against his own will and commands.'

Our services, which are matters of necessity [x], matters of expediency, and matters of praise: all which may be made the materials of a covenant.

1. Matter of duty and necessity. As David, by an oath, binds himself to keep God's righteous judgements [y]. And the people, in Nehemiah's time, enter into a curse and an oath, to walk in God's law, and to observe and to do all his commandments [z].

2. Matter of circumstantial expediency, which, in Christian wisdom, may be conducent unto the main end of a man's life, or may fit him for any special condition which God calleth him unto. So the Rechabites promised their father Jonadab, and held that promise obligatory in the sight of God, " Not to drink wine, nor to build houses[a] ;" because, by that voluntary hardship of life, they should be the better fitted to bear that captivity, which was to come upon them ; or because thereby they should the better express the condition of strangers amongst God's people, upon whose outward comforts they would not seem too much to encroach, that it might appear, that they did not incorporate with them for mere secular, but for spiritual benefits. It was lawful for Paul to have received wages and rewards for his work in the gospel, as well of the churches of Achaia, as of Macedonia, and others, as he proveth, 1 Cor. ix. 4, 14; yet he seemeth upon the case of expediency, that he " might cut off occasion from them that desired occasion," and might the better promote the gospel,—to bind himself by an oath (for so much those words, " The truth of Christ is in me," do import, as the learned have observed [b]) never to be burdensome in that kind unto those churches [c]. Lawful things, when inexpedient and gravaminous, may be forborne by the bonds of a covenant.

---

[x] Sunt quædam, quæ etiam non volentes debemus; quædam, etiam quæ nisi noverimus, non debemus; sed postquam ea Deo promittimus, necessario ea reddere constringimur. *Aug.* [y] Psalm cxix. 106. [z] Nehem. x. 29. [a] Jer. xxxv. 6, 7. [b] *Ambr.—Aquin.—Erasm.—Calv.—Beza,—Piscator,—Musc.— Estius,—Corn. A. Lap.—Tirinus.*—De hujusmodi votis, Vid. *Greg. Tholos.* de Rep. l. 3. c. 5. et Syntag Juris, l. 24. c. 10.—*Serarium* in l. Judic. c. 11. qu. 19. *Pined.* in Job xxii. 27.—*Seld.* of Tithes, c. 3.—*Brisson.* de formul. l. 1. [c] 2 Cor. xi. 7, 12.

3. Matter of thanksgiving and praises unto God, in which case it was usual to make and pay vows. "What shall I render to the Lord for all his benefits towards me?" saith David: " I will take the cup of salvation" (as the use of the Jews was in their feasts and sacrifices of thanksgiving [d];) " I will pay my vows unto the Lord." Whereby it appears, that godly men, when they prayed for mercies, did likewise, by vows and covenants, bind themselves to return tribute of praise in some particular kind or other, upon the hearing of their prayers [e]. So Jacob did [f]; and so Jephtha [g]; and so Hannah [h]; and so Hezekiah [i]; and so Jonah [k]; so Zaccheus, to testify his thankfulness unto Christ for his conversion, and to testify his thorough mortification of covetousness, which had been his master-sin, did not only out of duty make restitution where he had done wrong, but out of bounty, did engage himself to give the half of his goods to the poor [l].

The formal cause of a covenant is the plighting of our fidelity, and engaging of our truth unto God in that particular, which is the matter of our covenant; which is done two ways: either by a simple promise and stipulation, as that of Zaccheus; or in a more solemn way, by the intervention of an oath, or curse, or subscription, as that of Nehemiah, and the people there.

SECT. 11. The efficient cause is the person entering into the covenant: in whom these things are to concur:—

1. A clear knowledge, and deliberate weighing of the matter promised; because error [m], deception, or ignorance, are contrary to the formal notion of that consent, which in every covenant is intrinsecal, and necessary thereunto: "Non videtur consentire qui errat."

2. A free and willing concurrence [n]. " In omni pacto intercedit actio spontanea ;" and so in every promise. Not but that authority may impose oaths, and those as well pro-

---

[d] Luke xxii. 17.   [e] Psalm cxvi. 12, 13, 14. Psalm cxxiii. 2, 3.   [f] Gen. xxviii. 22.   [g] Judg. xi. 30, 31.   [h] 1 Sam. i. 11, 27, 28.   [i] Isai. xxxviii. 20.   [k] Isai. i. 9.   [l] Luke xxix. 8.   [m] L. 57. ff. de oblig. et Action. Nulla voluntas errantis est. l. 20. ff. de aqua. et aqu. l. 116. de Reg. juris.   [n] Votum voluntas est spontanea. *Tholos.* Syntag. Juris. l. 24. c. 10. Sect. 1. 219. de verborum significat.—Hostiæ ab animo libenti expostulantur. *Tert.* ad Scap. c. 2.

missory as assertory [o]; as Josiah made a covenant, and caused the people to stand unto it [p]. But that the matter of it, though imposed, should be such in the nature of the thing, as that it may be taken in judgement and righteousness, that so the person may not be hampered in any such hesitancy of conscience, as will not consist with a pious, spontaneous, and voluntary concurrence thereunto.

3. A power to make the promise, and bind oneself by it. For a man may have power to make a promise, which is not finally obligatory, but upon supposition [r]. As a woman might for her own part vow, and by that vow was bound up as to herself: but this bond was but conditional, as to efficacy and influence upon the effect, to wit, if her husband hear it, and held his peace [s].

4. A power, having made the promise, to perform it: and this depends upon the nature of the thing, which must be first possible ; for " Impossibilium nulla est obligatio [t]:" no man can bind himself to things impossible. And next, lawful [u], in regard either of the necessity, or expediency, or some other allowableness in the thing. For, " Turpe est jure impossibile ;" we can do nothing but that which we can do rightfully. Sinful things are, in construction of law, impossible, and so can induce no obligation. A servant can make no promise to the dishonour or disservice of his master [x], nor a child or pupil contrary to the will of his parent or guardian; nor a Christian, to the dishonour, or against the will of Christ, whom he serves. In every such sinful

---

p Gen. xxiv. 3. 1 Kings ii. 42. Ezra x. 3, 5.   q 2 Chron. xxxiv. 31, 32. r L. 5. de Cod. Legibus vide *Tholos.* Syntag. Juris l. 21. c. 5.—Vide *Peckium* de Reg. Juris Reg. 69. Sect. 4.   s Numb. xxx. 3, 14.   t L. 18. ff. de Reg. Juris, et l. 183. et de conditionibus institutionum, leg. 6. et 20. de conditionibus et demonstrat. l. 3. et 20. et de Obligat. et Action. l. 1. sect. 9.   u Quæ facta lædunt pietatem, existimationem, verecundiam nostram, et (ut generaliter dixerim) contra bonos mores fiunt, nec facere nos posse credendum est. *Papin.* l. 14, 15. ff. de Condition. Institut.—Pacta quæ contra bonos mores fiunt, nullam vim habere, indubitati juris est. l. 6. et 30. Cod. de pactis.—Generaliter novimus, turpes stipulationes nullius esse momenti. l. 26. ff. de verbor. obligat. et de legatis et fidei commiss. leg. 112. sect. 3, 4.—Impia promissio est quæ scelere adimpletur. Juramentum non est vinculum iniquitatis. Vid. *Caus.* 22. qu. 4.— Præstare fateor posse me fidem si scelere careat; interdum scelus est fides ; *Sen.* Hæ demum impositæ operæ intelliguntur, quæ sine turpitudine præstari possunt: ff. de operis libertorum, l. 38.   x Filius familias, vel servus, sine patris dominive auctoritate, voto non obligatur ; l. 2. sect. 1. ff. de pollicitationibus.

engagement, there is intrinsecally "dolus, error, deceptio;" the heart is blinded by the deceitfulness of lust ʸ. And these things are destructive to the nature of such an action, as must be deliberate and spontaneous. Promises of this kind bind to nothing but repentance.

From these considerations we may learn, what to judge of the promises which many men make of doing service unto God.

SECT. 12. 1. Some join in covenants, as the greatest part of that tumultuous concourse of people, who made an uproar against the apostle, were joined together, "they knew not wherefore ᶻ;" and do not understand the things they promise:—as if a man should set his hand and seal to an obligation, and not know the contents or condition of it. Such are all ignorant Christians, who have often renewed their covenant of new obedience and faith in Christ, and yet know not what the faith of Christ is, or what is the purity aud spiritualness of that law which they have sworn unto. As the apostle saith of the Jews, "If they had known, they would not have crucified the Lord of glory;" we may say of many of these, ' If they knew the purity and holiness of those things which they have vowed to keep, they either would not have entered into covenant with God at all, or would be more conscientious and vigilant in their observation of it.'—It is a sign of a man desperately careless, to run daily into debt, and never so much as remember or consider what he owes. If there were no other obligation to tie men unto the knowledge of God's will, this alone were sufficient, that they have undertaken to serve him; and therefore, by their own covenants, are bound to know him. For surely many men, who have promised repentance from their dead works, if they did indeed consider what that repentance is, and unto what a strict and narrow way of walking it doth confine them, would go nigh, if they durst, to plead an error in the contract,—and to profess that they had not thought their obligation had engaged them unto so severe and rigid a service, and so would repent of their repentance. But in this case, ignorance of what a man ought to know, cannot avoid the covenant which he is bound to make, and, having

---

ʸ Ephes. iv. 18, 22. Heb. iii. 13. 2 Pet. i. 9. 2 Cor. xi. 3.　　ᶻ Acts xix. 32.

made, to keep; but his covenant doth exceedingly aggravate his ignorance [a].

SECT. 13. 2. Some make many fair promises of obedience, but it is on the rack, and in the furnace, or as children under the rod :—" O if I might but recover this sickness, or be eased of this affliction, I would then be a new man, and redeem my misspent time."—And yet many of these, like Pharaoh, when they have any respite, find out ways to shift and delude their own promises, and, like melted metal taken out of the furnace, return again unto their former hardness. So a good divine [b] observes of the people of this land, in the time of the great sweat in king Edward's days, (I wish we could find even so much in these days of calamity which we are fallen into,) as long as the heat of the plague lasted, there was crying out " Peccavi," Mercy, good Lord, mercy, mercy.—Then, lords, and ladies, and people of the best sort, cried out to the ministers, " For God's sake tell us, what we shall do to avoid the wrath of God:—take these bags ; pay so much to such an one whom I deceived ; so much restore unto another, whom, in bargaining, I overreached ; give so much to the poor, so much to pious uses, &c." But after the sickness was over, they were just the same men as they were before. Thus, in time of trouble, men are apt to make many prayers, and covenants, to cry unto God, " Arise, and save us [c], Deliver us this time [d] :" they enquire early after God, and flatter him with their lips, and own him as their God, and rock of salvation, and presently "start aside, like a deceitful bow." As Austin [e] notes, that, in times of calamity, the very heathen would flock unto the Christian churches, to be safe amongst them. And when the Lord sent lions among the Samaritans, then they sent to enquire after the manner of his worship [f]. Thus many men's covenants are founded

---

[a] Qui per delictorum pœnitentiam instituerat Domino satisfacere, diabolo per aliam pœnitentiæ pœnitentiam satisfaciet; eritque tanto magis perosus Deo, quanto æmulo ejus acceptus. *Tertul.* de pœnitent. c. 5.   [b] *Dike*, of the deceitfulness of the heart, c. 20.   [c] Jer. ii. 27.   [d] Judges x. 15.   [e] Quos vides petulanter et procaciter insultare servis Christi, sunt in his plurimi, qui illum interitum clademque non evasissent, nisi servos Christi se esse finxissent: De Civit. Dei, l. 1. c. 1.—Ejecta in naufragio dominorum adhuc sunt, quia non eo animo ejiciuntur quod, ea habere nolunt, sed ut periculum effugiant; ff. l. 41. l. 9. sect. 8. et l. 44.—Semisaucium hac atque hac jactare voluntatem ; *Aug.* Confes. l. 8. c. 8.   [f] 2 Kings xvii. 25, 26.

only in terrors of conscience. They throw out their sins, as a merchant at sea his rich commodities in a tempest, but in a calm wish for them again. Neither do they throw away the property over them, but only the dangerous possession of them. This is not a full, cheerful, and voluntary action, but only a languid and inconstant velleity, contrary to that largeness of heart, and fixed disposition which Christ's own people bring unto his service; as David and the nobles of Israel " offered willingly, and with joy unto the Lord [g]."

SECT. 14. Since a covenant presupposeth a power in him that maketh it, both over his own will, and over the matter, thing, or action which he promiseth, so far as to be enabled to make the promise: and since we of ourselves have neither will nor deed, no sufficiency either to think or to perform [h]; we hence learn in all the covenants which we make, not to do it in any confidence of our own strength, or upon any self-dependence on our own hearts, which are false and deceitful, and may, after a confident undertaking, use us as Peter's used him; but still to have our eyes on the aid and help of God's grace, to use our covenants as means the better to stir up God's graces in us, and our prayer unto him for further supplies of it. As David, " I will keep thy statutes;" but then, " do not thou forsake me [i]." Our promises of duty must ever be supported by God's promises of grace, when we have undertaken to serve him. We must remember to pray as Hezekiah did, " Lord, I am weak, do thou undertake for me [k]." Our good works cannot come out of us, till God do first of all " work them in us [l]." He must perform his promises of grace to us, before we can ours of service unto him. Nothing of ours can go to heaven, except we first receive it from heaven. We are able to " do nothing, but in and by Christ which strengtheneth us [m]." So that every religious covenant which he makes, hath indeed a double obligation in it [n]; an obligation to the duty promised, that we may stir up ourselves to perform it; and an obliga-

[g] 1 Chron. xxix. 17.   [h] Rom. vii. 18. 2 Cor. iii. 5. Phil. ii. 12.   [i] Psalm cxix. 8.   [k] Isai. xxxviii. 14.   [l] Isai. xxvi. 12.   [m] John xv. 5. Phil. iv. 13.   [n] Quid tam congruum fidei humanæ, quam ea quæ inter eos placuerunt, servare? *Ulpian* L. 1. ff. de pactis.—Obligatio est juris vinculum, quo necessitate restringimur alicujus solvendæ rei: Instit. 1. 3. T. 14.—Vid. *Gregorium Tholos.* Repub. 1. 8. c. 8.

tion unto prayer, and recourse to God, that he would furnish
us with grace to perform it :—as he that hath bound himself
to pay a debt, and hath no money of his own to do it, is constrained to betake himself unto supplications, that he may
procure the money of some other friend.

Lastly, The final cause of a covenant is to induce an
obligation, where was none before; or else to double
and strengthen it, where was one before, to be 'vinculum
conservandæ fidei,' a bond to preserve truth and fidelity.
Being subject unto many temptations, and having backsliding and revolting hearts, apt, if they be not kept up to
service, to draw back from it; therefore we use ourselves, as
men do cowardly soldiers, set them there where they must
fight, and shall not be able to run away, or fall off from service.

III. This should serve to humble us upon a twofold consideration :—

SECT. 15. 1. For the falseness and unsteadfastness of our
hearts, which want such covenants to bind them, and, as it
were, fasten them to the altar with cords :—as men put locks
and fetters upon wild horses, whom otherwise no inclosure
would shut in. Our hearts (as Jacob said of Reuben[o]) are "unstable waters." Moist bodies (as water is) "non continentur
suis terminis[p]," do not set bounds to themselves, as solid and
compacted bodies do, but shed all abroad, if left to themselves: the way to keep them united and together, is to put
them into a close vessel :—so the heart of man can set itself
no bounds, but falls all asunder, and out of frame, εἰς ἀνάχυ-
σιν, as the apostle's expression is, (1 Pet. iv. 4) "instar aquæ
diffluentis," (Heb. xii. 1.) if it be not fastened and bound together by such strong resolutions. Sometimes men, either
by the power of the Word, or by the sharpness of some
afflictions, are quickened and inflamed unto pious purposes;
like green wood, which blazeth, while the bellows are blow-

---

o Gen. xlix. 4.   p Ὑγρὸν τὸ ἀόριστον οἰκείῳ ὅρῳ. Aristot. de Gener. et
Corrupt. l. c. 2.—Hinc qui vitam agunt mollem, remissam, voluptuariam, in
hanc et illam partem flexilem, dicuntur Βίον ζῆν τὸν ὑγρὸν καὶ διαῤῥέοντα,
Chrys. Rom. xiii. 14. et Suidæ ὑγρὸς dicitur ὁ εὐκατάφορος εἰς τὰς ἡδονάς.
Ejus animum, qui nunc luxuria et lascivia diffluit, retundam: Terent. Heauton.—
Messalina, facilitate adulterorum in fastidium versa, ad incognitas libidines pro-
fluebat : Tacit. Annal. l. 11.—Eruptiones lascivitatum, Tert. Apol. c. 31.—The
Scripture calleth it, "Weakness of heart," Ezek. xvi. 30.—and so the Philoso-
pher, Ἀκρασίας τὸ μὲν προπέτεια, τὸ δὲ ἀσθένεια, Ethic. l. 7, 8. Zell. p. 318.

ing: and now they think they have their hearts sure, and shall continue them in a good frame; to-morrow shall be as this day:—but presently, like an instrument in change of weather, they are out of tune again; and, like the chameleon, presently change colour; and, as Chrysostom [q] saith, the preacher, of all workmen, seldom finds his work as he left it. Nothing but the grace of God doth balance and establish the heart: and holy covenants are an ordinance or means which he hath pleased to sanctify unto this purpose, that by them, as instruments, grace, as the principal cause, might keep the heart steadfast in duty. If then Isaiah bewail the uncleanness of his lips, and Job suspected the uncleanness and wandering of his eyes, what reason have we to be humbled for this unsteadfastness of our hearts, from whence the diffluence and looseness of every other faculty proceeds!

2. If we must bewail the falseness of our hearts, that stand in need of covenants; how much more should we bewail their perfidiousness in the violation of covenants: that they take occasion, even by restraint, like a river [r] that is stopped in its course, to grow more unruly: or as a man after an ague, which took away his stomach, to return with stronger appetite unto sin again. To crucify our sins, and in repentance to 'put them,' as it were, ' to shame,' and then to take them down from the cross again, and fetch them to life, and repent of repentance;—to vow, and "after vows to make enquiry [s];" this is very ill requital unto Christ. He came from glory to suffer for us; and here met with many discouragements, not only from enemies, but from friends and disciples: Judas betrays him; Peter denies him; his disciples sleep; his kinsfolk stand afar off; yet he doth not look back from a cross to a crown: and though he be tempted to ' come down' from the cross, yet he stays it out, that he might ' love and save us to the uttermost.' But we, no sooner out of Egypt and Sodom, but we have hankering affections to return,—at the least, to look backwards again: engage ourselves to be ruled by the Word of the Lord, as

q Ὁ μὲν ἀργυροκόπος οἷον ἂν χαλκεύσῃ τὸ σκεῦος καὶ ἀπόθηται, τοιοῦτον ἐλθὼν τῇ ἐπιούσῃ πάλιν εὑρήσει· ἐπὶ δὲ ἡμῶν οὐχ οὕτως, &c. Homil. 13. ad Pop. Antioch.   r Spumeus, et fervens, et ab obice sævior ibit. Ovid.—Senec. Nat. Quæst. l. 6. c. 17.   s Prov. xx. 25.

the Jews did [t]; and with them [u], when we know his Word, cavil against it, and shrink away from our own resolutions. O how should this humble us, and make us vile in our own eyes! God is exceeding angry with the breach of but human covenants [x]; how much more with the breach of holy covenants between himself and us!—and threateneth severely to revenge the quarrel of his covenant [y]: and so doubtless he now doth, and will do still, except we take a penitent revenge upon ourselves for it. And therefore,

Lastly, having entered into covenant, we should use double diligence in our performance of it; quickening and stirring up ourselves thereunto,—

1. By the consideration of the stability of his covenant with us, even " the sure mercies of David [z]." To break faith with a false person, were a fault; but to deceive him that never fails nor forsakes us, increaseth both the guilt and the unkindness.

2. By consideration of his continued and renewed mercies. If he were a wilderness unto us, there might be some colour to repent us of our bargain, and to look out for a better service. But it is not only unthankfulness, but folly, to make a forfeiture of mercies, and to put God, by our breach of covenant with him, to break his with us too [b].

3. By consideration of our baptism, and the tenor thereof, wherein we solemnly promise to keep a good conscience, and to observe all things whatsoever Christ commandeth us [c]. From which engagement we cannot recede, without the note and infamy of greater perfidiousness [d]. To take Christ's pay, and to do sin service; to be a subject unto Michael, and a pensioner unto the dragon; to wear the livery of one master, and to do the work of another; to be an Israelite in title, and a Samaritan in truth;—this is either to forget or deride our baptism [e]: for therein we did, as it were, subscribe our name, and list ourselves in the register of

---

[t] Jer. xlii. 5, 6.   [u] Jer. xliii. 2.   [x] Jer. xxxiv. 18. Ezek. xvii. 18.
[y] Levit. vi. 25.   [z] Isai. liv. 8, 9. lv. 3.   [a] Vid. *Chrys.* in p. 113.
[b] Jer. ii. 5, 6, 7, 31. Numb. xiv. 34. Jon. ii. 8.   [c] 1 Pet. iii. 21. Matth.
xxviii. 19, 20.   [d] In fœderibus eosdem amicos atque inimicos habere solent
fœderati; quod ex Cicerone et Livio observavit *Briss.* de formul. l. 4.—Quis miles
ab infœderatis, ne dicam ab hostibus, regibus donativum et stipendium captat,
nisi plane desertor et transfuga? *Tert.* de Præscript. c. 12.—*Bern.* Serm. 3. de
Evang. septem panum.   [e] 2 Pet. i. 9.

Sion : and as it is a high honour to be enrolled in the ge-
nealogies of the church, so it is a great dishonour to be ex-
punged from thence, and to be written in the earth, and
have our names, with our bodies, putrefy in perpetual ob-
livion [f].

4. Consider the seal and witnesses, whereby this covenant
hath been confirmed. Sealed in our own consciences by
the seal of faith, believing the holiness of God's ways, and
the excellency of his rewards ; for, " he that believeth, hath
set to his seal [g] ;"—mutually attested by our spirits, feeling
the sweetness of duty, and by God's Spirit [h], revealing the
certainty of reward [i] : and this in the presence of angels and
saints, into whose communion we are admitted [k]. So that
we cannot depart from this covenant, without shaming ourselves to God, to angels, to men, and to our own consciences. Yea, the font where we were baptized,—and the
table where we have sacramentally eaten and drank the
body and blood of Christ,—and the very seats where we have
sat attending unto his voice, like Joshua's stone [l], will be
witnesses against us, if we deny our covenant :—though
there be no need of witnesses against those, who have to deal
with the Searcher of hearts, and the Judge of consciences ;
that consuming fire, whom no lead, no dross, no reprobate
silver, no false metal, can endure or deceive ; no Ananias or
Sapphira lie unto, without their own undoing.

Lastly, Let us consider the estate which these covenants
do refer unto, and our tenure whereunto these services are
annexed, which is " eternal life." After we have had patience to keep our short promises of doing God's will, he
will perform his eternal promises of giving himself unto us.
And who would forfeit an inheritance, for not payment of a
small homage or quit-rent reserved upon it ? If we expect
eternal life from him, there is great reason we should dedicate a mortal life unto him. Let us not pay our service in
dross, when we expect our wages in gold.

[f] Jer. xvii. 13. Nehem. vi. 64, 65.   [g] John iii. 33.   [h] Vid. *Bern.*
Serm. 1. in Annunc. Mariæ, et Ser. 2. de tribus testimoniis, et Ser. 2. in die Pent.—
Ser. 2. in festiv. Omnium Sanct.—Ser. 5. in dedic. Eccl.—Ser. de quatuor modis
orandi.—Ser. 8, 23. et 85. in Cant. de Natur. et Dignit. Divini Amoris, c. 11.—
Vid. etiam *Michaelis Medinæ* Apolog. pro Joanne Fero adversus Dom. Soto cri-
minationes, apud Sixt. Senensem, Biblioth. l. 6. Annot. 210.   [i] Rom. i. 16.
[k] 1 Cor. xi. 10. Heb. xii. 22.   [l] Josh. xxii. 24, 27.

THE

THIRD SERMON.*

HOSEA XIV. 2, 3.

So will we render the calves of our lips. Asshur shall not save us; we will not ride upon horses; neither will we say to the works of our hands, Ye are our gods, &c.

Sect. 1. Having handled the general doctrine of our entering into covenant with God, I shall now proceed unto the particulars, which they here engage themselves unto ; whereof the first, is a solemn thanksgiving, " *We will render the calves of our lips.*" All the sacrifices of the Jews were of two sorts [a]: some were ilastical, propitiatory, or expiatory, for pardon of sin, or impetration of favour: others were eucharistical sacrifices of praise, (as the peace-offerings [b],) for mercies obtained [c]. With relation unto these, the church here, having prayed for forgiveness of sin, and for the obtaining of blessings, doth hereupon, for the further enforcement of those petitions, promise to offer the peace-offerings of praise, not in the naked and empty ceremony, but with the spiritual life and substance, viz. " the calves of their lips," which are moved by the inward principles of hearty sincerity and thanksgiving.

From hence we learn, That sound conversion and repentance enlargeth the heart in thankfulness towards God, and disposeth it to offer up the sacrifice of praise. And this duty, here promised, cometh in this place under several considerations ; for we may consider it,—

Sect. 2.—I. 'Ut materiam pacti,' as the matter of a

---

* Folio edition, page 523.　　[a] Vid. *Gul. Stuck.* Antiq. Convival. l. 1. c. 33.
—*Weems.* exercit. Ceremonial. exercit. 13. quamvis alii aliter distinguunt.—
Cornel. A Lapid. in Synop. c. 1. Levit.—*Torniel.* An. 2545. sect. 21.—*Pined.* in Job i. 5.—*Aler. Hales*, p. 3. qu. 55. et memb. 4. art. 8. sect. 3.　　[b] Levit. vii. 12.　　[c] Psalm cvii. 22.

covenant or compact, which we promise to render unto
God, in acknowledgement of his great mercy in answering
the prayers, which we put unto him for pardon and grace.
It is observable, that most of those psalms wherein David [d]
imploreth help from God, are closed with thanksgiving unto
him, as Psalm vii. 17. xiii. 6. lvi. 12, 13. lvii. 7, 10, &c.
David thus, by a holy craft, insinuating into God's favour,
and driving a trade between earth and heaven, receiving and
returning, importing one commodity, and transporting another, letting God know that his mercies shall not be lost,—
that as he bestows the ' comforts ' of them upon him, so he
would return the ' praises' of them unto Heaven again.
Those countries that have rich and staple commodities to
exchange and return unto others [e], have usually the freest
and fullest traffic and resort of trade made unto them. Now
there is no such rich return from earth to Heaven as praise:
this is indeed the only tribute we can pay unto God,—to
value and to celebrate his goodness towards us. As, in the
flux and reflux of the sea, the water that in the one comes
from the sea unto the shore, doth, in the other, but run back
into itself again; so praises [f] are, as it were, the return of
mercies into themselves, or into that bosom and fountain of
God's love from whence they flowed. And therefore the
richer any heart is in praises, the more speedy and copious
are the returns of mercy unto it. God hath so ordered the
creatures amongst themselves, that there is a kind of natural
confederacy, and mutual negotiation amongst them, each
one receiving and returning, deriving unto others, and drawing from others what serves most for the conservation of
them all,—and every thing, by various interchanges and vicis-
situdes, flowing back into the original from whence it came :
thereby teaching the souls of men to maintain the like spiritual commerce and confederacy with Heaven, to have all

[d] David omnes fere Psalmos, in quibus Dei auxilium implorat, gratiarum
actione claudit. *Muis* in Psalm x. 16.   [e] Cives habent propinquam fructu-
osamque provinciam, quo facile excurrant, ubi libenter negotium gerant: quos
illa mercibus suppeditandis cum quæstu compendioque dimittit, &c. *Cicer.* in
Verr. Act. 2. lib. sec. 6.—Hujusmodi nobile emporeum erat Tyros, Phœniciæ urbs,
Ezek. xxvii. 12, 14. de qua regione *Lucanus*, " Primi docuere carinis Ferre cavis
orbis commercia."   [f] Gratiarum cessat decursus, ubi recursus non fuit.
Bern. Ser. 1. in cap. Jejunii.—Ad locum, unde exeunt gratiæ, revertantur. *Idem*
Ser. 3. in Vigil. Nativit. &c.

the passages between them and it open and unobstructed,—
that the mercies which they receive from thence, may not be
kept under and imprisoned in unthankfulness, but may have
a free way in daily praises, to return to their fountain again.
Thus Noah, after his deliverance from the flood, built an
altar, on which to sacrifice the sacrifices of thanksgiving;
that as his family by the ark was preserved from perishing,
so the memory of so great a mercy might, in like manner, by
the altar be preserved too [g]. So Abraham, after a weary
journey, being comforted with God's gracious appearing and
manifestation of himself unto him, built an altar, and "called
on the name of the Lord [h];" and after another journey out of
Egypt, was not forgetful to return unto that place again [i];—
God's presence drawing forth his praises, as the return of
the sun in a spring and summer, causeth the earth to thrust
forth her fruits and flowers, that they may, as it were, meet
and do homage to the fountain of their beauty. If Hezekiah may be delivered from death [k];—if David from guilt [l];—
they promise to sing aloud of so great mercy, and to take
others into the concert, " I will teach transgressors thy way,
and we will sing upon the stringed instruments." Guilt
stops the mouth, and makes it speechless [m]; that it cannot
answer for one of a thousand sins, nor acknowledge one of a
thousand mercies. When Jacob begged God's blessing on
him in his journey, he vowed a vow of obedience and thankfulness to the Lord, seconding God's promises of mercy,
with his promises of praise, and answering all the parts
thereof : "'If God will be with me, and keep me, I will be
his, and he shall be mine:'—if he single out me and my
seed, to set us up as marks for his angels to descend unto
with protection and mercy, and will indeed ' give this land
to us,' and return ' me unto my father's house;' then this
stone which I have set up for a pillar and monument, shall
be ' God's house,' for me and my seed to praise him in." And
accordingly we find he built an altar there, and changed the
name of that place, calling it the ' House of God,'—and God,
the ' God of Bethel.' And lastly, ' If God indeed will not
leave nor forsake me, but will give so rich a land as this unto

g Gen. viii. 20.   h Gen. xii. 7.   i Gen. xiii. 4   k Isai. xxxviii. 20.
l Psalm li. 14.   m Matth. xxii. 12.

me, I will surely return a homage back ; and of his own, I will give the tenth unto him again.'—So punctual is this holy man to restipulate for each distinct promise a distinct praise, and to take the quality of his vows, from the quality of God's mercies ; [Gen. xxviii. verses 20, 22. compared with verses 13, 15. Gen. xxxv. 6, 7, 14, 15.]   Lastly, Jonah, out of the belly of Hell, cries unto God, and voweth a vow unto him, that he would sacrifice with the voice of thanksgiving, and tell all ages, that salvation is of the Lord [n].—Thus we may consider praises as the matter of the church's covenant.

SECT. 3.—II. ' Ut fructum pœnitentiæ,' as a fruit of true repentance and deliverance from sin.   When sin is taken away, when grace is obtained, then indeed is a man in a right disposition to give praises unto God.   When we are brought out of a wilderness into Canaan [o]; out of Babylon, unto Sion [p];—then saith the prophet, "Out of them shall proceed thanksgiving, and the voice of them that make merry," &c.   When Israel had passed through the Red Sea, and saw the Egyptians dead on the shore, the great type of our deliverance from sin, death, and Satan,—then they sing that triumphant song ; Moses and the men singing the song, and Miriam and the women answering them, and repeating over again the burden of the song, " Sing to the Lord, for he hath triumphed gloriously ; the horse and his rider hath he thrown into the sea [q]."   When a poor soul hath been with Jonah in the midst of the seas, compassed with the floods, closed in with the depths, brought down to the bottom of the mountains, wrapped about head and heart, and all over with the weeds, and locked up with the bars of sin and death ; when it hath felt the weight of a guilty conscience, and been terrified with the fearful expectation of an approaching curse, lying as it were at the pit's brink, within the smoke of Hell ; within the smell of that brimstone, and scorchings of that unquenchable fire which is kindled for the Devil and his angels ;—and is then, by a more bottomless and unsearchable mercy, brought unto dry land,—snatched as a brand out of the fire,—translated unto a glorious condition, from a law to a gospel, from a

[u] Jonah ii. 9.   [o] Deut. viii. 10.   [p] Jer. xxx. 18, 19.   [q] Exod. xv. 1, 20, 21.

curse to a crown, from damnation to an inheritance, from a
slave to a son;—then, then only, never till then, is that soul
in a fit disposition to sing praises unto God, when God hath
forgiven all a man's 'iniquities,' and healed all the ' diseases'
of his soul, and redeemed his 'life from destruction,'—or
from ' Hell,' as the Chaldee rendereth it;—and crowned him
with loving kindness and tender mercies; turning away his
anger, and revealing those mercies which are "from everlasting in election unto everlasting[r]" in salvation; removing his sins from him as far as the east is from the west;—
then a man will call upon his soul over and over again, and
summon every faculty within him, and invite every creature
without him to "bless the Lord," and to ingeminate praises
unto his holy name, Psalm ciii. 1, 4, 20, 22.   And as David
there begins the Psalm, with " Bless the Lord, O my soul,"
and ends it with " Bless the Lord, O my soul;"—so the
apostle,—making mention of the like mercy of God unto him,
and of the exceeding abundant grace of Christ, in setting
forth him who was a blasphemer, a persecutor, and injurious,
as a pattern unto all that should believe on him unto eternal
life, begins this meditation with praises, "I thank Christ
Jesus our Lord;" and ends it with praises, "Unto the king
eternal, immortal, invisible, the only wise God, be honour
and glory for ever and ever, Amen[s]."   It is impossible that
soul should be truly thankful unto God, which hath no apprehensions of him, but as an enemy, ready to call in, or at
the least to curse, all those outward benefits which, in that
little interim and respite of time between the curse pronounced in the law, and executed in death, he vouchsafeth
to bestow.   And impenitent sinners can have no true notion
of God but such[t].   And therefore all the verbal thanks
which such men seem to render unto God for blessings, are
but like the music at a funeral, or the trumpet before a
judge,—which gives no comfortable sound to the mourning
wife, or to the guilty prisoner.

SECT. 4.—III. ' Ut medium impetrandi,' as an argument
and motive to prevail with God in prayer.   For the church

[r] Ab æterno per prædestinationem in æternum per glorificationem. *Ber.* Ser. 2.
in Ascens. Dom.   [s] 1 Tim. i. 12, 27.   [t] Qualem te putaveris Deo, talis
oportet appareat tibi Deus. *Bern.* in Cant. serm. 69.

here prays for pardon, for grace, for healing, not only with
an eye to its own benefit, but unto God's honour: " Lord,
when thou hast heard and answered us, then we shall glorify thee ⁿ." " I shall praise thee," saith David, " for thou
hast heard me, and art become my salvation ˣ." It is true, if
God condemn us, he will therein show forth his own glory ʸ,
as he did upon Pharaoh ᶻ.   In which sense the ' strong and
terrible ones ' are said to ' glorify ' him ᵃ, because his power
in their destruction is made the more conspicuous : but we
should not therein concur unto the glorifying of him.   " The
grave cannot praise him ; they that go down into the pit,
cannot celebrate his name ᵇ ;" " the living, the living, they
shall praise thee ᶜ."   This is a frequent argument with David
whereby to prevail for mercy, because else God would lose
the praise which,. by this means, he should render to his
name ᵈ, &c.   God indeed is all-sufficient to himself, and no
goodness of ours can extend unto him ᵉ :—yet as parents delight to use the labour of their children in things which are
no way beneficial unto themselves ᶠ ; so God is pleased to
use us, as instruments for setting forth his glory, though his
glory stand in no need of us, though we cannot add one
cubit thereunto.   He hath made all men " in usus profun-
darum cogitationum suarum ᵍ," unto the uses of his unsearchable counsels.—" He hath made all things for himself, yea, even the wicked for the day of evil ʰ."   Yet he is
pleased to esteem some men ' meet for uses,' which others
are not ⁱ ; and to ' set apart ' some for himself, and for those
uses ᵏ.   God, by his wisdom, ordereth ˡ and draweth the
blind and brute motions of the worst creatures unto his own
honour, as the huntsman doth the rage of the dog to his

ⁿ Psalm l. 15.   ˣ Psalm cxviii. 21.   ʸ 2 Thess. i. 9.   ᶻ Rom. ix. 17.
ᵃ Isai. xxv. 3.   ᵇ Psalm xxx. 9. lxxxviii. 10, 11.   ᶜ Isai. xxxviii. 19.
ᵈ Psalm vi. 4, 5. cxviii. 17.   ᵉ Job xxii. 2. xxxv. 7.   ᶠ Deus suam
gloriam quærit, non propter se, sed propter nos. *Aquin.* 22. qu. 3. art. 8. ad. 1. m.
ᵍ *Aug.* de Nuptiis et Concupis. l. 2. c. 16.—Omnia propter se ipsum fecit Deus,
omnia propter suos : *Bern.* Ser. 3. in die Pentecost.   ʰ Prov. xvi. 4.
ⁱ 2 Tim. ii. 21.   ᵏ Psalm iv. 3. Isai. xliii. 21.   ˡ Est in malorum potestate peccare : ut autem peccando, hoc vel hoc illâ malitiâ faciant, non est in
illorum potestate, sed Dei, dividentis tenebras et ordinantis eas ; ut hinc etiam
quod faciunt contra voluntatem Dei, non impleatur nisi voluntas Dei. *Aug.* de
prædest. Sanct. c. 16.—Vid. etiam ep. 69. q. 6. ep. 120. c. 2. ep. 141. l. 2. q. 1. sup.
Exod. qu. 18. l. 83. quæst. 27. de Civit. Dei, l. 11. c. 17.

pleasure, or the mariner the blowing of the wind unto his voyage, or the artist the heat of the fire unto his work, or the physician the blood-thirstiness of the leech unto a cure. But godly men are fitted to bring actually glory unto him, to glorify him doingly [m]. And this is that, which God chiefly takes pleasure in.

Our Saviour bids his disciples cast their net into the sea; and when they had drawn their net, he bids them bring of the fish which they had then caught: and yet we find, that there was a fire of coals, and fish laid thereon, and bread provided on the land before [n]:—thereby teaching us that he did not use their industry for any need that he had of it, but because he would honour them so far as to let them honour him with their obedience. And therefore even then when God tells his people that he needed not their services, yet he calls upon them for thanksgiving [o].

This then is a strong argument to be used in prayer for pardon, for grace, for any spiritual mercy :—" Lord, if I perish, I shall not praise thee, I shall not be meet for my master's uses. Thy glory will only be forced out of me with blows; like fire out of a flint, or water out of a rock. But thou delightest to see thy poor servants operate towards thy glory, to see them not forced by power, but by love, to show forth thy praises; and this we shall never do, till sin be pardoned."—God can bring light out of light, as the light of the stars out of the light of the sun; and he can bring light out of darkness, as he did at first: but in the one case, there is a meetness for such a use,—in the other, not. Now we are not meet subjects for God to reap honour from, till sin be pardoned, till grace be conferred :—then we shall give him the praise of his mercy in pitying such grievous sinners, —and the praise of his power and wisdom in healing such mortal diseases,—and the praise of his glorious and free grace, in sending salvation to those that did not enquire after it,—and the praise of his patience in forbearing us so long, and waiting that he might be gracious,—and the praise of his wonderful providence in causing all things to work together for our good,—and the praise of his justice by taking

[m] 1 Cor. x. 30, 31. Ephes. i. 11, 12.   [n] John xxi. 6, 9, 10.   [o] Psalm l. 9, 14.

part with him against our own sins, and joining with his grace to revenge the blood of Christ upon them. A potsherd is good enough to hold fire; but nothing but a sound and pure vessel is meet to put wine or any rich " depositum" into.

SECT. 5.—IV. ' Ut principium operandi,' as a principle of emendation of life, and of new obedience.—" Lord, take away iniquity, and receive us into favour, and then will we be thankful unto thee, and that shall produce amendment of life; ' Asshur shall not save us, neither will we ride upon horses,' " &c. A thankful apprehension of the goodness of God in forgiving, giving, saving, honouring us, is one of the principal foundations of sincere obedience. Then the soul will think nothing too good for God, that hath shown himself so good unto it. " What shall I render unto the Lord for all his benefits?" saith the prophet David q; and a little after it follows, " O Lord, truly I am thy servant; I am thy servant, and the son of thine handmaid ;" that is, ' a homeborn servant, thine from my mother's womb '—It is an allusion to those who were born of servants in the house of their masters, and so were in a condition of servants. " Partus sequitur ventrem." If the mother be a handmaid q, the child is a servant too; and so the Scripture calleth them ' filios domus,' children of the house r. His heart, being enlarged in thankfulness, presently minded him of the deep engagements, that did bind him unto service even from the womb. True filial and evangelical obedience ariseth from faith and love. Faith shows us God's love to us ; and thereby worketh in us a reciprocal love unto him. " We love him, because he first loved us s." This is the only thing, wherein a servant of God may answer him, and may, " de simili mutuam rependere vicem," as Bernard speaks, return back unto God what he gives him. " If he be angry with me t, I must

---

P Jure gentium, servi nostri sunt, qui ex ancillis nostris nascuntur. Leg. 5. D. de statu Hominis. et Leg. 28. de usuris et fructibus. *Ib.*   q Psalm cxvi. 12.
r Gen. xiv. 14, 15. iii. 17, 12. Lev. xxii. 11. Eccles. ii. 6.   s 1 John iv. 19.
t Si mihi irascatur Deus, num illi ego similiter redirascar ? non utique ; sed pavebo ; sed contremiscam ; sed veniam deprecabor. Ita si me arguat, non redarguetur à me ; sed ex me potius justificabitur : nec si me judicabit, judicabo ego eum, sed adorabo. Si dominatur, me oportet servire : si imperat, me oportet parere : nunc jam videas de amore quam aliter sit ; nam cum amat Deus, non aliud vult quam amari. *Bern.* Serm. 83. in Cantic.

not be angry again with him ; but fear and tremble, and beg
for pardon : if he reprove me, I must not reprove but justify him : if he judge me, I must not judge but adore him.
But if he love me, I must take the boldness to love him
again, for therefore he loves that he may be loved."—And
this love of ours unto Christ makes us ready to do every
thing, which he requires of us ; because we know, that he
hath done much more for us than he requireth of us.   "The
love of Christ," saith the apostle, "constraineth us,—because we thus judge, that if one died for all, then were all
dead ;" that is, ' either dead in and with him,' in regard of
the guilt and punishment of sin, so as to be freed from the
damnation of it,—or dead by way of conformity unto his
death, in dying unto sin, and crucifying the old man, so as
to shake off the power and strength of it.   And the fruit of
all, both in dying and in loving, is this, " That we should not
live unto ourselves, but unto him that died for us, and rose
again." Thus love argues from the greater to the lesser ;
from the greatness of his work for us, to the smallness of
ours unto him. If he died to give us life, then we must
live to do him service.

Fear [u] produceth servile and unwilling performances : as
those fruits which grow in winter, or in cold countries, are
sour, unsavoury, and unconcocted ; but those which grow in
summer, or in hotter countries, by the warmth and influence
of the sun, are sweet and wholesome : such is the difference
between those fruits of obedience, which fear and which
love produceth.   The most formal principle of obedience is
love ; and the first beginnings of love in us unto God, arise
from his mercies unto us being thankfully remembered.   And
this teacheth the soul thus to argue ; " ' God hath given deliverances unto me ; and should I break his command-

---

u Quis coram Deo innocens invenitur, qui vult fieri quod vetatur, si subtrahas
quod timetur ?   Qui gehennam metuit, non peccare metuit, sed ardere ; ille pu-
tem peccare metuit, qui peccatum ipsum sicut gehennas odit. *Aug.* ep. 144.—
Bern. ser. de Trip. Cohar.—Vere Christianus est, qui plus amat dominum quam
timet gehennam : ut etiamsi dicat illi Deus, ' Utere deliciis carnalibus sempiter-
nis, et quantum potes, pecca ; nec morieris, nec in gehennam mitteris, sed mecum tantummodo non eris ;'—exhorrescat, et omnino non peccet, non jam ut in
illud quod timebat, non incidat, sed ne illum quem sic amat, offendat. *Idem* de
Catech. Rudibus, c. 17. de Natur. et Grat. c. 57. cont. 2.   Et Pelag. l. 1. c. 9. et
l. 2. 9, 6.

ments ˣ?' Christ gave himself to redeem me from all iniquity, and to make me in a special manner his own ; therefore I must be ' zealous of good works ʸ :' therefore I must ' show forth the virtues of him, that called me out of darkness into his marvellous light ᶻ.' " No more frequent, more copious common place in all the Scriptures than this,—to call for obedience, and to aggravate disobedience, by the considera- tion of the great things, that God hath done for us ᵃ. In the law ᵇ, a ransomed man became the servant of him that bought and delivered him : and upon this argument, the apostle calls for obedience : " Ye are not your own, but ye are bought with a price : therefore glorify God in your body, and in your spirits, which are God's ᶜ." We have but the use of our- selves ; the property is his ᵈ ; and we may do nothing to violate that.

SECT. 6.—V. Ut instrumentum divinæ gloriæ, as a means and instrument of publishing God's praises. There is an emphasis in the word *lips*. Sometimes it is a diminutive word, taking away from the duty performed ; as Mat. xv. 8, " This people honour me with their lips, but their heart is far from me." But here is an augmentative word that enlargeth the duty, and makes it wider. " I will sacrifice unto thee," saith Jonah, " with the voice of thanksgiving ᵉ." God regard- eth not the sacrifice, if this be not the use that is made of it, to publish and celebrate the glory of his name. The outward ceremony is nothing without the thankfulness of the heart ; and the thankfulness of the heart is too little, ex- cept it have a voice to proclaim it abroad, that others may learn to glorify and admire the works of the Lord too. It is not enough to sacrifice ; not enough to sacrifice the sacri- fices of thanksgiving,—except withal we " declare his works with rejoicing ᶠ." There is a private thankfulness of the soul within itself, when, meditating on the goodness of God, it doth in secret return the tribute of an humble and obedient

---

ˣ Ezra xiii. 14.   ʸ Tit. ii. 14.   ᶻ 1 Pet. ii. 9.   ᵃ Deut. xiii. 20, 21.
xi. 7, 8. xxix. 32. vi. 7. Josh. xxiv. 2, 14. 1 Sam. xii. 24. Isai. i. 2. Jer. ii. 5, 6.
Hos. ii. 8. Mich. vi. 3, 5.   ᵇ Per modum pignoris, licet non per modum
mancipii. *Leg.* 2. Cod. de postliminio reversis, &c.—Nempe servi sunt quoad
solvatur pretium redemptori. Si quis servum captum ab hostibus redemerit,
protinus est redimentis. l. 12. sect. 7. F. de captivis.   ᶜ 1 Cor. vi. 19, 23.
ᵈ Fructuarius nihil facere debet in perniciem proprietatis. l. 13. sect. 4. F. de
usu fructu.   ᵉ Jonah ii. 9.   ᶠ Psalm cvii. 22.

heart back again unto him, which is to praise God on the
bed : and there is public thanksgiving, when men " tell of
the wondrous works of God in the congregation of his
saints[f]." Now here the church promiseth this public thanksgiving; it shall not be the thankfulness of the heart only,
but of the *lips* too. As it is noted of the thankful leper,
that " with a loud voice he glorified God[g]."—" The living,
the living shall praise thee," saith Hezekiah : but how should
they do it ? " The fathers to the children shall make known
thy truth[h]." There are some affections and motions of the
heart that do stop the mouth, are of cold, stupefactive, and
constringent nature ; as the sap stays and hides itself in the
root, while it is winter[i]. Such is fear and extremity of
grief. " Come," saith the prophet, " let us enter into our de-
fenced cities, and let us be silent there ; for the Lord our God
hath put us to silence[k]." Other affections open the mouth,
are of an expansive and dilating nature, know not how to be
straitened or suppressed ; and of all these, joy and sense
of God's mercy can least contain itself in the compass of
our narrow breast, but will spread and communicate itself to
others. A godly heart is, in this, like unto those flowers,
which shut when the sun sets, when the night comes,—and
open again, when the sun returns and shines upon them. If
God withdraw his favour, and send a night of affliction,
they shut up themselves, and their thoughts in silence : but
if he shine again, and shed abroad the light and sense of his
love upon them, then their heart and mouth is wide open towards Heaven, in lifting up praises unto him. Hannah prayed
silently, so long as she was in bitterness of soul, and of a
sorrowful spirit[l] : but as soon as God answered her prayers,
and filled her heart with joy in him, presently "her mouth
was enlarged" into a song of thanksgiving[m].

There is no phrase more usual in the Psalms, than to ' sing
forth praises' unto God ; and it is not used without a special
emphasis. For it is one thing to praise, and another to sing
praises[n].—This is, to publish, to declare, to speak of, abundantly to utter the memory of God's great goodness, that

[f] Psalm cxlix. 15. xxvi. 7, 12.   [g] Luke xvii. 15.   [h] Isai. xxxviii. 19.
[i] *Plutarch.* de capiend. ex hostibus utilitate.—*Arist.* Problem. sect. 27.   [k] Jer.
viii. 14. Isai. xx. 14.   [l] 1 Sam. i. 12, 15.   [m] 1 Sam. ii. 1.   [n] Psalm
cxlvi. 2.

' one generation may derive praises unto another,' as the expressions are, Psalm cxlv. 4, 7. And therefore we find in the most solemn thanksgivings[o], that the people of God were wont, in great companies, and with musical instruments, to sound forth the praises of God, and to cause their joy to be heard afar off[p]. This then is the force of the expression;— "Lord, when thou hast taken away iniquity, and extended thy grace and favour to us, we will not only have thankful hearts, every man to praise thee by himself; but we will have thankful lips to show forth thy praise; we will stir up and encourage one another; we will tell our children, that the generations to come may know the mercy of our God."

This is a great part of the communion of saints, to join together in God's praises. There is a communion of sinners, wherein they combine together to dishonour God, and encourage one another in evil[q]. Eve was no sooner caught herself; but she became a kind of serpent, to deceive and to catch her husband. A tempter had no sooner made a sinner, but that sinner became a tempter. As therefore God's enemies hold communion to dishonour him; so great reason there is that his servants should hold communion to praise him, and to animate and hearten one another unto duty, as men that draw at an anchor, and soldiers that set upon a service, use to do with mutual encouragements[r]. The holy oil for the sanctuary was made of many spices, compounded by the art of the perfumer[s], to note unto us, that those duties are sweetest which are made up in a communion of saints, each one contributing his influence and furtherance unto them: as in winds and rivers, where many meet in one, they are strongest,—and in chains and jewels where many links and stones are joined in one, they are richest. All good is diffusive, like leaven in a lump, like sap in a root: it will find the way from the heart to every faculty of soul and body, and from thence to the ears and hearts of others. Every living creature was made with the seed of life in it, to preserve itself

---

[o] Apud poetas clarissimos laudes heroum ac Deorum inter regalia convivia ad citharam canebantur. *Quint.* l. 1. c. 10. Spalding. i. 215.—Nec aliter veri Dei laudes in conviviis Christianorum. *Tert.* Apol. c. 19.—*Cypr.* l. 2. ep. 2.   [p] Jer. xii. 27, 31, 43. Isai. xii. 4, 5, 6. Jer. xxxi. 7.   [q] Psalm lxiv. 5. lxxxiii. 5, 8. Prov. i. 10, 11.   [r] Isai. ii. 3. Zach. viii. 21. Mal. iii. 16.   [s] Exod. xxiii. 24, 25.

by multiplying [t]. And of all seeds, that of the Spirit, and the Word [u], is most vigorous; and in nothing so much as in glorifying God, when the joy of the Lord, which is our strength, doth put itself forth to derive the praises of his name, and to call in others to the celebration of them.

SECT. 7. From all which we learn, 1. By what means (amongst many others) to try the truth of our conversions; namely, By the life and workings of true thankfulness unto God for pardon of sin, and accepting into favour. Certainly when a man is converted himself, his heart will be enlarged, and his mouth will be filled with the praises of the Lord; he will acquaint others, what a good God he is turned unto. If he have found Christ himself, as Andrew, and Philip, and the woman of Samaria did, he will presently report it to others, and invite them to ' come and see [x].' If Zaccheus be converted, he receiveth Christ joyfully [y]. If Matthew be converted, he entertains him with a feast [z]. If Cornelius be instructed in the knowledge of him, he will call his kinsfolk and friends to partake of such a banquet [a]. If David be converted himself, he will endeavour that other sinners may be converted too [b], and will show them what the Lord hath done for his soul. The turning of a sinner from evil to good, is like the turning of a bell from one side to another, you cannot turn it, but it will make a sound, and report its own motion. He that hath not a mouth open to report the glory of God's mercy to his soul, and to strengthen and edify his brethren, may justly question the truth of his own conversion. In Aaron's garments (which were types of holiness) there were to be golden bells and pomegranates; which (if we may make any allegorical application of it) intimateth unto us, that as a holy life is fruitful and active in the duties of spiritual obedience, so it is loud and vocal in sounding forth the praises of God, and thereby endeavouring to edify the church. Gideon's lamps and pitchers were accompanied with trumpets: when God is pleased to put any light of grace into these earthen vessels of ours, we should have mouths full of thankfulness, to return unto him the glory of his goodness.

[t] Gen. i. 1, 11, 12.   [u] 1 John iii. 29. 1 Pet. i. 23.   [x] John i. 41, 46. iv. 29.   [y] Luke xix. 6.   [z] Luke v. 29.   [a] Acts xviii. 24. [b] Psalm li. 13.

And as that repentance is unsound, which is not accompanied with thankfulness, so that thankfulness is but empty and hypocritical, which doth not spring out of sound repentance. We use to say, that the words of fools are 'in labris nata,' born [c] in their lips : but the words of wise men are 'è sulco pectoris,' drawn up out of an inward judgement. The *calves of the lips* are no better than the calves of the stall, in God's account, if they have not a heart in them. Without this, the promise here made to God would be no other than that, with which nurses deceive their little children, when they promise them a gay-golden-new-nothing. Praise in the mouth without repentance in the heart, is like a sea-weed that grows without a root:—like the pouring of balm and spices upon a dead body, which can never thoroughly secure it from putrefaction :—like a perfume about one sick of the plague, whose sweet smell carries infection along with it. It is not the mentioning of mercies, but the improving of them unto piety, which expresseth our thankfulness unto God. God sets every blessing upon our score, and expects an answer and return suitable. He compares Chorazin and Bethsaida with Tyre and Sidon ; and if their lives be as bad as these, their punishment shall be much heavier, because the mercies they enjoyed, were much greater. The not using of mercies is the being unthankful for them : and it is a heavy account which men must give for abused mercies [e]. Sins against mercy, and under mercy, are 'the first ripe fruit ;' when the sun shines hottest, the fruits ripen fastest. God doth not bear so long with the provocations of a church, as of those that are not a people ; the sins of the Amorites were longer in ripening, than the sins of Israel [f]. When judgement is abroad, it will begin at the house of God.

SECT. 8. II. We should be so much the more earnestly pressed unto this, by how much it is the greater evi-

---

[c] *Quint.* Instit. l. 10. c. 3.—*A. Gell.* l. 1. c. 15.—Βαθεῖαν ἄλοκα διὰ φρενὸς καρπούμενος, 'Εξ ἧς τὰ κεδνὰ βλαστάνει βουλεύματα. *Æsch.* ed. Blomfield, 590.—Dicta, factis deficientibus, erubescunt. *Tert.* de Patria, c. 1. [d] Μία ἀμοιβὴ κυριωτάτη, ταῦτα δρᾶν ἅπερ ἀρεστὰ τῷ Θεῷ. *Clem. Alex.* Strom. l. 7.— Deum colit, quisquis imitatus est. *Senec.* epist. 95.—Vid. *Chrysost.* Hom. 25. in Matth. [e] Deut. xxxii. 6. Amos ii. 9, 13. Luke iii. 7. Heb. vi. 7. [f] Amos viii. 1, 2. Jer. i. 11, 12.

dence of our conversion unto God, and by how much
more apt we are to call for mercies when we want
them, than, with the leper, to return praises when we do
enjoy them. Ten cried to be healed; but there was but one
that returned glory to God. Vessels will sound when they
are empty: fill them, and they are presently dumb. When
we want mercies, then with Pharaoh we cry out for pardon,
for peace, for supplies, for deliverance: but when prayers are
answered, and our turn served, how few remember the method which God prescribes, "Call upon me in the day of
trouble; I will hear thee, and thou shalt glorify me g?" Yea,
how many, like swine, trample on the meat that feeds them,
and tread under foot the mercies that preserve them! How
many are so greedily intent upon the things they desire h,
that they cannot see nor value the things they enjoy!
" Omnis festinatio cæca est." It is noted even of good king
Hezekiah, that he " did not render according to the benefits "
which he had received i. Therefore we should be exhorted
in our prayers for pardon and grace, to do as the church
here doth, to promise the sacrifices of thankfulness and obedience, not as a price to purchase mercy (for our good ex-
tends not unto God k), but as a tie and obligation upon ourselves, to acknowledge and return the praise of mercy to him
that gives it. And this the apostle exhorteth us unto, that
" our requests should be made known unto God," not only
with prayer and supplication, but "with thanksgiving l;"
which we find to have been his own practice m. We should
keep a catalogue n of God's mercies to quicken us unto duty,
as well as a catalogue of our own sins, to make us cry
for mercy. And unto this duty of thanksgiving we may be
excited,—

First, By the consideration of God's greatness. " Great
is the Lord ; and (therefore) greatly to be praised o." The

g Psalm l. 15.   h Seneca de Benefic. l. 3. c. 3.—Liv. l. 22.   i 2 Chron.
xxxii. 25.   k Psalm xvi. 2.   l Phil. iv. 6. 1 Thess. v. 17, 18. 1 Tim. ii. 1.
m Ephes. iii. 14, 20, 21.   n Vid. Field of the Church, l. 1. c. 1. Qui curat esse
nisi propter te, pro nihilo est, et nihil est. Qui vult esse sibi et non tibi, nihil
esse incipit inter omnia. Bern. serm. 20. in Cant.—Eo quisque pessimus, quo optimus, si hoc ipsum quod est optimus, adscribat sibi. Serm. 84. in Cantic.
o Psalm cxlv. 3.

praises of God should be according to his name [p]. All
things were made for no other end, but to return glory to
him that made them. Because all things are *of* him, therefore all must be *to* him [q]. And this the very figure of the
world teacheth us: for a circular line ends where it began,
and returns back into its original point,—by that means
strengthening and preserving itself. For things are usually
strongest, when nearest their original; and the more remote
from that, the weaker they grow. As a tree is strongest at
the root, and a branch or bough next the trunk or stock, and
the further out it goes from thence, the smaller and weaker
it grows too; and the further it is from the original of its
being, the nearer it is unto not being;—so all creatures are
hereby taught, both for preservation of that being they have,
and for supply of what perfections they want, and in both,
for the setting forth of the greatness of their Maker (out of
whose infinite Being all finite beings are sustained and perfected),—to run back unto God, for whose sake they are
and have been created. Rivers come from the sea, and
therefore run back into the sea again. The trees receive sap
from the earth; and, within a while, pay it back in those
leaves that fall down to the earth again. Now as God hath
made all creatures thus to show forth the glory of his greatness, so he will have them do it by these principles, and in
that manner of working which he hath planted in them. In-
animate and mere natural creatures are bid to praise the
Lord [r]; but this they do blindly and ignorantly, like the
arrow which flies toward the mark, but understandeth not its
own motion, being directed thither by an understanding
without and above itself. And thus when every thing, by
the natural weight and inclination of its own form, moveth
to the place where it may be preserved, or draweth to it
those further degrees of perfection, whereby it may be im-
proved, and have more of being communicated to it,—it may
truly be said to praise the Lord, in that it obeyeth the law
which he planted in it; and it is, by his wise providence,
carried back towards him, to derive its conservation and
perfection from the same fountain, from whence its being
did proceed. But now reasonable creatures being by God

p Psalm xlviii. 10. xcvi. 8.　　q Rom. xi. 36.　　r Psalm cxlviii. 8, 9.

enriched with internal knowledge, and that knowledge in
his church exceedingly raised by his manifestation of himself, as their uttermost blessedness, in the Word unto them,
he therefore requires that we should work actively, and with
intention of the end for which he made us,—guiding all our
aims and inclinations towards his glory by that internal
knowledge of his excellency, which he hath implanted in us,
and revealed to us.   And indeed all other creatures are,
in this sense, said to glorify God, because the infinite power,
wisdom, goodness, and perfection of God, which are in their
beings and workings so notably relucent, do become the object of reasonable creatures, to contemplate upon, and by
that means draw forth admiration and adoration of him.

SECT. 9. Secondly, By the consideration of God's goodness. He deserves it at our hands. He gives more to us
than we are able to render unto him. The sun shines on the
moon with his own glorious light ; the moon returns but a
faint and spotted light upon the world. We can return
nothing unto God, but that which is his own[s]; and it goes
not with that purity from us, as it came unto us. We cannot send forth a thought round about us, but it will return
with a report of mercy, and that mercy calls for a return of
praise.   But above all[t], the goodness of God mentioned in
the text, "*Taking away iniquity, and receiving graciously,*"
this calls for the "*calves of the lips*" to be offered, as in the
new moons, with trumpets and solemnity[u]. The beams of the
sun the more directly they fall on the body of the moon, do
fill it with the more abundant light : so the more copious and
notable God's mercies are unto us, the more enlarged should
our praises be unto him. Therefore true penitents that have
more tasted of mercy, are more obliged unto thanksgiving[x].
" Excellent speech is not comely in the mouth of fools[y];
but praise is comely for the upright[z]." For as God is most
dishonoured by the sins of holy men, when they are committed against light, and break forth into scandal,—as a

---

[s] 1 Chron. xxix. 16.   [t] Magna est gratia, quæ tribuitur hominibus vehe-
menter egentibus, et in rebus magnis et difficilibus, et cum quis beneficium alicui
dat aut solus, aut primus. Vid. *Arist.* Rhet. l. 2. c. 7. Itaque in hujusmodi benefac-
tores admissa gravius vindicantur. l. 1. de obsequiis parentibus et patronis præ-
stand. D. et l. 28. de pœnis, sect. 8.   [u] Numb. x. 10.   [x] Psalm cxlvii. 20.
[y] Prov. xvii. 7.   [z] Psalm xxxiii. 1.

spot in silk is a greater blemish than in sackcloth ᵃ;—so is
he most honoured by the confession and praises of holy
men, because they know more of his glory and goodness
than others, and can report greater things of him. Wicked
men speak of God by hearsay, and by notion only; but
holy men, by intimate experience ᵇ: as the queen of Sheba
knew more of Solomon's wisdom from his mouth, than from
his fame. He that sees but the outward court and building
of a palace, can say it is a glorious place: but he that, like
the ambassadors of the king of Babylon in Hezekiah's time,
shall be admitted to see the house of precious things, and all
the treasures of the palace,—can speak much more honour-
ably of it. Every one might see and admire the stones of
the temple without, who were not admitted to view the gold
and curious workmanship within. The more intimate communion a man hath with God as a redeemer, the more glorious and abundant praises can he render unto him. Besides,
praise is the language of Heaven ᶜ; the whole happiness of
the saints there is to enjoy God, and their whole business is
to praise him. And they who are to live in another country,
will be more solicitous to learn the language, and fore-
acquaint themselves with the manners and usages of that
country, than they who have no hopes nor assurance of
coming thither. As they who have hope to be like Christ
in glory, will purify themselves, that they may in the mean
time be like him in grace ᵈ; so they that have hope to praise
him for ever in Heaven, will study the song of Moses, and
of the Lamb, before they come thither. And indeed none
can praise God but they that can abase and deny themselves.
Wicked men, in all duties, serve and seek themselves; but the
very formality of praise is to seek God, and to make him the
end of our so doing. The apostle exhorts us "to offer our-

ᵃ Pretiosam vestem exigua quævis macula turpius decolorat; nobis ad immun-
ditiem minima quævis inobedientia sufficit, &c. *Bernard.* ser. de triplici custodia.
2 Sam. xii. 14.   ᵇ Est locus ubi vere quiescens et quietus cernitur Deus;
locus omnino non judicis, non magistri, sed sponsi; sed heu rara hora, et parva
mora! *Bern.* Ser. 23. in Cant.—Mens, ineffabili verbi illecta dulcedine, quodam-
modo se sibi furatur, imò rapitur atque elabitur a seipsa, ut verbo fruatur: dulce
commercium: sed breve momentum et experimentum rarum. *Ibid.* Serm. 85.
vid. etiam Serm. 83. et Serm. 1, 3, 31.   ᶜ Illa domus lætitiæ est; ista, mi-
litiæ:—Illa domus laudis;—ista, orationis. *Bern.* ser. 2. in Dedicat. Eccle.
ᵈ 1 John iii. 2, 3.

selves a living sacrifice[e];" that is to say, to separate ourselves for God, and for his uses.   The sacrifice, we know,
was God's; for his sake it was burnt, and broken, and destroyed.   We must, by such sacrifices, deny ourselves, be
lost to ourselves; not serve, nor seek, nor aim at ourselves;
but resolve to esteem nothing dear in comparison of God's
honour, and to be willing any way, whether by life or by
death, that he may be magnified in us [f].   Love of communion
in natural creatures, is stronger than self-love.   Stones will
move upward, fire downward, to preserve the universe from
a vacuity, and to keep 'the compages' of nature together.
How much more is, and ought the love of God himself in
the new creature to be stronger than self-love, whereby it
seeks and serves itself!   And without this, all other services
are but Ananias's lie, lies to the Holy Ghost, keeping to ourselves what we would seem to bestow upon him.   Lifting up
the eyes, beating the breast, spreading the hands, bending
the knee, hanging down the head, levelling the countenance,
sighing, sobbing, fasting, howling, all nothing else but
mocking of God.   And we may say of such men, as the
emperor of him that sold the glasses for pearl, (though in a
sadder sense,) "Imposturam faciunt, et patientur;"—they
deceive God, and fail in his precepts, and they shall be themselves deceived, and fail in their own expectation: for "the
hope of the wicked shall perish."

III.   By a double consideration of ourselves.

SECT. 10.   I. Of our natural torpor and sluggishness
unto this duty.   As the Dead Sea drinks in the river Jordan,
and is never the sweeter; and the ocean all other rivers,
and is never the fresher;—so we are apt to receive daily mercies from God, and still remain insensible of them, unthankful for them.   God's mercies to us are like the dew on the
ground; our thanks to him, like the dew on the fleece.   We
are like fishermen's weels, wide at that end which lets in the
fish, but narrow at the other end, so that they cannot get
out again: greedy to get mercy, tenacious to hold it; but
unthankful in acknowledging or right using of it.   The rain
comes down from heaven in showers; it goes up but in mists.
We sow in our land one measure, and receive ten:—yea,

e Rom. xii. 1.   f Acts xxi. 13. Phil. i. 20.

Isaac received a hundred fold [g]; but God sows ten, it may be, a hundred mercies amongst us, when we scarce return the praise and the fruit of one.   Our hearts in this case are like the windows of the temple [h], ' wide inward,' to let in mercies,—but ' narrow outward,' to let forth praises.   Now as Solomon says, " If the iron be blunt, we must put to the more strength :" and as husbandmen use where the nature of land is more defective, to supply it with the more importunate labour ; so having hearts so earthly for the performance of so heavenly a duty, we should use the more holy violence upon them : and as the widow did extort justice from an unjust judge by her continual coming [i], we should press and urge, and with ingeminated importunity charge this duty upon ourselves, as the psalmist doth ;—" O that men would praise the Lord for his goodness, and for his wonderful works to the children of men [k]."

II. Of our own benefit.   For indeed all the benefit which ariseth out of this duty, redounds to us, and none to God. His glory is infinite, and eternally the same ; there is, nor can be, no accession unto that by all our praises [l].   When a glass reflecteth the brightness of the sun, there is but an acknowledgment of what was, not any addition of what was not.   When an excellent orator makes a panegyrical oration in praise of some honourable person, he doth not infuse any dram of worth into the person, but only setteth forth and declareth that which is, unto others.   A curious picture praiseth a beautiful face, not by adding beauty to it, but by representing that which was in it before.   The window which lets in light into a house, doth not benefit the light, but the house into which the light shineth : so our praising of God doth serve to quicken, comfort, and refresh ourselves, who have interest in so good a God ; or to edify and encourage our brethren, that they may be ambitious to serve so honourable a Master ;—but they add no lustre or glory to God at all.

SECT. 11.   Now lastly, for the right performance of this duty.   It is founded on the due apprehensions of God's being good, and of his doing good [m];— or on his excellency in him-

[g] Gen. xxvi. 12.   [h] 1 Kings vi. 4.   [i] Luke xviii. 5,   [k] Psalm cvii. 8, 15, 21, 31.   [l] Ipse sibi omnia. *Tertul.* contra Praxeam, c. 5.   [m] Psalm cxix. 68.

self, and his goodness unto us. In the former respect, it
standeth in adoring and extolling the great name of God,
ascribing in our hearts and mouths blessedness unto him,
acknowledging his infinite majesty in himself, and his sovereignty over his poor creatures [n];—and so covering our faces,
and abhorring ourselves in his sight [o], not daring to question
any of his deep, absolute, and most unsearchable counsels ;
—but because all things are *of* him, to acknowledge that all
things ought to be *for* and *to* him, and are to be reduced to
the ends of his glory, by the counsel of his own will [p]. In
the latter respect, as he is the God in whom we live, and
move, and have our being, and hope for our blessedness ; so
it importeth, First, A glorying and rejoicing in him as our
alone felicity [q].—Secondly, A choosing and preferring him
above all other good things, making him our end and aim,
in life, in death, in doing, in suffering [r].—Thirdly, A thankful acknowledgment of all his mercies, as most beneficial
unto us, and most gratuitous and free in regard of him [s].—
Lastly, A constant endeavour of a holy life, so to bring forth
fruit, to do the will of God, and to finish his work which
he hath set us ; so to order our conversation aright before
him, as that he may have ascribed unto him the glory of his
authority over the consciences of men, and of the power of
his love shed abroad in their hearts ; and that all [t] that see
our conversation, may say, " Doubtless, the God whom these
men serve after so holy a manner, for whom they despise all
outward and sinful pleasures, is a holy and blessed God ;
infinitely able to comfort, satisfy, and reward all those, that so
conscionably and constantly give themselves up unto him [n]."

n Exod. xv. 11. Mic. vii. 18.   o Isai. vi. Job xlii. 5, 6.   p Difficul-
tatem quæstionis, ' Cur alius sic, alius vero sic mortuus est,' velut non solvendo
solvit Apostolus—Et hujus profunditatis horrorem usque ad hoc perduxit, ut di-
ceret, ' Etiam cujus vult miseretur, et quem vult obdurat.' *Aug.* contr. 2. ep. Pelag. l. 4. c. 7. et l. 4. c. 6.—Cur in diversa causa idem judicium nisi ' Hoc volo ;'
—de Dono Persev. c. 8.—De peccat. meritis et remiss. l. 2. c. 5.—Rom. ix. 20, 21.
xi. 33, 36. Matth. xi. 25, 26. Psalm cxxxv. 5, 6. Job ix. 12. Ephes. i. 11.
q Psalm xxxiii. 1. Hab. iii. 18. Phil. iv. 4.   r Rom. iv. 7, 8.   s 2 Sam.
vii. 18. Lam. iii. 22, 23.   t Justinus Martyr de se fatetur se, conspecta
Christianorum in morte constantiâ, collegisse veram esse quæ apud ipsos vigeret,
pietatem. Apol. 1. Illa ipsa obstinatis quam exprobratis, magistra est : quis enim
non contemplatione ejus concutitur ad requirendum quid intus in re sit ? Quis
non ubi requisivit, accedit ? ubi accessit, pati exoptat ? *Tert.* Apol. c. ult.
u John xv. 8. xvii. 4. Psalm l. 23. Deut. iv. 6, 7. Matth. lii. 16. 2 Cor. ix. 13.
1 Pet. xii.

SECT. 12. The second particular in their covenant is, Amendment of life, and a more special care against those sins of carnal confidence, and spiritual adultery, whereby they have formerly dishonoured and provoked God. From whence there are two observations which offer themselves:—

1. That true repentance and sound conversion, as it makes a man thankful for the pardon of sin past, so it makes him careful [x] against the practice of sin for the time to come ; especially those particular sins, whereby he had formerly most dishonoured God, and defiled his own conscience. This doctrine consisteth of two parts, which we will consider asunder.

And first, Of this care and purpose of amendment in general. When the poor converts, who had been guilty of the most precious and innocent blood that ever was shed, began to be convinced of that horrible sin, and found those nails wherewith they had fastened the Lord of Glory to a cross, pricking and piercing of their own hearts,—with what bleeding and relenting affections did they mourn over him! with what earnest importunities did they require after the way of salvation, wherein they might serve and enjoy him! Never were their hands more cruel in shedding that blood, than their hearts were now solicitous to be bathed in it, to be cleansed by it [y]. The poor prodigal, who is the emblem of a penitent sinner, when he ' came to himself again,' or ' bethought himself,' as the phrase is [z], (for we do never depart from God, but we do withal forsake and lose ourselves, and are transported with a spiritual madness from our right minds), immediately grew to a resolution of arising out of that base and brutish condition, and of going home to his father,—and, by that means, to his wit and senses again. So when by John's preaching of repentance, men were turned to the ' wisdom of the just' (for all unrighteousness is folly and madness), and were prepared for the Lord, we immediately find what a special care they had to be informed in the ways of duty, earnestly enquiring after that new course of obedience, which they were now to walk in [a]. All true peni-

---

[x] Oportebat quidem, si fieri posset, revivere me (ut ita loquar) denuo, quod male vixi ; sed faciam recogitando, quod reoperando non possum. *Bern.* Ser. de Cant. Ezek.   [y] Acts ii. 37.   [z] 1 Kings viii. 47.   [a] Luke iii. 10, 12. 14.

tents are of the mind of these in the text, "We will not say
any more, And what have I to do any more with idols?" or
as Ezra in his penitent prayer, "Should we now again
break thy commandments [b]?" When Christ rose from the
dead, he 'died no more:' and when we repent of sin, it
must be with a repentance, that must never any more be repented of[c]. The time past of our life must suffice us to
have wrought the will of the Gentiles[d].

This care ariseth from the nature of true repentance,
which hath two names usually given it, μετάνοια, 'a change
of the mind:' the heart is framed to have other and truer
notions of sin, of grace, of heaven, of hell, of conscience,
of salvation, than it had before: for the mind of wicked
men being defiled, they can frame to themselves none but
impure apprehensions of spiritual things, as a yellow eye
sees every thing yellow, and a bitter palate tastes every thing
bitter. 2. Μεταμέλεια, 'a change of the cares and endeavours of life:,—That whereas, before, a man made provision
for the flesh, and his study and care was how to satisfy the
lusts of his own heart[e], what he should eat, what he should
drink, wherewith he should be clothed;—now his care is
how he may be saved, how he may honour and enjoy God[f],
The first question in repentance is, "What have I done[g]?"
and the next question is, "What shall I do[h]?" And this
care repentance worketh[i];—

SECT. 13. First, By a godly sorrow for sin past. It brings
into a man's remembrance the history of his former life;
makes him, with heaviness of spirit, recount the guilt of so
many innumerable sins, wherewith he hath bound himself
as with chains of darkness; the loss of so much precious
time, mispent in the service of such a master, as had no
other wages to give but shame and death;—the horrible in-
dignities thereby offered to the majesty and justice of God;
—the odious contempt of his holy will, and sovereign authority;—the daring neglect of his threatenings, and under-
valuing of his rewards;—the high provocation of his jealousy
and displeasure;—the base corrivalry and contesting of

b Ezra ix. 13.   c Rom. vi. 9, 12. 1 Cor. vii. 10.   d 1 Pet. iv. 3.
e Rom. xiii. 14.   f Acts ii. 37. xvi. 30.   g Jer. viii. 6.   h Acts ix. 6.
i Consilium futuri ex præterito venit. Sen.

filthy lusts with the grace of the gospel, and the precious
blood of the Son of God;—the gainsaying, and wrestling,
and stubborn antipathy of a carnal heart to the pure motions
of the Spirit and Word of Christ;—the presumptuous re-
pulses of him that standeth at the door and knocks, waiting
that he may be gracious;—the long turning of his back, and
thrusting away from him the word of reconciliation, wherein
Christ, by his ambassadors, had so often beseeched him to
be reconciled unto God:—The remembrance of these things
makes a man look with self-abhorrency upon himself, and
full detestation upon his former courses.—And he now no
longer considers the silver or the gold, the profit or the pleasure of his wonted lusts:—though they be never so delectable
or desirable in the eye of flesh [i], he looks upon them as ac-
cursed things to be thrown away, as the converts did upon
their costly and curious books [k]. Sin is like a painted picture: on the one side of it, to the impenitent, appeareth
nothing but the beauty of pleasure, whereby it bewitcheth
and allureth them;—on the other side, to the penitent appeareth nothing but the horrid and ugly face of guilt and
shame, whereby it amazeth and confoundeth them. Thus
the remembrance of sin past (which they are very careful to
keep always in their sight [l]), doth, by godly sorrow, work
especial care of amendment of life for the time to come [m].

Secondly, By a present sense of the weight and burden of
remaining corruptions, which work, and move, and put forth
what strength they can, to resist the grace of God in us. As
the time past wherein sin reigned, so the present burden of
sin besetting us, is esteemed sufficient, and makes a man
careful not to load himself wilfully with more, being ready to
sink, and forced to cry out under the pain of those which he
unwillingly lieth under already. A very glutton [n] when he is
in a fit of the gout or stone, will forbear those meats which
feed so painful diseases:—a penitent sinner is continually in
pain under the body of sin; and therefore dares not feed so
dangerous and tormenting a disease. The more spiritual

---

[i] Πεινῶντι γὰρ ἀνδρὶ μᾶζα τιμιωτέρα Χρυσοῦ τε κᾀλέφαντος. Achæus Eretri-
ens. apud Athenæum, 6. c. 20.   [k] Acts xix. 19. Isai. xxx. 22. xxxi. 7.
[l] Psalm li. 3.   [m] 2 Chron. vi. 37. 38. Psalm cxix. 59. Ezek. xvi. 61, 63.
xx. 43.   [n] Εἰ τοῖς μεθυσκομένοις ἑκάστης ἡμέρας, Ἀλγεῖν συνέβαινε τὴν
κεφαλὴν πρὸ τοῦ πιεῖν Τὸν ἄκρατον, ἡμῶν οὐδὲ εἷς ἔπινεν ἄν. Clearchus apud
Athenæum, l. 14. c. 1.

any man is[o], the more painful and burdensome is corruption to him[p]. For sin to the new man is as sickness to the natural man. The more exquisite and delicate the natural senses are, the more are they sensible and affected with that which offends nature[q]. Contraries cannot be together without combat. The spirit will lust against the flesh, and not suffer a man to fulfil the lusts of it[r]. The seed of God will keep down the strength of sin[s].

Thirdly, By a holy jealousy, and godly fear of the falseness and backsliding of our corrupt heart[t], lest, like Lot's wife, it should look back towards Sodom; and, like Israel, have a mind hankering after the flesh-pots of Egypt, the wonted profits and pleasures of forsaken lusts. A godly heart prizeth the love of God, and the feelings of spiritual comfort, from thence arising, above all other things; and is afraid to lose them. It hath felt the burnings of sin; the stinging of these fiery serpents; and hath often been forced to befool itself, and to beshrew its own ignorance, and, with Ephraim, to smite upon the thigh. And the burnt child dreads the fire, and dares not meddle any more with it; considers the heaviness of God's frown,—the rigour of his law,—the weakness and fickleness of the heart of man,—the difficulty of finding Christ out when he hath withdrawn himself,—and of recovering light and peace again, when the soul hath wilfully brought itself under a cloud: and therefore will not venture to harden itself against God. Thus godly fear keeps men from sin[u].

Fourthly, By a love to Christ, and a sweet recounting of the mercies of God in him. The less a man loves sin, the more he shall love Christ. Now repentance works a hatred of sin, and thereupon a love of Christ; which love is evermore operative, and putting forth itself towards holiness of

[o] Conflictus miserabilis. *Aug.* de nup. et concup. l. 2. c. 1. [p] Rom. vii. 22. [q] Quo quis pejus se habet, minus sentit. *Sen.* ep. 52. [r] Gal. iii. 16, 17. [s] 1 John iii. 9. [t] Φόβος βουλευτικοὺς ποιεῖ. *Arist.* Rhet. l. 2. c. 5.—Solicitus incipit ambulare cum Deo suo, et ex omni parte scrutatur, ne vel in levissima re tremendæ illius Majestatis offendatur aspectus. Sic ardens et lucens nondum in domo se esse confidat, ubi, sine omni timore ventorum, accensum lumen soleat deportari, sed meminerit se esse sub die, et utrâque manu studeat operire quod portat, &c. *Bernard.* Serm. 3. in vigil. nativ. [u] Job xxxi. 23. Psalm cxix. 120. Prov. xxviii. 14. Eccles. ix. 2. Jer. xxxii. 40. Phil. ii. 12. Psalm iv. 4.

life. As the love of God in Christ towards us worketh forgiveness of sin; so our reciprocal love, wrought by the feeling and comfort of that forgiveness, worketh in us a hatred of sin. A direct love begets a reflect love, as the heat, wrought in the earth, strikes back a heat into the air again. The woman in the gospel, " having much forgiven her, loved much ˣ." " We love him because he loved us first :" and love will not suffer a man to wrong the things which he loves. What man ever threw away jewels or money, when he might have kept them, except when the predominant love of something better, made these things comparatively hateful ʸ? What woman would be persuaded to throw away her sucking child from her breast unto swine or dogs to devour it ? Our love to Christ and his law will not suffer us to cast him off, or to throw his law behind our backs. New obedience is ever joined unto pardon of sin and repentance for it, by the method of God's decrees, by the order and chain of salvation ; and ariseth out of the internal character and disposition of a child of God. We are not sons only by adoption, appointed to a new inheritance ; but we are sons by regeneration also, partakers of a new nature, designed unto a new life, joined unto a new head, descended from a new Adam ; unto whom, therefore, we are, in the power of his resurrection, and in the fellowship of his sufferings, to be made conformable ᶻ. And the apostle hath many excellent and weighty arguments to enforce this upon us ᵃ. " If then ye be risen with Christ, seek those things that are above, where Christ is sitting on the right hand of God. Set your affections on things above, not on things on the earth. For ye are dead, and your life is hid with Christ in God : when Christ, who is our life, shall appear, then shall ye also appear with him in glory."

1st. Our fellowship with Christ: "We are risen with him :" what he did corporally for us, he doth the same spiritually in us. As a Saviour and mediator, he died and rose alone ; but as a head and second Adam, he never did any thing, but his mystical body and seed were so taken into the fellowship of it, as to be made conformable unto it. Therefore if he

---

ˣ Luke vii. 47.   ʸ Luke xiv. 26.   ᶻ Phil. iii. 10.   ᵃ Col. iii. 1, 2, 3, 4.

rose as a Saviour to justify us,—we must, as members, be therein fashioned unto him, and rise spiritually by heavenly-mindedness, and a new life to glorify him.

2nd. We must have our affections in Heaven, because Christ is there. The heart ever turns toward its treasure: where the body is, thither will the eagles resort.

3rd. He is there in glory at God's right hand; and grace should move to glory, as a piece of earth to the whole. And he is there in our business, making intercession in our behalf, providing a place for us, sending down gifts unto us. And the client cannot but have his heart on his business, when the advocate is actually stirring about it.

4th. We are dead with Christ, as to the life of sin; and a dead man takes no thought nor care for the things of that life from whence he is departed. A man, naturally dead, looks not after food, or raiment, or land, or money, or labour, &c. And a man, dead to sin, takes no more care how to provide for it.

5th. In Christ we have a new life: therefore, we should have new inclinations suitable unto it, and new provisions laid in for it. A child in the womb is nourished by the navel; being born, it is nourished by the mouth. A natural man feeds on worldly things by sense; a spiritual man feeds on heavenly things by faith and conscience. We can have nothing from the first Adam, which is not mortal and mortiferous; nothing from the second, which is not vital and eternal. Whatever the one gives us, shrinks and withers unto death: whatever the other, springs and proceeds unto immortal life. Our life, therefore, being new, the affections that serve it and wait upon it, must be new likewise.

6th. This life is our own; not so any thing in the world besides. I can purchase in the world only to me and mine heirs for ever: but spiritual purchases are to myself for ever; and every man's affections are naturally most fixed upon that, which is most his own.

7th. It is a hidden life; the best of it is yet unseen [b]; and though the cabinet which is seen, be rich,—yet the jewel which is hidden in it, is much richer. As there is a sinful curiosity in lust, to look after the hidden things of iniquity,

[b] 1 John iii. 2.

and to hanker after forbidden pleasures ; so there is a spiritual curiosity or ambition in grace, to aspire toward hidden
treasures, to press forward towards things that are before us,
" to be clothed upon with our house that is from Heaven."
As Absalom, being brought from banishment, longed to see
the face of his father; so the soul [c], being delivered out of
darkness, never thinks it sees enough of light.   When God
did most intimately reveal himself unto Moses, Moses did
most earnestly beseech him to " show him his glory [d]."   The
more sweetness we find in the first-fruits, insomuch of Christ
as is revealed to us, the more strong are our affections to
the whole harvest, to that abundance of him which is hidden
from us.   A few clusters of grapes, and bunches of figs, will
inflame the desire of enjoying that Canaan, which abounds
with them.

8th. It is hidden with Christ ; so hidden as that we know
where it is : hidden, so that the enemy cannot reach it ; but
not hidden from the faith of the child.

9th. It is hidden in God. It is life in the fountain [e]. And
every thing is perfectest in its original and fountain. And
this is such a fountain of life, as hath in it fulness without
satiety, and purity without defilement, and perpetuity without decay, and all-sufficiency without defect.

Lastly, It is but hidden, it is not lost ; hidden like seed
in the ground. When Christ the Sun of Righteousness shall
appear, this life of ours in him will spring up and appear
glorious.

SECT. 14. Now next let us consider this care of repentance against a man's own more particular and special sins.
" Asshur shall not save us, we will not ride upon horses," &c.
Israel had been guilty of very many provocations ; but
when they come to covenant with God, and to renew their
repentance, their thoughts and cares are most set against

---

[c] Non quiesco, nisi osculetur me osculo oris sui. Gratias de osculo pedum,
gratias et de manus ; sed si cura est illi ulla de me, osculetur me osculo oris sui :
non sum ingrata, sed amo : accepi, fateor, meritis potiora, sed prorsus inferiora
votis ; desiderio feror, non ratione, &c. *Bern.* Ser. 9. in Cant.—Testimonium
credibile nimis gustatæ sapientiæ est esuries ipsa tam vehemens. *Serm.* 2. de dua-
bus mensis.—Non excudit desiderium sanctum felix inventio, sed extendit, &c.
ser. 84. in Cant.—Videsis *Claudi. Espencei* libellum de Languore Spirit. c. 3. et 4.
[d] Exod. xxxiii. 11, 18.   [e] Psalm xxxvi. 9.

272 SEVEN SERMONS ON THE [Serm. III.

their carnal confidence, and spiritual adultery : their most
unfeigned detestations, their most serious resolutions, were
against these their most proper sins.   True repentance
worketh indeed a general " hatred of every false way [f]," and
suffereth not a man to allow himself in the smallest sin.
Yet as the dog in hunting of the deer, though he drive the
whole herd before him, yet fixeth his eye and scent upon
some one particular, which is singled out by the dart of the
huntsman ; so though sound conversion do work a universal hatred of all sin, because it is sin,—for hatred is ever
against the whole kind [g] of a thing,—though every member of
the old man be mortified, and every grace of the new man
shaped and fashioned in us;—yet the severest exercise of
that hatred is against the sins whereunto the conscience
hath been more enslaved, and by which the name of God
hath been most dishonoured.   A man that hath many
wounds, if there be any of them more deep, dangerous, or
nearer any vital part than the other,—though he will tend
the cure of them all, yet his chiefest care shall be towards
that.   As the king of Syria gave command to his army to
single out the king of Israel in the battle [h] ; so doth repentance lay its batteries most against the highest and strongest
and most reigning sin of the heart; and by how much the
more a man prized it before, by so much the more doth he
detest it now.   They counted no silver nor gold too good
to frame their idols of before ; their ear-rings shall go to
make them a calf [i] : but when they repent, nothing can be
too base to compare them, or to cast them unto [j].

The human nature is the same in all men ; yet some faculties are more vigorous in some, and other in others :
some witty, others strong ; some beautiful, others proper;
some a quick eye, others a ready tongue ; some for learned,
others for mechanical professions.   As some grounds take
better to some kind of grain than to others ; so in the new
man, though all the graces of Christ are, in some degree and
proportion, shaped in every regenerate person, yet one ex-
cels in one grace, another in another.   Abraham in faith,

[f] Psalm cxix. 128.   [g] Ὀργὴ περὶ τὰ καθ᾽ ἕκαστα· τὸ δὲ μῖσος, πρὸς τὰ
γένη. *Arist.* Rhet. l. 2. c 4.   [h] 1 Kings xxii. 31.   [i] Exod. xxii. 3.   [j] Isai.
ii. 20. xxx. 22.

Job in patience, Moses in meekness, David in meditation, Solomon in wisdom, Phinehas in zeal, Mary Magdalen in love, Paul in labour, &c. And so it is in the old man too. Though, by nature, we have all the members of original corruption, yet these put themselves forth in actual vigour [k]differently. One man is more possessed by a proud devil,— another, by an unclean one; Ahaz, superstitious; Balaam, ambitious; Cain, envious; Korah, stubborn; Esau, profane; Ishmael, a mocker; the young man, a worldling. According to different complexions and tempers of body (by which habitual lust is excited and called forth into act), or according to the differences of education, countries [l], callings, converse, and interests in the world,—so men are differently assaulted with distinct kinds of sin; and most men have their ' peccatum in deliciis,' which they may more properly call " their own [m]." And as this sin is usually the special bar and obstacle that keeps men from Christ, as we see in the example of the young man [n], and of the Jews [o]; so when Christ hath broken this obstacle, and gotten the throne in a man's heart, then the chief work of repentance is to keep this sin from gathering strength again: for, as they say of some kind of serpents, that, being cut in pieces, the parts will wriggle towards one another, and close and get life again; so, of all sins, a man is in most danger of the reviving of his own proper corruption: as being like the nettle, whose roots are so crooked, so catching to the ground, that it is a work of much care to keep the ground clean of them, after they are weeded out.

And therefore repentance sets itself particularly against that sin, as a special argument of sincerity. " I was up-

[k] In eodem prato, bos herbam quærit, canis leporem, ciconia lacertum. *Senec.* ep. 128.   [l] Multæ gentes ob specialia quædam peccata infames ; unde illud τρία κάππα κάκιστα *Suid.* in κάππα διπλοῦν.—Bœoti, Pharsali, Thessali, ob voracitatem, Vid. Athen. 1. 40. Isauri et Arabes ob latrocinia. *Dion.* 1. 55.—*Ammian. Marcel.* l. 14.—*Theodos.* Cod de feriis, l. 10. &c.—*Plin.* l. 6. a. 28.—*Strabo* lib. 16.—*Diodor. Sicul.* l. 3.—Qui mancipia vendunt, nationem cujusque in venditione pronunciare debent : præsumptum etenim est quosdam servos malos videri, quia et natione sunt, quæ magis infamis est. Leg. 31. sect. 21. D. de Ædilitio Edicto.—Athenarum linguata civitas. *Tert.* l. de Anima c. 3.—Hinc adagia, " Cretensi mendacior, Pœno perfidior, Scytha asperior, Sybarita fastuosior, Milesiis effœminatior," &c. Vid. *Erasm.* in initio Chiliad.—et *Alex. ab Alex.* Genial. 4. cap. 13.—*Arist.* Rhet. l. 6. c. 7.—*Liv.* l. 45.   [m] Psalm xviii. 23. [n] Mark x. 22.   [o] John v. 44. xii. 42, 43.

right," saith David, "before him, and kept myself from mine iniquity[p]." And, "he that is begotten of God," saith the apostle, "keepeth himself[q];" which he doth certainly with most vigilancy there, where he is in most danger of being assaulted. So in David: he had, in that great and scandalous fall of his, stained his conscience with impure lust, with the guilt of blood; and that not out of ignorance or common infirmity, or sudden passion and surprisal of some hasty temptation (which might happily have consisted with uprightness), but seriously, and deliberately, using many cunning arts, and carnal shifts of sinful wisdom to colour and daub it over: and lastly, by this means, had given a great blow to the holy name of God, and "caused his enemies to blaspheme," as Nathan tells him[r]. Therefore in his penitential Psalm, these four things he principally insists upon: "A clean heart, pardon of blood-guiltiness, truth in the inward parts, and occasion to teach transgressors the way of God, that they may be converted[s]." See it in Zaccheus:—worldliness and defrauding had been his sin; restitution[t] and liberality are the evidences of his repentance in special for that sin[u]. So Mary Magdalen; her sin had been uncleanness, her eyes vessels and factors for adultery, her hair a net plaited and spread to catch sinners: she remembered her wanton kisses, her provoking perfumes: and now, in her conversion, where her sin had been most prevalent, there her sorrow was most penitent, and her repentance most vigilant: her eyes vessels of tears; her kisses humbled, or rather advanced unto the feet of Christ; her hair a towel to wipe off those tears, which she judged too unclean for so holy feet to be washed withal; her ointment poured out upon a new lover, who had anointed her with his grace[x]. The sin of the gaoler against Paul and Silas, was cruelty[y], and the first fruit of his repentance was courtesy to them: he brought them out of a dungeon into his own house;

[p] Psalm xviii. 23. [q] 1 John v. 18. [r] 2 Sam. xii. 14. [s] Psalm li. 6, 7, 10, 13, 14. [t] Quod quadruplum reddat Zaccheus, videtur quibusdam potius ex abundantia pietatis quam ex vi legis fecisse. Lex enim quadrupli pœnam in una tantum furti specie statuit. Exod. xxii. 1, 4. Vide Maldonat. et Lucam. Brugens. Sane quod ad edictum Prætoris attinet, videtur tantum in duplum teneri. l. 1. D. de Publicanis. [u] Luke xix. 8. [x] Luke vii. 37, 38. [y] Acts xvi. 24.

from the stocks, to his table; became a host instead of a gaoler, a surgeon instead of a tormentor, and washed their stripes [z]. This was Daniel's method of working repentance in Nebuchadnezzar, persuading a proud oppressing tyrant unto justice and mercy [a]; and Paul unto Felix, preaching before a corrupt and lascivious judge [b], "of righteousness, temperance, and judgement to come [c]:" and to the learned and superstitious philosophers, in a learned discovery, and making known unto them their 'unknown God [d].' So John, the preacher of repentance, laid his axe to the 'root of every tree,' to the radical and prevailing lust in every order of men ; to extortion in the publican, to covetousness in the people, to violence in the soldiers, to carnal confidence in the Pharisees [e]. And so Christ to the young man ;—" One thing thou wantest [f];"—and to the woman of Samaria, " Go, call thy husband [g]," when indeed he was an adulterer, and not a husband.

The reason of this care of repentance is, 1st. Because, in godly sorrow, this sin hath lain most heavy upon the conscience. Hereby God hath been most of all despised and dishonoured ; our consciences most wasted and defiled ; our hearts most hardened ; our affections most bewitched and entangled. It hath been a master-sin, that hath been able to command, and to draw in many other servile lusts to wait upon it. Many wounds, even after they have been healed, will, against change of weather, affect the part wherein they were, with pain and aching : and therefore men usually are more tender of that part, keep it warmer, fence it with furs and cerecloths : as the apostle saith, that "on our dishonourable parts, we bestow the more abundant honour :" so on such an infirm and tender part, we bestow the more abundant care : and the like do we in those wounds of the soul, which are aptest to bleed afresh.

---

[z] Acts xvi. 30, 33, 34.   [a] Dan. iv. 27.   [b] At non frater ejus, cognomento Felix, pari moderatione agebat, jampridem Judææ impositus, et cuncta malefacta sibi impune ratus, tanta potentia subnixo. *Tacit.* Annal. l. 2. Antonius Felix, per omnem sævitiam ac libidinem, jus regium servili ingenio exercuit, Drusilla, Cleopatræ et Antonii nepte, in matrimonium accepta. *Tacit.* Hist. l. 5, 9. Vide *Joseph.* Antiq. l. 20. c. 5. Liberti ejus, potestatem summam adepti, stupris, excitâ cæde, proscriptionibus, omnia fœdabant :—ex quibus Felicem legionibus Judææ præfecit. *Sext. Aur. Victor* in Claudio.   [c] Acts xxiv. 25.   [d] Acts xvii. 23.   [e] Matth. iii. 7. Luke iii. 9, 14.   [f] Mark x. 21.   [g] John iv. 16.

2nd. Hereby, as was said before, we testify our uprightness; when we will not spare our beloved sin, nor roll it
under our tongue, nor hide it in our tent; when we will not
muffle nor disguise ourselves, like Tamar; nor hide amongst
the bushes and trees, like Adam; or in the belly of the ship,
with Jonah; nor spare any wedge of gold, with Achan; or
any delicate Agag, any fatling sins, with Saul; but, with
David, will show that we "hate every false way," by throw-
ing the first stone at our first sin, that which lay nearest and
closest in our bosoms, which the Scripture calls "Cutting
off the right hand, and plucking out the right eye:"—as
Cranmer put that hand first into the fire, which had before
subscribed to save his life. The story of the Turkish emperor is commonly known, who, being reported so to dote
on one of his concubines, as, for love of her, to neglect the
affairs of his kingdom, caused her to be brought forth in
great pomp, and cut off her head before his Bashaws, to as-
sure them that nothing was so dear unto him, but that he
could willingly part from it, to attend the public welfare.
This was an act of cruelty in him; but the like is an act of
penitency in us, when we can sacrifice the dearest affections,
wherewith we served sin. Let Christ kill our Agag, though
delicately apparelled, and divide the richest of all our spoils.
If we be learned, we shall direct all our studies unto the fear
of God [g]. If rich, we shall lay up a foundation of good works
against the time to come, and consecrate our merchandise as
holy to the Lord [h]. If wise, if honourable, if powerful, if
adorned with any endowment,—our business will be, with
Bezaleel and Aholiab, to adorn the gospel with them all,
from our gold to our goat's hair, to lay out all upon the
sanctuary; to make those members and abilities, which had
been Satan's armour and weapons of unholiness, to be now
weapons of holiness, and dedicated unto Christ [i]. This is
the holy revenge, which godly sorrow taketh upon sin [k].

If any men who profess repentance, and think they are
already long ago converted unto God, would examine the
truth of their conversion by this touchstone, it would mi-

g Eccles. xii. 12, 13.   h 1 Tim. vi. 18. Isai. xxiii. 16.   i Rom. vi. 19.
k 2 Cor. vii. 11.

nister matter of much humiliation and fear unto them, when
their own heart would reply against them as Samuel against
Saul, "Hast thou indeed, as thou professest, done the work
of the Lord in destroying Amalek? 'What then meaneth
the bleating of the sheep, and the lowing of the oxen in mine
ears?'" What mean these worldly and covetous practices?
these lascivious or revengeful speeches? these earthly, sensual, or ambitious lusts? are these Agags spared and kept
delicately? and canst thou please thyself in the thoughts of
a sound repentance? Did Paul fear, that God would humble him for those that had not repented amongst the Corinthians, by this argument, because he should find "envy-
ings, strifes, and debates amongst them[k]?" And wilt thou
presume of thy repentance, and not be humbled, when thou
findest the same things in thyself? Hast thou never yet
proclaimed defiance to thy beloved sin, made it the mark of
thy greatest sorrows, of thy strongest prayers and com-
plaints unto God? Hast thou never stirred up a holy indignation and revenge against it? and, above all things,
taken off thy thoughts from the meditation and love of it,
and found pleasure in the holy severity of God's book,
and the ministry thereof against it? made no covenant
with thine eye,—put no knife to thy throat,—set no door
before thy lips,—made no friends of unrighteous Mam-
mon? Dost thou still retain hankering affections after
thy wonted delights, as Lot's wife after Sodom? and are the
flesh-pots of Egypt desirable in thy thoughts still? "Be
not high-minded, but fear." There is no greater argument
of an unsound repentance than indulgent thoughts, and reserved delight and complacency in a master-sin. The devil
will diligently observe, and hastily catch one kind glance of
this nature (as Benhadad's servants did[l]), and make use of it
to do us mischief. David had been free from some of his
greatest troubles, if he had not relented towards Absalom,
and called him home from banishment. He no sooner kissed
Absalom, but Absalom courted and kissed the people to
steal their hearts away from him. As there are, in points of
faith, fundamental articles,—so there are, in points of practice, fundamental duties; and, amongst them, none more

---

[k] 2 Cor. xii. 20, 21.   [l] 1 Kings xx. 33.

primary, and essential unto true Christians than self-denial [m]. And this is one special part and branch of self-denial, to keep ourselves from our own iniquity ; and to say to our most costly and darling lusts, " Get ye hence: Asshur, away ; idols, away ; I will rather be fatherless, than rely upon such helpers."

m Matth. xvi. 24.

THE

FOURTH SERMON.*

———

HOSEA XIV. 3, 4.

Asshur shall not save us; we will not ride upon horses; neither will we say any more to the work of our hands, Ye are our gods; for in thee the fatherless findeth mercy. I will heal their backsliding, I will love them freely; for mine anger is turned away from him.

SECT. 1. THERE remaineth the second point formerly mentioned, from the promise or covenant, which Israel here makes, which I will briefly touch, and so proceed unto the fourth verse; and that is this :—

That true repentance and conversion taketh off the heart from all carnal confidence, either in domestical preparations of our own, " *We will not ride upon horses ;*" or in foreign aid from any confederates, especially enemies of God and his church, though otherwise never so potent; *Asshur shall not save us.* Or lastly, in any superstitious and corrupt worship which sends us to God the wrong way, " *We will not say any more to the work of our hands, Ye are our gods ;*" and causeth the soul, in all conditions, be they never so desperate, so desolate, so incurable, to rely only upon God. It is very much in the nature of man fallen, to affect an absoluteness, and a self-sufficiency, to seek the good that he desireth within himself, and to derive from himself the strength, whereby he would repel any evil which he feareth. This staying within itself[a], reflecting upon its own power and

---

* Folio-edition, p. 539. a Sua potestate delectati, velut bonum suum sibi ipsi essent, è superiore communi omnium beatifico bono, ad propria defluxerunt, &c. *Aug.* de Civ. Dei, l. 2. c. 1.—Cum causa miseriæ malorum Angelorum quæritur, ea merito occurrit, quod ab illo, qui summè est, aversi, ad seipsos conversi sunt; qui non summè sunt, et *Ib.* c. 6. l. de vera Relig. c. 13. de Gen. ad Lit. l. 11. c. 14. et 23. *Aquin.* part. 1. qu. 63. art. 3. It seems there was no

wisdom, and, by consequence, affecting an independency
upon any superior virtue in being and working, making
itself the first cause and the last end of its own motions,
—is, by divines, conceived to have been the first sin by
which the creature fell from God; and it was the first temptation by which Satan prevailed to draw man from God too.
For since, next unto God, every reasonable created being
is nearest unto itself, we cannot conceive how it should turn
from God, and not, in the next step, turn unto itself; and,
by consequence, whatsoever it was, in a regular dependence
to have derived from God, being fallen from him, it doth,
by an irregular dependence, seek for from itself.   Hence it
is, that men of power are apt to deify their own strength,
and to frame opinions of absoluteness to themselves, and to
deride the thoughts of any power above them, as Pharaoh [b],
and Goliath [c], and Nebuchadnezzar [d], and Sennacherib [e]. And
men of wisdom to deify their own reason, and to deride any
thing that is above or against their own conceptions; as
Tyrus [f], and the Pharisees [g], and the philosophers [h].   And
men of morality and virtue, to deify their own righteousness,
to rely on their own merits and performances, and to deride
righteousness imputed and precarious, as the Jews [i], and
Paul before his conversion [k].   So natural is it for a sinful
creature, who seeketh only himself, and maketh himself the
last end, to seek only unto himself, and to make himself
the first cause and mover towards that end.

But because God will not give his glory to another, nor
suffer any creature to encroach upon his prerogative, or to
sit down in his throne; he hath therefore always blasted the
policies and attempts of such, as aspired unto such an absoluteness and independency, making them know in the end,
" that they are but men [l], and that the Most High ruleth over
all :" and that it is an enterprise more full of folly than it is

other way for angels to sin, but by reflex of their understanding upon themselves ; which being held with admiration of their own sublimity and honour,
the memory of their subordination to God, and their dependency on him, was
drowned in this conceit ; whereupon their adoration, love, and imitation of God,
could not choose but be also interrupted. *Hook*, l. l. sect. 4.   [b] Exod. v. 2.
[c] 1 Sam. xvii. 8, 10, 44.   [d] Dan. iii. 15.   [e] 2 Kings xviii. 33, 34, 35.
Isai. x. 8, 9, 10, 11, 13, 14.   [f] Ezek. xxxviii. 2, 6.   [g] Luke xvi. 14.
John vii. 48, 49, 52. Acts iv. 11. Isai. xlix. 7. liii. 3.   [h] Acts xvii. 18, 32.
1 Cor. i. 22, 23.   [i] Rom. x. 5.   [k] Rom. vii. 9. Phil. iii. 6, 9.
[l] Psalm ix. 19, 20.

of pride, for any creature to work its own safety and felicity out of itself. And as men usually are most vigilant upon their immediate interests, and most jealous and active against all encroachments thereupon ; so we shall ever find, that God doth single out no men to be so notable monuments of his justice, and their own ruin and folly, as those who have vied with him in the points of power, wisdom, and other divine prerogatives, aspiring unto that absoluteness, self-sufficiency, self-interest, and independency which belongeth only unto him. And as he hath, by the destruction of Pharaoh, Sennacherib, Herod, and divers others, taught us the madness of this ambition ; so doth he, by our own daily preservation, teach us the same. For if God have appointed that we should go out of ourselves unto a thing below for a vital subsistence, to bread for food, to house for harbour, to clothes for warmth, &c., much more hath he appointed, that we should go out of ourselves for a blessed and happy subsistence; by how much the more is required unto blessedness than unto life, and by how much the greater is our impotency unto the greatest and highest end.

SECT 2. Yet so desperate is the aversion of sinful man from God, that when he is convinced of his impotency, and driven off from self-dependence, and reduced unto such extremities, as should in reason lead him back unto God ; yet when he hath "no horses of his own" to ride upon, no means of his own to escape evil,—yet still he will betake himself unto creatures like himself, though they be enemies unto God, and enemies unto him too for God's sake (for so was the Assyrian unto Israel) ; yet if Ephraim see his sickness, and Judah his wound, Ephraim will go to the Assyrian and King Jareb for help [m]. If he must beg, he would rather do it of an enemy than a God ; yea, though he dissuade him from it, and threaten him for it. Ahaz would not believe, though a sign were offered him ; nor be persuaded to trust in God to deliver him from Rezin and Pekah, though he promise him to do it ; but under pretence of not tempting God in the use of means, will weary God with his provocation, and rob God to pay the Assyrian, " who was not a help, but a distress unto him [n].

[m] Hos. v. 13.   [n] 2 Kings xvi. 5, 8, 17, 18. 2 Chron. xxviii. 20, 21. Isai. vii. 8, 13. xxx. 5.

SECT. 3. Well; God is many times pleased to waylay human counsels [o], even in this case too, and so to strip them not only of their own provisions, but of their foreign succours and supplies, as that they have no refuge left but unto him. Their horses fail them, their Assyrians fail them [p]. Their hope hath nothing either 'sub ratione boni,' as really good to comfort them at home; or 'sub ratione auxilii,' as matter of help and aid to support them from abroad. They are brought, as Israel, into a wilderness, where they are constrained to go to God, because they have no second causes to help them. And yet even here, wicked men will make a shift to keep off from God, when they have nothing in the world to trust unto. This is the formal and intimate malignity of sin, to decline God, and to be impatient of him in his own way. If wicked men be necessitated to implore help from God, they will invent ways of their own to do it [q]. If horses fail, and Asshur fail, and Israel must go to God whether he will or no,—it shall not be to the God that made him, but to a god of his own making; and when they have most need of their glory, they will " change it into that which cannot profit [r]." So foolish was Jeroboam, as, by two calves at Dan and Bethel, to think his kingdom should be established, and by that means rooted out his own family, and at last ruined the kingdom [s]. So foolish was Ahaz, as to seek help of those gods, which were the ruin of him and all Israel [t]. Such a strong antipathy and averseness there is in the soul of natural men unto God, as that when they are in distress, they go to him last of all; they never think of him, so long as their own strength, and their foreign confederacies hold out. And when at last they are driven to him, they know not how to hold communion with him in his own way, but frame carnal and superstitious ways of worship to themselves; and so, in their very seeking unto him, do provoke him to forsake them; and the very things whereon they lean, go up into their hand to pierce it [u].

SECT. 4. Now then, the proper work of true repentance be-

---

[o] Fidentiam pariunt, τὸ σωτήριον ἐγγὺς καὶ βοήθεια. Vid. *Arist.* Rhet. l. 2. c. 5.   [p] Hos. vii. 11, 12. viii. 9, 10.   [q] Ex arbitrio, non ex imperio. *Tert.* contr. Psychich. c. 13. vide de Præscript. c. 6.   [r] Jer. ii. 11.   [s] 1 Kings xii. 28, 29. xiv. 10, 15, 29. 2 Kings xvii. 21, 23. Hos. viii. 4, 5. x. 5, 8, 18.   [t] 2 Chron. xxviii. 23.   [u] Isai. xv. 2. xvi. 12. 1 Kings xviii. 26.

ing to turn a man the right way unto God, it taketh a man off
from all this carnal and superstitious confidence, and directeth
the soul, in the greatest difficulties, to cast itself with comfort and confidence upon God alone. So it is prophesied of
the remnant of God's people, that is, the penitent part of
them (for the remnant are those that came up " with weeping and supplication, seeking the Lord their God, and
asking the way to Sion, with their faces thitherward ˣ,") that
they should " no more again stay themselves upon him that
smote them, but should stay upon the Lord, the Holy One
of Israel in truth, and should return unto the mighty God ʸ.
They resolve the Lord shall save them, and not the Assyrian. So say the godly in the Psalmist, "A horse is a
vain thing for safety, neither shall he deliver any by his
great strength," &c. " Our soul waiteth for the Lord ; he
is our help and shield ᶻ." They will not say any more, "We
will fly upon horses, we will ride upon the swift ᵃ." Lastly,
" At that day," saith the prophet, speaking of the penitent
remnant and gleanings of Jacob, " shall a man look to his
Maker, and his eyes shall have respect to the Holy One of
Israel ; and he shall not look to the altars, the work of his
hands, neither shall respect that which his fingers have
made, the groves or the images ᵇ." And again, " Truly, in
vain, is salvation hoped for from the hills, and from the multitude of mountains ;" that is, from the idols, whom they
had set up and worshipped in high places ; " Truly in the
Lord our God is the salvation of Israel ᶜ." They will not
say any more to the work of their hands, Ye are our
gods.

SECT. 5. So then, the plain duties of the text are these :
1. To trust in God, who is all-sufficient to help, who is Jehovah, the fountain of being, and can give being to any
promise, to any mercy which he intends for his people ;
cannot only work, but command ; not only command, but
create deliverance, and fetch it out of darkness and desolation. He hath 'everlasting strength ;' there is no time, no
case, no condition, wherein his help is not at hand, whenever he shall command it ᵈ.

ˣ Jer. xxxi. 7, 9. l. 4. 5.   ʸ Isai. x. 20, 21.   ᶻ Psalm xxxiii. 17, 20.
ᵃ Isai. xxx. 16.   ᵇ Isai. xvii. 7, 8.   ᶜ Jer. iii. 23.   ᵈ Isai. xxvi. 4.

2. We must not trust in any creature. 1. Not in Asshur, in any confederacy or combination with God's enemies, be they otherwise never so potent. Jehoshaphat did so, and his " ships were broken ᵉ." Ahaz did so, and his " people were distressed ᶠ." It is impossible for God's enemies to be cordial to God's people, so long as they continue cordial to their God. There is such an irreconcileable enmity between the seed of the woman, and the seed of the serpent, that it is incredible to suppose, that the enemies of the church will do any thing which may, ' per se,' tend to the good of it ; or that any end and design, by them pursued, can be severed from their own malignant interest. Let white be mingled with any colour which is not itself, and it loseth of its own beauty. It is not possible for God's people to join with any that are his enemies, and not to lose of their own purity thereby. He must be as wise, and as potent as God, that can use the rage of God's enemies, and convert it, when he hath done, to the good of God's church, and the glory of God's name, and be able at pleasure to restrain and call it in again. We must ever take heed of this dangerous competition between our own interests and God's, to be so tender and intent upon that, as to hazard and shake this. Jeroboam did so, but it was fatal to him, and to all Israel. The end of Judah's combining with the Assyrian, was, that they might " rejoice against Rezin and Remaliah's son ;" but the consequent of it, which they never intended, was, that the " Assyrian came over all the channels, and over all the banks," and overflowed, and went over, and reached to the very neck ; and, if it had not been Emmanuel's land, would have endangered the drowning of it ᵍ. If Israel, for his own ends, join with Asshur, it will hardly be possible for him in so doing, though against his own will, not to promote the ends of Asshur against God's church, and against himself too. And yet the prophet would not have, in that case, God's people to be dismayed, or to say, " A confederacy, a confederacy ;" but to " sanctify the Lord himself, and make him their fear and their dread," who will certainly be a sanctuary unto them, and will " bind up his testimony, and seal the law amongst his disciples ; " when others shall

---

ᵉ 2 Chron. xx. 35, 37.   ᶠ 2 Chron. xxviii. 21.   ᵍ Isai. viii. 6, 7, 8.

"stumble, and fall, and be broken, and be snared, and be taken." If we preserve Emmanuel's right in us, and ours in him, all confederacies against us shall be broken, all counsels shall come to nought.

2. Not in horses, or in any other human preparations and provisions of our own. "Some trust in chariots, and some in horses; but we," saith David, "will remember the name of the Lord our God[h]." That name can do more with a sling and a stone, than Goliath with all his armour[i]. It is a strong tower for protection and safety to all that fly unto it[k]; whereas horses, though they be "prepared against the day of battle, yet safety cometh only from the Lord[l]." "Horses are flesh, and not spirit; and their riders are men, and not God." And, "Cursed are they that make flesh their arm, and depart from the Lord[m]." No, not in variety of means and ways of help, which seemeth to be intimated in the word 'riding,' from one confederate unto another: if Asshur fail, I will post to Egypt; if one friend or counsel fail, I will make haste to another; a sin very frequently charged upon Israel[n]. These are not to be trusted in, 1. Because of the intrinsecal weakness and defect of ability in the creature to help. Every man is a liar, either by imposture, and so in purpose; or by impotency, and so in the event, deceiving those that rely upon him[o].

2. Because of ignorance and defect of wisdom in us, to apply that strength which is in the creature, unto the best advantage. None but an artificer can turn and govern the natural efficacy of fire, wind, water, unto the works of art. The wisdom whereby we should direct created virtues unto human ends, is not in, or of ourselves, but it comes from God[p].

SECT. 6.—3. Nor in idols, nor in corrupting the worship of God. Idols are lies[q], and teachers of lies, and promisers of lies to all that trust in them[r]. An idol is just nothing in

---

[h] Psalm xx. 7.   [i] 1 Sam. xvii. 45.   [k] Prov. xviii. 10.   [l] Prov. xxi. 31.   [m] Isai. xxxi. 1, 2, 3. Jer. xvii. 5.   [n] Hos. vii. 11. Isai. xx. 5. lvii. 10. Jer. ii. 36, 37.   [o] Psalm lxii. 9.   [p] James i. 5. Isai. xxviii. 26, 29. Exod. xxxvi. 1, 2. Eccles. vii. 24. ix. 1. 11.   [q] In Idololatriâ mendacium, cum tota substantia ejus mendax sit. *Tert.* de Idololat. Unde Idolatræ dicuntur συκοφαντεῖν τὴν ἀλήθειαν. *Clem. Alex.* in Protreptic.   [r] Jer. x. 8, 14, 15, 16. Hab. ii. 18. Rev. xxii. 15.

the world [s]; and that which is nothing, can do nothing for those that rely upon it. Whatever thing a man trusteth in, in time of trouble, must needs have these things in it to ground that confidence upon:—

First, A knowledge of him and his wants : therefore we are bid to trust in God's providence over us for all outward good things, because he knoweth that we have need of them [t].

Secondly, A loving and merciful disposition to help him. A man may sometimes receive help from such as love him not, out of policy, and in pursuance of other ends and intents; but he cannot confidently rely upon any aid, which is not first founded in love. I ever suspect and fear the gifts and succours, which proceed from an enemy : they will have their own ends only, even then when they seem to tender and serve me : therefore David singleth out God's mercy as the object of his trust [u].

Thirdly, A manifestation of that love in some promise or other, engaging unto assistance. For how can I, with assurance, and without hesitancy, expect help there, where I never received any promise of it ? Here was the ground of David's, Jehoshaphat's, Daniel's trust in God, the word and promise which he had passed unto them [x].

Fourthly, Truth and fidelity in the care to make these promises good. This is that which makes us so confidently trust in God's promises, because we know they are all " Yea and Amen ;" that it is " impossible for God to lie," or deceive, or for any to seek his face in vain [y].

Fifthly, Power to give being, and put into act whatsoever is thus promised. That which a man leans upon, must have strength to bear the weight which is laid upon it. This is the great ground of our trusting in God at all times, even then when all other helps fail; because he is 'I am,' that can create and give a being to every thing which he hath promised, because 'power belongeth unto him,' and in 'the Lord Jehovah is everlasting strength ;' and nothing is too hard, no help too great for him who made heaven and earth,

---

[s] אֱלִילִים Nihilitates, nomen generaliter 'nihil' sonat, quod apte idolis tribuitur. *Mercer.* 1 Cor. viii. 4.   [t] Matth. v. 32.   [u] Psalm lii. 8.   [x] 1 Chron. xvii. 25, 27. Psalm cxix. 42. 2 Chron. xx. 7, 8. Dan. ix. 2, 3.   [y] 2 Cor. i. 20. Josh. xxi. 45. Heb. vi. 18. Isai. xlv. 19.

and can command all the creatures which he made, to serve those whom he is pleased to help [z]. Now whosoever seeks for any of these grounds of trust in idols, shall be sure to fail of them. Knowledge they have none [a], and therefore love they have none: for how can that love any thing which knows nothing? Truth they have none, neither of being in themselves, nor of promise to those that trust in them: the very formality of an idol is to be a lie, to stand for that which it is not, and to represent that which it is most unlike [b]: and power they have none: either to hear or save [c]. And therefore that repentance which shaketh off confidence in idols, doth not only convert a man unto God, but unto himself; it is not only an impious, but a sottish thing, and below the reason of a man, first, to make a thing, and then to worship it, to expect safety from that, which did receive being from himself [d]. These are the great props of carnal confidence,—foreign interests, domestical treasures, superstitious devotions;—when men please themselves in the ' children of strangers,' and have their ' land full of silver, and gold, and treasures,' full of horses and chariots, and full of idols; hoard up provisions and preparations of their own; comply with the enemies of God abroad, and corrupt the worship of God at home [e]. These are the things for which God threateneth terribly to shake the earth, and to bring down, and to make low the loftiness of man,—if he do not (as Ephraim here, by long and sad experience, doth) penitently renounce and abjure them all.

SECT 7. And now this is matter, for which all of us may be humbled. There is no sin more usual amongst men than carnal confidence, to lean on our own wisdom, or wealth, or power, or supplies from others; to deify counsels and armies, or horses and treasures; and to let our hearts rise or fall, sink or bear up within us, according as the creature is helpful or useless, nearer or farther from us: as if God were not a God afar off, as well as near at hand. This we may justly fear, God has, and still will visit us for, because we do not " sanctify the Lord of hosts himself in our hearts, to make

---

[z] Psalm lxii. 8, 11. Exod. iii. 14. Isai. xxvi. 4. Gen. xviii. 14. Jer. xxxii. 17. Psalm cxxi. 2. Rom. v. 19, 21. Matth. viii. 2.   [a] Isai. xliv. 9.   [b] Isai. xliv. 20. xl. 18. Jer. x. 14, 15, 16.   [c] Isai. xlv. 20, xlvi. 7. xli. 23, 24, 28, 29: [d] Isai. xlvi. 7, 8.   [e] Isai. ii. 6, 7, 8.

him our fear and our defence:" and that he will blow upon all such counsels and preparations, as carnal confidence doth deify.

Therefore we must be exhorted to take off our hopes and fears from second causes, not to glory in an arm of flesh, or to dróop when that fails us; not to say in our prosperity, " Our mountain is so strong, that we shall not be shaken;" nor in our sufferings, that " Our wound is incurable, or our grave so deep, that we shall never be raised again :" but to make the ' name of the Lord our stronger tower;' for ' they who know thy name, will trust in thee:' and for direction herein, we must learn to trust in God.

First, Absolutely, and for himself, because he only is absolute, and of himself. Other things, as they have their being, so have they their working, and power of doing good or evil only from him [f]. And therefore[g] till he take himself away, though he take all other things away from us, we have matter of encouragement and rejoicing in the Lord still; as David and Habakkuk resolve, 1 Sam. xxx. 6. Hab. iii. 17, 18. All the world cannot take away any promise from any servant of God; and there is more reality in the least promise of God, than in the greatest performance of the creature.

Secondly, To trust him in the way of his commandments[h], not in any precipices or presumptions of our own; " Trust in him, and do good[i]." First, fear him, and then trust in him; he is a help and shield only unto such[k]. It is high insolence for any man to lean upon God without his leave; and he alloweth none to do it, but such as ' fear him, and obey the voice of his servants[l].'

Thirdly, To trust him in the way of his providence[m], and the use of such means as he hath sanctified and appointed. Though man liveth not by bread alone, but by the Word of blessing which proceedeth out of the mouth of God; yet

---

[f] Matth. iv. 4. John xix. 11.   [g] Nihil Rex majus minari male parentibus potest, quam ut abeat e regno. *Senec.* Epist. 80.—Tua me non satiant, nisi tecum. *Bern.* Soliloq.—Ubi bene erit sine illo? aut ubi male esse poterit cum illo? *Bern.* Ser. 1. de Adven. Dei.—Ditior Christi paupertas cunctis. *Id.* Ser. 4. in Vigil. Natal.—Bonum mihi, Domine, in camino habere te mecum, quam esse sine te, vel in cœlo. *Idem.*   [h] Nolite sperare in iniquitate, nolite peccare in spe. *Bern.* Ser. 2. de Advent. In viis custodiet; nunquid in præcipitiis? *Bern.* Serm. 14. Psal. ' Qui habitat.'   [i] Psalm xxxvii. 3.   [k] Psalm cxv. 11. [l] Isai. l. 10.   [m] Vid. *Aug.* de Opere Mona. et Qu. in Gen. l. 1. qu. 26.

that Word is by God annexed to bread, and not to stones:
and that man should not trust God, but mock and tempt
him, who should expect to have stones turned into bread. If
God hath provided stairs, it is not faith, but fury,—not confidence, but madness, to go down by a precipice: where
God prescribes means, and affords secondary helps, we must
obey his order, and implore his blessing in the use of them.
This was Nehemiah's way; he prayed to God, and he petitioned the king [n]. This was Esther's way; a fast to call upon
God, and a feast to obtain favour with the king [o]. This was
Jacob's way; a supplication to God, and a present to his
brother [p]. This was David's way against Goliath; the 'name
of the Lord' his trust, and yet a sling and a stone his weapon [q]. This was Gideon's way against the Midianites; his
sword must go along with the sword of the Lord, not as an
addition of strength, but as a testimony of obedience [r].
Prayer is called sometimes a lifting up of the 'voice,'—sometimes, a lifting up of the 'hands;' to teach us, that when we
pray to God, we must as well have a hand to work [s], as a
tongue to beg. In a word, we must use second causes in
obedience to God's order, not in confidence of their help;
the creature must be the object of our diligence, but God
only the object of our trust.

Sect. 8. Now lastly, from the ground of the church's
prayer and promise, we learn, that the way unto mercy [t] is to
be in ourselves fatherless. "The poor," saith David, "com-
mitteth himself unto thee; thou art the helper of the fatherless [u]." When Jehoshaphat knew not what to do, then was
a fit time to direct his eye unto God [x]. When the stones of
Sion are in the dust, then is the fittest time for God to favour
her [y]. When Israel was under heavy bondage, and had not
Joseph, as a tender father (as he is called [z]), to provide for
them, then God remembered that he was their father, and
Israel his first-born [a]. Nothing will make us seek for help
above ourselves, but the apprehension of weakness within

---

[n] Neh. ii. 4.   [o] Esther iv. 16. v. 4.   [p] Gen. xxxii. 9, 13.   [q] 1 Sam.
xvii. 45, 49.   [r] Judg. vii. 18.   [s] Dii prohibebunt hæc ; sed non propter me
de cœlo descendent : vobis dent mentem oportet, ut prohibeatis. *Liv.* l. 9.
[t] Patrem misericordiarum patrem esse necesse est etiam miserorum. *Bern.* Serm. 1.
in Fest. Omnium Sanct.   [u] Psalm x. 14. cxlvi. 9.   [x] 2 Chron. xx. 19.
[y] Psalm cii. 13.   [z] Gen. xli. 43.   [a] Exod. iv. 22.

ourselves. Those creatures that are weakest, nature hath
put an aptitude and inclination in them to depend upon those
that are stronger. The vine [b], the ivy, the hop, the wood-
bind, are taught by nature to clasp, and cling, and wind
about stronger trees. The greater sense we have of our own
vileness, the fitter disposition are we in to rely on God.
" I will leave in the midst of thee an afflicted and poor people, and they shall trust in the name of the Lord [c]." When a
man is proud within, and hath any thing of his own to lean
upon, he will hardly tell how to trust in God [d]. Israel never
thought of returning to her first husband, till her way was
hedged up with thorns, and no means left to enjoy her former lovers [e]. When the enemy should have shut up, and
intercepted all her passages to Dan and Bethel, to Egypt
and Assyria, that she hath neither friends nor idols to fly
to ; then she would think of returning to her first husband,
namely, to God again.

Now from hence we learn, First, The condition of the church
in this world, which is, to be as an orphan, destitute of all
succour and favour ; as an outcast, whom no man looketh
after [f]. Paul thought low thoughts of the world, and the
world thought as basely of him : " The world," saith he,
" is crucified unto me, and I unto the world [g]." Before conversion, the world is an Egypt unto us, a place of bondage :—
after conversion, it is a wilderness unto us, a place of emptiness and temptations.

Secondly, The backwardness of man towards grace; we go
not to God till we are brought to extremities, and all other
help fails us. The poor prodigal never thought of looking
after a father, till he found himself in a fatherless condition,
and utterly destitute of all relief [h].

Thirdly, The right disposition and preparation unto mercy,
which is to be an orphan, destitute of all self-confidence, and
broken off from all other comforts. " When the poor and
needy seeketh water, and there is none, I the Lord will help
him [i]." God will " repent for his people, when he seeth that

[b] Vites, arboribus applicitæ, inferiores prius apprehendendo ramos, in cacumina
evadunt. *Quntil.* lib. 1. 2. 26. Spalding, i. 48.—Hedera dicta, quod ' hæreat :'
Festus.   [c] Zeph. iii. 12. Isai. xiv. 32.   [d] Prov. iii. 5. xxviii. 25.   [e] Hos.
ii. 6, 7.   [f] Jer. xxx. 17.   [g] Gal. vi. 14.   [h] Luke xv. 17, 18.   [i] Isai.
xli. 17.

their power is gone [k];" when there is ' dignus vindice no-dus,' an extremity fit for divine power to interpose. Christ is set forth as a physician, which supposeth sickness; as a fountain, which supposeth uncleanness; as meat, which supposeth emptiness; as clothing, which supposeth nakedness. He never finds us, till we are lost sheep: when we have lost all, then we are fit to follow him, and not before.

Fourthly, The roots of true repentance. ' Nos pupilli, Tu misericors.' The sense of want and emptiness in ourselves, the apprehension of favour and mercy in God. Conviction of sin in us, and of righteousness in him [l];—of crookedness in us, and of glory in him [m].

Hereby room is made for the entertainment of mercy: "Where sin abounds, grace will more abound;" and the more the soul finds itself exceeding miserable, the more will the mercy of God appear exceeding merciful [n]. And hereby God showeth his wisdom in the seasonable dispensing of mercy then, when we are in greatest extremity; as fire is hottest in the coldest weather. God delights to be seen in the mount, at the grave, to have his way in the sea, and his paths in the deep waters. Mercies are never so sweet, as when they are seasonable; and never so seasonable as in the very turning and critical point, when misery weighs down, and nothing but mercy turns the scale.

This teacheth us how to fit ourselves for the mercy of God, namely, to find ourselves destitute of all inward or outward comforts, and to seek for it only there. Beggars do not put on scarlet, but rags [o], to prevail with men for relief: as Benhadad's servants put on ropes, when they would beg mercy of the King of Israel. In a shipwreck, a man will not load him with money, chains, treasure, rich apparel; but commit himself to the sea naked, and esteem it mercy enough to have ' tabulam post naufragium,' one poor plank to carry him to the shore. It is not exaltation enough unto Joseph, except he be taken out of a prison unto honour.

Secondly, We should not be broken with diffidence or distrust in times of trouble; but remember, it is the condition

---

[k] Deut. xxxii. 36. [l] John xvi. 9, 10. [m] Isai. xl. 4, 5. [n] Rom. v. 20.
[o] Mendici cum eleemosynam petunt, non pretiosas vestes ostendunt, sed seminu-da membra, aut ulcera, si habuerint; ut citius ad misericordiam videntis animus inclinetur: *Bern.* Serm. 4. de Advent.

of the church to be an orphan. It is the way, whereby Moses became to be the son of Pharaoh's daughter: when his own parents durst not own him, the mercy of a prince found him out to advance him; and when he was nearest unto perishing, he was nearest unto honour. In the civil law [p], we find provision made for such as were cast out, and exposed to the wide world, some hospitals to entertain them, some liberties to comfort and compensate their trouble. And alike care we find in Christ: the Jews had no sooner cast out the man, that was born blind, whose parents durst not be seen in his cause, for fear of the like usage, —but the mercy of Christ presently found him, and bestowed comfort upon him [q]. This is the true David [r], unto whom all helpless persons, that are in distress, in debt, in bitterness of soul, may resort, and find entertainment [s].

Lastly, We should learn to behave ourselves as pupils under such a guardian, to be sensible of our infancy, minority [t], disability to order or direct our own ways, and so deny ourselves, and not lean on our own wisdom; to be sensible how this condition exposeth us to the injuries of strangers,—for " because we are called out of the world, therefore the world hateth us"—and so to be vigilant over our ways, and not trust ourselves alone in the hands of temptation, nor wander from our guardian, but always to yield unto his wisdom and guidance. Lastly, to comfort ourselves in this, That while we are in our minority, we are under the mercy of a Father, a mercy of conservation by his providence, giving us all good things richly to enjoy, even all things necessary unto life and godliness:—a mercy of protection, defending us by his power from all evil:—a mercy of education and instruction, teaching us by his Word and Spirit:—a mercy of communion many ways, familiarly conversing with us, and manifesting himself unto us:—a mercy of guidance and government, by the laws of his family:—

---

[p] Leg. 19. Cod. de Sacros. Ecclesiis et leg. 46. Cod. de Episcopis et Cler. Sect. 1, 3.—Vid. Tholos. Syntag. Juris. l. 15. c. 28.   [q] John ix. 35.   [r] David homines, in angustia constitutos et oppressos ære alieno, in suam tutelam suscipiens, typus Christi est, publicanos et peccatores recipientis : *Glass.* Philolog. Sacr. lib. 2. page 424.—Parentum amor magis in ea quorum miseretur, inclinatur. *Sen.* Epist. 66. Ruhkopf, vol. 2. p. 303.   [s] 1 Sam. xxii. 2.   [t] Tutela vis est et potestas in capite libero ad tuendum eum, qui, propter ætatem suam, sponte se defendere nequit : D. de Tutelis, L. 1.

a mercy of discipline, fitting us, by fatherly chastisements, for those further honours and employments he will advance us unto. And when our minority is over, and we once are come to a perfect man; we shall then be actually admitted unto that inheritance immortal, invisible, and that fadeth not away, which the same mercy at first purchased, and now prepareth and reserveth for us. Now it followeth,

Verse IV. " *I will heal their backsliding, I will love them freely; for mine anger is turned away from him.*"

SECT. 9. In the former words, we have considered both Israel's petition in time of trouble, and the promise and co-venant, which thereupon they bind themselves in. In these and the consequent words, unto the end of the eighth verse, we have the gracious answer of God to both; promising in his free love both to grant their petition, and, by his free grace, to enable them unto the performance of the covenant which they had made.

The petition consisted of two parts: 1. That God would take away all iniquity. 2. That he would do them good, or receive them graciously. To both these, God giveth them a full and a gracious answer: 1. That he will take away all iniquity, by *healing their backsliding*. 2. That he would do them good, and heap all manner of blessings upon them, which are expressed by the various metaphors of fruitfulness, opposite to the contrary expressions of judgement, in the former part of the prophecy.

" *I will heal their backsliding.*"] This is one of the names by which God is pleased to make himself known unto his people, " I am the Lord that *healeth* thee [u];" and, " Return, O backsliding children, and I will *heal* your backslidings [x]."

Now God healeth sin four manner of ways:—

First, By a gracious pardon, burying, covering, not imputing them unto us. So it seems to be expounded, Psalm ciii. 3; and that which is called *healing* in one place, is called *forgiveness* in another, if we compare Matthew xiii. 15. with Mark iv. 12.

Secondly, By a spiritual and effectual reformation, purging the conscience from dead works, making it strong and able to serve God in new obedience; for that which health

[u] Exod. xv. 26.   [x] Jer. iii. 22.

is to the body, holiness is to the soul. Therefore the Sun of righteousness is said to " arise with *healing* in his wings [z]:"— whereby we are to understand the gracious influence of the Holy Spirit, conveying the virtue of the blood of Christ unto the conscience ; even as the beams of the sun do the heat and influence thereof unto the earth, thereby calling out the herbs and flowers, and healing those deformities which winter had brought upon it.

Thirdly, By removing and withdrawing of judgements, which the sins of a people had brought, like wounds or sicknesses, upon them. So *healing* is opposite to smiting and wounding [a].

Fourthly, By comforting against the anguish and distress, which sin is apt to bring upon the conscience. For as, in physic, there are purgatives to cleanse away corrupt humours, so there are cordials likewise, to strengthen and refresh weak and dejected patients : and this is one of Christ's principal works, " To bind and *heal* the broken in heart, to restore comforts unto mourners, to set at liberty them that are bruised, and to have mercy upon those whose bones are vexed [b]." I am not willing to shut any of these out of the meaning of the text.

First, Because it is an answer to that prayer, " Take away *all* iniquity ;" the *all* that is in it, the guilt, the stain, the power, the punishment, the anguish, whatever evil it is apt to bring upon the conscience ; let it not do us any hurt at all.

Secondly, Because God's works are perfect : where he forgives sin, he removes it ; where he convinceth of righteousness, unto pardon of sin,—he convinceth also of judgement, unto the casting out of the Prince of this world, and bringeth forth that judgement unto victory [c].

" *Their backsliding.*"] Their prayer was against " all iniquity ;" and God, in his answer thereunto, singleth out one kind of iniquity, but one of the greatest by name : and that, First, To teach them and us, when we pray against sin, not to content ourselves with generalities, but to bewail our great and special sins by name ; those especially that have

---

[a] Mal. iv. 2.   [a] Deut. xxxii. 39. Job v. 18. Hos. vi. 1, 2. Jer. xxxiii. 5, 6.
[b] Psalm cxlvii. 3. Isai. lvii. 18, 19. Luke iv. 18. Psalm vi. 2, 3.   [c] Matth. xii. 20.

been most comprehensive, and the seminaries of many others.

Secondly, To comfort them; for if God pardon by name the greatest sin, then surely none of the rest will stand in the way of his mercy: if he pardon the talents, we need not doubt but he will pardon the pence too. Paul was guilty of many other sins; but when he will magnify the grace of Christ, he makes mention of his great sins: a blasphemer, a persecutor, injurious; and comforts himself in the mercy which he had obtained against them [d].

Thirdly, To intimate the great guilt of apostasy and rebellion against God. After we have known him [e], and tasted of his mercy, and given up ourselves unto his service, and come out of Egypt and Sodom,—then to look back again, and to be false in his covenant; this God looks on, not as a single sin, but as a compound of all sins. When a man turns from God, he doth, as it were, resume and take home upon his conscience all the sins of his life again.

Fourthly, To proportion his answer to their repentance. They confess their apostasy: they had been in covenant with God; they confess he was their "first husband [f];" and they forsook him, and sought to horses, to men, to idols, to vanity and lies: this is the sin they chiefly bewail; and therefore this is the sin, which God chiefly singles out to pardon, and to heal them of. This is the great goodness of God towards those, that pray in sincerity, that he fits his mercy "ad cardinem desiderii [g]," answers them in the main of their desires; lets it be unto them, even as they will.

SECT. 10. "*I will love them* [h] *freely.*"] This is set down as the fountain of that remission, sanctification, and comfort, which is here promised. It comes not from our conversion unto

---

d 1 Tim. i. 13.   e Ut aqua, prius calefacta, dein in puteum demissa, fit frigidissima: *Casaub.* in Athenæum, l. 3. c. 35.—Et *Plutarch.* Symposiac. l. 6. q. 4. f Hos. ii. 7.   g *Aug.* Confes. lib. 5. cap. 8.   h Si vera fit gratia, id est, gratuita, nihil invenit in homine, cui merito debeatur, &c. *Aug.* lib. de patient. c. 20.— Vid. cont. Julian. lib. 6. cap. 19.—De peccato orig. cap. 24.—de grat. et lib. arbit. cap. 5.—De natur. et grat. cap. 4.—De corrept. et gr. c. 10.—Epist. 105 et 106, et alibi passim.—Temerè in tali negotio, vel prius aliquid tribuis tibi, vel plus et magis ; amat, et ante : *Bernard.* Serm. 69. in Can.—Ex se sumit materiam, et velut quoddam seminarium miserandi : miserendi causam et originem sumit ex proprio; judicandi vel ulciscendi magis ex nostro. *Idem.* Serm. 5. in natali Dom.

God, but from God's free love and grace unto us. And this
is added, First, To humble them, that they should not ascribe any thing to themselves, their repentance, their prayers,
their covenants and promises, as if these had been the means
to procure mercy for them; or as if there were any objective
grounds of loveliness in them, to stir up the love of God
towards them. It is not for their sake that he doth it, but
for his own : " The Lord sets his love upon them, because
he loved them [i]:" " Not for your sakes do I this," saith the
Lord God, " be it known unto you [k]:" " He will have mercy,
because he will have mercy [l]."

Secondly, To support them, above the guilt of their
greatest sins. Men think nothing more easy, while they live
in sin, and are not affected with the weight and heinousness
of it, than to believe mercy and pardon. But when the
soul, in conversion unto God, feels the heavy burden of
some great sins,—when it considers its rebellion, and apostasy, and backsliding from God,—it will then be very apt to
think, God will not forgive nor heal so great wickedness as
this. There is a natural Novatianism in the timorous conscience of convinced sinners, to doubt and question pardon
for sins of apostasy and falling, after repentance. Therefore,
in this case, God takes a penitent off from the consideration
of himself by his own thoughts, unto the height and excellency of his thoughts, who knows how to pardon abundantly [m]. Nothing is too hard for love ; especially free love,
that hath no foundation or inducement from without itself.

And because we read it before, Hos. viii. 5, that " God's
anger was kindled against them ;" therefore he here adds,
that this also should be " turned away" from them. Anger[n]
will consist with love. We find God angry with Moses, and
Aaron, and Miriam, and Asa ; and he doth sometimes " visit
with rods and scourges, where he doth not utterly take away
his loving kindness from a people [o]." A man may be angry
with his wife, or child, or friend, whom yet he dearly loveth.
And God is said to be thus angry with his people, when the
effects of displeasure are discovered towards them. Now

---

[i] Deut. vii. 7, 8.   [k] Ezek. xxxvi. 22, 23.   [l] Rom. ix. 15.   [m] Isai.
lv. 7, 8, 9. Jer. xxix. 11. Ezek. xxxvii. 3.   [n] *Arist.* Rhet. l. 2, c. 2.
[o] Psalm lxxxix. 32, 33.

upon their repentance and conversion, God promiseth not only to love them freely, but to clear up his countenance towards them; to make them, by the removal of judgements, to see and know the fruits of his free love and bounty unto them. When David called Absalom home from banishment, this was an effect of love; but when he said, " Let him not see my face," this was the continuation of anger: but at last, when he admitted him into his presence, and kissed him, here that anger was turned away from him too [p].

SECT. 11. These words then contain God's merciful answer to the first part of Israel's prayer, for the " taking away of all iniquity," which had been the fountain of those sad judgements, under which they languished and pined away: wherein there are two parts. 1. The ground of God's love. 2. A double fruit of that love. 1. In ' healing their backsliding,' in ' removing his anger' and heavy judgements from them. We will briefly handle them in the order of the text.

" *I will heal their backsliding.*"] When God's people do return unto him, and pray against sin,—then God, out of his free love, doth heal them of it. First, he teacheth them what to ask; and then he tells them what he will give. Thus we find ' conversion' and ' healing' joined together [q]. " They shall return even to the Lord, and he shall be entreated of them, and shall heal them [r]:" "Return, backsliding children; I will heal your backslidings [s]." Men [t], if they be injured and provoked by those whom they have in their power to undo, though they return and cry ' peccavi,' and are ready to ask forgiveness,—yet many times, out of pride and revenge, will take their time and opportunity to repay the wrong. But God doth not so; his pardons, as all his other gifts, are without his exprobration: as soon as ever his servants come back unto him with tears and confession, he looks not upon them with scorn, but with joy: his mercy makes more haste to embrace them, than their repentance to

---

p 2 Sam. xiv. 21, 24, 33.   q Psalm vi. 10.   r Isai. xix. 22.   s Jer. iii. 22.
t Εἴπερ γάρ τε χόλον γε καὶ αὐτῆμαρ καταπέψῃ, Ἀλλά γε καὶ μετόπισθεν ἔχει κότον, ὄφρα τελέσσῃ, Ἐν στήθεσσιν ἑοῖσι.   Hom. Il. i. 81.—Quæ in præsens Tiberius civiliter habuit, sed in animo revolvente iras, etiamsi impetus offensionis languerat, memoria valebat. *Tac.* Annal. l. 4. Non enim Tiberium, quamvis triennio post cædem Sejani, quæ cæteros mollire solent, tempus, preces, satis mitigabant, quin incerta et abolita pro gravissimis et recentibus puniret. Annal. l. 6.—Vid.*Aristot.* Ethic. l. 4. c. 11.

return unto him ᵘ. Then out comes the wine, the oil, the
balm, the cordials ; then the wounds of a Saviour do, as it
were, bleed afresh, to drop in mercy into the sores of such a
penitent. O though he be 'not a dutiful, a pleasant child,'
yet he is a ' child :' " though I spake against him, yet I remember him still, my bowels are troubled for him ; I will
surely have mercy upon him ˣ." The Lord greatly complains of the inclination of his people to backsliding, and
yet he cannot find in his heart to destroy them, but expresseth a kind of conflict ʸ between justice and mercy ; and
at last resolves, "'I am God, and not man ;' I can as well
heal their backsliding by my love, as revenge it by my justice ; therefore ' I will not execute the fierceness of mine
anger, but I will cause them to walk after the Lord ᶻ.'" Yea,
so merciful he is, that, even upon a hypocritical conversion, when his people did but flatter and lie unto him, and
their heart was not right towards him, nor they steadfast in
his covenant,—yet the text saith, he, "being full of compassion, forgave their iniquity," (not as to the justification of
their persons, for that is never without faith unfeigned, but
so far as to the mitigation of their punishment, that ' he destroyed them not, nor stirred up all his wrath against
them ᵃ :')—for so that place is to be expounded, as appeareth
by the like parallel place, Ezek. xxiii. 17 : " Nevertheless
mine eye spared them from destroying them ; neither did I
make an end of them in the wilderness."

Now the metaphorical word, both here, and so often elsewhere used in this argument, leadeth us to look upon sinners as patients, and upon God as a physician. By which
two considerations we shall find the exceeding mercy of
God in the pardon and purging away of sin, set forth
unto us.

SECT. 12. 'Healing' then is a relative word ; and leads
us first to the consideration of a patient, who is to be
healed ; and that is here a grievous sinner fallen into a relapse. Healing is of two sorts : the healing of a sickness
by a physician ; the healing of a wound by a surgeon :

<hr/>
ᵘ Luke xv. 20.   ˣ Jer. xxxii. 20.   ʸ Gravis quædam inter virtutes videtur
orta contentio : siquidem veritas et justitia miserum affligebant ; pax et miseri-
cordia judicabant magis esse parcendum, &c. vid. *Bern.* Ser. 1. in An.   ᶻ Hos.
xi. 7, 10.   ᵃ Psalm lxxviii. 34, 39.

and sin is both a sickness and a wound. " The whole head is sick, the whole heart faint: from the sole of the foot, even unto the head, there is no soundness in it, but wounds, and bruises, and putrefying sores ^c :"—a sickness that wants healing, a wound that wants binding ^d ;—a sick sinner that wants a physician to call to repentance ^e ;—a wounded sinner that wants a Samaritan (so the Jews called Christ^f) to bind up and pour in wine and oil ^g.

Diseases are of several sorts ; but those of all other most dangerous, that are in the vital parts ; as all the diseases of sin are, and from thence spread themselves over the whole man. Ignorance, pride, carnal principles, corrupt judgement, —diseases of the head :—hardness, stubbornness, atheism, rebellion,—diseases of the heart :—lust, a dart in the liver : —corrupt communication, the effect of putrefied lungs :— gluttony and drunkenness, the swellings and dropsies of the belly :—despair and horror, the grief of the bowels :—apostasy, a recidivation or relapse into all :—an ear that cannot hear God speak ^h :—an eye quite daubed up, that cannot see him strike ⁱ :—a palate out of taste, that cannot savour nor relish heavenly things^j :—lips poisoned ^k :—a tongue set on fire ^l :—flesh consumed, bones sticking out, sore vexed and broken to pieces ^m. Some diseases are dull, others acute ; some stupifying, others tormenting :—sin is all; a stupifying palsy, that takes away feeling ⁿ ; a plague in the heart, which sets all on fire ^o.

Let us consider, a little, the proper passions and effects of most diseases, and see how they suit to sin.

First, Pain and distemper. This, first or last, is in all sin ; for it begets in wicked and impenitent men the pain of guilt^p, horror, trembling of heart, anguish of conscience,

---

^c Isai. i. 3, 6.   ^d Ezek. xxxiv. 4.   ^e Matth. ix. 12, 13.   ^f John viii. 48.
^g Luke x. 34.   ^h Jer. vi. 10.   ⁱ Jer. lxiv. 18. Isai. xxvi. 11.   ^j Rom.
viii. 5.   ^k Rom. iii. 13.   ^l James iii. 6.   ^m Job xxxiii. 21. Psalm vi. 2.
li. 8.   ⁿ Ephes. iv. 19.   ^o 1 Kings viii. 38. Hos. vii. 4.   ^p Peccatum
quod inultum videtur, habet pedissequam pœnam suam, si nemo de admissi nisi
amaritudine doleat: *Aug.* de Continent. c. 6.—Memoria Testis, Ratio Index,
Timor Carnifex : *Bern.* Ser. de villico iniq.—Omne malum aut timore aut pudore
natura suffudit. *Tert.* Apol. c. 1.—Perturbatio animi, respicientis peccata sua ; re-
spectione perhorrescentis ; horrore erubescentis ; erubescentia corrigentis. *Aug.*
in Ps. 30. Con. 1.—Morbus est ἐναντία τῇ ὑγιείᾳ διάθεσις, ὑφ᾽ ἧς ἐνέργειαν λέγομεν
βλάπτεσθαι, *Galen.*—Habitus corporis contra naturam, usum ejus ad id facit

fear of wrath, expectation of judgement and fiery indignation, as in Cain, Pharaoh, Ahab, Felix, and divers others [q].
And in penitent men it begets the pain of shame and sorrow,
and inquietude of spirit, a wound in the spirit, a prick in the
very heart [r]. ' Penitency' and ' pain ' are words of one derivation, and are very near of kin unto one another :—never
was any wound cured without pain ; never any sin healed
without sorrow.

Secondly, Weakness and indisposedness to the actions of
life. Sin is like an unruly spleen, or a greedy wen in the
body, that sucks all nourishment, and converts all supplies
into its own growth, and so exhausts the strength and vigour of the soul, making it unfit and unable to do any good.
Whenever it sets about any duty, till sin be cured, it goes
about it like an arm out of joint [s]; which, when you would
move it one way, doth fall back another. It faints, and
flags, and is not able to put forth any skill, or any delight
unto any good duty. Naturally men are reprobate, or void
of judgement unto any good work [t]. Godliness is a mystery, a spiritual skill and trade ; there is learning, and use,
and experience, and much exercise required to be handsome
and dexterous about it [u]. To be sinners, and to be without
strength, in the apostle's phrase, is all one [x]. And look how
much flesh there is in any man, so much disability is there
to perform any thing that is good [y]. Therefore the hands of
sinners are said to hang down, and their knees to be feeble,
and their feet to be lame, that cannot make straight paths
till they be healed [z]. If they, at any time, upon natural dictates, or some sudden strong conviction, or pang of fear, or
stirrings of conscience, do offer at any good work, to pray,
to repent, to believe, to obey, they bungle at it, and are out
of their element : they are wise to do evil, but to do good
they have no knowledge. They presently grow weary of

deteriorem, cujus causâ natura nobis ejus corporis sanitatem dedit. Leg. 1. Sect. 7.
D. de Ædilitio Edict.   [q] Gen. iv. 13, 14. Exod. ix. 27, 28. 1 Kings xxi. 27.
Acts xxiv. 25. Isai. xxxiii. 14. Heb. ii. 15. Rom. viii. 15. Heb. x. 27.
[r] Rom. vi. 21. Ezek. xvi. 61. 2 Cor. vii. 10. Prov. xviii. 14. Acts ii. 37.
[s] Καθάπερ τὰ παραλελυμένα τοῦ σώματος μόρια εἰς τὰ δεξιὰ προαιρουμένων
κινῆσαι, τοὐναντίον εἰς τὰ ἀριστερὰ παραφέρεται. Arist. Eth. l. i. c.ult.   [t] Tit.
ii. 16.   [u] 1 Tim. iii. 16. Phil. iv. 11. Heb. iv. 13, 14.   [x] Rom. v. 6, 8.
[y] Rom. vii. 18.   [z] Heb. xii. 12, 13.

any essays and offers at well-doing, and cannot hold out or persevere in them.

Thirdly, Decay and consumption. Sin wastes [a] and wears out the vigour of soul and body; feeds upon all our time and strength, and exhausts it in the services of lust. Sickness is a chargeable thing; a consumption at once to the person and to the estate. The poor woman in the gospel, which had an issue of blood, "spent all that she had, on physicians, and was never the better [b]:"—so poor sinners empty all the powers of soul, of body, of time, of estate, every thing within their reach, upon their lusts; and are as unsatisfied [c] at last as at the first [d]. Like a silk-worm, which works out his own bowels into such a mass, wherein himself is buried; it weareth them out, and sucketh away the radical strength in the service of it; and yet never giveth them over, but, as Pharaoh's task-masters exacted the brick when they had taken away the straw, so lust doth consume and weaken natural strength, in the obedience of it; and yet when nature is exhausted, the strength of lust is as great, and the commands as tyrannous as ever before [e]. We are to distinguish between the vital force of the faculties, and the activity of lust which sets them on work: *that* decays and hastens to death, but sin retains its strength and vigour still: nothing kills *that* but the blood of Christ, and the decay of nature ariseth out of the strength of sin. The more any man, in any lust whatsoever, makes himself a servant of sin, and the more busy and active he is in that service,—the more will it eat into him, and consume him: as the hotter the fever is, the sooner is the body wasted and dried up by it.

Fourthly, Deformity. Sickness withereth the beauty of the body, maketh it, of a glorious, a ghastly and loathsome spectacle. Come to the comeliest person living, after a long and pining sickness, and you shall not find the man in his own shape: a wan countenance, a shrivelled flesh, a lean visage, a hollow and standing eye, a trembling hand, a stam-

---

[a] Tabificæ mentis perturbationes. *Cic.* 4. Tusc. 36.   [b] Luke viii. 43.   [c] Ἄπληστος ἡ τοῦ ἡδέος ὄρεξις. *Arist.* Eth. l. 3. c. ult. Πονηρία τῶν ἀνθρώπων ἄπληστόν τι· ἄπειρος ἡ τῆς ἐπιθυμίας φύσις, Polit. l. 2. Naturalia desideria finita sunt; ex falsa opinione nascentia, ubi desinant, non habent, &c. *Sen.* p. 16. Ex libidine orta, sine termino sunt. Ep. 39.   [d] Eccles. i. 8.   [e] Isai. lvii. 10. Jer. ii. 25.

mering tongue, a bowed back, a feeble knee, a swelled belly;
nothing left but the stakes of the hedge, and a few sinews to
hold them together. Behold here the picture of a sinner,
swelled [f] with pride [g], pined with envy, bowed [h] with earthli-
ness, wasted and eaten up with lust, made as stinking and
unsavoury as a dead carcase [i]. When thou seest an unmer-
ciful man, that hath no compassion left in him,—think thou
sawest Judas or king Jehoram, whose sore disease made his
bowels fall out [k]. When thou seest a worldly man, whose
heart is glued to earthly things,—think upon the poor woman, who was bowed together, and could not lift up herself [l]. When thou seest a hypocrite walking crooked and
unevenly in the ways of God, think upon Mephibosheth or
Asa, lame, halting, diseased in their feet. When thou seest
a proud ambitious man, think upon Herod, eaten up with
vermin. O! if the diseases of the soul could come forth
and show themselves in the body, and work such deformity
there (where it would not do the thousandth part so much
hurt) as they do within ;—if a man could, in the glass of the
Word, see the ugliness of the one, as plainly as, in a material
glass, the foulness of the other ; how would this make him
cry out, " My head, my head ; my bowels, my bowels ; my
leanness, my leanness ; unclean, unclean !" No man thinks
any shape ugly enough to represent a devil by : yet take
him in his naturals, and he was a most glorious creature ; it
is sin that turns him into a serpent or dragon. There is
something of the monster in every sin ; the belly or the feet,
set in the place of the head or heart ; sensual and worldly
lusts, set up above reason,—and corrupt reason, above
grace.

SECT. 13. Now because the sickness, here spoken of, is a
falling sickness, and that the worst kind of fall, not forward
in our way or race, as every good man sometimes falls,
where a man hath the help of his knees and hands to break
the blow, to prevent or lessen the hurt, and to make him to

[f] Inflatus et tumens animus in vitio est. Sapientis animus nunquam tur-
gescit, nunquam tumet. *Cic.* Tusc. Quæst. l. 3.   [g] Invidus alterius rebus
macrescit opimis. *Hor.* Ep. i. 2. 57.   [h] O curvæ in terras animæ et cœlestium
inanes. *Pers.* Ut corpora verberibus, ita sævitia, libidine, malis consultis animus
dilaceratur. *Tacit.* Annal. l. 6.   [i] Psalm xiv. 3. Ezek. xvi. 4.   [k] 2 Chron.
xxi. 19.   [l] Luke xiii. 11.

rise again; but old Eli's falls, a 'falling backward,' where a man can put forth no part to save the whole, and so doth more dangerously break and bruise himself thereby;—therefore as it is a sickness which requires curing, so it is a wound which requires healing and binding. The ancients compare it to falling into a pit full of dirt and stones [m], where a man doth not only defile, but miserably break and bruise himself. There is 'contritio, solutio continui, suppuratio, sanies,' &c. all the evils of a dangerous and mortal wound.

Add to all this, that, in this diseased and wounded condition, 1st. A man hath no power to heal or to help himself, but in that respect he must cry out with them in the prophet, " My wound is incurable, and refuseth to be healed [n]."

2d. He hath no desire, no will, no thought to enquire or send after a physician, who may heal him ; but is well contented rather to continue as he is, than to be put to the pain and trouble of a cure, and pleaseth himself in the goodness of his condition [o].

3rd. He is in the hands of his cruel enemy, who takes no pity on him ; but by flattery and tyranny, and new temptations, continually cherisheth the disease [p].

4th. When the true Physician comes, he shuts the door against him, refuses his counsel, rejecteth his receipts, quarrels with his medicines ; they are too bitter, or too strong and purging, or too sharp and searching ; he will not be healed at all, except it may be his own way [q].—Thus we have taken a view of the patient, sick, weak, pained, consumed, deformed, wounded, and sore bruised ; without power or help at home, without friends abroad : without sense of danger, no desire of change ; patient of his disease, impatient of his cure ; but one means in the world to help him, and he unable to procure it ; and, being offered to him, unwilling to entertain it : who can expect after all this, but to

---

[m] Cecidimus super acervum lapidum et in luto : unde non solum inquinati, sed graviter vulnerati et quassati sumus : *Bern.* Ser. 1. in Cœna Dom.—Cecidimus in carcerem, luto pariter et lapidibus plenum, captivi, inquinati, conquassati. *Idem* Ser. 2. in Octav. Paschæ.—Libens ægrotat, qui medico non credit, nec morbum declinat : *Arist.* Eth. l. 3.—O fortes, quibus medicis opus non est ! fortitudo ista non sanitatis est, sed insaniæ ; nam et phreneticis nihil fortius :—sed quanto majores vires, tanto mors vicinior. *Aug.* in Psal. 58.   [n] Jer. xv. 18.   [o] Rev. iii. 17. Matth. ix. 26.   [p] 2 Tim. ii. 12.   [q] Prov. i. 24, 25. 2 Chron. xxxvi. 16. Ezek. xxiv. 16. Matth. xxiii. 37. Jer. xiii. 11.

hear the knell ring, and to see the grave opened for such a
sick person as this ?

SECT. 14. Now let us take a view of the physician.
Surely an ordinary one would be so far from visiting such a
patient, that, in so desperate a condition as this, he would
quite forsake him ; as their use is to leave their patients,
when they lie a dying.   Here then observe the singular
goodness of this Physician :—

First, Though other physicians judge of the disease when
it is brought unto them, yet the patient first feels it, and
complains of it himself: but this Physician giveth the
patient the very feeling of his disease, and is fain to take
notice of that as well as to minister the cure.   " He went on
frowardly in the way of his heart," saith the Lord, and
pleased himself in his own ill condition ; " I have seen his
way, and will heal him r."

Secondly, Other patients send for the physician, and use
many entreaties to be visited and undertaken by him : here
the Physician comes unsent for, and entreats the sick person
to be healed.   The world is undone by falling off from God,
and yet God is the first that begins reconciliation ; and the
stick of it is in the world, and not in him: and therefore
there is a great emphasis in the apostle's expression, " God
was in Christ, reconciling the world to himself," not himself
unto the world.   " He entreats us to be reconciled s."   " He
is found of them that sought him not t;" and his office is not
only ' to save,' but ' to seek that which was lost.'

Thirdly, Other physicians are well used, and entertained
with respect and honour : but our patient here neglects and
misuseth his Physician, falls from him, betakes himself unto
mountebanks and physicians of no value : yet he insists on
his mercy, and comes when he is forsaken, when he is re-
pelled: " I have spread out my hands, all the day, unto a
rebellious people u."

Fourthly, Other physicians have usually ample and honourable rewards x for the attendance they give : but this
Physician comes out of love, heals freely ; nay, is bountiful
to his patient ; doth not only heal him, but bestows gifts

r Isai. lvii. 17, 18.   s 2 Cor v. 19, 20.   t Isai. lxv. 1.   u Isai. lxv. 2.
x Medicos civitate donavit Julius Cæsar. *Suet.* in Jul. c. 4.

upon him; gives the visit, gives the physic; sends the ministers and servants, who watch and keep the patient [y].

Lastly, Other physicians prescribe a " bitter potion for the sick person to take; this Physician drinketh of the bitterest himself:—others prescribe the sore to be lanced; this Physician is wounded and smitten himself:—others order the patient to bleed; here the Physician bleeds himself;—yea, he is not only the physician, but the physic; and gives himself, his own flesh, his own blood, for a purgative, a cordial, a plaister to the soul of his patient; dies himself, that his patient may live, and " by his stripes we are healed [z]."

SECT. 15. We should, from all this, learn, First, To admire the unsearchable riches of the mercy of our God, who is pleased in our misery to prevent us with goodness, and when we neither felt our disease, nor desired a remedy, is pleased to convince us of our sins, " Thou hast fallen by thine iniquity:"—To invite us to repentance; " O Israel, return unto the Lord thy God:"—To put words into our mouth, and to draw our petition for us; " Take with you words, and say unto him, Take away all iniquity," &c.—To furnish us with arguments; " We are fatherless, thou art merciful:"—To encourage us with promises; " I will heal, I will love:"—To give us his ministers to proclaim, and his Spirit to apply these mercies unto us. If he did not convince us, that iniquity would be a downfal and a ruin unto us [b]: we should hold it fast, and be pleased with our disease; like a madman that quarrels with his cure, and had rather continue mad than be healed [c].

If being convinced, he did not invite us to repentance, we should run away from him, as Adam did. No man loves to be in the company of an enemy; much less, when that enemy is a judge. They " have turned their back unto me, and not their face [d]." Adam will hide himself ' from the presence of the Lord [e];" and Cain will go out ' from the presence of the Lord [f].' Guilt cannot look upon majesty;

[y] Vis morborum pretia medentibus; fori tabes pecuniam advocatis fert. *Tacit.* Annal. l. 11. 6.   [z] Isai. liii. 5.   [c] Pol! me occidistis, amici; non servâstis, ait: *Horat.*—Molestus est somnium jucundum videnti qui excitat. *Sen.* ep. 102.   [b] Ezek. xviii. 30.   [d] Jer. ii. 27.   [e] Gen. iii. 8. [f] Gen. iv. 16.

stubble dares not come near the fire.   If we be in our sins,
we cannot stand before God [g].

If being invited [h], he did not 'put words into our mouths,' we
should not know what to say unto him.   We know not wherewith to come before the Lord, or to bow before the high God,
if he do not ' show us what is good [i].'   Where God is the judge,
who cannot be mocked or derided ; who knoweth all things;
and if our heart condemn us, he is greater than our hearts ; and
wherever we hide, can find us out, and make our sin to find
us too [k];—where, I say, this God is the judge, there guilt
stoppeth the mouth, and maketh the sinner speechless [l].
Nay, the best of us ' know not what to pray for as we ought,
except the Spirit be pleased to help our infirmities [m].'   When
we are taught what to say,—if God do not withdraw his
anger, we shall never be able to reason with him [n] : " Withdraw thine hand from me; let not thy dread make me afraid;
then I will answer, then I will speak [o]."   If he do not reveal
mercy ; if he do not promise love or healing ; if he do not
make it appear that he is a God that heareth prayers ; flesh
will not dare to come near unto him [p].   We can never pray,
till we can cry, ' Abba, Father;' we can never call unto him
but in the ' multitude of his mercies.'   As the earth is shut
and bound up by frost and cold, and putteth not forth her
precious fruits, till the warmth and heat of the summer call
them out ; so the heart, under the cold affections of fear and
guilt, under the dark apprehensions of wrath and judgement,
is so contracted, that it knows not to draw near to God: but
when mercy shines, when the love of God is shed abroad in
it, then also the heart itself is shed abroad and enlarged to
pour out itself unto God.   Even when distressed sinners
pray, their prayer proceeds from apprehensions of mercy :
for prayer is the child of faith [q], and the object of faith is
mercy.

SECT. 16. Secondly, The way to prize this mercy, is to
grow acquainted with our own sickness ; to see our face in

[g] Ezra ix. 15.   [h] Oratio de conscientia procedit : si conscientia erubescit,
erubescat oratio : si spiritus reus apud te sit, erubescit conscientia : *Tert.* exhort. castit. c. 10.   [i] Mic. vi. 6, 8.   [k] Gal. vi. 7. 1 John iii. 20. Numb.
xxxii. 23.   [l] Matth. xxii. 12. Rom. iii. 19.   [m] Rom. viii. 26.   [n] Job
ix. 13, 14.   [o] Job xiii. 21, 22.   [p] 2 Sam. vii. 27.   [q] Rom. x. 15.
James v. 15.

the glass of the law; to consider how odious it renders us to God, how desperately miserable in ourselves. The deeper the sense of misery, the higher the estimation of mercy. When the apostle looked on himself as the chief of sinners, then he accounted it a saying "worthy of all acceptation, That Christ Jesus came into the world to save sinners[r]." Till we be 'sick and weary,' we shall not look after a 'physician to heal and ease us[s];' till we be 'pricked in our hearts,' we shall not be hasty to enquire after the means of salvation[t]. Though the proclamation of pardon be made to 'all, that will[u],' yet none are willing, till they be brought to extremities: as men cast not their goods into the sea, till they see they must perish themselves, if they do not. Some men must be bound, before they can be cured. All that God doth to us in conversion, he doth most freely: but a gift is not a gift till it be received[x]; and we naturally refuse and reject Christ when he is offered[y], because he is not offered but upon these terms,—' that we deny ourselves, and take up a cross, and follow him :' therefore, we must be wrought upon by some terror or other[z]. When we find the wrath of God abiding upon us, and our souls shut under it as in a prison[a], and the fire of it working and boiling, like poison, in our consciences ; then we shall value mercy, and cry for it as the prophet doth, "Heal me, O Lord, and I shall be healed ; save me, and I shall be saved, for thou art my praise[b]." Things necessary are never to be valued to their uttermost, but in extremities. When there is a great famine in Samaria, an ass's head (which at another time is thrown out for carrion) will be more worth, than, in a plentiful season, the whole body of an ox. Nay, hunger shall, in such a case, overvote nature, and devour the very tender love of a mother : the life of a child shall not be so dear to the heart, as his flesh to the belly of a pined parent[c]. As soon as a man finds a shipwreck, a famine, a hell in his soul, till Christ save, feed, deliver it,—immediately Christ will be the desire of that soul, and nothing in Heaven or earth valued in comparison of him. Then that which was esteemed the 'foolishness of preaching'

---

[r] 1 Tim. i. 25.   [s] Matth. ix. 12. xi. 28.   [t] Acts ii. 37.   [u] Rev. xxii. 17.
[x] Rom. v. 17. John i. 12.   [y] Isai. liii. 3. John i. 11.   [z] 2 Cor. v. 11.
[a] John iii. 36. Gal. iii. 22.   [b] Jer. xvii. 14.   [c] 2 Kings vi. 25, 26.

before,-shall be counted ' the power of God, and the wisdom
of God :' then every one of Christ's ordinances (which are
the 'waters of the temple, for the healing of the sea,' that
is, of many people [d], and the 'leaves of the tree of life,' which
are for the 'healing of the nations [e],'—and the ' streams of that
fountain which is opened in Israel for sin and for uncleanness [f], and the ' wings of the Sun of Righteousness,' whereby he conveyeth ' healing, to his church [g], shall be esteemed,
as indeed they are, the riches, the glory, the treasure, the
feast, the physic, the salvation of such a soul [h].' And a man
will wait on them with as much diligence and attention, as
ever the impotent people did at the pool of Bethesda, when
the angel stirred the water : and endure the healing severity
of them, not only with patience, but with love and thankfulness ; suffer reason to be captivated, will to be crossed,
high imaginations to be cast down, every thought to be subdued, conscience to be searched, heart to be purged, lust to
be cut off and mortified ;—in all things, will such a sick soul
be contented to be dieted, restrained, and ordered, by the
counsel of this heavenly Physician.

SECT. 17. It is here next to be noted, That God promiseth
to heal their ' backslidings.' The word imports a departing
from God, or a turning away again. It is quite contrary,
in the formal nature of it, unto faith and repentance ; and
implies that which the apostle calls a ' repenting of repentance [i].' By faith we come to Christ [k], and cleave to him,
and lay hold upon him [l] ; but, by this, we depart, and draw
back from him, and let him go [m]. By the one, we prize
Christ as infinitely precious, and his ways as holy and
good [n]; by the other, we vilify and set them at nought,
stumble at them, as ways that do not profit [o]. For, a man
having approved of God's way, and entered into covenants

---

[d] Ezek. xlvii. 8.   [e] Rev. xxii. 2.   [f] Zach. xiii. 1.   [g] Mal. iii. 2.
[h] Rom. xi. 12. Ephes. iii. 8. 2 Cor. iii. 8, 11. iv. 6, 7. Isai. xxv. 6. Rev.
xix. 9. Luke iv. 18. Heb. ii. 3. James i. 21. John xii. 50. Acts xxviii. 28.
[i] 2 Cor. vii. 10.   [k] John vi. 37. Venire ad Christum, quid est aliud quam
credendo converti ? *Aug.* de grat. et lib. arbit. ca. 5.—Transfugas arboribus sus-
pendunt. *Tacit.* de morib. Germ.—Transfugas, ubicunque inventi fuerint, quasi
hostes interficere licet ; l. 3. s. 6. ad leg. Cornel. de Sicariis. D. ep. l. 38. D. de
pœnis, s. 2, et 19. captivis et postliminio, et l. 3. de Re militari, s. 11. l. 7.
[l] Heb. vi. 18. Isai. lvi. 2, 6.   [m] Heb. x. 13, 28, 29.   [n] Phil. iii. 8.
2 Pet. i. 4.   [o] Matth. xxi. 42. Acts iv. 11. 1 Pet. ii. 7, 8. John xxi. 14, 15.

with him, after this to go from his word, and fling up his
bargain, and start aside like a deceitful bow; of all other
dispositions of the soul, this is one of the worst, to deal
with our sins as Israel did with their servants [p], dismiss
them, and then take them again. It is the sad fruit of an
' evil and unbelieving heart [q];' and God threateneth such persons to ' lead them forth with the workers of iniquity [r],' as
cattle are led to slaughter, or malefactors to execution. And
yet we here see God promiseth healing unto such sinners.

For understanding whereof we are to know, that there is a
twofold apostasy; the one, out of impotency of affection
and prevalency of lust, drawing the heart to look towards the
old pleasures thereof again; and it is a recidivation or relapse into a former sinful condition, out of forgetfulness and
falseness of heart, for want of the fear of God to balance
the conscience, and to fix and unite the heart unto him.
Which was the frequent sin of Israel, to make many promises and covenants unto God, and to break them as fast [s].
And this falling from our first love [t], growing cold and slack
in duty, breaking our engagements unto God, and returning
again to folly,—though it be like a relapse after a disease,
exceeding dangerous,—yet God is sometimes pleased to forgive and heal it.

The other kind of apostasy is proud and malicious;
when, after the ' taste of the good Word of God, and the
powers of the world to come,' men set themselves to hate,
oppose, persecute godliness; to do despite to the Spirit of
grace; to fling off the holy strictness of Christ's yoke; to
swell against the searching power of his word; to ' trample
upon the blood of the covenant;' and when they know the
spiritualness and holiness of God's ways, the innocency and
piety of his servants, do yet, notwithstanding, set them-

---

[p] Jer. xxxiv. 10, 11.   [q] Heb. iii. 12.   [r] Psalm cxxv. 5.   [s] Judges
ii. 11, 12. Psalm cvi. 7, 8. ii. 12. 13.   [t] Eorum qui peccant ante quam Deum
noverint, antequam miserationes ejus experti sunt, antequam portaverint jugum
suave et onus leve, priusquam devotionis gratiam et consolationes acceperint
Spiritus Sancti ; eorum, inquam, copiosa redemptio est : at eorum qui, post con-
versionem suam, peccatis implicantur, ingrati acceptæ gratiæ, et post missam
manum ad aratrum retro respiciunt, tepidi et carnales facti ;—eorum utique
perpaucos invenias, qui post hæc redeunt in gradum pristinum: nec tamen, si
quis hujusmodi est, desperamus de eo, tantum et resurgere velit cito : quanto
enim diutius permanebit, tanto evadet difficilius. *Bern.* Serm. 3. in Vigil. —Vid.
Serm. 35. in Cant.—*Aug.* de Civ. Dei, lib. 6. cap. 30.—*Isid. Pelus.* l. 1. ep. 13.

selves against them for that reason, though under other pre-
tences. This is not a weak, but a wilful, and (if I may
so speak) a strong and a stubborn, apostasy; a sin which
wholly hardeneth the heart against repentance, and, by consequence, is incurable. ' To speak against the Son of Man [u],'
that is, against the doctrine, disciples, ways, servants of
Christ,—looking on him only as a man, the leader of a sect,
as master of a new way (which was Paul's notion of Christ
and Christian religion when he persecuted it, and ' for which
cause he found mercy;' for had he done that knowingly,
which he did ignorantly, it had been a sin incapable of
mercy [x],)—thus to sin is a blasphemy that may be pardoned;
but to ' speak against the Spirit [y],' that is, to oppose and
persecute the doctrine, worship, ways, servants of 'Christ,
knowing them, and acknowledging in them a spiritual holiness, and, ' eo nomine,' to do it, so that the formal motive of
malice against them, is the power and lustre of that spirit
which appeareth in them ; and the formal principle of it,
neither ignorance, nor self-ends, but very wilfulness, and immediate malignity.   Woe be to that man, whose natural enmity and antipathy against godliness do ever swell to so
great and daring a height ! " It shall not be forgiven him,
neither in this world, nor in that which is to come [z] :"
that is, say some [a], neither in the time of life, nor in the
point or moment of death, which translates them into the
world to come. Others [b], not in this life by justification,
nor in the world to come by consummate redemption,
and public judiciary absolution in the last day, which is
therefore called " the day of redemption," in which men
are said to ' find mercy of the Lord [c].' For that which
is here done in the conscience by the ministry of the
Word and efficacy of the Spirit, shall be then publicly and
judicially pronounced by Christ's own mouth before angels
and men [d]. Others [e], " shall not be forgiven ;" that is, shall
be plagued and punished both in this life, and in that to
come. Give me leave to add what I have conceived of the
meaning of this place, though no way condemning the expo-

---

[u] Vid. *Bezæ* Annotat. in Joan. 5. 16.   [x] Acts xxvi. 9. 1 Tim. i. 13.   [y] Vid.
Isidor. Pelus. lib. 1. ep. 59.   [z] Matth. xii. 32.   [a] *Beza, Calvin, Cartwright,*
against the Rhemists.   [b] *Chemnit. Diodati.*   [c] Ephes. iv. 30. 2 Tim. i. 18.
[d] 2 Cor. v. 10.   [e] *Chrysost.* et *Theophylact. Broughton* Explicat. of the Revelation, cap. 21. p. 301, 302.

sitions of so great and learned men: I take it, "By this world," we may understand the church which then was of the Jews,—or the present age, which our Saviour Christ then lived in. It is not, I think, insolent in the scripture, for the word 'age' or 'world' to be sometimes restrained to the 'church.' Now as Israel was God's first-born, and the first-fruits of his increase[f]; so the church of Israel is called the 'church of the first-born[g],' and the 'first tabernacle,' and a 'worldly sanctuary[h],' and 'Jerusalem that now is[i].' And then by the 'world to come,' we are to understand the 'Christian church,' afterwards to be planted: for so frequently in scripture is the 'evangelical church' called the 'world to come,' and the 'last days,' and the 'ends of the world;' and the things thereunto belonging, 'things to come,' which had been hidden from former ages and generations, and were by the ministry of the apostles made known unto the church in their time, which the prophets and righteous men of the former ages did not see nor attain unto. Thus it is said, "In these last days, God hath spoken to us by his Son[k];" and "unto angels he did not put in subjection the world to come[l]:" and, "Christ was made a High-priest of good things to come[m]:" and, "the law had a shadow of good things to come[n];" and the times of the gospel are called, "ages to come[o];" and, "the ends of the world[p]." Thus legal and evangelical dispensations are usually distinguished by the names of times past, and the last days, or times to come[q]:—The one, an earthly and temporary; the other, a heavenly and abiding administration:—and so the Septuagint render the original word, אבי עד [r], "everlasting Father," which is one of the names of Christ, by Πατὴρ τοῦ μέλλοντος αἰῶνος, "the Father of the world to come."

The meaning, then, of the place seems to be this,—That sins of high and desperate presumption, committed maliciously against known light, and against the evidence of God's spirit, as they had no sacrifice or expiation allowed for them in the former world, or state of the Jewish church, but they who in that manner despised Moses and his law, though delivered but by angels, "died without mercy[s];"—so

[f] Exod. iv. 22. Jer. xxxi. 9. ii. 3.　　[g] Heb. xii. 23.　　[h] Heb. ix. 1. 8.
[i] Gal. iv. 25.　　[k] Heb. i. 1.　　[l] Heb. ii. 5.　　[m] Heb. ix. 11.　　[n] Heb. x. 1.
[o] Ephes. ii. 7.　　[p] 1 Cor. x. 11.　　[q] Heb. i. 1. Ephes. iii. 9, 10. Col. i. 25, 26.
[r] Isai. ix. 6.　　[s] Numb. xv. 27, 30, 31. Heb. ii. 2, 3, 4.

in the world to come,' or in the 'evangelical church' (though grace therein should be more abundantly disco- vered and administered unto men), yet the same law should continue still, as we find it did [t]; neither the open enemies of Christ in the one, nor the false professors of Christ in the other, committing this sin, should be capable of pardon.

This doctrine of apostasy, or backsliding, though worthy of a more large explication, I shall here conclude, with add- ing but two words more :—

First, That we should beware, above all other sins, of this, of falling in soul as old Eli did in body, ' backward,' and so hazarding our salvation. If once we have shaken hands with sin, never take acquaintance with it any more; but say, as Israel here, "What have I to do any more with idols?" The church should be like Mount Sion, "that can- not be moved." It is a sad and sick temper of a church to toss from one side to another; and then especially, when she should be healed, to be " carried about with every wind."

Secondly, We should not be so terrified by any sin, which our soul mourns and labours under, and our heart turneth from, as thereby to be withheld from going to the physi- cian for pardon and healing. Had he not great power and mercy; did he not love freely, without respect of persons, and pardon freely without respect of sins; we might then be afraid of going to him: but when he extendeth forgiveness to all kinds, " iniquity, transgression, sin [u]," and hath ac- tually pardoned the greatest sinners, Manasses, Mary Mag- dalen, Paul, publicans, harlots, backsliders; we should, though not presume hereupon to turn God's mercy into poi- son, and his grace into wantonness (for mercy itself will not save those sinners that hold fast sin, and will not forsake it), yet take heed of despairing, or entertaining low thoughts of the love and mercy of God : for such examples as these are set forth for the encouragement of all " that shall ever believe unto eternal life [x];" and the thoughts and ways which God hath to pardon sin, are " above our thoughts and ways," whereby we look on them in their guilt and great- ness, many times, as unpardonable; and therefore are fit

[t] Heb. ii. 2, 3, 4, 5. vi. 4, 5, 6. x. 26, 27, 28.   [u] Exod. xxxiv. 6.
[x] 1 Tim. i. 16.

matter for our faith, even against sense, to believe and rely upon.

SECT. 18. Now followeth the fountain of this mercy; *" I will love them freely."*] God's love is a most free and bountiful love, having no motive or foundation [x] but within itself; and his free love and grace is the ground of all his other mercies to his people : *" he showeth mercy on whom, and because he will show mercy."* From the beginning to the end of our salvation, nothing is primarily active but free grace : *" freely loved* [z] ;" *" freely chosen* [a] ;" *" Christ, the gift of free love* [b] :" *" his obedience freely accepted for us, and bestowed upon us* [c] :" *" justification free* [d] ;" *" adoption free* [e] ;" *" faith and repentance free* [f] ;" *" good works free* [g] ;" *" salvation free* [h] ."* Thus the foundation of all mercies is *free love.* We do not first give to God, that he may render to us again. We turn, we pray, we covenant, we repent, we are holy, we are healed,—only because he loves us : and he loves us, not because he sees any thing lovely or amiable in us,—but because he will show the absoluteness of his own will, and the unsearchableness of his own counsel towards us. We are not originally denominated good by any thing which floweth from us, or is done by us; but by that which is bestowed upon us. Our goodness is not the motive of his love ; but his love the fountain of our goodness. None indeed are healed and saved, but those that repent and return ; but repentance is only a condition, and that freely given by God, disposing the subject for salvation; not a cause moving or procuring God to save us. It is necessary as the means to the end,—not as the cause to the effect. That which looks least free of any other act of God, his rewarding of obedience, is all and only mercy. When we sow in righteousness, we must reap in mercy [i] ; when he renders according to our works, it is because of his mercy [k].

This is the solid bottom and foundation of all Christian comfort, That God loves freely. Were his love to us to be measured by our fruitfulness or carriages towards him,

---

[x] Cum quis propter nullam aliam causam donat, quam ut libertatem et munificentiam exerceat, hæc proprie Donatio appellatur. *Julian.* D. de Donationib. lib. 1.   [y] Isai. lv. 57, 58.   [z] Deut. vii. 7, 8.   [a] Ephes. i. 5, 6.   [b] John iii. 16.   [c] Rom. v. 15, 18.   [d] Rom. iii. 24.   [e] Ephes. i. 5.   [f] Phil. i. 29. 2 Tim. ii. 25.   [g] Ephes. ii. 10.   [h] Tit. iii. 5. Acts xv. 1.   [i] Hos. x. 12.   [k] Psalm lxii. 12.

each hour and moment might stagger our hope: but he is therefore pleased to have it all " of grace, that the promise might be made sure[l]." This comforts us against the guilt of the greatest sins; for love and free grace can pardon what it will. This comforts us against the accusations of Satan, drawn from our own unworthiness—" 'Tis true, I am unworthy; and Satan cannot show me unto myself more vile, than, without his accusations, I will acknowledge myself to be: but that love that gave Christ freely, doth give in him more worthiness, than there is, or can be, unworthiness in me." This comforts us in the assured hope of glory; because when he loves, he loves to the end; and nothing can separate from his love. This comforts us in all afflictions,—That the free love of God, who hath predestinated us thereunto, will wisely order it all unto the good of his servants [m].

Our duty therefore it is, First, To labour for assurance of this free love: it will assist us in all duties; it will arm us against all temptations; it will answer all objections that can be made against the soul's peace; it will sustain us in all conditions, which the saddest of times can bring us unto. " If God be for us, who can be against us?" Though thousands should be against us to hate us, yet none shall be against us to hurt us.

Secondly, If God love us freely, we should love him thankfully[n]; and let love be the salt to season all our sacrifices. For as no benefit is saving unto us, which doth not proceed from love in him: so no duty is pleasing unto him, which doth not proceed from love in us[o].

Thirdly, Plead this free love and grace in prayer. When we beg pardon, nothing is too great for love to forgive; when we beg grace and holiness, nothing is too good for love to grant. There is not any one thing which faith can manage unto more spiritual advantages, than the free grace and love of God in Christ.

Fourthly, Yet we must so magnify the love of God, as that we turn not free grace into wantonness. There is a corrupt generation of men, who, under pretence of exalting grace, do put disgrace upon the law of God, by taking away

l Rom. iv.16.   m Rom. viii. 29. Heb. xii. 6.   n 1 John iv. 19.
o 1 John. v. 3.

the mandatory power thereof from those that are under grace; a doctrine most extremely contrary to the nature of this love. For God's love to us, works love in us to him; and our love to him is this, that we " keep his commandments:" and to keep a commandment, is to confirm and to subject my conscience, with willingness and delight, unto the rule and preceptive power of that commandment. Take away the obligation of the law upon conscience as a rule of life, and you take away from our love to God the very matter, about which the obedience thereof should be conversant. It is no diminution to love, that a man is bound to obedience; nay, it cannot be called ' obedience,' if I be not bound unto it: but herein the excellency of our love to God is commended, that whereas other men are so bound by the law, that they fret at it, and swell against it, and would be glad to be exempted from it,—they who love God[p], and know his love to them, delight to be thus bound,—and find infinitely more sweetness in the strict rule of God's holy law, than any wicked man can do in that presumptuous liberty, wherein he allows himself to shake off and break the cords of it.

SECT. 19. Now lastly, when we return with sound repentance unto God, then God is pleased to give more than ordinary tastes of the sweetness of his love, by removing judgements, which are the fruits of his anger, from us. This point falls in with what was handled before on the second verse. Therefore, I shall conclude with these two notes:—

First, That, in all judgements, God will have us look on them as fruits of his anger, and take more notice in them of his displeasure, than our own sufferings. When wrath is gone out, the sword drawn, thousands and ten thousands slain in our coasts, Israel given to the spoil, and Jacob unto robbers; a land set on fire with civil flames, and none able

---

[p] Sub lege est enim, qui timore supplicii quod lex minatur, non amore justitiæ, se sentit abstinere ab opere peccati, nondum liber nec alienus à voluntate peccandi. In ipsa enim voluntate reus est, qua mallet, si fieri posset, non esse quod timeat, ut libere faciat quod occulte desiderat. *August*. de nat. et grat. cap. 57. tom. 10. p. 103. Et infra, " Omnia fiunt facilia caritati," cap. 29. Non est terribile sed suave mandatum : De grat. Christi, lib. 1. cap. 13.—Suave fit quod non delectabat: De peccat. et merit. et remis. lib. 2. cap. 17.—Contr. 2. Epist. Pelag. lib. 1. cap. 9.—de doctr. Christi, lib. 1. cap. 15.—de Spiritu et lit. cap. 3.

to quench them; a kingdom divided against itself; a church, which was sometimes the asylum for other exiled and afflicted Christians to fly for shelter unto, miserably torn by the foolish and unnatural divisions of brethren, and dangerously threatened by the policy and power of the common enemy, who studies how to improve these divisions, to the ruin of those that torment them; our work is to make this conclusion,—" Our God is angry;" a God that loves freely, that is infinite in mercy and pity, who doth not afflict willingly, nor grieve the children of men; this should be our greatest affliction, and the removal of this anger by a universal reformation and conversion unto him, our greatest business. And I do verily believe, that England must never think of out-living or breaking through this anger of God, this critical judgement that is upon it, so as to return to that cold and formal complexion, that Laodicean temper that she was in before,—till she have so publicly and generally repented of all those civil disorders, which removed the bounds, and brought dissipation upon public justice: and of all those ecclesiastical disorders, which let in corruptions in doctrine, superstitions in worship, abuses in government, discountenancing of the power of godliness in the most zealous professors of it, as that our reformation may be as conspicuous, as our disorders have been; and it may appear to all the world, that God hath washed away the filth, and purged the blood of England from the midst thereof, " by the spirit of judgement, and by the spirit of burning."

Secondly, That God's love is the true ground of removing judgements in mercy from a people. Let all human counsels be never so deep, and armies never so active, and cares never so vigilant, and instruments never so unanimous; if God's love come not in, nothing of all these can do a nation any good at all. Those that are most interested in God's love, shall certainly be most secured against his judgements. Hither our eyes, our prayers, our thoughts must be directed.

Lord, love us, delight in us, choose us for thyself: and then, though counsels, and treasures, and armies, and men, and horses, and all second causes fail us; though Satan rage, and hell threaten, and the foundations of the earth be shaken ; though neither the vine, nor the olive, nor the fig-tree, nor the field, nor the pastures, nor the herds, nor the stall, yield any supplies ; yet we will rejoice in the Lord, and glory in the God of our salvation : sin shall be healed : anger shall be removed : " nothing shall be able to se-parate us from the love of God, which is in Christ Jesus our Lord."

FIFTH SERMON.*

HOSEA, XIV. 5, 6, 7.

I will be as the dew unto Israel: he shall grow as the lily, and cast forth his roots as Lebanon. His branches shall spread, and his beauty shall be as the olive-tree, and his smell as Lebanon. They that dwell under his shadow, shall return: they shall revive as the corn, and grow as the vine: the scent thereof shall be as the wine of Lebanon.

SECT. 1. In these verses, is contained God's answer unto the second part of Israel's petition, wherein they desired him to do them good, or to receive them graciously. And here God promiseth them several singular blessings, set forth by several metaphors and similitudes, all answering to the name of Ephraim, and the ancient promises made unto him [a], &c. opposite to the many contrary courses, threatened in the former parts of the prophecy, under metaphors of a contrary importance. Here is the ' dew of grace,' contrary to the ' morning cloud' and the ' earthly dew' that passeth away, cap. xiii. 3. " Lilies, olives, vines, spices," contrary to judgements of " nettles, thorns, thistles," chap. ix. 16, x. 8. " Spreading roots" contrary unto " dry roots," chap. ix. 16. " A fruitful vine" bringing forth excellent wine, contrary to an " empty vine," bringing fruit only to itself; that is, so sour and unsavoury, as is not worth the gathering, chap. x. 1. " Corn growing," instead of " corn taken quite away," chap. ii. 9, instead of " no stalk, no bud, no meal," chap. viii. 7. " Fruit" promised, instead of " no fruit," threatened, chap. ix. 16. " Wine promised in opposition to the " failing of wine," chap. ix. 2. ii. 9. " Sweet wine" opposite to " sour drink," chap. iv. 18. " Safe dwelling," instead

---

of " no dwelling," chap. ix. 3. " Branches growing" and
spreading, instead of " branches consumed," chap. xi. 6.
" Green tree" instead of " dry springs," chap. xiii. 5. And
all these fruits, " the fruits as of Lebanon," which was, of
all other parts of that country, the most fertile mountain,
full of various kinds of the most excellent trees, cedars, cy-
press, olive, and divers others, affording rich gums and bal-
sams; full also of all kinds of the most medicinal and aro-
matic herbs, sending forth a most fragrant odour, whereby
all harmful and venomous creatures were driven from har-
bouring there: and in the valleys of that mountain were
most rich grounds for pasture, corn, and vineyards, as the
learned in their descriptions of the Holy Land have observed [b].

The [c] original of all these blessings is the " heavenly dew"
of God's grace and favour (alluding to that abundance of
dew, which fell on that mountain), descending upon the
church, as upon a garden, bringing forth lilies,—as upon
a forest, strengthening the cedars,—as upon a vineyard,
spreading abroad the branches,—as upon an olive-yard, making the trees thereof green and fruitful,—and as on a rich
field, receiving the corn. Here is a spiritual beauty, the
beauty of the lily, exceeding that of Solomon in all his
glory; spiritual stability, the roots of the cedars, and other
goodly trees in that mountain; spiritual odours, and spices
of Lebanon; spiritual fruitfulness, and that of all sorts and
kinds, for the comfort of life. The fruit of the field, " bread
to strengthen,"—the fruit of the olive-trees, " oil to refresh,"
—the fruit of the vineyard, " wine to make glad," the heart
of man [d].

We esteem him a very rich man, and most excellently ac-
commodated [e], who hath gardens for pleasure,—and fields
for corn and pasture,—and woods for fuel, for structure, for
defence, for beauty, and delight,—and vineyards for wine
and oil; and all other conveniences, both for the necessi-
ties and delights of a plentiful life. Thus is the church here
set forth unto us as such a wealthy man, furnished with

---

[b] *Adrichomius* in Septalim 6.—*Brocard.*—*Hier.* in loc.   [e] Folio-edition,
page 558.   [d] Psalm civ. 15.   [e] Θεμιστοκλῆς ἀπὸ βασιλέως ἔλαβεν δωρεὰν
τὴν Λάμψακον εἰς οἶνον· Μαγνησίαν δ' εἰς ἄρτον, Μυοῦντα δ' εἰς ὄψον, Περκώ-
πηντε, καὶ Παλαισκήψιν εἰς στρωμνὴν καὶ ἱματισμόν. Athenæus, l. 1. e. 23.—
Casanbon, p. 29.—Vid. l. 4. ff. de Censibus.

the unsearchable riches of Christ, with all kind of blessings both for sanctity and safety; as the apostle praiseth God, the Father of our Lord Jesus Christ, who hath blessed us with " all spiritual blessings" in heavenly places in Christ, viz. election to eternal life,—adoption to the condition of sons, and to a glorious inheritance,—redemption from misery unto blessedness,—remission of sins,—knowledge of his will, —holiness and unblameableness of life,—and the seal of the Holy Spirit of promise; as we find them particularly enumerated, Ephes. i. 3, 13.

SECT. 2. The words, thus opened, do first afford us one general observation,—in that God singleth out so many excellent good things by name in relation to that general petition, " Do us good;" that God many times answereth prayer abundantly beyond the petitions of his people. They prayed at large only for good, leaving it (as it becometh us who know not always what is good for ourselves) to his holy will and wisdom, in what manner and measure to do good unto them; and he answers them in particular with all kind of good things: as, in the former petition, they prayed in general for the forgiveness of sin,—and God in particular promiseth the healing of their rebellions, which was the greatest of their sins. God many times answers the prayers of his people, as he did the " seed of Isaac[f]," with a hundred-fold increase. As God's word never returns empty unto him, so the prayers of his servants never return empty unto them; and usually the crop of prayer is greater than the seed out of which it grew; as the putting in of a little water into a pump, makes way to the drawing out of a great deal more. Isaac and Rebecca had lived twenty years together without any children, and he grew now in years; for he was forty years old before he married. Hereupon he solemnly prays to God in behalf of his wife, because she was barren; and God gave him more than it is probable he expected; for he gave him two sons at a birth[g]. As the cloud which riseth out of the earth many times in thin and insensible vapours, falleth down in great and abundant showers; so our prayers, which ascend weak and narrow, return with a full and enlarged answer. God deals in this point with his children, as Joseph

f Gen. xxvi. 12.   g Gen. xxv. 21, 22.

did with his brethren in Egypt: he did not only put corn into their sacks, but returned the money which they brought to purchase it [h]. So he dealt with Solomon: he did not only give him ' wisdom' and gifts of government, which he asked, but further gave him both ' riches and honour,' which he asked not [i]. The people of Israel, when they were distressed by the Ammonites, besought the Lord for help: he turns back their prayers, and sends them to their idols to help them: they humble themselves, and put away their idols; and pray again; and the highest pitch that their petitions mounted unto, was, "Lord, we have sinned; do unto us whatsoever seemeth good unto thee; only deliver us, we pray thee, this day [k]." And God did answer this prayer beyond the contents of it: he did not only deliver them from the enemy, and so save them, but subdued the enemy under them, and delivered him into their hands: he did not only give them the relief they desired, but a glorious victory beyond their desires [l]. God deals with his servants, as the prophet did with the woman of Shunem, when he bid her ask what she needed, and tell him what she would have him to do for the kindness she had done to him, and she found not any thing to request at his hands: he sends for her again, and makes her a free promise of that which she most wanted and desired, and tells her that God would give her a son [m]. So, many times, God is pleased to give his servants such things as they forget to ask,—or gives them the things which they ask [n], in a fuller measure than their own desires durst to propose them. David in his troubles asked life of God, and would have esteemed it a great mercy only to have been delivered from the fear of his enemies: and God doth not only answer him according to the desire of his heart in that particular, and above it too, for he gave him "length of days for ever and ever;" but further settled the crown upon his head, and added ' honour and majesty' unto his life [o].

And the reasons hereof are principally two:—

SECT. 3.—I. We beg of God according to the sense and knowledge which we have of our own wants, and according to the measure of that love, which we bear unto ourselves.

---

[h] Gen. xlii. 25.   [i] 1 Kings iii. 13.   [k] Judges x. 15.   [l] Judges xi. 12.
[m] 2 Kings iv. 16.   [n] Folio-Edition, p. 559.   [o] Psalm xxi. 2, 3, 4, 5.

The greater our love is to ourselves, the more active and importunate will our petitions be for such good things as we need: but God answers prayers according to his knowledge of us, and according to the love which he beareth unto us. Now God knows what things we want, much better than we do ourselves; and he loves our souls much better than we love them ourselves; and therefore he gives us more and better things, than our own prayers know how to ask of him. A little child will beg none but trifles and mean things of his father, because he hath not understanding to look higher, or to value things that are more excellent: but his father, knowing better what is good for him, bestows on him education, trains him unto learning and virtue, that he may be fit to manage and enjoy that inheritance which he provides for him:—so, " we know not what to ask, as we ought P;" and when we do know, our spirits are much straitened; we have but a finite and narrow love unto ourselves: but God's knowledge is infinite, and his love is infinite; and according unto these, are the distributions of his mercy. Even the apostle himself, when he was in affliction, and buffeted by the messenger of Satan, and vexed with a thorn in the flesh,—besought the Lord for nothing "but that it might depart from him :" but God had a far better answer in store to the apostle's prayer, and purposed to do more for him than he desired, namely, to give him a 'sufficiency of grace' to support him, and to 'magnify his strength in the infirmity of his servant q.' When the prophet had encouraged men to 'seek the Lord,' and to turn unto him, and that upon this assurance ; That he will not only hear petitions for mercy and forgiveness, but will 'multiply to pardon,'—that is, will pardon more sins than we can confess (for with him there is not only mercy, but 'plenteous redemption r;') he further strengtheneth our faith, and encourageth our obedience unto this duty, by the consideration of the 'thoughts of God ;'—to wit, his thoughts of love, mercy, and peace towards us: " My thoughts are not your thoughts, neither are your ways my ways, saith the Lord: for as the heavens are higher than the earth, so are my ways higher than your ways, and my thoughts than your thoughts." Isai. lv. 7, 8, 9. He can pardon beyond our petitions, be-

---

p Rom. viii. 26.   q 2 Cor. xii. 9.   r Psalm cxxx. 7.

cause his thoughts of mercy towards us are beyond our apprehensions. See the like place, Jer. xxix. 10, 11, 12.

SECT. 4.—2. God answers prayers not always with respect to the narrow compass of our weak desires, but with respect to his own honour, and to the declaration of his own greatness: for he promiseth "to hear us, that we may glorify him ⁵." Therefore he is pleased to exceed our petitions, and to do for us abundantly above what we ask or think, that our hearts may be more abundantly enlarged, and our mouths wide open in rendering honour unto him. When Perillus ᵗ, a favourite of Alexander, begged of him a portion for his daughter, the king appointed that fifty talents should be given unto him, and he answered that "ten would be sufficient:" the king replied, that "ten were enough for Perillus to ask, but not enough for Alexander to grant:"—so God is pleased many times to give more than we ask, that we may look upon it not only as an act of mercy, but as an act of honour; and to teach us in all our prayers to move God as well by his glory, as by his mercy. So Moses did, when he prayed for pardon unto Israel, lest God's 'Name should be blasphemed ᵘ.' So Joshua did, when Israel turned their backs before their enemies,— "What wilt thou do unto thy great name ˣ?" So Solomon in his prayer at the dedication of the Temple, "Hear thou in Heaven thy dwelling-place, and do according to all that the stranger calleth to thee for: that all the people of the earth may know thy name ʸ." So David in his, for Israel, and for the performance of God's promise to the seed of David, "Do as thou hast said; let it even be established, that thy name may be magnified for ever ᶻ." So Asa; "O Lord, thou art our God; let not man prevail against thee ᵃ." So Jehoshaphat; "Art not thou God in Heaven? and rulest not thou over all the kingdoms of the heathen? and in thine hand is there not power and might, so that none is able to withstand thee ᵇ?" &c. So Hezekiah, when he spread the blasphemies of Sennacherib before the Lord ᶜ, "O Lord our God, save us

---

ˢ Psalm l. 12.　ᵗ Περίλλου δέ τινος τῶν φίλων αἰτήσαντος τροῖκα τοῖς θυγατρίοις, ἐκέλευσε πεντήκοντα τάλαντα λαβεῖν· αὐτοῦ δὲ φήσαντος ἱκανά εἶναι δέκα, Σοί γε (ἔφη) λαβεῖν, ἐμοὶ δ' οὐχ ἱκανὰ δοῦναι. *Plut.* Apophtheg. Xylandr. ii. p. 179. ᵘ Numb. xiv. 15, 16, 17.　ˣ Josh. vii. 9.　ʸ 1 Kings viii. 43.　ᶻ 1 Chron. xvii. 23, 24.　ᵃ 2 Chron. xiv. 11.　ᵇ 2 Chron. xx. 6.　ᶜ Folio Edition. p. 560.

from his hand, that all the kingdoms of the earth may know that thou art the Lord, even thou only[d]." So the church of God in the time of distress; "Help us, O God of our salvation, for the glory of thy name;" and deliver and purge away our sins for thy name's sake: wherefore should the heathen say, "Where is their God[e]?" As every creature of God was made for his glory[f]; so every attribute of God doth work and put forth itself for his glory. If he show mercy, it is to shew the 'riches of his glory[g];'—If he execute justice, it is to make his ' power known[h].' When he putteth forth his power, and doth terrible things, it is to make his ' name known[i].' If he engage his truth, and make his promises Yea and Amen, it is for his own glory, and that his ' name may be magnified in doing what he hath said[k].' Whensoever therefore we pray unto God, and therein implore his mercy on us, his justice on his enemies, his truth to be fulfilled, his power, wisdom, or any other attribute to be manifested towards his people,—the highest and most prevailing medium we can use, is the 'glory of his own name:' God's ultimate end in working must needs be our strongest argument in praying, because therein it appears, that we seek his interest in our petitions, as well as, and above our own.

SECT. 5. This serveth, first, to encourage us unto prayer, because God doth not only hear and answer prayers, which is a sufficient motive unto his servants to call upon him, "O thou that hearest prayers, unto thee shall all flesh come[l];" but because he oftentimes exceedeth the modesty, the ignorance, the fearfulness of our requests, by giving unto us more than we ask. When poor men make requests unto us, we usually answer them as the echo doth the voice;—the answer cuts off half the petition. The hypocrite, in the apostle, (James ii. 15, 16,) when he saw a brother or sister naked or destitute of daily food, would " bid him be warmed or filled,"—but in the mean time "give him nothing" that was needful; and so did rather mock than answer their requests.

---

[d] Isai. xxxvii. 20.   [e] Psalm lxxix. 9, 10.   [f] Prov. xvi. 4. Rom. xi. 36. [g] Rom. ix. 23. Ephes. i. 11, 12.   [h] Rom. ix. 17, 22. 2 Thes. i. 9.   [i] Isai. lxiv. 1, 2, 3.   [k] 2 Cor. i. 20. 2 Sam. vii. 25, 26. Exod. iii. 14, 15. xii. 41. Josh. xxi. 45.   [l] Psalm lxv. 2. lxvi. 20. lxxxvi. 5, 6, 7. cii. 17.

We shall seldom find amongst men Jael's courtesies [m]: giving milk to those that ask water, except it be as hers was, δῶρον ἄδωρον, munus [cum hamo [n], an entangling benefit, the better to introduce a mischief. There are not many Naamans among us, that when you beg of them one talent, will force you to take two [o]. But God's answer to our prayers is like a multiplying-glass, which renders the request much greater in the answer than it was in the prayer. As when we cast a stone into the water, though it be but little in itself, yet the circles which come from it, spread wider and wider, till it fill the whole pond;—so our petitions, though very weak as they come from us, and craving but some one or other good thing, yet finding way to the fountain of life, and unsearchable treasure of mercy which is in Christ, are usually answered with many and more spreading benefits. The trumpet [p] exceedingly strengtheneth the voice which passeth through it: it goes in at a narrow passage, and the voice is but a silent breath, as it comes from the mouth; but it goes out wider with a doubled and multiplied vigour:—so our prayers usually go up narrow to God, but they come down with enlarged answers from him again: as the root is but of one colour, when the flower which groweth out of it, is beautified with variety.

Now this should be a great encouragement unto us to call upon God with sincerity of heart, because he multiplieth to pardon, because "we know not the numbers" of his salvation [q]; "we cannot count the sum" of his thoughts towards us [r]. If there were any man so wealthy, that it were all one with him to give pounds or pence, and who usually, when he were asked silver, would give gold,—every indigent and necessitous person would wait upon this man's mercy. Now, it is as easy with God to give talents as farthings, as easy to over-answer prayers, as to answer them at all. It is as easy to the sun to fill a vast palace, as a little closet, with light; as easy to the sea, to fill a channel, as a bucket, with water. "He can satisfy with goodness, and answer with wonderful and terrible things [s]." Oh! who would not make requests

---

[m] Judges v. 21.   [n] Seneca.   [o] 2 Kings v. 23.   [p] Spiritus noster clariorem sonum reddit, cùm illum tuba, per longi canalis angustias tractum, potentiorem novissimo exitu effudit. *Sen.* Epist. 108.—Ruhkopf, vol. iii. p. 315.   [q] Psalm lxxi. 15.   [r] Psalm cxxxix. 17, 18.   [s] Psalm lxv. 4, 5.

unto such a God, whose usual answer unto prayer is, "Be it
unto thee as thou wilt[t]!" Nay, who answers us beyond
"our wills and thoughts[u];" and measureth forth mercy by
the greatness of his own grace, and not the narrowness of
our desires. The shekel[x] belonging to the sanctuary was,
as many learned men think, in weight double to the common
shekel, which was used in civil matters:—to note unto us,
that as God expects from us double the care in things belonging unto him, above what we use in the things of the
world,—so he usually measureth back double unto us again:
"good measure, pressed down, shaken together, and running
over, into our bosoms." When the man, sick of the palsy,
was carried[y] unto Christ to be healed,—Christ did beyond
the expectation of those that brought him; for he not only
cured him of his disease, but of his sin ; gave him not only
health of body, but peace of conscience:—First, "Be of
good cheer, thy sins be forgiven thee;" and then, "Arise,
take up thy bed, and go to thy house[z]." The thief on the
cross besought Christ to remember him, when he came into
his kingdom; but Christ answers him far beyond his petition,
assuring him that, the very same day, he should be with
him in Paradise[a]. The poor man at the gate of the temple
begged for nothing of Peter and John but a small alms ;
but they gave him an answer to his request far more worth
than any other alms could be; namely, such an alms as
caused him to stand in need of alms no longer, restored him
in the name of Christ unto sound strength, that he "walked,
and leaped, and praised God[b]." In like manner[c], doth God
answer the prayers of his people, not always (it may be) in
the kind, and to the express will of him that asketh; but
for the better, and consequently more to his will than himself
expressed.

SECT. 6. Secondly, This should encourage us in prayer to
beg for an answer, not according to the defect and narrowness of our own low conceptions, but according to the ful-

---

[t] Matth. xv. 28.   [u] Ephes. iii. 20.   [x] *Hier.* in Ezek. 49.—*Pagnin.* in
Thesaur.—*Waserus* de mensur. Heb. lib. 1. c. 1. Sect. 6. 1.—*Bez.* on Mat. 17.
24.—*Jun.* in Gen. 23.—*Masius* in Josh. 7.—*Ainsworth* on Gen. 20.—*Serar.* in
Josh. 7, q. 5.   [y] Folio Edition, p. 561.   [z] Matth. ix. 2, 6.   [a] Luke
xxiii. 42, 43.   [b] Acts iii. 6.   [c] Si non secundum voluntatem, tamen ad
utilitatem. Πρόξω ἃ θέλετε· ἃ δὲ λέγετε, παραιτήσομαι. Acrot. apud *Plutarch.*
Laconic. Apophtheg. Xyland. tom. 2. p. 216.

ness of God's own abundant mercies. It would not please one of us, if a beggar should ask of us gold, or jewels, silk, or dainties; we should esteem such a petitioner fuller of pride and impudence than of want. But God delights to have his people beg great things of him, to implore the performance of " exceeding great and precious promises[d];" to pray for a share in the " unsearchable riches of Christ ;" to know things which pass knowledge, and to be filled " with the fulness of God[e];" to ask " things which eye hath not seen, nor ear heard, nor hath entered into the heart of man to conceive[f];" to ask not as beggars only for an alms, but as ' children for an inheritance[g] ;' not to ask some thing, or a few things, but " in every thing to let our requests be made known unto God[h]:" because, with Christ, he giveth us " freely all things[i];" even " all things richly to enjoy[k]." As Alexander the Great[1] was well pleased with Anaxarchus the philosopher, when he desired a hundred talents of his treasurer : " He doth well," saith he, " in asking it; and understands his friend aright, who hath one both able and willing to give him so great a gift." God allows his children a spiritual and heavenly ambition to " covet earnestly the best gifts[m] ;"—to aspire unto a kingdom ; and accordingly to put up great and honourable requests unto him ;—to think what great things Christ hath purchased, what great things God hath promised and proposed to us ; and to regulate our prayers more by the merits and riches of Christ, and by the greatness of God's mercies, than by those apprehensions which we cannot but have of our own unworthiness.

Sect. 7. Now next from the particulars of the text, though many particular observations might be raised, yet I shall reduce them unto one general, which may comprehend the particulars ; namely,—That whom God loves and pardons, upon them he poureth forth the benediction of his grace and Spirit, as the dew of heaven, to quicken them unto a holy and fruitful conversation. The general promises nakedly set down before, I ' will heal,' I ' will love,' are here further amplified by many excellent metaphors, and

[d] 2 Pet. i. 4.   [e] Ephes. iii. 8, 16, 18.   [f] 1 Cor. ii. 9.   [g] Rom. viii. 15, 17, 23. Gal. iv. 6, 7.   [h] Phil. iv. 6.   [i] Rom. viii. 32.   [k] 1 Tim. vi. 17   [l] *Plutarch.*   [m] 1 Cor. xii. 31.

elegant figures,—which are nine in number, multiplied into
so many particulars, partly, because of the difficulty of the
promise to be believed, which is therefore severally incul-
cated and represented ;—partly, because of the dejectedness
of the people under the variety of their former sufferings,
who are therefore by variety of mercies to be raised up and
revived ;—and, partly, to represent the perfection and completeness of the blessings intended, which should be of all
sorts, and to all purposes. And the foundation of all the
rest is this, that God promiseth to be as the ' dew ' unto
Israel : for Ephraim having been cursed with much drought
and barrenness ; now when God blesseth him again, he promiseth to be unto him, as dew is to the weary and thirsty
ground, which so refresheth it, that the fruits thereof do
grow and flourish again. Lilies, flowers, trees, vines, corn,
are very apt (especially in such hot countries as Judea),
without much refreshing dew and showers from heaven, to
dry up and wither away : so would Ephraim have been quite
consumed by the heavy wrath of God, if he should not, with
the supplies of his great and holy Spirit, and with his
heavenly refreshments and loving countenance, revive them
again.

'Dew,' in the natural signification of it, importeth a comforting, refreshing, encouraging, and calling forth the fruits of
the earth, as being of a gentle, insinuating virtue, which lei-
surely soaketh into the ground : and, in that sense, is mentioned as a blessing[n], Gen. xxviii. 39. In the mystical and spiritual
sense of it, it signifieth Christ[o] ; who, by his holy word and
heavenly grace dropping down and distilling upon the souls
of men[p],—by his princely favour and loving countenance,
which is as a cloud of the latter rain[q],—by his heavenly
righteousness, and most spiritual efficacy[r],—doth so quicken,
vegetate, and revive the hearts of men, that they, like " dew
from the womb of the morning," are born in great abundance unto him ;—as multitudes of men, and believers, use
to be expressed in the Scripture by ' drops of dew[s].' In
one word, that which dew is to the fields, gardens, vineyards, flowers, fruits of the earth, after a hot and a scorch-

[n] Folio-Edition, p. 562.   [o] *Chrys.* in Ps. li. 7. Psalm lxxii. 6.   [p] Deut.
xxxii. 2. Job xxix. 22, 23.   [q] Prov. xvi. 15. xix. 12.   [r] Isai. xxvi. 19,
xlv. 8.   [s] Psalm cx. 3. Mich. v. 7.

ing day ; that the favour, word, grace, loving countenance, and holy Spirit of Christ, will be to the drooping and afflicted consciences of his people.

From this metaphor then we learn,

1. That we are naturally dry, barren, fruitless,—and utterly unable to do any good, to bring forth any fruit unto God ;—like a heathy and parched land subject to the scorching terrors of the wrath of God, and to his burning indignation. So Christ compares Jerusalem unto a dry, withered tree, fitted unto judgement [t]. And he assureth us, that, " out of him, we can do nothing [u] ;" in us, of ourselves, there " dwelleth no good thing [x]." We are not of ourselves, as of ourselves, " sufficient unto any thing [y]." He is the sun that healeth us [z] ;—he the rain that disposeth us [a] ;—he the root that deriveth life and nourishment upon us [b]. As natural, so much more spiritual, fruitfulness hath its ultimate resolution into him, who alone is the ' father of the rain,' and ' begetteth the drops of dew [c].'

SECT. 8.—2. That the grace of God is like dew to the barren and parched hearts of men, to make them fruitful. And there are many things, wherein the proportion and resemblance stands :—

First, None can give it but God : it comes from above ; it is of a celestial original ; the nativity thereof is from " the womb of the morning." Are there any amongst the vanities of the Gentiles that can cause rain ? or can the heavens give showers ? " Art not thou he, O Lord our God ? for thou hast made all these things [d]." And the like we may say, in a more strict and peculiar sense, of regeneration, That it is a spiritual and ' heavenly birth;' it is " not of blood, nor of the will of the flesh, nor of the will of man, but of God."—There is no concurrence or active assistance of the flesh, or of any natural abilities unto a birth, which is merely spiritual [e]. Therefore Christ was pleased to go up into Heaven, before he shed forth his holy Spirit in abundance on the church [f]; —to teach us, first, that our conversion and sanctification

[t] Luke xxiii. 31.   [u] John xv. 4, 5.   [x] Rom. vii. 18.   [y] 2 Cor. iii. 5. [z] Mal. iv. 2.   [a] Psalm lxxii. 6.   [b] Revel. xxii. 16.   [c] Hos. ii. 21, 22. Job xxxviii. 28.   [d] Jer. xiv. 22.   [e] John i. 13. Job iii. 5, 6. James i. 17, 18.   [f] John vii. 39. xvi. 17. Acts i. 4, 5.

comes from above, by a divine teaching [g], by a spiritual conviction, by a supernatural and omnipotent traction, by a heavenly calling, by the will of him who alone can give a will
unto us.   No voice can be heard by those that are dead, but
" the voice of the Son of Man [h]." And withal to acquaint us,
whither the affections and conversations of men, thus sanctified, should tend,—namely, unto Heaven,—as every thing
works towards its original, and every part inclines unto the
whole [i].   With allusion unto this metaphor of dew or rain,
the holy Spirit is said to be 'poured' out upon the
churches [k]; and the ' word of grace ' is frequently compared
unto rain.   As it is the seed by which we are enabled to be
fruitful [l],—so it is the rain which softeneth the heart, that it
may be the better wrought upon by that seminal virtue;
(Isai. lv. 10, 11. Heb. vi. 7.) ; whereas false teachers are called
" clouds without water [m] :" they have no fructifying virtue in
them.   None can give grace but God : it is heavenly in its nature, therefore it is so in its original: "it stays not for man [n] :"
it depends not on the wills, concurrences, preparations, or
dispositions which arise out of us, but it wholly preventeth
us ; we are made active by it, but we are not at all antece-
dently active [o] in fitting or disposing ourselves for it.

Secondly, It is the fruit of a serene [p], clear, and quiet
Heaven: for dew never falleth either in scorching or tem-
pestuous weather, as philosophers have observed.   In [q] like

[g] Ita docet ut quod quisque didicerit, non tantum cognoscendo videat, sed
etiam volendo appetat, agendoque perficiat : *Aug.* de grat. Christi, cap. 14.—
Trahitur miris modis ut velit, ab illo qui novit intus in ipsis hominum cordibus
operari, non ut homines, quod fieri non potest, nolentes credant, sed ut volentes
ex nolentibus fiant : *Aug.* Cont. 2. Epist. Pelag. lib. 1. cap. 19. tom. 10. p. 283.
Interna, occulta, mirabilis, ineffabilis potestas :—*Aug.* de grat. Christi, cap. 24.—
Occultissima, efficacissima potestas : *Aug.* cont. 2. Ep. Pelag. li. 1. cap. 20.—
Omni potentissima potestas : *Aug.* de corrept. et grat. cap. 14.—' Modo mirabili
et ineffabili agens:' de prædestinat. sanct. cap. 20. ' Idque indeclinabiliter atque
insuperabiliter.' de corrept. et grat. cap. 12. ' Intus à patre audiunt atque discunt,
qui credunt ;' de prædest. sanct. cap. 8.—' Vocatio alta et secreta :' Epist. 107.—
Bernard. Serm. Parv. Serm. 66.   [h] John vi. 44, 45. xvi. 8, 9, 10, 11.   Heb.
iii. 1. James i. 18. Phil. ii. 13. John v. 25. Heb. xii. 25.   [i] Col. iii. 1, 2.
Phil. iii. 20.   [k] Acts ii. 17. Tit. iii. 6.   [l] Matth. xiii. 18.   [m] Jude
v. 12.   [n] Mic. v. 7.   [o] Pedissequa, non prævia voluntas ; *Aug.* Ep.
106.—' Gratiam Dei prævenire dicimus hominum voluntates ;' Epis. 107. ut velimus, sine nobis operatur ; cum autem volumus, nobiscum cooperatur ; *Aug.* de
grat. et lib. arbitr. ca. 7.   [p] *Arist.* Meteorolog. lib. 1. cap. 10.—Plin. lib. 2.
cap. 60. 1. 18. cap. 29.   [q] Folio-Edition, p. 563.

manner, the grace, favour, and blessings of God, are the
fruits of his reconciled affection towards us. Upon the
wicked he raineth " storm and tempest;" he showereth
down on them the fury of his wrath; and shows himself
dark, cloudy, gloomy, terrible unto them[r]. But unto those
that fear his name, he openeth a clear and a gracious countenance; and being reconciled unto them, shetdeth abroad
his love into their hearts, and his peace into their consciences, like Gideon's dew on the fleece and on the ground,
as a special evidence of his grace: and therefore the
Psalmist compares the love and peace that is amongst
brethren, unto dew, Psalm cxxxiii. 3. which ever falleth
from a calm, serene, and quiet sky.

SECT. 9. Thirdly, It is abundant and innumerable: who
can number the drops of dew on the ground, or the " *hairs*
of little rain?"—for so they are called in the original שעירים[s],
because of their smallness and number[t]. So Hushai expresseth the multitude of all Israel[u]: " We will light upon him,
as the dew falleth upon the ground." And the multitude of
believers are said to be born unto Christ by his sending forth
the rod of his strength, " as dew from the womb of the
morning[x]:" as we find historically verified[y]. Such is the
grace and favour of God unto his people after their conversion; unsearchable, it cannot be comprehended or measured,
nor brought under any number or account[z]. Christ is compared unto manna; he was the bread that came down from
Heaven[a]; and manna came in mighty abundance, so that there
was enough for every one to gather[b]. It had dew under it,
and dew over it, as we may conjecture by comparing Exod.
xvi. 14. with Numb. xi. 9; whereunto the Holy Ghost seemeth
to allude when he speaks of the " hidden manna[c]:"—though
that may likewise refer unto the pot of manna which was
kept in the tabernacle[d]; as our life is said to be " hid with
Christ," now he is in heaven[f]. By this dew coming along
with manna is intimated, that the mercies of God in Christ,

[r] Psalm xi. 6. lxxxiii. 15. Job xx. 23. Nah. i. 3, 8.   [s] *Duncan's* Stereotype Bible, vol. i. p. 292.   [t] Deut. xxx. 2.   [u] 2 Sam. xvii. 12.
[x] Psalm cx. 3.   [y] Acts ii. 41. v. 14, 16. vi. 7. ix. 31, 41.   xix. 20.
[z] Psalm lxxi. 15. cxxxix. 17, 18.   [a] John vi. 50, 51.   [b] Exod.
xvi. 16.   [c] Rev. ii. 17.   [d] Exod. xvi. 32, 33. Heb. ix. 4.   [e] *Lud.*
Capel. Spicileg. p. 132, 133.   [f] Col. iii. 3.

his ' daily mercies' (which are said with allusion, I suppose,
unto this manna, to be renewed ' every morning g,') and
his ' hidden mercies,' to wit, the inward comforts of his
grace and Spirit,—are all innumerable and past finding out.
We may say of his mercies, as the psalmist of his commandments,—" I have found an end of all perfection, but these
are ' exceeding broad ;'" more than eye hath seen, or ear
heard, or the heart itself is able to comprehend h.

Fourthly, It is silent, slow, insensible : while it is falling,
you cannot say, ' Here it is :'—it deceives the eye, and is too
subtile for that to see it : it deceives the ear, and is too silent for that to hear it : it deceives the face, and is too thin
and spiritual for that to feel it. You see it, when it is come ;
but you cannot observe, how it comes. In this manner was
God pleased to fill the world with the knowledge of his gospel, and with the grace of his Spirit, by quiet, small, and
(as it were) by insensible means. " The kingdom of God
came not with observation i ;" that is, with any visible notable splendour, or external pomp, as the Jews expected the
Messiah to come; but it came with spiritual efficacy, and
with internal power upon the consciences of men, and spread
itself over the world by the ministry of a very few despised
instruments. With respect unto which manner of working,
the Spirit is compared unto ' wind,' which we hear and feel,
but " know not whence it comes, nor whither it goes k." The
operations of grace are secret and silent upon the conscience:
you shall find mighty changes wrought, and shall not tell
how they were wrought. The same man, coming into the
church, one hour, a swine, a dog, a lion,—and going out
the next hour, in all visible respects the same, but invisibly
changed into a lamb.

Fifthly, It is of a soft and benign nature, which gently
insinuateth and worketh itself into the ground, and by degrees moisteneth and mollifieth it, that it may be fitted unto
the seed which is cast into it. In like manner, the Spirit,
the grace, the Word of God, is of a searching, insinuating,
softening quality: it sinks into the heart, and works itself
into the conscience ; and from thence makes way for itself
into the whole man, mind, thoughts, affections, words, actions, fitting them all unto the holy seed that is put into

g Lam. iii. 23.   h 1 Cor. ii. 9.   i Luke xvii, 20, 21.   k John iii. 8.

them :—as the earth, being softened and mingled with the dew, is the more easily drawn up into those varieties of herbs and fruits, that are fed by it.

Sixthly, It is of a vegetating and quickening nature; it causeth things to grow and revive again. Therefore the prophet calls it " the dew of herbs[1]," which are thereby refreshed, and recover life and beauty. Even so the Word and Spirit of[m] grace distilling upon the soul, " as small rain upon tender herbs, and as showers on the grass," cause it to live the life of God, and to bring forth the fruits of holiness and obedience[n]. Those parts of the world which are under either perpetual frosts, or perpetual scorchings,—are barren and fruitless, the earth being closed up, and the sap thereof dried away by such distempers:—such is the condition of a soul under wrath, that hath no apprehensions of God but in frost or fire; for who can stand " before his cold[o]?" Who can dwell with " everlasting burnings[p]?" Fear contracteth and bindeth up the powers of the soul: it is the greatest indisposer of all other unto regular action. But when the soul can apprehend God as love, find healing in his wings, and reviving in his ordinances,—this love is of an opening and expansive quality, calling forth the heart unto duty; love within (as it were) hastening to meet and close with love without; the love of obedience in us, with the love of favour and grace in God. I shut and bar my door against an enemy whom I fear, and look upon as armed to hurt me; but I open wide my doors, my bosom, unto a friend whom I love, and look upon as furnished with counsel, and comfort, and benefits to revive me. There is a kind of mutual love between dew and the earth: dew loves the earth with a love of beneficence, doing it good; and earth loves the dew with a love of concupiscence, earnestly desiring it, and opening unto it. Such is the love between Christ and the soul, when he appears as dew unto it. He visits the soul with a love of mercy, reviving it; and the soul puts forth itself towards him in a love of duty, earnestly coveting as well to serve as to enjoy him.

Lastly, It is of a refreshing and comforting nature, tempering the heat of those hotter countries, and so causing the

[1] Isai. xxvi. 19.   [m] Folio-Edition, p. 564.   [n] Isai. lv. 10, 11.
[o] Psalm cxlvii. 17.   [p] Isai. xxxiii. 14.

face of things to flourish with beauty and delight. So God promiseth to be unto his people in their troubles, "as a cloud of dew in the heat of harvest [q]." The spiritual joy and heavenly comfort, which the peace and grace of God ministereth to the consciences of believers [r], is said to make "the bones flourish like an herb [s]:" as on the other side, a broken spirit is said to "dry up the bones [t]." "Their soul," saith the prophet, "shall be as a watered garden, they shall sorrow no more; I will turn their mourning into joy, and will comfort them [u]."

Sect. 10. By all which we should learn, First, As to be sensible of our own personal and spiritual dryness, barrenness, emptiness of fruit and peace, hard hearts, with red consciences, guilty spirits, under our own particular sins; so, in regard of the whole land, to take notice of that tempest of wrath, which, like an east wind out of the wilderness, "drieth up our springs, and spoileth our treasures," as the prophet complains [x]; and to be humbled into penitent resolutions, as the church here is. If God, who was wont to be as dew to our nation, who made it heretofore like a paradise and a watered garden,—be now as a tempest, as a consuming fire unto it,—turning things upside down,—burning the inhabitants of the earth,—causing "our land to mourn, and our joy to wither," (as the prophet speaks [y];)—this is an evident sign, that "the earth is defiled under the inhabitants thereof [z]. Therefore as our sins have turned our dew into blood, so our repentance must turn our blood into dew again. If ever we look to have a happy peace, we must make it with God. Men can give peace only to our bodies, our fields, our houses, our purses;—nor that neither without his over-ruling power and providence, who alone manageth all the counsels and resolutions of men;—but he alone can give peace to our consciences by the assurance of his love, "which is better than life." And if there should be peace in a nation, made up only by human prudence and correspondences, without public repentance, and thorough reformation in church, in state, in families, in persons, in judgement, in manners,—it would be but like those short interims between the Egyp-

[q] Isai. xviii. 4. [r] Rom. xv. 13. v. 1. Phil. iv. 4. 1 Pet. 1. 8. [s] Isai. lxvi. 14. [t] Prov. xvii. 22. [u] Jer. xxxi. 12, 13. [x] Hos. xiii. 15, 16. [y] Joel i. 12. [z] Isai. xxiv. 4, 5.

tian plagues [a]; a respiting only, not a removing of our affliction ; like the shining of the sun on Sodom, before the fire
and brimstone fell upon it [b].   We all cry and call for peace ;
and while any thing is left, would gladly pay dear, very dear
to recover it again.   But there is no sure and lasting purchase of it, but by unfeigned repentance and turning unto
God : this is able to give peace in the midst of war.   In the
midst of storm and tempest, Christ is sufficient security to
the tossed ship [c].   " This man is the peace, even when the
Assyrian is in the land [d]."   Whereas impenitency, even when
we have recovered an outward peace, leaves us still in the
midst of most potent enemies: God, Christ, angels, scripture, creatures, conscience, sins, curses, all our enemies.
The apostle tells us, that " lusts war against the soul [e]."
There is a strong emphasis in the word *soul,* which is more
worth than all the world ; nothing [f] to be taken in exchange
for it [g].   So long as we have our lusts conquered, we are under the wofulest war in the world, which doth not spoil us
of our blood, our money, our coin, our cattle, our houses, our
children, but of the salvation of immortal souls.   Time will
repair the ruins of other wars ; but eternity itself will not deliver that poor soul, which is lost and fallen in the wars of
lust.

Therefore, if you would have peace as a mercy, get it
from God ; let it be a dew from heaven upon your conversion unto him.   A ' king's favour ' is said to be as ' dew on
the grass [h],' and as ' a cloud of the latter rain [i];' and it
would with all joyfulness be so apprehended, if by that
means the blessing of peace were bestowed upon these distressed kingdoms.   How much more comfortable would it
be to have it as a gift from God unto a repenting nation !
For God can give peace in anger, as well as he doth war.
A ship at sea may be distressed by a calm, as well as broken
by a tempest.   The cattle which we mean to kill, we do first
prefer unto some fat pasture : and sometimes God gives over
punishing, not in mercy, but in fury ; leaving men to go on
quietly in their own hearts' lusts, that they who are filthy, may

a Exod. viii. 15. ix. 34.   b Gen. xix. 23, 24.   c Matth. viii. 24, 27.
d Mic. v. 5.   e 1 Pet. ii. 11.   f Folio-Edition, p. 565.   g Matth.
xvi. 26.   h Prov. ix. 12.   i Prov. xvi. 15.

be filthy still [k]. God was exceeding angry with Israel, when he gave them their ' hearts' desire,' and sent them quails[l]. Many men get their wills from God's anger by murmuring, as others do theirs from his mercy by prayer; but then there comes a curse along with it. Now therefore when our own sword doth devour us, when our land is, " through the wrath of the Lord of Hosts, so darkened," that the people thereof are "as fuel of the fire, no man sparing his brother, every man eating the flesh of his own arm," (it is the sad character which the prophet gives of a civil war [m];) let us take heed of God's complaint, " In vain have I smitten your children, they receive no correction [n]." Let us make it our business to recover God. It is he that " causeth wars to cease in the earth [o];" and it is he " who poureth out upon men the strength of battle, and giveth them over to the spoilers [p]." A sinful nation gains nothing by any human treaties, policies, counsels, contributions, till by repentance they secure their interest in God, and make him on their side. God, being prevailed with by Moses in behalf of Israel, after the horrible provocation of the golden calf, sends a message to them : " I will send an angel before thee, and will drive out the Canaanite." And presently it follows, "When the people heard these evil tidings, they mourned [q]." What, were these evil tidings,—To have an angel to protect and lead them? to have their enemies vanquished? to have possession of a land, flowing with milk and honey? was there any thing lamentable in all this? Yes; To have all this and much more, and not to have God and his presence,—was heavy tidings unto God's people. And therefore Moses never gave God over, till he promised them his own presence again; with which he chose rather to stay in a wilderness, than without it to go into the land of Canaan ; " If thy presence go not along, carry us not up hence [r]."

SECT. 11. Secondly, We should from hence learn, whatever our spiritual wants are, to look up to Heaven for a supply of them. Neither gardens, nor woods, nor vineyards, nor fields, nor flowers, nor trees, nor corn, nor spices, will flourish or revive, without the dew and concurrence of hea-

---

[k] Psalm lxxxi. 12. Hos. iv. 14, 17. Isai. i. 5. Ezek. xxiv. 13.   [l] Numb. xi. 32, 33.   [m] Isai. ix. 19, 20.   [n] Jer. ii. 30.   [o] Psalm xlvi. 10.
[p] Isai. xlii. 24, 25.   [q] Exod. xxxiii. 2, 3, 4.   [r] Exod. xxxiii. 13, 14, 15.

venly grace : Christ alone is all in all unto his church. Though the instruments be earthly, yet the virtue which gives success unto them, comes from Heaven.

1. The ' beauty of the lilies,' or as the prophet David calls it, " the beauty of holiness," ariseth from the ' dew of the morning[s].' He is the ornament, the attire, the comeliness, of his spouse. For his people to forget him, is for a maid to forget her ornaments, or a spouse her attire[t]. The perfect beauty of the church, is that comeliness of his, which he communicates unto her[u]. Of ourselves, we are "wretched, miserable, poor, naked ;" our gold, our riches, our white raiment[x], we must buy of him[y]. He is "the Lord our righteousness, whom therefore we are said to " put on[z]." He hath made us kings and priests unto our God[a] ; and being such, he hath provided beautified robes for us, as once he appointed for the priests[b]. This spiritual beauty of holiness in Christ's church, is sometimes compared to the marriage-ornaments for a queen[c]: sometimes to the choice flowers of a garden, roses and lilies[d] : sometimes to a most glorious and goodly structure[e]: sometimes to the shining forth of the moon, and the brightness of the sun[f]. All the united excellences of the creatures[g] are too low to adumbrate and figure the glories of the church.

2. The[h] root and stability of the church is in and from him : he is the ' root of David[i].' Except he dwell in us, we cannot be rooted nor grounded[k]. All our strength and sufficiency is from him[l]. The graft is supported by another root, and not by its own. This is the reason of the stability of the church, because it is " founded upon a rock[m];" not upon Peter, but upon him whom Peter confessed[n]; upon

---

[s] Psalm cx. 3.   [t] Jer. ii. 32.   [u] Ezek. xvi. 14.   [x] Vide *Gul.* *Stuck.* Conviv. l. 2. c. 26.   [y] Rev. iii. 18.   [z] Rom. xiii. 14. [a] Rev. v. 10.   [b] Exod. xxviii. 2. Rev. iv. 4, 6. xi. 7, 9.   [c] Psalm xlv. 14. Rev. xviii. 7, 8. xxi. 2.   [d] Cant. ii. 1, 2.   [e] Rev. xxi. 11, 23. [f] Cant. vi. 10. Rev. xii. 1.   [g] Et quæ divisa beatos Efficiunt, collecta tenes. *Claud.* xxi. 34. Gesner, vol. i. p. 311.   [h] Folio-Edition, p. 566. [i] Rev. v. 5.   [k] Ephes. iii. 17.   [l] Phil. iv. 13. Ephes. vi. 10. 1 Pet. v. 10.   [m] Matth. xvi. 18.   [n] Ἀσφαλὴς ὁμολογία, ἣν ἐμπνευθεὶς ὁ Πέτρος παρ' αὐτοῦ ὡς κρηπῖδα καὶ βαθμὸν ἀπέθετο· ἐφ' ἧ τὴν ἑαυτοῦ ἐκκλησίαν ὁ Κύριος ᾠκοδόμησεν. *Isidor. Pelusiot.* l. 1. Ep. 235.—Ut ædificaretur Ecclesia super petram, quis factus est petra ? Paulum audi dicentem ; " Petra autem erat Christus:" *Aug.* in Psalm lx. vol. 4. p. 438. Super hanc petram quam con-

the apostles only doctrinally, but upon Christ personally, as
" the chief corner-stone, elect and precious," in whom whosoever believeth, shall not be confounded,—or, by failing in
his confidence, be any ways disappointed and put to shame °.
This is the difference between the righteousness of creation P, and the righteousness of redemption ; the state of the
world in Adam, and the state of the church in Christ.
Adam had his righteousness in his own keeping; and therefore when the power of hell set upon him, he fell from his
steadfastness. There was no promise given unto him, that
the gates of Hell should not prevail against him; being of
an earthly constitution, he had corruptibility, mutability, infirmity, belonging unto him out of the principles of his being. But Christ, the second Adam, is " the Lord from Heaven," over whom death hath no claim, nor power: and the
righteousness and stability of the church is founded and
hath its original in him. The powers of darkness must be
able to evacuate the virtue of his sacrifice,—to stop God's
ears unto his intercession,—to repel and keep back the
supply and influences of his Spirit,—to keep or recover
possession against his ejectment,—in one word, to kill him
again, and to thrust him away from the right hand of the
Majesty on High, before ever they can blow down or over-
turn his church. As Plato compared a man, so may we the
church, unto a tree inverted, with the root above, and the
branches below. And the root of the tree doth not only
serve to give life to the branches, while they abide in it,

---

fessus es, super hanc petram quam cognovisti, dicens, " Tu es Christus, Filius Dei
vivi," ædificabo Ecclesiam meam : de Verbis Dom. Serm. 13. vol. 5. p. 290. Quid
est ' super hanc petram ?' Super hanc fidem ; Super id quod dictum est, ' Tu es
Christus, Filius Dei :' Tract. 10. in Epist. 1. Joan.—Felix fidei Petra, Petri ore
confessi Tu es Christus Filius Dei. Hilar. de Trin. lib. 2. Super hanc confessionis
petram Ecclesiæ ædificatio est. lib. 6. Ἐπὶ ταύτῃ τῇ πέτρᾳ, τουτέστι, τῇ πίστει
τῆς ὁμολογίας. Chrysost. in loc.—Vid. Reynold. Conference with Hart. cap. 2.
divis. 1.—Casaub. Exercitat. ad. Annal. Eccles. xv. c. 12 et 13.—Sixt. Senen.
l. 6. Annot. 68. 69.   º Ephes. ii. 20, 21. 1 Pet. ii. 6.   P Istam gratiam
non habuit homo primus, qua nunquam vellet, malus esset : Sed sane habuit, in
qua si permanere vellet, nunquam malus esset. Sed deseruit et desertus est.——
Hæc prima est gratia, quæ data est primo Adam : sed hac potentior est in se-
cundo Adam. Prima est enim qua fit, ut habeat homo justitiam, si velit : secunda ergo plus potest qua fit etiam ut velit, et tantum velit, tantoque ardore diligat,
ut carnis voluntatem contraria concupiscentem voluntate Spiritus vincat, &c.
August. de corrept. et grat. cap. 11. et 12. vol. x. p. 507.

—but to hold them fast, that none can be able to cut them off[q].

SECT. 11.—3. The growth and spreading abroad the branches of the church, is from him, whose name is " the Branch [r]." Unto him are all the ends of the earth given for a possession, and " all the kingdoms of the world are to be the Lord's, and his Christ's." In regard of his dispensation towards Israel, God's first-born, so the land of Canaan is peculiarly called 'Emmanuel's land [s].' But in regard of his latter dispensation, when he sent the " rod of his strength out of Sion," and went forth " conquering and to conquer," and gave commission to preach the gospel unto every creature; so the whole world is now, under the gospel, become Emmanuel's land, and he is " King of all the earth[t];" " King of kings, and Lord of lords [u]." Gentiles come into the light of his church, and kings to the brightness of her rising, and " the nation and kingdom that will not serve her, shall perish[x]," &c. Now every country is Canaan; and every Christian church the Israel of God; and every regenerate person born in Sion; and every spiritual worshipper, the circumcision: now Christ is crucified in Galatia, and a passover eaten in Corinth, and manna fed on in Pergamus, and an altar set up in Egypt, and Gentiles sacrificed, and stones made children unto Abraham, and temples unto God [y]. In Christ's former dispensation, the church was only national amongst the Jews; but in his latter dispensation, it is œcumenical and universal, over all the world;— a spreading tree, under the shadow of the branches whereof shall dwell " the fowl of every wing [z]"

SECT. 12.—4. The graces of the Holy Spirit wherewith the church is anointed, are from him [a]. He is the olive-tree which emptieth ' the golden oil' out of himself [b]. " Of his fulness we all receive, grace for grace [c]." With the same

---

q John x. 28, 29.   r Isai. xi. 11. Zach. iii. 8.   s Isai. viii. 8.
t Psalm xlvii. 7.   u Rev. xix. 16.   x Isai. lx. 3, 12.   y See John
iv. 21. Mal. i. 11. Zeph. ii. 11. Gal. vi. 16. Isai. xliv. 5. xiv. 1. Zach. viii. 23.
Rom. ii. 29. Psalm lxxxvii. 4, 5. Phil. iii. 3. Col. ii. 11. Gal. iii. 1. 1 Cor.
v. 7, 8. Rev. ii. 17. Isai. xix. 19, 21, 23. Rom. xv. 16. Luke iii. 8. Ephes. ii. 11.
z Ezek. xvii. 23.   a Origo fontium et fluminum mare; virtutum et scientiarum Christus. Si quis callet ingenio, si quis nitet eloquio, si quis moribus placet; inde est. Bern. in Cant. Ser. 1.   b Zach. iv. 12.   c John i. 16.

Spirit are we anointed ; animated by the same life ; regenerated to the same nature ; renewed unto the same image;
reserved unto the same inheritance ; dignified, in some
respect, with the same offices ; made priests to offer spiritual sacrifices, and kings to subdue spiritual enemies, and
prophets to receive teaching from God, and to have a du-
plicate of his law written in our hearts [d].

5. The [e] sweet perfume and scent or ' smell of Lebanon,'
which ariseth out of holy duties, the grace which droppeth
from the lips of the people, the spiritual incense which
ariseth out of their prayers, the sweet savour [f] of the gospel
which spreadeth itself abroad in the ministry of his Word,
and in the lives of his servants,—they have all their original
in him, and from his heavenly dew. Of ourselves, without
him, as we are " altogether stinking and unclean [g]," so we
defile every holy thing which we meddle with [h]. Insomuch,
that God is said, as it were, to stop his nose that he ' may
not smell them [i] :' they are all of them, as they came from
us, " gall and wormwood, and bitter clusters [k]." But when
the Spirit of Christ bloweth upon us, and his grace is poured into our hearts and lips, then the spices flow out [l]: then
prayer goes up like incense and sweet odours [m] ; then, instead of corrupt, rotten, contagious communication, our discourses tend to edifying, and ' minister grace to the hearers [n],' then the ' savour of the knowledge of Christ' manifesteth itself in the mouths and lives of his servants in every
place where they come [o].

SECT. 13.—6. The shadow and refreshment, the refuge
and shelter of the church against storm and tempest, against
rain and heat, against all trouble and persecution,—is from
him alone. He is the only 'defence and covering' that is
over the 'assemblies and glory of Sion [p].' The name of the
Lord is ' a strong tower,' unto which the righteous fly and
are safe [q]. So the Lord promiseth, when his people should

---

[d] 2 Cor. i. 21. John xiv. 19. 1 Cor. xv. 48, 49. Rom. viii. 17. 1 Pet. i. 5.
Rev. i. 6. John vi. 45. Jer. xxxi. 33.   [e] Folio-Edition, p, 567.   [f] Τῶν
προσαγόντων πονήρια, τὸ θυμίαμα εὔωδες εἰς βδέλυγμα ὀσφραν θῆναι παρεσκεύασε.
Chrys. Ser. 27. in Gen.—Vid. Lud. Capell. Spicileg. p. 97, 98.—Weems. Exercit.
Cerem. l. 1. p. 62, 63.   [g] Psalm xiv. 1. Prov. xiii. 5.   [h] Hag. ii. 13, 14.
Prov. xxviii. 9. Isai. i. 11, 15.   [i] Amos v. 21.   [k] Deut. xxix. 18, 32, 33.
[l] Cant. iv. 16.   [m] Revel. v. 8.   [n] Ephes. iv. 29.   [o] 2 Cor. xii. 4.
[p] Isai. iv. 5.   [q] Prov. xviii. 10.

be exiles from his temple, and scattered out of their own land, that he would himself be a little sanctuary unto them in the countries, where they should come[r]. He is a dwelling-place[s] unto his church in all conditions[t]; a strength to the needy, a refuge from the storm, a shadow from the heat, a hiding place from the wind, a covert from the tempest, a chamber wherein to retire when indignation is kindled[u]. Every history of God's power, every promise of his love, every observation and experience of his providence, every comfort in his Word,—the knowledge which we have of his name by faith, and the knowledge which we have of it by experience,—are so many arguments to trust in him, and so many hiding places to fly unto him, against any trouble. " What time I am afraid, I will trust in thee[x]."—" Why art thou cast down, O my soul? still trust in God[y]."—" He hath delivered, he doth deliver, he will deliver[z]." Many times the children of God are reduced to such extremities, that they have nothing to encourage themselves withal but their interest in him; nothing to fly unto for hope but his great name, made known unto them by faith in his promises, and by experience of his goodness, power, and providence. This was David's case at Ziklag[a]; and Israel's, at the Red Sea[b]; and Jonah's, in the belly of the fish[c]; and Paul's, in the shipwreck[d]. God is never so much glorified by the faith of his servants, as when they can hold up their trust in him against sight and sense; and when reason saith, ' Thou art undone, for all helps fail thee,'—can answer in faith, ' I am not undone, for he said, *I will never fail thee, nor forsake thee.*'

7. The power which the church hath to rise up above her pressures, to outgrow her troubles, to revive after lopping and harrowing, to make use of affliction[e] as a means to flourish again,—all this is from him. That in trouble we are not overwhelmed, but can say with the apostle, " As dying, and

---

[r] Ezek. xi. 16.   [s] De domo suâ nemo extrahi debet aut in jus vocari, quia domus tutissimum cuique refugium atque receptaculum.—De in jus vocando. P. leg. 18 et 21.   [t] Psalm xc. 1. xci. 1, 2.   [u] Isai. xxv. 4. xxvi. 20. xxxii. 2.   [x] Psalm lxviii. 3.   [y] Psalm xlii. 5, 11.   [z] 2 Cor. i. 10.   [a] 1 Sam. xxx. 6.   [b] Exod. xiv. 10, 13.   [c] Jon. ii. 4. 7. [d] Acts xxvii. 20, 25.   [e] Medicamenta quædam prius affligunt, ut sanent ; et ipsa collyria, nisi sensum videndi prius claudant, prodesse non possunt : *Aug.* qu. in Matth. qu. 14.—Quo terreri deberet, illo ipso recreatur :——contumeliam tenet curationis pignus, &c. *Scult.* cap. 42.—Observat. in Matth. de muliere Syrophœnissa.—Plures efficimur, quoties metimur : *Tertul.* Apol. cap. ult.

behold we live[f]; as chastened, and not killed; as sorrowful,
yet always rejoicing; as poor, yet making many rich; as
having nothing, and yet possessing all things ;" like the
corn which dies, and is quickened again; like the vine that
is lopped, and spreads again ;—all this is from him who is
the resurrection and the life[g]; who was that grain of wheat
which, dying, and being cast into the ground, did bring
forth much fruit[h]; the branch which grew out of the roots of
Jesse, when that goodly family was sunk so low as from
David the king, unto Joseph the carpenter.

SECT. 14. Lastly, As God is the author of all these blessings unto his people, so when he bestows them, he doth it in
perfection: the fruits which this dew produceth, are the fruits
of Lebanon, the choicest and most excellent of any other.
If he plant a vineyard, it shall be in a ' very fruitful hill,'
and with the ' choicest plants [i] ;' ' a noble vine, a right seed[k].'
When, in any kind of straits, we have recourse to[l] the
creature for supply,—either we find it, like our Saviour's fig-
tree, without fruit,—or, like our prophet's vine, as good as
empty, the fruits thereof not worth the gathering, Hos. x. 1.
" Grapes of gall and bitter clusters ;" full of vanity, windi-
ness, vexation, disappointment. Friends fail either in their
love, or in their power. People cry ' Hosanna' to-day, and
' Crucify' to-morrow. Men of low degree are vanity, and men
of high degree a lie. Counsels clash, or are puzzled with
intricacies, and unhappy obstacles, like the wheels in Eze-
kiel's vision, that seem hampered in one another. Armies,
like Reuben, unstable as waters, that flow now, and anon
ebb, and sink away again. Treasures, like the mountains
out of which they were first digged, barren and fruitless;
better fuel to feed our sins, than water to quench our
flames ; matter of prey to the wicked, more than of help to
the miserable. In one word, take any creature-helps in the
world, and there will be something, nay very much of defect
in them. All being, but by God's, is mixed with not being.
And as every man, so every creature else which is nothing

[f] Ὀλίγοι καὶ πολλῶν δυνατώτεροι, αἰχμάλωτοι καὶ τοῦ βασιλέως ἰσχυρότεροι,
ἀπολέσαντες πατρίδα καὶ πίστιν μὴ ἀπολέσαντες, γυμνοὶ καὶ ἐνδεδυμένοι,
πτωχοὶ καὶ εὔποροι, καὶ ἐλευθέρων ἀμείνους, &c. Chrys. de Tribus Pueris,
Ser. 2. in Psalm 50.   [g] John xi. 25.   [h] John xii. 24.   [i] Isai.
v. 1, 2.   [k] Jer. ii. 21.   [l] Folio-Edition, p. 568.

but creature, is a 'liar,' like Job's brook, or friendship
which he compareth thereunto,—that vanisheth into nothing
when there is most need of it [m];—a liar, either by way of perfidiousness, which promiseth and then deceives,—or by way
of impotency, which undertaketh and then miscarries.   But
whenever God promiseth and undertaketh to bless any man
or any people, he carrieth on his work to perfection: his
blessings are all milk and honey, dew and fatness, wine and
oil, the fruits of Lebanon, full of sweetness and maturity.—
' He perfects that which he begins' concerning his servants [n].
There doth not one thing fail of all the good he speaks concerning his people; " they all come to pass, and not one
faileth [o]." The riches which are gotten by human lusts and
sinful resolutions, do come along with many and piercing
sorrows [p]: but when God blesseth a man with riches, he
takes away all the sorrow from it [q]. The gifts of God are
all of them like his works, " very good [r]," and bring after a
sabbath, a rest, and peace into the soul with them.

Sect. 15.   Thirdly, We should from hence learn to show
forth the fruits of this heavenly dew, in those several expressions, which the prophet here useth, drawn from the consideration of a " garden, forest, fruitful field," heavenly paradise; which is a similitude frequently used by the holy
Spirit, to note the beauty, sweetness, fruit, comfort, shelter, protection, which the church of Christ affordeth to the
members of it [s]; as, on the other side, the wicked are compared unto " a dry desert, and barren wilderness [t]." For
these things as they are promises in regard of God, and so
matter of comfort,—so are they duties in regard of us, and
so matter of obedience.

First, He promiseth, That his people shall " grow as the
lily," which is the most beautiful [u] of all flowers [x]. That they
shall be " gloriously clothed," like a king's daughter, with
the ' garments of praise,' and the Spirit of holiness [y], set
forth by various metaphors of ' broidered work,' and ' fine

---

[m] Job vi. 17, 21.   [n] Psalm cxxxviii. 8. Phil. i. 6.   [o] Josh. xxiii. 14.
[p] 1 Tim. vi. 10.   [q] Prov. x. 22.   [r] Gen. i. 31.   [s] Isai. xxxv. 1, 2.
lviii. 11. Cant. iv. 12. vi. 16.   [t] Isai. xxxv. 6, 7. xli. 18. Jer. xvii. 6.
[u] Tanta est floris lilii dignitas, ut Homerus omnes flores vocaverit λείρια;
Jul. Pollux.—Vid. *Plin.* lib. 21. chap. 1.   [x] Matth. vi. 28, 29.   [y] Isai.
lxii. 3.

linen,' and ' silk,' and ' ornaments,' and ' bracelets,' and
' chains,' and ' jewels,' and ' crowns ᶻ.'

And as it is his promise, so it ought to be our duty and
endeavour to adorn the gospel of Christ, to be in his garden as a lily, and not as a nettle or bramble; to walk as becometh godliness; to let our light shine before men, that
they may be won to admire the amiableness of the Lord's
tabernacle, and glorify God in the hour of their visitation;
to be as lights in the midst of a crooked generation ᵃ, or as
'lilies amongst briars ᵇ;' to make it appear that spiritual wisdom causeth the ' face to shine ᶜ,'—that holiness is indeed a
most beautiful thing, which commendeth us to the eyes of
God and angels: a robe worn by Christ the king of Saints,
and by which we are made like unto him, who is the " fairest
of ten thousand, and altogether lovely." We should take
heed of any thing whereby our holy profession may be
blemished, and the name of God defiled by our means: of
such levity, as is inconsistent with the majesty of holiness; of
such morosity, as is inconsistent with the meekness of holiness; of such drooping, as is inconsistent with the joy of
holiness; of such stiffness and sourness, as is inconsistent
with the lenity of holiness. In one word, we should labour
by the innocency, purity, elegancy, fragrancy, fruitfulness,—
by the winning ingenuity, the mild and humble condescen-
sion, the prudent insinuation, the meek, quiet, and graceful
managing of a holy life,—to " show forth the praises of
him that hath called us, and to put to silence the ignorance
of foolish men;" who, like blackmoors, despise beauty,—
like dogs, bark at the shining of the moon, and " speak evil
of the things they know not."

Sᴇᴄᴛ. 16. Secondly ᵈ, He promiseth That his church
should " cast out his roots as Lebanon:" though she should
have the beauty of the lily, yet she should be freed from the
infirmity of it, an aptness to fade and wither, beautiful to-
day, and to-morrow cast into the oven. But she should have
stability like the cedar ᵉ, which is one of the strongest of
trees, and least subject to putrefaction; and therefore the
church is compared to it ᶠ, and the temple is said to be built

---

ᶻ Ezek. xvi. 8, 13.   ᵃ Phil. ii. 15.   ᵇ Cant. ii. 2.   ᶜ Eccles.
viii. 1.   ᵈ Folio-Edition, p. 569.   ᵉ *Plin.* lib. 16. cap. 40.—*Theophrast.*
Hist. Plant. l. 3.   ᶠ Ezek. xvii. 22, 33.

of it [g]; to signify the strength and duration of the church, against which the gates of hell should not prevail : (and we may by the way observe, that most of the things here mentioned by our prophet, are also noted to have been in the temple, or in the services thereof; lilies, 1 Kings vii. 19, 22, 26; olive-trees, 1 Kings vi. 23, 32, 33; spices for incense, wheat and oil for meat-offerings, wine for drink-offerings.) God furnisheth his people with these blessings, which may be most properly dedicated unto him. Teaching us as often as we receive any gifts from God, presently to enquire what relation they have to his temple: how his name may be honoured, how his church may be served, how his gospel may be furthered, how his people may be edified and comforted by them, how all our enjoyments may be divided as spoils unto Christ [h];—the power of great men [i];—the swords of mighty men [k];—the wisdom of learned men [l];—the cunning of craftsmen [m];—the wealth of rich men [n]. Abraham gave of the spoils to Melchizedec [o]; and Israel of all their wealth, to the tabernacle [p]; and David and his people of their treasure, to the temple [q].

And as it is his promise, That the church should thus 'take root [r],' so we should account it our duty, to be firm, stable, constant, unmovable in the truth and in the work of the Lord, as a 'house built upon a rock.' To stand fast and be 'rooted in the truth,' that we may hold the profession thereof 'without wavering;' not being carried about with the 'wind of doctrine,' but knowing whom and what we have believed [s];—to stand fast and be rooted in the love of God, that we may be strengthened with might in his service, and may "with purpose of heart cleave unto him," being established by his grace [t]. In the civil law [u], till a tree hath taken root, it doth not belong to the soil on which it is

---

g 1 Kings vi. 15, 16.　　　h Τεύχεα συλήσας, οἴσω ποτὶ Ἴλιον ἱρὴν, Καὶ κρεμόω ποτὶ νηὸν Ἀπόλλωνος ἑκάτοιο. *Hom.* Iliad. H. 82.—Spolia in Templis suspendere antiqui moris erat. *Cic.* de Nat. Deor. lib. 2.—Liv. lib. 10.—*Virgil.* Æn. 7.　　i Isai. lx. 3.　　k 1 Sam. xviii. 17, 25, 28. Judg. vii. 8　　l 1 Kings iii. 9, 28.　　m Exod. xxviii. 3. xxxi. 6.　　n Isai. xxiii. 18. Prov. iii. 9. Psalm xlv. 12. Isai. lx. 69. 1 Tim. vi. 17, 18, 19.　　o Heb. vii. 4. p Exod. xxxv. 21.　　q 1 Chron. xxix. 2.　　r 2 Kings xix. 30. Jer. xvii. 8. s 1 Cor. xvi. 13. Ephes. iv. 14. Col. ii. 7. Heb. x. 23.　　t Ephes. iii. 17. Col. i. 11. Heb. xii. 28. xiii. 9.　　u P. de adquirendo rerum dominio, l. 7. Sect. 13. et Arborum furtim cæsarum, l. 3. Sect. 3. Cod. de Re. vindicatione, l. 11.

planted. It is not enough to be in the church,—except, like
the cedar of Lebanon, we cast forth our roots, and are so
planted that we flourish in the " courts of our God, and
bring forth fruit in our old age [x]."

SECT. 17. Thirdly, He promised, That the church should
' spread forth' her branches, and fill the earth, and grow into
a great compass and extent, and should send forth her
" boughs unto the sea, and her branches unto the river [y] ;"
—that his church should be a universal church over the
whole world : that as the whole world, in regard of sin, lieth
in mischief [z], so the whole world should have Christ for its
propitiation, through faith [a] ; " Totus in maligno propter zi-
zania, Christus propitiatio propter triticum [b]."   By one
Spirit we all are baptized into one body [c] ; and that one
body made up of all the churches of the saints [d], even
of all nations, kindreds, people, tongues [e].—No difference
of persons ; " neither Greek nor Jew, neither circumcision nor uncircumcision, barbarian, Scythian, bond nor
free, but Christ all, and in all [f] ;"—No difference of places ; all
that in every place call upon the name of the Lord Jesus,
both theirs and ours [g] ;—No difference of times : Christ
" yesterday, and to-day, and the same for ever [h]."

And as this is the promise, so we should endeavour ;

1. To grow ourselves in knowledge and grace ; to let our
profiting appear unto all men ; to abound in the work of the
Lord ; to let our graces from the heart, like leaven from the
middle of the lump, spread abroad, and find their way to all
the parts and powers of soul and body, that the whole man
may be " filled with the fulness of God, and grow up unto
the measure of the stature of the fulness of Christ [i]."

2. To labour and endeavour the growth and progress of
the gospel in others. This is the nature of Grace, to manifest itself, and, by that means, to allure and gather others to
its own quality. It is set forth, in scripture, by the names
of ' light,' which shines abroad ; of ' ointment and perfume,'
which cannot be hid ; of ' leaven and salt,' which deriveth

[x] Psalm xcii. 12, 13, 14.   [y] Psalm lxxx. 9, 10, 11. Dan. ii. 35.
[z] 1 John v. 19.   [a] 1 John ii. 2.   [b] *Aug.* Epist. 48.   [c] 1 Cor.
12, 13.   [d] 1 Cor. xiv. 33.   [e] Rev. vii. 9.   [f] Col. iii. 11.
[g] 1 Cor. i. 2.   [h] Heb. xiii. 8.   [i] Ephes. iv. 13, 15, 16. Phil.
iii. 12, 13. 2 Pet. iii. 18. Heb. vi. 1.

its own nature and relish upon a whole lump. Therefore
the Holy Ghost was given in "tongues, fiery tongues, and a
rushing wind ;" all which have a quality of[k] self-manifesta-
tion, and notifying themselves unto others. There is an excellent place to this purpose in the apostle, Ephes. iv. 15, 16:
"But, speaking the truth in love, may grow up into him in
all things, which is the head, even Christ : from whom the
whole body, fitly joined together and compacted by that
which every joint supplieth, according to the effectual working in the measure of every part, maketh increase of the
body unto the edifying of itself in love :"—where the apostle
showeth the manner of spiritual increase in the mystical
body of Christ, by the proportion of the growth of members
in the natural body.

And, first, there must be a fellowship between the head
and members, which in the mystical body here is twofold, εἰς αὐτὸν, and ἐξ αὐτοῦ; growing 'into him,' and receiving
'from him :'—looking, in this work of growth, upon Christ
first, as the end of that growth unto which it drives : secondly, as the fountain from whence it proceeds : that by
growth we may have a more intimate and strong communion
with him, by that virtue which we receive from him. So
here are two necessary requisites unto this duty of endeavouring the increase of the body ; to have Christ for our
end unto which we work,—and for our fountain, out of
which we derive our ability of working. Every true member of Christ is intent and vigilant upon the interest and honour of Christ ; and it belongs unto the honour of Christ to
have a perfect body. The church is his fulness ; he esteems
himself maimed and incomplete, if that should be finally deficient in any thing, requisite to the integral perfection of it[l]:
and hence it is that every true Christian puts forth the uttermost of his endeavours, in his place, to carry on the increase of his Master's body : as every true-hearted soldier
that loves his general, is exceeding desirous, and to his
power endeavours, that every company and regiment under
his general's command may be, in all the offices and members of it, complete. Again; every member of Christ, being
unto him united, doth from him receive of his fulness 'grace

---

[k] Folio Edition, p. 570.   [l] Vid. *Cameron.* de Eccles. p. 84, 85, 86.

for grace,' and so worketh unto the same ends as the head
doth.   And as the water which first riseth out of the fountain, doth not stand still there wherein it began, but goeth
forward till it grow into a great river ; so those who are
joined unto Christ as a fountain, do, by reason of that vital
communion which they have with the fountain, carry on the
growth of the whole body ; and the more vigorous the life of
Christ is in any part, the more actively doth that part work
towards the edification of the whole.

SECT. 18.—2. Here is further required a fellowship and
mutual communion of the members of the body, within and
amongst themselves : unto which is first presupposed the
organical and harmonious constitution and compacture of
the body into one, out of which ariseth the form and
beauty, the strength and firmness, the order and fitness that
is in it unto those works that are proper to it,—intimated in
those words, συναρμολογούμενον, and συμβιβαζόμενον, fitly joined
together and compacted.   It is a metaphor drawn from car-
penters and other artificers, who by several joints do so co-
aptate and fit the parts of their work unto one another, that
being put together and fastened, there may one whole structure or body grow out of them : and in that body this accu-
rate fitness and intimateness of the parts one with another,
produceth an excellent strength, a beautiful order, and a
ready serviceableness of each part to the other, and of all to
the whole[m].   So Jerusalem is said to be a city ' compacted '
within itself[n].   The ark (a type of the church) had the ribs,
and planks, and parts thereof so closely fastened into one another, that no water might get in to drown it.   And in the tabernacle, all the curtains thereof were to be 'coupled together'
into one another[o].   Christ is all for unity, and joining things
into one : two natures united in one person, two parties reconciled by one mediator, two people concorporated into
one church, one Father, one seed, one head, one faith, one
hope, one love, one worship, one body, one spirit, one end
and common salvation.   ' Christ is not,' loves not to be, ' divided.'   This is a fundamental requisite unto the growth of
the body, the preservation of its unity[p].   The building must

---

[m] Nulla multitudinis potentia nisi consentientis, id est, unum sentientis.
Aug. de Vera Relig. cap. 25.   [n] Psalm cxxii. 3.   [o] Exod. xxvi. 3.
[p] Possessionem bonitatis tanto latius, quanto concordius individua sociorum

be ' fitly framed together,' if you would have it ' grow into
a holy temple' to the Lord ᑫ. When there was most unity,
there was greatest increase in the church; when they were
' all of one accord,' of ' one heart,' and ' one soul,' then the
Lord ' added to the church daily such as should be saved ʳ.'
They that cause divisions and dissensions, do not serve the
Lord Jesus; and therefore they cannot but hinder the progress of his gospel ˢ. As in the natural, so in the mystical
body, ' solutio continui' tendeth to the paining and grieving
of that spirit by which the body lives ᵗ, and, by consequence,
hinders the growth of it. Our growth is, by the apostle,
distributed into growth in knowledge, and growth in grace ᵘ:
and divisions in the church are of themselves great hin-
drances unto ˣ both these; unto knowledge, because the
most usual breaches in the church arise out of diversities of
opinion, publicly asserted and insisted on by the authors
and followers of them. And though accidentally, where
truth is embraced, it is held with more care, and searched
into with more accurateness, because of the errors that oppose it, (as the fire is hottest in the coldest weather;) yet
corrupt doctrine being of the nature of a weed or canker, to
spread, and eat further and further, it must needs consequently hinder the spreading, and, in that kind, the growth
of knowledge. Nor doth it less hinder the growth of grace:
for while the people of God are all of one heart, and of one
way, then all their communion runs into this one design of
mutually edifying, comforting, supporting, encouraging one
another in their holy faith: but when they are divided and
broken into faction by different judgements, if there be not
a greater abundance of humility and spiritual wisdom, the
spirits of men run out into heats and passions ʸ, and into
perverse disputes, and mere notional contentions, which
have ever been diminutions unto the power of godliness ᶻ.
When there are schisms in the body, the members will not
have care one of another ᵃ. Greatly, therefore, even for his

possidet caritas.—Et tanto eam reperiet ampliorem, quanto amplius ibi potuerit
amare consortem; *Aug.* de Civ. Dei, l. 15. c. 5.   ᑫ Ephes. ii. 21. Col. ii. 19.
ʳ Acts ii. 46, 47.   ˢ Rom. xvi. 17, 18.   ᵗ Ephes. iv. 30, 31.
ᵘ 2 Pet. iii. 18.   ˣ Folio-Edition, p. 571.   ʸ Non tulit Cœlius assent-
tientem; sed exclamavit, Dic aliquid contra, ut duo simus.' *Senec.* de Ira, 3. lib.
c. 8. ed. Ruhkopf, vol. i. p. 106.   ᶻ 1 Cor. iii. 3, 4.   ᵃ 1 Cor. xii. 25.

own cause, are the sad and dangerous divisions of these
times to be lamented, when men make use of civil troubles
to disturb, yea, to tear asunder the unity of the church ;
when they set up, as in the times of the Donatists, altar
against altar, and church against church, and make secessions from the common body, and then one from another, to
the infinite content and advantage of the common enemies
of our religion, and hazard of it. It were a blessed thing [b]
if we were in a condition capable of the apostle's exhortation, " To speak all the same thing, to be perfectly joined in
the same mind, and in the same judgement, to be of one
mind, and to live in peace [c]." But if that cannot be attained
unto, let us yet all learn the apostle's other lesson, wherein
we are otherwise minded, to depend upon God for revealing
his will unto us, " and whereunto we have attained, to walk
by the same rule, to mind the same thing ;" to remember
that every difference in opinion doth not, ought not to, dis-
sipate or dissolve the unity of God's church.   Even in Corinth, where the people were divided into several parties, yet
they continued ' one church [d].'

The body thus constituted, and compacted for the increase thereof :—

SECT. 19.—1. Here are members severally distinct from
one another ; some principal, others ministerial, all concurring differently unto the service of the whole.   If the heart
should be in the head, or the liver in the shoulder,—if there
should be any unnatural dislocation of the vital or nutritive
parts,—the body could not grow, but perish.   The way for
the church to prosper and flourish, is for every member to
keep in his own rank and order, to remember his own measure, to act in his own sphere, to manage his particular condition and relations with spiritual wisdom and humility ; the
eye to do the work of an eye, the hand of a hand.   Say not
as Absalom, " If I were a judge, I would do justice [e] ;"—but
consider what state God hath set thee in ; and in that walk
with God, and adorn the profession of the gospel [f].   Remember Uzzah : it was a good work he did ; but because he did

<hr/>

[b] Unitas interior et unanimitas ipsam quoque multiplicitatem colligat et con-
stringit caritatis glutino et vinculo pacis ; *Bernard.* in Septuagesima, Serm. 2.
[c] 1 Cor. i. 10.   2 Cor. xiii. 11.   [d] 1 Cor. xi. 18.   [e] 2 Sam. xv. 4.
[f] Rom. xii. 3. 1 Cor. xii. 8. 11, 29, 30. 2 Cor. x. 13, 14. Ephes. iv. 7.

it out of order [g], having no call, God smote him for his error [h]. There are excellent works which, being done without the call of God, do not edify but disturb the body [i]. Every man must walk in the church, as God hath distributed and called; and every man must in the calling, wherein he was called, ' abide with God [k].'

2. Here are joints and ligaments so fastening these members together, that each one may be serviceable to the increase of the whole [l]. There are bands which join the body to the head, without which it can neither grow nor live, namely, the ' Spirit of Christ,' and ' faith' in him [m]. And there are bands which join the parts of the body unto one another; as, namely, the same ' holy Spirit [n];' which Spirit of grace stirreth up every member to seek the growth and benefit of the whole [o]. The same sincere love and truth which each member beareth unto all the rest, this is called ' a bond of perfectness [p],' and ' the bond of peace [q].' Now love is a most communicative grace; it will plant, and water, and feed, and spend itself for the good of the whole; it will deny itself to serve the body,—as Christ did [r].

3. Here is a measure belonging unto every part : some are in one office, others in another; some have one gift, others another; and all this ' for the perfecting of the saints [s].' One is able to teach, another to comfort, a [t] third to convince, a fourth to exhort, a fifth to counsel; and every one of these is to be directed unto the edification and growth of the whole [u]. The apostle saith, that ' we are fellow-citizens with the saints [x]' Now as, amongst fellow-citizens, there useth to be an intercourse of mutual negotiation [y], one man hath one commodity, and another another, and these they usually barter withal;—so amongst the saints, one man is eminent in one grace, another in another; and according to their mutual indigencies or abilities, they do interchangeably minister to one another towards the growth of the whole.

---

[g] Ut Ilus, Palladium ex incendio eripiens, dum arderet templum Minervæ, luminibus privatus est; *Plutarch.* Xylandr. vol. i. p. 309. E.   [h] 2 Sam. vi. 6, 7.   [i] Rom. x. 15. Heb. v. 4.   [k] 1 Cor. vii. 17, 20, 24.   [l] 1 Cor. ii. 19. [m] 1 Cor. vi. 17. Rom. viii. 9. Ephes. iii. 17.   [n] 1 Cor. xii. 13.   [o] 1 Cor. xii. 25, 26.   [p] Col. iii. 14.   [q] Ephes. iv. 3.   [r] Gal. v. 13. [s] Ephes. iv. 11, 12. 1 Cor. xii. 4, 11.   [t] Folio-Edition, p. 572.   [u] Rom. xii. 3, 8. Ephes. iv. 7.   [x] Ephes. ii. 19.   [y] Vid. *Aristot.* Ethic. l. 5. c. 8.

And this is that which is here further requisite to the increase
of the body, called,

4. Ἐπιχορηγία, the 'supply of service,' and the supply of
nourishment, which one part affords unto another, and so to
the whole. This is principally from the head to the members, called by the apostle, 'the supply of the Spirit of Jesus
Christ:ᶻ' of whose fulness we receive 'grace for graceᵃ;'
into whose image we are transformed from glory to gloryᵇ.
But it is proportionably between the members amongst themselves: for as several particular ingredients make up one
cordial,—and several instruments concur to the perfecting of
one ἀποτέλεσμα, or consummate work,—and the beauty of
every thing ariseth out of the variety, and order, and mutual
serviceableness that the parts thereof have unto one another;
so is it in the church too, which Christ hath so tempered together, that they might all stand mutually in need of one
another. Therefore we find the Saints, in Scripture, communicating to one another their experiences, temptations,
deliverances, comforts, for their mutual edificationᶜ. And
God's dealings with saints, in particular, are therefore registered in Scriptureᵈ; both that we might learn that way of
building up one another, and that, by their examples, we
might support our faith, and through patience and experience of the Scripture have hope: because what hath been
done unto one, is, in the like condition, applicable unto
every otherᵉ.

5. After all this there is ἐνέργεια, an 'effectual working,' a
vis πλαστικὴ, or a vis πεπτικὴ, a faculty to form, and to con-
coct the matter, which hath been subministered unto life and
nourishment:—which is the work of faith, and of the Spirit
of Christ, whereby the soul of a believer, being sensible of
want, desirous of supply, and pressing forward unto perfection, doth sweetly close with whatsoever the measure of any
other part hath communicated unto it, converting it into
growth and nourishment to itself, which the apostle calls
'the mixing of the Word with faithᶠ.' Now

ᶻ Phil. i. 19.   ᵃ John i. 16.   ᵇ 2 Cor. iii. 18.   ᶜ Psalm
xxxiv. 3, 6. John i. 41, 45. iv. 29. 2 Cor. i. 4, 6. Phil. i. 12, 13, 14. Col.
ii. 1. 2.   ᵈ Specialiter pronunciata generaliter sapiunt. Cum Deus Is-
raelitas admonet disciplinæ, vel objurgat, utique ad omnes habet: *Tert.* de
Spectac. c. 3.   ᵉ James v. 10, 11, 17. Rom. xv. 4. 1 Cor. x. 6. Heb. xiii. 5.
ᶠ Heb. iv. 2.

SECT. 20. Fourthly, He promiseth, That the beauty of his church shall be as the ' olive-tree ;' that as she should have the glory of the lily, the strength and extension of the cedar, so this spreading should not be a vain ostentation, but should have, joined with it, the flourishing and fruitfulness of the olive. Now the honour of the olive-tree standeth in two things: perpetual greenness, and most profitable fruit, which serveth both for light to cause the lamp to burn[g], and for nourishment to be eaten[h]: in the one respect, it is an emblem of peace; it maketh the face shine[i];—and in the other, it is an emblem of grace, and spiritual gifts[k]. These are the two most excellent benefits, which God promiseth unto his people. " He will speak peace unto them[l];" and he " will give them grace and glory[m]."

And as he promiseth, so should we practise these things, and learn to beautify the gospel of Christ, first, with our good works, as the fruits of his grace[n];—secondly, with our spiritual joy and comfort, as the fruits of his peace: that others, seeing the light and shining forth of a serene, calm, and peaceable conscience in our conversation, may thereby be brought in love with the ways of God. These two do mutually cherish and increase one another. The more conscience we make of fruitfulness, the more way do we make for peace ; when the waters of lust are sunk, the dove will quickly bring an olive-branch in:—and the more the peace of God rules in the heart, the more will it strengthen the conscience and care of obedience, out of these considerations : First, Out of thankfulness for so great a blessing. Secondly, Out of fear to forfeit it. Thirdly, Out of wisdom to improve and increase it.

SECT. 21. Fifthly, He promiseth, That his church shall be as ' the smell of Lebanon,' and that the ' scent of it' shall be as the ' wine of Lebanon ;' as elsewhere we find her compared to a garden of spices ;—she shall be filled with the

---

[g] Exod. xxvii. 20.   [h] Lev. vi. 15, 16.   [i] Psalm civ. 15.
[k] 1 John ii. 20.   [l] Psalm lxxxv. 8. Isai. xxxii. 17.   [m] Psalm lxxxiv. 11.
[n] John xv. 8.   [o] Ἔστι δέ τις οἶνος, ὃν δὴ σαπρίαν καλέουσι· Οὗ καὶ ἀπὸ στόματος στάμνων ἀνοιγομενάων Ὄζει ἴων, ὄζει δὲ ῥόδων, ὄζει δ' ὑακίνθου, &c. Hermippus apud Athenæum, l. 1. c. 23.—Casaub. p. 29.—Convivia, Ludi, Pocula crebra. Unguenta, Coronæ, Serta parantur. Lucret. l. 4. 1125.   [p] Cant. iv. 12, 14.

sweet savour of the gospel of Christ. " Thanks be unto
God," saith the apostle, "which always causeth us to triumph
in Christ, and maketh manifest the savour of his knowledge
by us in every place[r]; for we are unto God a sweet savour of
Christ[s]:"—where there are two metaphors, one of a sweet
ointment,—the other, of a triumph. The name of Christ is
compared to an ointment[t]; and preaching of the gospel,
which is making manifest the savour of this ointment, is
called the ' bearing of Christ's name[u].' Now, this sweet
savour is annexed unto a triumphal solemnity ; because, in
all times of public joy, they were wont to anoint themselves
with sweet oil, which is therefore called, ' Oleum lætitiæ,' the
oil of gladness[x]. (For in times of mourning, they did abstain
from sweet ointments[y].) The gospel therefore being a message of ' great joy[z],' a leading ' captivity captive,' and the
means whereby Christ rideth forth gloriously, ' conquering
and to conquer[a];' therefore they who brought these good
tidings, are said to be as a ' sweet savour[b],' whose lips drop
' sweet-smelling myrrh[c],' and whose doctrine is compared to
the powders of the merchant[d]. And the time of the gospel
is called an ' accepted time, a day of salvation[e];' that is, a
time of singular joy and solemnity, a continued Easter, or
festival[f]. And here withal he promiseth likewise, That his
people should offer up spiritual incense and services unto
him in prayers, thanksgivings, alms, and good works[g].

And as he promiseth, so we should practise these things :
our care should be to let our lips and lives breathe forth
nothing but grace and edification[h]; to be frequent in the
spiritual sacrifices of prayer, thanksgiving, and good works,
which may be as an ' odour of a sweet savour' in the nostrils of God[i];—to labour to leave behind us a good name,
not out of vain-glory, or an empty ambitious affectation of
honour; but out of the conscience of a holy life, which
makes the name ' smell better than sweet ointment[k].'

SECT. 22. Sixthly, He promiseth, That they " who dwell

[r] Folio-Edition, p. 573.   [s] 2 Cor. ii. 14, 15.   [t] Cant. i. 3.
[u] Acts ix. 15.   [x] Psalm xlv. 7, 8. Isai. lxi. 3.   [y] 2 Sam. xiv. 2. Dan.
x. 2, 3.   [z] Luke ii. 13.   [a] Psalm xlv. 3, 4. Psalm cx. 2. Rev. vi. 2.
[b] Aderant unguenta, coronæ; incendebantur odores. Cic. Tusc. Qu. l. 5.—vid.
Athenæum, l. 15. c. 11, 12.   [c] Cant. v. 13.   [d] Cant. iii. 6.
[e] 2 Cor. vi. 2.   [f] 1 Cor. v. 7, 8.   [g] Ezek. xx. 41.   [h] Col. iv. 6.
[i] Phil. iv. 18. Rev. viii. 4.   [k] Eccles. vii. 1.

under his shadow, shall return;" which words admit of a
double sense, and so infer a double promise and a double
duty :—1.We may, by a 'hysteron proteron,' understand the
words thus,—" When Israel have repented and are brought
home to God again, they shall then have security, defence,
protection, refreshment under the comforts of his grace,
against all the violence of temptation; as a spreading tree
doth afford a sweet shade unto the weary traveller, and
shelter him from the injuries of the heat[1]." Whereby is
signified the secure, quiet, and comfortable condition of
God's people under the protection of his providence and
promises.

And as he promiseth such a condition, so should we, in
all our troubles, not trust in an arm of flesh, or betake ourselves to mere human wisdom, and carnal counsels, which
are too thin shelters against God's displeasure, or the enemies of the church ;—but we must fly unto him to hide us ;
we must find spiritual refreshment in his ordinances, promises, and providence; get his wing to cover us, and his
presence to be a little sanctuary unto us, and the joy of the
Lord to be our strength[m]. When the Lord cometh out of
his place to punish the inhabitants of the land for their
iniquity; when flood and fire, storm and tempest, the fury
of anger, the strength of battle, are poured out upon a people; when a destroying angel is sent abroad with a commission to kill and slay[n]; when Death, the king of terrors,
rideth up and down in triumph, stripping men of treasures,
lands, friends, honours, pleasures, making them a house in
darkness, where master and servant, princes and prisoners,
are all alike;—to have then an ark with Noah, a Zoar with
Lot, a Goshen in Egypt,—to have one arm of this olive-tree
spread over us,—to have one promise out of God's Word, one
sentence from the mouth of Christ promising paradise unto
us,—is infinitely of more value to a languishing spirit, than
all the diadems of the earth, or the peculiar treasure of
princes.

2. If we take the words in order as they lie, then the
mercy here promised is, That when God shall restore and

---

[1] Job vii. 2. Isai. iv. 6. Mich. iv. 4. Zech. iii. 10.   [m] Psalm lvii. 2.
xci. 1. Isai. xxvi. 20. Nehem. viii. 10.   [n] Ezek. ix. 5, 6.

repair his church, they who dwell under the comforts of it, should return and be converted to the knowledge and obedience, which should be there taught them: When the 'Branch of the Lord is beautiful and glorious, and the fruit of the earth excellent and comely,' then he that remaineth in Jerusalem, 'shall be called holy [o];' then every vessel in Judah and Jerusalem shall be inscribed, 'holiness unto the Lord [p];' then 'the heart of the rash shall understand knowledge, and the tongue of the stammerers shall speak plainly [q].'

And this should be the endeavour of every one who liveth under the shade of this tree, under the purity of God's ordinances, under the pious government and constitution of such a church or family as is here described, (especially in such times, when [r], on the one side, the world is so much loosened and estranged from us; and, on the other side, reformation in the church is so much desired) to convert and turn unto the Lord. All endeavours of reformation in a church are miserably defective, when they come short of this end, which is the ultimate reason of them all,—namely, the repentance and conversion of those, that dwell under the shadow of it. When God promiseth to give unto his church 'the glory of Lebanon,' and the excellency of 'Carmel and Sharon,' the consequence of this beauty and reformation in the church is, "The eyes of the blind shall be opened, the ears of the deaf shall be unstopped, the lame shall leap, the dumb shall sing, the parched ground shall be a pool, the thirsty land springs of water [s]. The wolf, the leopard, the lion, the bear, the asp, the cockatrice, shall be so turned from the fierceness and malignity of their natures, that they shall not hurt nor destroy in all the holy mountain, but a little child shall lead them all [t]." It is a great happiness and advantage to live under the shade of a godly government. Many men have reason to bless God all their days, that they were, in their childhood, trained up in such a school, where piety was taught them as well as learning, and where they had means as well of conversion as of institution; that they lived in such a family, where the master of it was of Joshua's

[o] Isai. iv. 2, 3. [p] Zech. xiv. 20, 21. [q] Isai. xxxii. 2, 3, 4.
[r] Folio-Edition, p. 574. [s] Isai. xxxv. 2, 7. [t] Isai. xi. 6, 9.

mind, " I and my house will serve the Lord [u]." Salvation comes to a whole house, when the governor thereof is converted [x]. I shall never look upon a church as reformed to purpose, till I find reformation work conversion; till piety, and charity, and justice, and mercy, and truth, and humility, and gentleness, and goodness, and kindness, and meekness, and singleness of heart, and zeal for godliness and mutual edification, and the life and power of religion, are more conspicuous than before. When the very head-stone was brought forth, and the last work in the building of the temple was finished, yet the people must then cry, " Grace, grace unto it [y];" intimating that reformation is never indeed consummate, till the blessing of God make it effectual unto those uses, for which it was by him appointed. Church-reformation should be like Paul's epistles, which always close in duties of obedience.

SECT. 23. Seventhly, He promiseth, That they " shall revive as the corn, and grow as the vine:" in which two expressions, are set forth two excellent and wholesome consequents of affliction. 1. The corn, though it die first [z], and suffer much from frost, hail, snow, tempest,—yet when the spring comes, it revives and breaks through it all: so God promiseth to his church, in the saddest condition, a reviving again, and that it shall be brought forth into the light [a]. 2. The vine when it is pruned and lopped, will not only revive and spread again, but will bring forth the more fruit, and cast forth the more fragrant smell: so God promiseth unto his people not only a reviving out of their afflictions, (in which respect haply it was that Christ was buried in a garden, to note, that death itself doth not destroy our bodies, but only sow them; the dew of herbs will revive them again [b];) but further, a profiting by afflictions, that we may say with David, " It is good for us;" when we find it " bring forth the peaceable fruits of righteousness, after we have been exercised therein."

And as he promiseth these things, so we should learn to turn these promises into prayer and into practice. When [c]

---

[u] John xxiv. 15.   [x] Luke xix. 9. Acts xvi. 33, 34.   [y] Zech. iv. 7.
[z] Semina non, nisi corrupta et dissoluta, fœcundius surgunt : omnia pereundo servantur : omnia de interitu reformantur. *Tert.* Apol. c. 48.   [a] Ezek. xxxvii. 12. Mic. vii. 9.   [b] 1 Cor. xv. 41, 44.   [c] Nemo agonis præsidem sugillaverit,

we seem in our own eyes cast out of God's sight, yet we
must not cast him out of our sight; but, as Jonah in the
whale's belly, and as Daniel in Babylon, pray towards his
holy temple still. The woman of Canaan [d] would not be
thrust off with a seeming rejection, not utterly despond
under a grievous tentation, but, by a singular acumen and
spiritual sagacity, discerned matter of argument in that
which looked like a denial [e]. Soap and fuller's-earth, at the
first putting on, seem to stain and to foul clothes, when the
use and end is to purify them. And God's frowns and delays may seem to be the denials of prayer, when, haply, his
end is to make the granting of them the more comfort.
Therefore in all troubles we must not give-over looking towards God, but say with Job, "Though he slay me, I will
trust in him."

And, after all afflictions, we must learn to express the
fruit of them, to come out of them refined, as silver out of
the fire; to have thereby our faith strengthened, our hope
confirmed, our love inflamed, our fruit and obedience increased, our sin taken away, and our iniquities purged [f]; to
be 'chastened and taught [g];' to [h] be 'chastened and converted [i].' If we have run away from our duties, and been
cast into a whale's belly for it,—when we are delivered, let us
be sure to look better to our resolutions afterwards : "after
all that is come upon us for our sins, take heed of breaking
his commandments again [k]." As Job's riches after his, so we
should endeavour that our graces after our afflictions may
be doubled upon us ; and that the scent of our holy example
may, like spices bruised, or the grapes of Lebanon crushed
in the wine-press, give a more fragrant smell in the nostrils
of God and man, "as the smell of a field, which the Lord
hath blessed."

quod homines violentiæ objectat. Injuriarum actiones extra stadium. Sed quantum livores illi, et cruores et vibices negotiantur intendet : coronas scilicet, et gloriam, et dotem, privilegia publica, stipendia civica, imagines, statuas, et qualem
potest præstare seculum de fama æternitatem, de memoriâ resurrectionem. Pyctes
ipse non queritur dolere se, nam vult. Corona premit vulnera, palma sanguinem
obscurat ; plus victoria tumet quam injuria. Hunc tu læsum existimabis quem
vides lætum ? *Tert.* Scorpiac. c. 6. ed. Lut. 1675, p. 492.   [d] Vid. *Chrys.* Ser. 38.
in Gen. xvi. 3.   [e] Matth. xv. 27.   [f] Isai. xxvii. 9.   [g] Psalm
lxxxiv. 12.   [h] Folio-Edition, p. 575.   [i] Jer. xxxviii. 18.   [k] Ezra
ix. 13, 14.

Lastly, He promiseth, That all these should be 'fruits of Lebanon,' of the best and perfectest kind. There are many evidences of the goodness of God even in the lives of Pagan men. We read of Abimelech's forbearance to sin against God [1]; and of his and Ephron's singular kindness to Abraham [m]. No argument more common than this of the virtues, the temperance, prudence, justice, mercy, patience, fidelity, friendships, affability, magnanimity of many heathen men; insomuch that some have presumed so far as to make them 'ex congruo [n]' meritorious, or dispositive to salvation. But all these are but wild grapes, bitter clusters, the fruits of an empty vine, not worth the gathering in order to salvation: but the graces which God bestoweth upon his church, are of a more spiritual and perfect nature, proceeding from faith in Christ, from love of God, from a conscience cleansed from dead works, from an intention to glorify God and adorn the gospel, from a new nature, and from the Spirit of Christ, conforming his servants unto himself; they are not grapes of Sodom, but grapes of Lebanon.

And as he thus blesseth us, in the like manner should we serve him; not offer unto him the refuse, the halt, and blind, and maimed, for sacrifice; not give unto him of that which cost us nothing, but go to Lebanon for all our sacrifices, covet earnestly the best gifts, press forward and labour to perfect holiness in the fear of God; give unto him our lilies, the beauties of our minority; and our cedars, the strength of our youth; and our olives, and grapes, and corn, and wine: whatever gifts he hath bestowed on us, use them unto his service and honour again; not content ourselves with the form of godliness, with the morality of virtue, with the outside of duties, with the seeds and beginnings of holiness (he hath none, who thinks he hath enough); but strive who shall outrun one another unto Christ, as Peter and John did towards his sepulchre. It was a high pitch which Moses aimed at, when he said, "I beseech thee, show me thy glory [o]." Nothing would satisfy

---

[1] Gen. xx. 4, 6.　　　[m] Gen. xx. 14, 15. xxiii. 10, 11, 15.　　　[n] Vide *Vegam* de Justif. lib. 6. cap. 18, 19, 20.—*Andrad.* Orthodox. Explicat. 1. 3.— *Maldonat.* in Johan. v. 6.—*Sixt. Senens.* Bibliothec. 1. 6. annot. 51.—*Collium* de Animabus Pagan. 1. 1. cap. 11. et 20.—*Ban.* in secundam secundæ qu. 2. art. 8.— *Greg. Valent.* To. 3. disput. 1. Qu. 2. punct. 1 et 4.—*Erasm.* Præfat. in Qu. Tusc. Cic.—*Aug.* contra Julian. Pelag. 1. 4. c. 3.　　　[o] Exod. xxxiii. 18.

him but fulness and satiety itself.   Be sure that all your
graces come from Sion, and from Lebanon, that they grow
in Emmanuel's land : till Christ own them, God will not accept them.   Moral virtues and outward duties, grapes of
Sodom, may commend us unto men ; nothing but inward, spiritual, and rooted graces, the grapes of Lebanon, will commend us unto God.   To do only the outward works of duty, without the inward principle, is at best
but to make ourselves like those mixed beasts, elephants
and camels, in the civil law[q]; " operam præstant, natura fera
est ;" which, though they do the work of tame beasts, yet
have the nature of wild ones.   Moral virtue[r], without spiritual piety, doth not commend any man unto God; for we
are not accepted unto him, but in Christ; and we are not in
Christ but by the Holy Spirit.

[p] Reproba pecunia non liberat solventem, l. 24. Sect. 1. P. de pignoratitia
actione.   [q] Leg. 2. P. ad Leg. Aquil.—*Senec.* de Benefic. lib. 7. cap. 19.
[r] Vide *Aug.* de Civit. Dei, lib. 5. cap. 19. et lib. 19. cap. 4. et cap. 25.—Retract.
l. 1. cap. 3.—de Trin. lib. 14. cap. 1.—de nup. et concupis. l. 1. c. 3.—contra Julian.
Pelag. l. 4. c. 3. Ad Simplician. l. 1. qu. 2. contr. 2. Ep. Pelag. lib. 3. cap. de fide
et operibus, c. 7. Epist. 105, 107, 120.—*Prosper.* contra Collat. c. 13.—*Greg.*
Arimin. 1. dist. 1. q. 3. art. 2.

THE

SIXTH SERMON.*

HOSEA XIV. 8.

*Ephraim shall say, What have I to do any more with Idols?
I have heard him, and observed him.   I am like a green fir-
tree: from me is thy fruit found.*

Sect. 1. The conversion of Israel unto God in their trouble,
was accompanied with a petition and a covenant:—a petition
imploring mercy and grace from God ; and a covenant, promising thanksgivings and obedience unto him.   And God is
pleased, in his answer, to have a distinct respect unto both
these : for whereas they petition, first, for pardon, that God
would 'take away all iniquity ;' he promiseth ' to heal their
backslidings, and to love them freely :'—and whereas they
pray for blessings, ' Receive us into favour, do us good ;'
God likewise maketh promises of that in great variety, expressed by the several metaphors of fertility, answering to
the name and blessings promised formerly unto Ephraim.
And all this we have handled out of the four preceding
verses.

Now, in this eighth verse, God is pleased not only graciously to accept, but further to put to his seal, and to confirm the covenant which they make,—promising, that, by the
assistance of his Spirit, they should be enabled to do what
they had undertaken.   This is the greatest ground of confidence that we can have, to bind ourselves in holy covenants
unto God, even the promise of his strength and assistance,
enabling us to keep covenant with him.   Therefore when
David had said, " I have sworn, and will perform it, that I
will keep thy righteous judgements ;" it follows a little after,

* Folio-Edition, p. 577.

"Accept, I beseech thee, the freewill-offerings of my mouth,
O Lord, and teach me thy judgements [b]." David was confident, that God would not only accept his covenant, but
teach him how to keep it; and that made him the more confident to bind himself by it.

In the original, the words are only thus, "Ephraim, what
have I to do any more with idols?" which therefore some
would have to be the words of God spoken unto Ephraim :
but there is nothing more usual in Scripture, than an ellipsis [c]
of the verb. And we find this very verb omitted, and yet
necessary to be supplied, Isai. v. 9.; and in this place, the
Chaldee paraphrast, and from him the best interpreters, with
our translators [d], have supplied it. Thus, 'Ephraim shall
say:' and so it is God's confirmation of the promise which
penitent Ephraim had made, and his undertaking for him,
that he should indeed be enabled to perform his covenant.

"*What have I to do any more with idols?*"] It is 'interrogatio cum indignatione;' an interrogation not only importing a negative, ' I will *not* any more have to do with them,'
but also a vehement detestation of them, and indignation
against them: as that of David to Abishai [e], and that of
Elisha to Jehoram [f], and that of the devil to Christ [g].

"*With idols.*"] The original word signifieth likewise *sorrows*, and grief of mind, a fit word to express their sin and
repentance. ' What have we to do with these idols and sorrows any more? they can produce no good ; they can hear
no prayers ; they can work no deliverance ; they can bring
nothing but evil and anguish to us ; and therefore we will
not follow or seek unto them any more.'—Here then is a solemn detestation, as of all their other sins, so of that especially which had most dishonoured God, most wounded their
own consciences, and procured most sorrow unto themselves ; with God's confirmation of it.

Next, follow several promises of special mercies. 1.
Of hearing and answering their prayers : " I have heard" or
answered " him ;" or, as others render it, " I will hear him."
2. Of fatherly care and providence over them ; I have " observed him," or fixed mine eyes " upon him ;" I have strictly

---

[b] Psalm cxix. 106, 108.   [c] *Solom. Glassius* Grammat. Sacr. p. 380, 654.
[d] Folio-Edition, p. 578.   [e] *Glass.* Rhetor. Sacra, Tract. 2. cap. 5. 2 Sam.
xvi. 10.   [f] 2 Kings iii. 13.   [g] Matth. viii. 29.

considered his condition, that I might proportion my mercies thereunto. It is a symbol, First, Of vigilant care, and
most intent and solicitous inspection and providence : " The
eye of the Lord is upon them that fear him, upon them that
hope in his mercy, to deliver their soul from death, and to
keep them alive in famine ᵸ."—Secondly, Of direction and
counsel : " I will instruct thee, and teach thee in the way
that thou shalt go ;"—" I will guide (or counsel) thee with
mine eye ⁱ."—Thirdly, Of honour and exaltation : he " with-
draweth not his eyes from the righteous, but with kings are
they on the throne ;" yea, he doth establish them for ever,
and they " are exalted ᵏ." Lastly, It is an expression of
' hearing prayers :' God is said to have his " eye open to the
supplication of his servants," to hearken unto them in all
that they call upon him for ¹; and " the eyes of the Lord are
upon the righteous, and his ear open unto their cry ᵐ." The
church had before professed herself to be an orphan, that
stood in need of tuition and protection : and here God
promiseth to cast his eye, and to place his affection upon
her ; to look to her; to be her tutor and guardian ; to
govern her with his special providence and wisdom ; to
take notice of her wants, and supply them ; to take notice of
her desires, and fulfil them ; to take notice of her condition,
and, accordingly, in all respects to provide for her. 3. Of
refreshment from the heat and violence of temptations, or
any kind of afflictions, by the metaphor of a ' fir-tree,'
which, being ever green, and casting forth a large shade,
doth afford much comfort and reviving to the weary traveller. 4. Because the fir-tree, though comfortable in regard
of the shade, is yet unfruitful ; therefore he further promiseth to be " a root of blessings," and all kind of spiritual
graces unto them : " From me is thy fruit found ;" that is,
from me is, or shall be thy fruit ⁿ; though the word *found*
may here seem to imply and direct unto an enquiry after the
foundation and original of the fruit here mentioned: ' Though
all thy fruit of good works and new obedience may seem to
proceed from thyself, and to be thine own ; yet if thou be
careful to enquire after the root of them, thou wilt find that
they come from us, though they grow upon thee ; and that

ᵸ Psalm xiii. 18, 19. ⁱ Psalm xxxii. 8. ᵏ Job xxxvi. 7.
¹ 1 Kings viii. 52. ᵐ Psalm xxxiv. 15. ⁿ Mal. ii. 6. 1 Pet. ii. 22.
Zeph. iii. 13.

thou bringest them forth only by the help, supply, and vigour of my grace bestowed on thee. Thou dost them; but the power and strength whereby thou dost them, proceeds from me [o].'

SECT. 2.   These words then are the sum of God's answer which he makes unto the covenant of his people. They return ' the calves of their lips ;' God hears and accepts them.   They renounce carnal confidence in men, in horses, in idols; and when they look off, and turn away from these, then God looketh upon them with a fatherly eye of care, providence, counsel, and protection ; 'I have observed him.' They will not say any more to the work of their hands, 'Ye are our gods,'—nor any longer make lies their refuge; and God enables them to do as they have said, and affordeth comfort and refreshment unto them, as the shade of a fir-tree unto a weary traveller.   Lastly, They believe and acknowledge, that when they are fatherless and destitute of all help, there is mercy in God to comfort and provide for them; and this God makes good too.   Mercy of protection ; " I am as a great fir-tree ;"—and mercy of bounty and benediction; "from me is thy fruit found ;"—by the one, defending them against their fears,—by the other, enabling them unto their duties.   Thus God doth enlarge and proportion his [P] mercy to the uttermost extent of Israel's prayer or promise; and when they have no help or comfort out of him, he himself becomes all in all unto them, making a thorough compensation for every thing which they part with for his sake, and causing them to find in him alone all that comfort and satisfaction to their desires, which in vain they sought for in other things.

The parts are these two generals : First, God's promise enabling Israel to perform theirs ; "Ephraim shall say, What have I to do any more with idols ?"   Secondly, God's special regard to their prayers,—" I have heard him ;"—to their persons, and " observed him ;" illustrated by two metaphors, the one, importing protection and defence, " I am as a green fir-tree ;" the other, grace and benediction, " from me is thy fruit found."

---

o Certum est nos velle. cum volumus ; sed ille facit, ut velimus. Certum est nos facere, cum facimus ; sed ille facit, ut faciamus. *Aug.* Ipse facit, ut illi faciant quæ præcepit : illi non faciunt, ut ipse faciat quod promisit ;—de Prædestin. Sanct. cap. 10.   P Folio-Edition, p. 579.

Sect. 3. *" Ephraim shall say."*] This is God's speech
and promise, setting-to his seal and gracious ratification to
the covenant that Israel made, ver. 2, 3.; without the
which, it would have been null and evanid. For a man, by
believing, setteth-to his seal to the truth of God[q]; so God,
by assisting, setteth-to his seal to the purpose of man : but
with this great difference,—man's seal is but a subscription
and confession of that which was firm before ; for all God's
promises are Yea and Amen, and faith doth not put certainty
into the promise of God[r], but into the heart of man concerning the promises[s]. But God's seal is a confirmation
and making efficacious the promise of man, which otherwise
would vanish into a lie : all our sufficiency is from him : we
can neither will nor do any thing further than we receive
from him both to will and to do. Pharaoh made promise
after promise, and broke them as fast[t]. Israel makes promises one while, and quickly starts aside like a deceitful
bow, as ice which melts in the day, and hardens again in the
night[u] ; to-day they will, to-morrow they will not again ;
they repent to-day, and to-morrow they repent of their repenting ; like the sluggard in his bed, that puts out his arm
to rise, and then pulls it in again. So unstable and impotent
is man in all his resolutions, till God say Amen to what he
purposeth, and " establisheth the heart by his own grace[x]."
When the waters stood as a wall on the right-hand and on
the left of Israel, as they passed through the Red Sea, this
was a work of God's own power : for water is unstable, and
cannot keep together by its own strength, nor be contained
within any bounds of its own. So great a work is it to see
the mutable wills and resolutions of men, kept close to any
pious and holy purposes.

Sect. 4. The point we learn from hence, is this ;—That
our conversion and amendment of life is not sufficiently provided for by any band, obligation, or covenant of our own,
whereby we solemnly promise and undertake it,—except God
be pleased, by his free grace, to establish and enable the
heart unto the performance of it. Or thus, a penitent man's
conversion and covenant of new obedience, hath its firmness

[q] John iii. 33.   [r] Rom. iii. 3, 4. 2 Tim. ii. 13.   [s] Rom. iv. 16.
2 Tim. i. 12.   [t] Exod. viii. 8, 28. ix. 28.   [u] Psalm lxxviii. 34, 38.
Jer. xxxiv. 15, 16.   [x] Heb. xiii. 9.

in the promise and free grace of God. Israel here, in the
confidence of God's mercy, prays for pardon and blessings;
and in the confidence of his grace, maketh promise of reformation and amendment of life: but all this is but like a
written instrument or indenture, which is invalid and of no
effect, till the parties concerned have mutually sealed and
set-to their hands. Till God be pleased to promise us, that
we shall do that which we have promised unto him, and do,
as it were, make our own covenant for us,—all will prove
too weak and vanishing to continue. The grace of God
unto the purposes of men, is like grain to colours dyed, or
like oil to colours in a table or picture, which makes them
hold fresh and not fade away.

There is a necessary and indissolvable dependence of all
second causes upon the first, without whose influence and
concurrence they neither live, nor move, nor have, nor continue in their being [y]. He who is first of causes and last of
ends, doth use and direct the necessary, voluntary, contin-
gent motions and activities of all second causes unto whatsoever ends he himself is pleased to pre-ordain. And this
the natural and necessary concatenation of things doth require, that that which is the absolutest, supremest, first, and
most independent will, wisdom, and power of all others,—
should govern, order, and direct all other wills, powers, and
wisdoms that are subordinate to, and inferior under it, unto
whatsoever uses and purposes he who hath the absolute
dominion and sovereignty over all, is pleased to appoint. It
cannot be other than a marvellous diminution unto the greatness of God, and a too low esteem of the absoluteness of
that majesty which belongs unto him, to make any counsels,
decrees, purposes of his, to receive their ultimate form and
stamp from the previous and intercurrent casualties or conditions of the creature. This I have always looked on as the
principal cause of those dangerous errors concerning grace,
free-will, and the decrees of God, wherewith the churches [z]
of Christ have been so miserably, in the former ages, and in
this of ours, exercised by the subtilty of Satan, and by the
pride of corrupt-minded men; namely,—the too low and
narrow thoughts and conception which men have framed to

y Acts xvii. 28. Heb. i. 3.   z Folio-Edition, p. 580.

themselves, of God,—the not acquiescing in his sovereign dominion and absolute power of disposing all things which he made, unto whatsoever uses himself pleaseth[a] : into which, I am sure, the holy Scripture doth resolve all[b].

SECT. 5. Even in the sinful actions of men, God's influence and providence hath a particular hand ; as actions, his influence ; as sinful, his providence. His influence to the natural motion and substance of the action, though not to the wickedness of it : for this standeth not in being or perfection (else the fountain of being and perfection must needs be the first cause of it), but in defect and privation of perfection. As when a hand draweth a line by a crooked rule, the line is from the hand, but the crookedness of it is from the rule : or, as when a man goeth lamely, the motion, as motion, is from the natural faculty, but the lameness of the motion is from the defect and viciousness of the faculty. A swearer could not speak an oath, nor a murderer reach out his hand to strike a blow, but by the force of those natural faculties, which in and from God have all their being and working. But that these natural motions are, by profaneness or malice, directed unto ends morally wicked, this proceedeth from the vitiosity and defect which is in the second cause, making use of God's gifts unto his own dishonour. 2. The providence of God hath a notable hand in the guiding, ordering, and disposing of these actions, as sinful, unto the ends of his own glory, in the declaration of his power, wisdom, and justice,—unto which the sins of wicked men are perforce carried on, contrary to those ends which they themselves in sinning did propose unto themselves. As an artificer[c] useth the force of natural causes unto artificial effects ; as a huntsman useth the natural enmity of the

---

[a] Vid. *Aug.* Enchirid. ad Laurent. c. 95, 96, 97, 98. [b] Matth. xviii. 25, 26. Rom. ix. 18, 21. xi. 33, 36. Ephes. i. 5, 9, 11. Psalm cxxxv. 6. [c] Vid. *Aug.* de Civ. Dei, lib. 1. cap. 17. et lib. 14. cap. 26. qu. super Exod. li. et quæst. 18. de peccat. orig. l. 2. c. 34 et 40. Epist. 59. in solut. q. 6. contra Julian. Pelag. lib. 5. cap. 3 et 4 de Grat. et Lib. Arbit. cap. 20, 21. Epist. 130 et 141. Ut medici fœdorum animalium felle aut coagulo utuntur ad morbos sanandos ; vid. *Plut.* de sera numinis vindicta.—Quid tam elaboratum et distortum, quam est ille Discobolos Myronis ? Si quis tamen, ut parum rectum, improbet opus, nonne ab intellectu artis abfuerit ? *Quintil.* lib. 2. Instit. cap. 13. Spalding, vol. i. p. 333.—*Plutarch.* Sympos. l. 5. c. 1.—Vide *Field* of the Church, l. 1. cap. 1.—*Aug.* de Civ. Dei, l. 12. cap.

dog against the fox or wolf, unto the preservation of the
lands, which otherwise would be destroyed ; though the
dog himself by nature is as great an enemy to the lamb as
the fox.   As the Pharisees were as great enemies to religion
as the Sadducees, yet Paul wisely made use of their enmity
amongst themselves for his own preservation and deliverance
from them both.   Nothing more usual than for God to manage and direct the sins of men, to the bringing about of his
own purposes and counsels [d].   But now unto gracious actions, which belong not at all unto nature as nature, but
only as inspired and actuated with spiritual and heavenly
principles,—a more singular and notable influence of God is
required, not only to the substance of the action, but more
especially to the rectitude and goodness of it : for we have
no sufficiency of ourselves, not so much as unto the first
offers and beginnings of good in our thoughts [e].   When we
are bid " to work out our own salvation with fear and trembling," it must be in dependence on the power, and in confidence of the aid of God ; for " it is he that worketh in us,
both to will and to do [f]."   When we covenant to turn unto
God, we must withal "pray unto him to turn us [g]."   God
commands us " to turn ourselves, and to make us a new
heart and a new spirit, that we may live [h] ;" but withal he
telleth us, that it is " he who gives us one heart, and one
way, and a new spirit, that we may walk in his statutes [i]."
He giveth us ' posse, velle, agere, proficere ;' the power to
make us able,—the heart to make us willing,—the act to
walk,—the proficiency to improve,—the perseverance to finish and perfect holiness.   David cannot run in the way of
God's commandments, till he enlarge his heart [k].   Nothing
can find the way to Heaven, but that which comes first from
Heaven [l].   We cannot give unto God any thing but of his
own.   " Who am I," saith David, " and what is my people,
that we should be able to offer so willingly after this sort ?
For all things are of thee, and of thine own we have given
thee [m]."

d Gen. l. 20. 1 Sam. ii. 25, 1 Kings ii. 26, 27. 2 Sam. xii. 11. compared with
2 Sam. xvi. 22. Isai. x. 5, 6, 7. Acts iv. 28. Psalm lxxvi. 10.   e 2 Cor. iii. 5.
f Phil. ii. 11, 12, 13.   g Lam. v. 21. Jer. xxxi.   h Ezek. xviii. 30, 31, 32.
i Ezek. xi. 19, 20. Jer. xxxii. 39.   k Psalm cxix. 32.   l John ii. 13.
m 1 Chron. xxix. 14.

SECT. 6. For the further understanding of this point, and of the sweet concord and concurrence between the will of man converted, and the effectual grace of God converting, we shall set down these few propositions [n].

1. That there is in man, by nature, a power or faculty which we call free-will, whereunto belongeth such an indifferency and indeterminacy in the manner of working, that whether a man will a thing, or nill it,—choose it, or turn from it,—he doth in neither move contrary to his own natural principles of working. A stone, moving downward, doth move naturally; upward, contrary to its nature,—and so violently. But which way soever the will moves, it moves according to the condition of its created being,—wherein it was so made, as when it chose one part of a contradiction, it [o] retained an inward and fundamental habitude unto the other; like those gates, which are so made, as that they open both ways. So that as the tongue, which was wont to swear or blaspheme, when it is converted, doth, by the force of the same faculty of speaking, being newly sanctified, utter holy and gracious speeches;—so the will, which, being corrupted, did choose evil and only evil, being sanctified, doth use the same manner of operation in choosing that which is good; the created nature of it remaining still one and the same, being now guided and sanctified by different principles. This we speak only with respect to the natural manner of its working: for if we speak of liberty in a moral or theological sense [p], so it is certain, that the more the will of man doth observe the right order of its proper objects, and last end, the more free and noble it is; the very highest perfection of free-will standing in an immutable adherency unto God, as the ultimate end of the creature,—and all ability of receding or falling from him being the deficiency, and not the perfection, of free-will: and therefore the more the will of man doth

---

[u] Vid. *Calvin.* in Ezek. xi. 19, 20.—et *Aug.* contr. 2. Epist. Pelag. lib. 1. cap. 2. et lib. 2. cap. 5.   [o] Folio-Edition, p. 581.   [p] *Gibœuf.* de Libert. Creat. l. 1.—Melior est, cum totus hæret atque constringitur incommutabili Bono, quam cum inde vel ad seipsum relaxatur: *Aug.* de Doct. Christ. l. 5. c. 22.— Libero arbitrio male utens homo et se perdidit et ipsum. Sicut enim qui se occidit, utique vivendo se occidit, sed se occidendo non vivit, nec seipsum potest resuscitare, cum occiderit; ita cum libero peccaretur arbitrio, victore peccato amissum est et liberum arbitrium : *Aug.* Enchirid. c. 30. et Epist. 107.

cast off and reject God, the more base, servile, and captive it grows. In which sense we affirm against the papists, That by nature, man, since the fall of Adam, hath no free-will or natural power to believe and convert unto God, or to prepare himself thereunto.

2. In man fallen, and being thereby, universally, in all his faculties, leavened with vicious and malignant principles, there is a native pravity and corrupt force, which putteth forth itself in resisting all those powerful workings of the Word and Spirit of grace, that oppose themselves against the body of sin, and move the will unto holy resolutions: for the wisdom of the flesh cannot be subject to the law of God[q]. The flesh will lust against the spirit, as being contrary thereunto[r]. An uncircumcised heart will always resist the Holy Spirit[s]. There is such a natural antipathy between the purity of the Word, and the impurity of the will of man, that he naturally refuseth to hear, and snuffeth at it, and pulleth away the shoulder, and hardeneth the heart, and stoppeth the ears, and shutteth the eyes, and setteth up strong holds and high reasonings against the ways of God; and is never so well as when he can get off all sights and thoughts of God, and be, as it were, without God in the world[t].

3. According to the degrees and remainders of this natural corruption, so far forth as it is unmortified and unsubdued by the power of grace, this original force doth proportionably put forth itself in withstanding and warring against the Spirit of God[u], even in the regenerate themselves. A notable example whereof we have in Asa, of whom it is said, that he was wroth with Hanani the Seer, and put him in a prison-house, and was in rage with him, when he reproved him for his carnal confidence[x]. And the apostle doth, in many words, both state and bewail the warring of the law of his members against the law of his mind,—so that when he did, with the one, serve the law of God,—he did with the other

[q] Rom. viii. 7. [r] Gal. v. 17. [s] Acts vii. 51. [t] Jer. v. 3. vi. 10, 17, 23. xix. 15. Mal. i. 13. 2 Chron. xxxvi. 16. [u] Habitat in eis, et mentem resistentem repugnantemque solicitat, ut ipso conflictu etiamsi non sit damnabilis, quia non perficit iniquitatem,—sit miserabilis tamen, quia non habet pacem: *Aug.* de nupt. et concupis. lib. 2. cap. 2. contra Julian. Pelag. lib. 5. cap. 7. [x] 2 Chron. xvi. 10.

serve the law of sin, and was unable to do the thing which
he would; and the evil which he would not, he did do by
the strength of sin that dwelled in him [y].

Sect. 7.—4. We are to distinguish of the wills of God,
which are set forth in Scripture, two manner of ways. There is
' voluntas signi,' or that will of God, whereby he requires us
to work, and which he hath appointed to be observed by us;
his will signified in precepts and prohibitions. " This is the
will of God," saith the apostle, " even your sanctification [z]."
So we are said " to prove, to try, to do God's will, or that
which is pleasing in his sight [a]."—And there is ' voluntas
beneplaciti [b],' the will of his purpose and counsel; according unto which he himself, in his own secret and unsearchable good pleasure, is pleased to work; for he worketh all
things after the counsel of his own will [c]. Whatsoever the
Lord pleaseth, that he doth in heaven and earth [d]. And no
second causes can do any thing else, though they never so
proudly break the order of God's revealed will, but what his
hand and counsel had before determined [e]. The will of God's
precept and command is every day violated, resisted, and
broken through by wicked men unto their own destruction.
" How often would I, and ye would not [f]!" But the will of
God's counsel and purpose cannot be resisted nor withstood
by all the powers of the world; the counsel of the Lord must
stand; and [g] those very agents that work purposely to disappoint and subvert it, do, by those very workings of theirs,
bring it to pass:—and when by their own intentions they are
enemies to it, by God's wonderful ordering and directing
they [h] are executioners of it [i].

5. According unto this distinction of God's will, we are
to distinguish of his call. Some are called ' voluntate signi,'

[y] Rom. vii. 14, 15.   [z] 1 Thes. iv. 3.   [a] Matth. vii. 21. Rom. xii. 2.
John viii. 29.   [b] Aquin. Part. 1. qu. 19. art. 11.   [c] Ephes. i. 11.
[d] Psalm cxxxv. 6.   [e] Acts iv. 28.   [f] Matth. xxiii. 37. Jer. xiii. 11.
[g] Multa fiunt à malis contra voluntatem Dei, sed tantæ est ille sapientiæ tantæ-
que virtutis, ut in eos exitus sive fines, quos bonos et justos ipse præscivit, ten-
dant omnia, quæ voluntati ejus videntur adversa : Aug. de Civ. Dei, lib. 22. c. 1.
Alii obediunt, alligantur; nemo leges Omnipotentis evadit :—de Agone Christiano,
6, 7.—Vid. Bradwardin. de Causa Dei, lib. 1. cap. 32. et Hug. de Sanct. Victor.
Sum. Sentent. Tract. 1. cap. 13. et de Sacrament. lib. 1. part. 2. cap. 19, 20. et
part. 3. cap. 5, 6, 13, 14, 15.—Anselm. lib. 1. Cur Deus homo, c. 15. Lumbard,
lib. 1. dist. 17.   [h] Folio-edition, p. 582.   [i] Rom. ix. 19. Psalm xxxiii. 11.
cxv. 2. Prov. xix. 21. Isai. xlvi. 10. Josh. xxiv. 9, 10.

by the will of his precept, when they have the will of God
made known unto them, and are thereby persuaded unto the
obedience of it in the ministry of the gospel: in which sense
our Saviour saith, " Many are called, but few chosen[k]." And
unto those who refuse to come unto him, that they might
have life, he yet saith, " These things I say, that ye might
be saved[l] "—Others are called ' voluntate beneplaciti,'—ordained first unto eternal life by the free love and grace of
God, and then thereunto brought by the execution of that
his decree and purpose, in the powerful calling and transla-
ting them from darkness unto light. And this is to be called
κατὰ πρόθεσιν, "according unto purpose[m]," namely, the purpose
and counsel of showing mercy to whom he will show mercy[n].

6. They who are called, only as the hen calleth her
chicken, with the mere outward call or voice of Christ in the
evangelical ministry, may and do resist this call, and so
perish. Chorazin, and Bethsaida, and Capernaum, were outwardly called by the most powerful ministerial means that
ever the world enjoyed, both in doctrine and miracles; and
yet our Saviour tells them, that they shall be in a worse condition in the day of judgement, than Tyre, Sidon, or Sodom[o].
So the prophet complains, " Who hath believed our report,
or to whom is the arm of the Lord revealed[p] ?" which the
evangelist applies unto the argument of conversion[q] : for so
the hand or arm of the Lord is said to be with his ministers,
when, by their ministry, men do turn to the Lord[r]. And
the same prophet again, or Christ in him, complains, " All
the day long, have I stretched forth my hands unto a disobedient and gainsaying people[s] :" so disobedient and gainsaying, that we find them resolve sometimes point blank contrary to the call of God[t].

SECT. 8.—7. They who are called inwardly and spiritually with a heavenly call, ' vocatione alta et secundum
propositum,' with such a call as pursueth the counsel and
purpose of God for their salvation, though they do resist

---

[k] Matth. xx. 16.   [l] John v. 34, 40.   [m] Vocatio alta et secreta, quâ
fit ut legi atque doctrinæ accommodemus assensum : *Aug.* ep. 107.—Vocatio,
quâ fit credens : de Prædest. Sanct. c. 16, 17. Rom. viii. 28.   [n] Rom. viii. 19.
[o] Matth. xi. 21, 24.   [p] Isai. liii. 1.   [q] John xii. 37, 40.   [r] Acts
xi. 21.   [s] Isai. lxv. 2. Rom. x. 21.   [t] Jer. xliv. 16, 17. xviii. 11, 12.
ii. 25. Matth. xxiii. 27.

'quoad pugnam,' and corruption in them doth strive to bear up against the grace of Christ,—yet they do not resist finally and 'quoad eventum,' unto the repelling or defeating of the operation of God's effectual grace : but they are thereby framed to embrace, approve, and submit unto that call, God himself working a good will in them[u], captivating their thoughts unto the obedience of Christ, and working in them that which is pleasing in his own sight[x].

And this is done by a double act :—

SECT. 9.—1. An act of spiritual teaching, and irradiating the mind and judgement with heavenly light, called, by the prophet, 'the writing of the law in the heart, and putting it into the inward parts[y],'—and by our Saviour, 'the Father's teaching,' John. vi. 45. and the Holy Spirit's "convincing of sin, righteousness and judgement[z],"—and by the apostle, "a demonstration of the Spirit and power[a]," 'a spiritual revelation of wisdom out of the Word unto the conscience[b].' For though we are to condemn fanatic revelations besides the Word, and without it,—yet we must acknowledge spiritual revelation, or manifestation of the divine light and power of the Word, by the Holy Spirit, in the minds of men convert-ed : for the Word of God, being a spiritual object, doth, unto the salvifical knowledge of it, require such a spiritual quality[c] in the faculty which must know it, as may be able to pass a right judgement upon it ; for spiritual things are spiritually discerned[d]. It is true, the hypocrites and other wicked men may have very much notional and intellectual knowledge of the scriptures, and those holy things therein revealed[e]; but none of that knowledge amounteth unto that,

---

[u] Illud nescio quomodo dicitur, 'frustra Deum misereri nisi nos velimus.' Si enim Deus misereretur, etiam volumus ; ad eandem quippe misericordiam pertinet, ut velimus : *Aug.* ad Simplician. lib. 1. qu. 2.—Hæc gratia, quæ occulte humanis cordibus divina largitate tribuitur, à nullo duro corde respuitur : ideo quippe tribuitur, ut cordis duritia primitus auferatur :—De Prædestin. Sanct. c. 8. et contr. 2. ep. Pelag. l. 1. c. 10.   [x] Phil. ii. 13. 2 Cor. xix. 5. Heb. xiii. 21. [y] Jer. xxxi. 23. 2 Cor. iii. 3.   [z] John xvi. 8, 11.   [a] 1 Cor. ii. 4. [b] Ephes. i. 17.   [c] Cibus in somnis simillimus est cibis vigilantium, quo ta-men dormientes non aluntur : *Aug.* conf. l. 3. c. 6. Sol non omnes quibus lucet, etiam calefacit : sic sapientia multos, quos docet, non continuo etiam accendit : aliud est multas divitias scire, aliud possidere : nec notitia divitem facit, sed possessio : *Bern.* in Cant. Ser. 23.—Τήρησις ἐντολῶν γνῶσις τοῦ Θεοῦ. *Basil.* de Martyre manente.—Hominis sapientia pietas est : *Aug.* Enchir. c. 2. de Doctr. Christiana. l. 2. c. 6, 7. et l. l.c. 35.   [d] 1 Cor. ii. 14.   [e] Heb. vi. 4. 1 Pet. ii. 21.

which is called ' the teaching of God, and a spiritual demonstration:'—for the mysteries of the gospel were unto this end
revealed, that by them we might be brought unto the obedience of Christ; and therefore the knowledge of them is
never proportioned or commensurate to the object, till the
mind be thereby[f] made conformed unto Christ; till the conceptions which are framed in us touching God, and sin, and
grace, and heaven, and eternal things, be suitable to those
which were in the mind of Christ[g]. Evangelical truths are
not fitted unto mere intellectual, but unto practical judgement. It is such a knowledge of Christ, as may fill us with
the fulness of God[h]; a knowledge that must work communion with Christ, and conformity unto him[i]; a knowledge
that must produce a good conversation[k]. "He that saith
he knoweth him, and keepeth not his commandments, is a
liar, and the truth is not in him[l]." We do not know Christ,
till we know him as our chiefest good, as our choicest treasure, as our unsearchable riches, as elect, and precious, and
desirable, and altogether lovely, and the fairest of ten thousand, and worthy all acceptation; in comparison of whom,
all the world besides is as dung. The knowledge of Christ
is not seeing only, but seeing and tasting[m]. And therefore
they who, in one sense, are said to have known God, Rom.
i. 23. are yet in the same place, verse 28. said not to have
God in their knowledge. It is an excellent speech of the
philosopher, that " such as every man is in himself, such
is the end that he works unto, and such notions he hath of
that good which is his end."—And therefore it is impossible,
that a wicked frame of heart can ever look upon any supernatural object as his last end, or as principally desirable. If
I should see a man choose a small trifle before a rich jewel,
however he should profess to know the excellency, and to
value the richness, of that jewel; yet I should conclude, that
he did not indeed understand the worth of it aright. And
therefore unto the perfect and proper knowledge of supernatural things, there is required a special work of the grace
and spirit of Christ, opening the heart, and working it to a
spiritual constitution, proportionable to such kind of truths

f Folio-Edition, p. 583   g 1 Cor. ii. 16.   h Ephes. iii. 18, 19.
i Phil. iii. 10.   k James iii. 15.   l 1 John ii. 3, 4.   m Psalm
xxxiv. 8. cxix. 103.

about which it is conversant. The Scripture every where
attributeth this work unto God [n], and his Spirit. It is he
that giveth a heart to perceive, and eyes to see, and ears to
hear [o]. It is he that giveth a heart to know him [p]. It is
he that manifesteth himself unto those that love him [q]. It
is he that revealeth unto us by his Spirit the things of God [r].
It is he that giveth us an understanding [s], and that opens the
understanding to understand the scriptures [t]. It is he that
teacheth us to call Christ ' our Lord [u];' for the voice of carnal and corrupt reason is, " We will not have this man to
reign over us [x]." Every man naturally frameth and shapeth
his notions of doctrinal matters unto the manner of his conscience and conversation, embracing that which is consonant,
and rejecting that which is dissonant, thereunto [y]. " To the
unclean, every thing is unclean," because the very " mind
and conscience of such men is defiled [z]." This then is the
first work in effectual calling,—the opening of the eye of the
mind rightly to conceive of the things of God, of the guilt
of sin, of the heaviness of wrath, of the peril of perishing,
of the weight and moment of damnation and salvation, of the
things that concern its everlasting peace, of the righteousness of Christ, of the beauties of holiness, of the exceeding
abundant weight of glory, of the comforts of the Holy Spirit,
and the unspeakable and glorious joy, shed forth into the
heart by believing. These truths the heart is so convinced
of, as seriously to ponder them, and to fix its deepest and
saddest considerations upon them.

SECT. 10.—2. An act of spiritual inclining and effectual
determining the will of man to embrace the ultimate dictate
of a mind thus enlightened,—and to make a most free, spontaneous, and joyful choice of supernatural good things thus
rightly apprehended, upon a clear and deliberate consideration of their excellency above all other things [a]. This act of
' choosing' the Lord for our portion and chiefest good, and
of ' cleaving' unto him, we find often mentioned in the

---

[n] Deum scire nemo potest, nisi Deo docente : sine Deo, non cognoscitur
Deus : *Iren.* l. 4. c. 14.—A Deo discendum est quid de Deo intelligendum sit ;
quia non, nisi se Auctore, cognoscitur : *Hil.* de Trin. l. 5.   [o] Deut. xxix. 5.
[p] Jer. xxiv. 7.   [q] John xv. 21.   [r] 1 Cor. ii. 10.   [s] 1 John v 20.
[t] Luke xxiv. 45. Acts xvi. 14.   [u] Matth. xvi. 17. 1 Cor. xii. 3.
[x] Luke xix. 14.   [y] Mic. ii. 11 Isai. xxx. 10, 11.   [z] Tit. i. 15.
[a] Phil. iii. 8.

Scripture [b]. For when the soul of a man is so thoroughly, by
God's teaching [c], convinced of the danger and misery of sin,
wherein, so long as a man continueth, he lives only to dishonour God, and to undo himself; of the benefit of righteousness in Christ, whereby he is reconciled unto God, and
adopted unto a glorious inheritance; and of the beauty of
holiness, whereby he is conformed unto Christ his head, and
fitted for the inheritance; these previous acts of heavenly
teaching, are always seconded with effectual operations upon
the will, suitable unto themselves: for the liberty of the will
doth not stand in a peremptory indifferency unto any object whatsoever; else there should be no liberty in heaven;
—this is a defect and imperfection, not any matter of power
or freedom. "Misera vis est valere ad nocendum." But
the liberty of will standeth in this,—that, being a reasonable
appetite, it is apt to be led one way or another, to choose
one thing or another [d], according to the dictates of reason,
and 'servato ordine finis,' with subjection to that which is
made appear to be the supreme end and happiness of the
soul: for every faculty is naturally subservient to the ultimate good of that nature whereof it is a faculty, and should
monstrously exorbitate from its use and end, if it should put
forth itself to the destruction, or refuse to close with that
which is the happiness of the soul unto which it pertains.
As soon as ever therefore the Spirit of grace doth, by such a
spiritual and practical demonstration as hath been described,
set forth God in Christ as the supreme and most unquestion-
able end and happiness of the soul, there are consequently
suitable impressions upon the will, determining it unto
operations conform unto such a beautiful and glorious object,
and enlarging it to run into this centre, to renounce all
other things, and to cleave only unto this.

And these acts upon the will are:—

1. By preventing grace, it is bended and excited unto
heavenly apparitions, and unto the choice of such spiritual

[b] Deut. xxx. 19. Josh. xxiv. 22. Psalm lxxxiv. 10. Heb. xi. 25. Acts xi. 23.
Psalm cxix. 30, 31, 173.   [c] Operatur Deus in cordibus quid aliud quam voluntatem? *Aug.* ep. 107.   Certum est nos velle cum volumus; sed ipse facit ut
velimus, præbendo vires efficacissimas voluntati :—De Grat. et Lib. Arbit. c. 16.
Folio-Edition. p. 584.

good things, the sovereign excellencies whereof have been so sweetly represented. Good is the object of the will: we cannot will evil under the notion of evil: and amongst good things, that which is by the practical judgement resolved to be best, and that, by the teaching of God himself, who neither is deceived nor can deceive, is the object of the will's election. And thus God, by his exciting grace, worketh in us 'ipsum velle,' that every act whereby we choose Christ and subscribe our name in the call of his soldiers and servants, answering the call of God by a most cheerful consent thereunto.

2. By assisting and co-operating grace [e], it is further enabled to put forth this good will into deed, and so to work towards its salvation [f].

Lastly, By subsequent grace, it is carried on towards perfection, to finish what was begun; and so to proceed from the beginning of faith in vocation, to the end of faith in salvation,—the Spirit of Christ working in us, as he himself did work for us, unto a 'consummatum est,' saving to "the uttermost those that come unto God by him [g]."

And, by this means, the native obstinacy of the will, both in and after conversion, is subdued; so that it neither doth nor can overcome the grace of God, working effectually with his Word: First, Because of the purpose of God, to show mercy where he will show mercy, which can in nowise be resisted. Secondly, Because of the power of God, in the effectual applying of that mercy unto the souls of men with admirable sweetness, with undeniable evidence, with ineffable persuasion, with omnipotent and invincible energy; which no hardness of heart is able to refuse, because the proper operation of it is to take away that hardness which would refuse it, and that by an act of equal power with that "whereby Christ was raised from the dead," which all the world was not able to hinder or prevent [h]. Thus we see, though we desire, and endeavour, and purpose, and cove-

---

[e] Cooperando perficit, quod operando incipit: ut velimus, sine nobis operatur; cum volumus, nobiscum cooperatur: *Aug.* de Grat. et Lib. Arbit. c. 17.—Enchirid. c. 32.—de nat. et grat. cap. 31. contr. 2. ep. Pelag. l. 2. c. ult.—Non mihi sufficit, quod semel donavit, nisi semper donaverit: Peto ut accipiam; et cum accepero, rursus peto, &c. *Hier.* ep. [f] Isai. xxvi. 12. 1 Cor. xv. 10. [g] Phil. i. 6. 1 Pet. ii. 10. Ephes. iv. 13. Heb. vii. 25. [h] Ephes. i. 19. Col. ii. 12. 1 Pet. i. 5.

nant conversion and amendment of life ; yet the whole progress of conversion, our promises, our covenants, our abilities, our sufficiences to make good any thing, do all receive
their stability from the grace of God.

SECT. 11. From whence we learn, First, Not to put confidence in our own studies, vows, purposes, promises of new
obedience. "Every man is a liar;" no sooner left unto
himself, but he becomes a miserable spectacle of weakness
and mutability. Even Adam in innocency [i], when he was
to be supported and persevere by his own strength, though
he had no sin or inward corruption to betray him, how suddenly was he thrown down from his excellency by Satan
with a poor and slender temptation! how strangely did a
creature of so high and noble a constitution exchange God
himself for the fruit of a tree, believe a serpent before a
Maker, and was so miserably cheated as to suppose, that, by
casting away God's image, he should become the more like
him! Who could have thought, that David, a man after
God's own heart, with one miscarrying glance of his eye,
should have been plunged into such a gulf of sin and misery
as he fell into? that so spiritual and heavenly a soul should
be so suddenly overcome with so sensual a temptation? that
so merciful and righteous a man should so greatly wrong a
faithful servant, as he did Uriah, and then make the innocent blood of him whom he wronged, a mantle to palliate
and to cover the wrong, and make use of his fidelity to convey the letters [j] and instructions for his own ruin? Who
could have thought, that Lot, so soon after he had been delivered from fire and brimstone, and vexed with the filthy
conversation of the Sodomites, should be himself inflamed
with unnatural incestuous lust? Who could have suspected,
that Peter, who had his name from a rock, should be so
soon shaken like a reed,—and after so solemn a protestation
not to forsake Christ, though all else should, to be driven [k]
with the voice of a maid from his steadfastness, and with
oaths and curses to be the first that denied him? Surely
"every man," in his best estate, "is altogether vanity."

Therefore it behoveth us to be always humbled in the
sight of ourselves, and to be jealous, 1st. Of our original

i Vid. *Aug.* de correp. et grat. c. 11.   j Ut Bellerophon literas in seipsum
scriptas ferebat. *Hom.* ll. 2. et *Plut.* de Curiositate.   k Folio-Edition, p. 585.

impotency unto the doing of any good, unto the forbearing
of any evil, unto the repelling of any temptation by our own
power. "In his own might, shall no man be strong [k]." To
be a 'sinner,' and to be 'without strength,' are terms equivalent in the apostle [l]. Nay, even where there is a will to do
good, there is a defect of power to perform it [m]: our
strength is not in ourselves, but in the Lord, and in the
power of his might, and in the working of his Spirit in our
inner man [n]. If but a good thought arise in our mind, or a
good desire and motion be stirring in our heart, or a good
word drop from our lips,—we have great cause to take notice of the grace of God that offered it to us, and wrought it
in us, and to admire how any of the fruit of Paradise could
grow in so heathy a wilderness.

2d. Of our natural antipathy and reluctancy unto holy
duties: our aptness to draw back towards perdition; to refuse and thrust away the offers and motions of grace; our
rebellion which ariseth from the law of the members against
the law of the mind; the continual droppings of a corrupt
heart upon any of the tender buds and sproutings of piety
that are wrought within us; our aptness to be weary of
the yoke, and to shake off the burden of Christ from our
shoulders [o]; our natural levity [p] and inconstancy of spirit in
any holy resolutions, continuing as a morning dew, which
presently is dried up; beginning in the spirit, and ending in
the flesh, having interchangeable fits of the one and the
other; like the polypus, now of one colour, and anon of
another; now hot with zeal, and anon cold with security;
now following Moses with songs of thanksgiving for deliverance out of Egypt, and, quickly after, thrusting Moses
away, and in heart returning unto Egypt again. Such a
discomposedness and natural instability there is in the spirit of a man, that, like strings in an instrument, it is apt to
be altered with every change of weather: nay, while you are
playing on it, you must ever and anon be new tuning it;
like water heated, which is always offering to reduce itself
to its own coldness. No longer sun, no longer light; no

---

[k] 1 Sam. ii. 9.   [l] Rom. v. 6, 8.   [m] Rom. vii. 18.   [n] Ephes.
vi. 10. iii. 19. Phil. iv. 13.   [o] Isai. xliii. 22.   [p] Hoc habent inter
cætera boni mores, placent sibi et permanent. Levis est malitia, sæpe mutatur.
Senec. Epist. 47. Maximum indicium est malæ mentis, fluctuatio. Epist. 120.

longer Christ, no longer grace: if his back be at any time
upon us, our back will immediately be turned from him;
like those forgetful creatures in Seneca, who even while they
are eating, if they happen to look aside from their meat,
immediately lose the thoughts of it, and go about seeking
for more.

3d. Of the manifold decays and abatements of the grace
of God in us, our aptness to leave our first love q. How did
Hezekiah fall into an impolitic vain-glory r, in showing all
his treasures unto the ambassadors of a foreign prince,
thereby kindling a desire in him to be master of so rich a
land, as soon as God left him unto himself s. How quickly,
without continual husbandry, will a garden or vineyard be
wasted and overgrown with weeds! How easily is a ship,
when it is at the very shore, carried with a storm back into
the sea again! How quickly will a curious watch, if it lie
open, gather dust into the wheels, and be out of order!
Though, therefore, thou have found sweetness in religion,
joy in the Holy Spirit, comfort, yea, heaven in good duties,
power against corruptions, strength against temptations,
triumph over afflictions, assurance of God's favour, vigour,
life, and great enlargement of heart in the ways of godliness;
yet for all this, be not high-minded, but fear. Remember
the flower that is wide open in the morning, when the sun
shines upon it, may be shut up in the evening before night
come. If the sun had not stood still, Joshua had not taken
vengeance on the enemy t; and if the Sun of righteousness do not constantly shine upon us, and supply us, we
shall not be able to pursue and carry on any victorious
affections. While God ' openeth his hand,' thou art ' filled;'
but if he ' withdraw his face,' thou wilt be ' troubled' again u.
Therefore take heed of resting on thine own wisdom or
strength. Thou mayest, after all this, grieve the Spirit of God,
and cause him to depart and hide himself from thee: thou
mayest fall from thy steadfastness, and lose thy wonted comforts: thou mayest have a dead winter upon the face of thy

q Rev. ii. 4.   r Lege Imperiali, interdicta vini, olei, liquaminis exporta-
tio; ne Barbari, gustu illecti, promptius invaderent fines Romanorum, Leg. 1.
Cod. quæ res exportari non debeant.—Et apud Chineses, exteri in loca regni in-
teriora non admittuntur, tantum in oris maritimis conceditur commercium.—
Boterus in Catalog. Imperiorum.   s 2 Kings xx. 12, 13.   t Josh. x. 13.
u Psalm civ. 28, 29.

conscience, and be brought to such a sad and disconsolate condition, as to conclude that God hath cast thee out of his sight, that he hath forgotten to be gracious, and hath shut up his loving-kindness in displeasure; to roar out for anguish of spirit, as one whose bones are broken: thy soul may draw nigh to the grave, and thy life to the destroyers, and thou mayest find it a woful and a most insuperable difficulty to recover thy life and strength again.   It was so with Job[w].   It was so with David[x].   It[y] was so with Heman[z], and divers others[a].   Therefore we should still remember in a calm to provide for a storm ; to stir up the graces of God continually in ourselves, that they be not quenched[b]; so to rejoice in the Lord, as withal to work out our own salvation with fear and trembling[c] ; never to let the grace of God puff us up, or make us forgetful of our own weakness; but, as the apostle saith of himself in regard of God's grace, " When I am weak, then am I strong[d] ;" so to say of ourselves in regard of our own natural corruption, " When I am strong, then I am weak."

SECT. 12. Secondly, This must not so humble us, as to deject and dismay us, or make us give over the hope of holding out to the end, when our nature is so weak, our enemies so strong, our temptations so many ; but we must withal be quickened by these considerations, with prayer to implore, and with faith to rely on and draw, strength from the Word and grace of God; to have always the window of the soul open towards the Sun of righteousness, whereby the supplies of his grace to prevent, excite, assist, follow, establish us, and carry on every good thing which he hath begun for us, may be continually admitted.   This is one of the most necessary duties for a Christian, To hold constant and fixed purposes in godliness: the Scripture frequently calls upon us for them, that "with purpose of heart we should cleave unto God[e] :" that we should " continue in the grace of God[f]:" that we should be " rooted and grounded in love[g] :"   that we would " hold fast the pro-

---

[w] Job x. 16, 17.   xiii. 26, 27, 28.   xvi. 9, 13.   xxx. 15, 31.   [x] Psalm li. 8. lxxvii. 2, 3, 4.   [y] Folio-Edition, p. 586.   [z] Psalm lxxxviii. [a] See Job xxxiii. 19, 22.   Psalm x. 3, 11.   Isai. liv. 6, 11.   John ii. 3, 4. [b] 2 Tim. i. 6.   [c] Psalm ii. 11. Phil. ii. 12, 13.   [d] 2 Cor. xii. 10. [e] Acts xi. 23.   [f] Acts xiii. 43.   [g] Ephes. iii. 17.

fession of our faith without wavering [h]:" that we would
be "steadfast and unmovable, always abounding in the
work of the Lord [i]:" that we would look to ourselves, that
we may not "lose the things which we have wrought [k]:"
that we would "hold fast and keep the works of Christ
unto the end [l]." And it is that which godly men are most
earnestly solicitous about, and do strive unto with greatest
importunity. "I have purposed that my mouth shall not
transgress [m]." "Unite my heart to fear thy name [n]." "My
heart is fixed to God, my heart is fixed; I will sing and
give praise [o]." Therefore in this case it is necessary for us
to draw nigh unto God, who only can ratify all our pious
resolutions; "who giveth power to the faint, and to them
that have no power, increaseth strength [p];" who only can
"settle and stablish the hearts of men [q]." The conscience
of our duty, the sense of our frailty, the power, malice, and
cunning of our enemies, the obligation of our covenant,
should direct the soul perpetually unto God for the supply
of his grace,—that that may, in all our weaknesses, be sufficient for us, and "hold us up, that we may be safe," as the
psalmist speaks [r]; and may never, through infirmity or un-
stableness of spirit, violate our own resolutions.

SECT. 13.—3. This is matter of great comfort unto the
godly, That, in the midst of so many temptations, snares, impediments, amongst which we walk,—not only the safety of
our souls, and security of our eternal salvation, but even our
present condition in this life, our conversion, our obedience,
all our pious purposes of heart, all the progress we make in
a holy conversation,—do not depend upon the weakness and
uncertainty of a human will, but upon the infallible truth,
the constant promise, the immutable purpose, the invincible
power, the free love, the absolute grace, the omnipotent
wisdom and working of God, who doth whatsoever he
pleaseth both in heaven and earth, and worketh all things
by the counsel of his own will. "I, the Lord, change not;
therefore the sons of Jacob are not consumed [s]." We, poor
and weak men, change with every wind; strong to-day, and

---

[h] Heb. x. 23.   [i] 1 Cor. xv. 58.   [k] 2 John verse 8.   [l] Rev.
ii. 25, 26.   [m] Psalm xvii. 3.   [n] Psalm lxxxvi. 11.   [o] Psalm
lvii. 7.   [p] Isai. xl. 29.   [q] 1 P t. v. 10.   [r] Psalm cxix. 117.
[s] Mal. iii. 6.

weak to-morrow; fixed and resolute to-day, shaken and
staggering to-morrow; running forward to-day, and revolting
as fast to-morrow; no hold to be taken of our promises, no
trust to be given to our covenants; like Peter on the water,
we walk one step, and we sink another. All our comfort
is this,—our strength and standing is not founded in
ourselves, but in the rock whereon we are built,—and
in the power of God, by which we are kept through
faith unto salvation,—out of whose hands none are able to
pluck us. Our very actions are wrought in us, and carried on
unto their end by the power of Christ, who hath mercy,
wisdom, and strength enough to rescue us, as from the
power of hell and death, so from the danger of our own
sickly and froward hearts. To see a man, when he is half
a mile from his enemy, draw a sword to encounter him, or
take up a stone to hit him, would be but a ridiculous spectacle; for what could he do with such weapons, by his own
strength, at such a distance? But if he mount a cannon,
and point that level against the enemy; this we do not
wonder at, though the distance be so great; because,
though the action be originally his, yet[t] the effect of it
proceedeth from the force of the materials and instruments
which he useth, to wit, the powder, the bullet, the fire, the
cannon. It seemed absurd, in the eye of the enemy, for
little David, with a shepherd's bag and a sling, to go
against Goliath, an armed giant, and it produced in his proud
heart much disdain and insultation[u]: but when we hear
David mention the name of God, in the strength and confidence whereof he came against so proud an enemy, this
makes us conclude weak David strong enough to encounter
with great Goliath. It is not our own strength, but the love
of God, which is the foundation of our triumph over all
enemies[x].

But some will then say[y], Since we may be secure, if God's

[t] Folio-Edition, p. 587.   [u] 1 Sam. xvii. 41, 42, 43.   [x] Rom.
viii. 38, 39.   [y] Doctrina istius modi apta nata est ad securitatem, omnis re-
ligionis pestem et perniciem, hominibus ingenerandam, &c. Remonstr. in Script.
Dogmaticis circa artic. 5. p. 299.—Nos autem dicimus, humanam voluntatem
sic divinitus adjuvari ad faciendam justitiam, ut accipiat Spiritum Sanctum, quo
fiat in animo ejus delectatio dilectioque summi illius et incommutabilis Boni——
Cum id præstiterit gratia ut moreremur peccato, quid aliud faciemus si vivimus in
eo, nisi ut gratiæ simus ingrati? neque enim qui laudat beneficium medicinæ,

grace and power alone be our strength, let us then commit
ourselves and our salvation unto him, and, in the mean time,
give over all thoughts and care of it ourselves, and live as
we list; no act of ours can frustrate the counsel of the love
of God.—To this we answer with the apostle, " God forbid."
Though the enemies of free grace do thus argue, yet they
who indeed have the grace of God in their hearts, have better learned Christ. For it is against the formal nature of the
grace and Spirit of Christ to suffer those in whom it dwelleth,
to give over themselves unto security and neglect of God:
for grace is a vital and active principle ; and doth so work
in us, as that it doth withal dispose and direct us unto working too. The property of grace is to fight against and to
kill sin, as being most extremely contrary unto it: and therefore it is a most irrational way of arguing, to argue from the
being of grace to the life of sin. " How shall we that are
dead to sin, live any longer therein ᶻ?" If we be dead to
sin, this is argument enough, in the apostle's judgement,
why we should set our affections on things above ᵃ. The
grace of God doth not only serve to bring salvation, but to
" teach us to deny ungodliness and worldly lusts, and to live
soberly, righteously, and godly in this present world ᵇ." He
who hath decreed salvation as the end, hath decreed also
the antecedent means unto that end to be used in manner,
suitable to the condition of reasonable and voluntary agents,
—unto whom it belongs, having their minds by grace enlightened, and their wills by grace prevented, to co-operate
with the same grace in the further pursuance of their salvation. And if at any time corruption should, in God's children, abuse his grace and efficacy unto such presumptuous
resolutions, they would quickly rue so unreasonable and carnal a way of arguing, by the woful sense of God's displeasure in withdrawing the comforts of his grace from them,
which would make them ever after take heed how they turned
the grace of God into wantonness any more. Certainly, the
more the servants of God are assured of his assistance, the
more careful they are in using it unto his own service. Who
more sure of the grace of God than the apostle Paul, who

prodesse morbos dicit, &c. Quos præscivit ut prædestinaret, prædestinavit ut vo-
caret : vocavit ut justificaret ; justificavit ut glorificaret: *Aug.* de Spiritu et Liter.
c. 3, 5, 6, 30.   ᶻ Rom. vi. 2.   ᵃ Col. iii. 2, 3.   ᵇ Tit. ii. 11, 12.

gloried of it as that that made him what he was? " By the
grace of God, I am that I am ;" who knew that God's grace
was sufficient for him, and that nothing could separate him
from the love of Christ; who knew whom he had believed,
and that the grace of the Lord was exceeding abundant towards him ; and yet who more tender and fearful of sin?
who more set against corruption, more abundant in duty,
more pressing unto perfection, than he? This is the nature
of grace, To animate and actuate the faculties of the soul in
God's service, to ratify our covenants, and to enable us to
perform them.

SECT. 14. Fourthly, As it is singular comfort to the servants of God, that their own wills and purposes are in God's
keeping, and so they cannot ruin themselves ; so it is also,
that all other men's wills and resolutions are in God's keeping too, so that they shall not be able to purpose or resolve
on any evil against the church, without leave from him. So
then, first, When the rage and passions of men break out,
tribe divided against tribe, brother against brother, father
against child, head against body ; when the band of unity,
which was wont to knit together this flourishing kingdom,
is broken like the prophet's staff, and there withal the
beauty of the nation miserably withered and decayed, (for
these two go still together, beauty and bands [c],) we must
look on all this as God's own work. It was he that sent an
evil spirit between Abimelech and the men of Shechem, for
the mutual punishment of the sins of one another. It was
he who turned the hearts of the Egyptians to hate his people, and to deal subtilely with them [d]. He sent the Assyrian
against his people, giving them a charge to take the spoil
and the prey, and to tread them down like the mire of the
streets [e]. He appointed the sword of the King of Babylon,
by his overruling direction, to go against Judah, and not
against the Ammonites [f]. He, by the secret command of
his providence, marked some for safety, and gave commission to kill and slay others [g]. It is he who giveth Jacob for
a spoil, and Israel to the robbers, and poureth out upon
them the strength of battle [h]. If there be evil in a city, in

[c] Zach. xi. 10, 14.   [d] Psalm cv. 25.   [e] Isai. x. 6, 16.   [f] Ezek.
xxi. 19, 22.   [g] Folio-Edition, p. 588. Ezek. ix. 4, 5.   [h] Isai. xlii. 24, 25.

a kingdom, the Lord hath done it [i]. This consideration is very useful both to humble us, when we consider that God hath a controversy against the land; and that it is he whom we have to do withal in these sad commotions, that are in the kingdoms; and to quiet and silence us, that we may not dare to murmur at the course of his wise and righteous proceedings with us; and to direct us with prayer, faith, and patience to implore, and in his good time to expect, such an issue and close, as we are sure shall be for his own glory, and for the manifestation of his mercy towards his people, and his justice towards all that are implacable enemies unto Sion.

2. In the troubles of the church, this is matter of singular comfort, that however enemies may say, 'this and that we will do, hither and thither we will go,'—though they may combine together, and be mutually confederate [k], and gird themselves, and take counsel, and speak the word; yet, in all this, God hath the casting voice. There is little heed to be given unto what Ephraim saith, except God say the same: without him, whatsoever is counselled, shall come to nought; whatsoever is decreed or spoken, shall not stand [l]. We have a lively hypotyposis or description of the swift, confident, and furious march of the great host of Sennacherib towards Jerusalem, with the great terrors and consternation of the inhabitants in every place where they came, weeping, flying, removing their habitations [m]; and when he was advanced unto Nob, from which place the city Jerusalem might be seen, he there shook his hand against Jerusalem, threatening what he would do unto it. And then when the waters were come to the very neck, and the Assyrian was in the height of pride and fury, God sent forth a prohibition against all their resolutions; and that huge army, which was, for pride and number, like the thick trees of Lebanon, were suddenly cut down by a mighty one, to wit, by the angel of the Lord, verse 33, 34. compared with Ezek. xxxi. 3, 10. Isai. xvii. 12, 13, 14, 37, 36. Therefore,

3. Our greatest business is to apply ourselves to God, who alone is the Lord that healeth us, who alone can join

---

[i] Amos iii. 6. Isai. xlv. 7.　　　[k] Psalm lxxxiii. 2, 5.　　　[l] Is. viii. 9, 10.
[m] Isai. x. 28, 29, 30, 31.

the two sticks of Ephraim and Judah, and make them one[n]—
that he would still the raging of the sea, and command a
calm again. He can say, 'Ephraim shall say thus and
thus;'—he hath the hearts of kings, and consequently of all
other men, in his hands [o], and he can turn them as rivers of
water, which way soever he will; as men by art can derive
waters, and divert them from one course to another;—as
they did in the siege of Babylon, as historians tell us[p], whereunto the Scripture seemeth to refer[q]. He can sway, alter,
divert, overrule the purposes of men as it pleaseth him, reconciling lambs and lions unto one another[r], making Israel,
Egypt, and Assyria agree together[s]. He can say to Balaam,
'bless,'—when his mind was to curse[t]. He can turn the
wrath of Laban into a covenant of kindness with Jacob[u];
and when Esau had advantage to execute his threats against
his brother, he can then turn resolutions of cruelty into
kisses[x]. And when Saul had compassed David and his men
round about, and is most likely to take them, he can even
then take him off by a necessary diversion[y]. This is the
comfort of God's people, That whatever men say, except God
say it too, it shall come all to nothing. He can restrain the
wrath of men whensoever it pleaseth him, and he will do it
when it hath proceeded so far as to glorify his power, and to
make way for the more notable manifestation of his goodness to his people[z]. And thus far of God's answer to the
covenant of Ephraim; they promised to renounce idols, and
here God promiseth that they should renounce them.

SECT. 15. Now there are two things more to be observed
from this expression, "What have I to do any more with
idols?" 1. That, in true conversion, God maketh our special sin to be the object of our greatest detestation; which
point hath been opened before. 2. From those words, "any
more," that the nature of true repentance is to 'break sin
off,' as the expression is, Dan. iv. 27; and not to suffer a
man to continue any longer in it[a]. It makes a man esteem

[n] Exod. xv. 26. Ezek. xxvii. 19.　　[o] Prov. xxi. 1.　　[p] *Herodot.* lib. 1.—
Xenophon. Cyropæd. lib. 7.—*Salianus.* Anno mundi. Sect. 5 et 35. Sect. 22.—
Sir *W. Raleigh*, lib. 3. cap. 3. Sect. 5.　　[q] Isai. xliii. 15, 16. xliv. 23, 28.
Jer. l. 23. Jer. li. 36.　　[r] Isai. xi. 6.　　[s] Isai. xix. 24, 25.　　[t] Josh.
xxiv. 10.　　[u] Gen. xxxi. 24, 44.　　[x] Gen. xxxiii. 4.　　[y] 1 Sam.
xxiii. 26, 27, 28.　　[z] Psalm lxxvi. 10.　　[a] Rom. vi. 1, 2.

the time past sufficient to have wrought the will of the Gen-
tiles^a; and is exceeding thrifty of the time to come, so to
redeem it, as that God may have all; doth not linger, nor
delay, nor make objections, or stick at inconveniences, or
raise doubts whether it be seasonable to go out of Egypt and
Sodom or no; is not at the sluggard's language, " modo et
modo," a little more sleep, a little more slumber; nor at
Agrippa's language, " Almost thou persuadest^b me ;" nor
at Felix's language, " When I have a convenient^c season, I
will send for thee ;" but immediately resolves with Paul,
" not to confer with flesh and blood^d," and makes haste " to
fly from the wrath to come," while it is yet to come, before
it overtake us^e: doth not make anxious or cavilling questions, " What shall I do for the hundred talents?" how
shall I maintain my life, my credit, my family? how shall I
keep my friends? how shall I preserve mine interests, or
support mine estate? but ventures the loss of all for the
' excellency of the knowledge of Christ^f;' is contented to
part with a sky full of stars for one Sun of righteousness.
The converts that return to Christ, come like ' dromedaries,'
like ' doves,' like ' ships;' no wings, no sails can carry them
fast enough from their former courses unto him^g. Abraham
is up betimes in the morning, though it be to the sacrificing
of a son^h. David makes haste, and delays not, when he is
to keep God's commandmentsⁱ. When Christ called his disciples, immediately they left their nets, their ship, their father, and followed him^k. This is the mighty power of repentance: it doth not give dilatory answers, it doth not say
to Christ, ' Go away now, and come to-morrow, then I will
hear thee; I am not yet old enough, or rich enough; I have
not gotten yet pleasure, or honour, or profit, or preferment
enough by my sins ;'—but presently it hears and entertains
him:—' I have sinned enough already to condemn, to shame,
to slay me; I have spent time and strength enough already
upon it, for such miserable wages as shame and death come

<hr>

^a 1 Pet. iv. 2, 3.   ^b Folio-Edition, p. 589.   ^c Non erat omnino quod
responderem veritate convictus, nisi tantum verba lenta et somnolenta, ' modo,
ecce modo, sine paululum.' Sed ' modo et modo' non habebant modum. *Aug.*
Confess. lib. 8. c. 5. Da mihi castitatem et continentiam, sed noli modo ; timebam
ne me cito exaudires, et cito sanares. Ibid. cap. 7.   ^d Gal. i. 16.   ^e Luke
iii. 7.   ^f Matth. xiii. 46. Phil. iii. 7, 8.   ^g Isai. lx. 6, 7, 8, 9.   ^h Gen.
xxii. 3.   ⁱ Psalm cxix. 60.   ^k Matth. iv. 20, 22.

to; therefore I will never any more have to do with it.' This is the sweet and most ingenuous voice of repentance: " The thing which I see not, teach me; and if I have done iniquity, I will do no more [1]." There is no sin more contrary to repentance than apostasy; " for godly sorrow worketh repentance unto salvation," which the soul never finds reason to repent of [m]. " Let us therefore take heed of an evil heart of unbelief, in departing from the living God [n], and of drawing back unto perdition [o];" of dismissing our sins, as the Jews did their servants [p], and calling them back again: for Satan usually returns with seven more wicked spirits, and maketh the last state of such a man worse than the first [q]. Ground which hath been a long time laid down from tillage unto pasture, if afterwards it be new broken, will bring a much greater crop of corn than it did formerly, when it was a common field: and so the heart which hath been taken off from sin, if it return to it again, will be much more fruitful than before. As lean bodies have many times the strongest appetite, so lust, when it hath been kept lean, returns with greater hunger unto those objects which feed it. A stream which hath been stopped, will run more violently being once opened again. Therefore, in repentance, we must shake hands with sin for ever, and resolve never more to tamper with it.

SECT. 16. Now in that the Lord saith, " I have heard him, and observed him," we learn hence, First, That God heareth and answereth the prayers only of penitents. When a man resolves, ' I will have no more to do with sin,' then, not till then, doth his prayer find way to God. Impenitency clogs the wing of devotion [r], and stops its passage unto Heaven. The person must be accepted before the petition; Christ Jesus is the priest that offereth, and the altar which sanctifieth, all our services [s]. And Christ will not be their advocate in heaven, who refuse to have him their king on earth. The Scripture is in no point more express than in this, " If I regard iniquity in my heart, the Lord will not

---

[1] Job xxxiv. 32.   [m] 2 Cor. vii. 10, 11.   [n] Heb. iii. 12.   [o] Heb. x. 39.   [p] Jer. xxxiv. 16.   [q] Luke xi. 26.   [r] Solenne erat eos, quibus puræ manus non erant, sacris arceri. *Brisson.* de formul. l. 1.—Etiam impiæ initiationes arcent profanos: *Tert.* Apol.—Quantum à præceptis, tantum ab auribus Dei longe sumus. *Tert.*   [s] 1 Pet. ii. 5. Isai. lvi. 7.

hear me ᵗ." Prayer is a pouring out of the heart; if iniquity be harboured there, prayer is obstructed; and if it
do break out, it will have the scent and savour of that
iniquity upon it. " The sacrifice of the wicked is an
abomination to the Lord ᵘ," both because it is impure
in itself, and because it hath no altar to sanctify it. " He
that turneth away his ear from hearing the law, even his
prayer shall be an abomination ˣ ". Great reason that God
should refuse to hear him, who refuseth to hear God; that
he who will not let God beseech him, (as he doth in his
Word ʸ,) should not be allowed to beseech God ᶻ. His ear is
not heavy that it cannot hear; but iniquity separates between us and him, and hides his face that he will not hear ᵃ.
God heareth not sinners ᵇ. The prevalency of prayer is this,
That it is the prayer of a ' righteous' man ᶜ. And indeed no
wicked man can pray in the true and proper notion of prayer.
It is true, there is a kind of prayer of nature, when men cry
in their distress unto the God and author of nature, for
such good things as nature feeleth the want of; which
God, in the way of his general providence, and common mercies, is sometimes pleased to answer suitably to the natural
desires of those that ask them. But the prayer of faith
(which is the ᵈ true notion of prayer ᵉ) goes not to God as the
author of nature, but as the God of grace, and the Father of
Christ; and doth not put up mere natural, but spiritual requests unto him as to a heavenly Father,—which requests proceed from the Spirit of grace and supplication, teaching us
to pray as we ought ᶠ. So that they who have not the Spirit
of Christ, enabling them to cry " Abba, Father," are not
able to pray a prayer of faith. Prayer hath two wills concurring in it, whenever it is right; our will put forth in desires ᵍ, and God's will respected as the rule of those desires:
for we are not allowed to desire what we will ourselves of
God, but we must ask according to his will ʰ. Now when-

ᵗ Psalm lxvi. 18.   ᵘ Prov. xv. 8.   ˣ Prov. xxviii. 9.   ʸ 2 Cor.
v. 20.   ᶻ Prov. i. 24, 28. Isai. i. 15.   ᵃ Isai. lix. 1, 2. Ezek. viii. 18.
ᵇ John ix. 31.   ᶜ James v. 16.   ᵈ Folio-Edition, p. 590.   ᵉ Rom.
x. 14. James i. 15.   ᶠ Zach. xii. 10. Rom. viii. 26, 27. Gal. iv. 6.
ᵍ Gemendi et interpellandi inspirans affectum. *Aug.* ep. 105. Inspirans desiderium etiam adhuc incognitæ tantæ rei, quam per patientiam expectamus. Ep.
121. c. 15.   ʰ 1 John v. 14.

soever impenitent sinners pray for spiritual things, they do ever pray contrary to one of these two wills: when they pray for mercy and pardon, they pray against God's will, for that which God will not give ; for mercy is proposed to, and provided for, those that forsake sin [i]. He who chooseth to hold fast sin, doth, by his own election, forsake mercy : for the goodness of God leads to repentance [k]. God's mercy is a holy mercy, it will pardon sin forsaken, but it will not protect sin retained.—Again, when they pray for grace, they pray against their own will, for that which they [l] themselves would not have.   It is impossible that a man should formally will the holding fast and continuing in sin (as every impenitent man doth), and, with the same will, should truly desire the receiving of grace, which is destructive to the continuance of sin : and if a wicked man do truly will the grace of God when he prays for it, why doth he refuse the same grace when he heareth it in the ministry of the Word offered unto him ? If God offer it, and he desire it, how comes it not to be received ?   Certainly there is not any thing in the corrupt heart of man, by nature, which can willingly close with any sanctifying grace of the Spirit of Christ.   Self-denial is a concomitant in all acts of grace, and self-seeking, in all acts of lust : and therefore when there is nothing but lust, there can be no real volition of grace, which can be so contrary unto it.

This teacheth us to have penitent resolutions, and spiritual aims in all our prayers, if we would have them prevail at the throne of grace.   We are now under the calamity of a civil war, and very desirous we are it should be removed : we suffer, and languish, and fret, and pine away, and we complain every where of want and violence.   But who sets themselves to cry mightily to God, and call upon their soul as the mariners did upon Jonah, " O thou sleeper, what meanest thou ? arise, call upon God."   Haply we go so far; we pray too, and yet receive no answer, because we ask amiss [m].   We are troubled, that our lusts are abridged of their fuel, or that our nature is deprived of her necessaries ; and for these

---

Prov. xxviii. 13.   k Rom. ii. 4.   l Interdum obnixe petimus, id quod recusaremus, si quis offerret——multa videri volumus velle, sed nolumus.—— Sæpe aliud volumus, aliud optamus ; et verum ne Diis quidem dicimus. Sen. ep. 95. 2.   m James iv. 1, 2, 3.

things we pray. But till our troubles bring us to seek God more than ourselves, make us more sensible of his wrath than of our wants ; more displeased at what offends him, than at what pincheth and oppresseth ourselves ; we cannot promise ourselves an answer of peace. The mariners cried, and the tempest continued still,—Jonah was to be cast over ; so long as there was a fugitive from God in the ship, the storm would not cease. Never can we promise ourselves any comfortable fruit of our prayers, till the aim of them is spiritual, that God may be honoured ; that his church may be cleansed and reformed ; that our lives may be amended ; that whatsoever forsakes God in us, may be cast away. Till " God's whole work be performed upon Mount Sion and upon Jerusalem," we cannot promise ourselves that he will call—in his commission and charge to take the spoil and the prey [n]. And therefore our greatest wisdom is, to consider what God calls for ; to make it our prayer and endeavours that his will and counsel may be fulfilled :—the more we make God our end, the sooner we shall recover our peace again.

Secondly, We learn, That our performance of duty doth depend much upon God's hearing and answering of prayer. Ephraim will have no more to do with idols, because God hath heard him. Prayer is the key of obedience, and the introduction unto duty. The principles of duty are,—wisdom, to know and order them ; will, to desire and intend them ; strength, to perform and persevere in the doing of them : and all these are the product of prayer. " If any want wisdom, let him ask it of God [o]." So Solomon did [p] : " And who am I, and what is my people, saith David, that we should be able to offer so willingly ? for all things come of thee [q]." And the apostle prays for the Ephesians, that God would grant them to be " strengthened with might by his Spirit in the inward man [r]." The principles of duty are the fruits of prayer ; and, therefore, the performance of duty doth much depend on the hearing and answering of prayer.

SECT. 19. Thirdly [s], We learn from God's " observing," or having a careful and vigilant eye upon Ephraim, that when we renounce all carnal and sinful confidence, and cast our-

---

[n] Isai. x. 12.   [o] James i. 5.   [p] 1 Kings iii. 9.   [q] 1 Chron.
xxix. 14.   [r] Ephes. iii. 16.   [s] Folio-Edition, p. 591.

selves wholly upon God, engaging his eye of favour and providence unto us,—this will be a most sufficient protection
against all the cruelties of men. One would think, when
we hear a sword threatened, dashing of infants, ripping of
women, the prophet should have called upon them to take
unto them weapons to make resistance, (and certainly the
use of means in such cases is necessary; the sword of the
Lord doth not exclude the sword of Gideon.) One would
think, "Take to you words," were but a poor preparation
against a destroying enemy; yet this is all that the prophet insists on:—When the Assyrian comes against you,
do you take with you words; your lips shall be able to defend more, than his armies can annoy.—Words, uttered from
a penitent heart, in time of trouble, unto God, are stronger
than all the preparations of flesh and blood, because that
way as prayer and repentance go, that way God goeth too.
Amalek fights, and Moses speaks unto God in the behalf of
Israel; and the lifting up of his hands prevails more than
the strength of Israel besides [t]. One man of God, that
knows how to manage the cause of Israel with him, is the
chariots and horsemen of Israel [u]. What huge armies did
Asa and Jehoshaphat vanquish by the power of prayer [x]!
Till God forbid prayer, as he did to Jeremy [y], and take off
the hearts of his servants from crying unto him in behalf of
a people, we have reason to hope, that he will at last think
thoughts of mercy towards them [z]. And in the mean time,
when they are reduced to the condition of 'fatherless children,' he will be a guardian unto them; his eye of providence and tuition will observe them, and take care of them:
" He is the father of the fatherless, and judge of the widow,
even God in his holy habitation [a]."

SECT. 20. Now in that he saith, " I am a green fir-tree,"
it is a promise made in opposition to all the vain succours
which they relied on before; intimating, that instead of
them, he would be their defence and shelter, that they
should not need to hide themselves under such narrow refuges. Whatsoever human wisdom, wealth, power, or other
outward means men have to defend themselves withal, yet
they shall never find any true and solid protection but in

[t] Exod. xvii. 11, 12.   [u] 2 Sam. ii. 12.   [x] 2 Chron. xiv. 11. xx. 23, 25.
[y] Jer. vii. 16. xi. 14.   [z] Exod. xxxii, 10, 14   [a] Psalm lxviii. 3.

and from God, after sound conversion unto him. The fir-tree (Pliny saith) casteth not its leaves, and so yields a per-petual shade both in winter and summer;—to note, that sound conversion yieldeth comfort in all conditions of life. "Though the earth be removed, and the mountains carried into the midst of the sea ͣ," &c. "However it be, God is good to Israel; and it shall go well with the righteous: he will be for a sanctuary to his people, that they need not be afraid ᵇ." If you would have your hearts above all the trou-bles of the world, get under this fir-tree; cast yourselves under this protection; get into the chamber of God's provi-dence and promises; and then, though the troubles of the world may strip you of all outward comforts, yet God will be all unto you.

Lastly, in that he saith, "From me is thy fruit found," we learn, That though good works be ours, when they are done by us, yet they come from God, who enableth us to do them; we bear them, but God worketh and produceth them in us: the duty is ours, but the efficacy and blessing is his. This falleth in with what hath been handled in the first doc-trine, and therefore I shall say no more of it.

ͣ Psalm xlvi. 2, 3. Hab. iii. 16, 17, 18.   ᵇ Isai. viii. 12, 13, 14.

THE

SEVENTH SERMON.*

HOSEA XIV. 9.

Who is wise, and he shall understand these things? prudent, and he shall know them? for the ways of the Lord are right, and the just shall walk in them: but the transgressors shall fall therein.

THESE words are a most pathetical close, and, as it were, a seal which the prophet setteth to all the doctrine of his whole book, and to the course of his ministry: implying, First, A strong asseveration of the truth of all those things which he had, in the name of God, delivered unto them ;— Secondly, An elegant and forcible excitation of the people unto a sad and serious pondering of them, laying to heart the sins therein charged, the duties therein required, the judgements therein threatened, the blessings therein promised ;—And withal, Thirdly, A tacit complaint of the paucity of those who were wise unto salvation, and of the desperate use which wicked men make of the Word of God, and the ministry of his grace ; namely, to stumble at it, and to turn it unto themselves into an occasion of ruin.

" *Who is wise, and he shall understand?" &c.*] The interrogation is, First, A secret exprobration of folly unto his hearers, or the greatest part of them ; for so this kind of interrogation doth frequently in Scripture intimate either a negation [b], or at least the rareness and difficulty of the thing spoken of; as, " Who hath known the mind of the Lord [c] ?" " Who shall lay any thing to the charge of God's elect [d] ?" These are negatives. " Who knoweth the power of thine anger [e] ?" " Who amongst you will give ear to this [f] ?" " Who hath

---

* Folio-Edition, p. 592. [b] Vid. *Glass.* Rhetor. Sacr. Tract. 2. c. 5.
[c] 1 Cor. ii. 16. [d] Rom. viii. 33. [e] Psalm xc. 11. [f] Isai. xlii. 23.

believed our report? or to whom is the arm of the Lord revealed ᵍ?" These are restrictives.—Who? that is, few or
none are such.—Secondly, An earnest wish and desire of the
prophet. O that men were wise to understand these things,
and lay them to heart: as, "Who shall deliver me from this
body of death?" that is, O that I were delivered ʰ! "Who
will show us any good ⁱ?" that is, O that any could do it.—
Thirdly, A strong affirmation, or demonstration, wherein true
wisdom doth indeed consist, and what men, that are truly
wise, will do, when the ways of God are, by the ministry of
his servants, set forth before them; namely, ponder and
consider the great weight and consequence of them: as,
"Who is the wise man, that may understand this ᵏ?"
namely, as it ˡ followeth, "For what the land perisheth, and
is burnt up like a wilderness, that none passeth through?"
and the Lord saith, "Because they have forsaken my law
which I set before them," &c. This is the character of a
wise man, to resolve the judgements that are upon a people,
into their proper original, and not to allege 'non causam
pro causa.'—Fourthly, A vehement awakening and quickening of the people unto this duty of sad attendance on the
words, which he had spoken unto them; as "Who is on the
Lord's side? let him come unto me ᵐ;" and "Who is on my
side? who ⁿ?" So it is, as if the prophet should have said,
—"There are none of you who have been my hearers, but
would willingly retain the reputation of wise and understanding men, and would esteem it a high indignity to be
recorded unto all ages for fools and madmen. Well, I have
preached amongst you many years together," (sixty are the
fewest that we can well compute, some say seventy, others
above eighty:) "but alas! what entertainment hath mine
embassage received? what operation or success hath it had
amongst you? Are there not the calves still standing at
Dan and Bethel? Do not carnal policies prevail still
against the express will of God? O! if there be any wise,
any prudent men amongst you, (and oh! that all God's people were such,) let them now at length, in the close of my
ministry towards them, show their wisdom, by giving heed
to what I have declared from the Lord, that they may learn

ᵍ Isai. liii. 1.   ʰ Rom. vii. 24.   ⁱ Psalm iv. 7.   ᵏ Jer. ix. 12, 13.
ˡ Folio-Edition, p. 593.   ᵐ Exod. xxxii. 26.   ⁿ 2 Kings ix. 32.

to walk in God's righteous ways, and may not stumble and perish by them."

SECT. 2. Here are two words used to express the wisdom which God requireth in those who would fruitfully hear his Word; the one importing a mental knowledge of the things, and the other a practical and prudential judgement [o] in pondering them, and in discerning the great moment and consequence of them unto our eternal weal or woe. So the apostle prays for the Colossians, that they might be filled with the knowledge of God's will "in all wisdom and spiritual understanding [p]." In mere notional things, which are only to be known for themselves, and are not further reducible unto use and practice, it is sufficient that a man knows them. But in such things, the knowledge whereof is ever in order unto a further end, there is required besides the knowledge itself [q], a faculty of wisdom and judgement to apply and manage that knowledge respectively to that end, and for the advancement of it. Now we know that theological learning is all of it practical, and hath an intrinsecal respect and order unto worship and obedience [r]: therefore it is called "the knowledge of the truth which is after godliness [s]." "The fear of the Lord is the beginning of wisdom," and "a good understanding have all they, that do his commandments [t]." Keep his judgements, and do them; "for this is your wisdom and understanding [u]." Therefore, besides the bare knowledge of the truth, there is required wisdom, and spiritual understanding to direct that knowledge unto those holy uses and saving ends, for which it was intended.

The doubling of the sentence it is the augmenting of the sense; to note, that it is the supreme and most excellent act of wisdom and prudence so to know the word and ways of God, as with a practical judgement to ponder them in order to salvation.

---

[o] Duæ sunt partes rationis secundum Philosophum; una ἐπιστημονική, altera λογιστική, qua ratiocinamur et deliberamus in ordine ad mores. Vide *Arist.* Ethic. lib. 6. c. 2. et cap. 8. [p] Col. i. 9. [q] Οὐ τῷ εἶναι μόνον φρόνιμος, ἀλλὰ καὶ τῷ πρακτικὸς, *Arist.* Ethic. l. 7, c. 11. [r] Οἱ δ᾽ ἂν μὴ εὑρίσκωνται βιοῦντες ὡς ἐδίδαξε, γνωριζέσθωσαν μὴ ὄντες Χριστιανοὶ, κἂν λέγωσι διὰ γλώτ]ης καὶ τοῦ Χριστοῦ διδάγματα, *Justin. Martyr.* Apol. 2.—Qui Christiani nominis opus non agit, Christianus non esse videtur: *Salvian.* de Gubern. Dei, lib. 4. [s] Tit. i. 1. [t] Psalm cxi. 10. [u] Deut. iv. 6.

SECT. 3. By the 'ways of the Lord' we are to understand, 1. The ways of his judgements, and of his wonderful
providence towards men; which, however, to the proud and
contentious spirit of the wicked they may seem perverse and
inordinate, and are to the eye of all men unsearchable[u],—
are yet, by spiritual wisdom, acknowledged to be most
righteous and holy, to have no crookedness or disorder in
them, but to be carried on in an even and straight way, unto
the ends whereunto his holy counsel doth direct them.
"His works are perfect, and all his ways are judgement[x]."
When Jeremy had a mind to plead with the Lord concerning his judgements, yet he premiseth this as a matter un-
questionable, That ' God was righteous in them all[y].'

2d. The ways of his will, word, and worship; so the 'word'
is often taken in Scripture, to signify the doctrine which men
teach; as Matth. xxii. 16. Acts xiii. 10. xviii. 25. xxii. 4.
And damnable heresies are called ' pernicious ways,' in opposition to the way of ' truth[z];' and the rites or rules of
corrupt worship are called by the prophet ' the way of Beer-
sheba[a].' And these ways of God are likewise very straight,
which carry men on in a sure line unto a happy end[b]:
whereas wicked ways have crookedness and perverseness in
them[c]. And this way seems here chiefly to be meant, because it follows, "The just will walk in them[d];" that is,
They will so ponder and judge of the righteous ways of God
in his Word, as to make choice of them for their way of
happiness, wherein they intend to walk; as the psalmist
speaks, " I have chosen the way of thy truth[e]." Whereas
wicked men, being offended at the purity of divine truth, do
stumble and fall into perdition;—as the Chaldee paraphrast
expresseth this place.

The words are a powerful and pathetical stirring up of the
people of Israel unto the consideration and obedience of the
doctrines, taught by the prophet in his whole prophecy.
The arguments which he useth, are drawn, First, From the

---

[u] Judicia Dei plerumque occulta, nunquam injusta : *Aug.* Serm. 88. de Tem-
pore. Ἀγαθὴ ἡ τοῦ Θεοῦ δικαιοσύνη. *Clem. Alex.*—Vid. *Tertul.* contr. Marcion.
l. 2. c. 11, 12, 13, 14, 15, 16.   [x] Deut. xxxii. 4.   [y] Jer. xii. 2.
[z] 2 Pet. ii. 2.   [a] Amos viii. 14.   [b] Psalm xix. 8.   [c] Psalm
cxxv. 5.   [d] Folio-Edition, p. 594.   [e] Psalm cxix. 30. xxv. 12.

character of the persons, "Who is wise, he shall understand," &c.   Secondly, From the nature of the doctrine
taught, "For the ways of the Lord are right."   Thirdly,
From a double use and fruit of it made by different sorts of
men: to the "just," it is a way of happiness; they will
"walk:" to the "wicked," it is an occasion of stumbling;
they will "fall therein."

Touching the persons, we observe two things; the one
intimated, their paucity; the other expressed, their prudence.

SECT. 4. From the former consideration we may note,
That there are few men who are wise unto salvation, and
who do seriously attend and manage the ministry of the
Word unto that end.   If there be any kind of accidental
'Lenocinium' to allure the fancies, or curiosities, or cus-
tomary attendances of men on the ordinances; elegancy in
the speaker, novelty and quaintness in the matter, credit or
advantage in the duty; upon such inducements, many will
wait on the Word, some to hear a sweet song[f]; others to
hear some new doctrine[g]; some for loaves, to promote their
secular advantages[h]; having one and the self-same reason of
following Christ, which the Gadarenes had, when they entreated him to depart from their coasts.   But very few[i]
there are who do it 'propter se,' and with respect to the
primary use and intention of it.   Our prophet seems to do
as the philosopher did, who lighted a candle at noon to find
out a wise man indeed; "to run to and fro through the
streets, and in the broad places, to find out a man that
seeketh the truth," as the Lord commanded the prophet
Jeremy[k].   How doth the most elegant of all the prophets
complain, "Who hath believed our report[l]?"   How doth
the most learned of the apostles complain, that the preaching of the gospel was esteemed 'foolishness[m]?'   Noah was
a preacher of righteousness to a whole world of men, and
yet but eight persons saved from the flood, and some of
them rather for the family's sake than their own[n].   Paul
preached to a whole academy at Athens, and but a very few

---

f Ezek. xxxiii. 32.   g Acts xvii. 19.   h John vi. 26.   i Rari sunt
qui philosophantur, Ulpian. P. de Excusationibus Leg. 5.—Rari quippe boni, nu-
mero vix sunt totidem quot Thebarum portæ vel divitis ostia Nili ; *Juven.* Sat. 13.
k Jer. v. 1.   l Isai. liii. 1. xlix. 4.   m 1 Cor. i. 23.   n 1 Pet. iii. 20.

converted °; some disputed, and others mocked; but few believed the things which they were not able to gainsay. Hezekiah sent messengers unto all Israel, to invite them unto the true worship of God at Jerusalem ; but they were mocked and laughed to scorn, and a remnant only humbled themselves, and came to Jerusalem P; whereunto the prophet seemeth to allude ᑫ. Though a gun be discharged at a whole flight of birds, there are but few killed ; though the net be spread over the whole pond, but few fishes are taken ; many thrust their heads into the mud, and the net passeth over them : and so most hearers do busy their heads with their own sensual or worldly thoughts, and so escape the power of the Word. In the richest mine that is, there is much more earth and dross digged out, than pure metal. Christ's flock in every place is but a 'little flock ᴿ;' 'few chosen ˢ;' 'few saved ᵗ;' few that find 'the narrow way which leadeth unto life ᵁ.' The basest creatures are usually the most numerous, as flies and vermin; those that are more noble ˣ, are more rare too. The people of the God of Abraham are, in the scripture-style, 'princes and nobles ʸ;' and how few are such kind of men in comparison of the vulgar sort ! They are indeed many in themselves ᶻ; but very few and thin, being compared with the rest of the world.

SECT. 5. We must learn therefore not to be offended or discouraged by the paucity of sincere professors, no more than we are in a civil state by the paucity of wise counsellors and politicians, in comparison of the vulgar people. It is no strange thing at all in any societies of men, to see the weaker part more than the wiser. If but few attend the right ways of the Lord, and walk in them,—remember it is a work of wisdom ; and such wisdom as cometh from above, and hath no seeds or principles in corrupt nature out of which it might be drawn ; nay, against which, all the vigour of carnal reason doth exalt itself; so that the more natural

° Acts xvii. 34.   P 2 Chron. xxx. 10, 11.   ᑫ Isai. xvii. 6. xxiv. 13. ᴿ Luke xii. 32.   ˢ Matth. xx. 16.   ᵗ Luke xiii. 23.   ᵁ Matth. vii. 13, 14.   ˣ Τὰ μέγιστα μονοτόκα τῶν ζώων ἐστι. Arist. de Generat. Anima. lib. 4. cap. 4.—Unum pario, sed Leonem : vid. Aul. Gell. l. 13. c. 7.— Gesner. de quadruped. in Elephanto, et Leone. C.   ʸ Psalm xlvii. 9. Acts xvii. 11. 1 Pet. ii. 9.   ᶻ Heb. ii. 10. Rev. vii. 9.

wisdom men have ª, the more in danger they are to despise and undervalue the ways of God, as being better able to reason and to cavil against them ᵇ. Therefore, First, In the ministry of the word, we ᶜ must continue our labour, though Israel be not gathered ᵈ. We must stretch out our hands, though it be 'to a disobedient and gainsaying people ᵉ.' 'Whether they will hear, or whether they will forbear, we must speak unto them, be they never so rebellious ᶠ;' and the reason is, because the Word is never in vain, but it doth ever 'prosper in the work, whereunto God sends it ᵍ.' If men be righteous, they walk; if wicked, they stumble ʰ; and in both, there is a sweet savour unto God ⁱ. God's work is accomplished, his glory promoted, the power of his gospel commended, in the one and the other ᵏ;—as the virtue of a sweet savour is seen as well by the antipathy which one creature hath unto it, as by the refreshment which another receiveth from it;—the strength of a rock, as by holding up the house that is built upon it, so by breaking in pieces the ship that doth dash against it;—the force of the fire, as well by consuming the dross, as by refining the gold;—the power of water, as well in sinking the ship that leaks, as in supporting the ship that is sound. The pillar of the cloud was as wonderful in the darkness which it cast upon the Egyptians, as in the light which it gave unto the Israelites ˡ: the power of the angel as great in striking terror into the soldiers, as in speaking comfort unto the women ᵐ. Secondly, In attendance on the Word, we must resolve rather to walk with the wise, though few, than to follow a multitude to do evil, and to stumble with the wicked, though they be many; rather enter the ark with a

---

ª Pudet doctos homines ex discipulis Platonis fieri discipulos Christi, &c. vid. *Aug.* de Civ. Dei. l. 10. c. 29. et l. 13. c. 16. et Ep. 102.   ᵇ Matth. xi. 25. Acts iv. 11. John vii. 48. 1 Cor. xx. 28. ii. 8. 2 Cor. x. 5, 6.   ᶜ Folio-Edition, p. 595.   ᵈ Isai. xlix. 4, 5.   ᵉ Isai. xlix. 4, 5.   ᶠ Ezek. ii. 7.   ᵍ Isai. lv. 11.   ʰ Ὑπακούουσιν εὐαγγέλιον, παρακούσασιν κριτήριον. *Clem. Alex.* Protrept. ed. Potter, vol. 1. p. 90.   ⁱ 2 Cor. ii. 15.   ᵏ Vultures unguento fugantur, et scarabæi rosa. *Plin.* et *Ælian.* Κανθάρους ῥοδίνῳ χρισθέντας μύρῳ τελευτᾶν λέγουσι. *Clem. Pædag.* l. 2. c. 8. Ὁ γὰρ Στωϊκὸς ἔρως, ὥσπερ οἱ κάνθαροι λέγονται τὸ μὲν μύρον ἀπολιπεῖν τὰ δὲ δυσώδη διώκειν. *Plut.* Quod Stoici doceant absurdiora poetis. Xyland. tom. ii. p. 1058. Μύρον τῇ περιστερᾷ ῥώμη, τῷ δὲ κανθάρῳ φθορά. *Nissen.* Hom. 3. in Cantic. Τὸν αἴλουρον ὀδμῇ μύρου ἐκταράττεσθαι καὶ μαίνεσθαι λέγουσι. *Plut.* in Conjugalib. præcept.   ˡ Exod. xiv. 20.   ᵐ Matth. xxviii. 4, 5.

few, than venture the flood with a world of sinners; rather
go three or four out of Sodom, than be burnt for company.
We must not affect a humorous singularity in differing un-
necessarily from good men, being one for Paul against
Apollos,—another for Apollos, against Cephas; but we must
ever affect a holy and pious singularity in walking contrary
unto evil men, in shining as lights in the midst of a crooked
and perverse nation [n]. For 'the righteous is more excellent
than his neighbour [o].' Though there be but few in the way,
there will be many in the end of the journey: as the tribes
and families went up divided towards Jerusalem; but when
they were come thither, they 'appeared, every one of them,
before God in Sion [p].'

SECT. 6. Secondly, In that the prophet calleth upon his
hearers to attend unto his doctrine by this argument, because it will be an evidence of their prudence and wisdom,
we learn, That true and solid wisdom doth draw the heart to
know aright; namely, to consider and ponder the judgements, blessings, ways, and Word of God, in order to the
chief ends, and accordingly to direct all their conversation:
for, in God's account, that knowledge which doth not edify,
is no knowledge at all [q]. None are his wise men, which are
not wise unto salvation [r]; who do not draw their wisdom
from his Word, and from his commandments [s].

There is a twofold wisdom [t], as the philosopher distin-
guisheth, σοφία ὅλως and κατὰ μέρος; wisdom in some particulars
—as we esteem every man who is excellent in his profession,
to be a wise man ' eo usque,' so far as concerns the managing of that profession;—as when a man knows all the
necessary principles and maxims of that way wherein he is,
the right ends thereof, and the proper conclusions deducible
from those principles, and dirigible unto those ends. And
next, wisdom in general, and in perfection; which is of those
principles, ends, and conclusions, which are universally and
most transcendently necessary unto a man's chiefest and most
general good: and this the philosopher calleth the knowledge
of the most excellent and honourable things [u], or of the last

---

[n] Phil. ii. 15.   [o] Prov. xii. 26.   [p] Psalm viii. 4, 7.   [q] 1 Cor.
viii. 2.   [r] 2 Tim. iii. 15.   [s] Psalm xix. 7. cxix. 98, 99. Jer. viii. 9.
[t] Eth. l. 6. c. 7.   [u] Ἐπιστήμη τῶν τιμιωτάτων. Eth. l. 6. c. 7. Ἡ ἀρχι-
κωτάτη καὶ ἡγεμονικωτάτη, καὶ ἡ ὥσπερ δούλας οὐδ' ἀντειπεῖν τὰς ἄλλας ἐπιστή-

end and chief good of man. Now the end, by how much
the more supreme, perpetual, and ultimate it is, by so much
the more it hath of excellency and goodness in it, as bearing
thereby most exact proportion and conveniency to the soul
of man [x]. For the soul, being immortal itself, can have no
final satisfaction from any good, which is mortal and perishable; and being withal so large and unlimited, as that the
reasonings and desires thereof extend unto the whole latitude of goodness, being not restrained unto this or that
kind, but capable of desiring and judging of all the different
degrees of goodness which are in all the whole variety of
things, it can never therefore finally acquiesce in any but
the most universal and comprehensive goodness, in the
nearer or more remote participation whereof consisteth the
different goodness of all other things.

SECT. 7. This supreme and absolute goodness can, indeed, be but one, all other things being good by the participation of that. 'There is none good but One, that is God [y].'
But because there are two sorts of men in the world,
righteous and wicked, the seed of the woman, and the
seed of the serpent; therefore, consequently, there are two
sorts of ends, which these men do differently pursue. The
end of wicked men is a happiness, which they, out of their
own corrupt judgements, do shape themselves, and unto
which they do finally carry all the motions of their souls,
called in Scripture, 'the pleasures of sin,' and 'the wages of
iniquity [z]:' that thing, whatsoever it is, for obtaining whereof
men do direct all their other endeavours, as profit, pleasure,
and honour, or power; and there are mediums exactly proportionable unto these ends, namely, the lusts of the flesh,
the lusts of the eyes, and the pride of life [a]. And there is a
wisdom, consonant unto these ends and means, and fit to
direct and manage these lusts unto the attaining of those
ends; which therefore the apostle calleth 'the wisdom of
the flesh,' or corrupt nature [b], and St. James, a wisdom
'earthly, sensual, and devilish [c];' 'earthly,' managing the
lusts of the eyes unto the ends of gain; 'sensual,' managing

μας δίκαιον, ἡ τοῦ τέλους καὶ τἀγαθοῦ τοιαύτη. Arist. Metaphys. edit. Du Val
vol. 4. p. 288. Πολλῶν καὶ θαυμαστῶν ἐπιστήμη. Rhet. l. 1. c. 37.   x Vide
Field of the Church, l. 1. c. 1.   y Matth. xix. 17.   z Heb. xi. 25.
2 Pet. ii. 15.   a 1 John ii. 16.   b Rom. viii. 7.   c James iii. 15.

the lusts of the flesh unto ends of pleasure; and 'devilish,' managing the pride of life unto ends of power.   But
such wisdom as this, God esteems very foolishness.   " My
people are foolish, sottish children, they have no understanding :" why?   " They are wise to do evil; but to do
good they have no knowledge d."   Wisdom is only unto
that which is good :—he is the wisest man, who is simple and
ignorant in the trade of evil e.   " If any man amongst you
seemeth to be wise in this world, let him become a fool, that
he may be wise f."

On the other side, the true and ultimate end of righteous
man, is Almighty God g, as most glorious in himself, and
most good unto us ; or the seeking of his glory, that he may
be honoured by us ; and of our own salvation, that we may
be glorified by him.   The fruition of him as the highest and
first 'in genere veri,' and the greatest and last 'in genere
boni,' the chiefest object for the mind to rest in by knowledge, and the heart by love : this must needs be the best of
all ends, both in regard of the excellency of it h, as being
infinitely and most absolutely good ; and in regard of eternity,—so that the soul, having once the possession of it, can
never be to seek of that happiness which floweth from it i.
The proper means for the obtaining of this end, is the knowledge of God in Christ, as in his Word he hath revealed himself, to be known, worshipped, and obeyed; for there only he
doth teach us the way unto himself ; and true wisdom is the
pursuing of this means in order unto that end.   For though
many approaches may be made towards God by the search
and contemplation of the creature; yet, in his Word, he hath
showed us a more full and excellent way, which only can
make us wise unto salvation through faith in Christ Jesus k.

SECT. 8. All the thoughts and wisdom of men is spent
upon one of these two heads, either the obtaining of the
good which we want, or avoiding and declining the evil
which we fear.   And by how much the more excellent and

d Jer. iv. 22.   e Rom. xvi. 19.   f 1 Cor. iii. 18.   g Fecisti nos
ad te ; et inquietum est cor nostrum, donec requiescat in te : *Aug.* Conf. l. 1. c. 1.
Omnis mihi copia, quæ Deus meus non est, egestas est. l. 13. c. 8. vid. de Trin.
l. 8. c. 3. de Civ. Dei, l. 22. c. 1.   h Beatitudo hæc duo requirit, fruitionem
incommutabilis boni, et certitudinem æternæ fruitionis. Vid. *Aug.* de Civ. Dei,
l. 11. c. 13.   i John vi. 27, 28.   k 2 Tim. iii. 15. Prov. ix. 10. Eccles.
xii. 12, 13. Jer. ix. 23, 24.

difficult the good is which we want, and by how much the
more pernicious and imminent the evil is which we fear,—
by so much greater is the wisdom, which, in both these,
procures the end at which we aim. Now then, what are the
most excellent good things which we want? Food is common to us with other creatures ; raiment, houses, lands,
possessions, common to us with the worst men : take the
most admired perfections which are not heavenly, and we
may find very wicked men excel in them. All men will confess the soul to be more excellent than the body, and therefore the good of that to be more excellent than of the other :
and the chief good of it to be that, which doth most advance it towards the fountain of goodness, where is fulness
of perfection, and perpetuity of fruition. The [1] excellency of
every thing standeth in two things : the perfection of
beauty wherein it was made,—and the perfection of use, for
which it was made. The beauty of man, especially in his
soul, consists in this, that he was made like to God, after
his image [m] : and his end and use in this, that he was made
for God, first to serve him, and after to enjoy him ; for " the
Lord hath set apart him that is godly, for himself [n]." " This
people have I formed for myself ; they shall show forth my
praise [o]." Therefore to recover the image of God, which is
in knowledge, righteousness, and true holiness [p] ; to work to
the service and glory of God [q] ; to aspire and to enjoy the
possession and fruition of God [r] ; must needs be man's
greatest good ; and, by consequence, to attend on the means
hereof, must needs be his greatest wisdom.

What is the most pernicious and destructive evil, which a
man is in danger of ? not the loss of any outward good
things whatsoever ; for they are all, in their nature, perishable ; we enjoy them upon these conditions,—to part with
them again :—no wisdom can keep them. " Meat for the
belly, and the belly for meats ; but God shall destroy both [s]
it and them [t]." Not the suffering of any outward troubles,
which the best of men have suffered, and triumphed over :
but the greatest loss is, the loss of a precious soul, which is

[1] Vid. *Arist.* de iis quæ bona sunt, et quæ meliora et majora. Rhet. l. i. c. 6, 7.
[m] Gen. i. 26, 27.   [n] Psalm iv. 3.   [o] Isai. xliii. 21.   [p] Col. iii. 10.
Ephes. iv. 24.   [q] John xv. 8.   [r] Exod. xxxiii. 18. Phil. i. 23.
[s] Folio-Edition, p. 597.   [t] 1 Cor. vi. 13.

more worth than all the world [t]; and the greatest suffering
is the wrath of God upon the conscience [u]. Therefore to
avoid this danger, and to snatch this darling from the paw
of the lion, is, of all other, the greatest wisdom. It is wisdom to deliver a city [x], much more to deliver a soul [y]: an-
gelical, seraphical knowledge without this, is all worth
nothing [z].

SECT. 9. Therefore we should learn to show ourselves wise
indeed, by attendance on God's Word. If the most glorious
creatures for wisdom and knowledge that ever God made, the
blessed angels [a], were employed in publishing the law of
God [b],—and did, with great admiration, look into the mysteries of the gospel, and stoop down with their faces towards
the mercy-seat [c],—it cannot but be also our chiefest wisdom
to hide the Word in our hearts, and to make it our companion and counsellor, as David did [d]. We esteem him the
wisest man, who followeth the best and safest counsel [e], and
that which will most preserve and promote his interest, his
honour, and his conscience.   Herein was Rehoboam's weakness, that, by passionate and temerarious counsels, he suffered his honour to be stained, his interest to be weakened,
and his conscience to be defiled with resolutions of violence
and injustice. Now, there is no counsel to that of God's
Word: it enlighteneth the eyes ; it maketh wise the simple [f];
it is able to make a man wise for himself [g], and unto salvation,—which no other counsel can do [h]. There is no case
that can be put, though of never so great intricacy and perplexity, no doubt so difficult, no temptation so knotty and
involved, no condition whereinto a man can be brought so
desperate, no employment so dark and uncouth, no service
so arduous or full of discouragements ; in all which, so far
as respecteth conscience and salvation, there are not most

---

[t] Matth. xvi. 26.   [u] Psalm xc. 11. Isai. xxxiii. 14. Heb. x. 31. Matth.
x. 28.   [x] Eccles. ix. 15.   [y] Prov. xi. 10.   [z] 1 Cor. xiii. 1, 2.
[a] Videntur ipsi Angeli ex scriptis Evangelicis et ministerio Apostolico plurima
didicisse. Vid. *Chrysos.* Hom. 1. in Johan.—*Gregor. Nissen.* Hom. 8. in Cantic.—
Theophylact. et *Oecum.* in Eph. 3. alios apud *Sixt. Senens.* l. 6. Annot. 165. 182,
et 199.   [b] Acts vii. 53. Gal. iii. 19.   [c] 1 Pet. i. 22. Ephes. iii. 10.
Exod. xxxvii. 9.   [d] Psalm cxix. 24.   [e] Vide *Greg. Tholosan.* de Repub.
l. 24.   [f] Psalm xix. 7, 8.   [g] Μισῶ σοφιστὴν, ὅστις οὐδ' αὑτῷ σοφός.
Eurip. Fragm. iii. Priestley's edition, vol. 7. p. 696. *Plut.* de occulte vivendo.
[h] 2 Tim. iii. 15, 16.

clear and satisfactory expedients to be drawn out of God's
Word, if a man have his judgement and senses, after a spiritual manner, exercised in the searching of it. That we are
so often at a stand how to state such a question, how to
satisfy such a scruple, how to clear and expedite such
a difficulty, how to repel such a temptation, how to
manage such an action, how to order our ways, with an
even and composed spirit, in the various conditions whereinto we are cast in this world,—doth not arise from any defect in the Word of God, which is perfect, and able to furnish
us unto every good work; but only from our own ignorance
and unacquaintance with it, who know not how to draw the
general rule, and to apply it to our own particular cases. And
this cannot but be matter of great humiliation unto us in
these sad and distracted times, when, besides our civil
breaches which threaten desolation to the state, there should
be so many and wide divisions in the church;—that after so
long enjoyment of the Word of God, the Scripture should be
to so many men as a sealed book, and they, like the Egyptians, have the dark side of this glorious pillar towards them
still; that men should be tossed to and fro like children,
and carried about with every wind of doctrine; and suffer
themselves to be bewitched, devoured, brought into bondage,
spoiled, led away captive, unskilful in the word of righteousness, unable to discern good and evil, to prove and try
the spirits whether they be of God; always learning, and
never able to come to the knowledge of the truth;—and this
not only in matters problematical, or circumstantial, wherein
learned and godly men may differ one from another [i], and
yet still the peace and unity of the church be preserved—
(for things of this nature ought not to be occasions of
schism, or secessions from one another; but in matters
which concern life and godliness, touching the power of
God's law, the nature of free grace, the subjection of the
conscience unto moral precepts, confession of sin in prayer
unto God, and begging pardon of it; the differencing of
true Christian liberty, from loose, profane, and wanton li-

---

[i] Sunt quædam falsæ opiniones, quæ ulcus non gignunt; sunt etiam errores
venenati, qui animam depascuntur. Vid. *Plut.* de superstit.

centiousness, and a liberty to vent and publish what perverse
things soever men please; the very being of churches, of
ministers, of ordinances in the world; the necessity of humiliation and solemn repentance in times of public judgements; the tolerating of all kind of religions in Christian
commonwealths; the mortality of the reasonable soul, and
other the like pernicious and perverse doctrines of men of
corrupt minds, the devil's emissaries, purposely by him
stirred up to hinder and puzzle the reformation of the
church :—these things, I say, cannot but be matter of humiliation unto all that fear God, and love the prosperity of
Sion, and occasions the more earnestly to excite them unto
this wisdom in the text, to hear what God the Lord says,
and to lay his righteous ways so to heart [i], as to walk stead-
fastly in them, and never to stumble at them, or fall from
them.

SECT. 10. Now there are two things, which, I take it, the
prophet, in this close of his prophecy, seems principally to
aim at; namely, the judgements and the blessings of God.
His righteous ways in his threatenings against impenitent,
and in his promises made unto penitent sinners. These are
the things which wise and prudent men will consider in
times of trouble.

For judgements, there is a twofold knowledge of them :
the one natural, by sense; the other spiritual, by faith. By
the former way, wicked men do abundantly know the afflictions which they suffer, even unto vexation and anguish of
spirit; they fret themselves [k]; they are grey-headed with
very trouble and sorrow [l]; they gnaw their tongues for pain [m];
they pine away in their iniquities [n]; they are mad in their
calamities; have trembling hearts, failing of eyes, and sorrow of mind [o], &c. And yet for all this they are said, in
the Scripture, when they burn, when they consume, when
they are devoured, not to know any of this, or to lay it to
heart [p] :—and the reason is, because they knew it not by
faith, nor in a spiritual manner in order unto God. They
did not see his name; nor hear his rod; nor consider his
hand and counsel in it; nor measure his judgements by his

---

i Folio-Edition, p. 598.   k Isai. viii. 21.   l Hos. vii. 9   m Rev.
xvi. 10.   n Levit. xxvi. 39.   o Deut. xxviii. 34, 65.   p Isai.
xlii. 25. Hos. vii. 9. Jer. xii. 11.

word; nor look on them as the fruits of sin, leading to repentance, and teaching righteousness, nor as the arguments
of God's displeasure, humbling us under his holy hand, and
guiding us to seek his face, and to recover our peace with
him. This is the spiritual and prudent way of knowing
judgements [q]. ' Scire est per causam scire:' true wisdom
looks on things in their causes, resolves judgements into the
causes of them, our sins to be bewailed, God's wrath to be avert-
ed; makes this observation upon them,—' Now I find, by experience, that God is a God of truth: often have I heard judgements threatened against sin; and now I see that God's threatenings are not empty wind, but that all his words have truth
and substance in them.'—The first part of wisdom is, to see
judgements in the Word before they come, and to hide from
them:—for as faith, in regard of promises, is the substance
of things hoped for, and seeth a being in them while they
are yet but to come; so is it, in regard of threatenings, the
substance of things feared, and can see a being in judgements before they are felt. The next part of wisdom is, to
see God in judgements, in the rods when they are actually
come, and to know them in order unto him. And that
knowledge stands in two things: First, To resolve them unto
him as their author; for nothing can hurt us without a commission from God [r]. Satan spoils Job of his children,—the
Sabeans and Chaldeans, of his goods: but he looks above
all these unto God, acknowledging his goodness in giving,
his power in taking away, and blesseth his name [s]. Joseph
looks from the malice of his brethren, unto the providence
of God; " He sent me before you to preserve life [t]." If the
whale swallow Jonah, God prepares him [u]: and if he vomit
him up again, God speaks unto him [x]. Secondly, To direct
them unto him as the end [y], to be taught by them to seek the
Lord, and wait on him in the way of his judgements,—to be
more penitent for sin, more fearful and watchful against it,
—to study and practise the skill of suffering as Christians,
according to the will of God, that he may be glorified [z].

q Mic. vi. 9. Isai. xxvi. 8, 9. xxvii. 9. Levit. xxvi. 40, 41, 42.   r John xix. 11.
s Job i. 21.   t Gen. xlv. 5.   u John i. 17.   x John ii. 10.   y Perdidistis
utilitatem calamitatis, et miserrimi facti estis; et pessimi permansistis. *Aug.*
de Civ. Dei, l. 1. c. 13.   z Psalm xciv. 12. cxix. 67, 71. Zach. xiii. 9.
Isai. xxvi. 9. Heb. xii. 11. Deut. viii. 16. 1 Pet. iv. 16, 19.

So likewise for blessings, there is a double knowledge of them,—one, sensual by the flesh,—the other, spiritual in the conscience. The former is but a brutish and epicurean feeding on them without fear; as Israel, upon quails in the wilderness; as swine which feed on the fruit that falls down, but never look up to the tree whereon it grew ; to use blessings as Adam did the forbidden fruit, being drawn by the beauty of them to forget God; as our prophet complains, Hos. xiii. 6. But spiritual knowledge of blessings, as to taste and see the goodness of the Lord in them; to look up to him as the author of them, acknowledging that it is he who giveth us power to get wealth, and any other good thing [a]; and to be drawn by them unto him as their end, to the adoring of his bounty, to the admiration of his goodness, to more cheerfulness and stronger engagements unto his service ; to say with Jacob, " He gives me bread to eat, and raiment to put on, therefore he shall be my God [b];" " he giveth me all things richly to enjoy, therefore I will trust in him [c]." Catalogues of mercy should beget resolutions of obedience [d].

SECT.[e] 11. Thirdly, We have here a singular commendation of the doctrine, which the prophets had delivered unto the people of God; namely, that it was altogether right, and the way which God required them to walk in, whatever judgement carnal and corrupt minds might pass upon it. Now the doctrine of God's judgements, precepts, and promises, are said to be right divers ways :—

1. In regard of their equity and reasonableness, there is nothing more profoundly and exactly rational than true religion ; and therefore conversion is called by our Saviour ' conviction [f].' There is a power in the Word of God to stop the mouths, and dispel the cavillations of all contradictors, so that they shall not be able to resist or speak against the truth that is taught [g]. And the apostle calleth his ministry, ' a declaration and a manifestation of the truth of God unto the consciences of men [h];' and Apollos is said

[a] Deut. viii. 17, 18. Psalm cxxvii. 1. Prov. x. 22.   [b] Gen. xxviii. 40.
[c] 1 Tim. vi. 17.   [d] Josh. xxiv. 2, 14.   [e] Folio-Edition, p. 599.
[f] Elenchus est syllogismus cum contradictione conclusionis. *Arist.* Elench. l. 8. c. 1. Et ἐλέγχειν est certa argumentatione disputantem vincere. *Steph.* ex Platone.   [g] John xvi. 8. Tit. i. 9, 10. Acts vi. 10. Matth. xxii. 34.   [h] Demonstratio est syllogismus scientificus. *Arist.* poster. Analyt. lib. 1. c. 2.—Nul-

' mightily to have convinced the Jews, showing or demon-
strating by the Scripture, that Jesus was Christ [h].' Therefore the apostle calleth the devoting of ourselves unto God,
' a reasonable service [i] :' and those that obey not the Word,
are called ' unreasonable and absurd men,' that have not
wisdom to discern the truth and equity of the ways of God[k].
What can be more reasonable, than that he who made all
things for himself, should be served by the creatures which
he made? that we should live unto him who gave us our
being? that the supreme will should be obeyed, the infallible truth believed? that he who can destroy, should be
feared? that he who doth reward, should be loved and trusted in? that absolute justice should vindicate itself against
presumptuous disobedience, and absolute goodness extend
mercy unto whom it pleaseth? It is no marvel that the
Holy Spirit doth brand wicked men throughout the Scripture, with the disgraceful title of ' fools,' because they reject that which is the supreme rule of wisdom, and hath the
greatest perfection and exactness of reason in it [l].

2. In regard of their consonancy and harmony within
themselves [m]; as that which is right and straight, hath all its
parts equal and agreeing one unto another; so all the parts
of divine doctrine are exactly suitable and conform to each
other. The promises of God are not ' Yea and Nay, but Yea
and Amen [n].' However there may be seeming repugnances
to a carnal and captious eye,—which may seem of purpose
allowed for the exercise of our diligence in searching, and
humility in adoring, the profoundness and perfection of the
Word,—yet the Scriptures have no obliquity in them at all;
but all the parts thereof do most intimately consent with one
another, as being written by the Spirit of truth, who cannot
lie nor deceive; who is the same yesterday, to-day, and
for ever.

3. In regard of their directness unto that end for which
they were revealed unto men, being the straight road unto

---

lum scelus rationem habet. *Liv.* lib. 21.   1 Cor. ii. 4.   2 Cor. iv. 2.   [h] Acts
xviii. 28.   [i] Rom. xii. 1.   [k] 2 Thes. iii. 2.   [l] Jer. viii. 9.
[m] Οὐδεμία γραφὴ τῇ ἑτέρᾳ ἐναντία ἐστιν· αὐτὸς μὴ νοεῖν μᾶλλον ὁμολογήσω τὰ
εἰρημένα, &c. *Just. Mart.* Dialog. cum Tryphon.—Quod de suo codice Justini-
anus, verius de sacro codice affirmetur, ' contrarium aliquid, in hoc codice positum,
nullum sibi locum vindicabit,' &c.   Cod. de vetere Jure enucleando, l. 2. sect.
15. et. l. 3. Sect. 15.   [n] 2 Cor. i. 19, 20.

eternal life, able to build us up, and to give us an inheritance [o]. In which respect the Word is called the 'Word of
life [p],' and the 'gospel of salvation [q],' yea, 'salvation itself [r],'
as being the 'way' to it, and the 'instrument' of it [s].

4. In regard of their conformity to the holy nature and
will of God, which is the original rule of all rectitude and perfection [t]. Law is nothing but the will of the law-giver, revealed with an intention to bind those that are under it, and
for the ordering of whom it was revealed. That will being
in God most holy and perfect, the law or word which is but
the patefaction of it, must needs be holy and perfect too;
therefore it is called the 'acceptable and perfect will of
God [u].' It is also called 'a word of truth,' importing a conformity between the mind and will of the speaker, and the
word which is spoken by him; in which respect it is said to
be 'holy, just, and good [x].'

5. In regard of the smoothness, plainness, and perspicu-
ousness of them, in the which men may walk surely, easily,
without danger of wandering, stumbling, or miscarriage: as
a man is out of danger of missing a way, if it be straight
and direct, without any turnings,—and in no great danger
of falling in it, if it be plain and smooth, and no stumbling-
block left in it. Now such is the Word of God to those
who make it their way, a straight way, which looketh directly forward [y]; 'an even and smooth way,' which hath no
offence or stumbling-block in it [z]. [a] It is true, there are
δυσνόητα, hard things, to exercise the study and diligence,
the faith and prayers of the profoundest scholars; waters
wherein an elephant may swim.—But yet as nature hath
made things of greatest necessity to be most obvious and
common, as air, water, bread, and the like; whereas things
of greater rarity, as gems and jewels, are matters of honour
and ornaments, not of daily use;—so the wisdom of God
hath so tempered the Scriptures, as that from thence the
wisest Solomon may fetch jewels for ornament, and the poorest Lazarus, bread for life: but these things which are of com-

---

[o] Acts xx. 32.   [p] Acts v. 20.   [q] Ephes. i. 13.   [r] John iv. 22.
xii. 50. Acts xxviii. 28.   [s] 2 Tim. iii. 15, 16, 17. James i. 21.   [t] Non
idcirco juste voluit, quia futurum justum fuit quod voluit; sed quod voluit, idcirco justum fuit, quia ipse voluit, &c. *Hug.* de Sacrament. lib. 1. part. 4. cap. 1.
[u] Rom. xii. 2. Col. i. 2.   [x] Rom. vii. 14.   [y] Psalm v. 8. Heb. xii. 13.
[z] Psalm xxvi. 12. cxix. 165.   [a] Folio-Edition, p. 600.

mon necessity, as matters of faith, love, worship, obedience, which are universally requisite unto the common salvation, (as the apostle expresseth it[a],) are so perspicuously set down in the Holy Scriptures[b], that every one who hath the Spirit of Christ, hath therewithal a judgement to discern so much of God's will, as shall suffice to make him believe in Christ for righteousness, and, by worship and obedience, to serve him unto salvation. The way of holiness is so plain, that simple men are made wise enough to find it out; and wayfaring men, though fools, do not err therein[c].

SECT. 12. From all which we learn, First, To take heed of picking quarrels at any word of God, or presuming to pass any bold and carnal censure of ours upon his righteous ways. When God doth set his Word in the power and workings of it upon the spirit of any wicked man, making his conscience to hear it as the voice of God, it usually worketh one of these two effects: either it subdues the soul to the obedience of it, by convincing, judging, and manifesting the secrets of his heart, so that he falleth down on his face, and worshippeth God[d]; or else it doth, by accident, excite and enrage the natural love which is in every man to his lusts, stirring up all the proud arts and reasonings, which the forge of a corrupt heart can shape in defence of those lusts against the sword of the Spirit, which would cut them off; as that which hindereth the course of a river, doth accidently enrage the force of it, and cause it to swell and overrun the banks:—and from hence ariseth gainsaying and contradiction against the Word of grace, and the ways of God, as unequal and unreasonable, too strict, too severe, too hard to be observed[e], snuffing at it[f]; gathering odious consequences from it; replying against it[h]; casting reproaches upon it[i]; enviously swelling at it[k]. There are few sins more dangerous than this of picking quarrels at God's Word, and taking up weapons against it. It will prove a burthensome stone to those, that burthen themselves with it[l]. Therefore, whenever our crooked and corrupt reason doth offer to except

---

[a] Jude, verse 3. Tit. i. 4.   [b] In iis quæ aperte in Scripturis posita sunt, inveniuntur illa omnia quæ continent fidem, moresque vivendi. *Aug.* de doct. Christian. lib. 2. cap. 9. et Ep. 3. ad Volusian. et contr. Ep. Petilian. cap. 5.— Vid. *Theodoret.* Serm. 8. de Martyrib.   [c] Psalm xix. 7. Isai. xxxii. 4. xxxv. 8. Matth. xi. 25.   [d] 1 Cor. xiv. 25.   [e] Ezek. xviii. 25. [f] Mal. i. 13.   [g] Rom. iii. 8.   [h] Rom. ix. 19, 20.   [i] Jer. xx. 8, 9. [k] Acts xiii. 45.   [l] Zach. xii. 3. Matth. xxi. 44.

against the ways of God as unequal, we must presently conclude as God doth [m], that the inequality is in us, and not in
them. When a lame man stumbleth in a plain path, the
fault is not in the way, but in the foot: nor is the potion but
the palate to blame [n], when a feverish distemper maketh that
seem bitter, which indeed was sweet. He that removeth in a
boat from the shore, in the judgement of sense, seeth the
houses or trees on the shore to totter and move, whereas the
motion is in the boat, and not in them. Unclean and corrupt
hearts, have unclean notions of the purest things, and conceive of God as if he were such a one as themselves [o].

SECT. 13. Secondly, It should teach us to come to
God's Word always as to a rule, by which we are to
measure ourselves, and take heed of wresting and wrying
that to the corrupt fancies of our own evil hearts [p], as the
apostle saith some men do, " to their own destruction [q]."
Every wicked man doth, though not formally and explicitly,
yet really and in truth, set up his own will against God's,
resolving to do what pleaseth himself, and not that which
may please God, and consequently followeth that reason
and counsel which wait upon his own will; and not that
Word which revealeth God's. Yet because he that will serve
himself, would fain deceive himself too (that so he may not
do it with less regret of conscience), and would fain seem
God's servant, but be his own, therefore corrupt reason sets
itself on work to excogitate such distinctions and evasions [r],
as may serve to reconcile God's Word and a man's own lust

m Ezek. xviii. 25.   n Ut vernula illa apud Senecam quæ cum cæca
esset, cubiculum esse tenebrosum querebatur. 'Εν τῷ πυρέτῳ πικρὰ πάντα
καὶ ἀηδῆ φαίνεται γενομένοις· ἀλλ' οὐκέτι τὸ πότον, ἀλλὰ τὴν νόσον αἰτιώμεθα.
Plutarch. de Animi Tranquillitate.   o Psalm l. 21.   p Cesset voluntas
propria, et non erit infernus, &c. Vid. Bernard. Serm. 3. de Resurrect.   q 2 Pet.
iii. 16. Acts xiii. 10.   r Βιάζονται πρὸς τὰς ἐπιθυμίας τὴν γραφήν. Clem.
Alex. Strom. 1. 7. Εἰς τὰς ἰδίας μετάγουσι δόξας. Ibid. Κλέπτουσι τὸν κανόνα
τῆς ἐκκλησίας, ταῖς ἰδίαις ἐπιθυμίαις καὶ φιλοδοξίαις χαριζόμενοι. Ibid. p. 897.
Ἕλκοντες πρὸς τὴν ἑαυτῶν ὀργὴν τὸ εὐαγγέλιον. Justin. Martyr. Ep. ad
Zenam.—Simplicitatem sermonis Ecclesiastici id volunt significare, quod ipsi
sentiunt. Hieron. ep. Vid. Aug. de Doct. Christian. lib. 3. cap. 10.—Scripturas
tenent ad speciem, non ad salutem:—de Baptism. contr. Donat. lib. 3. cap. ult.
Eas secundum suum sensum legunt:—de Grat. Christ. lib. 1. cap. 14. Sequitur
voluntatem non quam audit sed quam attulit; et vitia sua cum cœpit putare
similia præceptis, indulget illis non timide nec obscure: luxuriantur etiam
inoperto capite. Ser. de vita beata, cap. 13.—Nondum hæc negligentia Deum
venerat: nec interpretando sibi quisque jusjurandum et leges aptas faciebat,
sed suos potius mores ad ea accommodabat. Liv. lib. 3. 20.

together. Lust says, Steal; God says, No[s], ' Thou shalt not
steal :' carnal reason, the advocate of lust, comes in and dis-
tinguisheth, " I may not steal from a neighbour; but I may
weaken an enemy, or pay myself the stipend that belongs to
my service, if others do not :"—and under this evasion, most
innocent men may be made a prey to violent soldiers, who
use the name of public interest to palliate their own greediness. Certainly it is a high presumption to tamper with the
word of truth, and make it bear false witness in favour of
our own sins ; and God will bring it to a trial at last, whose
will shall stand, his or ours.

SECT. 14. Lastly, This serveth as an excellent boundary,
both to the ministration of the preacher, and to the faith of
the hearer, in the dispensing of the Word ; First, To us in
our ministry, that we deliver nothing unto the people but the
right ways of the Lord, without any commixtures or contem-
perations of our own[t]. Mixtures are useful only for these two
purposes,—either to slacken and abate something that is ex-
cessive, or to supply something that is deficient, and to col-
lect a virtue and efficacy out of many things, each one of
which alone would have been ineffectual : and so all hetero-
geneous mixtures do plainly intimate, either a viciousness to
be corrected, or a weakness to be supplied, in every one of
the simples, which are, by human wisdom, tempered together, in order unto some effect to be wrought by them.
Now, it were great wickedness to charge any one of these
upon the pure and perfect Word of God, and, by consequence, to use deceit and insincerity, by adulterating of it,
either by such glosses as diminish and take away from the
force of it, as the Pharisees did in their carnal interpre-

---

[s] Folio-Edition, p. 601.   [t] Πᾶν τὸ κρεῖτον ἐν τῇ τοῦ χείρονος ἐπιμιξίᾳ
δολοῦσθαι λέγεται—ὡς οἶνος τῷ ὕδωρ αὐτῷ παρακίρνασθαι, &c. Basil. in Psalm
xiv. Ἀναμίγνυναι τὸν οἶνον ὕδατι. Naz. Orat. 1.—Qui frumento arenam immis-
cuit, quasi de corrupto agi potest. l. 26. ad Leg. Aquil. P. Sect. 20.—Aurum
accepisti, .aurum redde : nolo mihi pro aliis alia subjicias ; nolo pro auro aut
impudenter plumbum, aut fraudulenter æramenta supponas ; nolo auri speciem,
sed naturam planè. Vincent. Lirin.—Lege Cornelia cavetur, ut qui in aurum
vitii quid addiderit, qui argenteos nummos adulterinos flaverit, falsi crimine
teneatur. l. 9. P. Leg. Cornel. de falsis.—Qui tabulam legis refixerit, vel quid
inde immutaverit, lege Julia peculatûs tenetur, l. 8. P. id leg. Jul. peculat.
Instrumentum rem principalem sequitur :—vid. Locati conducti. A. 19. Sect.
2. In itinere non debet exstrui ædificium, lib. 9. P. si servitus vindicetur.
[g] Ne quis vela regia aut titulum audeat alienis rebus imponere, Cod. l. 2. Tit. 16.
—Qui rem depositam in usus suos, invito domino, converterit, furti reus est :
Leg. 3. Cod. Deposit. vel contra.

tations (confuted by our Saviour[u];) or by such super-induce-
ments of human traditions as argue any defect, as they also
did use[x]. Human arts and learning are of excellent use, as
instruments in the managing and searching, and as means
and witnesses in the explication of Holy Writ, when piously
and prudently directed unto those uses. But to stamp any
thing of but a human original with a divine character, and
obtrude it upon the consciences of men (as papists do their
unwritten traditions), to bind unto obedience ; to take any
dead child of ours (as the harlot did[y]), and lay it in the bosom of the Scripture, and father it upon God ; to build any
structure of ours in the road to heaven, and stop up the
way;—is one of the highest and most dangerous presumptions that the pride of man can aspire unto. To erect a
throne in the consciences of his fellow-creatures, and to
counterfeit the great seal of heaven for the countenancing
of his own forgeries,—is a sin, most severely provided
against by God, with special prohibitions and threatenings[z].
This therefore must be the great care of the ministers of the
gospel, to show their fidelity in delivering only the counsel
of God unto his people[a]; to be as the two golden pipes,
which received oil from the olive-branches, and then
emptied it into the gold[b] ; first, to receive from the Lord,
and then to deliver to the people[c].—Secondly, The people
are hereby taught, first, to examine the doctrines of men by
the rule and standard of the Word ; and to measure them
there, that so they may not be seduced by the craftiness of
deceivers, and may be the more confirmed and comforted by
the doctrine of sincere teachers : for though the judgement
of interpretation belong principally to the ministers of the
Word, yet God hath given unto all believers a judgement of
discretion, to try the spirits and to search the Scriptures,
whether the things which they hear, be so or no[d]: for no man
is to pin his own soul and salvation, by a blind obedience,
upon the words of a man, who may mislead him ; nay, not
upon the words of an angel, if it were possible for an angel
to deceive[e] ; but only and immediately upon the Scripture ;
—except when the blind lead the blind, the leader only

[u] Matth. v. 21, 27, 38, 43.   [x] Matth. xv. 2, 9.   [y] 1 Kings iii. 20.
[z] Deut xii. 32. xviii. 20. Jer. xxvi. 2. Prov. xxx. 6.   [a] Acts xx. 27.   [b] Zach.
iv. 15.   [c] Ezek. ii. 7. Isai. xxi. 10. Ezek. iii. 4. 1 Cor. xi. 23. 1 Pet. iv. 11.
[d] 1 John iv. 1. Acts xvii. 11. 1 Thes. v. 21.   [e] Gal. i. 8. 1 Kings xiii. 18, 21.

should fall into the ditch, and the other go to heaven for his blind obedience in following his guides towards hell; whereas our Saviour tells us, that both shall fall, though but one be the leader [f]. Secondly, Having proved all things, to hold fast that which is good ; with all readiness to receive the righteous ways of God, and submit unto them, how mean soever the [j] instruments be in our eyes, how contrary soever his message be to our wills and lusts. When God doth manifest his Spirit and Word in the mouths of his ministers, we are not to consider the vessel, but the treasure,—and to receive it as from Christ, who, to the end of the world, in the dispensation of his ordinances, speaketh from heaven unto the church [k].

SECT. 15. Fourthly, In that it is said, that ‘ the just will walk in them,’ we may observe two things. 1. That obedience, and walking in the right ways of the Lord, is the end of the ministry ; that the saints might be perfected ; that the body of Christ might be edified ; that men might grow up into Christ in all things [l]; that their eyes might be opened, and they turned from darkness to light, and from the power of Satan unto God [m]. The prophet concludeth, that he hath laboured in vain, if Israel be not gathered [n]. Without this, the law is vain ; the pen of the scribe in vain [o]. Better not know the way of righteousness, than, having known it, to turn from the holy commandment which was delivered unto us [p]. We should esteem it a great misery to be without preaching without ordinances ; and so indeed it is : of all famine, that of the Word of the Lord is the most dreadful : better be with God’s presence in a wilderness, than in Canaan without him [q] : better bread of affliction and water of affliction, than a famine of hearing the Word ; to have our teachers removed [r]. This is mischief upon mischief, when the law perisheth from the priest, and there is no vision [s]. And yet it is much better to be, in this case, without a teaching priest and without the law, than

---

[f] Matth. xv. 14. xxiii. 15.   [h] Vid. *Davenant.* de indice et norma fidei, chap. 25, 31.   [i] *Isid. Pelut.* lib. 3. Ep. 165.   [j] Folio-Edition, p. 602.
[k] 1 Thes. ii. 13. 2 Cor. v. 20. Heb. xii. 25. Matth. xxviii. 20.   [l] Ephes. iv. 11, 15.   [m] Acts xxvi. 16. xvii. 11.   [n] Isai. xlix. 4, 5.   [o] Jer. viii. 8.
[p] 2 Pet. ii. 12.   [q] Exod. xxxiii. 15.   [r] Amos viii. 11. Isai. xxx. 20.
[s] Ezek. vii. 26.

to enjoy them, and not to walk answerably unto them [t].
Where the Word is not a savour of life, it is a savour of
death unto death, exceedingly multiplying the damnation of
those that do despise it [u]. First, It doth ripen those sins
that it finds, making them much more sinful than in other
men, because committed against greater light, and more
mercy. One and the same sin in a heathen is not so
heinous and hateful as in a Christian. Those trees on
which the sun constantly shines, have their fruit grow riper
and greater, than those which grow in a shady and cold
place. The rain will hasten the growth as well of weeds as
of corn, and make them ranker than in a dry and barren
ground [x]. Secondly, It doth superadd many more and
greater: for the greatest sins of all are those, which are
committed against light and grace; sins against the law and
prophets, greater than those that are committed against the
glimmerings of nature [y]; and sins against Christ and the
gospel, greater than those against the law [z]: such are, unbelief, impenitency, apostasy, despising of salvation, preferring death and sin before Christ and mercy, judging ourselves unworthy of eternal life, &c. Thirdly, It doth, by
these means, both hasten and multiply judgements. The
sins of the church are much sooner ripe for the sickle, than
the sins of Amorites; they are near unto cursing [a]. Summer fruits sooner shaken off than others [b]. Christ comes
quickly to remove his candlestick from the abusers of it [c].
The Word is a rich mercy in itself, but nothing makes it effectually, and, in the event, a mercy unto us, but our
walking in it.

SECT. 16.—2. We learn from hence, That we never make

[t] Nihil est aliud scientia nostra quam culpa, qui ad hoc tantummodo legem novimus, ut majore offensione peccemus : *Salvian.* lib. 4.—Criminosior culpa ubi
status honestior. Qui Christiani dicimur, si simile aliquid barbarorum impurita-
tibus facimus, gravius erramus : atrocius enim suo sancti nominis professione
peccamus : ubi sublimior est prerogativa, major est culpa; *Salvian.* lib. 4.
Possunt nostra et Barbarorum vitia esseparia : sed in his tamen vitiis necesse est
peccata nostra esse graviora.——Nunquid dici de Hunnis potest, ' Ecce quales
sunt qui Christiani esse dicuntur ?' nunquid de Saxonibus et Francis, ' Ecce quid
faciunt qui se asserunt Christi esse cultores ?' Nunquid propter Maurorum efferos
mores Lex Sacro-sancta culpatur ?——Evangelia legunt, et Impudici sunt ; Apos-
tolos audiunt, et inebriantur ; Christum sequuntur, et rapiunt, &c. Ibid.
[u] 2 Cor. ii. 15. Matth. xi. 22, 24.   [x] John ix. 41. xv. 22, 24.   [y] Ezek.
ii. 3, 5, 6, 7.   [z] Heb. ii. 2. x. 28, 29.   [a] Heb. vi. 8.   [b] Amos
viii. 1. Jer. i. 11, 12.   [c] Rev. ii. 5.

the Scriptures our rule to live and walk according unto them, till we be first justified, and made righteous : our obedience to the rule of the law written in the Scriptures, proceedeth from those suitable impressions of holiness, wrought in the soul by the Spirit of regeneration, which is called " the writing of the law in our hearts [d] ;" or the casting of the soul into the mould of the Word, as the phrase of the apostle seemeth to import, Rom. vi. 7 : We are never fit to receive God's truth in the love and obedience of it, till we repent and be renewed :—If God (saith the apostle) will " give repentance for the acknowledgement of the truth [e]." " The wise in heart," that is, those that are truly godly, (for none but such are the Scriptures' wise men) these " will receive commandments, but a prating fool will fall [f] ;" where [g] by " prating " I understand cavilling, contradiction, taking exceptions, making objections against the commandment, and so falling and stumbling at it ;—according to that of the apostle [h] ; " Let every man be swift to hear ;" that is, ready to learn the will of God, and to receive the commandment : but " slow to speak, slow to wrath ;" that is, careful that he suffer no pride and passion to rise up and speak against the things which are taught ;—according as Job says, " Teach me, and I will hold my peace [i]." For the only reason why men fret, and swell, and speak against the truth of God, is this,—because they will not work righteousness.   " The wrath of man worketh not the righteousness of God :" therefore men are contentious, because they " love not to obey the truth [j]." Disobedience is the mother of gainsaying [k]. When we once resolve to lay apart all filthiness, then we will receive the Word with meekness, and not before. None hear God's words, but they who are of God [l]. None hear the voice of Christ, but the sheep of Christ [m]. Christ preached is the power of God, and the wisdom of God ; but it is only to them that are called, to others a stumbling-block and foolishness [n].   " We speak wisdom," saith the apostle, but it is " amongst them that are perfect [o]." He that is subject unto one prince, doth not greatly

d Jer. xxxi. 33. 2 Cor. iii. 3.   e 2 Tim. ii. 5.   f Prov. x. 8.
g Folio-Edition, p. 603.   h James i. 19, 20, 21.   i Job. vi. 24.
j Rom. ii. 8.   k Rom. x. 21.   l John viii. 47.   m John x. 4, 5.
n 1 Cor. i. 24.   o 1 Cor. ii. 6.

care to study the laws of another; or if he do, it is in order
to curiosity, and not unto duty. So long as men resolve of
Christ, "We will not have this man to reign over us," so
long either they study not his Word at all; or it is in order
to some carnal and corrupt ends, and not either to obedience
or salvation.

Hereby we may try our spiritual estate, whether we be
just men or no; if we make God's Word our way, our rule,
our delight, laying it up in our hearts, and labouring to be
rich in it, that we may walk with more exactness. It was an
ill sign of love to Christ, the master of the feast, when men
chose rather to tend their cattle and grounds, than to wait
on him P:—an ill sign of valuing his doctrine, when the loss
of their swine made the Gadarenes weary of his company q.
There was much work to do in the house, when Mary neglected it all, and sat at his feet to hear his doctrine, and yet
was commended by him for it: he was better pleased to see
her hunger after the feast that he brought, than solicitous to
provide a feast for him; more delighted in her love to his
doctrine, than her sister's care for his entertainment r. This
is one of the surest characters of a godly man, that he makes
the Word, in all things, his rule and counsellor, labouring
continually to get more acquaintance with God and his holy
will thereby s. It is his way: and every man endeavours to
be skilful in the way which he is to travel.—It is his tool
and instrument: every workman must have that in a readiness, to measure and carry on all the parts of his work.—It
is his wisdom: every one would be esteemed a wise man in
that, which is his proper function and profession t.—It is the
mystery and trade unto which he is bound: and every man
would have the reputation of skill in his own trade.—It is
his charter, the grant of all the privileges and immunities
which belong unto him: and every citizen would willingly
know the privileges which he hath a right in.—It is the
testament and will of Christ, wherein are given unto us

P Luke xiv. 18.   q Luke viii. 37.   r Luke x. 41, 42.   s Prov.
x. 14. Col. iii. 16. John xv. 7.   t Turpe est patricio, et nobili, et causas
oranti, jus in quo versaretur, ignorare. Pompon. P. de origine Juris. leg. 234.
Sect.—Itaque in medicum, imperite secantem, competit actio. l. 7. P. ad Leg.
Aquil. Sect. 8. quia imperitia culpæ adnumeratur Instit. lib. 4. de Leg. Aquil.
Sect. 7. et l. 132. de Regulis Juris.

exceeding great and precious promises: and what heir or child would be ignorant of the last will of his father?— Lastly, It is the law of Christ's kingdom: and it concerns every subject to know the duties, the rewards [u], the punishments that belong unto him in that relation.

SECT. 17. Fifthly, In that he saith that the "transgressors shall fall therein," we learn, That the holy and right ways of the Lord, in the ministry of his Word, set forth unto us, are, unto wicked men, turned into matter of falling; and that two manner of ways;—1. By way of 'Scandal;' they are offended at it. 2. By way of 'Ruin;' they are destroyed by it.

1. By way of 'Scandal;' they are offended at it. So it is prophesied of Christ, that as he should be for a sanctuary unto his people,—so to others, who would not trust in him, but betake themselves to their own counsels, he should be for a 'stone of stumbling,' and for a 'rock of offence;' for 'a gin, and for a snare [x];' 'for the fall and rising again of many in Israel, and for a sign to be spoken against [y].' So he saith of himself,—" For judgement, am I come into this world [z], that they which see not, might see; and that they which see, might be made blind [a]." And this offence [b] which wicked men take at Christ, is from the purity and holiness of his Word, which they cannot submit unto. 'A stone of stumbling' he is, and 'a rock of offence,' to them which stumble at the Word, 'being disobedient [c].' Thus Christ preached was 'a sanctuary' to Sergius Paulus the deputy, and a 'stumbling-block' to Elymas the sorcerer; a 'sanctuary' to Dionysius and Damaris, and a 'stumbling-block' to the wits and philosophers of Athens; a 'sanctuary' to the Gentiles that begged the preaching of the gospel, and a 'stumbling-block' to the Jews that contradicted and blasphemed [d]: the former primarily and 'per se,' for salvation was the purpose of his coming; there was sin enough to condemn the world before: "I came not," saith he, "to judge the world, but to save the world [e]." The other occa-

---

[u] Juris ignorantia cuique nocet. 1. 9. P. de juris et facti ignor.—*Arist.* Ethic. lib. 3. cap. 7.—*Greg. Tholos.* syntag. Jur. 1. 30. c. 10.   [x] Isai. viii. 14. [y] Luke ii. 34, 35.   [z] Folio-Edition, p. 604.   [a] John ix. 39.   [b] Bonæ res neminem scandalizant, nisi malam mentem: *Tert.* de veland. virg. c. 3. [c] 1 Pet. ii. 8. 2 Cor. ii. 14, 15.   [d] Acts xiii. 42, 45.   [e] John xii. 47.

422   SEVEN SERMONS ON THE   [Serm. VII.

sionally [f], not by any intrinsecal evil quality in the Word,
which is 'holy, just, good,' and dealeth with all meekness
and beseechings, even towards obstinate sinners [g]; but by
reason of the pride and stubbornness of these men who dash
against it:—as that wholesome meat which ministereth
strength to a sound man, doth but feed the disease of
another that sits at the same table with him; the same light
which is a pleasure to a strong eye, is a pain to a weak one;
the same sweet smells that delight the brain, do afflict the
matrix when it is distempered; and none of this by the
infusion of malignant qualities, but only by an occasional
working upon and exciting of those which were there
before.

Sect. 18. And there are many things in the Word of God,
at which the corrupt hearts of wicked men are apt to stumble and be offended: as First, The profoundness and depth of
it, as containing great mysteries, above the discovery or
search of created reason. Such is the pride and wantonness of sinful wit, that it knows not how to believe what it
cannot comprehend; and must have all doctrines tried at
her bar, and measured by her balance. As if a man should
attempt to weigh out the earth in a pair of scales, or to empty
the waters of the sea with a bucket. As soon as Paul mentioned the resurrection, presently the Athenian wits mocked
his doctrine [i]; and it was a great stumbling-block to Nicodemus to hear that a man must be born again [k]. Sarah hath
much ado to believe 'beyond reason [l];' and Moses himself
was a little staggered by this temptation [m]. A very hard
thing it is for busy and inquisitive reason to rest in an
ὦ βάθος, in the depth of the wisdom and counsel of God,
and to adore the unsearchableness of his judgements, though
even human laws tell us [n], that reason of law is not always
to be enquired into. The first great heresies [o] against the

---

[f] Vid. *Iren.* in l. 5. c. 27.   [g] Οὐχ αἱ γραφαὶ γεγόνασιν αὐτοῖς αἰτίαι,
ἀλλ' ἡ σφῶν αὐτῶν κακοφροσύνη. *Athan.* de Syn. Arim. et Seleuc.   [h] Δεῖ
μὴ λογισμοῖς ἀνθρωπίνοις διευθύνειν τὰ θεῖα, ἀλλὰ πρὸς τὸ βούλευμα τῆς διδασ-
καλίας τοῦ πνεύματος τῶν λόγων ποιεῖσθαι τὴν ἔκθεσιν. *Just.* Exposit. Fidei.
[i] Acts xvii. 32.   [k] John iii. 4.   [l] Gen. xviii. 12.   [m] Numb.
xi. 21, 22.   [n] Οὐδὲ γὰρ οὓς ἄνθρωποι νόμους τίθενται, τὸ εὔλογον ἁπλῶς
ἔχουσι καὶ πάντοτε φαινόμενον. *Plut.* de sera numinis vindicta.—Non omnium
quæ à majoribus constituta sunt, ratio reddi potest; et ideo rationis eorum, quæ
constituuntur, inquiri non oportet. P. lib. 1. T. 4. Leg. 20, 21.   [o] Vid.
Hooker. l. 5. 3.—Mater omnium hæreticorum superbia.—*Aug.* de Gen. contr.

highest mysteries of Christian religion, the Trinity,—the two natures of Christ,—the hypostatical union,—the deity of the Holy Spirit,—had their first rise amongst the Grecians, who were then the masters of wit and learning, and esteemed the rest of the world barbarous ; and the old exception which they were wont to take at the doctrine of Christianity, was the ' foolishness ' of it, as the apostle notes [p].

SECT. 19. Secondly, The sanctity and strictness of it is contrary to the carnal wills and affections of men : for as corruption doth deify reason in the way of wisdom, not willingly allowing any mysteries above the scrutiny and comprehension of it ; so doth it deify will in a way of liberty and power, and doth not love to have any authority set over that which may pinch or restrain it. As Joshua said to Israel, " Ye cannot serve the Lord, for he is a holy God [q] ; " we may say of the law,—We cannot submit to the law, because it is a holy law. " The carnal mind is not," cannot be, " subject to the law of God [r]." Heat and cold will ever be offensive unto one another, and such are flesh and spirit [s]. Therefore ordinarily the arguments against the ways of God, have been drawn from politic or carnal interests. Jeroboam will not worship at Jerusalem, for fear lest Israel revolt to the house of David [t]. Amos must not prophesy against the idolatry of Israel, for ' the land is not able to bear all his words [u].' The Jews conclude, Christ must not be ' let alone, lest the Romans come and take away their place and nation [x].' Demetrius and the craftsmen will by no means have Diana spoken against, because, by making shrines [y] for her, ' they got their wealth [z].' Corruption [a] will close with religion a great way, and ' hear gladly,' and do ' many things' willingly, and part with much to escape damnation : but there is a particular point of rigour and strictness in every unregenerate man's case, which, when it is set on close upon him, causeth him to ' stumble,' and to be offended, and to break the treaty. The hypocrites, in the prophet, will give " rams,

---

Manichæos, l. 2. c. 8.   p 1 Cor. i. 23.   q Josh. xxiv. 19.   r Rom. viii. 17.   s Gal. v. 17.   t 1 Kings xii. 27.   u Amos vii. 10. x Rom. xi. 48.   y Folio-Edition, p. 605.   z Acts xix. 24, 25. a See *Perkins'* Works, Tom. 1. p. 356, 362.—*Bolton's* Course of True Happiness.— *Sanderson's* Sermon, 1 Kings xxi. 29.—*Dan. Dykes'* Deceit of the Heart, c. 6, 7, 8.—*Downham* of Christian Warfare, part 4, l. 1. c. 13. sect. 3. et l. 2, 11.

and rivers of oil, and the first-born of their body, for the sin
of their soul:" but " to do justly, to love mercy, to walk
humbly with God ; to do away the treasures of wickedness,
the scant measure, the bag of deceitful weights, violence,
lies, circumvention, the statutes of Omri, or the counsels of
the house of Ahab;"—'durus sermo,' this is intolerable; they
will rather venture smiting and desolation, than be held to
so severe terms [b]. The young man will come to Christ, yea,
run to him, and kneel, and desire instruction touching the
way to eternal life, and walk with much care in observation
of the commandments : but if he must ' part with all,' and,
instead of great possessions, ' take up a cross and follow
Christ,' and fare as he fared ;—' durus sermo,' this is indeed a
hard saying:—he that came ' running,' went away ' grieving'
and displeased [c] ; and upon this one point doth he and
Christ part [d]. Herod will hear John gladly, and do many
things, and observe and reverence him as a just and holy
man ; but, in the case of Herodias, he must be excused;
upon this issue, doth he and salvation shake hands [e]. This
is the difference between hypocritical and sincere conversion; that goes far, and parts with much, and proceeds to
almost : but when it comes to the very turning point, and
ultimate act of regeneration, he then plays the part of an
" unwise son, and stays in the place of the breaking forth of
children [f],"—as a foolish merchant, who, in a rich bargain of
a thousand pounds, breaks upon a difference of twenty shil-
lings :—but the other is contented to part with all, to suffer
the loss of all, to carry on the treaty to a full and final conclusion, to have all the armour of the strong man taken from
him, that Christ may divide the spoils [g] ; to do the hardest
duties if they be commanded [h].

SECT. 20. Thirdly, The searching, convincing, and penetrating quality which is in the Word, is a great matter of
offence unto wicked men, when it ' cuts them to the heart,'
as Stephen's sermon did his hearers [i]. Light is of a discovering and manifesting property [k] ; and for that reason is

---

b Mic. vi. 6, 16.   c Vid. *Basil.* Homil. in Ditescentes,—statim ab initio.
d Mark x. 17, 22.   e Mark vi. 20, 27.   f Hos. xiii. 13.   g Luke
xi. 22. Psalm cxix. 128.   h Fides famem non timet. *Hier.*—Perquam durum,
sed ita lex scripta est. Ulpian. P. Qui et à quibus manumissi liberi non fiunt.
12. sect. 2. Gen. xxii. 3.   i Acts vii. 54.   k Ephes. v. 13.

" hated by every one that doth evil[1]." For though the pleasure of sin unto a wicked man be sweet, yet there is bitterness in the root and bottom of it; he who loves to enjoy the
pleasure, cannot endure to hear of the guilt.

Now the work of the Word is to take men in their own
heart[m]; to make manifest to a man the secrets of his own
heart[n]; to pierce, like arrows, the heart of God's enemies[o];
to divide asunder the soul and spirits, the joints and marrow, and to be a discerner of the thoughts and intents of the
heart[p]. This act of discovery cannot but exceedingly gall
the spirits of wicked men: it is like the voice of God unto
Adam in Paradise, " Adam, where art thou?" or like the
voice of Ahijah to the wife of Jeroboam[q], " I am sent unto
thee with heavy tidings."

Fourthly, The plainness and simplicity of the gospel, is
likewise matter of offence to these men[r]; and that partly
upon the preceding reason; for the more plain the Word is,
the more immediate access it hath unto the conscience, and
operation upon it. So much as is merely human elegancy,
fineness of wit, and delicacy of expression, doth oftentimes
stop at fancy, and take that up, as the body of Asahel
caused the passers-by to stand still and gaze[s]. And wicked
men can be contented to admit the Word any whither, so
they can keep it out of their conscience, which is the only
proper subject of it[t]. When I hear men magnify quaint and
polite discourses in the ministry of the Word, and speak
against sermons that are plain and wholesome; I look upon
it, not so much as an act of pride, (though the wisdom of
the flesh is very apt to scorn the simplicity of the gospel,)
but indeed is an act of fear and cowardice; because where
all other external trimmings and dresses are wanting to
tickle the fancy, there the Word hath the more downright
and sad operation upon the conscience, and must consequently the more startle and terrify.

SECT. 21. Fifthly, The great difficulty, and indeed impossibility of obeying it in the strictness and rigour of it, is another
ground of scandal, that God in his Word should command men

[1] John iii. 20. [m] Ezek. xiv. 5. [n] 1 Cor. xiv. 25. [o] Psalm
xlv. 5. [p] Heb. iv. 12. Isai. xlix. 2. [q] 1 Kings xiv. 6. [r] 2 Cor.
x. 10. [s] 2 Sam. ii. 23. [t] 2 Cor. iv. 2.

to do that which indeed cannot be done. This was matter of ^u
astonishment to the disciples themselves, when our Saviour
told them, that it was "easier for a camel to go through
the eye of a needle, than for a rich man to enter into
the kingdom of God ^x." This was the cavil of the dis-
putant in the apostle, against the counsels of God, " Why
doth he yet find fault?" if he harden whom he will,
why doth he complain of our hardness, which it is impossible
for us to prevent, because none can resist his will ^y? Now
to this scandal we answer, First, That the law of God was
not originally ^z, nor is it intrinsecally, or in the nature of the
thing impossible, but accidentally, and by reason of natural
corruption which is enmity against it. A burden may be
very portable in itself, which he who is a cripple, is not able
to bear : the defect is not in the law, but in us ^a.—Secondly,
That of this impossibility ^b there may be made a most excellent use ;—that, being convinced of impotency in ourselves, we may have recourse to the perfect obedience and
righteousness of Christ, to pardon all our violations upon
it ^c.—Thirdly, Being regenerated and endued with the Spirit
of Christ, the law becomes evangelically possible ^d unto us
again; yea, not only possible, but sweet and easy ^e ; though
impossible to the purpose of justification and legal covenant,
which requireth perfection of obedience under pain of the
curse ^f : in which sense it is a yoke which cannot be borne ^g;
a commandment which cannot be endured ^h;—yet possible to

---

^u Folio-Edition, p. 606.   ^x Mark x. 25.   ^y Rom. ix. 1.   ^z Censores di-
vinitatis, dicentes 'Sic non debuit Deus, et sic magis debuit,' consultiores sibimet
videntur Deo : *Tert.* in Marcion. l. 2. C. 2.   ^a Rom. viii. 3.   ^b Non fuit impossibile, quando præceptum est ; sed stultitia peccantis impossibile sibi fecit. *Gul.
Paris.* de vitiis et peccat. cap. 10.—Neque enim suo vitio non implebatur Lex,
sed vitio prudentiæ carnis. *Aug.* de spir. et lit. cap. 19.   ^c Gal. iii. 21, 24.
^d Nec latuit præceptorem præcepti pondus hominum excedere vires : sed judicavit
utile ex hoc ipso suæ illos insufficientiæ admoneri—Ergo, mandando impossibilia,
non prævaricatores homines fecit sed humiles, ut omne os obstruatur et subditus
fiat omnis mundus Deo, quia ex operibus legis non justificabitur omnis caro coram illo : accipientes quippe mandatum, et sentientes defectum, clamabimus in
Cœlum, et miserabitur nostri Deus. *Bern.* Ser. 50. in Cantic. Lex data ut
gratia quæreretur, gratia data ut Lex impleretur.—*Aug.* de spir. et lit. c. 10.—Omnia fiunt caritati facilia : De nat. et grat. cap. 69.—de nat. Christ. cap. 9—de grat.
et lib. arb. cap. 15.—Cor lapideum non significat nisi durissimam voluntatem et
adversus Deum inflexibilem. *Aug.* de grat. et lib. arb. cap. 14.   ^e Rom.
vii. 2. 1 John v. 2. Matth. xi. 30.   ^f Gal. iii. 10.   ^g Acts xv. 13.
^h Heb. xii. 20.

the purpose of acceptation of our services done in the obedience of it, the spiritual part of them being presented by
the intercession, and the carnal defects covered by the
righteousness, of Christ, in whom the Father is always well
pleased.—Fourthly, If any wicked man presume to harden
himself in the practice of sins, under this pretence, that it
is impossible for him to avoid them, because God hardeneth
' whom he will;' though the apostolical increpation be answer sufficient, " Who art thou, that repliest against God?"
yet he may further know, that he is not only hardened judicially by the sentence of God, but most willingly also by his
own stubborn love of sin, and giving himself over unto
greediness in sinning; and thereby doth actively bring upon
himself those indispositions unto duty; so that the law, being
impossible to be performed by him, is indeed no other than
he would himself have it to be, as bearing an active enmity
and antipathy unto it.

SECT. 22. Sixthly, The mercy and free grace of God in
the promises, is unto wicked men an occasion of stumbling
while they turn it into lasciviousness, and continue in sin
that grace may abound [i], and venture to make work for the
blood of Christ, not being led ' by the goodness of God
unto repentance,' but hardening themselves in impenitency,
because God is good [k]. There is not any thing at which
wicked men do more ordinarily stumble, than at mercy,—as
gluttons surfeit most upon the greatest dainties ;—venturing
upon this ground to go on in sin, because they cannot out-
sin mercy; and to put off repentance from day to day, because they are still under the offers of mercy; making mercy
not a sanctuary unto which to fly from sin, but a sanctuary
to protect and countenance sin ; and so, by profane and desperate presumption, turning the very mercy of God into a
judgement [l] and savour of death unto themselves [m]; pretending liberty from sin, that they may continue in it, and abuse
God by his own gifts.

Lastly, The threatenings of God set forth in his Word,
and executed in his judgements upon wicked men, are great

[i] Rom. vi. 1. Jude verse iv.   [k] Rom. ii. 4.   [l] Fructum ex eo quis
consequi non debet, quod impugnat: *Golofrid.*—Nemo fit liber in fraudem fisci :
Marcian. P. Qui et à quibus manumissi, l. 11.   [m] Deut. xxix. 19, 20.
Numb. xv. 30.

occasions of stumbling unto them, when they are not thereby, with Manasses, humbled under God's mighty hand,—but, with Pharaoh, hardened the more in their stubbornness against him. There is such desperate wickedness in the hearts of some men[n], that they can even sit down and rest in the resolutions of perishing, resolving to enjoy the pleasures of sin while they may :—" To-morrow we shall die ;" therefore, in the mean time, " let us eat and drink [o]."—" This evil is of the Lord; why should we wait for the Lord any longer [p] ?"—There are three men in the Scripture that have a special brand or mark of ignominy set upon them, Cain, Dathan, and Ahaz : " The Lord set a mark upon Cain [q] ;"—" This is that Dathan," and " This is that Ahaz [r] :" and if we examine the reasons, we shall find that the sin of stubbornness had a special hand in it. Cain's offering was not accepted ; upon this he grew wrath and sullen, and ' stubborn' against God's gentle warning, and slew his brother. Dathan and his companions, sent for by Moses, return a proud and ' stubborn' answer, " We will not come up." Ahaz greatly distressed by the King of Syria, by the Edomites, by the Philistines, by the Assyrian ; and in the midst of all this distress, ' stubborn' still, and trespassing more against the Lord. It is one of the saddest symptoms in the world, for a man or a nation not to be humbled under the correcting hand of God ; but, like an anvil, to grow harder under blows ;—and a most sure argument, that God will not give over, but go on to multiply his judgements still : for he will overcome when he judgeth, and therefore will judge till he overcome. In musical notes, there are but eight degrees ; and then the same returns again : and philosophers, when they distinguish degrees in qualities, do usually make the eighth degree to be the highest : but in the wrath of God against those, who impenitently and stubbornly stand out against his judgements, we shall find no fewer than eight and twenty degrees threatened by God himself, " I will punish seven times more ;" and yet " seven times more;" and again " seven times more ;" and once more " seven times more for your sins [s]."

---

n Vide quæ de Sardanapalo, Nino, Bacchida, Xanthia, aliis, congessit *Athenæus*, lib. 8. c. 3. et lib. 12. c. 7.—Contumacia cumulat pœnam, l. 4. P. de pæri.
o 1 Cor. v. 32.   p 2 Kings vi. 33.   q Gen. iv. 15.   r Folio-Edition, p. 607. Numb. xxvi. 9. 2 Chron. xxii. 22.   s Levit. xxvi. 18, 21, 24, 28.

Thus wicked men do not only stumble at the Word by way
of scandal, but also—

SECT. 23.—2. By way of ruin, because they are sure, in
the conclusion, to be destroyed by it: for the rock stands
still; the ship only is broken, that dasheth against it.
God's Word is, and will be, too hard for the pride of men;
the more they resist it, the mightier will it appear in their
condemnation. The weak corn which yields to the wind, is
not harmed by it; but the proud oak which resists it, is
many times broken in pieces^t. The soul which submits to
the Word, is saved by it; the soul which rebels against it, is
sure to perish. Therefore since the Word comes not to any
man in vain, but returns glory to God, either in his conversion, or in his hardening; it greatly concerneth every man
to come unto it, with meek, penitent, docile, tractable, believing, obedient resolutions;—and to consider how vain
and desperate a thing it is for a potsherd to strive with a
rod of iron; for the pride and wrath of man to give a chal-
lenge to the justice and power of God; for briars and thorns
to set themselves in battle against fire. As our God is a
consuming fire himself, so his law "is a fiery law^u," and his
Word in the mouth of his ministers 'a fire^x.' If we be gold,
it will purge us; if thorns, it will devour and feed upon us.
"This is the condemnation," saith our Saviour, "that light
is come into the world, and men love darkness rather than
light^y." There was damnation in the world before, while it
lay in darkness, and in mischief, and knew not whither it
went; but not so heavy damnation as that, which groweth
out of light. When physic, which should remove the
disease, doth co-operate with it, then death comes with the
more pain and the more speed. The stronger the conviction
of sin is, the deeper will be the wrath against it, if it be not,
by repentance, avoided. No surfeit more dangerous than
that of bread; no judgement more terrible than that, which
grows out of mercy, known and despised. "The word
which I have spoken," saith Christ, "the same shall judge
you at the last day^z." Every principle of truth which is,

---

^t ʿΩν ἄμαχος ἡ δύναμίς ἐστιν, ὑπὸ τούτων ἧτlον ἀδικεῖται τὰ εἴκοντα
τῶν ἀνθισταμένων. *Plut.* Sympos. lib. 4. qu. 2. Xylandr. vol. 2. p. 666. B.
^u Deut. xxxiii. 2.   ^x Jer. v. 14, 23, 29.   ^y John iii. 19.   ^z John
xii. 48.

by the Word, begotten in the hearts of disobedient sinners,
and is held down and suppressed by unrighteousness, lies
there like fire raked up under ashes, which, at that great
day, will kindle into an unquenchable flame. The Word can
bring much of hell upon the spirit of impenitent sinners
here : it can hew, and cut, and pierce, and burn, and torment, and root out, and pull down, and destroy, and strike
with trembling and amazement, the proudest and securest
sinners [a]. We need no messengers from the dead to tell us
of the torments there : all the rhetoric in hell cannot set forth
hell more to the life, than Moses and the prophets have
done already [b]. But O ! what a hell will it be at last, when
the Word, which warned us of it, shall throw us into it!
When every offer of mercy which we have refused, and every
threatening of wrath which we have despised, shall accom-
pany us unto the tribunal of Christ, to testify against us,
and into the fire of hell, to upbraid us with our own perdition ! O the doleful condition of impenitent sinners ! If
they have not the Word, they perish for the want ; and, if
they have it, they perish double for the contempt of it. O
that men would consider the terror of the Lord, and be persuaded! and that they would learn so much wisdom, as not
to arm the very mercy of God against themselves! A
bridge is made to give us a safe passage over a dangerous
river ; but he who stumbles on the bridge, is in danger to
fall into the river. The Word is given as a means to carry
us over hell unto heaven; but he who stumbles and quarrels
at this means, shall fall in thither, from whence otherwise
he had been delivered by it.

a Hos. vi. 5. Acts vii. 54. Heb. iv. 12. Isai. xlix. 2. Psalm xlv. 5. Rev.
xi. 5, 10. Jer. i. 10. 2 Cor. x. 4. Acts xxiv. 25.   b Luke xvi. 31.

END OF VOL. III.

LONDON:
PRINTED BY S. AND R. BENTLEY, DORSET STREET.